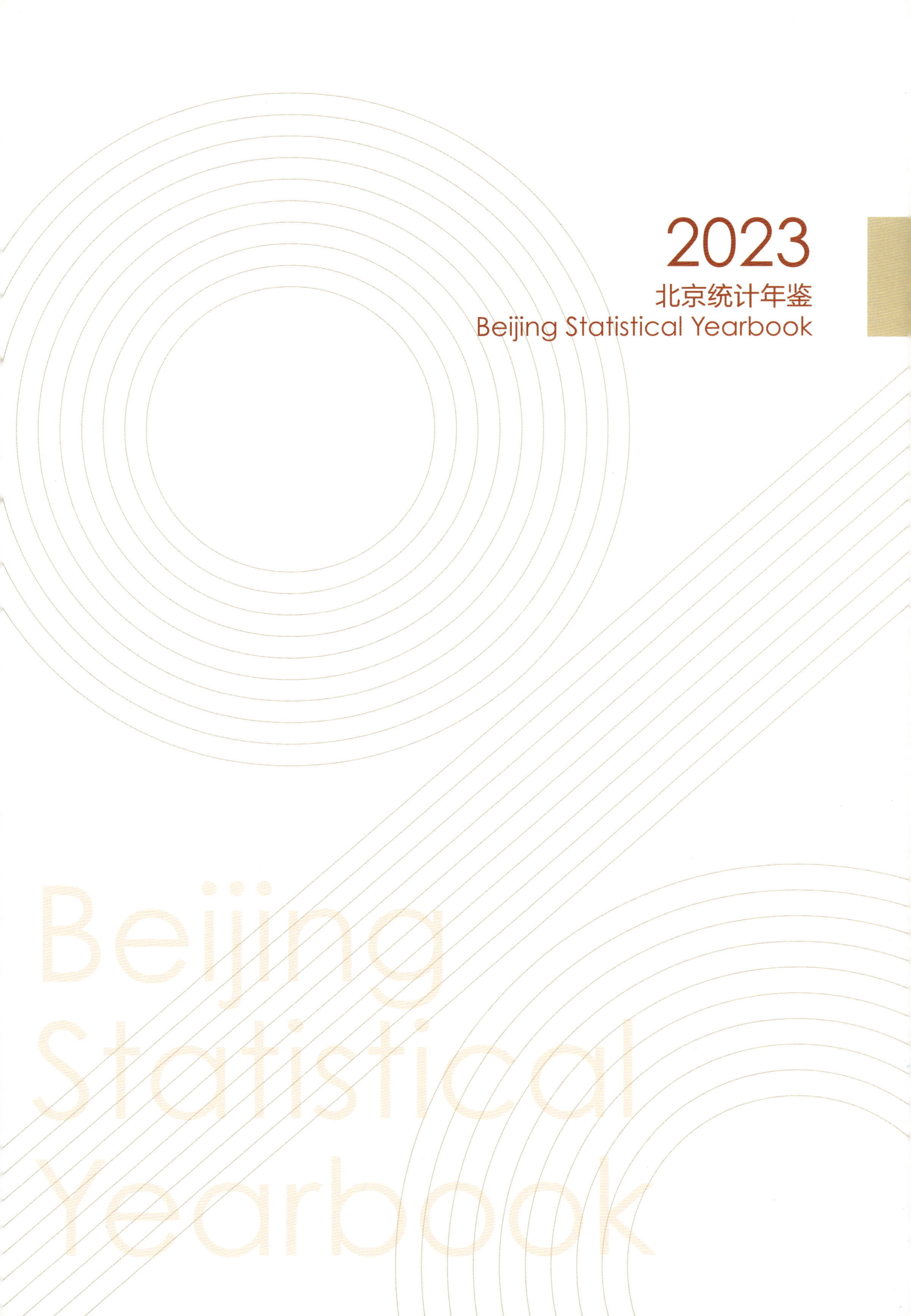
2023
北京统计年鉴
Beijing Statistical Yearbook
Beijing
Statistical
Yearbook

图书在版编目(CIP)数据

北京统计年鉴. 2023 = Beijing Statistical Yearbook 2023 : 汉英对照 / 北京市统计局, 国家统计局北京调查总队编. -- 北京 : 中国统计出版社, 2023.10
ISBN 978-7-5230-0265-0

Ⅰ. ①北… Ⅱ. ①北… ②国… Ⅲ. ①统计资料－北京－2023－年鉴－汉、英 Ⅳ. ①C832.1-54

中国国家版本馆CIP数据核字(2023)第184683号

北京统计年鉴2023

作　　者/北京市统计局 国家统计局北京调查总队
责任编辑/李 冲
封面设计/高 立
出版发行/中国统计出版社有限公司
通信地址/北京市丰台区西三环南路甲6号 邮政编码/100073
发行电话/邮购 (010) 63376909 书店 (010) 68783171
网　　址/http://www.zgtjcbs.com
印　　刷/河北鑫兆源印刷有限公司
经　　销/新华书店
开　　本/880mm×1230mm 1/16
字　　数/1200千字
印　　张/34.5印张 彩插/1.5印张
版　　别/2023年10月第1版
版　　次/2023年10月第1次印刷
定　　价/350.00元

2022年的北京
BEIJING IN 2022

41610.9
地区生产总值(亿元)
Gross Domestic Product(100 million yuan)

2843.3
研究与试验发展
(R&D)经费内部支出(亿元)
Internal R&D Expenditures(100 million yuan)

83.9
第三产业增加值占地区生产总值比重(%)
Added Value of Tertiary Industry as % of GDP(%)

363399
社会劳动生产率(元/人)
Overall Labor Productivity(yuan/person)

5714.4
一般公共预算收入(亿元)
General Public Budget Revenue (100 million yuan)

190313
人均地区生产总值(元)
Per Capita Gross Domestic Product(yuan)

77415
全市居民人均可支配收入(元)
Per Capita Disposable Income of Households of the Whole City (yuan)

101.8
居民消费价格指数(上年=100)
Consumer Price Index(preceding year=100)

2022年的北京
BEIJING IN 2022

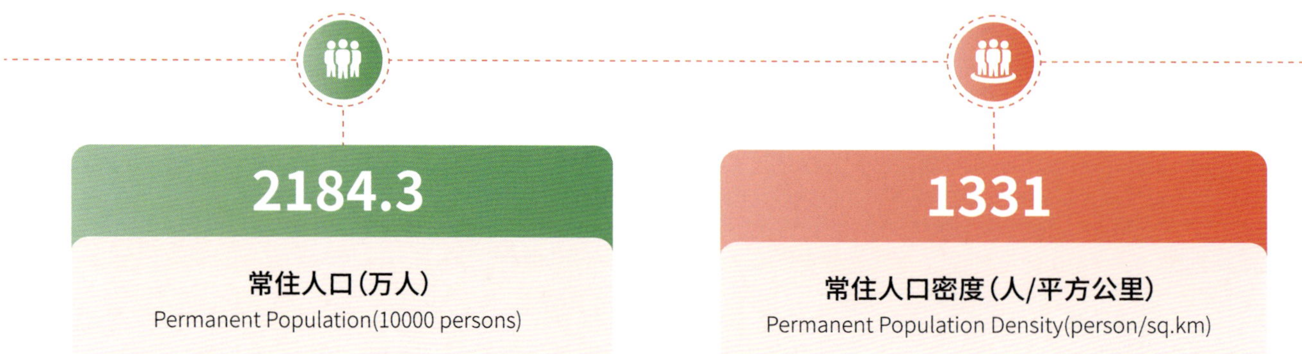

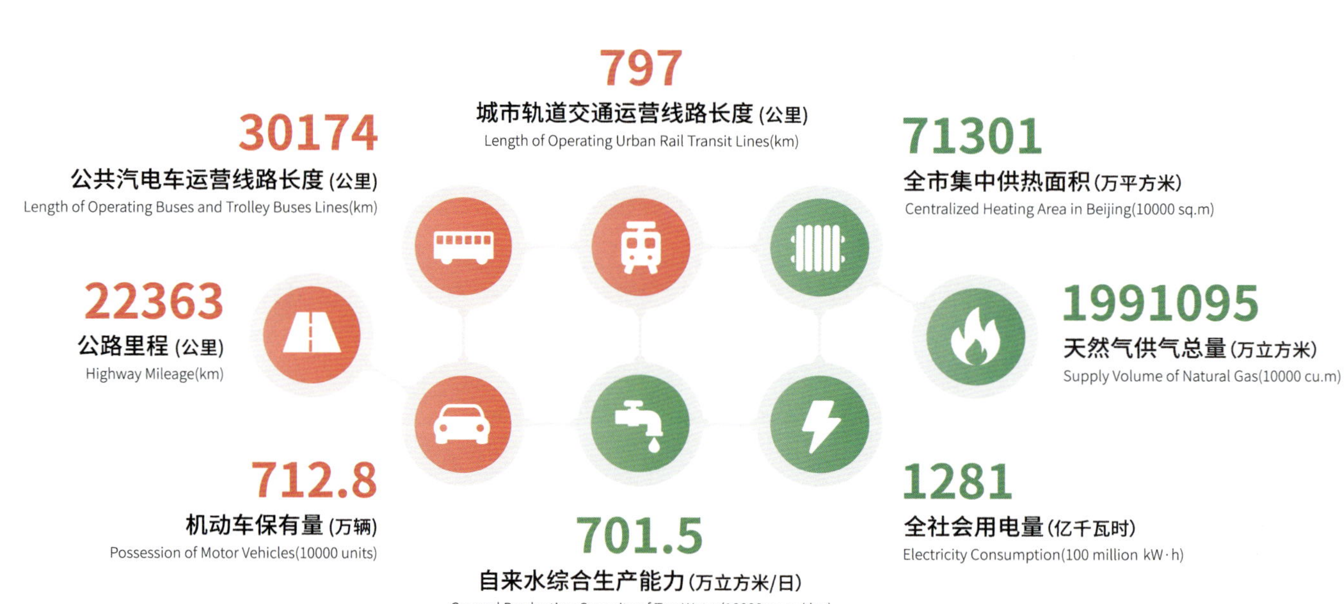

6.83

研究与试验发展经费内部支出相当于地区生产总值比例(%)
Internal R&D Expenditures as % of GDP(%)

218

万人发明专利拥有量(件)
Invention Patent Ownership per 10000 persons(unit)

7947.5

技术合同成交总额(亿元)
Total Volume of Transaction of Technological Contracts(100 million yuan)

2.79

每十万常住人口公共图书馆书刊文献外借册次 (万册次)
Volume-times of Borrowed books,Magazines and Documents of Public Libraries per 100000 Permanent Population(10000 Volume-times)

5.78

每千常住人口医院床位数 (张)
Number of Ward Beds per 1000 Permanent Population(unit)

0.98

每十万常住人口博物馆数 (个)
Number of Museums per 100000 Permanent Population(unit)

5.72

每千常住人口执业(助理)医师数 (人)
Number of Certified (Assistant) Doctors per 1000 Permanent Population(person)

9.1

每十万常住人口幼儿园数 (个)
Number of Kindergartens per 100000 Permanent Population(unit)

14.1

平均每一专任教师负担小学生数 (人)
Average Number of Students in Primary School Instructed by a Full-time Teacher(person)

30.0

$PM_{2.5}$年平均浓度
(微克/立方米)
Annual Average Concentration of $PM_{2.5}$(μg/cu.m)

108.6

人均水资源
(立方米)
Per Capita Water Resource
(cu.m)

16.9

人均公园绿地面积
(平方米)
Per Capita Park Green Area
(sq.m)

49.8

城市绿化覆盖率
(%)
Urban Green Coverage
(%)

北京一日
A DAY IN BEIJING

每日创造
Daily Production

156557.8
一般公共预算收入
(万元)
General Public Budget Revenue(10000 yuan)

204634.4
一般公共预算支出
(万元)
General Public Budget Expenditure(10000 yuan)

12326.6
发电量
(万千瓦时)
Electricity Generated (10000 kW·h)

2386
汽车生产量
(辆)
Output of Motor Vehicles(vehicle)

258343
移动电话机生产量
(台)
Output of Mobile Telephones(set)

4769.2
实际利用外商直接投资额
(万美元)
Actual Use of Foreign Direct Investment (USD 10000)

6401
显示器生产量
(台)
Output of Display Devices (set)

3056.2
第一产业
Primary Industry

837136.5
地区货物进口值
(万元)
Total Imports of Local Enterprises (10000 yuan)

1140026.0
地区生产总值(万元)
Gross Domestic Product (10000 yuan)

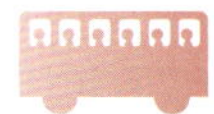

472.8
公共汽电车客运量
(万人次)
Passenger Traffic of Buses and Trolley Buses(10000 person-times)

161370.5
地区货物出口值
(万元)
Total Exports of Local Enterprises (10000 yuan)

180960.8
第二产业
Secondary Industry

956009.0
第三产业
Tertiary Industry

620.1
城市轨道交通客运量
(万人次)
Passenger Traffic of Rail Transit (10000 person-times)

68244.4
国内旅游收入
(万元)
Revenue from Domestic Tourism (10000 yuan)

120.8
国际旅游收入
(万美元)
Revenue from Inbound Tourism (USD 10000)

8.2
民航客运量
(万人次)
Passenger Traffic of Civil Aviation (10000 person-times)

57.8
公路客运量
(万人次)
Passenger Traffic of Highway (10000 person-times)

10.7
铁路客运量
(万人次)
Passenger Traffic of Railway (10000 person-times)

每日生活
Daily Life

340
常住出生人口
(人)
Births (Permanent Residence)
(person)

343
常住死亡人口
(人)
Deaths (Permanent Residence)
(person)

250
登记结婚对数
(对)
Registered Marriages
(couple)

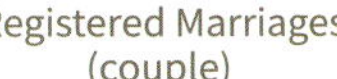

121
离婚对数
(对)
Divorces
(couple)

212.1
全市居民人均
可支配收入(元)
Per Capita Disposable Income
of Residents of the Whole City
(yuan)

2.0
生活垃圾清运量
(万吨)
Domestic Waste Removed and
Transported
(10000 tons)

77599.7
吃类商品(万元)
Food
(10000 yuan)

18000.3
穿类商品(万元)
Clothing
(10000 yuan)

377924.5
社会消费品
零售总额 (万元)
Total Retail Sales of
Consumer Goods
(10000 yuan)

266401.0
用类商品(万元)
Daily Use Articles
(10000 yuan)

15923.5
烧类商品(万元)
Fuels
(10000 yuan)

116.9
全市居民人均
消费支出(元)
Per Capita Consumption Expenditure
of Residents of the Whole City
(yuan)

608.5
污水处理能力
(万立方米)
Treatment Volume of
Sewage
(10000 cu.m)

489.0
法人单位从业人员
平均工资(元)
Average Wages of Employed
Person in Legal Entities
(yuan)

337.7
自来水销售总量
(万立方米)
Total Sales Volume
of Tap Water
(10000 cu.m)

560.8
居民家庭用天然气销售量
(万立方米)
Sales Volume of Natural Gas
for Household Consumption
(10000 cu.m)

8792.4
城乡居民生活用电量
(万千瓦时)
Household Electricity
Consumption of Urban and
Rural Residents Household
(10000 kW·h)

536.0
特快专递业务量
(万件)
Express Mail Services
(10000 pcs)

7201
电影放映场次
(场次)
Show Times of Films
(times)

总体经济
OVERALL ECONOMY

地区生产总值(亿元)
Gross Domestic Product (100 million yuan)

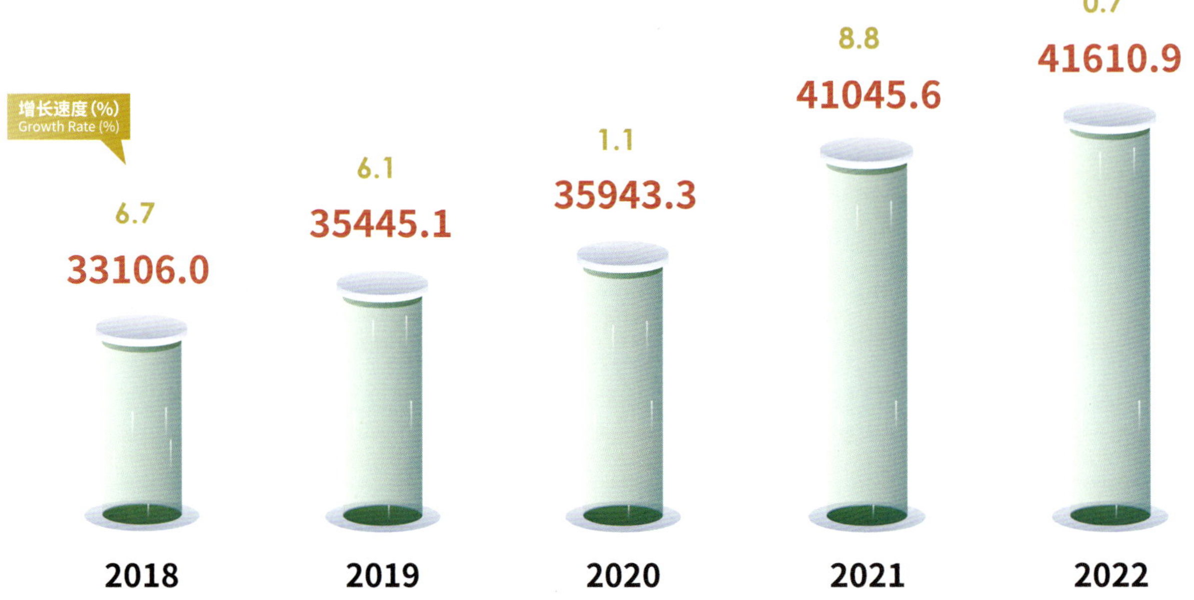

人均地区生产总值(元)
Per Capita Gross Domestic Product (yuan)

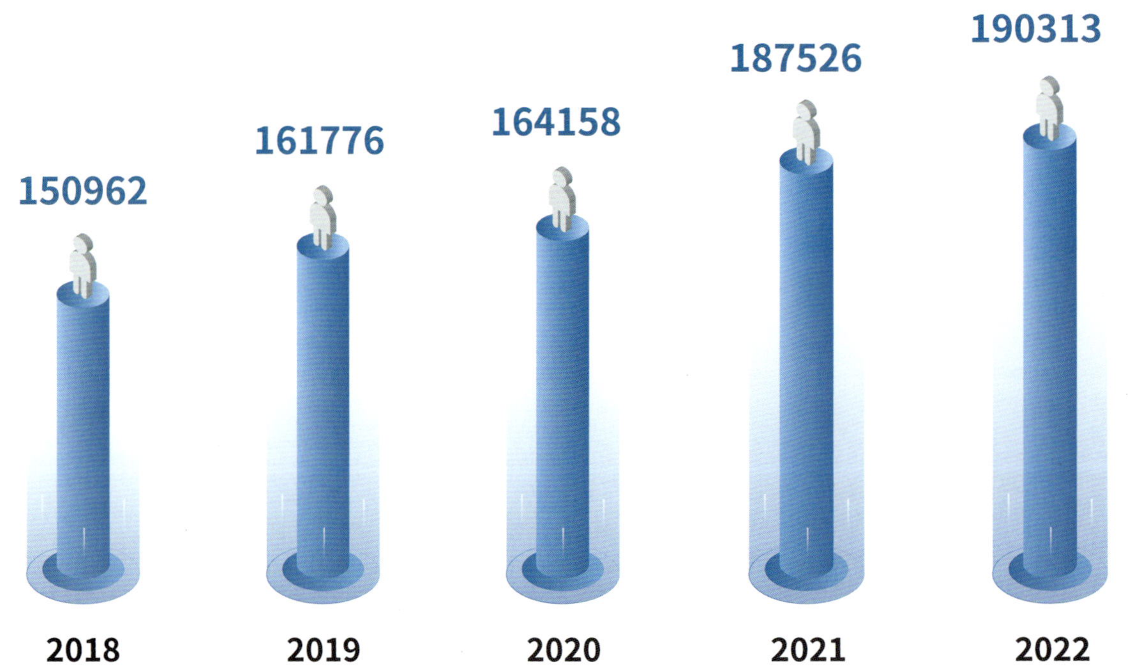

一般公共预算收入(亿元)
General Public Budget Revenue (100 million yuan)

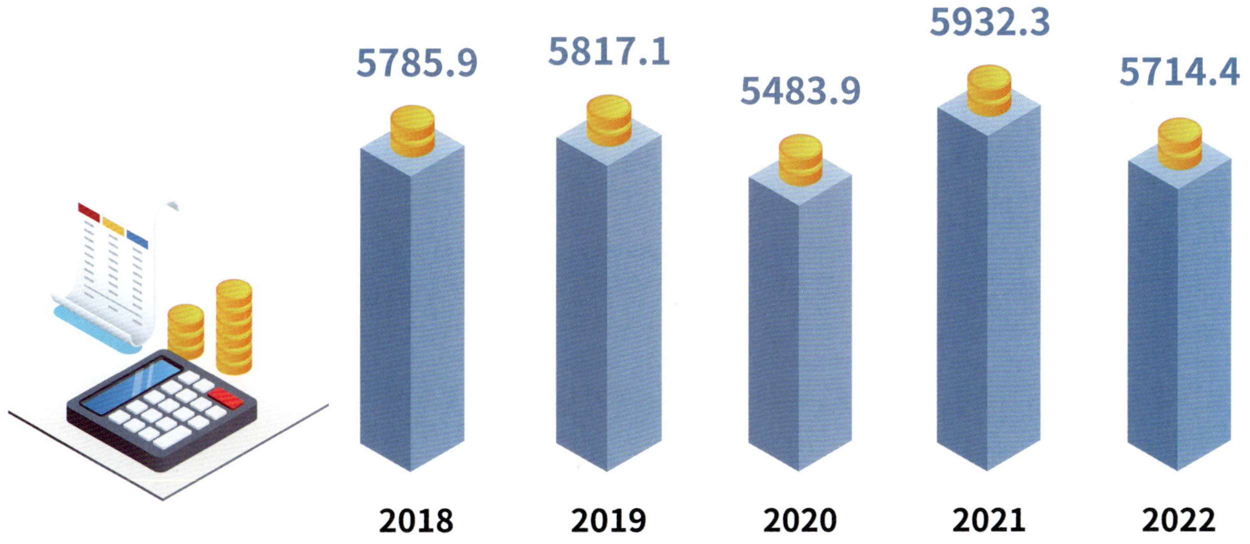

一般公共预算支出(亿元)
General Public Budget Expenditure (100 million yuan)

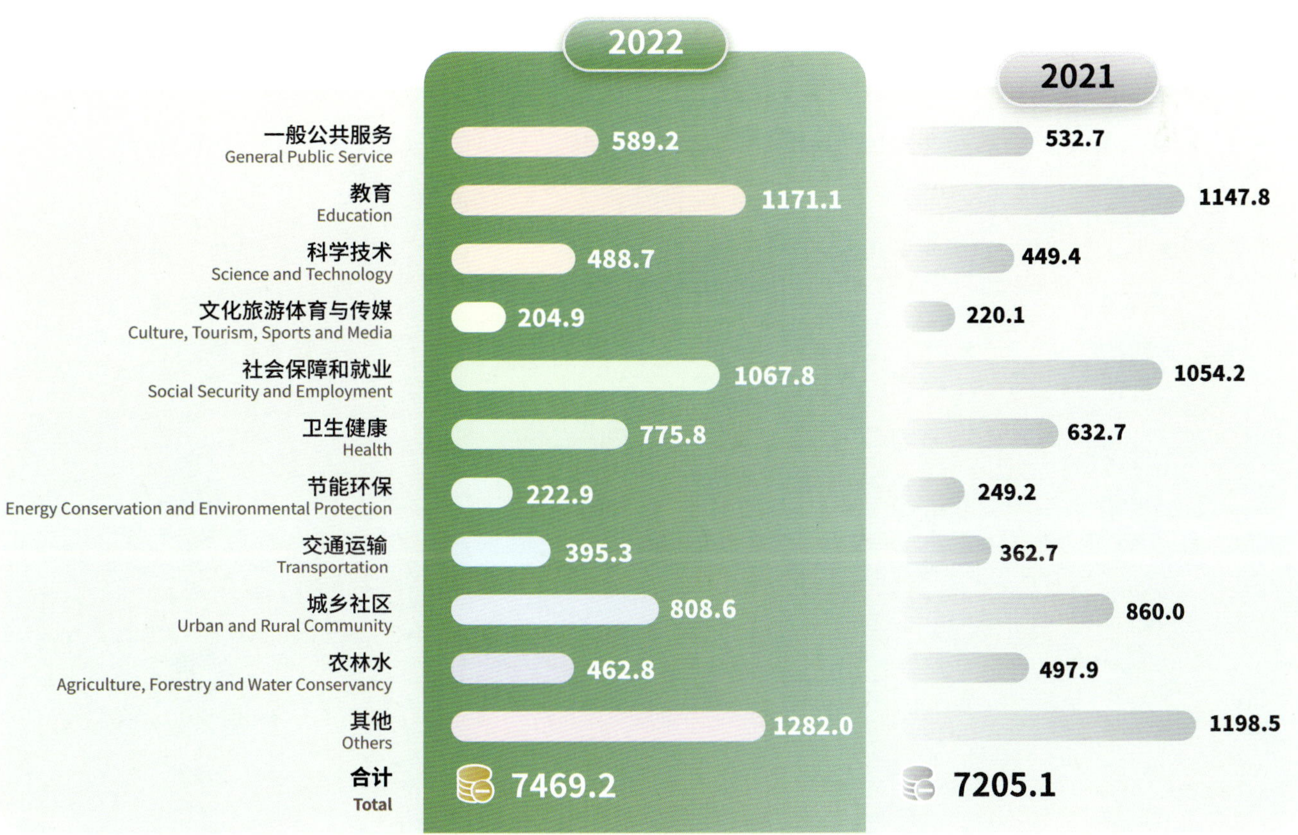

人口与就业
POPULATION AND EMPLOYMENT

常住人口(万人)
Permanent Population (10000 persons)

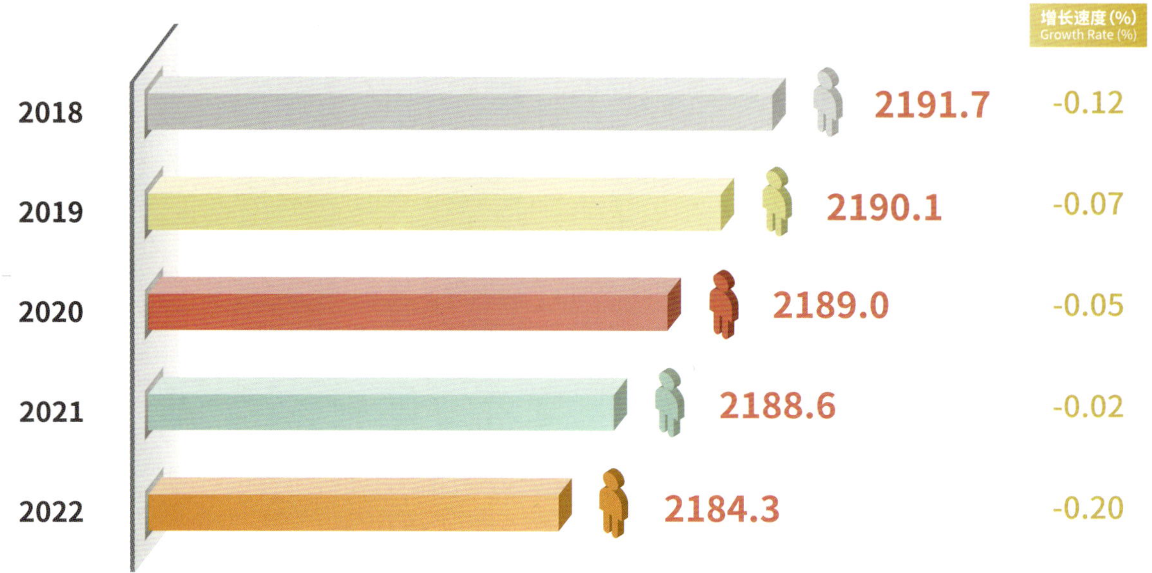

2022年常住人口分布(万人)
Distribution of Permanent Population in 2022 (10000 persons)

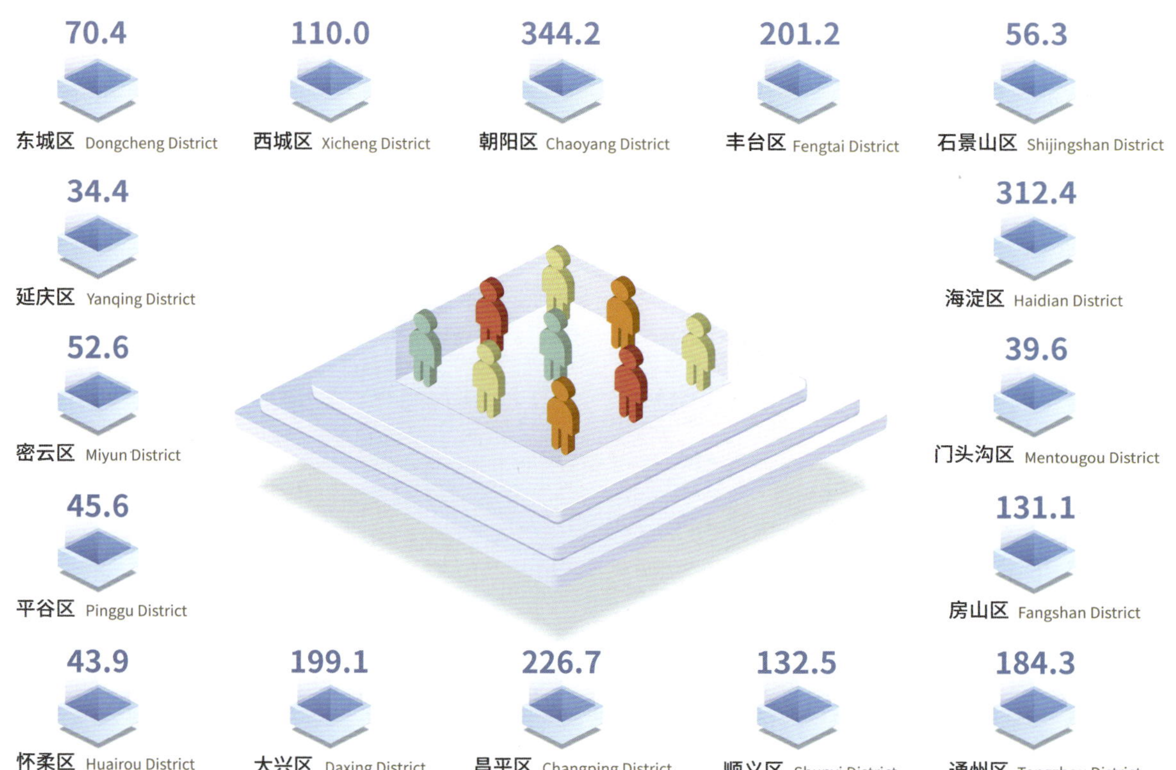

法人单位从业人员年末人数(万人)
Year-end Employed Persons in Legal Entities(10000 persons)

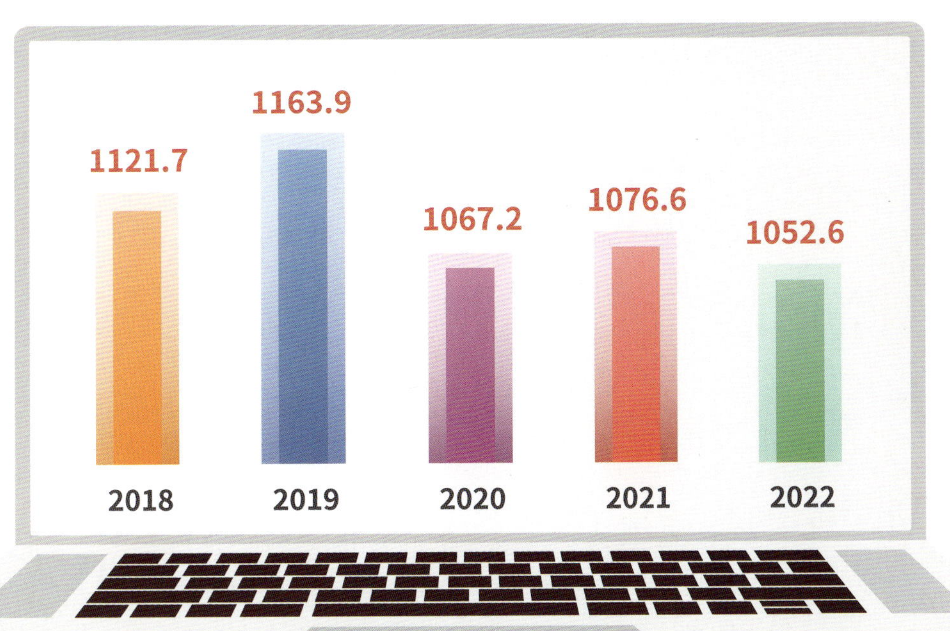

法人单位从业人员平均工资(元)
Average Wages of Employed Persons in Legal Entities(yuan)

价格指数
PRICE INDEX

价格指数（上年=100）
Price Index (preceding year=100)

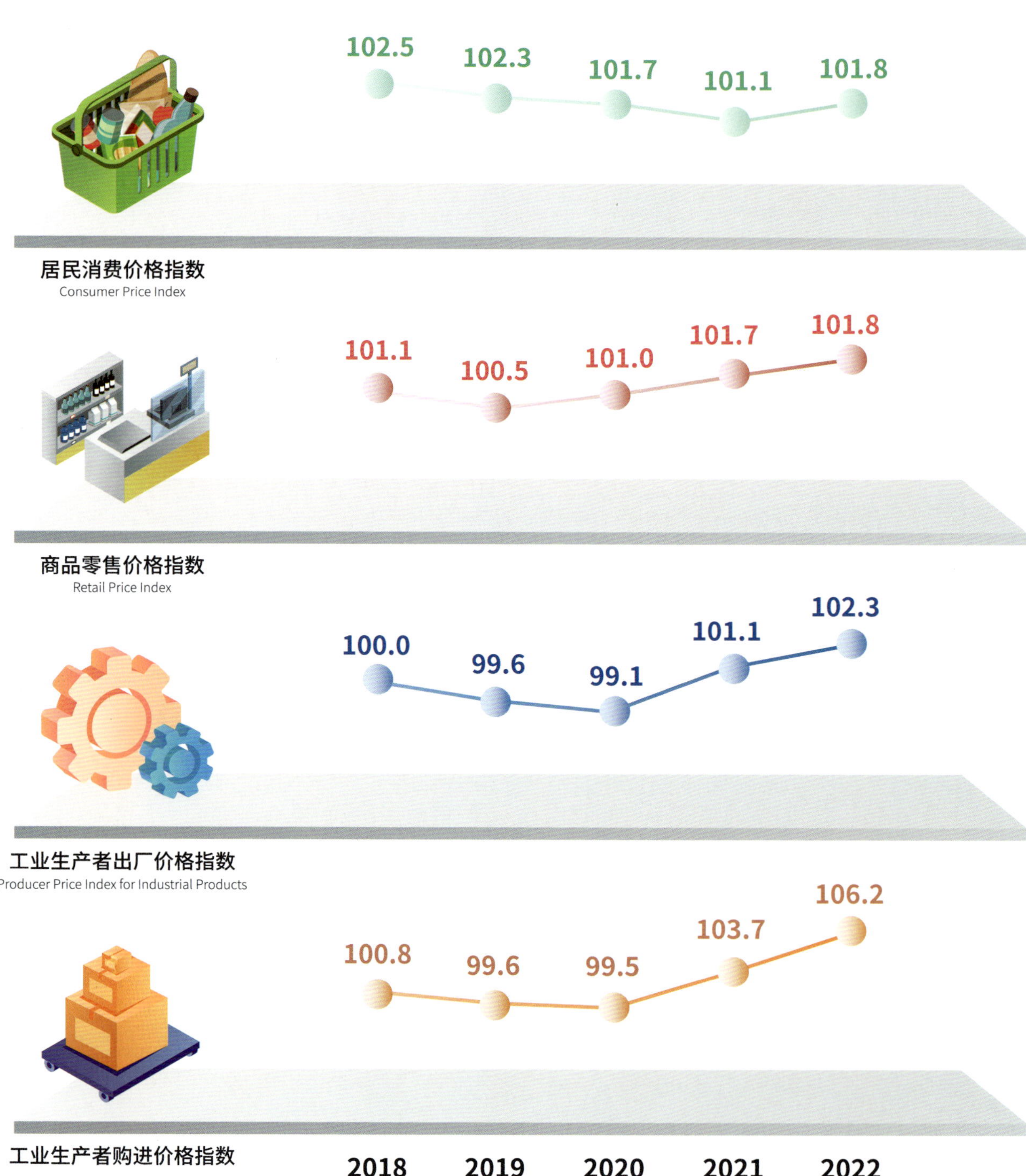

人民生活
PEOPLE'S LIVING CONDITIONS

居民人均可支配收入(元)
Per Capita Disposable Income of Residents (yuan)

城镇居民
Urban Residents

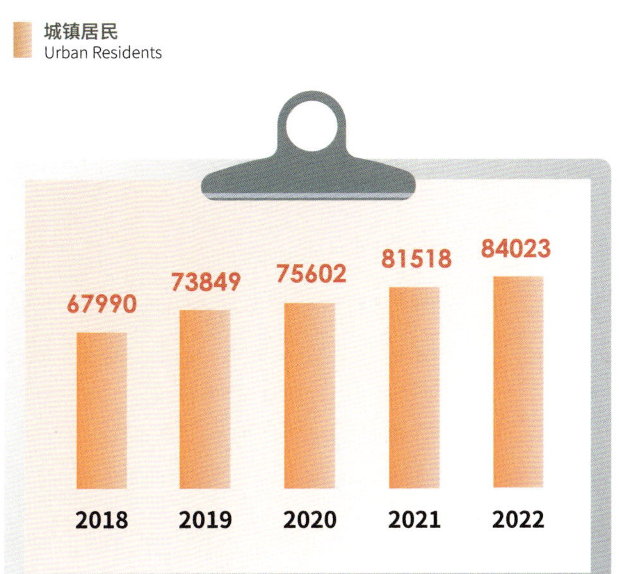

农村居民
Rural Residents

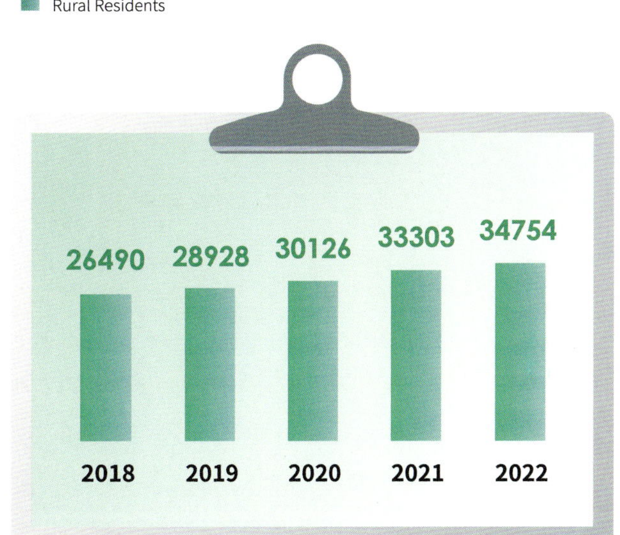

居民人均消费支出(元)
Per Capita Consumption Expenditure of Residents (yuan)

城镇居民
Urban Residents

农村居民
Rural Residents

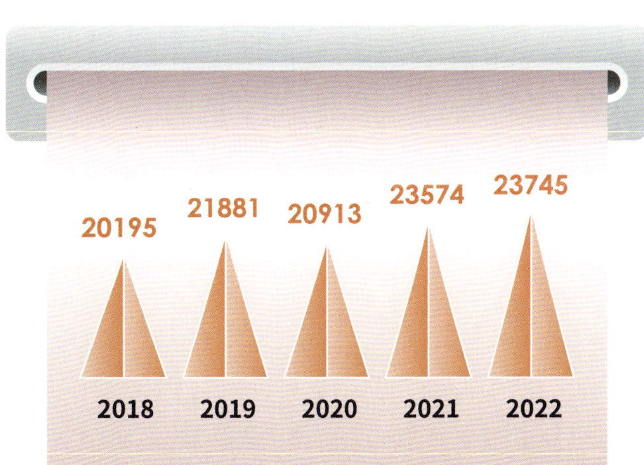

产业发展
INDUSTRY DEVELOPMENT

三次产业增加值结构(%)
Structure of Added Value of Three Industries (%)

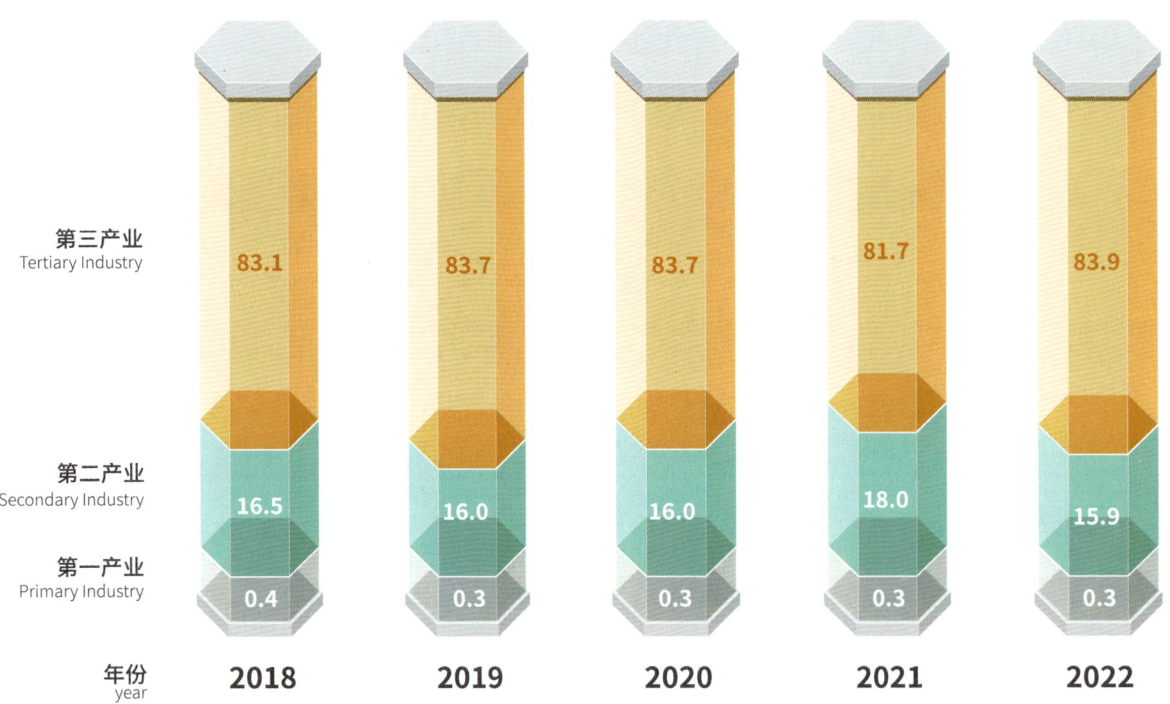

2022年数字经济和部分新兴产业增加值(亿元)
Added Value of Digital Economy and Some Emerging Industries (100 million yuan)

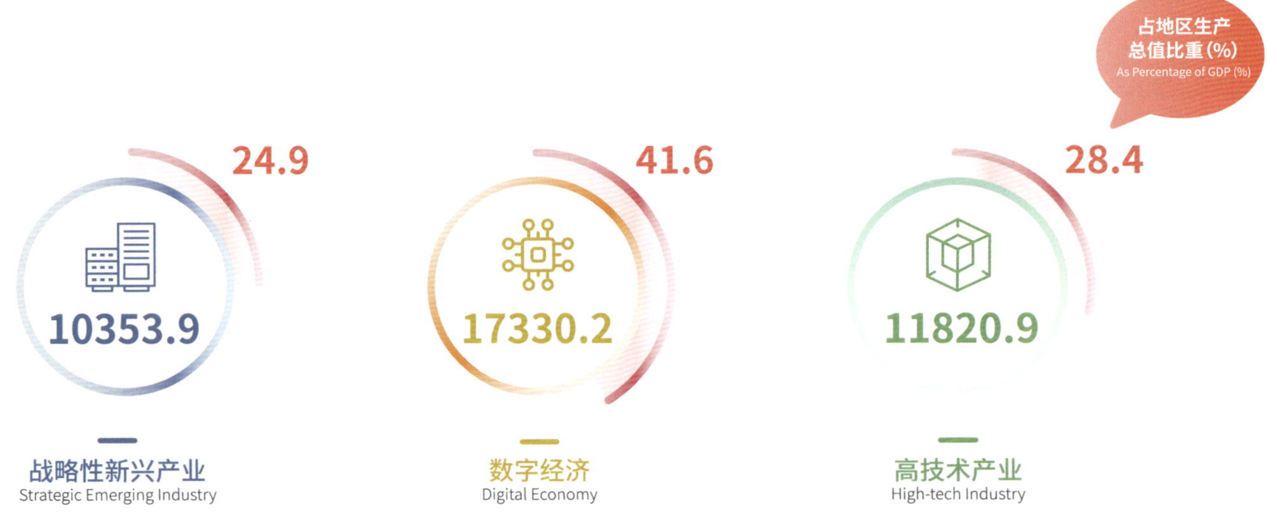

投资与消费
INVESTMENT AND CONSUMPTION

固定资产投资增长速度(%)
Growth Rate of Investment In Fixed Assets (%)

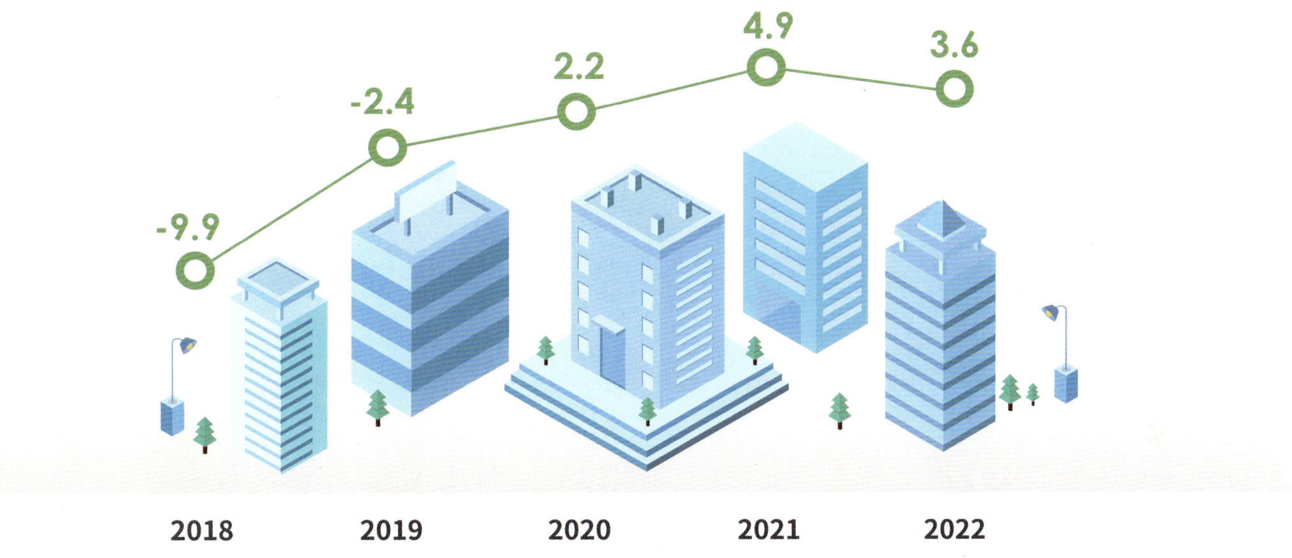

注:2018年为全社会口径,自2019年起为不含农户口径。
Note:In 2018,the data on fixed asset investment were those of full coverage.Since 2019, the data were those that excluding rural households.

社会消费品零售总额(亿元)
Total Retail Sales of Consumer Goods (100 million yuan)

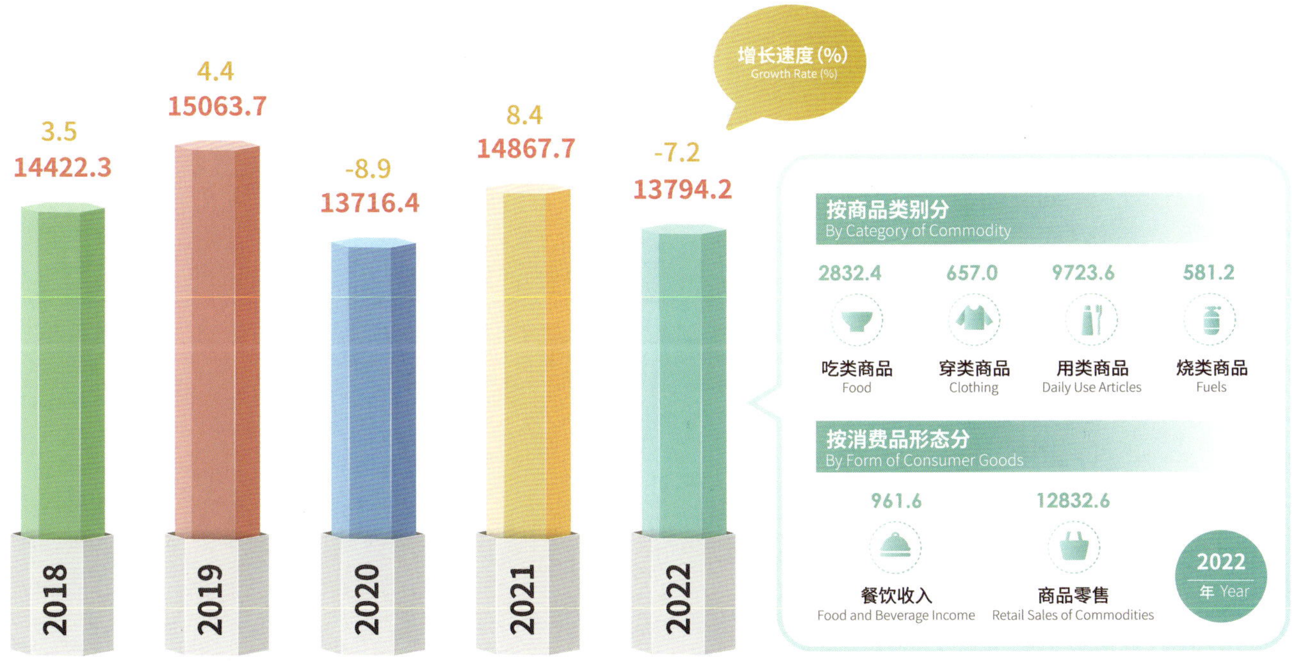

对外开放

OPENING TO THE OUTSIDE WORLD

进出口总值（亿元）
Total Value of Imports and Exports (100 million yuan)

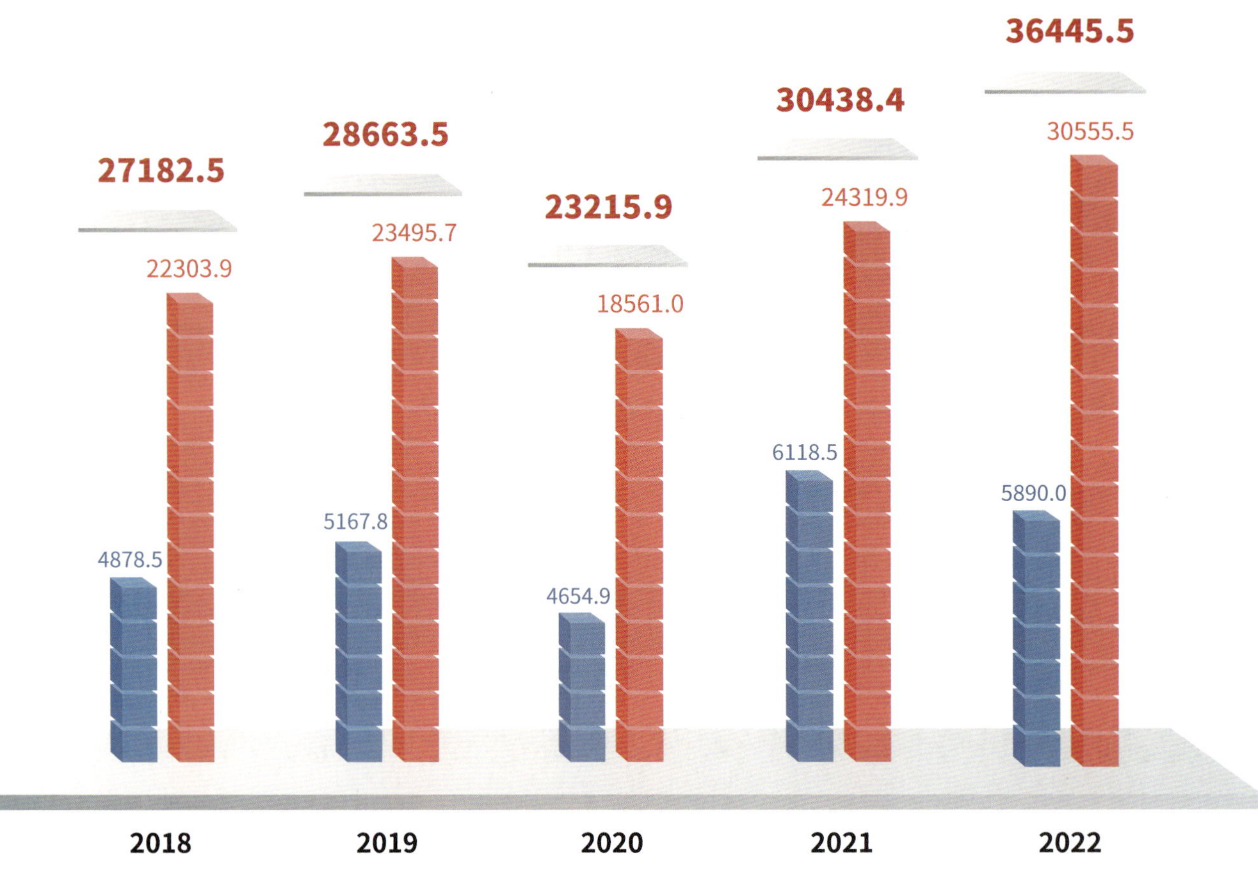

实际利用外商直接投资额(亿美元)
Actual Use of Foreign Direct Investment (USD 100 million)

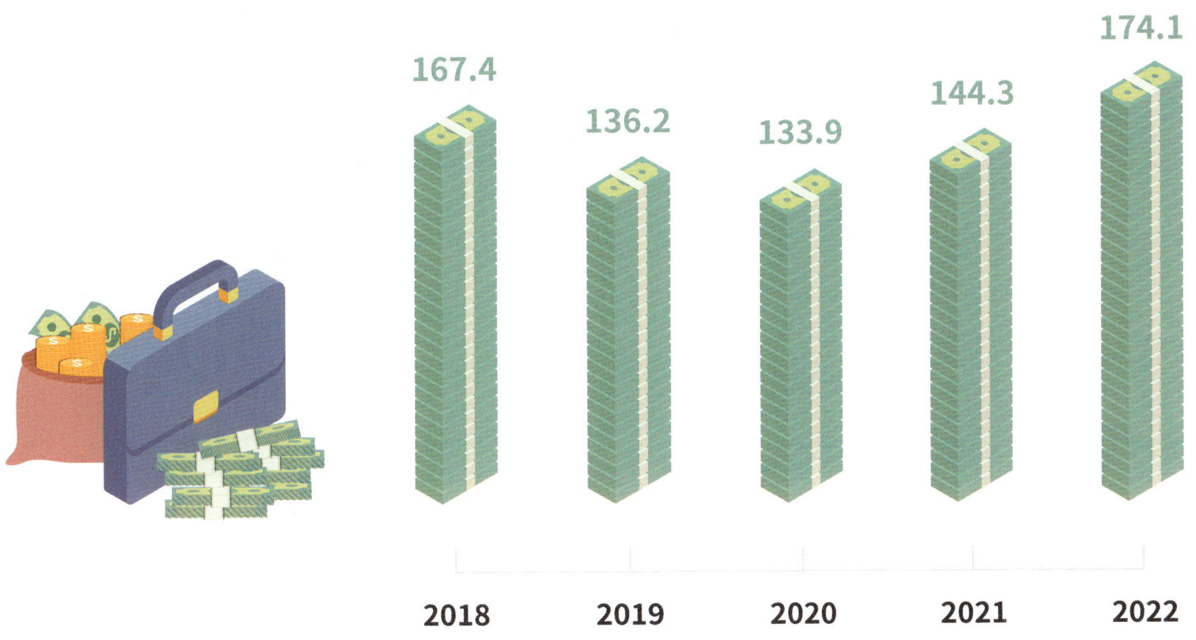

对外直接投资额(亿美元)
Amount of Outward Direct Investment (USD 100 million)

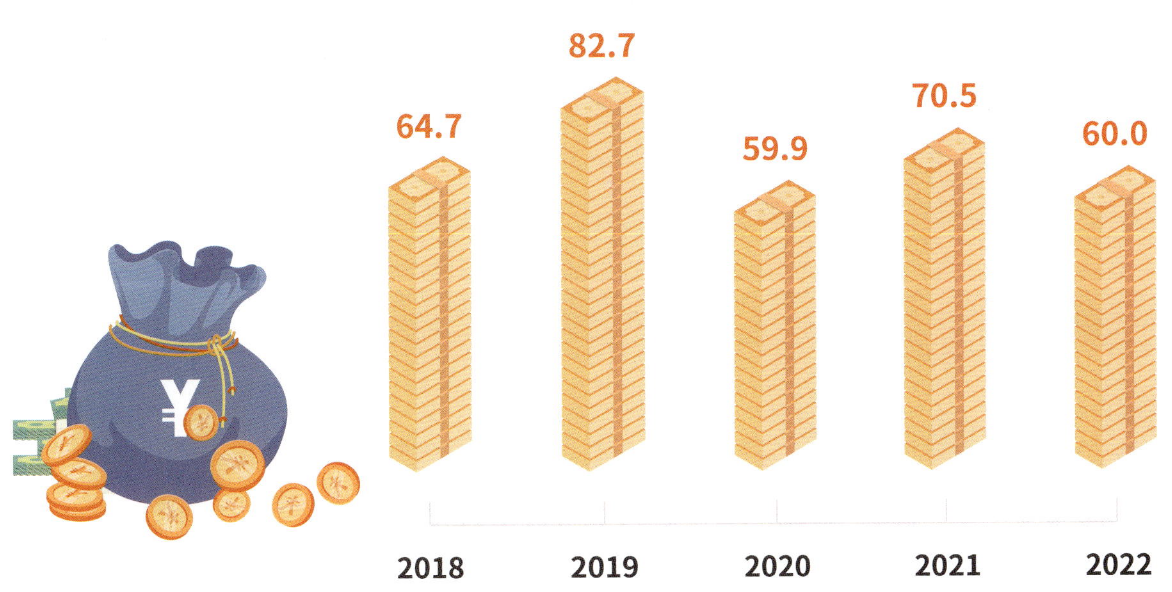

资源与环境

RESOURCE AND ENVIRONMENT

万元地区生产总值能耗（吨标准煤）
Energy Consumption per 10000 yuan of GDP (ton of SCE)

万元地区生产总值水耗(立方米)
Water Consumption per 10000 yuan of GDP (cu.m)

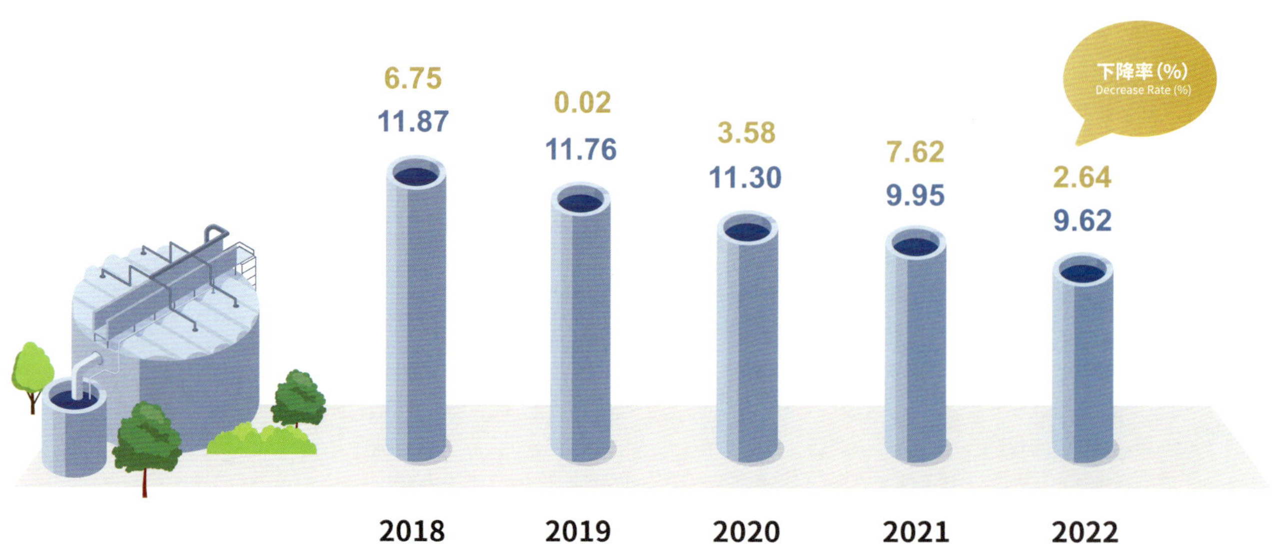

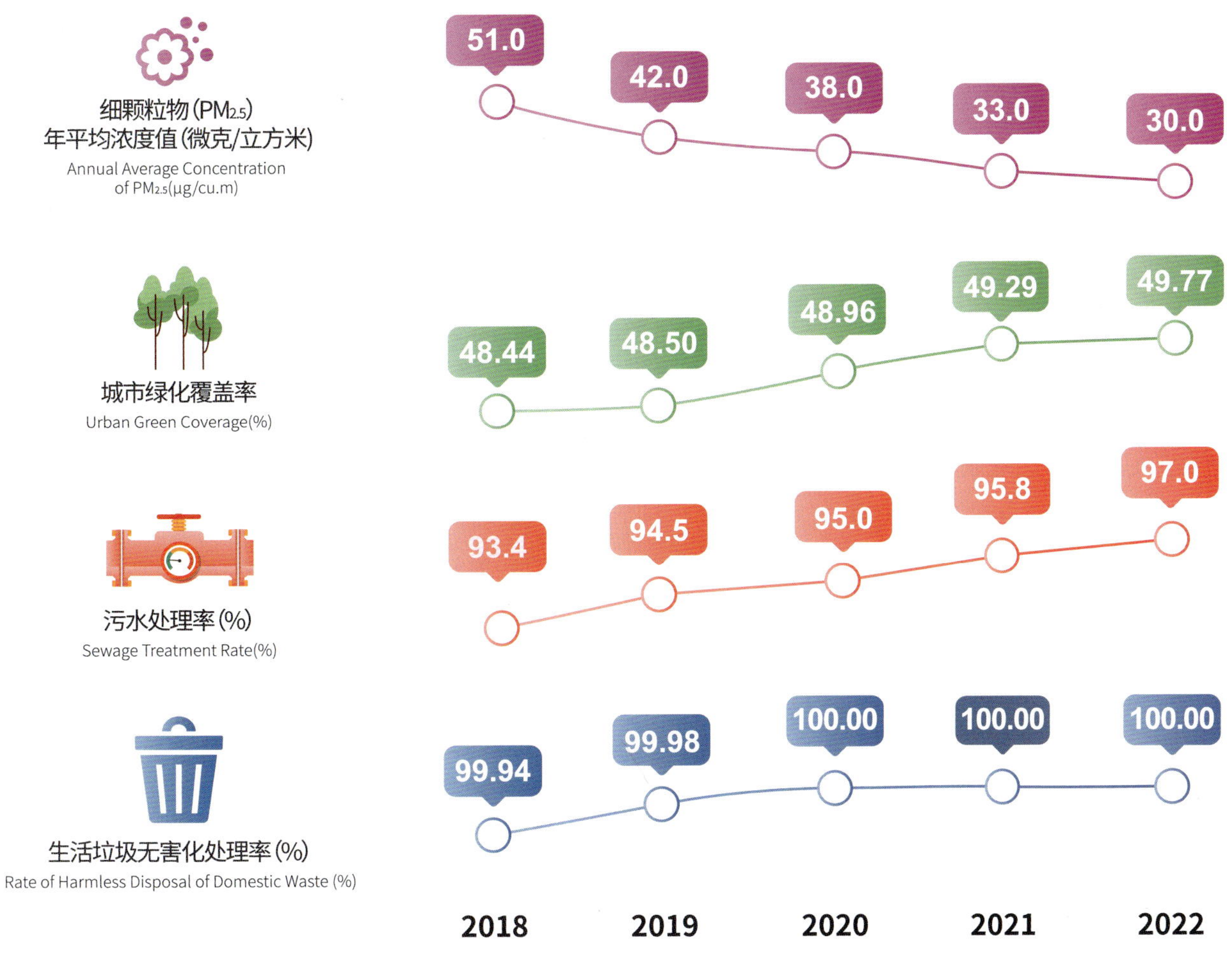
细颗粒物(PM2.5)
年平均浓度值(微克/立方米)
Annual Average Concentration
of PM2.5(μg/cu.m)
51.0
42.0
38.0
33.0
30.0
城市绿化覆盖率
Urban Green Coverage(%)
48.44
48.50
48.96
49.29
49.77
污水处理率(%)
Sewage Treatment Rate(%)
93.4
94.5
95.0
95.8
97.0
生活垃圾无害化处理率(%)
Rate of Harmless Disposal of Domestic Waste (%)
99.94
99.98
100.00
100.00
100.00
2018
2019
2020
2021
2022

科技创新

TECHNOLOGY INNOVATION

研究与试验发展(R&D)经费内部支出(亿元)

Internal R&D Expenditures (100 million yuan)

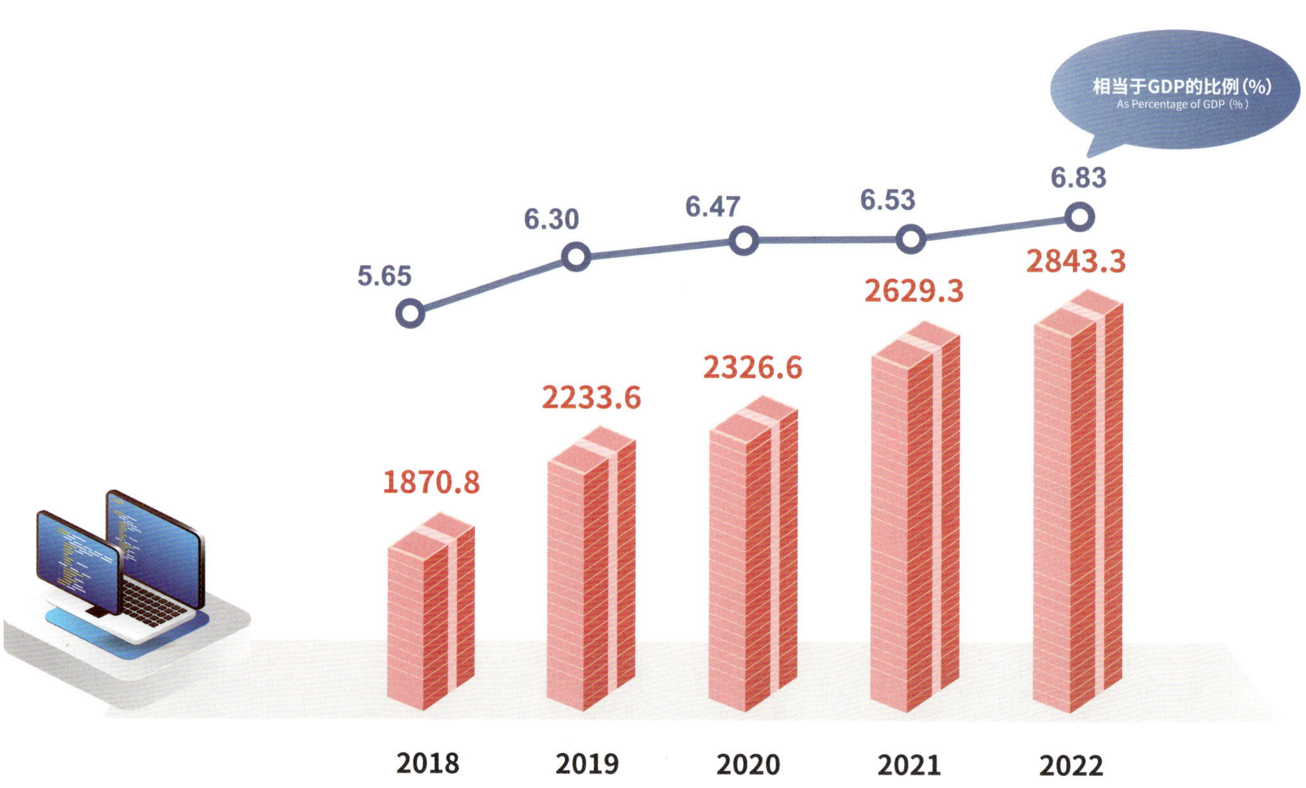

技术合同成交总额(亿元)

Total Volume of Transaction of Technical Contracts (100 million yuan)

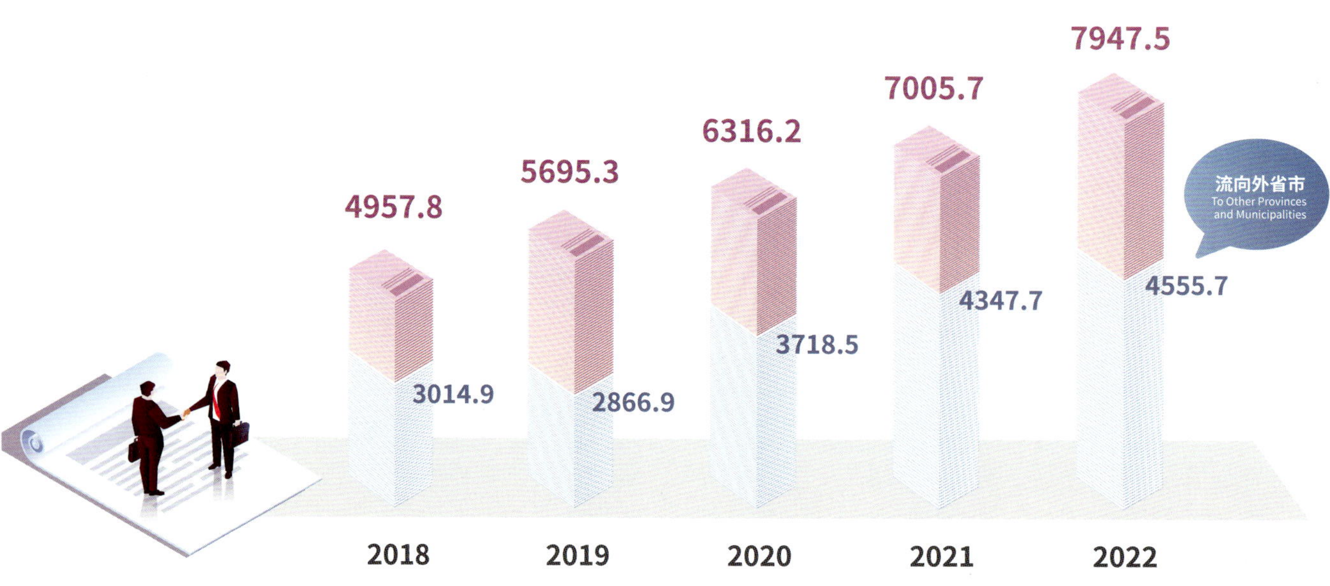

专利和发明专利授权量（件）
Patent and Invention Patent Granted (unit)

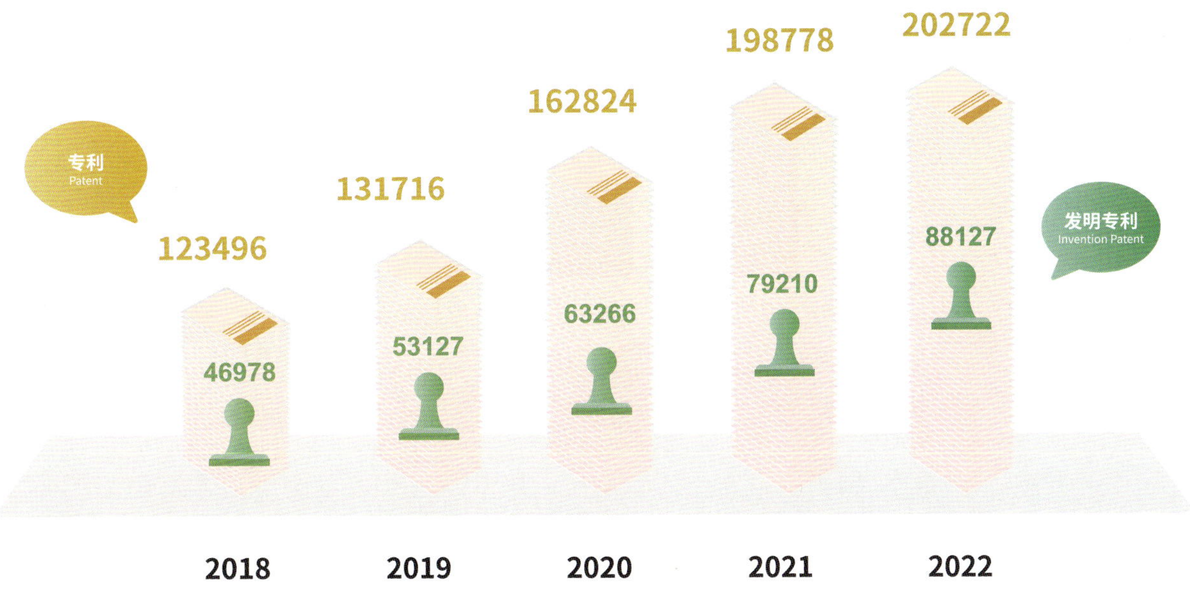

中关村国家自主创新示范区企业收入（亿元）
Revenue of Enterprise in Zhongguancun National Independent Innovation Demonstration Zone (100 million yuan)

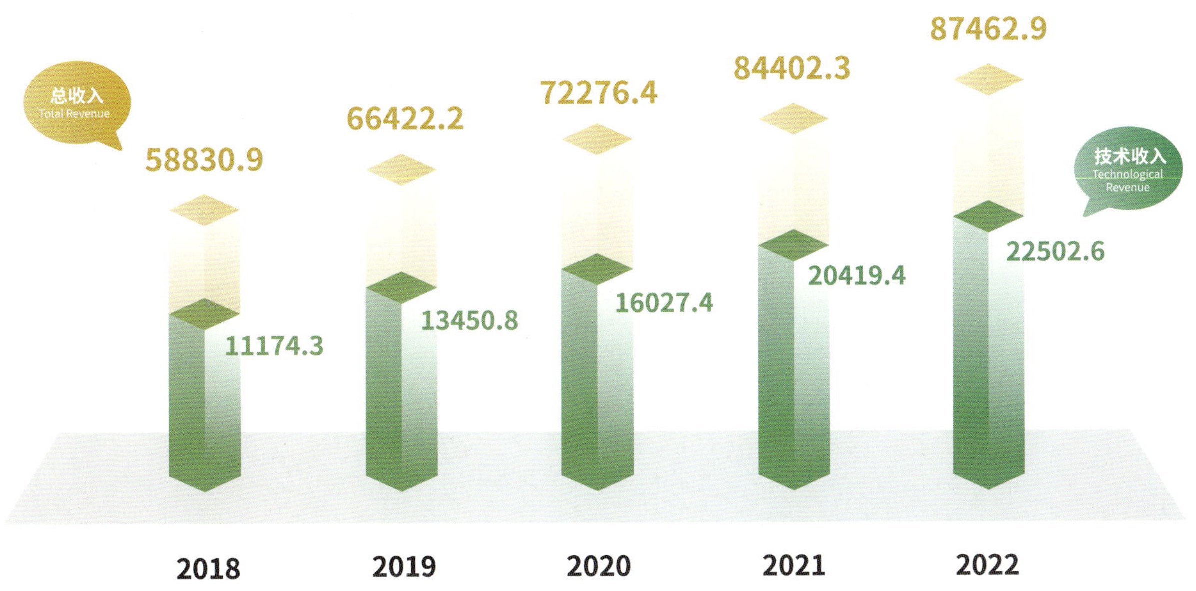

公共服务
PUBLIC SERVICE

教育
Education

学校数(个)
Number of Schools (unit)

在校生数(万人)
Enrolled Students in Schools (10000 persons)

专任教师数(万人)
Full-Time Teachers (10000 persons)

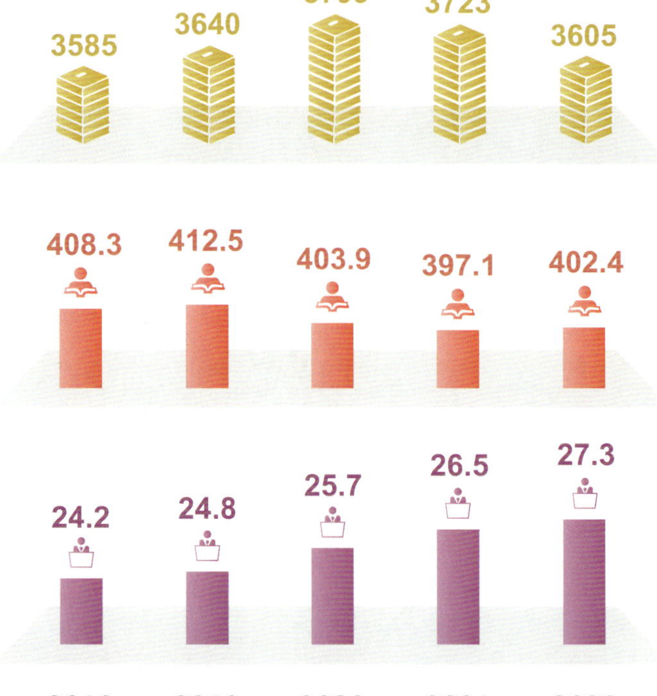

卫生
Health

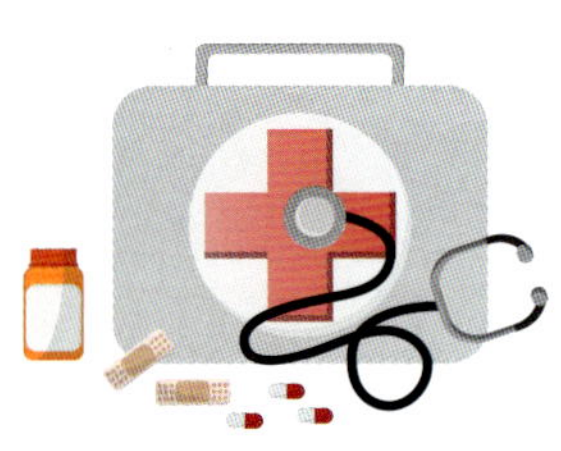

每千常住人口执业(助理)医师数(人)
Number of Certified (Assistant) Doctors per 1000 Permanent Population (person)

每千常住人口医院床位数(张)
Number of Ward Beds per 1000 Permanent Population (unit)

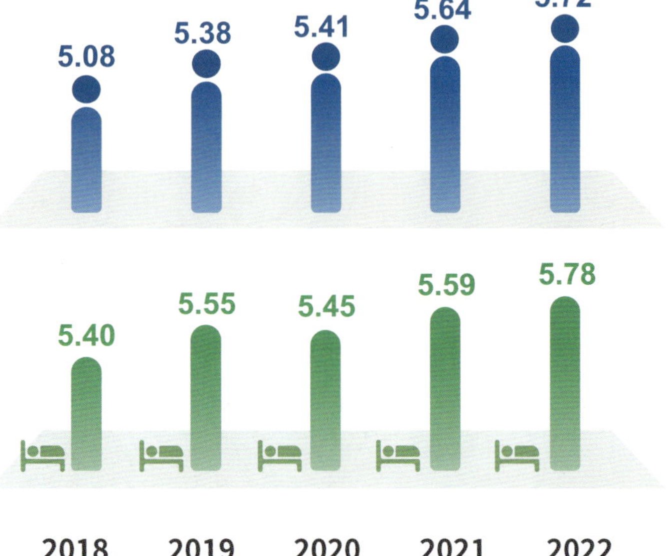

文化
Culture

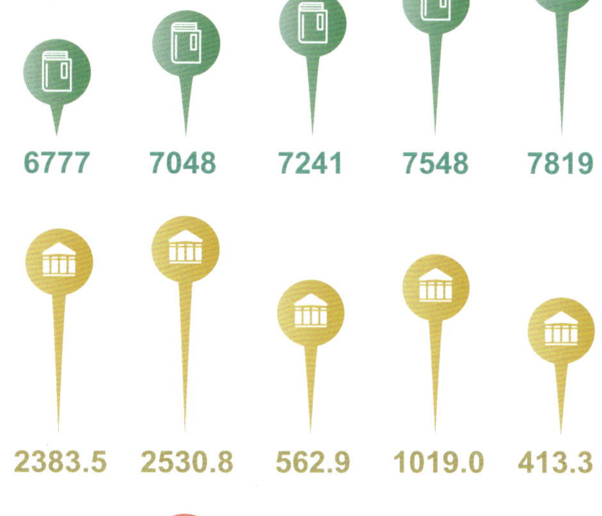

公共图书馆总藏书（万册、万件）
Total Collections of Public Libraries (10000 volumes)

文物局系统内博物馆及文物保护管理机构参观人次（万人次）
Visitors of Museums and Other Cultural Relic Protection and Administration Organizations under the Municipal Administration of Cultural Heritage (10000 person-times)

电影放映场次（万场次）
Show Times of Films (10000 Times)

交通
Traffic

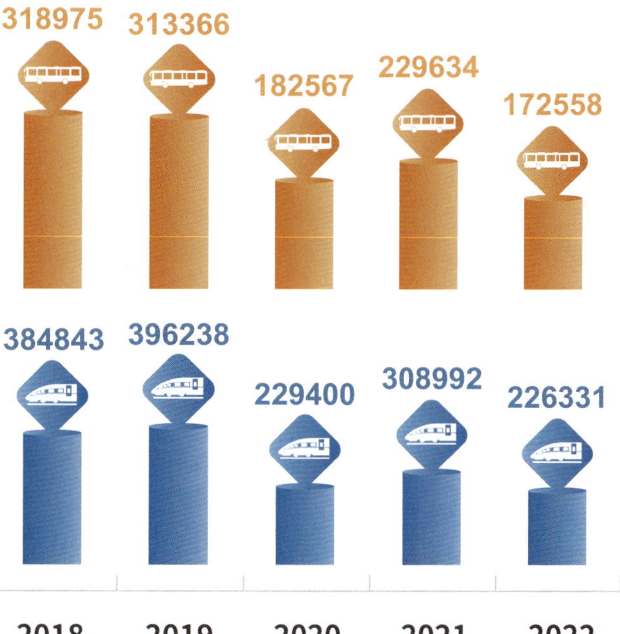

公共汽电车客运量（万人次）
Passenger Traffic of Buses and Trolley Buses (10000 person-times)

城市轨道交通客运量（万人次）
Passenger Traffic of Urban Rail Transit (10000 person-times)

社会保障
SOCIAL SERVICE

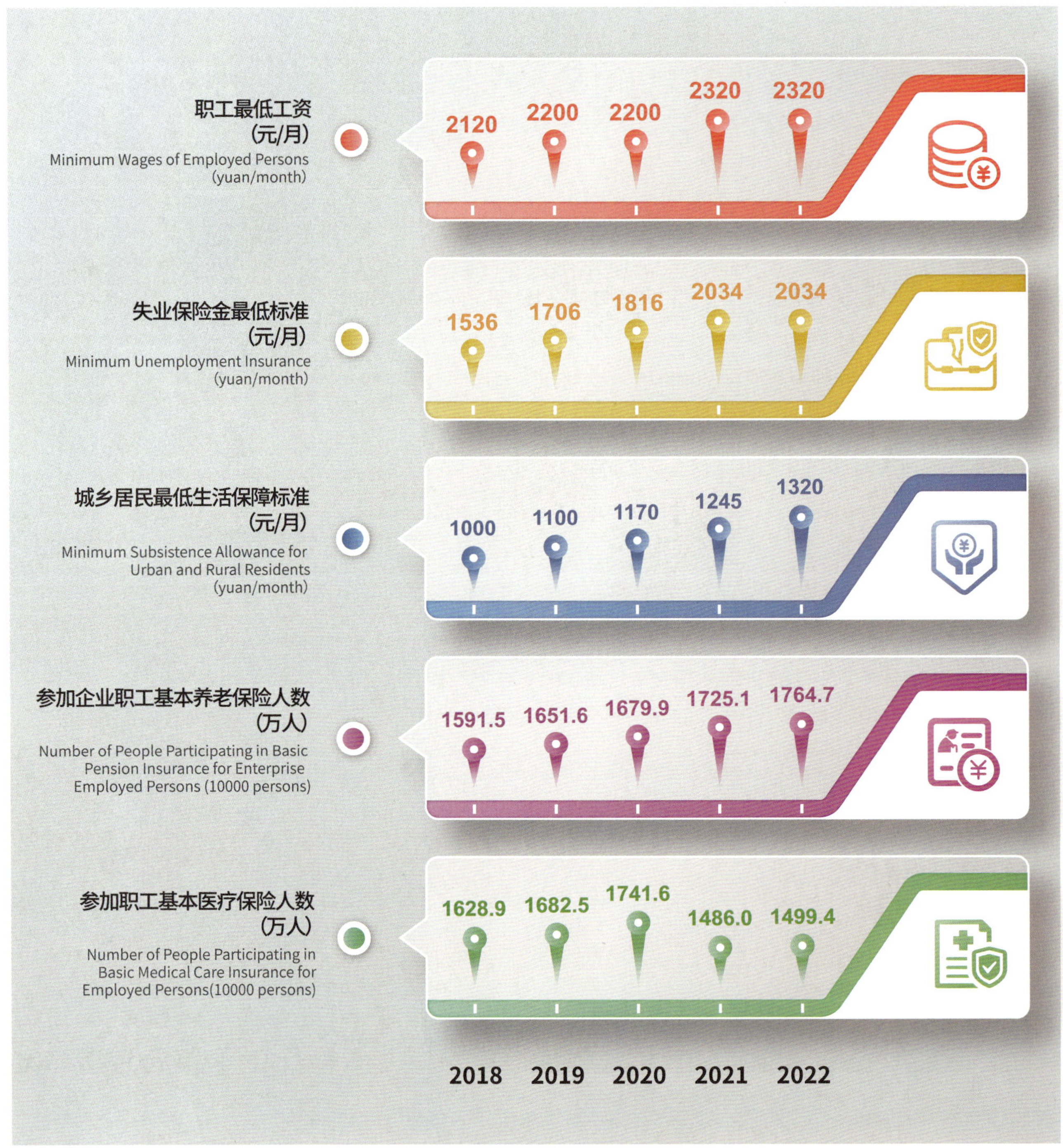

注：自2021年9月起，“参加职工基本医疗保险人数”统计口径进行调整，去除6个月及以上未缴费人员，按调整后口径计算，2020年参加职工基本医疗保险人数为1450.7万人。

Note:Since September 2021, the statistical coverage of the “number of people participating in basic medical care insurance for employed persons”was adjusted and removed those who failed to make payment for 6 months or more. Calculated according to the adjusted coverage, the number of people participating in basic medical care insurance for employed persons totaled 14.507 million in 2020.

《北京统计年鉴 2023》
编辑委员会及编辑工作人员

编 委 会

编辑工作人员

使用指南

《北京统计年鉴》是一部按年连续出版的大型统计资料书，通过大量的统计数据记录北京市一年来经济社会发展变化情况，是国内外各界人士了解北京、认识北京的重要资料工具书。

一、关于框架结构

（一）总体结构

本年鉴整体框架保持稳定，彩页部分以图文并茂的形式反映北京市主要经济社会指标发展变化趋势；统计表是年鉴的主体内容，主要包括综合，国民经济核算，人口与就业，价格指数，人民生活，财政与税收，能源、资源和环境，城市公用事业，固定资产投资和房地产开发，对外经济贸易，农业及农村经济，工业，建筑业，第三产业，交通运输邮电业，批发和零售业、住宿和餐饮业，旅游业，金融业，科技，教育，卫生及社会服务，文化和体育，公共管理、社会保障和社会组织，开发区等 24 个章节，从多领域、多行业反映北京市经济和社会发展情况。

（二）章节结构

章节内结构：每一章节由简要说明、统计表和主要统计指标解释三部分组成。其中，简要说明在每一章节首页，主要介绍该章节的主要内容、统计范围、指标口径和历史数据调整方法；统计指标解释在每章节尾页，主要对本章节内所涉及的主要指标、计算方法等做简要解释。

统计表排列：每一章节从反映该领域主要情况出发编排统计表内容。统计表的排列顺序一般先是主要指标历史数据表，后为当年数据表。

二、关于使用方法

（一）年份

书名中标注的年份为出版年份，年鉴中最新数据为上一年数据。例如，《北京统计年鉴 2023》表示该年鉴为 2023 年出版，年鉴中最新数据年份截至 2022 年。

统计表名中的“年份”主要有三种标识方法，分别代表三种含义：一是“表格名称（****-****年）”表示表内所列数据是包含了这两个年份之间的各年资料；二是统计表名中未显示年份，表示表内所列数据为当年和上年两年数据；三是“表格名称（****年）”表示表内所列数据仅为某一年资料。

（二）符号

统计表中常见符号如下：

：表示总计中的其中项；有“#”号的分组指标表示总计的部分项目，无“#”号的分组指标则表示其中项之和等于总计。

‖ ：宾栏中的“‖”为分组符号，代表某个指标存在几种分组数据。

… ：表示该数据不足该表最小计量单位数。

空格：表示该项指标数据不详或没有数据。

*** ：在可能根据数据识别或者推断单个统计调查对象身份时，予以屏蔽处理，以“***”表示。

（三）数据

1.本年鉴各章节均包含历史数据表和当年数据表两部分。历史数据表中的历史数据原则上可以连续使用，部分历史数据有调整的，以最新出版的年鉴为准，使用时需留意简要说明、表下注释中对制度方法、口径范围等变化情况的说明。当年数据表中如指标的口径范围、计算方法以及与上年度数据相比变化较大时，会在表下注释中进行说明。

2.与 2022 年版统计年鉴相比，主要做了如下修订：在综合章节中，增加“城镇调查失业率”有关数据；在旅游业章节中增加重点住宿业有关数据；在文化和体育章节中，增加“馆藏电子档案”数据；在公共管理、社会保障和社会组织章节中，增加“公安机关治安案件查处情况”；对国民经济核算、城市公共事业、工业、交通运输邮电业、金融业、科技、教育、开发区等部分章节内容进行了调整。

（四）电子光盘

《北京统计年鉴》配有电子光盘，包括中文和英文两种语言的版本，辅助用户对数据进行加工处理。

（五）本年鉴中部分数据合计数或相对数由于单位取舍不同而产生的计算误差，均未作机械调整。

USER GUIDE

Beijing Statistical Yearbook is a large statistical book published continuously on a chronological basis. With a great deal of statistical data, this Yearbook gives a reflection of the economic and social development and changes in Beijing over the past year. It serves as an important reference book for domestic and foreign personnel in all circles to understand and know Beijing.

I. Framework Structure

(I) Overall Structure

The overall structure of *Beijing Statistical Yearbook* remains stable. In color pages, the development and changing trends of main economic and social indicators of Beijing have been presented with both illustration and pictures; statistical tables are the main part of this Yearbook, mainly including 24 chapters, i.e. General Survey; National Accounts; Population and Employment; Price Index; People's Living Conditions; Government Finance and Taxation; Energy, Resources and Environment; Public Utilities; Investment in Fixed Assets and Real Estate Development; Foreign Economic Relations and Trade; Agriculture and Rural Economy; Industry; Construction; Tertiary Industry; Transport, Post and Telecommunication Services; Wholesale and Retail Trade, Accommodation and Restaurants; Tourism; Finance; Science and Technology; Education; Health and Social Services; Culture and Sports; Public Management, Social Security and Social Organization; and Development Zones, reflecting the economic and social development situation across the city through multiple fields and industries.

(II) Structure of Chapters

Internal structure of chapters in this Yearbook: Each chapter is composed of the Brief Introduction, Statistical Tables and Explanatory Notes to Main Statistical Indicators. Thereinto, Brief Introduction appears on the first page of each chapter, mainly introducing the main content, statistical scope, indicator standards, method of adjustment to historical data in each chapter; Explanatory Notes to Statistical Indicators come on the last page of each chapter, mainly giving a brief explanation to the main indicators and calculation method, etc. involved in the chapter.

Arrangement of statistical tables: In each chapter, statistical tables are arranged for the purpose of reflecting the main conditions in the field. Generally speaking, main indicators historical data tables come before current year data tables.

II. How to Use

(I) Years

The year indicated in the title of the book is the year of publication. The latest data indicated in this Yearbook are data in the previous years. For example, this book is titled *2023 Beijing Statistical Yearbook*, which means it will be published in 2023 while the latest data in the book is by the end of 2022.

"Years" in the statistical tables are marked in three ways, each indicating a different meaning. Firstly, the statistical table is named "****** (AAAA- BBBB)", which refers to that the data listed in the table are those from the year of AAAA to BBBB; Secondly, the statistical table contains no years, indicating that the data listed in the table are those of current year and last year; Thirdly, the statistical table is named "****** (AAAA)", indicating that the data listed in the table are those of the year of AAAA.

(II) Symbols

Symbols in statistical tables include:

#: means that the item is included in the total. Grouped indicators marked with "#" are part of the total, while those without "#" mean that sum of included items equals to the total.

||: grouping symbol, means that there are multiple ways of grouping the indicators.

…: means that the figure is less than the minimum measurement unit of the table.

Blank: means that the figure is unknown or unavailable.

: When it is possible to identify or infer the identity of the individual statistical respondent based on the data, it shall be shielded and indicated with "".

(III) Data

1. Each chapter in this Yearbook consists of two parts: historical data tables and current year data tables. In principle, historical data that are shown in the historical data tables can be used continuously; for some historical data that have been adjusted, please refer to the latest yearbook; When using the data, it is necessary to refer to the Brief Introduction and the explanations on the change in method system, standards and scope in the Notes under the statistical tables. In the current year data tables, if the standards and scope, calculation method for the corresponding indicators, and certain data greatly differ from that of the previous year, they shall be explained in the Notes under the statistical tables.

2. Compared with *Beijing Statistical Yearbook 2022*, the following major revisions have been made: data on "surveyed unemployment rate in urban area" are added in the chapter of General Survey; data on key accommodation services are added in the chapter of Tourism; data on "electronic archives" are added in the chapter of Culture and Sports; "investigation and handling of public security cases by public security organs" are added in the chapter of Public Administration, Social Security and Social Organization; and adjustments have been made to the content of some chapters including the national accounts, public utilities, industry, transport, post and telecommunication services, finance, science and technology, education, and development zones.

(IV) Electronic CD-ROM

Beijing Statistical Yearbook is provided with a CD-ROM, which contains Chinese and English versions of this Yearbook. The CD-ROM helps users in working with and processing the data.

(V) The sum of some statistics or some relative numbers in this Yearbook might have certain calculation errors because of the choice of different units of measurement. All the statistics have not undergone mechanical adjustment.

目　　录

Contents

一、综合
GENERAL SURVEY

二、国民经济核算
NATIONAL ACCOUNTS

三、人口与就业
POPULATION AND EMPLOYMENT

四、价格指数
PRICE INDEX

五、人民生活
PEOPLE'S LIVING CONDITIONS

六、财政与税收

GOVERNMENT FINANCE AND TAX REVENUES

七、能源、资源和环境
ENERGY, RESOURCES AND ENVIRONMENT

八、城市公用事业
PUBLIC UTILITIES

九、固定资产投资和房地产开发
INVESTMENT IN FIXED ASSETS AND REAL ESTATE DEVELOPMENT

十、对外经济贸易
FOREIGN ECONOMIC RELATIONS AND TRADE

十一、农业及农村经济
AGRICULTURE AND RURAL ECONOMY

十二、工业
INDUSTRY

十三、建筑业

CONSTRUCTION

十四、第三产业
TERTIARY INDUSTRY

十五、交通运输邮电业
TRANSPORT, POST AND TELECOMMUNICATION SERVICES

十六、批发和零售业、住宿和餐饮业
WHOLESALE AND RETAIL TRADE, ACCOMMODATION AND RESTAURANTS

十七、旅游业
TOURISM

十八、金融业
FINANCE

十九、科技
SCIENCE AND TECHNOLOGY

二十、教育
EDUCATION

二十一、卫生及社会服务
HEALTH AND SOCIAL SERVICES

二十二、文化和体育
CULTURE AND SPORTS

二十三、公共管理、社会保障和社会组织
PUBLIC MANAGEMENT, SOCIAL SECURITY AND SOCIAL ORGANIZATION

二十四、开发区
DEVELOPMENT ZONES

综 合
GENERAL SURVEY

简要说明

一、主要内容

本章资料包括北京市行政区划，全市社会经济发展主要指标以及“十四五”时期监测指标，法人及产业活动单位数，私营个体、非公经济、中小微型企业基本情况等。

二、有关统计标准的变化说明

（一）《国民经济行业分类》（GB/T 4754-2002）与《国民经济行业分类》（GB/T 4754-94）主要框架结构变化：

1.增加的门类：(1)信息传输、计算机服务和软件业；(2)租赁和商务服务业；(3)住宿和餐饮业；(4)水利、环境和公共设施管理业；(5)教育；(6)国际组织。

2.名称或范围进行调整的门类：(1)农、林、牧、渔业；(2)采矿业；(3)制造业；(4)交通运输、仓储和邮政业；(5)批发和零售业；(6)金融业；(7)科学研究、技术服务和地质勘查业；(8)居民服务和其他服务业；(9)卫生、社会保障和社会福利业；(10)文化、体育和娱乐业；(11)公共管理和社会组织。

3.取消的门类：(1)地质勘查、水利管理；(2)其他行业。

（二）《国民经济行业分类》（GB/T 4754-2011）与《国民经济行业分类》（GB/T 4754-2002）主要框架结构变化：

1.门类名称调整：(1)“电力、燃气及水的生产和供应业”更名为“电力、热力、燃气及水生产和供应业”；(2)“信息传输、计算机服务和软件业”更名为“信息传输、软件和信息技术服务业”；(3)“科学研究、技术服务和地质勘查业”更名为“科学研究和技术服务业”；(4)“居民服务和其他服务业”更名为“居民服务、修理和其他服务业”；(5)“卫生、社会保障和社会福利业”更名为“卫生和社会工作”；(6)“公共管理和社会组织”更名为“公共管理、社会保障和社会组织”。

2.门类顺序调整：(1)“批发和零售业”调至“交通运输、仓储和邮政业”之前；(2)“住宿和餐饮业”调至“交通运输、仓储和邮政业”之后。

3.门类范围调整：(1) 农、林、牧、渔业；(2) 制造业；(3) 交通运输、仓储和邮政业；(4) 信息传输、软件和信息技术服务业；(5) 金融业；(6) 租赁和商务服务业；(7) 科学研究和技术服务业；(8) 居民服务、修理和其他服务业；(9) 教育；(10) 卫生和社会工作；(11) 文化、体育和娱乐业；(12) 公共管理、社会保障和社会组织。

（三）《国民经济行业分类》（GB/T 4754-2017）与原（GB/T 4754-2011）门类名称和门类位次无调整。

Brief Introduction

I. Main Content

Statistics in this chapter mainly show the basic information of administrative divisions of Beijing, main indicators for social and economic development of the city, and monitoring indicators for the 14th Five-Year Plan, number of corporate and industrial entities, non-public economy, small-, medium- and micro-sized enterprises, etc.

II. Adjustment to Historical Statistics According to New Industrial Standards

(I) Changes to the main framework of the *Classification and Codes of National Economic Sectors* (GB/T 4754-2002) as compared with the previous version (GB/T 4754-94):

1. Sectors added: (1) information transmission, computer service and software; (2) renting and leasing activities and business services; (3) accommodation and restaurants; (4) management of water conservancy, environment and public facilities; (5) education; (6) international organizations.

2. Sectors with name or range changed: (1) agriculture, forestry,animal husbandry and fishery; (2) mining; (3) manufacturing; (4) transport, storage and post; (5) wholesale and retail trade; (6) finance; (7) scientific research, technical service, geological prospecting; (8) resident service and other service; (9) health, social security, and social welfare; (10) culture, sports and recreation; (11) public administration and social organizations.

3. Sectors cancelled: (1) geological prospecting, water conservancy management; (2) other sectors.

(II)Compared with the previous (GB/T 4754-2002) version, the *Classification of National Economic Sectors* (GB/T 4754-2011) mainly involves the following framework changes:

1. Changes to the name of categories: (1) The "electric power, gas and water production and supply" is renamed "production and supply of electricity, heating , gas and water"; (2) the "information transmission, computer service and software" is renamed "information transmission, software and information technology services"; (3) the "scientific research, technical service and geological prospecting" is renamed "scientific research and development, technical services"; (4) the "resident service and other service" is renamed "resident services, repair and other services"; (5) the "health, social security and social welfare" is renamed "health and social works"; (6) "public administration and social organization" is renamed "public administration, social security and social organizations".

2. Changes to the order of categories: (1) the "wholesale and retail trade" is put before the "transport, storage and post"; (2) the "accommodation and catering" is put after the "transport, storage and post".

3. Changes to the scope of categories: (1) agriculture, forestry,animal husbandry and fishery; (2) manufacturing; (3) transport, storage and post; (4) information transmission, software and information technology services; (5) finance; (6) leasing and business services; (7) scientific research and technical service; (8) resident services, repair and other services; (9) education; (10) health and social works; (11) culture, sports and entertainment; (12) public administration, social security and social organizations.

(III) Compared with the previous (GB/T 4754-2011) version, no adjustment has been made in the name of categories and the order of categories in the *Classification of National Economic Sectors* (GB/T 4754-2017) version.

1−1 行政区划(2022年)
ADMINISTRATIVE DIVISIONS (2022)

单位：个 (unit)

地 区	District	街道办事处 Sub-district	建制镇 Designated Town	建制乡 Designated Township	社区居委会 Community Neighborhood Committee	村民委员会 Villagers' Committee
全 市	**Total**	**165**	**143**	**35**	**3431**	**3783**
东 城 区	Dongcheng District	17			168	
西 城 区	Xicheng District	15			263	
朝 阳 区	Chaoyang District	24		19	544	144
丰 台 区	Fengtai District	24	2		352	56
石景山区	Shijingshan District	9			151	
海 淀 区	Haidian District	22	7		590	53
门头沟区	Mentougou District	4	9		122	178
房 山 区	Fangshan District	8	14	6	191	459
通 州 区	Tongzhou District	11	10	1	155	470
顺 义 区	Shunyi District	6	19		152	426
昌 平 区	Changping District	8	14		255	298
大 兴 区	Daxing District	8	14		254	437
怀 柔 区	Huairou District	2	12	2	36	284
平 谷 区	Pinggu District	2	14	2	49	272
密 云 区	Miyun District	2	17	1	96	330
延 庆 区	Yanqing District	3	11	4	53	376

资料来源：中共北京市委社会工作委员会北京市民政局。
Source: Social Work Committee of Beijing Municipal Committee of the Communist Party of China Beijing Municipal Civil Affairs Bureau.

1-2 主要经济指标增长速度(1979-2022年)

单位：%

年 份 Year	地区生产总值比上年增长 YoY Growth Rate of Gross Domestic Product	农林牧渔业总产值比上年增长 YoY Growth Rate of Gross Output Value of Agriculture, Forestry, Anima Husbandry and Fishery	规模以上工业总产值比上年增长 YoY Growth Rate of Gross Output Value of Industrial Enterprises Above Designated Size	固定资产投资比上年增长 YoY Growth Rate of Fixed Asset Investment	社会消费品零售总额比上年增长 YoY Growth Rate of Retail Sales of Consumer Goods
1979	9.7	7.0		17.3	20.6
1980	11.8	16.3		25.3	17.8
1981	-0.5	4.2		10.2	12.6
1982	7.4	12.8		5.5	6.6
1983	16.4	16.7		32.9	14.6
1984	17.4	13.3		29.2	22.5
1985	8.7	16.7	17.4	41.8	27.0
1986	8.0	8.5	3.8	13.0	15.3
1987	9.6	22.4	15.2	28.2	21.9
1988	12.8	52.9	27.9	19.7	35.5
1989	4.4	14.8	21.6	-14.4	15.2
1990	5.2	16.2	3.8	28.5	17.1
1991	9.9	9.0	16.7	7.1	18.3
1992	11.3	10.5	17.8	38.5	23.2
1993	12.3	18.8	35.7	54.3	22.4
1994	13.7	43.7	35.1	58.1	26.4
1995	12.0	13.9	-5.3	29.7	24.9
1996	9.8	2.7	6.5	4.2	12.5
1997	10.2	0.9	14.4	9.6	14.7
1998	9.6	2.5	7.0	20.2	14.5
1999	11.0	3.3	12.1	1.3	10.7
2000	12.0	4.4	30.2	10.8	10.7
2001	11.8	7.2	15.1	18.0	11.2
2002	11.8	5.6	10.7	18.5	10.3
2003	11.1	5.2	21.8	18.9	15.4
2004	13.3	4.5	30.0	17.2	15.7
2005	12.3	1.9	21.2	11.8	11.7
2006	12.8	0.4	18.2	19.3	14.0
2007	14.4	13.4	17.5	17.6	17.3
2008	9.0	11.6	7.9	-3.0	22.1
2009	10.0	3.6	6.0	26.2	16.8
2010	10.4	4.1	24.1	13.1	18.5
2011	8.1	10.7	5.9	13.3	14.6
2012	7.7	9.0	7.5	9.3	13.3
2013	7.7	6.6	11.4	8.8	10.0
2014	7.4	-0.4	6.2	7.5	9.4
2015	6.9	-12.3	-5.4	5.7	8.1
2016	6.9	-8.2	3.7	5.9	7.0
2017	6.8	-8.8	4.5	5.7	6.1
2018	6.7	-3.7	4.1	-9.9	3.5
2019	6.1	-5.1	3.6	-2.4	4.4
2020	1.1	-6.5	2.4	2.2	-8.9
2021	8.8	2.3	19.7	4.9	8.4
2022	0.7	-0.5	-4.5	3.6	-7.2

注：1.地区生产总值增长速度按不变价格计算。
2.2018年及以前，固定资产投资数据为全社会口径，自2019年起为不含农户口径，下同。
3.进出口总值增长速度为以美元计价的进出口总值增长速度，以人民币计价，2022年进出口总值增长19.7%。

YOY GROWTH RATE OF MAIN INDICATORS (1979-2022)

(%)

进出口总值比上年增长 YoY Growth Rate of Gross Value of Imports & Exports	居民消费价格指数(上年=100) Consumer Price Index (Previous year=100)	城镇居民人均可支配收入 Per-capita Disposable Income of Urban Households		农村居民人均可支配收入 Per-capita Disposable Income of Rural Households	
		比上年名义增长 Nominal Growth Rate as Compared with That in the Last year	比上年实际增长 Real Growth Rate as Compared with That in the Last year	比上年名义增长 Normal Growth Rate as Compared with That in the Last year	比上年实际增长 Real Growth Rate as Compared with That in the Last year
	101.8	13.6	11.6	11.2	9.2
	106.0	20.8	14.0	16.2	9.6
	101.3	10.7	9.3	20.7	19.2
	101.8	1.1	-0.7	23.4	21.2
	100.5	5.2	4.7	20.1	19.5
16.3	102.2	17.5	15.0	27.9	25.2
-8.6	117.6	30.8	11.2	16.7	-0.8
-6.0	106.8	17.6	10.1	6.2	-0.6
-12.7	108.6	10.7	1.9	11.3	2.5
11.9	120.4	21.6	1.0	16.0	-3.7
-4.3	117.2	11.1	-5.2	15.8	-1.2
-17.4	105.4	19.1	13.0	5.4	-0.04
2.5	111.9	14.1	2.0	9.7	-2.0
3.1	109.9	17.8	7.2	10.5	0.6
11.7	119.0	38.8	16.6	19.8	0.7
3.5	124.9	43.4	14.8	27.5	2.1
28.2	117.3	22.6	4.5	34.3	14.5
-20.8	111.6	17.6	5.4	10.5	-1.0
3.7	105.3	6.6	1.2	2.8	-2.4
0.4	102.4	9.3	6.7	7.4	4.9
12.6	100.6	9.2	8.5	6.4	5.8
43.8	103.5	13.6	9.8	8.4	4.7
4.2	103.1	12.7	9.3	8.6	5.3
2.0	98.2	8.5	10.5	6.9	8.9
30.5	100.2	12.2	12.0	3.2	3.0
38.1	101.0	13.5	12.4	9.6	8.5
32.7	101.5	13.8	12.1	18.4	16.7
25.9	100.9	14.1	13.1	12.0	11.0
22.1	102.4	10.9	8.3	13.4	10.7
40.8	105.1	13.3	7.8	12.3	6.9
-20.9	98.5	9.0	10.7	8.9	10.6
40.4	102.4	9.6	7.0	13.0	10.4
29.1	105.6	13.2	7.2	11.1	5.2
4.8	103.3	10.8	7.3	11.8	8.2
5.4	103.3	10.6	7.1	11.3	7.7
-3.4	101.6	8.9	7.2	10.3	8.6
-23.1	101.8	8.9	7.0	9.0	7.1
-11.6	101.4	8.4	6.9	8.5	7.0
14.6	101.9	9.0	7.0	8.7	6.7
27.4	102.5	8.9	6.2	9.3	6.6
0.9	102.3	8.6	6.2	9.2	6.7
-19.5	101.7	2.4	0.7	4.1	2.4
40.6	101.1	7.8	6.6	10.5	9.3
16.0	101.8	3.1	1.3	4.4	2.6

Note: a) The growth rates of GDP are calculated at constant price.

b) In and before 2018, the data on fixed asset investment were those of full coverage. Since 2019, the data were those that excluding rural households, the same below.

c) The Growth Rate of Gross Value of Imports & Exports shall be the growth rate of gross value of imports & exports calculated in USD. Calculated in RMB, the growth rate of gross value of imports & exports is 19.7% in 2022.

1−3 主要年份国民经济和社会发展总量指标

项 目		Item		1990
人口与就业		**Population and Employment**		
年末全市常住人口	(万人)	Year-end Permanent Population	(10000 persons)	1086.0
#城镇人口		Urban Population		798.0
年末户籍人口	(万人)	Year-end Registered Population	(10000 persons)	1032.2
常住就业人口	(万人)	Permanent Employed Population	(10000 persons)	
城镇非私营单位在岗职工平均工资	(元)	Average Wages of Employed Persons in Urban Non-Private Units	(yuan)	2653
年末实有城镇登记失业人员	(万人)	Year-end Number of Actual Registered Unemployed Persons in Urban Areas	(10000 persons)	1.67
国民经济核算		**National Accounts**		
地区生产总值	(亿元)	Gross Domestic Product	(100 million yuan)	500.8
人均地区生产总值	(元)	Per Capita Gross Domestic Product	(yuan)	4635
价格指数(上年=100)		**Price Indices (Preceding Year=100)**		
居民消费价格指数		Consumer Price Index		105.4
工业生产者出厂价格指数		Producer Price Index for Industrial Products		107.9
人民生活		**People's Living Conditions**		
全市居民人均可支配收入	(元)	Per Capita Disposable Income of Households of the Whole City	(yuan)	1741
全市居民人均消费支出	(元)	Per Capita Living Expenditures of Households of the Whole City	(yuan)	1469
财 政		**Government Finance**		
一般公共预算收入	(亿元)	General Public Budget Revenue	(100 million yuan)	
一般公共预算支出	(亿元)	General Public Budget Expenditure	(100 million yuan)	
能源、资源和环境		**Energy, Resources and Environment**		
能源消费总量	(万吨标准煤)	Total Energy Consumption	(10000 tons of SCE)	2709.7
水资源总量	(亿立方米)	Total Volume of Water Resource	(100 million cu.m)	36.9
城市绿化覆盖率	(%)	Urban Green Coverage	(%)	28.0
城市公用事业		**Public Utilities**		
全社会用电量	(亿千瓦时)	Electricity Consumption	(100 million kW·h)	150.5
自来水销售总量	(亿立方米)	Total Sales Volume of Tap Water	(100 million cu.m)	5.3
居民燃气用户	(万户)	Households Gas Users	(10000 households)	176.1
公共交通客运量	(亿人次)	Passengers Traffic of Public Transport	(100 million person-times)	33.5
污水处理率	(%)	Sewage Treatment Rate	(%)	7.3

注：1.2015年常住人口数据根据第七次全国人口普查结果进行了修订，下同。
2.2014年以前年末实有登记失业人员为城镇口径，2014—2019年调整为全市口径。自2020年9月起，对城镇登记失业人员相关统计口径进行调整，将离校未就业高校毕业生、领取失业补助金人员和领取一次性生活补助农民工纳入登记失业人员范围，下同。
3.地区生产总值绝对值按当年价格计算。2015年人均地区生产总值数据根据第七次全国人口普查结果进行了修订，2022年为初步核算数据，下同。
4.城镇非私营单位在岗职工平均工资2000年及以前数据为职工口径，职工包括在岗职工和不在岗职工；自2001年起，调整为在岗职工口径。2007年及以前城镇单位在岗职工工资包括乡及乡以上独立核算法人单位，不包括乡镇企业和个体工商户；自2008年起不包括个体工商户的独立核算法人单位。
5.自2012年起，自来水数据口径调整为城镇公共供水。

AGGREGATE INDICATORS ON NATIONAL ECONOMIC AND SOCIAL DEVELOPMENT IN KEY YEARS

1995	2000	2005	2010	2015	2020	2021	2022
1251.1	1363.6	1538.0	1961.9	2188.3	2189.0	2188.6	2184.3
946.2	1057.4	1286.1	1686.4	1897.5	1916.4	1916.1	1912.8
1070.3	1107.5	1180.7	1257.8	1345.2	1400.8	1413.5	1427.7
			1067.3	1164.4	1163.8	1158.0	1132.1
8144	15726	34191	65683	113073	185026	201504	215143
2.19	3.32	10.57	7.73	9.16	29.02	37.19	36.39
1516.2	3277.8	7149.8	14964.0	24779.1	35943.3	41045.6	41610.9
12762	25014	47182	78307	113692	164158	187526	190313
117.3	103.5	101.5	102.4	101.8	101.7	101.1	101.8
107.3	102.5	101.3	102.2	96.9	99.1	101.1	102.3
5501	9230	16853	29228	48458	69434	75002	77415
4366	7644	13289	21834	33803	38903	43640	42683
	345.0	919.2	2353.9	4723.9	5483.9	5932.3	5714.4
	443.0	1058.3	2717.3	5737.7	7116.2	7205.1	7469.2
3533.3	4144.0	5049.8	6359.5	6802.8	6762.1	7103.6	6896.9
30.3	16.9	23.2	23.1	26.8	25.8	61.3	23.7
32.7	36.5	42.0	45.0	48.4	49.0	49.3	49.8
222.6	384.4	570.5	809.9	952.7	1140.0	1232.9	1280.8
6.8	7.5	7.2	8.9	10.4	11.2	12.1	12.3
219.8	291.9	462.6	634.2	885.7	902.2	950.4	973.6
37.2	40.7	51.8	69.0	73.8	41.2	53.9	39.9
19.4	39.4	62.4	81.0	87.9	95.0	95.8	97.0

Note: a)The data on permanent population for 2015 have been revised according to the results of the seventh national population census, the same below.

b) The year-end number of actual registered unemployed persons before 2014 referred to the statistic in urban area and was adjusted to the statistic of the whole city from 2014 to 2019. The relevant statistical coverage of the registered unemployed persons in urban area was adjusted since September 2020, the unemployed college graduates, the personnel receiving unemployment compensation and the rural migrant workers receiving lump-sum living allowance were included in the list of registered unemployed persons; the same below.

c) The absolute values of GDP are calculated at current prices. The data on per capita GDP for 2015 have been revised according to the results of the seventh national population census, and the data for 2022 are the preliminary accounting data,the same below.

d) Figures on average wages of employed persons in urban non-private entities in and before 2000 referred to that of staff and workers which included both fully employed staff and workers and the off-the-job ones. Since 2001, the figures were adjusted to statistical range of fully employed staff and workers. In and before 2007, figures on wages of employed persons in urban entities covered that of the legal entities with independent accounting at and above township level, excluding township enterprises and self-employed businesses;since 2008,such figures have excluded that of the legal entities with independent accounting of self-employed businesses.

e) Since 2012, the statistical coverage of tap water data was adjusted to urban public water supply.

1-3 续表 1

项　目		Item		1990
固定资产投资		**Investment In Fixed Assets**		
固定资产投资	(亿元)	Total Investment In Fixed Assets	(100 million yuan)	179.2
#基础设施投资		Infrastructure Investment		31.6
#房地产开发投资		Investment in Real Estate Development		22.5
对外经济贸易		**Foreign Economic Relations and Trade**		
地区货物进出口总值	(亿美元)	Gross Value of Imports and Exports of Local Goods	(USD 100 million)	236.4
地区货物进出口总值	(亿元)	Gross Value of Imports and Exports of Local Goods	(100 million yuan)	
实际利用外商直接投资额	(亿美元)	Actual Use of Foreign Direct Investment	(USD 100 million)	
农　业		**Agriculture**		
农林牧渔业总产值(当年价格)	(亿元)	Gross Output Value of Agriculture, Forestry,Animal Husbandry and Fishery(at current prices)	(100 million yuan)	70.2
工　业		**Industry**		
规模以上工业总产值(当年价格)	(亿元)	Gross Output Value of Industry Above Designated Size (at current prices)	(100 million yuan)	625.9
规模以上工业主要财务指标		Principal Financial Indicators of Industrial Enterprises Above Designated Size		
资产总计	(亿元)	Total Assets	(100 million yuan)	498.3
负债总额	(亿元)	Total Liabilities	(100 million yuan)	
营业收入	(亿元)	Businesses Revenue	(100 million yuan)	
利润总额	(亿元)	Total Profits	(100 million yuan)	48.9
建 筑 业		**Construction**		
建筑业总产值	(亿元)	Gross Output Value	(100 million yuan)	94.7
建筑业企业年末从业人员	(万人)	Year-end Employed Persons	(10000 persons)	60.2
交通运输邮电业		**Transport, Post and Telecommunication Services**		
运　输		Transport		
货物周转量	(亿吨公里)	Total Freight Turnover	(100 million ton-km)	268.8
旅客周转量	(亿人公里)	Total Passenger Turnover	(100 million passenger-km)	119.8
邮　电		Post and Telecommunication Services		
邮电业务总量	(亿元)	Business Volume of Post and Telecommunication	(100 million yuan)	11.9
固定电话用户	(万户)	Fixed Telephone Subscribers	(10000 subscribers)	33.3
移动电话用户	(万户)	Mobile Telephone Subscribers	(10000 subscribers)	0.3
批发和零售业、住宿和餐饮业		**Wholesale and Retail Trade, Accommodation and Restaurants**		
社会消费品零售总额	(亿元)	Total Retail Sales of Consumer Goods	(100 million yuan)	345.1
旅游业		**Tourism**		
入境游客人数	(万人次)	Inbound Tourists	(10000 person-times)	100.0
国内游客人数	(万人次)	Domestic Tourists	(10000 person-times)	
国际旅游收入	(亿美元)	Revenue from Inbound Tourism	(USD 100 million)	6.6
国内旅游收入	(亿元)	Revenue from Domestic Tourism	(100 million yuan)	

注：1.自2011年起，固定资产投资统计起点由50万元调整至500万元。
2.2018年及以前固定资产投资为全社会口径，自2019年起为不含农户口径。
3.邮电业务总量2000年及以前按1990年不变价格计算，2001—2010年按2000年不变价格计算，2011—2016年按2010年不变价格计算。2017—2020年，邮政行业业务总量按2010年不变价格计算，电信业务总量按2015年不变价格计算。自2021年起，邮政行业业务总量按2020年不变价格计算，电信业务总量按上年不变价格计算。

1—3 Continued 1

1995	2000	2005	2010	2015	2020	2021	2022
841.5	1297.4	2827.2	5493.5	7990.9			
156.1	351.9	610.7	1403.5	2174.5			
352.8	522.1	1525.0	2901.1	4226.3			
370.4	494.0	1255.1	3016.6	3194.2	3350.4	4710.2	5465.0
3108.2	4090.1	10331.9	20478.2	19827.7	23215.9	30438.4	36445.5
	16.8	35.3	53.4	127.2	133.9	144.3	174.1
164.4	188.6	239.3	328.0	368.2	263.4	269.5	268.2
1493.3	2842.0	6946.2	13699.8	17449.6	20879.3	24988.1	23870.0
2582.6	4612.7	12829.8	22750.6	38609.8	55167.0	61056.0	66052.5
1528.8	2676.4	4706.7	11548.1	18102.4	24193.8	26371.6	29327.9
			14807.1	19256.1	23849.0	28745.1	27713.6
85.3	127.1	413.5	1028.3	1597.7	1729.5	3684.4	1998.7
426.6	812.5	1894.0	5196.0	8436.7	12905.9	13987.7	13866.1
82.6	56.6	67.2	59.9	59.0	52.7	56.8	58.3
323.1	299.6	457.7	513.7	623.7	842.8	880.4	881.2
207.7	314.0	838.1	1399.5	1747.7	1015.0	1047.2	573.3
56.1	214.7	413.0	1174.2	1181.9	3727.9	796.0	840.0
150.5	451.2	943.5	885.6	784.7	480.6	485.2	474.2
16.9	347.2	1459.8	2129.8	4051.6	3906.4	3972.0	3926.9
971.8	1760.3	3221.4	7273.0	12271.9	13716.4	14867.7	13794.2
207.0	282.1	362.9	490.1	420.0	34.1	24.5	24.1
6320.0	10186.0	12500.0	17900.0	26859.0	18352.4	25488.3	18206.7
21.8	27.7	36.2	50.4	46.1	4.8	4.3	4.4
352.6	683.0	1300.0	2425.1	4320.0	2880.9	4138.5	2490.9

Note: a) Since 2011,the statistical starting point of fixed asset investment is changed from RMB 500,000 to RMB 5 million.

b)The data on investment in fixed assets in and before 2018 referred to that of the whole city; since 2019, the data refer to that excluding peasant households.

c)The business volume of post and telecommunication services in and before 2000 was calculated at 1990's constant prices; that of 2001-2010 was calculated at 2000's constant prices; that of 2011-2016 was calculated at 2010's constant prices; since 2017 until 2020, the business volume of post services was calculated at 2010's constant prices, and that of telecommunication services was calculated at 2015's constant prices. Since 2021,The business volume of post service was calculated at 2020's constant prices,and that of telecommunication services was calculated at constant prices of last year.

1-3 续表 2

项目	Item	1990
金融业	**Finance**	
金融机构(含外资)本外币存款余额 (亿元)	Deposits of Financial Institutions (Including Foreign Institutions) (100 million yuan)	
金融机构(含外资)本外币贷款余额 (亿元)	Loans of Financial Institutions (Including Foreign Institutions) (100 million yuan)	
原保险保费收入 (亿元)	Premiums Revenue (100 million yuan)	
证券市场交易额 (亿元)	Trading Volume of Stock Market (100 million yuan)	
科　技	**Science and Technology**	
研究与试验发展经费内部支出 (亿元)	Internal R&D Expenditures (100 million yuan)	
技术合同成交总额 (亿元)	Total Volume of Transaction of Technological Contracts Concluded (100 million yuan)	20.3
专利授权量 (件)	Patents Granted (unit)	2268
教　育	**Education**	
在校生数 (万人)	Students Enrollment (10000 persons)	
专任教师数 (万人)	Full-time Teachers (10000 persons)	
卫生及社会服务	**Health and Social Services**	
卫　生	Public Health	
医疗卫生机构个数 (个)	Medical and Health Institutions (unit)	4953
医疗机构实有床位数 (万张)	Beds in Medical Institutions (10000 beds)	5.9
医疗卫生技术人员数 (万人)	Medical Technical Personnel (10000 persons)	11.2
#执业(助理)医师	Licensed (Assistant) Physicians	5.1
注册护士	Registered Nurses	3.5
婚　姻	Marriage and Divorce	
登记结婚对数 (万对)	Number of Registered Marriages (10000 couples)	9.3
离婚对数 (万对)	Number of Registered Divorces (10000 couples)	1.5
文　化	**Culture**	
公共图书馆总藏数 (万册、万件)	Collection of Public Libraries (10000 volumes)	2205
博物馆及其他文物保护机构 (个)	Museums and Other Cultural Relic Protection and Administration Organizations (unit)	
电影放映场次 (万场次)	Show Times of Films (10000 times)	20.7
社会保障	**Social Security**	
参加企业职工基本养老保险人数 (万人)	Number of People Participating in Basic Pension Insurance for Enterprise Employed Persons (10000 persons)	
参加职工基本医疗保险人数 (万人)	Number of People Participating in Basic Medical Care Insurance for Enterprise Employed Persons (10000 persons)	

注：1.离婚对数包括在民政部门登记的对数以及经法院调离和判离的对数。
2.2010年及以前，医疗卫生机构数据均不含村卫生室及驻京部队医院情况。自2011年起，包含村卫生室情况。自2012年起，除床位数外均包含驻京部队医院数据。
3."博物馆及其他文物保护机构"数据为北京市文物局系统内数据。
4.自2016年起，对专利相关数据的统计范围进行了调整。
5.自2021年9月起，对参加职工基本医疗保险人数统计口径进行调整，去除6个月及以上未缴费人员，按调整后的口径计算，2020年参加职工基本医疗保险人数为1450.7万人。历史年份数据未按新口径进行调整。

1–3 Continued 2

1995	2000	2005	2010	2015	2020	2021	2022
	11526.0	28969.9	66584.6	128573.0	188081.6	199741.5	218628.8
	6407.9	15335.5	36479.6	58559.4	84308.8	89032.9	97819.9
	93.4	498.2	966.5	1403.9	2302.9	2526.9	2758.5
	14727.2	12930.0	129495.2	918064.8	1259914.7	1800772.3	1846185.7
	155.7	379.5	821.8	1384.0	2326.6	2629.3	2843.3
41.2	140.3	434.4	1579.5	3452.6	6316.2	7005.7	7947.5
4025	5905	10100	33511	94031	162824	198778	202722
238.0	229.9	226.4	330.0	373.4	403.9	397.1	402.4
17.7	16.7	17.5	20.7	22.6	25.7	26.5	27.3
4955	6176	7536	9511	10425	11211	11727	12211
6.7	7.1	7.9	9.3	11.2	12.7	13.0	13.4
11.6	11.6	12.0	17.1	25.7	30.4	31.8	32.2
5.4	5.2	5.1	6.6	9.6	11.9	12.4	12.5
3.7	4.0	4.3	6.7	11.4	13.5	14.2	14.3
8.6	8.0	9.7	13.8	16.6	11.4	10.3	9.1
2.0	2.7	3.4	4.4	8.2	8.2	5.3	4.4
2629	3020	3626	4613	5943	7241	7548	7819
51	53	73	79	77	80	80	58
9.2	12.2	22.6	74.3	198.1	146.0	335.4	262.9
261.1	391.6	520.0	982.5	1424.2	1679.9	1725.1	1764.7
		574.8	1063.7	1475.7	1741.6	1486.0	1499.4

Note: a) Number of registered divorces includes those registered with civil affair authorities and those mediated and ruled in courts.

b) In and before 2010, figures on health centers were emerged with other health institutions such as community health service centers (stations). Since 2011, health care institutions included village health centers. Since 2012, all the other data except for the data on beds have included the data of hospitals of troops stationed in Beijing.

c) Figures of museums and other cultural relic protection and administration organizations were the one under the jurisdiction of Beijing Municipal Administration of Cultural Heritage.

d) The statistical range of patent-related data was adjusted since 2016.

e)Since September 2021, the statistical coverage of the "number of people participating in basic medical care insurance for employed persons" was adjusted and removed those who failed to make payment for 6 months or more. Calculated according to the adjusted coverage, the number of people participating in basic medical care insurance for employed persons totaled 14.507 million in 2020.Data for the previous years were not adjusted according to the new caliber.

1-4 主要年份国民经济和社会发展结构指标
COMPOSITION INDICATORS ON NATIONAL ECONOMIC AND SOCIAL DEVELOPMENT IN KEY YEARS

单位：% (%)

项　　目	Item	1990	1995	2000	2005	2010	2015	2020	2021	2022
人口与就业	**Population and Employment**									
常住人口	**Permanent Population**									
按性别分	By Gender									
男	Male	50.2	50.1	52.1	50.6	51.6	51.5	51.1	51.1	51.0
女	Female	49.8	49.9	47.9	49.4	48.4	48.5	48.9	48.9	49.0
按城乡分	By Urban Area and Rural Area									
城　镇	Urban	73.5	75.6	77.5	83.6	86.0	86.7	87.5	87.5	87.6
乡　村	Rural	26.5	24.4	22.5	16.4	14.0	13.3	12.5	12.5	12.4
就　业	**Employment**									
常住就业人口	Permanent Employed Population									
第一产业	Primary Industry					5.5	3.7	2.4	2.3	2.2
第二产业	Secondary Industry					23.6	18.9	16.7	16.7	16.4
第三产业	Tertiary Industry					70.9	77.4	80.9	81.0	81.4
国民经济核算	**National Accounts**									
地区生产总值	Gross Domestic Product									
第一产业	Primary Industry	8.7	4.8	2.4	1.2	0.8	0.6	0.3	0.3	0.3
第二产业	Secondary Industry	52.3	42.1	31.2	26.7	21.6	17.8	16.0	18.0	15.9
第三产业	Tertiary Industry	39.0	53.1	66.4	72.1	77.6	81.6	83.7	81.7	83.9
人民生活	**People's Living Conditions**									
城镇居民人均消费支出	Per Capita Consumption Expenditure of Urban Residents									
#食品烟酒	Food, Tobacco and Liquor	54.2	48.5	35.8	29.4	26.8	22.1	21.0	20.8	21.1
衣　着	Clothing	14.7	15.1	8.7	8.1	8.5	7.2	4.6	4.8	4.3
医疗保健	Health and Medical Services	1.4	2.9	7.0	9.8	6.4	6.5	9.0	9.9	9.4
交通通信	Transport and Communications	1.5	4.7	7.0	13.1	13.7	13.3	9.4	9.3	9.3
教育文化娱乐	Education, Cultural and Entertainment	11.6	10.2	14.8	14.7	11.5	11.0	7.2	7.8	7.2
农村居民人均消费支出	Per Capita Consumption Expenditure of Rural Residents									
#食品烟酒	Food, Tobacco and Liquor	50.7	49.6	37.5	30.3	26.6	27.7	28.5	28.3	27.4
衣　着	Clothing	9.5	10.9	7.0	6.4	5.9	6.3	5.0	5.4	4.7
医疗保健	Health and Medical Services	3.8	4.8	7.3	9.4	8.4	8.4	9.4	9.4	8.0
交通通信	Transport and Communications	1.7	4.1	7.0	11.9	11.7	13.5	14.0	14.4	13.8
教育文化娱乐	Education, Cultural and Entertainment	6.6	10.6	13.6	12.9	7.5	7.2	5.5	5.6	5.5
财　政	**Government Finance**									
一般公共预算收入	General Public Budget Revenue									
#增值税	Value-added Tax			13.3	10.6	8.9	15.2	30.1	29.4	23.0
个人所得税	Individual Income Tax			16.3	9.2	9.1	10.1	11.2	12.5	13.7
企业所得税	Corporate Income Tax			16.8	17.9	21.8	21.7	21.6	23.5	25.4

1-4 续表 1 Continued 1

单位：% (%)

项 目	Item	1990	1995	2000	2005	2010	2015	2020	2021	2022
能源消费总量	**Total Energy Consumption**									
第一产业	Primary Industry	3.9	3.4	2.5	1.7	1.5	1.2	0.8	0.7	0.7
第二产业	Secondary Industry	63.5	65.9	58.5	46.8	37.2	28.0	25.9	23.8	24.2
第三产业	Tertiary Industry	19.0	17.9	26.1	35.1	41.7	48.7	48.0	49.8	48.1
生活消费	Living Consumption	13.6	12.8	12.9	16.4	19.5	22.1	25.3	25.7	27.0
投 资	**Investment**									
固定资产投资资金来源	Source of Capital for Investment in Fixed Assets									
中央预算资金	Central Budgetary Fund	25.3	7.7	7.4	2.8	1.2	1.7	1.1	1.1	1.7
国内贷款	Domestic Loans	16.7	13.4	26.0	23.2	26.6	22.2	22.2	14.8	17.0
利用外资	Utilization of Foreign Investment	11.2	20.5	3.6	1.6	0.5	0.1	0.1	0.2	0.1
债券、自筹和其他资金	Securities, Self-raised Funds and Others	46.8	58.5	63.0	72.4	71.6	76.0	76.6	84.0	81.3
对外经济贸易	**Foreign Economic Relations and Trade**									
海关出口商品(以美元计价)	Commodities Exported at Customs (Calculated in USD)									
#一般贸易	General Trade		70.6	65.9	54.5	45.0	54.8	79.8	81.1	81.3
加工贸易	Processing Trade		21.3	29.6	39.6	42.1	28.0	5.4	5.1	4.4
海关进口商品(以美元计价)	Commodities Imported at Customs (Calculated in USD)									
#一般贸易	General Trade		84.4	87.3	85.2	88.7	85.7	87.8	88.1	88.8
加工贸易	Processing Trade		5.2	3.5	8.2	5.9	7.7	3.9	3.4	3.9
农 业	**Agriculture**									
农林牧渔业产值	Gross Output Value of Agriculture, Forestry, Animal Husbandry and Fishery									
农 业	Farming	55.6	52.8	46.7	38.0	47.0	42.0	40.9	45.6	48.4
林 业	Forestry	1.3	1.6	2.8	5.2	5.1	15.6	37.1	32.9	32.3
牧 业	Animal Husbandry	39.9	41.8	46.4	50.5	42.6	36.9	17.2	17.2	15.8
渔 业	Fishery	3.3	3.7	4.1	3.6	3.5	3.2	1.6	1.6	1.4
农林牧渔专业及辅助性活动	Professional and Supporting Activities of Farming, Forestry, Animal Husbandry, Fishery				2.7	1.8	2.4	3.3	2.6	2.1
工 业	**Industry**									
规模以上工业总产值	Gross Output Value of Industry Above Designated Size									
#医药制造业	Manufacture of Medicines	1.8	1.5	2.1	1.9	2.7	4.2	6.3	15.7	7.3
汽车制造业	Manufacture of Motor Vehicles	7.8	11.6	3.9	11.8	15.9	22.3	19.8	13.7	14.2
计算机、通信和其他电子设备制造业	Manufacture of Computer, Communication Equipment and Other Electronic Equipment	6.0	10.4	32.9	25.6	16.3	12.1	13.8	15.0	14.7
电力、热力生产和供应业	Production and Distribution of Electricity and Heating Power	2.6	2.8	2.9	8.6	15.5	23.4	26.8	24.7	30.7
建筑业	**Construction**									
建筑业总产值	Gross Output Value of Construction									
房屋建筑业	Construction of Buildings						51.3	54.2	54.4	55.5
土木工程建筑业	Civil Engineering Construction						32.7	33.6	32.2	31.7
建筑安装业	Construction Installation						7.9	6.3	6.5	6.3
建筑装饰和其他建筑业	Building Decoration and Other Construction						8.1	5.9	6.9	6.5
交通运输业	**Transport**									
货运量(按运输方式分)	Freight Traffic (By Means of Transportation)									
铁 路	Railway	11.4	9.2	8.5	6.1	6.6	4.3	1.4	1.1	1.4
公 路	Highway	87.5	90.4	91.2	92.4	85.1	82.0	82.7	82.0	77.2
民 航	Civil Aviation	0.04	0.05	0.11	0.24	0.55	0.68	0.56	0.57	0.53
管 道	Pipeline	1.0	0.3	0.2	1.2	7.7	13.0	15.4	16.3	20.8

注：1.自2017年起，将固定资产投资中原“国家预算内资金”调整为“中央预算资金”。
2.根据《国民经济行业分类》(GB/T 4754—2017)标准，自2018年起，将原“农林牧渔服务业”调整为“农林牧渔专业及辅助性活动”。

Note: a) Since 2017, under the Investment in Fixed Assets, the original State Budgets was adjusted to Central Budgetary Fund.
b) According to the standards in the *Classification of National Economic Sectors* (GB/T 4754-2017), Since 2018,the original Service Activities for Agriculture, Forestry, Animal Husbandry and Fishing is adjusted to Professional and Supporting Activities of Agriculture, Forestry, Animal Production and Hunting, Fishing.

1-4 续表 2 Continued 2

单位：% (%)

项目	Item	1990	1995	2000	2005	2010	2015	2020	2021	2022
客运量(按运输方式分)	Passenger (By Means of Transportation)									
铁　路	Railway	50.4	45.1	24.2	9.5	6.3	18.3	17.6	20.2	13.9
公　路	Highway	46.7	47.7	70.7	85.3	89.7	71.4	67.7	66.3	75.3
民　航	Civil Aviation	2.9	7.2	5.1	5.2	4.0	10.3	14.7	13.5	10.7
消　费	**Consumption**									
社会消费品零售总额	Total Retail Sales of Consumer Goods									
吃类商品	Food	39.6	41.8	26.1	24.9	20.9	18.1	20.4	20.0	20.5
穿类商品	Clothing	13.2	14.3	9.2	8.4	7.6	6.1	5.1	5.6	4.8
用类商品	Daily Use Articles	44.8	42.0	59.7	59.0	64.9	71.4	71.2	70.4	70.5
烧类商品	Fuels	2.3	1.9	5.0	7.7	6.6	4.5	3.3	4.0	4.2
入境旅游	**Inbound Tourism**									
接待海外旅游人数	Inbound Tourist									
外国人	Foreigners	63.8	80.4	84.4	85.9	86.0	85.1	77.4	71.2	78.6
港澳台同胞	Compatriots from Hong Kong, Macao and Taiwan	34.7	17.5	15.6	14.1	14.0	14.9	22.6	28.8	21.4
科　技	**Science and Technology**									
研究与试验发展(R&D)人员折合全时当量	Full-time Equivalents of R&D Professionals									
基础研究	Basic Research				12.9	15.2	16.8	22.3	22.3	22.6
应用研究	Applied Research				29.8	27.1	25.1	28.3	28.7	29.5
试验发展	Experimental Development				57.3	57.7	58.1	49.4	49.0	47.8
研究与试验发展(R&D)经费内部支出	Internal R&D Expentures									
基础研究	Basic Research				10.1	11.6	13.8	16.0	16.1	16.6
应用研究	Applied Research				27.8	26.4	23.0	24.5	25.0	25.7
试验发展	Experimental Development				53.1	62.0	63.2	59.4	58.9	57.7
教　育	**Education**									
在校学生	Students Enrollment									
#普通本专科	Regular Undergraduates and College Students		7.7	12.3	23.7	17.5	15.9	14.6	15.0	15.0
中等教育	Secondary Education		35.1	42.3	37.9	22.1	15.7	14.0	14.4	15.1
小学教育	Primary Education		42.3	32.3	21.8	19.8	22.8	24.6	26.1	26.9
专任教师	Full-time Teachers									
#高等教育	Higher Education		22.7	22.2	32.7	35.9	30.3	28.5	27.9	28.2
中等教育	Secondary Education		38.6	40.5	33.6	29.1	32.0	31.6	31.1	31.3
小学教育	Primary Education		37.9	36.8	25.3	23.9	22.1	22.0	22.3	22.2
卫　生	**Public Health**									
卫生技术人员	Medical Personnel									
#执业(助理)医师	Certified (Assistant) Doctors	45.6	46.7	44.6	42.4	38.6	37.6	39.0	38.9	38.8
注册护士	Registered Nurses	31.0	31.7	34.5	35.7	39.3	44.6	44.3	44.6	44.3

1-5 国民经济和社会发展主要比例和效益指标
MAIN INDICATORS ON PROPORTIONS AND EFFICIENCY IN NATIONAL ECONOMIC AND SOCIAL DEVELOPMENT

项　　目		Item		2022	2021
人口与就业		**Population and Employment**			
出生率(常住人口)	(‰)	Birth Rate (Permanent Population)	(‰)	5.67	6.35
死亡率(常住人口)	(‰)	Death Rate (Permanent Population)	(‰)	5.72	5.39
自然增长率(常住人口)	(‰)	Natural Growth Rate (Permanent Population)	(‰)	-0.05	0.96
少儿抚养比(常住人口)	(%)	Child-age Dependency Rate (Permanent Population)	(%)	16.60	16.42
老年抚养比(常住人口)	(%)	Old-age Dependency Rate (Permanent Population)	(%)	20.76	19.33
城镇调查失业率	(%)	Surveyed Unemployment Rate in Urban Areas	(%)	4.7	4.3
国民经济核算		**National Accounts**			
人均地区生产总值	(元)	Per Capita Gross Domestic Product	(yuan)	190313	187526
社会劳动生产率	(元/人)	Overall Labor Productivity	(yuan/person)	363399	353567
第一产业		Primary Industry		42821	40513
第二产业		Secondary Industry		348553	381862
第三产业		Tertiary Industry		375410	356902
人民生活		**People's Living Conditions**			
城镇与农村居民收入比例		Urban and Rural Income Ratio		2.42	2.45
(以农村居民人均可支配收入为1)		(Per Capita Disposable Income of Rural Residents = 1)			
能源消费		**Energy Consumption**			
能源消费弹性系数		Energy Consumption Elasticity Coefficient		0.00	0.57
电力消费弹性系数		Electricity Consumption Elasticity Coefficient		5.62	0.92
万元地区生产总值能耗		Energy Consumption per 10000 yuan of GDP		0.175	0.182
(可比价格)	(吨标准煤)	(Comparable Price)	(ton of SCE)		
万元地区生产总值水耗		Water Consumption per 10000 yuan of GDP		9.62	9.95
(当年价格)	(立方米)	(Current Price)	(cu.m)		
对外经济贸易		**Foreign Economic Relations and Trade**			
进出口总值与地区生产总值之比		Ratio of Total Value of Imports and Exports to		87.59	74.16
(按人民币计算)	(%)	Gross Domestic Product (calculated in RMB)	(%)		
工业(规模以上企业)		**Industry(Enterprise Above Designated Size)**			
资产负债率	(%)	Asset-liability Ratio	(%)	44.40	43.19
流动资产周转率	(次)	Turnover Rate of Current Assets	(time)	1.01	1.15
成本费用利润率	(%)	Ratio of Profits to Cost	(%)	7.64	14.53
建筑业		**Construction**			
产值竣工率	(%)	Rate of Buildings Completed (by Output Value)	(%)	49.8	44.1
面积竣工率	(%)	Rate of Buildings Completed (by Floor Space)	(%)	15.4	14.5
邮电通信业		**Post and Telecommunication Services**			
移动电话普及率	(户/百人)	Penetration Rate of Mobile Phone	(subscriber/100 persons)	179.8	181.5
固定电话主线普及率	(线/百人)	Penetration Rate of Main Line of Fixed Telephone	(line/100 persons)	21.7	22.2
科　技		**Science and Technology**			
研究与试验发展经费内部支出		Internal R&D Expenditures as % of GDP	(%)	6.83	6.41
相当于地区生产总值比例	(%)				
教　育		**Education**			
平均每一专任教师负担学生数		Average Number of Students Instructed by a Full-time Teacher			
#普通中学	(人)	Ordinary Secondary Education	(person)	8.8	8.6
小学学校	(人)	Primary Education	(person)	14.1	13.9
文　化		**Culture**			
每万人拥有公共图书馆	(个)	Public Libraries per 10000 persons	(unit)	0.01	0.01
每万人拥有博物馆	(个)	Museums per 10000 persons	(unit)	0.10	0.09
卫　生		**Public Health**			
每千常住人口医院床位数	(张)	Ward Beds per 1000 Permanent Population	(unit)	5.78	5.59
每千常住人口执业(助理)医师数	(人)	Licensed (Assistant) Physicians per 1000 Permanent Population	(person)	5.72	5.64

注：城镇调查失业率数据为年度均值。
Note:The data on surveyed unemployment rate in urban areas are annual averages.

1-6 北京一日
A DAY IN BEIJING

项目		Item		2022	2021
每日创造		**Daily Production**			
地区生产总值	(万元/日)	Gross Domestic Product	(10000 yuan/day)	1140026.0	1124537.8
第一产业		Primary Industry		3056.2	3052.3
第二产业		Secondary Industry		180960.8	202439.2
第三产业		Tertiary Industry		956009.0	919046.3
一般公共预算收入	(万元/日)	General Public Budget Revenue	(10000 yuan/day)	156557.8	162529.0
一般公共预算支出	(万元/日)	General Public Budget Expenditure	(10000 yuan/day)	204634.4	197400.6
发电量	(万千瓦时/日)	Electricity Generated	(10000 kW·h/day)	12326.6	12575.2
汽车生产量	(辆/日)	Output of Motor Vehicles	(vehicle/day)	2386	3712
移动电话机生产量	(台/日)	Output of Mobile Telephones	(set/day)	258343	318479
显示器生产量	(台/日)	Output of Display Devices	(set/day)	6401	14197
公共汽电车客运量	(万人次/日)	Passenger Traffic of Buses and Trolley Buses	(10000 person-times/day)	472.8	629.1
城市轨道交通客运量	(万人次/日)	Passenger Traffic of Urban Rail Transit	(10000 person-times/day)	620.1	846.6
铁路客运量	(万人/日)	Passenger Traffic of Railway	(10000 persons/day)	10.7	23.4
公路客运量	(万人/日)	Passenger Traffic of Highway	(10000 persons/day)	57.8	76.9
民航客运量	(万人/日)	Passenger Traffic of Civil Aviation	(10000 persons/day)	8.2	15.6
国际旅游收入	(万美元/日)	Revenue from Inbound Tourism	(USD 10000/day)	120.8	118.1
国内旅游收入	(万元/日)	Revenue from Domestic Tourism	(10000 yuan/day)	68244.4	113382.6
地区货物出口值	(万元/日)	Value of Exports of Local Goods	(10000 yuan/day)	161370.5	167629.3
地区货物进口值	(万元/日)	Value of Imports of Local Goods	(10000 yuan/day)	837136.5	666298.6
实际利用外商直接投资额	(万美元/日)	Paid-in Foreign Direct Investment	(USD 10000/day)	4769.2	3954.6
每日生活		**Daily Life**			
社会消费品零售总额	(万元/日)	Total Retail Sales of Consumer Goods	(10000 yuan/day)	377924.5	407335.4
吃类商品		Food		77599.7	81267.9
穿类商品		Clothing		18000.3	22664.9
用类商品		Daily Use Articles		266401.0	286918.7
烧类商品		Fuels		15923.5	16483.8
常住出生人口	(人/日)	Births (Permanent Residence)	(person/day)	340	381
常住死亡人口	(人/日)	Deaths (Permanent Residence)	(person/day)	343	323
登记结婚对数	(对/日)	Registered Marriages	(couple/day)	250	283
离婚对数	(对/日)	Divorces	(couple/day)	121	144
全市居民人均可支配收入	(元/日)	Per Capita Disposable Income of Residents of the Whole City	(yuan/day)	212.1	205.5
全市居民人均消费支出	(元/日)	Per Capita Consumption Expenditure of Residents of the Whole City	(yuan/day)	116.9	119.6
法人单位从业人员平均工资	(元/日)	Average Wages of Employed Persons in Legal Entities	(yuan/day)	489.0	456.2
电影放映场次	(场次/日)	Show Times of Fimls	(times/day)	7201	9189
特快专递业务量	(万件/日)	Express Mail Services	(10000 pcs/day)	536.0	605.6
城乡居民生活用电量	(万千瓦时/日)	Household Electricity Consumption of Urban and Rural Residents	(10000 kW·h/day)	8792.4	7846.2
居民家庭用天然气销售量	(万立方米/日)	Sales Volume of Natural Gas for Household Consumption	(10000 cu.m/day)	560.8	481.0
自来水销售总量	(万立方米/日)	Total Sales Volume of Tap Water	(10000 cu.m/day)	337.7	332.4
污水处理量	(万立方米/日)	Treatment Volume of Seweage	(10000 cu.m/day)	608.5	592.5
生活垃圾清运量	(万吨/日)	Domestic Waste Removed and Transported	(10000 tons/day)	2.0	2.1

注：离婚对数包括在民政部门登记的对数以及经法院调离和判离的对数。
Note: Divorces include those registered with civil affair authorities and those mediated and ruled in courts.

1-7 “十四五”时期经济社会发展主要监测指标
MAIN MONITORING INDICATORS OF SOCIAL AND ECONOMIC DEVELOPMENT IN THE FOURTEENTH FIVE-YEAR PLAN PERIOD

项 目	Item	“十四五”时期监测发展目标	Target in the 14th Five-year Plan	2022
常住人口规模 (万人)	Permanent Population (10000 persons)	≤2300	≤2300	2184.3
地区生产总值年均增速 (%)	Average Annual Growth Rate of GDP (%)	5左右	5 or so	【4.7】
城市副中心和平原新城增加值占地区生产总值比重 (%)	Added Value of Beijing Municipal Administrative Center and Plain New Towns as % of GDP (%)	>23	>23	21.8
全员劳动生产率 (万元/人)	Overall Labor Productivity (10000 yuan/person)	35左右	35 or so	36.3
全社会研究与试验发展经费支出占地区生产总值的比例 (%)	R&D Expenditure as % of GDP (%)	6左右	6 or so	6.83
每万人口高价值发明专利拥有量 (件)	High-value Invention Patent Ownership per 10000 Persons (unit)	82左右	82 or so	112.0
数字经济增加值年均增速 (%)(当年价格)	Average Annual Growth Rate of added value of Digital Economy(Current Year's Prices) (%)	7.5左右	7.5 or so	【9.8】
全市居民人均可支配收入年均实际增速 (%)	Average Annual Real Growth Rate of Per Capita Disposable Income of Residents of the Whole City (%)	与经济增长基本同步	keeping pace with economic growth	【4.1】
实际利用外资规模 (亿美元)	Actual Use of Foreign Capital (USD 100 million)	累计830左右	accumulated 830 or so	318.4
生产生活用水总量 (亿立方米)	Total Volume of Water Consumed for Production and Domestic Use (100 million cu.m)	<30	<30	24.6
地表水质量达到或好于Ⅲ类水体比例 (%)	Surface Water as % of Category-III Water Body in Terms of Same or Better Quality (%)	达到国家要求	meeting the national requirements	76
细颗粒物($PM_{2.5}$)年均浓度值 (微克/立方米)	Average Annual Concentration of $PM_{2.5}$ (μg/cu.m)	达到国家要求	meeting the national requirements	30
森林覆盖率 (%)	Forest Coverage Rate (%)	45	45	44.8
单位地区生产总值能耗降幅 (%)	Decrease of Energy Consumption per Unit of GDP (%)	达到国家要求	meeting the national requirements	3.58
每千常住人口执业(助理)医师数 (人)	Number of Licensed (Assistant) Physicians per 1000 of Permanent Population (person)	5.6左右	5.6 or so	5.72
单位地区生产总值生产安全事故死亡率 (人/百亿元)	Death Rate of Work Accidents per Unit of GDP (person/10 billion yuan)	<0.9	<0.9	0.96
食品安全抽检合格率 (%)	Up-to-standard Rate of Food Security Spot Checks (%)	>98.5	>98.5	98.52
药品抽验合格率 (%)	Up-to-standard Rate of Drug Spot Checks (%)	>99	>99	100.00

注：【】内数值为“十四五”时期以来年均增速。
Note: Figures in [ ] refer to the average annual growth rate since the 14th five-year plan period.

1-8 四次经济普查法人单位基本情况

项　　目	Item	法人单位数(个) Total Number of Legal Entities (unit)			
		2004	2008	2013	2018
合　计	**Total**	**220947**	**267890**	**630545**	**988619**
按登记注册类型分	**By Registration Type**				
内　资	Domestially-Invested Enterprises	213857	258238	617359	973887
国　有	State-owned Enterprises	20722	15672	22094	17953
集　体	Collectively-owned Enterprises	15879	9936	13845	15366
股份合作	Joint-equity Cooperative Enterprises	22180	10666	14456	6005
联　营	Associated Enterprises	614	403	1363	350
有限责任公司	Limited Liability Corporations	31480	49555	149881	76162
股份有限公司	Corporations Limited by Shares	3798	4602	5011	4475
私　营	Private Enterprises	110531	161288	390809	835891
其　他	Others	8653	6116	19900	17685
港澳台商投资	Hong Kong, Macao and Taiwan-invested	2257	2986	4960	5511
外商投资	Foreign-invested Enterprises	4833	6666	8226	9221
按隶属关系分	**By Affiliation**				
中　央	Central	10484	8728	9747	8732
地　方	Local	210463	259162	620798	979887
按行业分	**By Sector**				
农、林、牧、渔业	Agriculture, Forestry, Animal Husbandry and Fishery				413
采矿业	Mining	564	142	127	78
制造业	Manufacturing	30870	28786	33055	25684
电力、热力、燃气及水生产和供应业	Production and Supply of Electricity, Heating, Gas and Water	271	359	638	1193
建筑业	Construction	5878	9164	18486	35130
批发和零售业	Wholesale and Retail Trade	65084	85054	190704	273395
交通运输、仓储和邮政业	Transport, Storage and Post	3889	6022	14290	19176
住宿和餐饮业	Accommodation and Catering	8705	10695	16323	34458
信息传输、软件和信息技术服务业	Information Transmission, Software and Information Technology Services	11611	15776	47602	77152
金融业	Finance	672	1025	3811	12796
房地产业	Real Estate	8782	10955	17805	26885
租赁和商务服务业	Leasing and Business Services	32527	45003	134926	184764
科学研究和技术服务业	Scientific Research and Technical Services	13828	20451	71206	154187
水利、环境和公共设施管理业	Management of Water Conservancy, Environment and Public Facilities	1476	1719	3964	7346
居民服务、修理和其他服务业	Resident Services, Repair and Other Services	13001	10239	18735	36756
教　育	Education	5423	6242	11145	21236
卫生和社会工作	Health and Social Works	1745	2270	3810	6607
文化、体育和娱乐业	Culture, Sports and Entertainment	5856	7369	26784	53885
公共管理、社会保障和社会组织	Public Management, Social Security and Social Organizations	10765	6619	17134	17478

注：1.本表2004年、2008年行业划分执行《国民经济行业分类》(GB/T 4754—2002)标准，2013年执行《国民经济行业分类》(GB/T 4754—2011)标准，2018年执行《国民经济行业分类》(GB/T 4754—2017)标准。
2.表中2018年资产总计、收入总计、企业利润、年末从业人员合计数包括铁路部门数据，分组数据不含。

BASIC STATISTICS FOR LEGAL ENTITIES IN THE FOURTH ECONOMIC CENSUS

资产总计(亿元) Total Assets (100 million yuan)				收入总计 (亿元) Total Income (100 million yuan)			
2004	2008	2013	2018	2004	2008	2013	2018
216316.9	**646673.0**	**1220785.2**	**2119561.6**	**30942.0**	**66702.8**	**140828.4**	**199152.1**
206314.5	623894.6	1166922.3	1985481.9	25986.1	52376.6	114828.6	162106.2
92836.4	280476.4	318572.3	828238.3	7729.4	11678.0	16652.3	24528.0
1711.4	1468.7	2684.0	5463.1	665.0	682.7	614.3	677.1
2953.8	625.6	1098.2	1359.5	387.2	310.8	446.6	322.6
130.8	101.9	107.7	62.6	63.0	29.5	45.6	14.7
45133.1	111630.9	225521.5	432145.1	8661.3	21588.4	62577.8	81395.9
58244.2	219733.8	587253.5	585069.2	4634.1	10644.3	18133.4	20911.1
4951.7	9085.3	29471.4	130690.4	3769.7	7155.3	15808.7	33206.9
353.2	772.2	2213.7	2453.5	76.4	287.7	550.0	1049.8
3558.1	7515.9	16959.1	38758.3	1110.0	3722.8	6725.3	15675.8
6444.2	15262.4	36903.9	56531.1	3845.8	10603.3	19274.5	20542.2
168110.5	532422.7	918654.6	1551884.8	13037.9	26806.7	58770.4	72168.2
48206.4	114250.3	302130.6	528886.5	17904.1	39896.0	82058.0	126156.0
			28.0				5.6
69.0	433.1	2927.1	3983.7	152.7	384.6	1419.2	553.3
6531.1	9981.8	17827.4	26713.7	5259.5	9703.6	14565.1	17012.0
6851.8	7317.3	13204.4	21867.4	813.1	1780.8	4070.5	5759.3
3199.9	7283.4	18021.1	35232.6	2083.4	4140.5	10244.9	15415.5
8103.0	17832.9	40399.0	62339.8	9636.2	24305.8	55353.5	66771.0
2494.3	4999.9	15176.9	54752.4	751.0	2378.1	4878.5	6396.0
777.7	1204.6	2048.6	2559.2	361.4	662.0	1020.8	1412.3
8734.8	11120.3	28206.2	55834.3	1347.0	2953.3	5719.9	13749.1
141269.9	474100.4	873336.5	1486292.5	4117.1	6199.0	16762.4	24901.7
10016.4	20042.3	47129.9	96972.5	1760.1	2518.3	4964.0	6526.8
19440.6	74670.8	117957.3	194326.7	1203.5	3575.7	10240.0	12313.4
2932.3	9569.2	24304.6	43862.1	1132.9	3785.8	6722.1	11717.8
714.0	929.3	2870.9	5839.4	88.9	216.5	413.9	1093.7
822.7	252.7	897.7	1075.3	266.8	137.5	316.2	535.0
1120.8	1990.3	3710.9	6591.7	490.1	852.0	692.0	2913.4
464.6	741.9	1338.2	2513.1	323.4	621.0	1146.7	2526.6
1083.2	1747.0	4367.3	9011.1	446.6	826.8	1360.7	2653.1
1690.9	2455.8	7061.4	9765.9	708.2	1661.5	938.0	6896.5

Note: a) In 2004 and 2008, the sectors in this table were classified in accordance with the standards in *the Classification of National Economic Sectors* (GB/T 4754-2002); in 2013, the classification was carried out in accordance with the standards in *the Classification of National Economic Sectors* (GB/T 4754-2011); and in 2018, the classification was carried out in accordance with the standards in *the Classification National Economic Sectors* (GB/T 4754-2017).

b) In 2018, the data on total assets, total income, enterprise profits and year-end total number of persons employed included that of the railway sector; however, the grouped data did not cover the data of the railway sector.

1-8 续表 Continued

项目	Item	企业利润(亿元) Profit of Enterprises (100 million yuan) 2004	2008	2013	2018	年末从业人员(万人) Employed Persons (10000 persons) 2004	2008	2013	2018
合 计	**Total**	**1989.0**	**5488.1**	**20566.8**	**24842.9**	**705.2**	**816.9**	**1111.3**	**1361.0**
按登记注册类型分	**By Registration Type**								
内 资	Domestially-Invested Enterprises	1460.7	4602.9	17673.4	19658.5	639.3	704.7	965.1	1199.4
国 有	State-owned Enterprises	806.5	1332.1	2880.4	4161.7	195.2	195.0	194.9	178.8
集 体	Collectively-owned Enterprises	23.2	14.7	18.5	-19.4	43.6	26.5	21.7	16.7
股份合作	Joint-equity Cooperative Enterprises	26.2	6.8	6.6	7.8	28.6	14.0	12.2	5.9
联 营	Associated Enterprises	1.2	-0.9	-0.4	0.3	2.4	1.3	1.1	0.5
有限责任公司	Limited Liability Corporations	393.4	1536.3	8916.4	9953.8	155.2	221.1	331.1	343.2
股份有限公司	Corporations Limited by Shares	134.6	1630.4	5645.9	5682.8	39.3	62.4	80.8	92.1
私 营	Private Enterprises	75.6	65.2	191.9	-139.9	162.4	170.6	300.6	537.5
其 他	Others	0.1	18.4	14.1	11.4	12.7	13.9	22.6	24.5
港澳台商投资	Hong Kong, Macao and Taiwan-invested	188.0	113.1	649.4	910.8	20.4	39.0	55.1	73.6
外商投资	Foreign-invested Enterprises	340.2	772.1	2244.0	3915.5	45.4	73.2	91.2	79.7
按隶属关系分	**By Affiliation**								
中 央	Central	1083.5	3475.3	14647.9	16544.0	134.6	168.3	178.3	185.4
地 方	Local	905.5	2012.8	5918.9	7940.8	570.5	648.6	933.1	1167.2
按行业分	**By Sector**								
农、林、牧、渔业	Agriculture, Forestry,Animal Husbandry and Fishery				-0.4				0.2
采矿业	Mining	16.8	44.9	18.6	-69.9	4.1	5.1	6.9	3.6
制造业	Manufacturing	268.7	301.8	860.4	1095.6	148.8	134.7	138.5	96.8
电力、热力、燃气及水生产和供应业	Production and Supply of Electricity, Heating, Gas and Water,	104.3	192.6	377.5	535.5	7.8	6.7	9.3	10.8
建筑业	Construction	46.9	87.7	436.5	498.0	69.7	54.7	65.5	96.5
批发和零售业	Wholesale and Retail Trade	221.7	726.5	1026.1	1456.0	83.2	94.3	147.8	161.4
交通运输、仓储和邮政业	Transport, Storage and Post	76.0	-3.3	275.2	776.3	43.0	69.5	68.6	71.5
住宿和餐饮业	Accommodation and Catering	-0.3	7.1	-24.2	20.2	38.4	44.9	50.6	56.3
信息传输、软件和信息技术服务业	Information Transmission, Software and Information Technology Services	550.3	651.4	1830.7	2998.0	28.5	46.6	93.0	138.9
金融业	Finance	237.6	1356.6	10964.5	12027.4	15.0	25.1	43.3	80.6
房地产业	Real Estate	126.2	316.2	819.7	899.4	31.9	41.0	56.4	73.0
租赁和商务服务业	Leasing and Business Services	244.8	1484.9	3192.2	4318.9	63.8	95.9	141.7	187.2
科学研究和技术服务业	Scientific Research and Technical Services	58.4	280.0	668.8	291.6	38.9	56.4	95.2	140.4
水利、环境和公共设施管理业	Management of Water Conservancy, Environment and Public Facilities	-0.3	5.2	21.2	9.0	7.5	9.3	12.9	18.4
居民服务、修理和其他服务业	Resident Services, Repair and Other Services	15.1	6.2	-1.0	-22.0	19.6	14.1	21.5	30.6
教 育	Education	-0.8	0.5	11.2	-26.1	38.7	43.1	53.1	67.1
卫生和社会工作	Health and Social Works	-0.3	0.5	0.5	-35.3	16.0	20.0	27.8	36.4
文化、体育和娱乐业	Culture, Sports and Entertainment	23.8	29.4	89.0	70.6	16.2	18.6	27.6	37.5
公共管理、社会保障和社会组织	Public Management, Social Security and Social Organizations					34.1	36.6	51.8	54.1

1—9 规模(限额)以上法人单位基本情况(2022年)
NUMBER OF LEGAL ENTITIES ABOVE DESIGNATED SIZE(2022)

单位：个 (unit)

项 目	Item	法人单位数合计 Total Number of Legal Entities	单产业法人 Single-industry Legal Entities	多产业法人 Multi-industry Legal Entities
合 计	**Total**	**47276**	**36268**	**11008**
按登记注册类型分	**By Registration Type**			
内 资	Domestically-invested Enterprises	42802	33433	9369
国 有	State-owned Enterprises	3448	3287	161
集 体	Collectively-owned Enterprises	347	314	33
股份合作	Joint-equity Cooperative Enterprises	333	287	46
联 营	Associated Enterprises	16	14	2
有限责任公司	Limited Liability Corporations	16854	12423	4431
股份有限公司	Corporations Limited by Shares	1092	556	536
私 营	Private Enterprises	20451	16296	4155
其 他	Others	261	256	5
港澳台商投资	Hong Kong, Macao and Taiwan-invested Enterprises	1586	1030	556
与港澳台商合资经营	Joint Ventures	383	266	117
与港澳台商合作经营	Cooperative Enterprises	49	41	8
港澳台商独资	Solely-funded Enterprises	1082	685	397
港澳台商投资股份有限公司	Companies Limited by Shares	50	24	26
其他港澳台商投资	Others	22	14	8
外商投资	Foreign-invested Enterprises	2888	1805	1083
中外合资经营	Joint Ventures	773	523	250
中外合作经营	Cooperative Enterprises	59	45	14
外资企业	Solely-funded Enterprises	1941	1167	774
外商投资股份有限公司	Companies Limited by Shares	103	61	42
其他外商投资	Others	12	9	3
按机构类型分	**By Organization Type**			
企 业	Enterprises	43562	32685	10877
事业单位	Institutions	3213	3096	117
机 关	Government Agencies and Organizations	2	1	1
社会团体	Social Organizations	10	9	1
其他机构	Others	489	477	12

1-10 国民经济各行业规模(限额)以上法人单位情况(2022年)
NUMBER OF LEGAL ENTITIES IN DIFFERENT SECTORS OF THE NATIONAL ECONOMY ABOVE DESIGNATED SIZE (2022)

单位：个 (unit)

行　业	Sector	法人单位数 合　计 Total Number of Legal Entities	单产业法人 Single-industry Legal Entities	多产业法人 Multi-industry Legal Entities
合　计	**Total**	**47276**	**36268**	**11008**
农、林、牧、渔业	**Agriculture, Forestry, Animal Husbandry and Fishery**			
采矿业	**Mining**	**9**	**3**	**6**
煤炭开采和洗选业	Mining and Washing of Coal			
石油和天然气开采业	Extraction of Petroleum and Natural Gas	2		2
黑色金属矿采选业	Mining and Processing of Ferrous Metal Ores	2	1	1
有色金属矿采选业	Mining and Processing of Non-Ferrous Metal Ores			
非金属矿采选业	Mining and Processing of Non-metal Ores			
开采专业及辅助性活动	Professional and Support Activities for Mining	5	2	3
其他采矿业	Mining of Other Ores			
制造业	**Manufacturing**	**2906**	**2055**	**851**
农副食品加工业	Processing of Food from Agricultural Products	101	64	37
食品制造业	Manufacture of Foods	114	77	37
酒、饮料和精制茶制造业	Manufacture of Wine, Beverage and Refined Tea	36	24	12
烟草制品业	Manufacture of Tobacco	1	1	
纺织业	Manufacture of Textile	10	6	4
纺织服装、服饰业	Manufacture of Textile, Wearing Apparel and Ornament	70	45	25
皮革、毛皮、羽毛及其制品和制鞋业	Manufacture of Leather, Fur, Feather and Its Products, and Footwear	2	1	1
木材加工和木、竹、藤、棕、草制品业	Processing of Timbers, Manufacture of Wood, Bamboo, Rattan, Palm and Straw Products	5	4	1
家具制造业	Manufacture of Furniture	32	17	15
造纸和纸制品业	Manufacture of Paper and Paper Products	27	23	4
印刷和记录媒介复制业	Printing, Reproduction of Recording Media	91	82	9
文教、工美、体育和娱乐用品制造业	Manufacture of Articles for Culture, Education, Arts and Crafts, Sport and Entertainment Activities	21	15	6
石油、煤炭及其他燃料加工业	Processing of Petroleum, Coal and Other Fuels	14	12	2
化学原料和化学制品制造业	Manufacture of Chemical Raw Materials and Chemical Products	134	101	33
医药制造业	Manufacture of Medicines	263	190	73
化学纤维制造业	Manufacture of Chemical Fibres	1		1
橡胶和塑料制品业	Manufacture of Rubber and Plastics Products	50	40	10
非金属矿物制品业	Manufacture of Non-metallic Mineral Products	172	124	48
黑色金属冶炼和压延加工业	Smelting and Pressing of Ferrous Metals	5	4	1

注：行业划分执行《国民经济行业分类》(GB/T 4754—2017)标准。
Note: Sectors in this table are classified in accordance with the Standard for *Industrial Classification for National Economic Activities* (GB/T 4754-2017).

1-10 续表 1 Continued 1

单位：个 (unit)

行 业	Sector	法人单位数 合 计 Total Number of Legal Entities	单产业法人 Single-industry Legal Entities	多产业法人 Multi-industry Legal Entities
有色金属冶炼和压延加工业	Smelting and Processing of Non-ferrous Metals	21	17	4
金属制品业	Manufacture of Metal Products	143	112	31
通用设备制造业	Manufacture of General-Purpose Machinery	198	133	65
专用设备制造业	Manufacture of Special-Purpose Machinery	368	265	103
汽车制造业	Manufacture of Motor Vehicles	195	151	44
铁路、船舶、航空航天和其他运输设备制造业	Manufacture of Railway, Ships, Aerospace and Other Transport Equipments	74	51	23
电气机械和器材制造业	Manufacture of Electrical Machinery and Equipment	215	140	75
计算机、通信和其他电子设备制造业	Manufacture of Computers, Communication Equipment and Other Electronic Equipment	313	204	109
仪器仪表制造业	Manufacture of Measuring Instrument and Meter	192	128	64
其他制造业	Other Manufacturing	6	6	
废弃资源综合利用业	Waste Rrecycling and Recovery	11	8	3
金属制品、机械和设备修理业	Repair of Fabricated Metal Products, Machinery and Equipment	21	10	11
电力、热力、燃气及水生产和供应业	**Production and Supply of Electricity, Heating, Gas and Water**	**165**	**131**	**34**
电力、热力生产和供应业	Production and Supply of Electric Power and Heat Power	110	92	18
燃气生产和供应业	Production and Supply of Gas	21	15	6
水的生产和供应业	Production and Supply of Water	34	24	10
建筑业	**Construction**	**2808**	**1910**	**898**
房屋建筑业	Construction of Building	528	291	237
土木工程建筑业	Civil Engineering Construction	630	417	213
建筑安装业	Construction Installation	630	428	202
建筑装饰、装修和其他建筑业	Building Decoration, Finishing and Other Construction	1020	774	246
批发和零售业	**Wholesale and Retail Trade**	**10749**	**8674**	**2075**
批发业	Wholesale	8173	6967	1206
零售业	Retail Trade	2576	1707	869
交通运输、仓储和邮政业	**Transport, Storage and Post**	**843**	**558**	**285**
铁路运输业	Transport via Railway	17	8	9
道路运输业	Transport via Road	338	247	91
水上运输业	Water Transport	4	3	1
航空运输业	Air Transport	33	14	19
管道运输业	Transport via Pipeline	3		3
多式联运和运输代理业	Multimodal Transport and Transport Agent Service	301	177	124
装卸搬运和仓储业	Loading, Unloading, Portage and Storage	109	88	21
邮政业	Post	38	21	17
住宿和餐饮业	**Accommodation and Catering**	**3319**	**2528**	**791**
住宿业	Accommodation	1142	955	187
餐饮业	Catering	2177	1573	604
信息传输、软件和信息技术服务业	**Information Transmission, Software and Information Technology Services**	**4330**	**2859**	**1471**
电信、广播电视和卫星传输服务	Telecommunications, Broadcasting, Television and Satellite Transmission Services	257	165	92
互联网和相关服务	Internet and Related Services	799	587	212
软件和信息技术服务业	Software and Information Technology Services	3274	2107	1167

1-10 续表 2 Continued 2

单位：个 (unit)

行业	Sector	法人单位数 合计 Total Number of Legal Entities	单产业法人 Single-industry Legal Entities	多产业法人 Multi-industry Legal Entities
金融业	**Finance**	**2494**	**1998**	**496**
货币金融服务	Monetary Financial Services	727	621	106
资本市场服务	Capital Market Services	942	833	109
保险业	Insurance	574	345	229
其他金融业	Other Financial Services	251	199	52
房地产业	**Real Estate**	**4119**	**3320**	**799**
租赁和商务服务业	**Leasing and Business Services**	**5485**	**4181**	**1304**
租赁业	Leasing	202	148	54
商务服务业	Business Services	5283	4033	1250
科学研究和技术服务业	**Scientific Research and and Technical Services**	**3896**	**2636**	**1260**
研究和试验发展	Research and Experimental Development	630	538	92
专业技术服务业	Professional Technique Services	2004	1176	828
科技推广和应用服务业	Technique Generalization and Application Services	1262	922	340
水利、环境和公共设施管理业	**Management of Water Conservancy, Environment and Public Facilities**	**525**	**397**	**128**
水利管理业	Management of Water Conservancy	38	35	3
生态保护和环境治理业	Ecological Protection and Environmental Control	105	66	39
公共设施管理业	Management of Public Facilities	371	287	84
土地管理业	Management of Land	11	9	2
居民服务、修理和其他服务业	**Resident Services, Repair and Other Services**	**711**	**544**	**167**
居民服务业	Resident Services	208	143	65
机动车、电子产品和日用产品修理业	Repair of Motor Vehicles, Electronics and Household Appliances	206	161	45
其他服务业	Other Services	297	240	57
教　育	**Education**	**1915**	**1758**	**157**
卫生和社会工作	**Health and Social Works**	**898**	**802**	**96**
卫　生	Health	805	716	89
社会工作	Social Work Activities	93	86	7
文化、体育和娱乐业	**Culture, Sports and Entertainment**	**2103**	**1913**	**190**
新闻和出版业	Journalism and Publishing	513	451	62
广播、电视、电影和录音制作业	Radio Broadcasting, Television, Movies and Sound Recording	681	636	45
文化艺术业	Cultures and Arts	303	284	19
体　育	Sports Activities	200	167	33
娱乐业	Entertainments	406	375	31
公共管理、社会保障和社会组织	**Public Administration, Social Security and Social Organizations**	**1**	**1**	
中国共产党机关	Organs of Communist Party of China			
国家机构	Organs of State			
人民政协、民主党派	Peole's Political Consultative Conference and Democratic Parties			
社会保障	Social Security			
群众团体、社会团体和其他成员组织	Mass Communities, Social Organizations and Other Membership Organizations	1	1	
基层群众自治组织及其他组织	Grass Roots Self-Government Organization and Other Organizations			
国际组织	**International Organizations**			

1-11 规模(限额)以上企业法人单位情况(2022年)
NUMBER OF CORPORATE ENTERPRISES ABOVE DESIGNATED SIZE (2022)

单位：个 (unit)

项目	Item	法人单位合计 Total Number of Legal Entities	项目	Item	法人单位合计 Total Number of Legal Entities
合计	**Total**	**43562**	与港澳台商合资经营	Joint Ventures	383
按成立时间分	**By Establishment Time**		与港澳台商合作经营	Cooperative Enterprises	49
1949年以前	Before 1949	23	港澳台商独资	Solely-funded Enterprises	1081
1950-1965	From 1950 to 1965	180	港澳台商投资股份有限公司	Corporations Limited by Shares	50
1966-1979	From 1966 to 1979	103	其他港澳台商投资	Others	22
1980-1989	From 1980 to 1989	1187	外商投资企业	Foreign-invested Enterprises	2885
1990年以后	After 1990	42069	中外合资经营	Joint Ventures	773
按登记注册类型分	**By Registration Type**		中外合作经营	Cooperative Enterprises	58
内资企业	Domestically-invested Enterprises	39092	外资企业	Solely-funded Enterprises	1939
国有企业	State-owned Enterprises	235	外商投资股份有限公司	Corporations Limited by Shares	103
集体企业	Collectively-owned Enterprises	302	其他外商投资	Other	12
股份合作企业	Joint-equity Cooperative Enterprises	332	**按控股情况分**	**By Share Holding Status**	
联营企业	Associated Enterprises	16	国有控股	State-owned Enterprises	7753
有限责任公司	Limited Liability Corporations	16852	集体控股	Collectively-controlled Enterprises	1070
股份有限公司	Corporations Limited by Shares	1092	私人控股	Privately-controlled Enterprises	30904
私营企业	Private Enterprises	20256	港澳台商控股	Hong Kong, Macao and Taiwan-controlled Enterprises	1523
其他内资企业	Other Domestically-invested Enterprises	7	外商控股	Foreign-controlled Enterprises	2245
港澳台商投资企业	Hong Kong, Macao and Taiwan-invested Enterprises	1585	其他	Others	67

1-12 全市私营个体经济基本情况
STATISTICS FOR PRIVATE AND INDIVIDUAL ECONOMY

项目	Item	私营 Private			个体 Individual		
		2022	2021	2022年为2021年% 2022 as % of 2021	2022	2021	2022年为2021年% 2022 as % of 2021
登记注册*	**Registered at Administration**						
户数 (户)	Number of Business Entities (unit)	1739843	1621086	107.3	420195	423217	99.3
注册资本 (亿元)	Registered Capital (100 million yuan)	236941.8	224055.3	105.8	216.0	200.7	107.7
税收情况	**Taxes**						
税收收入合计 (亿元)	Total Tax Revenue (100 million yuan)	1907.1	2057.9	92.7	3.4	5.0	68.8

注：*为期末时点数。
资料来源：北京市市场监督管理局、国家税务总局北京市税务局。
Note: Figures with * indicate the accumulative figures at end of the year.
Source: Beijing Municipal Administration of Market Supervision,Beijing Municipal Tax Service of State Taxation Administration.

1-13 规模以上非公经济主要指标(2022年)
MAIN INDICATORS OF NON-PUBLIC SECTORS OF THE ECONOMY ABOVE DESIGNATED SIZE (2022)

项目	Item	单位数 (个) Number of Enterprises (unit)	收入合计 (亿元) Total Income (100 million yuan)	利润总额 (亿元) Total Profits (100 million yuan)	应交税金合计 (亿元) Taxes Payable (100 million yuan)	从业人员平均人数 (万人) Average Number of Persons Employed (10000 persons)
合　计	**Total**	**35452**	**101795.3**	**7078.8**	**2682.4**	**449.1**
按登记注册类型分	**Grouped by Registration Type**					
内　资	Domestic-funded	31263	52572.6	1471.4	1418.0	319.1
港澳台商投资	Hong Kong, Macao and Taiwan-funded	1518	23842.2	2560.9	459.3	57.8
外商投资	Foreign-funded	2671	25380.4	3046.5	805.2	72.3
按规模分	**Grouped by Size**					
#大型企业	Large-sized Enterprises	1248	44049.1	4915.2	1054.8	171.6
中小微型企业	Mini-, Small-, Mediume-sized Enterprises	30390	51491.2	1126.5	1285.1	233.2
中　型	Medium Size	6449	30415.7	809.8	739.8	125.8
小　型	Small Size	18861	16091.1	371.9	430.6	102.1
微　型	Mini Size	5080	4984.4	-55.1	114.6	5.3
按行业分	**Grouped by Sector**					
#制造业	Manufacturing	2411	10967.3	917.6	345.4	44.3
建筑业	Construction	2332	2697.3	39.4	74.8	16.5
批发和零售业	Wholesale and Retail Trade	9342	42171.8	1150.3	585.3	50.3
交通运输、仓储和邮政业	Transport, Storage and Post	649	3789.9	27.1	35.9	14.6
住宿和餐饮业	Accommodation and Restaurants	2782	834.3	-63.8	18.9	28.8
信息传输、软件和信息技术服务业	Information Transmission,Software and Information Technology Services	3820	21908.3	3062.9	660.5	97.5
金融业	Finance	1616	4266.6	1017.8	211.7	22.5
房地产业	Real Estate	2453	3094.1	-10.3	360.7	30.7
租赁和商务服务业	Renting and Leasing Activities and Business Services	4462	6521.1	559.6	195.9	76.3
科学研究和技术服务业	Scientific Research and Development, Technical Services	2641	2846.0	291.3	125.0	29.5
水利、环境和公共设施管理业	Management of Water Conservancy, Environment and Public Facilities	202	228.4	7.6	9.2	2.9
居民服务、修理和其他服务业	Resident Services, Repair and Other Services	631	203.7	0.2	8.4	10.3
教　育	Education	444	763.2	25.3	17.0	12.5
卫生和社会工作	Health and Social Works	363	417.4	-3.1	5.6	6.3
文化、体育和娱乐业	Culture, Sports and Entertainment	1229	540.8	7.5	20.3	4.7

注：1.本表不包含个体经营户数据。
2.按规模分组中的数据为非公企业法人单位数据。
3.行业划分执行《国民经济行业分类》(GB/T 4754—2017)标准。

Note: a) Data of the self-employed are not included in this table.
b) Data in the groups by size refer to those of the non-public corporate legal entities.
c) The sectors in this table are classified in accordance with the Standard in the Classification of National Economic Sectors(GB/T4754-2017).

1–14 规模以上中小微企业主要指标(2022年)
MAIN INDICATORS OF MICRO- SMALL- AND MEDIUM-SIZED ENTERPRISES ABOVE DESIGNATED SIZE (2022)

项 目	Item	单位数 (个) Number of Enterprises (unit)	收入合计 (亿元) Total Income (100 million yuan)	利润总额 (亿元) Total Profits (100 million yuan)	应交税金合计 (亿元) Total Tax Payable (100 million yuan)	从业人员平均人数 (万人) Average Number of Employed Persons (10000 persons)
合 计	**Total**	**36981**	**79054.1**	**3611.3**	**2281.4**	**309.6**
按规模分	**Grouped by Size**					
中 型	Medium Size	8929	51009.7	2348.9	1362.9	177.7
小 型	Small Size	22078	21383.3	430.0	653.1	124.4
微 型	Micro Size	5974	6661.1	832.5	265.3	7.4
按登记注册类型分	**Grouped by Registration Type**					
内 资	Domestic-funded	33563	63887.5	2687.2	1846.4	268.6
港澳台商投资	Hong Kong, Macao and Taiwan-funded	1174	3820.4	213.7	143.8	14.9
外商投资	Foreign-funded	2244	11346.3	710.5	291.1	26.1
按行业分	**Grouped by Sector**					
#制造业	Manufacturing	2816	8406.2	672.8	378.1	43.6
建筑业	Construction	2543	2541.2	98.2	85.4	17.7
批发和零售业	Wholesale and Retail Trade	10371	39560.3	692.9	608.4	37.6
交通运输、仓储和邮政业	Transport, Storage and Post	783	2681.8	108.8	47.2	10.3
住宿和餐饮业	Accommodation and Restaurants	3207	530.0	-83.4	16.8	16.3
信息传输、软件和信息技术服务业	Information Transmission, Software and Information Technology Services	3778	11230.8	1134.8	306.9	42.9
房地产业	Real Estate	2414	2579.7	-103.8	296.9	22.0
租赁和商务服务业	Renting and Leasing Activities and Business Services	5163	6654.9	595.1	294.4	77.9
科学研究和技术服务业	Scientific Research and Development, Technical Services	3034	2628.7	350.3	125.4	22.8
水利、环境和公共设施管理业	Management of Water Conservancy, Environment and Public Facilities	300	353.9	18.6	14.0	2.7
居民服务、修理和其他服务业	Resident Services, Repair and Other Services	612	163.5	4.2	7.9	4.7
卫生和社会工作	Health Care and Social Works	28	9.3	-1.6	1.3	0.3
文化、体育和娱乐业	Culture, Sports and Entertainment	1771	1046.2	81.2	48.2	8.2

注：1. 本表中的企业规模划型标准执行《统计上大中小微型企业划分办法(2017)》。根据该《办法》的适用范围，在统计单位规模时，不含以下行业的单位：交通运输、仓储和邮政业中的铁路运输业，金融业，房地产业中的房地产租赁经营，教育，卫生和社会工作中的卫生。因此中小微企业数据不含以上行业数据。

2. 行业划分执行《国民经济行业分类》(GB/T 4754—2017)标准。

Note: a) In this table, enterprise size is identified in accordance with the *provisions stated in the Statistical Division Standards of Large, Medium-sized, Small and Micro Enterprises(2017)*. According to the scope of application of the measures, enterprises in the following sectors are not covered in the statistics of the size of enterprises: transport via railway in the sector of transport, storage and post; finance; real estate leasing management in the sector of real estate; education; health in the sector of health care and social works. Therefore, the data on micro, small and medium-sized enterprises do not include those related to the abovementioned sectors.

b) The sectors in this table are classified in accordance with the standards in *the Classification of National Economic Sectors* (GB/T4754-2017).

主要统计指标解释

法人单位 指有权拥有资产、承担负债，并独立从事社会经济活动（或与其他单位进行交易）的组织。法人单位应同时具备以下条件：(1) 依法成立，有自己的名称、组织机构和场所，能够独立承担民事责任；(2) 独立拥有（或授权使用）资产或者经费，承担负债，有权与其他单位签订合同；(3) 具有包括资产负债表在内的账户，或者能够根据需要编制账户。

单产业法人 指仅包含一个产业活动单位的法人单位，该法人单位同时也是一个产业活动单位。

多产业法人 指由两个及以上产业活动单位组成的法人单位，这些产业活动单位接受法人单位的管理和控制。

登记注册类型 企业法人或企业产业活动单位的登记注册类型，按其在工商行政管理机关登记注册的类型填写。如企业登记注册类型发生变化，但未及时到工商部门变更登记，企业应根据变化后的实际情况填写。其他法人和产业活动单位的登记注册类型，按其主要经费来源和管理方式，根据实际情况，比照《企业登记注册类型与代码》填写。

国有企业 指企业全部资产归国家所有，并按《中华人民共和国企业法人登记管理条例》规定登记注册的非公司制的经济组织。不包括有限责任公司中的国有独资公司。

集体企业 指企业资产归集体所有，并按《中华人民共和国企业法人登记管理条例》规定登记注册的经济组织。

股份合作企业 指以合作制为基础，由企业职工共同出资入股，吸收一定比例的社会资产投资组建，实行自主经营，自负盈亏，共同劳动，民主管理，按劳分配与按股分红相结合的一种集体经济组织。

联营企业 指两个及两个以上相同或不同所有制性质的企业法人或事业单位法人，按自愿、平等、互利的原则，共同投资组成的经济组织称为联营企业。联营企业包括国有联营企业、集体联营企业、国有与集体联营企业和其他联营企业。

有限责任公司 指根据《中华人民共和国公司登记管理条例》规定登记注册，由两个以上，五十个以下的股东共同出资，每个股东以其所认缴的出资额对公司承担有限责任，公司以其全部资产对其债务承担责任的经济组织。有限责任公司包括国有独资公司、其他有限责任公司。

私营企业 指由自然人投资设立或由自然人控股，以雇佣劳动为基础的营利性经济组织。包括按照《公司法》《合伙企业法》《私营企业暂行条例》《个人独资企业法》规定登记注册的私营独资企业、私营合伙企业、私营有限责任公司、私营股份有限公司和个人独资企业。

其他企业 指上述类型之外的其他内资经济组织。

港澳台商投资企业 指港澳台地区投资者依照中华人民共和国有关涉外经济的法律、法规成立的企业，包括与港澳台商合资经营企业、与港澳台商合作经营企业、港澳台商独资经营企业、港澳台商投资股份有限公司、其他港澳台商投资企业。

外商投资企业 指外国企业或外国人依照中华人民共和国有关涉外经济的法律、法规成立的企业，包括中外合资经营企业、中外合作经营企业、外资企业、外商投资股份有限公司、其他外商投资企业。

非公经济 指资产由我国私人控股、港澳台商控股、外商控股的“非公有控股”经济成分的企业法人单位，以及主要经费来源于私人、港澳台资和外资的非企业法人单位和个体工商户。其中，私人、港澳台及外商控股是指由其绝对控股和相对控股的经济成分。

Explanatory Notes on Main Statistical Indicators

Legal Entity refers to any organization that has the right to own assets and bear liabilities, and conducts social and economic activities independently (or conducts transactions with other entities). A legal entity shall meet all of such conditions as: (1) established in accordance with law, having its own name, organization and site, capable of assuming civil responsibilities independently; (2) independently owning (or using under authorization) assets or outlays, assuming liabilities, having the right to sign contracts with other entities; (3) maintaining accounts including balance sheet, or capable of preparing accounts as needed.

Single-industry Legal Entity refers any legal entity conducting only one industrial activity. Such legal entity is also an industrial activity entity.

Multi-industry Legal Entity refers to any legal entity composed of two or more industrial activity entities which are managed and controlled by the legal entity.

Registration Type of an enterprise as legal person or as enterprise industrial activity entity shall be completed according to the type registered at the administration for industry and commerce. In the event of any change in registration type, and no registration alteration is made with the administration for industry and commerce in good time, the registration type shall be completed according to the actual situation. Registration type for other legal persons and industrial activity entities shall be completed according to the main source of outlays and management manner, pursuant to the actual conditions, and by referring to the *Type of Enterprise Registration and Code*.

State-owned Enterprise refers to non-corporation economic organizations where the entire assets are owned by the state and which have been registered in accordance with the *Regulation of the People's Republic of China on the Management of Registration of Corporate Enterprises*, excluding solely state-funded corporations in limited liability companies.

Collectively-owned Enterprise refer to economic organizations where the assets are owned collectively and which have been registered in accordance with the *Regulation of the People's Republic of China on the Management of Registration of Corporate Enterprises*.

Joint-equity Cooperative Enterprise refers to a form of collective economic organizations based on cooperative system, where capitals come mainly from employees as their shares, with certain proportion of capital from the public, where production is organized on the basis of independent operation, independent accounting for profits and losses, joint work, democratic management, and where the distribution system integrates distribution according to work with distribution according to capital share.

Associated Enterprise refers to organizations established by two or more corporate legal persons or institutional legal persons of the same or different ownership, through joint investment on the basis of voluntary participation, equality, and mutual benefits. They include state-owned associated enterprises, collectively-owned associated enterprises, state-collective associated enterprises and other associated enterprises.

Limited Liability Company refers to economic organizations established with investment from 2-50 shareholders and registered in accordance with the *Regulation of the People's Republic of China on the Management of Registration of Corporations*, each shareholder bearing limited liability to the corporation depending on its share of investment, and the corporation bearing liability to its debt to the maximum of its total assets. Limited liability companies include solely state-funded limited liability companies and other limited liability companies.

Private Enterprise refers to profit-making economic organizations established by natural persons or controlled by natural persons using employed labor. Private enterprises include solely private-funded enterprises, private partnership enterprises, private limited liability companies, private companies limited by shares, and private-funded enterprises registered in accordance with provisions in the *Company Law*, the *Partnership Enterprises Law*, the *Interim Regulations on Private Enterprises*, and the *Sole Proprietorship Enterprise Law*.

Other Enterprise refers to domestically funded economic organizations other than those mentioned above.

Hong Kong, Macao and Taiwan-invested Enterprise refers to enterprises established by investors from Hong Kong, Macao and Taiwan in accordance with laws and rules of the People's Republic of China on foreign-related businesses. They include joint ventures with investors from Hong Kong, Macao and Taiwan, cooperative enterprises with investors from Hong Kong, Macao and Taiwan, enterprises wholly funded by investors from Hong Kong, Macao and Taiwan, companies limited by shares and funded by investors from Hong Kong, Macao and Taiwan, and other enterprises funded by investors from Hong Kong, Macao and Taiwan.

Foreign-invested Enterprise refers to enterprises established by foreign enterprises or foreigners in accordance with laws and regulations of the People's Republic of China on foreign-related businesses. They include Sino-foreign joint ventures, Sino-foreign cooperative enterprises, foreign wholly-funded enterprises, foreign-funded companies limited by shares, and other foreign-funded enterprises.

Non-public Economy means corporate legal entities of "non-public sector of the economy" whose assets are controlled by Chinese individuals, investors from Hong Kong, Macao and Taiwan, and foreign investors, along with the non-corporate legal entities and self-employed operators whose main funds are from individuals, investors from Hong Kong, Macao and Taiwan, and foreign investors. Thereinto, enterprises controlled by individuals, investors from Hong Kong, Macao and Taiwan, and foreign investors mean economic sectors with absolute or relative control by such companies.

国民经济核算
NATIONAL ACCOUNTS

简要说明

一、主要内容

本章资料包括历年北京市地区生产总值、部分新兴产业增加值、各行业增加值、三次产业及三大需求贡献率、居民消费水平、社会劳动生产率等内容。

二、统计调查方法说明

地区生产总值是统计部门根据统计资料、财政决算资料、行政管理部门的行政记录资料和部门财务资料采用不同方法核算的数据。

三、关于历史数据调整的问题

按照国家统计局部署，2016 年开始实施地区研发支出核算方法改革，将研发支出未计入地区生产总值部分进行补充核算，并对历史数据进行了修订。

2018 年数据为北京市第四次全国经济普查数据，并根据普查结果对历史数据进行了修订。

2022 年的地区生产总值为初步核算数据，待最终核实数据确定后将在次年年鉴中进行更新。

四、有关统计标准的变化说明

（一）关于行业划分标准。本章行业划分执行《国民经济行业分类》（GB/T 4754-2017）标准。

（二）关于三次产业划分。三次产业分类依据国家统计局 2018 年修订的《三次产业划分规定》。第一产业是指农、林、牧、渔业（不含农、林、牧、渔专业及辅助性活动）。第二产业是指采矿业（不含开采专业及辅助性活动），制造业（不含金属制品、机械和设备修理业），电力、热力、燃气及水生产和供应业，建筑业。第三产业即服务业，是指除第一产业、第二产业以外的其他行业。

本章三次产业的分类均执行调整后的划分规定。

Brief Introduction

I. Main Content

Statistics in this chapter include the GDP of Beijing, added value of some emerging sectors, added value of different sectors, contribution rate of three industries and three demands, residents' consumption level and social labor productivity in previous years.

II. Statistical Survey Methods

The GDP of Beijing is calculated by the statistics department using different methods according to the statistical data and final financial account data as well as the administrative records of the administrative departments and the financial data of departments.

Ⅲ. Adjustment to Historical Statistics

In accordance with the deployment of the National Bureau of Statistics of the People's Republic of China (NBS), the reform of calculation method of regional R&D expenditure has been implemented since 2016, according to which supplementary accounting was carried out on the part of R&D expenditure not included in GDP data, and historical data were revised.

The data for 2018 were collected from the fourth national economic census in Beijing, and historical data were revised according to the census results.

The GDP data for 2022 were the preliminary accounting data and shall be updated in the yearbook of the following year after the final data verification and confirmation.

IV. Explanation on Changes of Statistical Standards

(I) Standard for Classification of Sectors.The standards in the *Classification of National Economic Sectors* (GB/T 4754-2017) have been implemented.

(II) Classification of Three Industries. The classification of three industries is based on the *Regulations on Three Industries Classification (2012)* revised by the National Bureau of Statistics in 2018. The primary industry refers to agriculture, forestry, animal production and hunting, fishing (excluding professional and supporting activities of agriculture, forestry, animal production and hunting, fishing). The secondary industry refers to mining and quarrying (excluding professional and support activities for mining), manufacturing (excluding repair of fabricated metal products, machinery and equipment), production and distribution of electricity, heating power, gas and water and construction. The tertiary industry refers to others excluding the primary and secondary industries.

The classification of three industries since 1978 as mentioned in this chapter has all been subject to the classification provisions after adjustment.

2-1 地区生产总值(1978-2022年)
GROSS DOMESTIC PRODUCT (1978-2022)

单位：亿元 (100 million yuan)

年份 Year	地区生产总值 Gross Domestic Product	按产业分 By Three Industries 第一产业 Primary Industry	第二产业 Secondary Industry	第三产业 Tertiary Industry	按行业分 By Sector #工业 Industry	#建筑业 Construction	人均地区生产总值(元) Per Capita Gross Domestic Product (yuan)	人均地区生产总值(美元) Per Capita Gross Domestic Product (USD)
1978	108.8	5.6	77.2	26.0	70.2	7.2	1257	797
1979	120.1	5.2	85.0	29.9	77.4	7.8	1358	908
1980	139.1	6.1	95.6	37.4	86.9	8.9	1544	1009
1981	139.2	6.6	92.3	40.3	82.7	9.8	1526	895
1982	154.9	10.2	99.6	45.1	89.3	10.5	1671	883
1983	183.1	12.7	112.5	57.9	98.8	13.9	1943	983
1984	216.6	14.7	130.5	71.4	114.0	16.7	2262	972
1985	257.1	17.7	153.5	85.9	130.7	23.0	2643	900
1986	284.9	19.0	165.6	100.3	141.2	24.6	2836	821
1987	326.8	24.2	182.2	120.4	154.5	28.1	3150	846
1988	410.2	36.9	220.9	152.4	189.5	31.8	3892	1046
1989	456.0	38.3	251.8	165.9	212.8	39.4	4269	1134
1990	500.8	43.7	262.0	195.1	219.3	43.1	4635	969
1991	598.9	45.5	290.5	262.9	255.6	35.9	5494	1032
1992	710.2	48.7	343.4	318.1	291.3	53.2	6468	1173
1993	888.9	53.2	416.3	419.4	336.5	81.2	8030	1393
1994	1149.8	66.8	512.7	570.3	413.4	100.9	10280	1193
1995	1516.2	72.2	638.3	805.7	520.7	119.8	12762	1529
1996	1819.4	75.0	709.2	1035.2	570.0	141.6	14495	1743
1997	2118.1	77.2	774.8	1266.2	627.6	149.7	16949	2045
1998	2439.1	77.9	834.1	1527.1	661.5	175.1	19625	2371
1999	2759.8	78.4	900.0	1781.5	713.3	189.5	22054	2664
2000	3277.8	79.3	1023.7	2174.9	831.0	196.6	25014	3022
2001	3861.5	80.8	1127.2	2653.6	920.2	212.3	28097	3395
2002	4525.7	82.4	1235.1	3208.2	999.6	239.7	32231	3894
2003	5267.2	84.1	1456.4	3726.7	1195.1	276.1	36583	4420
2004	6252.5	85.4	1773.7	4393.4	1483.2	308.9	42402	5123
2005	7149.8	86.9	1907.4	5155.5	1600.5	326.8	47182	5760
2006	8387.0	87.2	2072.1	6227.7	1713.8	379.4	53438	6703
2007	10425.5	99.4	2413.4	7912.8	1989.1	448.5	63629	8368
2008	11813.1	111.4	2526.7	9175.1	2030.8	520.4	68541	9869
2009	12900.9	116.8	2736.4	10047.7	2182.6	580.3	71059	10402
2010	14964.0	122.8	3233.1	11608.1	2607.5	656.9	78307	11568
2011	17188.8	134.5	3563.3	13491.0	2859.6	738.1	86246	13353
2012	19024.7	148.4	3856.0	15020.3	3090.1	803.0	92758	14694
2013	21134.6	159.8	4168.3	16806.5	3336.6	872.0	100569	16240
2014	22926.0	159.2	4433.0	18333.9	3522.8	952.7	106732	17375
2015	24779.1	140.4	4419.8	20218.9	3458.9	1002.6	113692	18253
2016	27041.2	129.8	4665.8	22245.7	3635.5	1074.5	123391	18577
2017	29883.0	121.9	5049.4	24711.7	3885.9	1210.9	136172	20168
2018	33106.0	120.6	5477.4	27508.1	4139.9	1387.8	150962	22813
2019	35445.1	114.4	5667.4	29663.4	4243.3	1477.4	161776	23451
2020	35943.3	108.3	5739.1	30095.9	4255.1	1528.2	164158	23799
2021	41045.6	111.4	7389.0	33545.2	5855.1	1591.4	187526	29067
2022	41610.9	111.5	6605.1	34894.3	5036.4	1614.2	190313	28295

注：1.本表数据按当年价格计算。
2.人均地区生产总值按年平均常住人口计算。
3.2022年为初步核算数，下同。

Note: a) Figures in this table are calculated at current year's prices.
b) Per capita GDP is calculated at average permanent population.
c) The data for 2022 are the preliminary accounting data, the same below.

2-2 地区生产总值指数(1978-2022年)
INDICES OF GROSS DOMESTIC PRODUCT(1978-2022)

(上年=100) (preceding year=100)

年份 Year	地区生产总值 Gross Domestic Product	按产业分 By Three Industries 第一产业 Primary Industry	第二产业 Secondary Industry	第三产业 Tertiary Industry	按行业分 By Sector #工业 Industry	#建筑业 Construction	人均地区生产总值 Per Capita Gross Domestic Product
1978	110.5	109.0	116.5	97.7	112.4	153.0	109.1
1979	109.7	105.0	109.1	113.2	110.1	108.4	107.4
1980	111.8	109.3	109.6	118.5	110.1	110.3	109.8
1981	99.5	109.2	96.3	106.0	95.3	106.4	98.3
1982	107.4	113.4	105.8	109.9	105.8	106.1	105.6
1983	116.4	107.5	113.6	124.2	111.5	132.3	114.5
1984	117.4	106.8	116.1	121.8	115.7	118.8	115.6
1985	108.7	106.3	111.0	104.4	109.1	124.7	106.9
1986	108.0	100.1	104.8	115.7	105.0	103.7	104.6
1987	109.6	113.4	105.6	116.7	105.5	106.3	106.1
1988	112.8	111.2	112.1	114.1	113.0	106.5	111.0
1989	104.4	101.1	108.9	97.3	108.4	112.2	103.1
1990	105.2	103.3	101.1	113.3	101.9	95.6	104.0
1991	109.9	103.7	107.5	114.5	112.6	81.6	108.9
1992	111.3	103.1	111.8	112.3	109.6	126.4	110.5
1993	112.3	103.2	112.8	113.3	110.2	128.8	111.4
1994	113.7	102.8	113.9	115.4	113.2	117.3	112.5
1995	112.0	92.0	107.4	120.7	107.3	107.8	105.4
1996	109.8	96.8	106.3	115.2	106.0	107.5	103.9
1997	110.2	103.0	107.7	113.4	108.2	105.3	110.7
1998	109.6	101.1	109.3	110.6	108.3	114.3	110.2
1999	111.0	102.5	111.7	111.0	112.4	108.3	110.2
2000	112.0	103.2	111.1	113.5	112.8	102.4	107.0
2001	111.8	103.6	109.0	113.4	109.0	106.7	106.6
2002	111.8	103.0	107.8	113.9	107.1	111.1	109.4
2003	111.1	98.5	110.2	111.9	111.4	110.7	108.4
2004	113.3	99.6	115.4	112.8	117.8	105.4	110.6
2005	112.3	98.4	109.7	113.8	110.4	106.6	109.3
2006	112.8	100.8	109.9	114.1	108.7	115.8	108.9
2007	114.4	102.0	111.9	115.5	112.1	111.0	109.6
2008	109.0	101.6	100.3	112.1	99.6	103.7	103.6
2009	110.0	104.6	110.0	110.1	108.2	118.3	104.5
2010	110.4	98.4	113.4	109.6	114.6	108.6	104.9
2011	108.1	100.9	106.6	108.6	107.5	102.9	103.6
2012	107.7	103.2	106.8	108.0	106.1	109.4	104.7
2013	107.7	103.0	107.7	107.8	107.3	109.4	105.2
2014	107.4	100.0	106.8	107.6	105.9	110.3	105.1
2015	106.9	89.2	102.8	108.2	100.2	112.4	105.4
2016	106.9	91.3	105.3	107.4	104.5	108.1	106.3
2017	106.8	95.2	104.2	107.4	105.0	101.7	106.7
2018	106.7	98.0	103.9	107.3	104.0	103.5	106.8
2019	106.1	95.0	103.9	106.5	103.0	105.4	106.2
2020	101.1	91.6	102.5	100.8	101.9	104.3	101.1
2021	108.8	102.8	123.2	106.1	131.5	100.1	108.9
2022	100.7	98.4	88.6	103.4	85.4	100.1	100.8

注：本表数据按不变价格计算。
Note: Figures in this table are calculated at constant prices.

2-3 地区生产总值指数(1978−2022年)
INDICES OF GROSS DOMESTIC PRODUCT(1978-2022)

(1978年=100) (year of 1978=100)

年 份 Year	地区生产总 值 Gross Domestic Product	按产业分 By Three Industries			按行业分 By Sector		人均地区生产总值 Per Capita Gross Domestic Product
		第一产业 Primary Industry	第二产业 Secondary Industry	第三产业 Tertiary Industry	#工业 Industry	#建筑业 Construction	
1978	100.0	100.0	100.0	100.0	100.0	100.0	100.0
1979	109.7	105.0	109.1	113.2	110.1	108.4	107.4
1980	122.6	114.8	119.6	134.1	121.2	119.6	117.9
1981	122.0	125.4	115.2	142.1	115.5	127.3	115.9
1982	131.0	142.2	121.9	156.2	122.2	135.1	122.4
1983	152.5	152.9	138.5	194.0	136.3	178.7	140.1
1984	179.0	163.3	160.8	236.3	157.7	212.3	162.0
1985	194.6	173.6	178.5	246.7	172.1	264.7	173.2
1986	210.2	173.8	187.1	285.4	180.7	274.5	181.2
1987	230.4	197.1	197.6	333.1	190.6	291.8	192.3
1988	259.9	219.2	221.5	380.1	215.4	310.8	213.5
1989	271.3	221.6	241.2	369.8	233.5	348.7	220.1
1990	285.4	228.9	243.9	419.0	237.9	333.4	228.9
1991	313.7	237.4	262.2	479.8	267.9	272.1	249.3
1992	349.1	244.8	293.1	538.8	293.6	343.9	275.5
1993	392.0	252.6	330.6	610.5	323.5	442.9	306.9
1994	445.7	259.7	376.6	704.5	366.2	519.5	345.3
1995	499.2	238.9	404.5	850.3	392.9	560.0	363.9
1996	548.1	231.3	430.0	979.5	416.5	602.0	378.1
1997	604.0	238.2	463.1	1110.8	450.7	633.9	418.6
1998	662.0	240.8	506.2	1228.5	488.1	724.5	461.3
1999	734.8	246.8	565.4	1363.6	548.6	784.6	508.4
2000	823.0	254.7	628.2	1547.7	618.8	803.4	544.0
2001	920.1	263.9	684.7	1755.1	674.5	857.2	579.9
2002	1028.7	271.8	738.1	1999.1	722.4	952.3	634.4
2003	1142.9	267.7	813.4	2237.0	804.8	1054.2	687.7
2004	1294.9	266.6	938.7	2523.3	948.1	1111.1	760.6
2005	1454.2	262.3	1029.8	2871.5	1046.7	1184.4	831.3
2006	1640.3	264.4	1131.8	3276.4	1137.8	1371.5	905.3
2007	1876.5	269.7	1266.5	3784.2	1275.5	1522.4	992.2
2008	2045.4	274.0	1270.3	4242.1	1270.4	1578.7	1027.9
2009	2249.9	286.6	1397.3	4670.6	1374.6	1867.6	1074.2
2010	2483.9	282.0	1584.5	5119.0	1575.3	2028.2	1126.8
2011	2685.1	284.5	1689.1	5559.2	1693.4	2087.0	1167.4
2012	2891.9	293.6	1804.0	6003.9	1796.7	2283.2	1222.3
2013	3114.6	302.4	1942.9	6472.2	1927.9	2497.8	1285.9
2014	3345.1	302.4	2075.0	6964.1	2041.6	2755.1	1351.5
2015	3575.9	269.7	2133.1	7535.2	2045.7	3096.7	1424.5
2016	3822.6	246.2	2246.2	8092.8	2137.8	3347.5	1514.2
2017	4082.5	234.4	2340.5	8691.7	2244.7	3404.4	1615.7
2018	4356.0	229.7	2431.8	9326.2	2334.5	3523.6	1725.6
2019	4621.7	218.2	2526.6	9932.4	2404.5	3713.9	1832.6
2020	4672.5	199.9	2589.8	10011.9	2450.2	3873.6	1852.8
2021	5083.7	205.5	3190.6	10622.6	3222.0	3877.5	2017.7
2022	5119.3	202.2	2826.9	10983.8	2751.6	3881.4	2033.8

注：本表数据按不变价格计算。
Note: Figures in this table are calculated at constant prices.

2-4 地区生产总值指数(2000-2022年)
INDICES OF GROSS DOMESTIC PRODUCT(2000-2022)

(2000年=100) (year of 2000=100)

年份 Year	地区生产总值 Gross Domestic Product	按产业分 By Three Industries			按行业分 By Sector		人均地区生产总值 Per Capita Gross Domestic Product
		第一产业 Primary Industry	第二产业 Secondary Industry	第三产业 Tertiary Industry	#工业 Industry	#建筑业 Construction	
2000	100.0	100.0	100.0	100.0	100.0	100.0	100.0
2001	111.8	103.6	109.0	113.4	109.0	106.7	106.6
2002	125.0	106.7	118.8	129.2	116.7	118.5	116.6
2003	138.9	105.1	129.5	144.6	130.0	131.2	126.4
2004	157.4	104.7	141.2	163.1	153.1	138.3	139.8
2005	176.8	103.0	153.9	185.6	169.0	147.4	152.8
2006	199.4	103.8	167.8	211.8	183.7	170.7	166.4
2007	228.1	105.9	182.9	244.6	205.9	189.5	182.4
2008	248.6	107.6	199.4	274.2	205.1	196.5	189.0
2009	273.5	112.5	217.3	301.9	221.9	232.5	197.5
2010	301.9	110.7	236.9	330.9	254.3	252.5	207.2
2011	326.4	111.7	258.2	359.4	273.4	259.8	214.7
2012	351.5	115.3	281.4	388.2	290.1	284.2	224.8
2013	378.6	118.8	306.7	418.5	311.3	310.9	236.5
2014	406.6	118.8	334.3	450.3	329.7	342.9	248.6
2015	434.7	106.0	364.4	487.2	330.4	385.4	262.0
2016	464.7	96.8	397.2	523.3	345.3	416.6	278.5
2017	496.3	92.2	432.9	562.0	362.6	423.7	297.2
2018	529.6	90.4	471.9	603.0	377.1	438.5	317.4
2019	561.9	85.9	490.3	642.2	388.4	462.2	337.1
2020	568.1	78.7	502.6	647.3	395.8	482.1	340.8
2021	618.1	80.9	619.2	686.8	520.5	482.6	371.1
2022	622.4	79.6	548.6	710.2	444.5	483.1	374.1

注：本表数据按不变价格计算。
Note: Figures in this table are calculated at constant prices.

2-5 地区生产总值构成(1978-2022年)
COMPOSITION OF GROSS DOMESTIC PRODUCT (1978-2022)

单位：% (%)

年份 Year	地区生产总值 Gross Domestic Product	按产业分 By Three Industries			按行业分 By Sector	
		第一产业 Primary Industry	第二产业 Secondary Industry	第三产业 Tertiary Industry	#工业 Industry	#建筑业 Construction
1978	100.0	5.1	71.0	23.9	64.5	6.6
1979	100.0	4.3	70.8	24.9	64.4	6.5
1980	100.0	4.4	68.7	26.9	62.5	6.4
1981	100.0	4.7	66.3	29.0	59.4	7.0
1982	100.0	6.6	64.3	29.1	57.7	6.8
1983	100.0	6.9	61.4	31.6	54.0	7.6
1984	100.0	6.8	60.2	33.0	52.6	7.7
1985	100.0	6.9	59.7	33.4	50.8	8.9
1986	100.0	6.7	58.1	35.2	49.6	8.6
1987	100.0	7.4	55.8	36.8	47.3	8.6
1988	100.0	9.0	53.9	37.2	46.2	7.8
1989	100.0	8.4	55.2	36.4	46.7	8.6
1990	100.0	8.7	52.3	39.0	43.8	8.6
1991	100.0	7.6	48.5	43.9	42.7	6.0
1992	100.0	6.9	48.4	44.8	41.0	7.5
1993	100.0	6.0	46.8	47.2	37.9	9.1
1994	100.0	5.8	44.6	49.6	36.0	8.8
1995	100.0	4.8	42.1	53.1	34.3	7.9
1996	100.0	4.1	39.0	56.9	31.3	7.8
1997	100.0	3.6	36.6	59.8	29.6	7.1
1998	100.0	3.2	34.2	62.6	27.1	7.2
1999	100.0	2.8	32.6	64.6	25.8	6.9
2000	100.0	2.4	31.2	66.4	25.4	6.0
2001	100.0	2.1	29.2	68.7	23.8	5.5
2002	100.0	1.8	27.3	70.9	22.1	5.3
2003	100.0	1.6	27.7	70.8	22.7	5.2
2004	100.0	1.4	28.4	70.3	23.7	4.9
2005	100.0	1.2	26.7	72.1	22.4	4.6
2006	100.0	1.0	24.7	74.3	20.4	4.5
2007	100.0	1.0	23.1	75.9	19.1	4.3
2008	100.0	0.9	21.4	77.7	17.2	4.4
2009	100.0	0.9	21.2	77.9	16.9	4.5
2010	100.0	0.8	21.6	77.6	17.4	4.4
2011	100.0	0.8	20.7	78.5	16.6	4.3
2012	100.0	0.8	20.3	79.0	16.2	4.2
2013	100.0	0.8	19.7	79.5	15.8	4.1
2014	100.0	0.7	19.3	80.0	15.4	4.2
2015	100.0	0.6	17.8	81.6	14.0	4.0
2016	100.0	0.5	17.3	82.3	13.4	4.0
2017	100.0	0.4	16.9	82.7	13.0	4.1
2018	100.0	0.4	16.5	83.1	12.5	4.2
2019	100.0	0.3	16.0	83.7	12.0	4.2
2020	100.0	0.3	16.0	83.7	11.8	4.3
2021	100.0	0.3	18.0	81.7	14.3	3.9
2022	100.0	0.3	15.9	83.9	12.1	3.9

注：本表数据按当年价格计算。
Note: Figures in this table are calculated at current year's prices.

2-6 三次产业贡献率(1982—2022年)
CONTRIBUTION RATE OF THREE INDUSTRIES TO THE INCREASE OF GDP (1982-2022)

单位：% (%)

年份 Year	地区生产总值 Gross Domestic Product	按产业分 By Three Industries			按行业分 By Sector	
		第一产业 Primary Industry	第二产业 Secondary Industry	第三产业 Tertiary Industry	#工业 Industry	#建筑业 Construction
1982	100.0	8.7	52.8	38.4	47.2	5.6
1983	100.0	2.3	54.6	43.1	41.3	13.2
1984	100.0	1.8	59.2	39.0	51.0	8.2
1985	100.0	3.1	80.6	16.3	58.5	22.1
1986	100.0	0.1	39.0	61.0	34.8	4.1
1987	100.0	5.4	36.8	57.8	31.2	5.6
1988	100.0	3.5	57.5	39.0	53.3	4.2
1989	100.0	1.0	121.1	-22.1	99.6	21.5
1990	100.0	2.4	12.8	84.8	19.8	-7.0
1991	100.0	3.3	39.8	56.9	55.8	-16.0
1992	100.0	2.2	53.6	44.1	37.9	14.9
1993	100.0	2.0	53.7	44.4	36.7	17.0
1994	100.0	1.5	52.3	46.3	41.7	10.5
1995	100.0	-4.3	31.9	72.2	26.3	5.6
1996	100.0	-1.7	31.7	70.0	25.5	6.3
1997	100.0	1.3	36.3	62.4	32.1	4.2
1998	100.0	0.5	45.5	54.0	34.0	11.6
1999	100.0	0.9	49.7	49.4	43.6	6.1
2000	100.0	1.0	43.4	55.6	41.9	1.5
2001	100.0	0.7	23.8	75.5	19.4	3.4
2002	100.0	0.6	20.2	79.2	14.8	5.4
2003	100.0	-0.3	27.0	73.3	24.4	5.5
2004	100.0	…	33.7	66.4	31.7	2.3
2005	100.0	-0.2	23.3	76.9	20.8	2.8
2006	100.0	0.1	20.7	79.2	15.2	5.7
2007	100.0	0.2	21.5	78.3	18.2	3.6
2008	100.0	0.2	0.8	99.0	-1.0	1.8
2009	100.0	0.4	23.4	76.2	15.8	7.9
2010	100.0	-0.1	30.2	70.0	26.6	3.9
2011	100.0	0.1	17.6	82.3	16.3	1.6
2012	100.0	0.3	18.7	81.0	13.8	5.1
2013	100.0	0.3	21.0	78.7	16.1	5.2
2014	100.0	…	19.4	80.6	13.5	6.0
2015	100.0	-1.0	8.5	92.6	0.5	7.9
2016	100.0	-0.7	13.8	86.9	9.2	4.7
2017	100.0	-0.3	10.8	89.5	9.9	1.0
2018	100.0	-0.1	10.0	90.2	8.0	2.1
2019	100.0	-0.3	10.7	89.6	6.5	3.4
2020	100.0	-2.9	38.2	64.6	23.0	15.3
2021	100.0	0.1	41.9	58.0	42.1	
2022	100.0	-0.7	-297.7	398.4	-302.5	0.7

注：1.本表数据按不变价格计算。
2.产业贡献率指各产业增加值增量与地区生产总值增量之比。

Note: a) Figures in this table are calculated at constant prices.
b) Share of the contributions of the three industries to the increase of the GDP refers to the proportion of the increment of the value-added of each industry to the increment of GDP.

2-7 按产业、行业分地区生产总值(2001-2022年)

单位：亿元

项 目	Item	2001	2002	2003	2004	2005	2006
地区生产总值	**Gross Domestic Product**	**3861.5**	**4525.7**	**5267.2**	**6252.5**	**7149.8**	**8387.0**
按产业分	**By Three Industries**						
第一产业	Primary Industry	80.8	82.4	84.1	85.4	86.9	87.2
第二产业	Secondary Industry	1127.2	1235.1	1456.4	1773.7	1907.4	2072.1
第三产业	Tertiary Industry	2653.6	3208.2	3726.7	4393.4	5155.5	6227.7
按行业分	**By Sector**						
农、林、牧、渔业	Agriculture, Forestry, Animal Husbandry and Fishery	81.8	82.9	84.6	87.4	88.7	88.8
工 业	Industry	920.2	999.6	1195.1	1483.2	1600.5	1713.8
建筑业	Construction	212.3	239.7	276.1	308.9	326.8	379.4
批发和零售业	Wholesale and Retail Trade	442.8	485.3	542.4	607.9	718.9	894.9
交通运输、仓储和邮政业	Transport, Storage and Post	227.6	249.2	271.1	303.4	333.9	373.5
住宿和餐饮业	Accommodation and Catering	103.3	130.5	121.0	172.9	190.8	230.2
信息传输、软件和信息技术服务业	Information Transmission, Software and Information Technology Services	233.0	309.3	415.9	492.8	637.4	751.0
金融业	Finance	519.7	600.8	683.9	755.9	879.9	1036.1
房地产业	Real Estate	233.6	346.3	402.3	508.7	573.4	775.0
租赁和商务服务业	Leasing and Business Services	146.4	230.1	250.4	294.6	379.9	474.4
科学研究和技术服务业	Scientific Research and Technical Services	195.2	230.4	273.1	305.3	373.3	459.7
水利、环境和公共设施管理业	Management of Water Conservancy, Environment and Public Facilities	27.3	29.8	33.6	37.5	43.5	50.9
居民服务、修理和其他服务业	Resident Services, Repair and Other Services	45.5	59.4	70.0	85.7	85.5	91.7
教 育	Education	160.8	174.5	225.7	288.5	312.9	347.3
卫生和社会工作	Health and Social Works	73.6	80.8	96.2	115.3	127.5	152.7
文化、体育和娱乐业	Culture, Sports and Entertainment	101.6	117.6	132.2	148.5	174.9	195.2
公共管理、社会保障和社会组织	Public Management, Social Security and Social Organizations	137.0	159.8	193.8	256.2	302.0	372.6
国际组织	International Organizations						

注：本表数据按当年价格计算。

GROSS DOMESTIC PRODUCT BY INDUSTRY AND SECTOR(2001-2022)

(100 million yuan)

2007	2008	2009	2010	2011	2012	2013	2014	2015	2016	2017	2018	2019	2020	2021	2022
10425.5	**11813.1**	**12900.9**	**14964.0**	**17188.8**	**19024.7**	**21134.6**	**22926.0**	**24779.1**	**27041.2**	**29883.0**	**33106.0**	**35445.1**	**35943.3**	**41045.6**	**41610.9**
99.4	111.4	116.8	122.8	134.5	148.4	159.8	159.2	140.4	129.8	121.9	120.6	114.4	108.3	111.4	111.5
2413.4	2526.7	2736.4	3233.1	3563.3	3856.0	4168.3	4433.0	4419.8	4665.8	5049.4	5477.4	5667.4	5739.1	7389.0	6605.1
7912.8	9175.1	10047.7	11608.1	13491.0	15020.3	16806.5	18333.9	20218.9	22245.7	24711.7	27508.1	29663.4	30095.9	33545.2	34894.3
101.3	112.8	118.3	124.6	136.5	150.4	162.0	161.5	142.8	132.2	124.3	122.6	116.9	110.7	113.4	113.1
1989.1	2030.8	2182.6	2607.5	2859.6	3090.1	3336.6	3522.8	3458.9	3635.5	3885.9	4139.9	4243.3	4255.1	5855.1	5036.4
448.5	520.4	580.3	656.9	738.1	803.0	872.0	952.7	1002.6	1074.5	1210.9	1387.8	1477.4	1528.2	1591.4	1614.2
1155.1	1502.0	1606.6	1995.4	2256.9	2356.3	2483.2	2579.0	2506.7	2544.3	2703.7	2824.1	2867.5	2840.3	3126.7	3110.3
412.5	408.4	449.2	570.4	637.3	635.5	670.6	724.8	739.8	790.8	901.0	1015.9	1010.8	844.4	900.9	879.2
265.0	297.7	285.7	346.3	380.6	408.8	413.1	404.4	441.7	447.0	470.4	515.3	538.1	360.8	429.8	372.6
959.7	1117.6	1165.3	1314.1	1611.7	1758.8	2015.8	2283.0	2600.0	3003.9	3508.2	4290.1	4879.6	5601.5	6770.5	7456.2
1410.2	1648.5	1744.4	2038.1	2421.6	2783.2	3247.5	3736.8	4365.5	4784.7	5299.6	5951.3	6544.2	7057.1	7683.1	8196.7
999.6	1037.8	1319.1	1261.4	1358.2	1588.1	1731.5	1745.2	1899.2	2241.2	2420.5	2481.5	2603.8	2459.0	2603.6	2594.5
679.4	836.1	886.2	1055.7	1285.5	1488.1	1746.9	1917.2	1987.1	2079.7	2226.4	2421.0	2599.3	2286.2	2591.0	2581.4
591.8	720.3	808.2	940.2	1106.6	1245.9	1442.0	1628.9	1765.4	1980.0	2260.5	2578.3	2823.3	2973.9	3373.3	3465.0
57.7	66.1	75.5	85.2	97.9	115.5	138.7	159.6	211.2	239.2	269.2	287.0	305.6	303.9	299.2	304.5
90.5	83.0	82.3	111.0	125.6	139.9	158.5	177.4	163.3	184.3	201.1	220.8	229.2	187.7	201.1	200.7
406.7	451.0	498.0	594.5	694.4	788.0	886.0	1000.1	1119.3	1263.9	1459.0	1603.4	1803.6	1899.2	1960.9	1927.4
181.9	211.1	240.7	290.0	355.9	417.6	481.0	547.0	675.5	750.2	835.0	938.1	1015.1	1002.7	1103.3	1260.1
236.3	262.4	275.4	313.9	361.6	430.1	482.4	508.1	568.5	612.7	657.4	728.1	749.7	651.7	795.0	784.3
440.2	507.0	583.1	658.9	760.7	825.6	866.8	877.6	1131.7	1277.1	1450.1	1600.9	1637.8	1581.0	1647.4	1714.1

Note:Figures in this table are calculated at current year's prices.

2-8 按产业、行业分地区生产总值指数(2001-2022年)

(上年=100)

项目	Item	2001	2002	2003	2004	2005
地区生产总值	**Gross Domestic Product**	**111.8**	**111.8**	**111.1**	**113.3**	**112.3**
按产业分	**By Three Industries**					
第一产业	Primary Industry	103.6	103.0	98.5	99.6	98.4
第二产业	Secondary Industry	109.0	107.8	110.2	115.4	109.7
第三产业	Tertiary Industry	113.4	113.9	111.9	112.8	113.8
按行业分	**By Sector**					
农、林、牧、渔业	Agriculture, Forestry, Animal Husbandry and Fishery	103.7	102.7	98.9	99.4	98.1
工　业	Industry	109.0	107.1	111.4	117.8	110.4
建筑业	Construction	106.7	111.1	110.7	105.4	106.6
批发和零售业	Wholesale and Retail Trade	112.5	109.2	111.3	111.1	117.8
交通运输、仓储和邮政业	Transport, Storage and Post	102.5	102.8	102.6	106.4	104.6
住宿和餐饮业	Accommodation and Catering	109.3	117.5	90.9	135.8	107.2
信息传输、软件和信息技术服务业	Information Transmission, Software and Information Technology Services	113.5	119.8	124.4	112.0	121.8
金融业	Finance	113.4	112.1	110.9	106.0	113.3
房地产业	Real Estate	132.4	131.6	111.9	119.3	109.3
租赁和商务服务业	Leasing and Business Services	106.7	132.6	103.5	109.5	122.0
科学研究和技术服务业	Scientific Research and Technical Services	127.6	113.2	112.2	108.6	115.3
水利、环境和公共设施管理业	Management of Water Conservancy, Environment and Public Facilities	95.2	102.5	104.3	104.2	113.5
居民服务、修理和其他服务业	Resident Services, Repair and Other Services	103.2	112.2	109.0	114.4	97.8
教　育	Education	125.6	109.7	128.1	124.5	107.6
卫生和社会工作	Health and Social Works	116.2	106.8	112.6	116.2	111.8
文化、体育和娱乐业	Culture, Sports and Entertainment	104.5	107.8	106.9	107.8	115.6
公共管理、社会保障和社会组织	Pulic Administration,Social Security and Social Organizations	107.0	109.9	114.1	125.9	115.4
国际组织	International Organizations					

注：本表数据按不变价格计算。

INDICES OF GROSS DOMESTIC PRODUCT BY INDUSTRY AND BY SECTOR(2001-2022)

(preceding year=100)

2006	2007	2008	2009	2010	2011	2012	2013	2014	2015	2016	2017	2018	2019	2020	2021	2022
112.8	**114.4**	**109.0**	**110.0**	**110.4**	**108.1**	**107.7**	**107.7**	**107.4**	**106.9**	**106.9**	**106.8**	**106.7**	**106.1**	**101.1**	**108.8**	**100.7**
100.8	102.0	101.6	104.6	98.4	100.9	103.2	103.0	100.0	89.2	91.3	95.2	98.0	95.0	91.6	102.8	98.4
109.9	111.9	100.3	110.0	113.4	106.6	106.8	107.7	106.8	102.8	105.3	104.2	103.9	103.9	102.5	123.2	88.6
114.1	115.5	112.1	110.1	109.6	108.6	108.0	107.8	107.6	108.2	107.4	107.4	107.3	106.5	100.8	106.1	103.4
100.6	102.2	101.1	104.6	98.6	100.9	103.2	103.0	100.1	89.4	91.5	95.3	97.7	95.1	92.3	102.3	98.2
108.7	112.1	99.6	108.2	114.6	107.5	106.1	107.3	105.9	100.2	104.5	105.0	104.0	103.0	101.9	131.5	85.4
115.8	111.0	103.7	118.3	108.6	102.9	109.4	109.4	110.3	112.4	108.1	101.7	103.5	105.4	104.3	100.1	100.1
118.1	122.5	125.4	109.3	121.5	109.2	103.7	105.3	105.4	98.4	103.0	107.0	100.8	101.9	97.9	107.6	98.9
106.2	106.7	102.8	101.5	111.1	104.7	105.3	105.6	105.7	102.8	105.4	110.9	105.9	100.8	87.5	103.0	95.4
115.8	108.0	98.3	97.0	115.7	102.7	99.7	97.2	99.5	100.5	100.5	102.3	102.2	99.9	72.4	115.0	86.3
111.6	116.8	115.4	104.9	109.8	123.0	106.9	108.9	112.2	111.9	112.3	113.5	119.0	112.9	114.5	111.3	109.8
111.1	121.9	108.0	106.7	109.4	108.1	112.5	112.5	113.2	118.4	109.3	107.7	107.6	109.5	104.9	105.1	106.4
123.1	106.3	95.7	123.2	86.8	94.3	114.5	103.1	98.8	105.2	106.7	99.5	100.8	106.2	99.1	103.3	98.8
117.6	124.3	123.6	111.8	111.4	118.4	109.5	109.9	106.5	98.5	101.8	103.7	103.7	104.4	85.9	103.8	98.7
115.5	118.5	119.1	118.8	108.6	107.6	107.8	111.5	110.3	112.4	108.6	109.8	108.9	106.4	100.3	106.8	101.8
110.7	104.8	115.1	120.4	105.6	106.0	106.9	106.7	112.8	113.6	109.3	110.7	103.8	103.8	99.1	94.4	101.5
101.0	92.3	92.1	104.5	126.1	112.9	104.4	103.6	113.5	102.5	109.7	103.4	104.4	100.7	86.2	102.9	97.6
106.9	111.6	110.3	109.4	111.2	103.7	106.0	106.3	110.4	111.8	108.8	108.6	106.8	109.6	105.3	100.4	97.1
113.7	109.2	114.4	114.1	112.7	108.5	108.7	112.1	111.4	114.3	107.7	108.1	109.2	105.8	94.3	106.6	113.7
107.9	109.9	113.7	107.5	106.6	106.4	109.4	106.3	102.2	103.7	106.9	102.8	106.0	102.1	89.5	113.8	97.8
118.5	111.4	110.0	112.5	107.5	103.8	104.8	103.9	99.2	110.3	109.1	108.8	107.5	98.6	98.6	101.7	103.5

Note: Figures in this table are calculated at constant prices.

2-9 数字经济和部分新兴产业增加值(2016−2022年)
ADDED VALUE OF DIGITAL ECONOMY AND SOME EMERGING INDUSTRIES(2016-2022)

单位：亿元 (100 million yuan)

项　目	Item	2016	2017	2018	2019	2020	2021	2022
地区生产总值	**Gross Domestic Product**	**27041.2**	**29883.0**	**33106.0**	**35445.1**	**35943.3**	**41045.6**	**41610.9**
#数字经济	Digital Economy	9674.7	10852.6	12515.9	13609.2	14370.4	16596.3	17330.2
#战略性新兴产业	Strategic Emerging Industry	5654.7	6619.8	7831.5	8441.9	8739.8	10597.1	10353.9
#高技术产业	High-tech Industry	5888.8	6834.5	7996.0	8689.4	9514.9	11482.2	11820.9
#生产性服务业	Producer Service Industry	13032.2	14549.2	16449.9	17806.1	18581.0	20741.9	
#生活性服务业	Consumer Service Industry	6205.3	6839.0	7475.9	8043.5	7660.0	8637.6	

注：本表数据按当年价格计算。
Note: Figures in this table are calculated at current year's prices.

2-10 支出法地区生产总值(1978-2022年)
GROSS DOMESTIC PRODUCT BY EXPENDITURE APPROACH (1978-2022)

单位：亿元 (100 million yuan)

年份 Year	地区生产总值 Gross Domestic Product	最终消费支出 Final Consumption Expenditure	居民消费 Households Consumption	政府消费 Government Consumption	资本形成总额 Gross Capital Formation	固定资本形成总额 Completed Fixed Assets	存货增加 Changes in Inventories	货物和服务净流出 Net Outflow of Goods and Services	最终消费率(消费率)(%) Final Consumption Rate (%)	资本形成率(投资率)(%) Capital Formation Rate (%)
1978	108.8	53.0	28.6	24.4	31.7	24.9	6.8	24.1	48.7	29.1
1979	120.1	55.4	31.5	23.9	37.0	29.1	7.9	27.7	46.1	30.8
1980	139.1	57.3	39.6	17.7	45.1	36.5	8.6	36.7	41.2	32.4
1981	139.2	61.8	44.2	17.6	50.5	40.2	10.3	26.9	44.4	36.3
1982	154.9	68.6	48.8	19.8	51.8	42.3	9.5	34.5	44.3	33.4
1983	183.1	77.6	54.6	23.0	62.9	56.1	6.8	42.6	42.4	34.4
1984	216.6	96.5	64.8	31.7	84.7	72.5	12.2	35.4	44.6	39.1
1985	257.1	127.1	88.7	38.4	150.6	102.7	47.9	-20.6	49.4	58.6
1986	284.9	161.1	109.9	51.2	178.8	116.0	62.8	-55.0	56.5	62.8
1987	326.8	181.5	124.3	57.2	201.2	148.6	52.6	-55.9	55.5	61.6
1988	410.2	222.6	161.9	60.7	251.1	177.7	73.4	-63.5	54.3	61.2
1989	456.0	244.0	176.1	67.9	271.5	151.9	119.6	-59.5	53.5	59.5
1990	500.8	269.7	194.1	75.6	296.5	195.0	101.5	-65.4	53.9	59.2
1991	598.9	302.6	225.7	76.9	327.3	208.8	118.5	-31.0	50.5	54.7
1992	710.2	342.2	261.2	81.0	415.5	289.2	126.3	-47.4	48.2	58.5
1993	888.9	446.7	355.5	91.2	537.3	446.1	91.2	-95.1	50.3	60.4
1994	1149.8	616.3	505.5	110.8	792.6	705.2	87.4	-259.1	53.6	68.9
1995	1516.2	848.4	675.1	173.2	1045.0	914.6	130.5	-377.2	56.0	68.9
1996	1819.4	1016.2	819.1	197.1	1074.9	981.5	93.4	-271.6	55.8	59.1
1997	2118.1	1207.5	998.9	208.7	1287.7	1080.5	207.2	-377.1	57.0	60.8
1998	2439.1	1318.0	1075.2	242.8	1439.3	1313.0	126.3	-318.3	54.0	59.0
1999	2759.8	1496.7	1184.5	312.2	1624.7	1334.9	289.9	-361.7	54.2	58.9
2000	3277.8	1654.4	1288.8	365.6	1836.0	1512.9	323.1	-212.6	50.5	56.0
2001	3861.5	1889.8	1417.4	472.4	2095.8	1728.3	367.4	-124.0	48.9	54.3
2002	4525.7	2279.3	1738.4	540.9	2541.8	2117.1	424.7	-295.4	50.4	56.2
2003	5267.2	2615.8	1977.5	638.3	2989.9	2635.0	354.9	-338.5	49.7	56.8
2004	6252.5	3054.4	2260.3	794.1	3478.3	3086.1	392.2	-280.3	48.9	55.6
2005	7149.8	3432.6	2521.1	911.5	3955.5	3494.8	460.7	-238.3	48.0	55.3
2006	8387.0	4112.5	2982.5	1130.1	4365.9	3880.8	485.1	-91.4	49.0	52.1
2007	10425.5	5087.3	3566.9	1520.4	4996.9	4428.7	568.2	341.3	48.8	47.9
2008	11813.1	6045.3	4137.3	1908.0	5335.7	4461.5	874.2	432.1	51.2	45.2
2009	12900.9	6991.8	4784.4	2207.4	5681.6	4910.1	771.5	227.5	54.2	44.0
2010	14964.0	8048.2	5634.1	2414.1	6873.2	5956.4	916.8	42.6	53.8	45.9
2011	17188.8	9516.9	6568.5	2948.4	7631.9	6670.1	961.8	40.0	55.4	44.4
2012	19024.7	10749.9	7398.0	3352.0	8508.4	7866.5	641.9	-233.5	56.5	44.7
2013	21134.6	12296.2	8471.5	3824.7	9218.1	8642.2	575.9	-379.7	58.2	43.6
2014	22926.0	13565.2	9219.9	4345.3	9633.4	8954.2	679.3	-272.6	59.2	42.0
2015	24779.1	14793.1	10118.8	4674.3	9910.8	9225.8	685.0	75.2	59.7	40.0
2016	27041.2	16134.7	11002.0	5132.6	10690.2	9951.8	738.4	216.4	59.7	39.5
2017	29883.0	17875.8	12064.4	5811.4	11784.3	10766.3	1018.0	222.9	59.8	39.4
2018	33106.0	20206.7	13478.1	6728.7	12527.8	11488.2	1039.7	371.5	61.0	37.8
2019	35445.1	21571.8	14536.2	7035.6	13463.4	12692.4	771.0	409.9	60.9	38.0
2020	35943.3	20722.2	13759.7	6962.5	14229.9	13542.8	687.1	991.2	57.7	39.6
2021	41045.6	23268.5	15804.9	7463.6	16198.3	15373.2	825.1	1578.8	56.7	39.5
2022	41610.9	23167.0	15434.5	7732.6	17134.5	16405.5	729.0	1309.4	55.7	41.2

注：本表数据按当年价格计算。
Note: Figures in this table are calculated at current year's prices.

2-11 支出法地区生产总值
GROSS DOMESTIC PRODUCT BY EXPENDITURE APPROACH

单位：亿元 (100 million yuan)

项　目	Item	2022	2021	指数(2021=100) Index(2021=100)
地区生产总值	**Gross Domestic Product**	**41610.9**	**41045.6**	**100.7**
最终消费支出	**Final Consumption Expenditure**	**23167.0**	**23268.5**	**98.0**
居民消费	Households Consumption	15434.5	15804.9	95.9
城镇居民	Urban Resident	14379.1	14750.5	95.8
农村居民	Rural Resident	1055.4	1054.4	96.6
政府消费	Government Consumption	7732.6	7463.6	102.5
资本形成总额	**Gross Fixed Capital Formation**	**17134.5**	**16198.3**	**104.9**
固定资本形成总额	Completed Fixed Asset	16405.5	15373.2	105.2
存货增加	Changes in Inventories	729.0	825.1	99.7
货物和服务净流出	**Net Outflow of Goods and Services**	**1309.4**	**1578.8**	**99.1**

注：本表总量数据按当年价格计算，指数按不变价格计算。
Note: Absolute values are calculated at current year's prices, whereas indices are calculated at constant prices.

2-12 三大需求贡献率(1982—2022年)
CONTRIBUTION RATE OF THREE DEMANDS TO THE INCREASE OF GDP (1982—2022)

单位：% (%)

年 份 Year	最终消费支出 Final Consumption Expenditure	资本形成总额 Gross Capital Formation	货物和服务净流出 Net Outflow of Goods and Services
1982	52.8	5.9	41.3
1983	18.3	44.6	37.1
1984	53.1	69.1	-22.2
1985	115.4	337.5	-352.9
1986	154.5	51.1	-105.5
1987	33.8	69.0	-2.8
1988	46.7	-10.8	64.1
1989	86.9	180.5	-167.4
1990	165.0	128.7	-193.7
1991	61.5	42.9	-4.4
1992	18.2	83.8	-1.9
1993	41.0	73.3	-14.2
1994	54.0	106.8	-60.8
1995	69.3	42.2	-11.5
1996	50.2	-25.2	75.1
1997	87.1	108.1	-95.1
1998	19.8	41.3	39.0
1999	56.1	68.9	-25.0
2000	30.5	46.2	23.2
2001	33.9	45.6	20.5
2002	72.2	68.9	-41.1
2003	40.0	69.4	-9.3
2004	39.7	43.5	16.8
2005	33.3	49.3	17.5
2006	63.0	27.6	9.4
2007	60.6	26.8	12.6
2008	87.4	10.1	2.5
2009	78.9	43.4	-22.3
2010	61.7	55.7	-17.4
2011	80.8	16.9	2.3
2012	74.0	50.9	-24.9
2013	67.0	43.4	-10.5
2014	73.3	25.0	1.7
2015	65.7	26.4	7.9
2016	62.2	31.3	6.5
2017	63.8	38.9	-2.7
2018	72.4	13.3	14.3
2019	56.1	37.9	6.0
2020	-327.2	218.6	208.6
2021	59.5	27.5	13.0
2022	-166.7	271.5	-4.9

注：1. 三大需求指支出法地区生产总值的三大构成项目，即最终消费支出、资本形成总额、货物和服务净流出。
2. 贡献率指三大需求增量与支出法地区生产总值增量之比。
3. 本表数据按不变价格计算。

Note: a) Three demands of GDP by expenditure method are final consumption expenditure, gross capital formation and net outflow of goods and services.
b) Contribution rate of the three demands to GDP growth refers to the proportion of the increment of the each component of GDP by expenditure method to the increment of GDP.
c) Figures in this table are calculated at constant prices.

2-13 居民消费水平(1978-2022年)
HOUSEHOLDS CONSUMPTION LEVEL (1978-2022)

年份 Year	居民消费水平(元) Households Consumption Level(yuan)			城乡消费水平对比(农村居民=1)	指数(1978年=100) Index(1978=100)			指数(上年=100) Index(Preceding Year=100)		
	全市 All Households	城镇居民 Urban Households	农村居民 Rural Households	Urban/Rural Consumption Ratio(Rural Households=1)	全市 All Households	城镇居民 Urban Households	农村居民 Rural Households	全市 All Households	城镇居民 Urban Households	农村居民 Rural Households
1978	330	451	185	2.4	100.0	100.0	100.0	112.3	110.1	122.6
1979	356	464	221	2.1	117.5	114.5	120.8	117.5	114.5	120.8
1980	440	562	280	2.0	147.6	140.0	159.0	125.6	122.1	131.5
1981	485	590	338	1.7	160.3	144.8	189.4	108.6	103.6	119.2
1982	526	622	384	1.6	170.6	149.7	211.2	106.4	103.4	111.5
1983	579	674	432	1.6	175.4	151.2	222.6	102.8	101.0	105.4
1984	677	789	494	1.6	201.4	173.9	250.4	114.8	115.0	112.5
1985	912	1101	585	1.9	263.2	235.3	289.2	130.7	135.3	115.5
1986	1094	1284	749	1.7	312.9	272.0	365.8	118.9	115.6	126.5
1987	1198	1391	827	1.7	316.7	272.0	375.3	101.2	100.0	102.6
1988	1536	1779	1046	1.7	367.7	313.3	435.7	116.1	115.2	116.1
1989	1648	1874	1169	1.6	398.2	337.1	472.7	108.3	107.6	108.5
1990	1797	2045	1186	1.7	466.7	393.4	527.5	117.2	116.7	111.6
1991	2071	2330	1345	1.7	528.3	440.2	587.1	113.2	111.9	111.3
1992	2379	2701	1458	1.9	554.7	466.2	583.6	105.0	105.9	99.4
1993	3211	3749	1637	2.3	620.7	530.1	589.4	111.9	113.7	101.0
1994	4520	5321	2120	2.5	719.4	620.2	631.8	115.9	117.0	107.2
1995	5682	6520	3113	2.1	776.2	659.3	739.2	107.9	106.3	117.0
1996	6525	7508	3437	2.2	817.3	696.9	744.4	105.3	105.7	100.7
1997	7993	9341	3659	2.6	1001.2	866.9	795.0	122.5	124.4	106.8
1998	8652	10097	3900	2.6	1031.2	892.9	801.4	103.0	103.0	100.8
1999	9466	11032	4196	2.6	1123.0	970.6	860.7	108.9	108.7	107.4
2000	9835	11445	4314	2.7	1137.6	981.3	866.7	101.3	101.1	100.7
2001	10313	11903	4740	2.5	1147.8	981.3	923.0	100.9	100.0	106.5
2002	12380	14404	5073	2.8	1345.2	1159.9	961.8	117.2	118.2	104.2
2003	13734	15992	5336	3.0	1419.2	1223.7	964.7	105.5	105.5	100.3
2004	15328	17820	5786	3.1	1522.8	1309.4	1012.0	107.3	107.0	104.9
2005	16636	18877	6693	2.8	1591.3	1336.9	1120.3	104.5	102.1	110.7
2006	19003	21173	7613	2.8	1771.1	1459.9	1241.3	111.3	109.2	110.8
2007	21769	24103	9124	2.6	1930.5	1581.1	1411.4	109.0	108.3	113.7
2008	24005	26435	10548	2.5	2063.7	1680.7	1573.7	106.9	106.3	111.5
2009	26353	28871	12125	2.4	2247.4	1821.9	1773.6	108.9	108.4	112.7
2010	29483	32171	13642	2.4	2429.4	1962.2	1933.2	108.1	107.7	109.0
2011	32960	36032	13961	2.6	2584.9	2091.7	1877.1	106.4	106.6	97.1
2012	36076	39451	14912	2.6	2758.1	2229.8	1993.5	106.7	106.6	106.2
2013	40313	43674	19064	2.3	2940.1	2356.9	2380.2	106.6	105.7	119.4
2014	42918	46355	21001	2.2	3090.0	2470.0	2594.4	105.1	104.8	109.0
2015	46423	50085	22745	2.2	3287.8	2625.6	2752.7	106.4	106.3	106.1
2016	50195	54043	25031	2.2	3498.2	2788.4	2967.4	106.4	106.2	107.8
2017	54965	59189	27072	2.2	3690.6	2939.0	3130.6	105.5	105.4	105.5
2018	61458	66067	30575	2.2	3930.5	3121.2	3418.6	106.5	106.2	109.2
2019	66348	71235	32989	2.2	4201.7	3330.3	3654.5	106.9	106.7	106.9
2020	62842	67038	33611	2.0	3907.6	3077.2	3647.2	93.0	92.4	99.8
2021	72208	76976	38686	2.0	4939.2	3895.7	4471.5	126.4	126.6	122.6
2022	70592	75108	38803	1.9	4741.6	3736.0	4328.4	96.0	95.9	96.8

注：1.本表居民消费水平数据按当年价格计算，指数按不变价格计算。
2.居民消费水平指按平均常住人口计算的人均居民消费支出。

Note: a) Figures of households comsumption level are calculated at current year's prices, whereas indices are calculated at constant prices.
b) Households consumption level refers to the per capita households consumption expenditure on the basis of average permanent population.

2-14 社会劳动生产率(1978-2022年)
OVERALL LABOR PRODUCTIVITY (1978-2022)

单位：元/人 (yuan/person)

年 份 Year	社会劳动生产率 Overall Labor Productivity	第一产业 Primary Industry	第二产业 Secondary Industry	第三产业 Tertiary Industry
1978	2504	444	4484	1911
1979	2626	421	4556	2033
1980	2914	510	4750	2391
1981	2795	561	4316	2420
1982	2959	878	4437	2467
1983	3368	1094	4799	2998
1984	3909	1287	5347	3646
1985	4580	1671	6040	4268
1986	5002	1932	6331	4783
1987	5669	2569	6917	5501
1988	7046	4084	8309	6745
1989	7742	4270	9432	7140
1990	8203	4810	9564	7941
1991	9498	5014	10351	10145
1992	11068	5556	12236	11637
1993	13921	7111	14841	14808
1994	17798	9666	18590	18940
1995	22807	10036	23501	25077
1996	27453	10479	26708	31789
1997	32190	10757	29930	38674
1998	38170	10928	34495	46851
1999	44485	10733	40704	54598
2000	52958	10753	48241	65302
2001	61874	11212	53157	78046
2002	69194	11879	54745	89352
2003	76198	12910	63171	94215
2004	80294	13749	77352	90158
2005	82556	14049	82234	90091
2006	93308	14232	90784	102203
2007	111958	16399	106434	122898
2008	122823	17977	116034	134512
2009	130364	18653	134467	138876
2010	147436	19877	160731	154363
2011	159347	23018	142416	175197
2012	172529	26051	160635	186426
2013	187654	30155	181427	199247
2014	201194	32753	195932	212038
2015	214891	31339	198730	228231
2016	229942	30611	213048	243228
2017	251234	30354	233174	264934
2018	278096	32107	256310	292888
2019	298724	33740	267834	315216
2020	306252	36519	283482	319642
2021	353567	40513	381862	356902
2022	363399	42821	348553	375410

注：1．本表数据按当年价格计算。
2．2010年及以前，社会劳动生产率为地区生产总值(增加值)与从业人员平均人数之比；自2011年起，社会劳动生产率为地区生产总值(增加值)与平均常住就业人口之比。

Note: a) Figures in this table are calculated at current year's prices.
b) In and before 2010, the social labor productivity referred to the ratio of GDP (the value added) to the average number of employed persons; since 2011, it refers to the ratio of GDP (the value added) to the average permanent employed population.

主要统计指标解释

国内（地区）生产总值　是一个地区所有常住单位在一定时期内生产活动的最终成果。地区生产总值有三种表现形式，即价值形态、收入形态和产品形态。从价值形态看，它是所有常住单位在一定时期内所生产的全部货物和服务价值与同期投入的全部非固定资产货物和服务价值的差额，即所有常住单位的增加值之和；从收入形态看，它是所有常住单位在一定时期内创造的各项收入之和，包括劳动者报酬、生产税净额、固定资产折旧和营业盈余；从产品形态看，它是所有常住单位在一定时期内最终使用的货物和服务价值与货物和服务净出口（净流出）价值之和。在实际核算中，地区生产总值有三种计算方法，即生产法、收入法和支出法。三种方法分别从不同的方面反映地区生产总值及其构成。

最终消费率(消费率)　通常指一定时期内最终消费支出占国内（地区）生产总值的比重，一般按现行价格计算。

$$\text{最终消费率（消费率）}=\frac{\text{最终消费支出}}{\text{国内（地区）生产总值}}\times 100\%$$

资本形成率(投资率)　通常指一定时期内资本形成总额占国内（地区）生产总值的比重，一般按现行价格计算。

$$\text{资本形成率（投资率）}=\frac{\text{资本形成总额}}{\text{国内（地区）生产总值}}\times 100\%$$

数字经济及部分新兴产业统计划分标准：

1. **数字经济**　是指以数据资源作为关键生产要素、以现代信息网络作为重要载体、以信息通信技术的有效使用作为效率提升和经济结构优化的重要推动力的一系列经济活动。本分类将数字经济产业范围确定为：01 数字产品制造业、02 数字产品服务业、03 数字技术应用业、04 数字要素驱动业、05 数字化效率提升业等 5 个大类。数字经济是以《国民经济行业分类》(GB/T 4754-2017）为基础，对国民经济行业分类中符合数字经济产业特征的和以提供数字产品（货物或服务）为目的的相关行业类别活动进行再分类。

2. **战略性新兴产业**　是以重大技术突破和重大发展需求为基础，对经济社会全局和长远发展具有重大引领带动作用，知识技术密集、物质资源消耗少、成长潜力大、综合效益好的产业，包括：新一代信息技术产业、高端装备制造产业、新材料产业、生物产业、新能源汽车产业、新能源产业、节能环保产业、数字创意产业、相关服务业等9大领域。战略性新兴产业是以《国民经济行业分类》(GB/T 4754-2017）为基础，对其中符合“战略性新兴产业”特征的有关活动进行再分类。

3. **高技术产业**　包括高技术制造业和高技术服务业。高技术制造业是指国民经济行业中 R&D 投入强度相对高的制造行业，包括：医药制造，航空、航天器及设备制造，电子及通信设备制造，计算机及办公设备制造，医疗仪器设备及仪器仪表制造，信息化学品制造等 6 大类。高技术服务业是采用高技术手段为社会提供服务活动的集合，包括信息服务、电子商务服务、检验检测服务、专业技术服务业的高技术服务、研发与设计服务、科技成果转化服务、知识产权及相关法律服务、环境监测及治理服务和其他高技术服务等 9 大类。高技术产业是以《国民经济行业分类》（GB/T 4754-2017）为基础，对国民经济行业分类中符合高技术产业范畴相关活动的再分类。

4. **生产性服务业**　指为生产活动提供的研发设计与其他技术服务，货物运输、通用航空生产、仓储和邮政快递服务，信息服务，金融服务，节能与环保服务，生产性租赁服务，商务服务，人力资源管理与职业教育培训服务，批发与贸易经纪代理服务，生产性支持服务。生产性服务业是以《国民经济行业分类》(GB/T 4754-2017）为基础，对国民经济行业分类中符合生产性服务业特征有关活动的再分类。

5. **生活性服务业**　是指满足居民最终消费需求的服务活动。分类范围包括十二大领域：居民和家庭服务，健康服务，养老服务，旅游游览和娱乐服务，体育服务，文化服务，居民零售和互联网销售服务，居民出行服务，住宿餐饮服务，教育培训服务，居民住房服务，其他生活性服务等。生活性服务业是以《国民经济行业分类》(GB/T 4754-2017) 为基础，对国民经济行业分类中符合生活性服务业特征有关活动的再分类。

Explanatory Notes on Main Statistical Indicators

Gross Domestic (Regional) Product represents the final results of all resident units in an area from their productive activities over a given period of time. It is expressed in three different perspectives respectively, namely value, income, and product. From the value perspective, it refers to the total value of all goods and services produced by all resident units during a certain period of time, minus the total value of input of goods and services of the nature of non-fixed assets; in other words, it is the sum of added value of all resident units. From the income perspective, it is the sum of incomes created by all resident units during a certain period of time, including compensation for labors, net taxes on production, depreciation of fixed assets and operating surplus. From the product perspective, it refers to the value of all goods and services for final demand by all resident units plus the net exports (net outflow) value of goods and services during a certain period of time. In actual national accounting, gross regional product is calculated in three methods, namely production method, income method and expenditure method, which reflect the gross regional product and its composition from different angles.

Final Consumption Rate (Consumption Rate) It usually refers to the proportion of final consumption in GDP (GRP) within a certain period, and is generally calculated at current price.

Final Consumption Rate (Consumption Rate) = Final Consumption / GDP (GRP) × 100%

Capital Formation Rate (Investment Rate) It usually refers to the proportion of total capital formation in GDP (GRP) within a certain period, and is generally calculated at current price.

Capital Formation Rate (Investment Rate) = Total Capital Formation / GDP (GRP) ×100%

Standards for the Statistical Classification of Digital Economy and Some Emerging Industries:

1. Digital Economy refers to a series of economic activities that take data resources as the key production factors, modern information network as the important carrier, and the effective use of information and communication technology as the important driving force for efficiency improvement and economic structure optimization. The industrial scope of digital economy is determined as the following 5 categories in this classification: 01 Digital product manufacturing industry, 02 Digital product service industry, 03 Digital technology application industry, 04 Digital elements driving industry, 05 Digital efficiency promotion industry. Digital economy is the re-classification of activities in related industry categories in the national economic sectors that are in line with the characteristics of digital economy and aim at providing digital products (goods or services) based on the *Classification of National Economic Sectors* (GB/T 4754-2017).

2. Strategic Emerging Industries refer to the industries that are based on major technological breakthroughs and major development needs, play important leading and driving role in the overall economic and social situation and in the long-term development, are knowledge and technology intensive, consume little material resources, with great growth potential and good comprehensive benefits. The strategic emerging industries include 9 major areas which are respectively the new generation of information and technology industry, high-end equipment manufacture industry, new material industry, bioindustry, new-energy automobile industry, new energy industry, energy conservation and environmental protection industry, digital creative industry and related services industry. The strategic emerging industries are the re-classification of related activities that are in line with the characteristics of "strategic emerging industries" based on the *Classification of National Economic Sectors* (GB/T 4754-2017).

3. High-tech Industry includes high-tech manufacturing industry and high-tech service industry. High-tech manufacturing industry refers to the manufacturing industry with a relatively high intensity of R&D input among the national economic sectors. It includes 6 major categories which are respectively manufacture of medicines, manufacture of aircrafts and spacecrafts, manufacture of electronic and communication equipment, manufacture of computers and office equipment, manufacture of medical equipment and appliance and measuring instrument and meter, and manufacture of information chemical products. High-tech service industry means the collection of services provided to society by adopting high-tech means. It includes 9 categories which are respectively information services, e-commerce services, inspection and testing services, high-tech service in professional technique services, R&D and design services, services for transformation of scientific and technological achievements, intellectual property right and related legal services, environmental monitoring and governance services, and other high-tech services. The high-tech industry is the re-classification of related activities that are in line with the categories of high-tech industry in the national economic sectors based on the *Classification of National Economic Sectors* (GB/T 4754-2017).

4. Producer Service Industry refers to the R&D and design and other technology services, cargo transportation, general aviation production, storage and express mail services, information services, financial services, energy conservation and environmental protection services, productive leasing services, business services, human resource management and vocational education and training services, wholesale and trading agency services, and the productive support services provided for production activities. The producer service industry is the re-classification of related activities that are in line with the characteristics of producer service industry in the national economic sectors based on the *Classification of National Economic Sectors* (GB/T 4754-2017).

5. Consumer Service Industry refers to the service activities to meet the final consumption demands of residents. The scope of classification covers 12 areas which are respectively resident and household services, healthcare services, pension services, tourism, sightseeing and entertainment services, sport services, cultural services, resident retail and Internet sales services, resident trip services, accommodation and restaurants services, education and training services, resident housing services, and other consumer-oriented services, etc. The consumer service industry is the re-classification of related activities that are in line with the characteristics of consumer service industry in the national economic sectors based on the *Classification of National Economic Sectors* (GB/T 4754-2017).

人口与就业
POPULATION AND EMPLOYMENT

简要说明

一、主要内容

人口部分包括历年北京市常住人口和户籍人口的分组资料、新中国成立以来已开展的七次人口普查数据、1990年以后的人口变动情况抽样调查数据。就业部分包括分三次产业的常住就业人口数据、法人单位从业人员及工资情况、城镇非私营单位在岗职工人数及工资的分组情况、城镇登记失业及新增就业情况等。

二、统计调查方法说明

（一）关于人口数据。1953年、1964年、1982年、1990年、2000年、2010年和2020年分别进行了七次人口普查，1987年、1995年、2005年、2015年进行了1%人口抽样调查，从1982年开始进行人口变动抽样调查。

（二）关于劳动工资数据。劳动工资统计采用全面调查和抽样调查相结合的方法。

三、有关行业划分的变化说明

2011年以前执行《国民经济行业分类》（GB/T 4754-2002）标准，2012-2017年执行《国民经济行业分类》（GB/T 4754-2011）标准，2018年起执行《国民经济行业分类》（GB/T 4754-2017）标准。

四、“城镇人口”和“乡村人口”口径变化情况

本章中1978-1989年“城镇人口”和“乡村人口”数据为户籍管理统计中的“非农业人口”和“农业人口”口径；1990-1999年根据1990年、2000年两次人口普查数据进行调整；2000年为国家统计局1999年发布的《关于统计上划分城乡的规定(试行)》中的“城镇人口”和“乡村人口”口径，2001-2005年为该口径的推算数；2006-2008年为国家统计局2006年发布的《关于统计上划分城乡的暂行规定》中的“城镇人口”和“乡村人口”口径的推算数；2009年及以后国家统计局每年对《统计用区划代码和城乡分类代码》进行更新维护，“城镇人口”和“乡村人口”的划分均按当年的城乡分类标准进行推算。

Brief Introduction

I. Main Content

Population statistics include classified data for permanent population and registered population in Beijing in previous years, statistics of population from seven population censuses since the founding of the People's Republic of China, and statistics of sample survey on population changes after 1990. Employment statistics include data on permanent employed population in three industries, employed persons and wages in legal entities, classified statistics for the number and wage of fully employed staff and workers in urban non-private entities, registered unemployment and new employment in urban areas.

II. Statistical Survey Methods

(I) Data on Population. Seven population censuses were conducted respectively in 1953, 1964, 1982, 1990, 2000, 2010 and 2020; 1% population sample surveys were conducted respectively in 1987, 1995, 2005 and 2015; and sample surveys on population changes have been conducted since 1982.

(II) Data on Employment Wage. The combined method of comprehensive survey and sample survey is adopted in the employment wage statistics.

III. Changes in the Classification of Sectors

The standards in the *Classification of National Economic Sectors* (GB/T 4754-2002) were implemented before 2011. The standards in the *Classification of National Economic Sectors* (GB/T 4754-2011) were implemented from 2012 to 2017. The standards in the *Classification of National Economic Sectors* (GB/T 4754-2017) are implemented since 2018.

IV. Changes in the Terms of Urban Population and Rural Population

The data on urban population and rural population for the period from 1978 to 1989 as mentioned in this chapter refer to the non-agricultural population and agricultural population in the household registration statistics; the data had been adjusted from 1990 to 1999 in accordance with the data on two population censes which were conducted respectively in 1990 and 2000; that of 2000 referred to the urban population and rural population in the *Regulations on the Statistical Division of Rural and Urban Areas (Trial)* issued by the National Bureau of Statistics in 1999; the data of 2001 to 2005 were estimated on the same basis; the data of 2006 to 2008 were the estimated figures of the urban population and rural population in the *Provisional Regulations on the Statistical Division of Rural and Urban Areas* issued by the National Bureau of Statistics in 2006; the National Bureau of Statistics of China has carried on update and maintenance of the *Division Codes and Urban-rural Classification Codes for Statistical Use* since 2009; the division of urban population and rural population had all been estimated and calculated in accordance with the urban-rural classification standards for each year.

3-1 七次人口普查人口基本情况
BASIC STATISTICS ON POPULATION IN SEVEN CENSUSES

项目	Item	1953	1964	1982	1990	2000	2010	2020
常住人口 （万人）	**Permanent Population (10000 persons)**	**276.8**	**759.7**	**923.1**	**1081.9**	**1356.9**	**1961.2**	**2189.3**
按城乡分	**By Urban Area and Rural Area**							
城镇人口	Urban Population	205.8	425.8	597.0	794.5	1052.2	1685.9	1916.6
乡村人口	Rural Population	71.0	333.9	326.1	287.4	304.7	275.3	272.7
按性别分	**By Gender**							
男	Male	159.8	391.1	467.1	559.3	707.4	1012.6	1119.5
女	Female	117.0	368.6	456.0	522.6	649.5	948.6	1069.8
常住人口性别比(女=100)	**Sex Ratio of the Permanent Population (Female=100)**	**136.5**	**106.1**	**102.4**	**107.0**	**108.9**	**106.8**	**104.7**
家庭户规模 （人/户）	**Family Household Size (person/household)**			**3.7**	**3.2**	**2.9**	**2.5**	**2.3**
各年龄组人口比重 （%）	**Proportion of Population by Age Group (%)**							
0-14	Age 0-14	30.1	41.5	22.4	20.2	13.6	8.6	11.9
15-59	Age 15-59	64.3	51.9	69.1	69.7	73.9	78.9	68.5
60岁及以上	Age 60 and Above	5.6	6.6	8.5	10.1	12.5	12.5	19.6
#65岁及以上	Age 65 and Above	3.3	4.1	5.6	6.3	8.4	8.7	13.3
总抚养比 （%）	**Gross Dependency Ratio (%)**	**50.2**	**83.8**	**38.9**	**36.1**	**28.2**	**20.9**	**33.6**
老年抚养比	Old-age Dependency Ratio	5.0	7.5	7.8	8.6	10.8	10.5	17.8
少儿抚养比	Child Dependency Ratio	45.2	76.3	31.1	27.5	17.4	10.4	15.8
民族人口	**Population by Ethnic Group**							
汉族 （万人）	Han Nationality (10000 persons)	260.0	731.2	890.8	1040.5	1298.4	1881.1	2084.5
占常住人口比重 （%）	Percentage in Permanent Population (%)	93.9	96.2	96.5	96.2	95.7	95.9	95.2
少数民族 （万人）	Ethnic Minority (10000 persons)	16.8	28.5	32.3	41.4	58.5	80.1	104.8
占常住人口比重 （%）	Percentage in Permanent Population (%)	6.1	3.8	3.5	3.8	4.3	4.1	4.8
每十万人口拥有的各种受教育程度人口 （人）	**Population with Various Education Attainment Per 100000 Persons (person)**							
大专及以上	Junior College and Above		4359	4866	9300	16839	31499	41980
高中和中专	Senior Secondary/Secondary Technical School		4513	17646	18978	23165	21220	17593
初中	Junior Secondary School		11768	29086	30551	34380	31396	23289
小学	Primary School		31883	26197	22579	16963	9956	10503
文盲人口及文盲率	**Illiterate Population and Illiteracy Rate**							
文盲人口 （万人）	Illiterate Population (10000 persons)		168.9	114.7	94.3	57.8	33.3	17.2
文盲率 （%）	Illiteracy Rate (%)		34.2	16.0	10.9	4.9	1.9	0.9
平均预期寿命 （岁）	**Average Life Expectancy (year old)**			**71.9**	**72.9**	**76.1**	**80.2**	**82.5**

注：1.1953年数据按当年区划统计。
2.1964年的文盲人口数为12周岁及以上文盲和半文盲人口，1982年、1990年、2000年、2010年、2020年的文盲人口数为15周岁及以上文盲和半文盲人口。文盲率是指15周岁及以上人口中，文盲人口和半文盲人口所占比重。
3.本表常住人口与表3-2相同的年份数据不同，是因为本表数据为普查时点数，表3-2为年末时点数。1953年、1964年、1982年、1990年普查时点为7月1日零时；2000年、2010年、2020年普查时点为11月1日零时。

Note: a) Data for 1953 are statistics by district division of the year.
b) Statistics on illiterate population in 1964 covered the illiterate and semi-illiterate people at 12 and above,and statistics in 1982,1990,2000, 2010 and 2020 covered those at 15 and above. Illiteracy rate refers to the proportion of illiterate and semi-illiterate people in the population at 15 and above.
c) This table has different figures from Table 3-2 in terms of the permanent population, because this table uses the data at the time point of the census, while in Table 3-2, the year end is taken as the time point for statistics. The time point of the census in 1953,1964,1982 and 1990 was 12 o'clock midnight, July 1st; the time point of the census in 2000, 2010 and 2020 was 12 o'clock midnight, November 1st.

3-2 常住人口(1978-2022年)
PERMANENT POPULATION (1978-2022)

单位：万人 (10000 persons)

年份 Year	常住人口 Permanent Population	#常住外来人口 Permanent Migrant Population	按性别分 By Gender		按城乡分 By Urban Area and Rural Area		常住人口密度(人/平方公里) Permanent Population Density (person/sq.km)	常住人口出生率(‰) Birth Rate (‰)	常住人口死亡率(‰) Death Rate (‰)	常住人口自然增长率(‰) Natural Growth Rate (‰)
			男 Male	女 Female	城镇人口 Urban Population	乡村人口 Rural Population				
1978	871.5	21.8	443.2	428.3	479.0	392.5	519	12.93	6.12	6.81
1979	897.1	26.5	454.6	442.5	510.3	386.8	534	13.67	5.92	7.75
1980	904.3	18.6	457.8	446.5	521.1	383.2	538	15.56	6.30	9.26
1981	919.2	18.4	465.9	453.3	533.3	385.9	547	16.93	6.02	10.91
1982	935.0	17.2	474.0	461.0	544.0	391.0	556	20.04	5.68	14.36
1983	950.0	16.8	483.0	467.0	557.0	393.0	565	15.63	5.49	10.14
1984	965.0	19.8	491.0	474.0	570.0	395.0	574	16.74	5.53	11.21
1985	981.0	23.1	500.0	481.0	586.0	395.0	584	15.45	5.75	9.70
1986	1028.0	56.8	524.0	504.0	621.0	407.0	612	15.82	4.47	11.35
1987	1047.0	59.0	525.0	522.0	637.0	410.0	623	17.29	5.40	11.89
1988	1061.0	59.8	534.0	527.0	650.0	411.0	631	14.43	5.08	9.35
1989	1075.0	53.9	538.0	537.0	664.0	411.0	640	12.84	5.35	7.49
1990	1086.0	53.8	545.0	541.0	798.0	288.0	646	13.04	5.81	7.23
1991	1094.0	54.5	547.0	547.0	808.0	286.0	651	8.03	5.82	2.21
1992	1102.0	57.1	554.0	548.0	819.0	283.0	656	9.22	6.11	3.11
1993	1112.0	60.8	559.0	553.0	831.0	281.0	662	9.35	6.16	3.19
1994	1125.0	63.2	564.0	561.0	846.0	279.0	669	8.96	5.76	3.20
1995	1251.1	180.8	627.0	624.1	946.2	304.9	744	7.92	5.12	2.80
1996	1259.4	181.7	639.0	620.4	957.9	301.5	749	8.02	5.34	2.68
1997	1240.0	154.5	628.7	611.3	948.3	291.7	738	7.91	6.02	1.89
1998	1245.6	154.1	630.6	615.0	957.7	287.9	741	6.00	5.30	0.70
1999	1257.2	157.4	636.4	620.8	971.7	285.5	748	6.50	5.60	0.90
2000	1363.6	256.1	710.9	652.7	1057.4	306.2	811	6.20	5.30	0.90
2001	1385.1	262.8	722.1	663.0	1081.2	303.9	824	6.10	5.30	0.80
2002	1423.2	286.9	743.1	680.1	1118.0	305.2	847	6.60	5.73	0.87
2003	1456.4	307.6	761.2	695.2	1151.3	305.1	867	5.06	5.15	-0.09
2004	1492.7	329.8	779.9	712.8	1187.2	305.5	910	6.13	5.39	0.74
2005	1538.0	357.3	778.7	759.3	1286.1	251.9	937	6.29	5.20	1.09
2006	1601.0	403.4	817.6	783.4	1350.2	250.8	976	6.22	4.94	1.28
2007	1676.0	462.7	850.8	825.2	1416.2	259.8	1021	8.16	4.83	3.33
2008	1771.0	541.1	900.2	870.8	1503.6	267.4	1079	7.89	4.59	3.30
2009	1860.0	614.2	949.8	910.2	1581.1	278.9	1133	7.66	4.33	3.33
2010	1961.9	704.7	1013.0	948.9	1686.4	275.5	1196	7.27	4.29	2.98
2011	2023.8	749.9	1044.1	979.7	1744.6	279.2	1233	8.28	4.26	4.02
2012	2077.5	792.1	1073.7	1003.8	1792.7	284.8	1266	9.02	4.30	4.72
2013	2125.4	831.6	1097.9	1027.5	1836.1	289.3	1295	8.89	4.50	4.39
2014	2171.1	858.3	1118.8	1052.3	1878.0	293.1	1323	9.69	4.89	4.80
2015	2188.3	862.5	1126.2	1062.1	1897.5	290.8	1333	7.89	4.91	2.98
2016	2195.4	858.8	1126.1	1069.3	1904.8	290.6	1338	9.23	5.16	4.07
2017	2194.4	855.5	1123.9	1070.5	1907.7	286.7	1337	8.97	5.24	3.73
2018	2191.7	848.2	1122.2	1069.5	1908.8	282.9	1336	8.13	5.50	2.63
2019	2190.1	843.5	1120.5	1069.6	1913.1	277.0	1335	7.98	5.40	2.58
2020	2189.0	839.6	1119.4	1069.6	1916.4	272.6	1334	6.98	4.59	2.39
2021	2188.6	834.8	1117.7	1070.9	1916.1	272.5	1334	6.35	5.39	0.96
2022	2184.3	825.1	1114.2	1070.1	1912.8	271.5	1331	5.67	5.72	-0.05

注：1978—1981年为户籍统计数，含暂住人口。自1990年起为人口变动情况抽样调查推算数。其中，1982年、1990年、2000年、2010年、2020年为人口普查推算数；1995年、2005年、2015年为1%人口抽样调查推算数；1983—1989年数据根据1983年、1990年两次人口普查数据进行了修订；2006—2009年数据根据2010年人口普查结果进行了修订；2011—2019年数据根据2010年、2020年两次人口普查结果进行了修订。

Note: Statistics for 1978-1981 were figures of registered residents, including temporary residents. Data since 1990 were estimated from sample surveys on population changes. Specifically, data for 1982,1990,2000,2010 and 2020 were estimated from the population censuses; data for 1995,2005,2015 were estimated from sample surveys on 1% of the population; data for 1983-1989 were revised in accordance with the data from the population censuses in 1983 and 1990; data for 2006-2009 were revised in accordance with the results of the population census in 2010 and data for 2011-2019 were revised in accordance with the results of the population censuses in 2010 and 2020.

3-3 常住人口年龄构成情况(2010-2022年)
PERMANENT POPULATION BY AGE COMPOSITION (2010-2022)

单位：万人 (10000 persons)

年 份 Year	0-14	15-59	60岁及以上 60 and Above	#65岁及以上 65 and Above
2010	168.7	1547.2	246.0	171.0
2011	186.8	1564.2	272.8	184.7
2012	200.7	1581.5	295.3	196.7
2013	208.8	1610.5	306.1	205.0
2014	226.5	1601.5	343.1	227.5
2015	234.7	1587.4	366.2	241.2
2016	243.8	1572.8	378.8	252.6
2017	249.1	1550.7	394.6	264.7
2018	252.0	1532.1	407.6	273.0
2019	253.4	1518.4	418.3	280.4
2020	259.1	1500.0	429.9	291.2
2021	264.7	1482.3	441.6	311.6
2022	264.0	1455.2	465.1	330.1

注：表中2010年数据为北京市第六次全国人口普查推算数，2020年数据为北京市第七次全国人口普查推算数；2011—2019年数据根据年度人口抽样调查数据推算，并根据2010年和2020年两次人口普查结果进行了修订；2021年和2022年数据为年度人口抽样调查推算数。

Note: Data for 2010 in this table are estimated from the sixth national population census in Beijing, and data for 2020 are estimated from the seventh national population census in Beijing; data for 2011-2019 are estimated based on the sample surveys data on population and have been revised in accordance with the results of the population censuses in 2010 and 2020.Data for 2021 and 2022 are the estimates from the sample survey on population.

3-4 常住人口总量及人口密度(按地区分)(2022年)
TOTAL NUMBER AND DENSITY OF PERMANENT POPULATION (BY DISTRICT) (2022)

地 区	District	常住人口 (万人) Permanent Population (10000 persons)	#常住外来人口 Permanent Migrant Population	城镇人口 Urban Population	乡村人口 Rural Population	常住人口密度 (人／平方公里) Permanent Population Density (person/sq.km)
全 市	**Total**	**2184.3**	**825.1**	**1912.8**	**271.5**	**1331**
东城区	Dongcheng District	70.4	14.9	70.4		16818
西城区	Xicheng District	110.0	22.0	110.0		21769
朝阳区	Chaoyang District	344.2	124.3	343.3	0.9	7564
丰台区	Fengtai District	201.2	62.8	199.9	1.3	6579
石景山区	Shijingshan District	56.3	15.6	56.3		6677
海淀区	Haidian District	312.4	105.9	305.4	7.0	7253
门头沟区	Mentougou District	39.6	11.5	36.2	3.4	273
房山区	Fangshan District	131.1	43.8	102.6	28.5	659
通州区	Tongzhou District	184.3	89.9	137.3	47.0	2034
顺义区	Shunyi District	132.5	60.1	87.8	44.7	1299
昌平区	Changping District	226.7	131.9	185.9	40.8	1687
大兴区	Daxing District	199.1	101.6	161.6	37.5	1921
怀柔区	Huairou District	43.9	15.2	32.8	11.1	207
平谷区	Pinggu District	45.6	7.2	27.9	17.7	480
密云区	Miyun District	52.6	10.8	34.9	17.7	236
延庆区	Yanqing District	34.4	7.6	20.5	13.9	173

注：本表数据为人口抽样调查推算数据，为年末数。
Note: Figures in this table are the year-end estimated figures from the sample survey on population.

3-5 常住人口自然变动(按地区分)(2022年)
NATURAL CHANGE OF PERMANENT POPULATION (BY DISTRICT) (2022)

地　区	District	出生人数(人) Number of Births (person)	死亡人数(人) Number of Deaths (person)	自然增加人数(人) Natural Increase of Population (person)	出生率(‰) Birth Rate (‰)	死亡率(‰) Death Rate (‰)	自然增长率(‰) Natural Growth Rate (‰)
全　市	**Total**	**124063**	**125036**	**-973**	**5.67**	**5.72**	**-0.05**
东城区	Dongcheng District	2956	7028	-4072	4.19	9.95	-5.76
西城区	Xicheng District	5569	10678	-5109	5.05	9.69	-4.64
朝阳区	Chaoyang District	18880	17800	1080	5.48	5.17	0.31
丰台区	Fengtai District	11017	13703	-2686	5.47	6.81	-1.34
石景山区	Shijingshan District	3592	4239	-647	6.36	7.51	-1.15
海淀区	Haidian District	15101	13851	1250	4.83	4.43	0.40
门头沟区	Mentougou District	1846	3316	-1470	4.66	8.37	-3.71
房山区	Fangshan District	8383	9852	-1469	6.39	7.51	-1.12
通州区	Tongzhou District	11079	7929	3150	6.01	4.30	1.71
顺义区	Shunyi District	7264	6560	704	5.48	4.95	0.53
昌平区	Changping Ddistrict	14796	10937	3859	6.52	4.82	1.70
大兴区	Daxing District	14663	7280	7383	7.36	3.65	3.71
怀柔区	Huairou District	2027	1741	286	4.61	3.96	0.65
平谷区	Pinggu District	2800	3913	-1113	6.13	8.57	-2.44
密云区	Miyun District	2531	3722	-1191	4.81	7.07	-2.26
延庆区	Yanqing District	1559	2487	-928	4.52	7.21	-2.69

注：本表数据为人口抽样调查推算数据。
Note: Figures in this table are estimated figures from the sample survey on population.

3-6 常住人口年龄构成(2022年)
PERMANENT POPULATION BY AGE COMPOSITION (2022)

年龄组 Age Group	常住人口数 (万人) Permanent Population (10000 persons)	占常住人口比重 (%) as Percentage of Permanent Population (%)
合 计 Total	**2184.3**	**100.0**
0-4	82.3	3.8
5-9	104.8	4.8
10-14	76.9	3.5
15-19	51.9	2.4
20-24	116.6	5.3
25-29	173.9	8.0
30-34	230.5	10.6
35-39	220.7	10.1
40-44	180.1	8.2
45-49	145.0	6.6
50-54	172.8	7.9
55-59	163.7	7.5
60-64	135.0	6.2
65-69	133.7	6.1
70-74	82.7	3.8
75-79	46.4	2.1
80-84	34.3	1.6
85岁及以上 85 and Above	33.0	1.5

注：本表数据为人口抽样调查推算数据，为年末数。
Note: Figures in this table are the year-end estimated figures from the sample survey on population.

3-7 常住人口受教育程度(2022年)
EDUCATION ATTAINMENT OF PERMANENT POPULATION (2022)

单位：人 (person)

项　目	Item	调查人口合计 Total Surveyed Population	男 Male	女 Female
15岁及以上人口	**Population at 15 and above**	**475497**	**236345**	**239152**
#小　学	Primary School	24851	9758	15093
初　中	Junior Secondary School	92537	47979	44558
普通高中	Senior Secondary School	83271	42631	40640
大学专科	Junior College	105675	53286	52389
大学本科	Undergraduates	126621	62645	63976
硕士研究生	Postgraduate with Master's Degree	30241	14806	15435
博士研究生	Postgraduate with Doctor's Degree	4600	2800	1800

注：本表数据为人口抽样调查样本数据。
Note: Figures in this table are the sample figures from the sample survey on population.

3-8 常住人口家庭户规模(2022年)
FAMILY SIZE OF PERMANENT POPULATION (2022)

地　区	Area	调查家庭总户数(户) Total Number of Surveyed Households (household)	家庭户规模所占比重(%) Percentage of Various Sized Family (%)				
			一人户 One-person Family	二人户 Two-person Family	三人户 Three-person Family	四人户 Four-person Family	五人及以上户 Five-person and above Family
全　市	**Total**	**210288**	**26.6**	**34.0**	**22.7**	**9.9**	**6.9**
城　镇	Urban	176965	26.7	33.7	23.6	9.9	6.1
乡　村	Rural	33323	25.8	35.6	17.6	9.7	11.2

注：本表数据为人口抽样调查样本数据。
Note: Figures in this table are the sample figures from the sample survey on population.

3-9 常住就业人口规模及构成(2010-2022年) PERMANENT EMPLOYED POPULATION AND ITS COMPOSITION (2010-2022)

单位：万人 (10000 persons)

年份 Year	常住就业人口 Permanent Employed Population	第一产业 Primary Industry	第二产业 Secondary Industry	第三产业 Tertiary Industry	构成(%)(合计=100) Composition (%) (Total=100) 第一产业 Primary Industry	第二产业 Secondary Industry	第三产业 Tertiary Industry
2010	1067.3	58.3	252.1	756.9	5.5	23.6	70.9
2011	1090.1	58.6	248.3	783.2	5.4	22.8	71.9
2012	1115.3	55.3	231.8	828.2	5.0	20.8	74.3
2013	1137.2	50.7	227.7	858.8	4.5	20.0	75.5
2014	1141.8	46.5	224.8	870.5	4.1	19.7	76.2
2015	1164.4	43.1	220.0	901.3	3.7	18.9	77.4
2016	1187.6	41.7	218.0	927.9	3.5	18.4	78.1
2017	1191.3	38.6	215.1	937.6	3.2	18.1	78.7
2018	1189.6	36.5	212.3	940.8	3.1	17.8	79.1
2019	1183.5	31.3	210.9	941.3	2.6	17.8	79.5
2020	1163.8	28.0	194.0	941.8	2.4	16.7	80.9
2021	1158.0	27.0	193.0	938.0	2.3	16.7	81.0
2022	1132.1	25.1	186.0	921.0	2.2	16.4	81.4

注：表中数据根据2010年、2020年两次人口普查数据以及人口抽样调查和劳动力调查数据推算。

Note: Figures in this table are estimated on the basis of the two population censuses respectively in 2010 and 2020 as well as the sample survey on population and the labor force survey.

3-10 户籍人口(1978-2022年)
REGISTERED POPULATION (1978-2022)

单位：万人 (10000 persons)

年份 Year	户籍户数(万户) Registered Households (10000 households)	户籍人口 Registered Population	#60岁及以上人口 Population at 60 and above	按性别分 By Genger 男 Male	女 Female	按户籍性质分 By Type of Household Register 非农业户 Non-Agricultural	农业户 Agricultural	户籍人口出生人数 Births of Registered Population	户籍人口死亡人数 Deaths of Registered Population	户籍人口自然增加人数 Natural Increase of Registered Population
1978	205.5	849.7		432.1	417.5	467.0	382.6	10.9	5.2	5.7
1979	214.6	870.6		441.1	429.4	495.2	375.4	11.8	5.1	6.7
1980	223.2	885.7		448.4	437.3	510.4	375.3	13.7	5.5	8.2
1981	234.8	900.8		456.6	444.2	522.6	378.2	15.1	5.4	9.7
1982	245.0	917.8		465.5	452.3	534.0	383.8	18.2	5.2	13.1
1983	255.1	933.2		474.7	458.5	547.1	386.0	14.5	5.1	9.4
1984	263.1	945.2		481.2	464.0	558.1	387.0	13.2	5.1	8.1
1985	274.1	957.9		488.0	469.9	572.5	385.4	11.8	5.2	6.6
1986	284.6	971.2		495.5	475.7	586.8	384.4	12.9	5.2	7.8
1987	299.4	988.0		504.1	483.9	601.0	387.0	16.9	5.3	11.6
1988	310.8	1001.2		510.4	490.8	614.3	387.0	15.3	5.5	9.8
1989	322.5	1021.1		520.3	500.8	630.6	390.5	19.0	5.7	13.3
1990	335.0	1032.2		525.3	507.0	640.2	392.1	14.0	6.3	7.7
1991	343.1	1039.5		528.5	511.1	648.4	391.2	9.2	5.7	3.5
1992	349.3	1044.9		530.8	514.1	656.3	388.6	8.3	6.2	2.2
1993	354.6	1051.2		533.9	517.3	668.7	382.5	7.9	6.3	1.6
1994	360.3	1061.8		538.9	522.8	683.8	377.9	8.5	6.3	2.2
1995	365.7	1070.3		543.0	527.3	696.9	373.5	8.5	6.2	2.3
1996	370.9	1077.7		546.8	530.9	709.7	368.0	7.8	6.7	1.2
1997	375.7	1085.5		550.4	535.1	722.7	362.9	7.6	6.7	0.9
1998	383.4	1091.5		552.6	538.9	733.6	357.8	6.7	7.5	-0.8
1999	390.3	1099.8		556.7	543.1	747.2	352.6	6.3	6.2	0.1
2000	397.9	1107.5		560.1	547.4	760.7	346.8	7.2	7.8	-0.5
2001	405.3	1122.3		567.3	555.0	780.2	342.2	6.0	5.3	0.7
2002	416.3	1136.3		574.7	561.6	806.9	329.4	6.0	5.2	0.8
2003	427.6	1148.8		581.0	567.9	830.8	318.0	4.5	5.8	-1.3
2004	439.8	1162.9		587.2	575.7	854.7	308.2	6.6	6.2	0.4
2005	451.7	1180.7		596.0	584.7	880.2	300.5	7.5	7.0	0.5
2006	463.7	1197.6		604.2	593.4	905.4	292.2	7.7	5.1	2.6
2007	473.0	1213.3	210.3	612.0	601.3	929.0	284.3	9.9	5.2	4.8
2008	481.2	1229.9	218.6	620.0	609.9	950.7	279.2	10.6	5.1	5.5
2009	488.7	1245.8	228.7	627.5	618.9	971.9	273.9	10.9	6.2	4.7
2010	496.1	1257.8	237.2	632.8	625.0	989.5	268.3	10.2	9.1	1.1
2011	503.1	1277.9	250.5	642.4	635.6	1013.8	264.2	12.5	5.3	7.2
2012	509.2	1297.5	266.1	651.7	645.8	1039.3	258.2	14.5	5.7	8.8
2013	516.2	1316.3	283.2	660.4	655.9	1065.0	251.4	13.6	5.7	7.9
2014	522.6	1333.4	301.0	668.3	665.1	1089.8	243.6	17.2	7.6	9.6
2015	529.2	1345.2	318.0	673.3	671.9	1111.3	233.8	12.3	7.3	4.9
2016	538.2	1362.9	334.4	681.5	681.4	1132.0	230.9	20.5	8.9	11.6
2017	543.1	1359.2	336.4	676.8	682.4	1131.7	227.5	18.6	26.5	-7.9
2018	548.8	1375.8	352.3	684.2	691.6	1152.3	223.5	15.7	10.1	5.6
2019	554.4	1397.4	371.1	694.7	702.7	1176.3	221.2	15.3	4.9	10.4
2020	557.6	1400.8	378.8	694.9	705.9	1185.0	215.8	11.7	15.8	-4.1
2021	560.7	1413.5	388.6	700.9	712.7	1200.7	212.8	10.3	11.7	-1.4
2022	564.1	1427.7	414.4	708.1	719.6	1216.3	211.4	8.6	3.0	5.6

资料来源：北京市公安局。
Source: Beijing Municipal Bureau of Public Security.

3-11 户籍人口年龄构成(2022年)
AGE COMPOSITION OF REGISTERED POPULATION (2022)

年龄组 Age Group	户籍人口(人) Registered Population (person)			占人口比重(%) Percentage (%)		
	合计 Total	男 Male	女 Female	合计 Total	男 Male	女 Female
合计 Total	**14277092**	**7081255**	**7195837**	**100.0**	**49.6**	**50.4**
0-4	587228	304103	283125	4.1	2.1	2.0
5-9	829931	428428	401503	5.8	3.0	2.8
10-14	615962	318340	297622	4.3	2.2	2.1
15-19	444993	228876	216117	3.1	1.6	1.5
20-24	546034	279385	266649	3.8	2.0	1.9
25-29	637267	322723	314544	4.5	2.3	2.2
30-34	964156	481922	482234	6.8	3.4	3.4
35-39	1189751	591681	598070	8.3	4.1	4.2
40-44	1164761	586019	578742	8.2	4.1	4.1
45-49	884875	436945	447930	6.2	3.1	3.1
50-54	1118897	556709	562188	7.8	3.9	3.9
55-59	1149372	576981	572391	8.1	4.0	4.0
60-64	1122259	558984	563275	7.9	3.9	3.9
65-69	1143151	550544	592607	8.0	3.9	4.2
70-74	743776	354373	389403	5.2	2.5	2.7
75-79	432280	197865	234415	3.0	1.4	1.6
80-84	336947	146115	190832	2.4	1.0	1.3
85-89	246692	109308	137384	1.7	0.8	1.0
90岁及以上 90 and above	118760	51954	66806	0.8	0.4	0.5

资料来源：北京市公安局。
Source: Beijing Municipal Bureau of Public Security.

3-12 户籍人口变动情况
CHANGES OF REGISTERED POPULATION

单位：人 (person)

项　目	Item	2022	2021
自然变动	**Natural Changes**		
自然增加	Natural Increase	55772	-14169
非农业人口	Non-agricultural Population	60721	731
农业人口	Agricultural Population	-4949	-14900
出　生	Births	86044	103148
非农业人口	Non-agricultural Population	79166	94502
农业人口	Agricultural Population	6878	8646
死　亡	Deaths	30272	117317
非农业人口	Non-agricultural Population	18445	93771
农业人口	Agricultural Population	11827	23546
机械变动	**Non-natural Changes**		
机械增加	Non-natural Increase	85649	141404
非农业人口	Non-agricultural Population	84917	137833
农业人口	Agricultural Population	732	3571
市外迁入	Inflow	139923	204770
非农业人口	Non-agricultural Population	139091	200763
农业人口	Agricultural Population	832	4007
迁往市外	Outflow	54274	63366
非农业人口	Non-agricultural Population	54174	62930
农业人口	Agricultural Population	100	436

资料来源：北京市公安局。
Source: Beijing Municipal Bureau of Public Security.

3-13 全市法人单位按登记注册类型分从业人员年末人数(2008-2022年)

单位：万人

年 份 Year	合 计 Total	内 资 Domestically-invested Enterprises	国有单位 State-owned Enterprises	集体单位 Collectively-owned Enterprises	股份合作 Joint-equity Cooperative Enterprises
2008	812.0	705.7	187.8	24.8	14.3
2009	822.3	714.5	185.7	24.3	12.7
2010	865.3	748.0	189.0	22.7	12.0
2011	907.7	767.0	188.8	20.1	7.7
2012	951.4	804.4	188.3	19.8	7.2
2013	981.9	829.7	189.5	17.5	6.8
2014	1010.5	857.3	188.6	18.8	6.6
2015	1050.7	900.4	182.9	16.9	5.2
2016	1089.7	946.9	188.1	13.9	5.2
2017	1120.6	975.7	183.4	14.3	4.4
2018	1121.7	977.3	177.8	13.1	3.7
2019	1163.9	1018.3	170.9	14.9	3.8
2020	1067.2	922.1	155.9	9.4	4.4
2021	1076.6	927.8	155.6	9.4	4.8
2022	1052.6	904.9	150.3	9.0	4.4

YEAR-END EMPLOYED PERSONS IN LEGAL ENTITIES BY TYPE OF REGISTRATION(2008-2022)

(10000 persons)

联营单位 Associated Enterprises	有限责任公司 Limited Liability Corporations	股份有限公司 Corporations Limited by Shares	私营 Private Enterprises	其他 Others	港澳台商投资 Hong Kong, Macao and Taiwan-invested	外商投资 Foreign-invested
2.2	196.4	46.4	223.0	10.8	33.5	72.8
0.9	215.7	58.4	202.9	13.9	36.6	71.2
0.9	228.2	64.7	218.7	11.8	42.4	74.9
0.7	243.0	75.9	221.8	9.0	50.6	90.1
0.7	261.6	83.2	234.0	9.6	54.3	92.7
0.7	278.0	85.4	239.6	12.2	56.1	96.1
0.5	290.6	86.2	254.6	11.4	58.7	94.5
0.4	300.3	103.5	273.3	17.9	59.7	90.6
0.3	305.1	116.9	298.2	19.2	61.2	81.6
0.3	318.3	124.4	307.7	22.9	65.2	79.7
0.4	330.2	128.2	302.5	21.4	67.7	76.7
0.2	327.0	112.6	372.6	16.3	71.1	74.5
0.3	319.7	93.2	327.2	12.0	73.3	71.8
0.3	335.8	93.7	317.1	11.1	73.5	75.3
0.2	340.3	85.1	305.5	10.1	70.5	77.2

3-14 全市法人单位从业人员年末人数及工资情况(2022年) YEAR-END EMPLOYED PERSONS IN LEGAL ENTITIES AND THEIR WAGES(2022)

项目	Item	从业人员年末人数(万人) Year-end Employed Persons (10000 persons)	从业人员工资总额(亿元) Total Wages of Employed Persons (100 million yuan)	从业人员平均工资(元) Average Wage of Employed Persons (yuan)
合计	**Total**	**1052.6**	**19123.8**	**178476**
按登记注册类型分	**By Registration Type**			
内资	Domestically-invested Enterprises	904.9	15094.7	164047
国有	State-owned Enterprises	150.3	3278.7	218765
集体	Collectively-owned Enterprises	9.0	69.3	76067
股份合作	Joint-equity Cooperative Enterprises	4.4	35.4	77240
联营	Associated Enterprises	0.2	3.1	144198
有限责任公司	Limited Liability Corporations	340.3	6092.2	174951
股份有限公司	Corporations Limited by Shares	85.1	2211.9	260976
私营	Private Enterprises	305.5	3271.6	104542
其他	Others	10.1	132.5	126812
港、澳、台商投资	Hong Kong, Macao and Taiwan-invested Enterprises	70.5	1997.5	275541
外商投资	Foreign-invested Enterprises	77.2	2031.6	257593
按城镇非私营、城镇私营分	**By Urban Non-private Units and Urban Private Units**			
城镇非私营	Urban Non-private Units	747.1	15852.2	208977
城镇私营	Urban Private Units	305.5	3271.6	104542
按国民经济行业分	**By Sector**			
农、林、牧、渔业	Agriculture, Forestry, Animal Husbandry and Fishery	1.9	15.0	75707
采矿业	Mining	2.6	44.4	166524
制造业	Manufacturing	76.1	1267.3	165269
电力、热力、燃气及水生产和供应业	Production and Distribution of Electricity, Heating Power, Gas and Water	10.3	197.8	195797
建筑业	Construction	70.3	896.7	123082
批发和零售业	Wholesale and Retail Trade	99.0	1457.9	144309
交通运输、仓储和邮政业	Transport, Storage and Post	58.1	823.6	139043
住宿和餐饮业	Accommodation and Catering	38.5	259.1	63996
信息传输、软件和信息技术服务业	Information Transmission, Software and Information Technology Services	137.2	3945.3	281796
金融业	Finance	60.5	2019.3	329406
房地产业	Real Estate	58.9	676.8	111167
租赁和商务服务业	Leasing and Business Services	132.6	1857.9	137752
科学研究和技术服务业	Scientific Research and Technical Services	109.1	2046.9	187588
水利、环境和公共设施管理业	Management of Water Conservancy, Environment and Public Facilities	14.6	164.1	108600
居民服务、修理和其他服务业	Resident Services, Repair and Other Services	19.9	125.1	60843
教育	Education	55.4	1165.7	204512
卫生和社会工作	Health and Social Works	38.6	845.5	220658
文化、体育和娱乐业	Culture, Sports and Entertainment	25.7	502.1	191839
公共管理、社会保障和社会组织	Public Management, Social Security and Social Organizations	43.3	813.3	188568
国际组织	International Organizations			

3-15 规模以上企业法人单位按岗位分就业人员平均工资(2017-2022年) AVERAGE WAGES OF EMPLOYED PERSONS IN CORPORATE LEGAL ENTITIES ABOVE DESIGNATED SIZE BY POSITION(2017-2022)

单位：元 (yuan)

项　目	Item	2017	2018	2019	2020	2021	2022
就业人员平均工资	Average Wage of Employed Persons	114379	126476	138978	150380	169410	180797
中层及以上管理人员	Management Personnel at Middle Level and Above	288654	319343	332942	350464	386650	411034
专业技术人员	Professional and Technical Personnel	156876	175614	189165	201236	225668	239333
办事人员和有关人员	Office Clerks and Related Personnel	95130	100722	110416	115603	132097	136881
社会生产服务和生活服务人员	Social Production Services and Life Services Personnel	68611	73836	82255	86132	95832	101667
生产制造及有关人员	Production, Manufacturing and Related Personnel	74063	82620	90090	99493	109340	114621

注：统计范围包括全市规模以上工业(含采矿业，制造业，电力、热力、燃气及水生产和供应业)、有资质的建筑业、限额以上批发和零售业、限额以上住宿和餐饮业、有开发经营活动的全部房地产开发经营业、规模以上服务业(含交通运输、仓储和邮政业，信息传输、软件和信息技术服务业，租赁和商务服务业，科学研究和技术服务业，水利、环境和公共设施管理业，居民服务、修理和其他服务业，教育，卫生和社会工作，文化、体育和娱乐业，以及物业管理、房地产中介服务等行业)共16个行业门类的4.1万家企业法人单位。不包括农、林、牧、渔业，金融业，公共管理、社会保障和社会组织三个行业门类。

Note: The statistical scope covers 41,000 corporate legal entities in 16 classes of sectors in the industry above designated size in Beijing (including mining ; manufacturing; production and supply of electricity, heating, gas and water), qualified construction, wholesale and retail trade above designated size, accommodation and catering above designated size, all real estate development business with development and operating activities , and service sector above designated size (including transport, storage and post; information transmission, software and information technology services; leasing and business services; scientific research and technical services; management of water conservancy, environment and public facilities; resident services, repair and other services; education; health and social works; culture, sports and entertainment; property management and real estate agency service, etc.). The following three classes of sectors are excluded: agriculture, forestry,animal husbandry and fishery; finance; public management, social security and social organization.

3-16 城镇非私营单位在岗职工年末人数及工资总额(1978-2022年) YEAR-END NUMBER AND TOTAL WAGES OF EMPLOYED PERSONS IN URBAN NON-PRIVATE UNITS(1978-2022)

年份 Year	在岗职工年末人数(万人) Year-end Number of Fully Employed Staff and Workers (10000 persons)	国有单位 State-owned Enterprises	集体单位 Collectively-owned Enterprises	其他单位 Others	在岗职工工资总额(亿元) Total Wages of Fully Employed Staff and Workers (100 million yuan)	国有单位 State-owned Enterprises	集体单位 Collectively-owned Enterprises	其他单位 Others
1978	291.6	240.9	50.7		18.7	16.2	2.5	
1979	311.9	254.2	57.7		22.4	19.4	3.0	
1980	326.5	269.4	57.1		26.9	23.3	3.6	
1981	344.4	283.1	61.3		28.3	24.2	4.1	
1982	360.1	293.0	67.1		30.5	25.9	4.6	
1983	371.9	303.4	68.5		33.8	28.5	5.3	
1984	375.4	302.5	71.6	1.3	40.4	33.7	6.6	0.1
1985	382.3	308.1	72.6	1.6	50.7	41.5	9.0	0.3
1986	397.9	324.4	71.1	2.4	58.0	48.5	9.1	0.4
1987	405.2	331.8	70.7	2.7	66.7	56.0	10.1	0.6
1988	410.4	336.4	69.9	4.1	81.2	68.1	12.1	1.0
1989	418.4	343.8	67.4	7.2	96.3	81.0	13.4	1.9
1990	454.9	357.9	86.8	10.2	118.9	96.1	19.7	3.1
1991	470.0	367.8	89.0	13.2	132.2	106.1	21.5	4.6
1992	476.6	371.5	90.5	14.6	158.5	128.6	23.9	6.0
1993	467.3	362.3	79.6	25.4	218.9	176.6	28.5	13.8
1994	471.8	363.5	73.4	34.9	306.5	243.4	36.2	26.9
1995	470.9	358.2	72.1	40.6	382.0	295.6	46.5	39.9
1996	460.6	349.0	64.8	46.8	442.4	339.4	46.2	56.8
1997	465.3	348.7	65.0	51.6	514.8	383.6	53.8	77.4
1998	450.1	321.7	50.8	77.6	558.2	391.9	45.0	121.3
1999	438.0	303.0	49.6	85.4	614.5	420.0	44.8	149.7
2000	434.2	283.0	46.0	105.2	695.5	453.6	46.7	195.2
2001	400.3	235.9	40.0	124.4	777.3	477.8	44.8	254.7
2002	434.2	212.6	32.7	188.9	950.9	508.8	40.0	402.1
2003	436.3	197.6	26.1	212.6	1098.9	565.5	35.0	498.4
2004	446.4	183.7	24.8	237.9	1315.1	625.7	34.0	655.4
2005	448.4	178.5	20.7	249.2	1520.1	694.9	30.8	794.4
2006	453.1	172.9	16.4	263.8	1805.5	738.0	30.5	1037.0
2007	478.9	172.7	15.4	290.8	2194.3	862.4	31.2	1300.7
2008	526.1	171.0	22.7	332.4	2874.3	1008.8	48.2	1817.3
2009	560.4	170.9	22.4	367.1	3227.2	1074.3	53.3	2099.6
2010	587.7	175.1	21.1	391.5	3789.1	1221.2	56.7	2511.2
2011	640.3	177.1	18.7	444.5	4778.6	1421.1	62.3	3295.2
2012	670.4	177.3	18.6	474.5	5657.9	1582.5	71.6	4003.8
2013	695.5	178.4	16.5	500.6	6502.0	1724.7	70.2	4707.1
2014	708.8	177.7	17.8	513.3	7293.3	1884.5	81.5	5327.3
2015	724.8	172.8	16.0	536.0	8225.2	2059.0	81.5	6084.7
2016	733.5	178.0	13.1	542.4	9005.0	2299.0	80.1	6625.9
2017	756.4	174.3	13.5	568.6	10182.8	2611.0	80.9	7490.9
2018	762.1	168.9	12.4	580.8	11562.8	2812.6	84.2	8666.0
2019	727.8	162.7	14.0	551.1	12627.3	3166.3	97.3	9363.7
2020	687.4	149.8	8.9	528.7	12692.8	3044.2	62.8	9585.8
2021	708.4	148.7	8.8	550.9	14283.2	3101.8	65.8	11115.6
2022	704.3	143.7	8.4	552.2	15356.5	3223.7	65.3	12067.5

注：1.2007年及以前城镇非私营单位是指乡及乡以上独立核算法人单位，不包括乡镇企业和个体工商户。自2008年起是指不包括个体工商户的独立核算法人单位，下同。

2.表中2000年及以前数据为职工口径，职工包括在岗职工和不在岗职工，下同。

Note: a) Urban non-private entities in and before 2007 referred to legal entities with independent accounting at and above township level, excluding township enterprises and self-employed businesses. Since 2008, they referred to legal entities with independent accounting excluding self-employed businesses, the same below.

b) Figures in and before 2000 in this table were counted by the statistical range of employees which included both the fully employed staff and workers and the off-the-job ones, the same below.

3-17 城镇非私营单位在岗职工平均工资(1978-2022年)
AVERAGE WAGES OF EMPLOYED PERSONS IN URBAN NON-PRIVATE UNITS (1978-2022)

单位：元 (yuan)

年份 Year	在岗职工平均工资 Average Wages of Employed Persons	国有单位 State-owned Enterprises	集体单位 Collectively-owned Enterprises	其他单位 Others
1978	673	703	471	
1979	742	778	556	
1980	848	889	635	
1981	837	880	685	
1982	863	896	715	
1983	931	964	785	
1984	1086	1127	946	1170
1985	1343	1367	1231	1768
1986	1488	1530	1287	2080
1987	1670	1712	1449	2267
1988	2000	2048	1738	2661
1989	2312	2366	1992	2761
1990	2653	2713	2334	3243
1991	2877	2937	2504	3713
1992	3402	3500	2828	4289
1993	4780	4920	3834	5469
1994	6540	6695	5009	8179
1995	8144	8237	6516	10278
1996	9579	9645	7133	13851
1997	11019	10917	8259	15370
1998	12285	11971	8800	15989
1999	13778	13483	8928	17748
2000	15726	15483	9844	19165
2001	19155	19776	11063	20594
2002	21852	23754	11997	21432
2003	25312	28464	13580	23769
2004	29674	34009	13422	28026
2005	34191	39067	14695	32324
2006	40117	43298	17781	39513
2007	46507	50524	20379	45508
2008	54913	59361	20990	54983
2009	58140	63239	23553	57911
2010	65683	70320	26607	65755
2011	75834	81215	32469	75584
2012	85307	90456	38596	85234
2013	93997	97356	42482	94513
2014	103400	106097	45772	104473
2015	113073	119046	49969	113066
2016	122749	129542	59507	122096
2017	134994	150622	58900	132062
2018	149843	166977	66776	146730
2019	173205	195783	69344	169239
2020	185026	203896	70124	181636
2021	201504	209851	75023	201278
2022	215143	224757	76485	214794

3-18 城镇非私营单位在岗职工年末人数和工资情况(2022年)
YEAR-END NUMBER AND WAGES OF EMPLOYED PERSONS IN URBAN NON-PRIVATE UNITS(2022)

项　目	Item	年末人数(人) Year-end Number (person)	工资总额(亿元) Total Wages (100 million yuan)	平均工资(元) Average Wages (yuan)
合　计	**Total**	**7043491**	**15356.5**	**215143**
按登记注册类型分	**By Registration Type**			
内　资	Domestically-invested Enterprises	5688856	11506.7	200069
国　有	State-owned Enterprises	1437508	3223.7	224757
集　体	Collectively-owned Enterprises	84106	65.3	76485
股份合作	Joint-equity Cooperative Enterprises	40320	31.4	77734
联　营	Associated Enterprises	2050	3.0	145116
有限责任公司	Limited Liability Corporations	3262547	5963.3	178810
股份有限公司	Corporations Limited By Shares	772095	2104.7	276166
其　他	Others	90229	115.3	125126
港、澳、台商投资	Hong Kong, Macao and Taiwan-invested Enterprises	645493	1935.6	292108
外商投资	Foreign-invested Enterprises	709142	1914.2	264464
按国民经济行业分	**By Sector**			
农、林、牧、渔业	Agriculture, Forestry, Animal Husbandry and Fishery	13703	11.0	80082
#农　业	Farming	2704	1.9	67544
采矿业	Mining	25778	44.1	167262
制造业	Manufacturing	561881	1030.1	182181
电力、热力、燃气及水生产和供应业	Production and Distribution of Electricity, Heating Power, Gas and Water	92402	190.5	208131
建筑业	Construction	441414	685.2	153310
批发和零售业	Wholesale and Retail Trade	493523	988.7	194297
批发业	Wholesale	323593	774.6	234485
零售业	Retail Trade	169930	214.1	119941
交通运输、仓储和邮政业	Transport, Storage and Post	516711	776.1	147103
#铁路运输业	Transport via Railway	97616	156.1	159408
道路运输业	Transport via Road	201900	234.6	111769
邮政业	Post	92356	124.8	131595
住宿和餐饮业	Accommodation and Catering	197177	168.8	81321
住宿业	Accommodation	69885	65.6	90188
餐饮业	Catering	127292	103.2	76538
信息传输、软件和信息技术服务业	Information Transmission, Software and Information Technology Services	999457	3248.0	319550
金融业	Finance	436223	1787.6	413725
房地产业	Real Estate	429769	567.9	127894
租赁和商务服务业	Leasing and Business Services	684990	1193.8	173232
租赁业	Leasing Activities	11434	23.2	191202
商务服务业	Business Services	673556	1170.6	172910
科学研究和技术服务业	Scientific Research and Technical Services	596586	1406.6	234723
水利、环境和公共设施管理业	Management of Water Conservancy, Environment and Public Facilities	112220	140.2	121869
居民服务、修理和其他服务业	Resident Services, Repair and Other Services	55377	47.2	83101
#居民服务业	Resident Services	16412	17.2	99909
教　育	Education	466130	1055.5	220707
卫生和社会工作	Health and Social Works	337029	791.0	236398
#卫　生	Health	317979	771.0	244747
文化、体育和娱乐业	Culture, Sports and Entertainment	179915	420.9	231090
#文化艺术业	Cultures and Arts	32300	58.2	178871
体　育	Sports Activities	16115	23.9	147651
公共管理、社会保障和社会组织	Public Management, Social Security and Social Organizations	403205	803.3	199796
国际组织	International Organizations			

3-19 国民经济各行业城镇非私营单位在岗职工平均工资(2022年) AVERAGE WAGES OF EMPLOYED PERSONS IN URBAN NON-PRIVATE UNITS IN DIFFERENT SECTORS OF NATIONAL ECONOMY (2022)

单位：元 (yuan)

项　目	Item	平均工资 Average Wages	国有单位 State-owned Enterprises	集体单位 Collectively-owned Enterprises	其他单位 Others
合　计	**Total**	**215143**	**224757**	**76485**	**214794**
农、林、牧、渔业	**Agriculture, Forestry, Animal Husbandry and Fishery**	**80082**	**189885**	**51945**	**87359**
#农、林、牧、渔专业及辅助性活动	Professional and Supporting Activities for Agriculture, Forestry, Animal Husbandry and Fishery	92301	168407	43396	70339
采矿业	**Mining**	**167262**			**167262**
煤炭开采和洗选业	Mining and Washing of Coal				
石油和天然气开采业	Extraction of Petroleum and Natural Gas	322668			322668
黑色金属矿采选业	Smelting and Pressing of Ferrous Metals	160177			160177
有色金属矿采选业	Mining and Processing of Non-Ferrous Metal Ores				
非金属矿采选业	Mining and Processing of Non-metal Ores				
开采专业及辅助性活动	Professional and Support Activities for Mining	162430			162430
其他采矿业	Mining of Other Ores	152926			152926
制造业	**Manufacturing**	**182181**	**127535**	**67801**	**183456**
农副食品加工业	Processing of Food from Agricultural Products	108883		60915	109063
食品制造业	Manufacture of Foods	123318		70323	123371
酒、饮料和精制茶制造业	Manufacture of Wine, Beverage and Refined Tea	111761		69881	112052
烟草制品业	Manufacture of Tobacco	324856			324856
纺织业	Manufacture of Textile	89957		61966	90687
纺织服装、服饰业	Manufacture of Textile, Wearing Apparel and Ornament	84991	143941	67488	85507
皮革、毛皮、羽毛及其制品和制鞋业	Manufacture of Leather, Fur, Feather and Its Products, and Footwear	67072		70653	56760
木材加工和木、竹、藤、棕、草制品业	Processing of Timbers, Manufacture of Wood, Bamboo, Rattan, Palm and Straw Products	83269		48855	93815
家具制造业	Manufacture of Furniture	114553		64956	115421
造纸和纸制品业	Manufacture of Paper and Paper Products	120056	121000	50540	126671
印刷和记录媒介复制业	Printing, Reproduction of Recording Media	135280	131535	65152	139423
文教、工美、体育和娱乐用品制造业	Manufacture of Articles for Culture, Education, Artwork, Sport and Entertainment Activities	102020	78114	64024	104290
石油、煤炭及其他燃料加工业	Processing of Petroleum, Coal and Other Fuels	208770			208770
化学原料和化学制品制造业	Manufacture of Chemical Raw Materials and Chemical Products	151193		61333	151679
医药制造业	Manufacture of Medicines	223390	142475	76615	223822
化学纤维制造业	Manufacture of Chemical Fibers	107535			107535
橡胶和塑料制品业	Manufacture of Rubber and Plastics Products	105960		52342	109383
非金属矿物制品业	Manufacture of Non-metallic Mineral Products	123470		66815	125108
黑色金属冶炼和压延加工业	Manufacture and Pressing of Ferrous Metals	127845		74115	129295

3-19 续表 1 Continued 1

单位：元 (yuan)

行业	Sector	平均工资 Average Wages	国有单位 State-owned	集体单位 Collectively-Owned	其他单位 Others
有色金属冶炼和压延加工业	Smelting and Processing of Non-ferrous Metals	158463			158463
金属制品业	Manufacture of Metal Products	125705	68368	76484	128889
通用设备制造业	Manufacture of General-Purpose Machinery	169559	75768	71019	171926
专用设备制造业	Manufacture of Special-Purpose Machinery	193991	64714	81774	194766
汽车制造业	Manufacture of Motor Vehicles	168381		52315	168732
铁路、船舶、航空航天和其他运输设备制造业	Manufacture of Railway, Ships, Aerospace and Other Transport Equipments Transportation Equipment	206086		50316	206362
电气机械和器材制造业	Manufacture of Electrical Machinery and Equipment	192711	96845	63103	194222
计算机、通信和其他电子设备制造业	Manufacture of Computers, Communication Equipment and Other Electronic Equipment	247713	177677	84098	247875
仪器仪表制造业	Manufacture of Measuring Instruments and Meters	195384	173285	103119	196579
其他制造业	Other Manufacturing	125263		56267	130110
废弃资源综合利用业	Waste Rrecycling and Recovery	131690		50140	137134
金属制品、机械和设备修理业	Repair of Fabricated Metal Products, Machinery and Equipment	183797		50269	184297
电力、热力、燃气及水生产和供应业	**Production and Supply of Electricity, Heating, Gas and Water**	**208131**	**28183**	**86760**	**210320**
电力、热力生产和供应业	Production and Supply of Electricity and Heating Power	228231	26219	87566	231088
燃气生产和供应业	Production and Supply of Gas	181028			181028
水的生产和供应业	Production and Supply of Water	137463	57152	85580	138404
建筑业	**Construction**	**153310**	**209001**	**86709**	**153853**
房屋建筑业	Construction of Buildings	165154	92789	95646	166353
土木工程建筑业	Civil Engineering Construction	164280	230919	80412	164225
建筑安装业	Construction Installation	141512	89151	56199	142186
建筑装饰、装修和其他建筑业	Building Decoration, Finishing and Other Construction	98995		54407	99324
批发和零售业	**Wholesale and Retail Trade**	**194297**	**200510**	**75230**	**195108**
批发业	Wholesale	234485	286446	83647	234552
零售业	Retail Trade	119941	94026	70217	121053
交通运输、仓储和邮政业	**Transport, Storage and Post**	**147103**	**192294**	**45259**	**147196**
铁路运输业	Transport via Railway	159408	221421		159068
道路运输业	Transport via Road	111769	80741	40553	112634
水上运输业	Water Transport	290906			290906
航空运输业	Air Transport	215906	241935	98706	215932
管道运输业	Transport via Pipeline	267711	335991		258364
多式联运和运输代理业	Multimodal Transport and Transport Agent Service	190024	155056	77154	190159
装卸搬运和仓储业	Loading, Unloading, Portage and Storage	140524	128905	84607	141565
邮政业	Post	131595	110661		131925
住宿和餐饮业	**Accommodation and Catering**	**81321**	**91005**	**83378**	**80785**
住宿业	Accommodation	90188	91516	95296	89769
餐饮业	Catering	76538	75693	56330	76705
信息传输、软件和信息技术服务业	**Information Transmission, Software and Information Technology Services**	**319550**	**226137**	**85705**	**320553**
电信、广播电视和卫星传输服务	Telecommunications, Broadcasting, Television and Satellite Transmission Services	275454	229304	89982	276872
互联网和相关服务	Internet and Related Services	364949	240329	116071	366599
软件和信息技术服务业	Software and Information Technology Services	313985	218875	84247	314789

3-19 续表 2 Continued 2

单位：元 (yuan)

行业	Sector	平均工资 Average Wages	国有单位 State-owned	集体单位 Collectively-Owned	其他单位 Others
金融业	**Finance**	**413725**	**306116**		**415594**
货币金融服务	Monetary Financial Services	396593	321526		397878
资本市场服务	Capital Market Services	518381	295756		526166
保险业	Insurance	330320	156133		331089
其他金融业	Other Financial Services	493752	341523		495963
房地产业	**Real Estate**	**127894**	**138973**	**85117**	**129463**
租赁和商务服务业	**Leasing and Business Services**	**173232**	**96603**	**64977**	**193169**
租赁业	Leasing Activities	191202	113942	73075	195632
商务服务业	Business Services	172910	96587	64803	193116
科学研究和技术服务业	**Scientific Research and Technical Services**	**234723**	**274307**	**108570**	**224887**
研究和试验发展	Research and Experimental Development	280682	289661	100605	272469
专业技术服务业	Professional Technique Services	216462	254993	115546	212052
科技推广和应用服务业	Technique Generalization and Application Services	223631	241328	92020	222221
水利、环境和公共设施管理业	**Management of Water Conservancy, Environment and Public Facilities**	**121869**	**137122**	**64233**	**114262**
水利管理业	Management of Water Conservancy	210915	216386	139423	168816
生态保护和环境治理业	Ecological Protection and Environmental Control	186924	228485	42679	178994
公共设施管理业	Management of Public Facilities	103618	116872	61319	97003
土地管理业	Management of Land	246661	232253	109552	269891
居民服务、修理和其他服务业	**Resident Services, Repair and Other Services**	**83101**	**104003**	**54194**	**81597**
居民服务业	Resident Services	99909	108169	53640	101971
机动车、电子产品和日用产品修理业	Repair of Motor Vehicles, Electronics and Household Appliances	100383	88096	55238	106063
其他服务业	Other Services	66562	102523	54012	63088
教　育	**Education**	**220707**	**254268**	**95282**	**124826**
卫生和社会工作	**Health and Social Works**	**236398**	**270540**	**100990**	**137833**
卫　生	Health	244747	274498	110831	146323
社会工作	Social Works	101903	135652	71356	84549
文化、体育和娱乐业	**Culture, Sports and Entertainment**	**231090**	**276267**	**87998**	**196845**
新闻和出版业	Journalism and Publishing	244701	242803	143580	247333
广播、电视、电影和录音制作业	Radio Broadcasting, Television, Movies and Sound Recording	302156	448445	62855	192601
文化艺术业	Culture and Arts	178871	195192	104406	136743
体　育	Sports Activities	147651	169909	44038	142208
娱乐业	Entertainment	173867	222710	89915	172981
公共管理、社会保障和社会组织	**Public Management, Social Security and Social Organizations**	**199796**	**200351**	**124813**	**148767**
中国共产党机关	Organs of Communist Party of China	209402	209402		
国家机构	Organs of State	199827	200102	183448	105064
人民政协、民主党派	Peole's Political Consultative Conference and Democratic Parties	217264	217264		
社会保障	Social Security	217242	217242		
群众团体、社会团体和其他成员组织	Mass Communities, Social Organizations and Other Membership Organizations	174168	181938	115871	165080
基层群众自治组织	Grass Roots Self-Government Organization				
国际组织	**International Organizations**				

3-20 城镇登记失业率和城镇新增就业人数(1979-2022年)
REGISTERED UNEMPLOYMENT RATE IN URBAN AREA AND NEWLY EMPLOYED PERSONS IN URBAN AREA (1979-2022)

单位：万人 (10000 persons)

年份 Year	年末实有登记失业人员 Year-end Number of Actual Registed Unemployed Persons	年末城镇登记失业率(%) Year-end Registered Unemployment Rate in Urban Area(%)	城镇新增就业人数 Newly Employed Persons in Urban Area
1979	4.96	1.60	
1980	8.67	1.60	
1981	8.36	1.28	
1982	7.03	1.62	
1983	4.20	1.09	
1984	2.03	0.54	
1985	1.61	0.40	
1986	1.25	0.30	
1987	2.24	0.45	
1988	1.58	0.40	
1989	1.71	0.40	
1990	1.67	0.30	
1991	1.92	0.40	
1992	1.72	0.36	
1993	1.92	0.41	
1994	1.91	0.41	
1995	2.19	0.46	
1996	2.80	0.58	
1997	3.29	0.73	
1998	2.95	0.66	
1999	2.80	0.62	
2000	3.32	0.76	
2001	5.19	1.18	
2002	6.02	1.35	
2003	6.96	1.43	
2004	6.46	1.30	
2005	10.57	2.11	24.85
2006	10.40	1.98	27.24
2007	10.63	1.84	30.48
2008	10.33	1.82	32.99
2009	8.16	1.44	34.33
2010	7.73	1.37	37.42
2011	7.89	1.39	37.75
2012	7.20	1.27	35.77
2013	6.81	1.21	33.23
2014	8.77	1.31	33.62
2015	9.16	1.39	34.65
2016	9.14	1.41	36.93
2017	9.22	1.43	35.35
2018	10.24	1.40	33.27
2019	9.35	1.30	35.10
2020	29.02	2.56	26.10
2021	37.19	3.23	26.90
2022	36.39	3.12	26.10

注：1.2014年以前年末实有登记失业人员为城镇口径，自2014年起调整为全市口径。
2.自2020年9月起，对城镇登记失业人员相关统计口径进行调整，将离校未就业高校毕业生、领取失业补助金人员和领取一次性生活补助农民工纳入登记失业人员范围。

资料来源：北京市人力资源和社会保障局。

Note: a) The year-end number of actual registered unemployed persons before 2014 refers to the statistic in urban area and was adjusted to the statistic of the whole city Since 2014.
b) The relevant statistical coverage of the registered unemployed persons in urban area was adjusted since September 2020,the unemployed college graduates, the personnel receiving unemployment compensation and the rural migrant workers receiving lump-sum living allowance were included in the list of registered unemployed persons.

Source: Beijing Municipal Human Resource and Social Security Bureau.

主要统计指标解释

户籍人口 指公民依照《中华人民共和国户口登记条例》已在其经常居住地的公安户籍管理机关登记了常住户口的人。

常住人口 指在某地区实际居住半年以上的人口。

常住外来人口 指不具有本市户籍户口，来自北京市行政区划以外的省、自治区、直辖市，且在京居住半年以上的人口。

出生率 指在一定时期内（通常为一年）出生人数与同期平均人数(或期中人数)之比，一般用千分比表示。计算公式：

$$出生率=\frac{年出生人数}{年平均人数}\times 1000‰$$

出生人数是指活产，即脱离母体时（不管怀孕月数），有过呼吸或其他生命现象的活婴儿总和。年平均人数是年初、年末人口数的平均数，也可用年中人口数代替。

死亡率 指在一定时期内（通常为一年）死亡人数与同期平均人数（或期中人数）之比，一般用千分比表示。计算公式：

$$死亡率=\frac{年死亡人数}{年平均人数}\times 1000‰$$

自然增长率 指在一定时期内（通常为一年）人口自然增加数（出生人数减死亡人数）与该时期内平均人数（或期中人数）之比，一般用千分比表示。计算公式：

$$自然增长率=\frac{年出生人数-年死亡人数}{年平均人数}\times 1000‰$$

人口自然增长率=人口出生率－人口死亡率

常住就业人口 指在常住人口中，年满 16 周岁，为取得报酬或经营利润，在调查周内从事了 1 小时（含 1 小时）以上劳动的人口；或由于在职学习、休假等原因在调查周内暂时未工作的人口；或由于停工、单位不景气等原因临时未工作的人口。

从业人员 指在各级国家机关、党政机关、社会团体及企业、事业单位中工作，取得工资或其他形式的劳动报酬的全部人员。包括：在岗职工、聘用的离退休人员以及在单位中工作的港澳台及外籍人员、兼职人员、借用的外单位人员和第二职业者。不包括本单位的不在岗职工。

在岗职工 指在本单位工作并由单位支付工资的人员，以及有工作岗位，但由于学习、病伤产假（六个月以内）等原因暂未工作，仍由单位支付工资的人员。

在岗职工工资总额 与在岗职工指标相对应，根据 1990 年 1 月 1 日的国家统计局令（一号）修订，指单位在报告期内直接支付给本单位在岗职工的劳动报酬总额。包括基础工资、职务工资、级别工资、工龄工资、计件工资、奖金、各种津贴和补贴、交通补贴、洗理费、书报费、旅游费、过节费、伙食补助、住房补贴、住房提租补贴、由单位从个人工资中直接为其代扣或代缴的个人所得税、房水电费以及住房公积金和社会保险基金个人缴纳部分等。

在岗职工平均工资 指企业、事业、机关等单位的在岗职工在一定时期内的人均劳动报酬。它表明一定时期在岗职工工资收入的高低程度，是反映在岗职工工资水平的主要指标。计算公式为：

$$\begin{matrix}在岗职工\\平均工资\end{matrix}=\frac{报告期实际支付的全部在岗职工工资总额}{报告期全部在岗职工平均人数}$$

从业人员平均工资 指企业、事业、机关等单位的从业人员在一定时期内的人均劳动报酬。计算公式为：

$$从业人员平均工资=\frac{报告期实际支付的全部从业人员劳动报酬总额}{报告期全部从业人员平均人数}$$

年末实有登记失业人员 指年末实有的登记失业人员总数，包括城镇登记失业人员和城市化建设地区的登记失业农民（失地农民）。

年末城镇登记失业率 指年末城镇登记失业人数与城镇从业人数和城镇登记失业人数二者之和的比。计算公式如下：

$$城镇登记失业率=\frac{年末实有登记失业人数}{城镇从业人数+年末实有登记失业人数}\times 100\%$$

Explanatory Notes on Main Statistical Indicators

Registered Population refers to persons who have registered their permanent residence with the public security register authority of their habitual residence according to the *Households Registration Regulations of PRC.*

Permanent Population refers to persons actually living for more than half a year at a place.

Permanent Migrant Population refers to persons who have no permanent residence registration in Beijing, come from other provinces, autonomous regions and municipalities, and have stayed in Beijing for more than half a year.

Birth Rate refers to the ratio of the number of births to the average population (or mid-period population) during a certain period of time (usually a year), which is often expressed in ‰. The following formula is used:

Birth Rate = Annual Number of Births/Annual Average Number of Population×1,000‰

Number of births refers to live births, i.e. the births when babies has breathed or shown any vital phenomena regardless of the length of pregnancy. Annual average number of population is the average of the number of population at the beginning of the year and that at the end of the year. Sometimes it is substituted with the mid-year population.

Death Rate refers to the ratio of the number of deaths to the average population (or mid-period population) during a certain period of time (usually a year), which is often expressed in ‰. The following formula is used:

Death Rate= Annual Number of Deaths/Annual Average Number of Population×1,000‰

Natural Growth Rate refers to the ratio of the natural growth of population (births minus deaths) to the average population (or mid-period population) during a certain period of time (usually a year), which is often expressed in ‰. The following formula is used:

Natural Growth Rate = (Annual Number of Births - Annual Number of Deaths)/Annual Average Number of Population×1,000‰

Natural Growth Rate of Population = Birth Rate - Death Rate

Permanent Employed Population refers to persons aged 16 and over, among the permanent population, who perform some work for compensation or business gains for one hour or more during the reference period; or persons temporarily out of work for the reasons of in-service study or on holiday, etc.; or persons temporary out of work for the reasons of shutdown or recession of the entity, etc.

Employed Persons refer to all persons working in government agencies, Party and political organs, social groups, enterprises and public institutions at all levels, and receiving wages or labor remuneration in other forms. They include: fully employed staff and workers, retired persons employed, persons from Hong Kong, Macao, Taiwan and foreign countries who are employed, part-time employees, employees transferred from other entities, and employees with a second job. They exclude employees that are not on the job in the entity.

Fully Employed Staff and Workers refer to persons working in the entity and paid by the entity, as well as persons having a job in the entity, but not working temporarily due to study, illness, injury or maternity leaves (less than 6 months) and other reasons, and still paid by the entity.

Total Wages of Fully Employed Staff and Workers correspond to the indicator of Fully Employed Staff and Workers. The indicator was revised in accordance with No. 1 Decree of the National Bureau of Statistics dated January 1, 1990, referring to the total wages directly paid by an entity to fully employed staff and workers of the entity during the reporting period. It consists of basic wage, post wage, wage of a rank, seniority wage, piece rate wage, bonus, allowances and subsidies, traffic subsidy, washing and haircutting allowance, books and newspaper allowance, travel benefit, festival bonus, food subsidy, housing subsidy, subsidy for incremental house rent, as well as personal income tax, water and electricity fees and the personally payable portion of housing accumulation fund and social security fund withheld directly by the employer from the employee's wage.

Average Wage of Fully Employed Staff and Workers refers to the per-capita labor remuneration of fully employed staff and workers in enterprises, public institutions and government agencies within a given period of time. It shows the level of wage income of fully employed staff and workers within a given period of time, serving as a main indicator reflecting the level of wage of fully employed staff and workers. The following formula is used:

Average Wage of Fully Employed Staff and Workers = Total Wages of All Fully Employed Staff and Workers Actually Paid in the Reporting Period / Average Number of All Fully Employed Staff and Workers in the Reporting Period

Average Wage of Employed Persons refers to the per-capita labor remuneration of employed persons in enterprises, public institutions and government agencies within a given period of time. The following formula is used:

Average Wage of Employed Persons = Total Labor Remuneration of All Employed Persons Actually Paid in the Reporting Period / Average Number of All Employed Persons in the Reporting Period

Period-end Actual Registered Unemployed Persons refer to the total number of actual unemployed persons registered at the end period, including unemployed persons registered in urban regions and the unemployed peasants registered in urbanization regions (land-lost peasants).

Year-end Registered Unemployment Rate in Urban Area refers to the ratio of urban registered unemployed persons at year end to the sum of urban employed persons and urban registered unemployed persons. The following formula is used:

Registered Unemployment Rate in Urban Area
=Number of Actual Registered Unemployed Persons at Year End / (Urban Employed Persons + Number of Actual Registered Unemployed Persons at Year End) × 100%

价格指数
PRICE INDEX

简要说明

一、主要内容

本章价格指数资料，反映生产、流通、消费与投资的价格变动趋势和变动幅度。主要包括居民消费价格指数、商品零售价格指数、农产品生产者价格指数、工业生产者出厂价格指数、工业生产者购进价格指数、固定资产投资价格指数、住宅销售价格指数。

二、调查方法

（一）居民消费价格指数和商品零售价格指数

编制居民消费价格指数、商品零售价格指数的资料采用抽样调查和重点调查相结合的方法取得，即在全市选择不同的区域，按照布局合理的原则抽选价格调查点，由国家确定调查商品和服务项目，在此基础上按照消费量大、价格变动趋势有较强代表性的原则选择调查样本，对其市场价格进行定期调查，以样本推算总体。

抽选价格调查点。按照布局合理等原则，将不同区域各种类型的商场、农贸市场、服务网点分别按销售额、成交额和经营规模为标志，从高到低排队，依据所需调查点的数量进行等距抽样。

选择代表规格品。代表商品和服务项目由国家确定，代表规格品由各省市按照有关原则选择。选择原则：（1）消费量较大；（2）价格变动趋势和变动程度有较强的代表性，即选中规格品的价格变动特征与未选中规格品之间价格变动的相关性愈高愈好；（3）选中的规格品之间，性质相隔愈远愈好，价格变动特征的相关性愈低愈好；选中的工业消费品必须是合格产品，产品包装上有注册商标、产地、规格等级等标识。

目前，居民消费价格调查按用途划分为 8 个大类，268 个基本分类，国家规定大城市调查规格品数量应在 670 种以上，北京市代表规格品数量为 1507 种。商品零售价格指数划分为 16 个大类，197 个基本分类，北京市代表规格品数量为 1135 种。

价格资料的采集。采取定人、定点、定时直接调查的方法采集价格资料或者由选中的调查对象协助填报。

权数资料来源与计算。居民消费价格指数的权数根据城市居民家庭生活消费支出调查资料整理计算。商品零售价格指数的权数根据商业统计中社会消费品零售总额计算。

按照国家统计局统一要求，自 2021 年 1 月起，北京流通消费价格统计专业执行新的《流通和消费价格统计报表制度》，其中居民消费价格和商品零售价格调查项目目录均重新进行了修订调整。

（二）工业生产者出厂价格指数和工业生产者购进价格指数

工业生产者出厂价格是工业品第一次出售时的出厂价格。该项调查采用重点调查与典型调查相结合的调查方法。根据代表性原则，抽选年主营业务收入 2000 万元以上的企业作为调查对象。经国家统计局审定，可酌情补充部分年主营业务收入 2000 万元以下的企业。

工业生产者购进价格是工业企业作为中间投入的价格。调查对象主要从填报工业生产者出厂价格的企业中选择。

选择代表企业的原则：（1）按工业行业选择调查企业，原则上应覆盖重点中类行业；（2）优先选择大型企业作为调查对象，并适当选择一些其他企业；（3）选择生产正常、稳定的企业作为调查对象。

选择代表产品的原则：（1）按工业行业选择基本分类和代表产品；（2）选择对国计民生影响大的产品；（3）选择生产较为稳定的产品；（4）选择有发展前景的产品；（5）选择具有地方特色的产品。

权数的确定。编制工业生产者出厂价格小类及以上的权数资料来源于工业统计中分行业工业销售产值数据资料；基本分类的权数资料来源于独立的工业生产者出厂价格权数专项调查。购进价格大类权数主要参考分行业的投入产出数据，其他分类权数来源于独立的工业生产者购进价格权数专项调查。一般情况下，工业生产者权数专项调查每五年进行一次。

根据国家统计制度要求，2021 年开始使用 2020 年作为新一轮的对比基期，新基期的调查分类目录、代表规格品和调查企业均有调整，分类权数也有变化，以反映工业生产结构的最新变动。

（三）固定资产投资价格指数

固定资产投资价格调查采用重点调查、典型调查和非传统数据替代相结合的方法。固定资产投资价格调查所涉及的价格是构成固定资产投资额实体的实际购进价格（或结算价格）。调查的内容包括构成当年建筑工程实体的钢材、木材、水泥、地方建筑材料、电料、化工材料等主要建筑材料价格，投入的劳动力价格（单位工资）和各种施工机械使用费用；设备工器具购置和其他费用投资价格。

选择建筑安装工程调查点的原则：（1）样本单位应具有一定覆盖面；（2）投资经济活动代表性强；（3）兼顾不同经济类型；（4）选择重点工程；（5）兼顾不同工程类别。

选择其他费用调查点的原则：在选择其他费用调查点时，所遵循的原则与建筑安装工程调查点的原则基本相同，特别是要注意选择那些投资额大的工程。但由于其他费用不易取得，所以在实际操作过程中，应同时在建设单位、施工单位开展重点调查，并辅以典型调查（从有关管理部门取得资料）。

权数的确定。固定资产投资价格指数的计算权数是建筑安装工程、设备工器具购置和其他费用三者前三年投资完成额的平均比重。

（四）住宅销售价格指数

住宅销售价格调查包括新建商品住宅销售价格和二手住宅销售价格调查。

新建商品住宅销售价格的调查方法：新建商品住宅销售面积、金额等资料直接采用当地房地产管理部门的网签数据。新建商品住宅的网签数据内容主要包括：住宅项目（楼盘）名称、项目地址、幢号、总层数、所在层数、房屋结构、建筑面积、成交总价（合同金额）、签约时间等。

二手住宅销售价格的调查方法：二手住宅销售价格调查为非全面调查，采用重点调查与典型调查相结合的方法，按照房地产经纪机构上报的方式收集基础数据。

（五）农产品生产者价格指数

农产品生产者价格调查采取抽样调查和重点调查相结合的调查方法。抽取 360 个农产品生产和出售的农业生产经营单位及行政村作为调查对象。对一些区域性比较强的农产品采取在主产区主观选样的方法选择农业生产经营单位及行政村作为调查对象。

由于北京市林业产品（树苗）产值比重较少，不足 1%，根据国家统计局统计制度要求，不需要进行林业产品生产者价格调查。

Brief Introduction

I. Main Content

Price indexes in this chapter reflect the trend and rate of changes in prices of production, circulation, consumption and investment, mainly consisting of consumer price index (CPI), retail price index (RPI), producer price index for farm products, producer price index for industrial products (PPI), purchasing price index for industrial producers, price index for investment in fixed assets, and selling price index for residential houses.

II. Survey Methods

(I) Consumer Price Index (CPI) and Retail Price Index (RPI)

Data for compilation of the consumer price index and retail price index are collected through a combination of sample surveys and surveys of key units. Different areas are selected across the city, and price survey sites are selected in accordance with the principle of reasonable layout. Commodity and service items for survey are determined by the country. On this basis, survey samples are selected according to the principle of large quantity of consumption, and strong representativeness in price change trend. Regular surveys are conducted to collect data on their market prices. General indexes are inferred on the basis of the sample data.

The selection of price survey sites: By adopting the principle of reasonable layout, an equidistant sampling is conducted for department stores, agricultural product trade markets and service outlets in different types and in different areas by their sales value, transaction value and operational scale, which will be ranked in a descending order based on the number of survey sites required.

The selection of representative specifications: Representative commodities and service items are determined by the country. Representative specifications are selected by provinces and cities according to relevant principles. Principles for selection: (1) large quantity of consumption; (2) strongly representative trend and extent of price changes, which means the characteristics of price changes of selected specifications shall be highly correlated with price changes of those that are not selected; (3) selected specifications shall be different in their nature and least correlated in the characteristics of price changes between each other; the selected industrial consumer goods must be qualified products, with registered trademark, origin, specifications, grade and other marks on the their package.

At present, data are collected under 268 basic headings in 8 categories in the consumer price surveys according to their specific purposes. The quantity of specifications for survey in big cities should be above 670 according to state regulations. In Beijing, the quantity of representative specifications is 1507. Retail price index consists of 197 basic headings in 16 categories. The quantity of representative specifications in Beijing is 1135.

Collection of price data: Price data are collected through direct surveys by designated personnel at designated sites on periodic basis.

Source and calculation of the weights: CPI weights are calculated according to survey information on living expenditures of urban residents. RPI weights are calculated according to the total retail sales of consumer goods in business statistics.

According to the uniform requirement of the National Bureau of Statistics, since January 2021, the new *Circulation and Consumption Price Statistical Reporting System* has been implemented for statistics of circulation and consumption price in Beijing, of which, the survey catalogues of consumer prices of household and retail prices of commodities have been revised and adjusted.

(II) Producer Price Index for Industrial Products (PPI) and Purchasing Price Index for Industrial Producers

The producer price for industrial products refers to the producer's price of industrial products when sold for the first time. This survey program is a combined use of the methods of surveys of key units and surveys of typical units. According to the principle of representativeness, enterprises with annual main business income of more than RMB 20 million are selected as the enterprises for survey. After the examination and approval by the National Bureau of Statistics, some enterprises with annual main business income below RMB 20 million may be supplemented as appropriate.

Purchasing price for industrial producers refers to the price of intermediate inputs of industrial enterprise. Enterprises for survey are selected among those that have submitted the producer price for industrial products.

Principles for selecting the representative enterprises: (1) Enterprises to be covered in the survey are selected by industrial sectors. In principle, the key branch should be covered; (2) Large-sized enterprises should be preferred to be selected for the survey, with appropriate selection of some other enterprises at the same time; (3) Enterprises selected should be those with normal and stable production.

Principles for selecting representative products: (1) basic headings and representative products shall be selected by industrial sectors; (2) the selected products should have significant impact on the national economy and people's livelihood; (3) the production of the goods selected should be relatively more stable; (4) the prospects of the goods selected should be promising; (5) the products selected should be representative to the localities.

Determination of weights: Weights data used for compiling producer price for industrial products of small class and above come from data of industrial sales value collected by sectors in industrial statistics; weights data in basic headings come from independent special survey on the weights of producer price for industrial products. Weights data of purchasing price of large class are mainly with reference to the input-output data by sectors, and the weights data of other headings come from independent special survey on the weights of purchasing price for industrial producers. In general, the special survey on the weights of industrial producers is conducted once every five years.

According to the requirements of the national statistical system, since 2021, 2020 shall be taken as a new round of comparison base period; in the new base period, the survey classification catalogues, the representative specifications and the enterprises for survey have all been adjusted, and the classification weights have been changed as well so as to reflect the latest changes in the industrial production structure.

(III) Price Index for Investment in Fixed Assets

A combined method of key survey, typical survey and nontraditional data substitution is used for the survey of data on prices of investment in fixed assets. The prices collected in the surveys on prices of investment in fixed assets are the actual purchasing prices (or settlement prices) of entities of investment in fixed assets. The survey covers the prices of main construction materials that constitute the architectural engineering entities in the year, such as steel, timber, cement, local construction materials, electric parts and chemical materials; the prices of labor input (wages) and costs of use of construction machines; the purchasing price of equipment, tools and instruments as well as other expenditures.

Principles for selecting survey sites of construction and installation projects: (1) the sample unit shall have certain coverage; (2) the economic activity of investment should have strong representativeness; (3) different economic types should be considered; (4) key projects shall be selected; (5) attention should be given to various types of projects.

Principles for selecting survey sites of other expenditures: in the selection of survey sites of other expenditures, the same principles shall be followed as in the selection of survey sites of construction and installation projects. Especially projects with larger amount of investment shall be selected. Since it is not easy to obtain data on other expenditures, during the actual data gathering operations, survey on key builders and construction units is to be conducted concurrently with survey on typical units (with information from administration units).

Determination of weights: Weights used for calculating the fixed assets investment price index are determined according to the average proportion of investment amount of construction and installation projects, purchase of equipment, tools and instruments and other expenditures completed in the previous three years.

(IV) Selling Price Index for Residential Houses

The surveys on selling price of residential houses include the surveys on new commercial residential house selling price and the second-hand residential house selling price.

Survey method of new commercial residential house selling price: Data of area and amount, etc. of new commercial residential houses are taken directly from the online contract signing data recorded by local real estate authorities. Online contract signing data of new commercial residential house transaction mainly consist of the name of residential project (building), project location, building number, total number of floors, floor number, house structure, building area, total price of transaction (contractual amount), and date of contract signing, etc.

Survey method of second-hand house selling price: Survey of second-hand house selling price is incomplete survey conducted with the combined method of key survey and typical survey. Basic data are collected in accordance with the manner of reporting by real estate brokerage agencies.

(V) Producer Price Index for Farm Products

A combined method of sample survey and key survey was used for the survey of producer prices of farm products. 360 entities and administrative villages producing and selling farm products are sampled. For some regional farm products, data on farm entities and administrative villages are collected with the method of subjective sampling in main production areas.

As the proportion of output value of forestry products (saplings) in Beijing is relatively small, taking no more than 1%, so no survey on producer price for forestry products is conducted according to statistical requirements of National Bureau of Statistics.

4-1 各种价格指数(1978-2022年) PRICE INDEXES (1978-2022)

(上年=100) (preceding year=100)

年份 Year	居民消费价格指数 Consumer Price Index	商品零售价格指数 Retail Price Index	农产品生产者价格指数 Producer Price Index for Agriculture Products	工业生产者出厂价格指数 Producer Price Index for Industrial Products (PPI)	工业生产者购进价格指数 Purchasing Price Index for Industrial Producers	固定资产投资价格指数 Price Index for Investment in Fixed Assets
1978	100.6	100.6				
1979	101.8	101.8	109.5			
1980	106.0	106.7	105.5			
1981	101.3	101.4	109.4			
1982	101.8	102.0	101.9			
1983	100.5	100.6	101.8			
1984	102.2	102.1	102.3			
1985	117.6	118.6	117.6			
1986	106.8	106.7	108.1			
1987	108.6	108.7	116.1			
1988	120.4	121.9	123.2			
1989	117.2	118.5	106.8			
1990	105.4	104.1	101.9	107.9	114.8	
1991	111.9	108.5	101.7	105.8	111.7	107.3
1992	109.9	108.3	102.4	100.9	103.3	112.2
1993	119.0	116.9	107.0	121.8	133.2	126.6
1994	124.9	117.9	133.4	112.9	118.7	116.2
1995	117.3	112.6	130.6	107.3	106.7	113.9
1996	111.6	107.3	101.5	100.7	100.3	108.2
1997	105.3	103.8	92.8	101.1	103.4	102.7
1998	102.4	98.3	93.6	95.1	98.1	100.8
1999	100.6	98.8	97.5	97.7	95.8	99.9
2000	103.5	98.9	95.0	102.5	100.0	101.0
2001	103.1	98.8	102.0	99.4	100.5	100.6
2002	98.2	98.4	92.4	96.6	97.1	100.4
2003	100.2	98.2	102.5	101.5	104.7	102.2
2004	101.0	99.2	106.2	103.0	114.2	104.3
2005	101.5	99.7	102.9	101.3	111.4	100.7
2006	100.9	100.2	99.1	99.1	105.5	100.4
2007	102.4	100.8	114.4	99.7	105.0	102.8
2008	105.1	104.4	112.3	103.3	115.8	107.8
2009	98.5	97.8	98.3	94.4	88.6	97.1
2010	102.4	100.4	106.5	102.2	110.5	102.5
2011	105.6	103.2	110.7	102.3	108.4	105.7
2012	103.3	100.6	104.7	98.4	98.7	101.3
2013	103.3	99.8	104.7	97.4	97.8	99.9
2014	101.6	99.1	99.7	99.1	98.8	100.0
2015	101.8	98.5	99.8	96.9	93.7	97.6
2016	101.4	98.1	99.7	98.1	98.5	99.7
2017	101.9	99.2	96.2	100.7	104.4	104.7
2018	102.5	101.1	103.6	100.0	100.8	103.8
2019	102.3	100.5	109.9	99.6	99.6	102.1
2020	101.7	101.0	110.9	99.1	99.5	
2021	101.1	101.7	98.2	101.1	103.7	
2022	101.8	101.8	102.7	102.3	106.2	

注：1.自2011年起，“工业品出厂价格指数”更名为“工业生产者出厂价格指数”，“原材料、燃料、动力购进价格指数”更名为“工业生产者购进价格指数”，下同。

2.自2013年起，“农产品生产价格指数”更名为“农产品生产者价格指数”。

3.自2020年起，国家统计局取消固定资产投资价格统计，下同。

Note: a) From 2011 ,"the Ex-factory Price Index for Manufactured Products" has been renamed as "Producer Price Index for Industrial Products (PPI)", and "the Purchasing Price Index for Raw Materials, Fuels and Power" has been renamed as "Purchasing Price Index for Industrial Producers", the same below.

b) From 2013, the "Production Price Index For Agricultural Products" has been renamed as "Producer Price Index For Farm Products".

c) From 2020, the National Bureau of Statistics cancelled the statistics for fixed assets investment price, the same below.

4-2 各种价格定基指数(1978-2022年)
FIXED-BASE PRICE INDEXES (1978-2022)

年份 Year	居民消费价格指数 Consumer Price Index (1978=100)	商品零售价格指数 Retail Price Index (1978=100)	工业生产者出厂价格指数 Producer Price Index for Industrial Products (1990=100)	工业生产者购进价格指数 Purchasing Price Index for Industrial Producers (1990=100)	固定资产投资价格指数 Price Index for Investment in Fixed Assets (1990=100)
1978	100.0	100.0			
1979	101.8	101.8			
1980	107.9	108.6			
1981	109.3	110.1			
1982	111.3	112.3			
1983	111.8	113.0			
1984	114.3	115.4			
1985	134.4	136.8			
1986	143.5	145.9			
1987	155.8	158.6			
1988	187.6	193.3			
1989	219.9	229.1			
1990	231.8	238.5	100.0	100.0	100.0
1991	259.4	258.8	105.8	111.7	107.3
1992	285.1	280.3	106.8	115.4	120.4
1993	339.3	327.7	130.0	153.7	152.4
1994	423.8	386.4	146.8	182.4	177.1
1995	497.1	435.1	157.5	194.7	201.7
1996	554.8	466.9	158.6	195.2	218.3
1997	584.2	484.6	160.4	201.9	224.2
1998	598.2	476.4	152.5	198.0	226.0
1999	601.8	470.7	149.0	189.7	225.7
2000	622.9	465.5	152.7	189.7	228.0
2001	642.2	459.9	151.8	190.7	229.4
2002	630.6	452.5	146.6	185.1	230.3
2003	631.9	444.4	148.8	193.8	235.3
2004	638.2	440.8	153.3	221.4	245.5
2005	647.8	439.5	155.3	246.6	247.2
2006	653.6	440.4	153.9	260.2	248.2
2007	669.3	443.9	153.5	273.3	255.1
2008	703.4	463.4	158.6	316.3	275.0
2009	692.8	453.2	149.8	280.3	266.9
2010	709.4	455.0	153.1	309.7	273.6
2011	749.1	469.6	156.6	335.7	289.2
2012	773.8	472.4	154.1	331.3	293.0
2013	799.3	471.5	150.1	324.0	292.7
2014	812.1	467.3	148.7	320.1	292.7
2015	826.7	460.3	144.1	299.9	285.7
2016	838.3	451.6	141.4	295.4	284.8
2017	854.2	448.0	142.4	308.4	298.2
2018	875.6	452.9	142.4	310.8	309.5
2019	895.7	455.2	141.9	309.5	316.0
2020	910.9	459.8	140.6	307.8	
2021	920.9	467.6	142.2	319.0	
2022	937.2	476.0	145.5	338.9	

4-3 居民消费价格分类指数(2022年)
CONSUMER PRICE INDEX BY CATEGORY (2022)

项 目	Item	2021 =100	项 目	Item	2021 =100
居民消费价格指数	**Consumer Price Index**	**101.8**	家用纺织品	Home Textiles	100.5
#非食品价格指数	Non-food Price Index	101.4	家庭日用杂品	Daily Groceries for Households	101.7
#服务项目价格指数	Price Index for Services	100.7	个人护理用品	Personal Care Products	101.0
#消费品价格指数	Price Index for Consumer Goods	102.8	家庭服务	Home Services	102.9
食品烟酒	**Food, Tobacco and Liquor**	**103.1**	**交通通信**	**Transport and Communication**	**105.0**
食 品	Food	103.9	交 通	Transport	106.7
粮 食	Grain	101.2	交通工具	Vehicles	98.1
薯 类	Tubers	107.2	交通工具用燃料	Fuels for Vehicles	121.2
豆 类	Beans	102.6	交通工具使用和维修	Vehicle Use and Maintenance	101.5
食用油	Edible Oil	104.1	交通费	Transportation Fee	103.0
菜及食用菌	Vegetables and Edible Mushrooms	101.4	通 信	Communication	99.2
#鲜 菜	Fresh Vegetables	101.2	通信工具	Communication Devices	97.1
畜肉类	Livestock Meat	97.7	通信服务	Communication Services	100.3
禽肉类	Poultry Meat	103.9	邮递服务	Mail Service	99.8
水产品	Aquatic Products	103.5	**教育文化娱乐**	**Education, Culture and Entertainment**	**100.6**
蛋 类	Eggs	106.1			
#鸡 蛋	Egg	106.4	教 育	Education	100.9
奶 类	Milk and Other Diary Products	101.8	教育用品	Educational Supplies	100.6
干鲜瓜果类	Dried and Fresh Melons and Fruits	113.7	教育服务	Education Services	100.9
			文化娱乐	Culture and Entertainment	100.3
#鲜 果	Fresh Fruits	115.4	文娱耐用消费品	Durable Consumer Goods for Cultural and Recreation Use	99.8
糖果糕点类	Confectionery	102.3			
调味品	Condiment	106.1	其他文娱用品	Other Recreational Supplies	102.9
其他食品类	Other Foods	104.5	文化娱乐服务	Cultural and Recreational Services	96.7
茶及饮料	Tea and Drinks	104.7	旅 游	Tourism	101.2
烟 酒	Tobacco and Liquor	102.2	**医疗保健**	**Medical Care**	**100.7**
卷 烟	Cigarettes and Cigars	101.7	药品及医疗器具	Medicine and Medical Equipment	101.5
酒 类	Liquor	102.7	中 药	Traditional Chinese Medicine	106.6
在外餐饮	Outside Food and Drinks	101.5	西 药	Western Medicine	99.4
衣 着	**Clothing**	**100.6**	滋补保健品	Nourishing Health Care Products	101.4
服 装	Garments	100.6	医疗卫生器具	Medical and Health Equipment	98.6
鞋 类	Footwear	100.7	保健器具	Health Care Equipment	100.2
居 住	**Living**	**100.6**	医疗服务	Medical Service	100.3
租赁房房租	Rental	100.6	**其他用品及服务**	**Other Supplies and Services**	**101.6**
住房保养维修及管理	Housing Maintenance and Management	102.3	其他用品类	Other Supplies	102.2
			首饰手表	Jewelry and Watches	101.8
水电燃料	Utilities and Fuels	100.1	母婴用品	Maternal and Infant Supplies	107.2
自有住房	Own Housing	100.4	其他杂项用品	Other Miscellaneous	100.5
生活用品及服务	**Daily Necessities and Services**	**101.6**	其他服务	Other Services	101.1
家具及室内装饰品	Furniture and Interior Decorations	101.4	在外住宿	Outside Accommodation	101.9
			美容美发洗浴	Beauty Salon and Bath	101.1
家 具	Furniture	101.7	养老服务	Pension Services	102.1
室内装饰品	Interior Decorations	99.4	金融及保险服务	Financial and Insurance Services	100.4
家用器具	Domestic Appliances	101.9	中介法律及其他服务	Intermediary Legal and Other Services	101.1
大型家用器具	Large Domestic Appliances	101.6			
小家电	Small Domestic Appliances	103.6			

4-4 商品零售价格分类指数(2022年)
RETAIL PRICE INDEX BY CATEGORY (2022)

项　　目	Item	2021 =100	项　　目	Item	2021 =100
商品零售价格指数	**Retail Price Index**	**101.8**	**文化办公用品**	**Cultural Office Supplies**	**100.5**
食　品	**Food**	**103.1**	**日用品**	**Daily Necessities**	**101.5**
粮　食	Grain	101.1	日用百货	Articles of Daily Use	105.1
薯　类	Tubers	107.2	厨具餐具茶具	Kitchen Utensils, Tableware and Teaware	101.1
豆　类	Beans	102.6			
食用油	Edible Oil	104.1	清洗用品	Cleaning Supplies	98.7
菜及食用菌	Vegetables and Edible Mushrooms	101.4	其他日用品	Other Daily Necessities	98.7
			体育娱乐用品	**Sports and Entertainment Supplies**	**102.3**
畜肉类	Livestock Meat	97.7	体育户外用品	Sports and Outdoor Supplies	106.1
禽肉类	Poultry Meat	103.9	娱乐用品	Entertainment Supplies	101.4
水产品	Aquatic Products	103.5	**交通、通信用品**	**Transportation and Communication Supplies**	**97.9**
蛋　类	Eggs	106.1			
奶　类	Milk and Other Diary Products	101.9	交通运输机械	Transportation Machinery	98.3
干鲜瓜果类	Dried and Fresh Melons and Fruits	113.8	通信器材	Communication Equipment	97.4
			家　具	**Furniture**	**101.7**
糖果糕点类	Confectionery	102.3	**化妆品**	**Cosmetic**	**101.1**
调味品	Condiment	106.1	**金银饰品**	**Gold and Silver Jewelry**	**102.9**
其他食品类	Other Food	104.5	**中西药品及医疗保健用品**	**Chinese Traditional Medicine, Western Medicines and Health Care Products**	**100.9**
餐饮业零售	Retail of Restaurants	101.5			
饮料、烟酒	**Drinks, Tobacco and Liquor**	**103.0**			
茶及饮料	Tea and Drinks	104.6	医疗卫生器具	Medical and Health Equipment	98.6
卷　烟	Cigarettes and Cigars	101.7	中　药	Traditional Chinese Medicine	106.6
酒　类	Liquor	102.7	西　药	Western Medicine	99.4
服装、鞋帽	**Clothing, Shoes and Hats**	**100.6**	保健器具及用品	Health Care Equipment and Supplies	101.2
服　装	Garments	100.6	**书报杂志及电子出版物**	**Books, Newspapers, Magazines and Electronic Publications**	**106.8**
鞋帽袜	Footgear and Hats	100.6			
其他衣着配件	Other Clothing Accessories	100.0	教材及参考书	Teaching Materials and Reference Books	100.6
纺织品	**Textile**	**100.3**	书报杂志及音像制品	Books, Newspapers, Magazines and Audiovisual Products	109.3
服装材料	Clothing Materials	100.6			
床上用品	Bedding	100.3	计算机办公软件	Computer Office Software	100.0
家用电器及音像器材	**Domestic Appliances, Audio & Video Equipment**	**100.5**	**燃　料**	**Fuel**	**117.3**
			煤炭及制品	Coal and Coal Products	100.0
家庭设备	Home Equipment	102.0	石油及制品	Petroleum and Oil Products	117.4
文娱用耐用消费品	Durable Consumer Goods for Cultural and Recreation Use	100.4	**建筑材料及五金电料**	**Building Materials and Hardware**	**102.6**
			建筑装潢材料	Building Decoration Materials	103.2
专业音像器材	Professional Audio Equipment	96.2	五金水暖	Hardware and Plumbing	101.2

4-5 农产品生产者价格指数
PRODUCER PRICE INDEX FOR FARM PRODUCTS

(上年=100) (preceding year=100)

项 目	Item	2022	2021
总 指 数	**General Index**	**102.7**	**98.2**
农业产品	Agricultural Products	103.3	104.7
#粮 食	Grain	116.1	131.7
蔬菜及食用菌	Vegetable and Edible Fungus	99.5	99.2
林业产品	Forestry Products		
畜牧业产品	Animal Husbandry Products	102.0	90.3
#肉 牛	Beef Cattle	101.1	99.3
肉 羊	Mutton Sheep	94.2	107.0
奶产品	Milk Products	99.1	104.8
猪	Hogs	100.7	70.0
肉禽(毛重)	Poultry (Gross Weight)	106.3	101.4
禽 蛋	Eggs	105.4	109.5
渔业产品	Fishing	99.3	109.5

4-6 工业生产者出厂价格及购进价格指数(2000-2022年)

(上年=100)

年　份 Year	工业生产者出　厂价格指数 Producer Price Index for Industrial Products (PPI)	轻工业 Light Industry	重工业 Heavy Industry	生产资料 Means of Production	生活资料 Comsumer Goods	工业生产者购　进价格指数 Purchasing Price Index for Industrial Products	燃　料、动力类 Fuels and Power
2000	102.5	98.0	104.2	103.4	98.8	100.0	104.3
2001	99.4	99.6	99.4	99.4	99.6	100.5	101.7
2002	96.6	97.6	96.4	96.4	97.9	97.1	102.3
2003	101.5	98.0	104.5	102.2	99.1	104.7	109.6
2004	103.0	100.2	105.3	103.7	100.6	114.2	120.0
2005	101.3	98.7	103.3	101.9	99.1	111.4	117.1
2006	99.1	97.9	99.6	99.0	99.3	105.5	113.1
2007	99.7	100.7	99.2	99.3	101.3	105.0	105.1
2008	103.3	101.8	104.0	103.8	101.3	115.8	132.3
2009	94.4	96.2	93.6	93.3	99.1	88.6	85.1
2010	102.2	98.7	103.8	102.7	100.3	110.5	121.3
2011	102.3	104.6	102.0	102.5	101.6	108.4	117.8
2012	98.4	101.1	98.0	97.8	101.0	98.7	99.0
2013	97.4	100.7	96.9	96.7	100.5	97.8	96.4
2014	99.1	100.8	98.8	98.7	100.9	98.8	99.4
2015	96.9	100.0	96.4	96.1	99.9	93.7	85.6
2016	98.1	101.8	97.6	98.0	98.3	98.5	98.0
2017	100.7	99.3	100.9	101.5	99.4	104.4	108.4
2018	100.0	99.9	100.0	100.4	99.3	100.8	102.0
2019	99.6	103.6	99.1	99.6	99.6	99.6	99.5
2020	99.1	103.8	98.5	98.9	99.5	99.5	98.5
2021	101.1	99.9	101.4	102.1	99.1	103.7	106.1
2022	102.3	99.2	102.9	104.3	98.1	106.2	115.7

注：根据统计制度规定，我国工业生产者价格统计调查每五年进行一次基期轮换，2021年1月开始编制和发布以2020年为基期的价格指数。与上轮基期相比，新基期的调查分类目录、代表规格品和调查企业均有调整，分类权数也有变化，以反映工业生产结构的最新变动。

PRODUCER PRICE INDEX AND PURCHASING PRICE INDEX FOR INDUSTRIAL PRODUCTS (2000-2022)

(preceding year=100)

黑色金属材料类 Ferrous Metal Materials	有色金属材料和电线类 Nonferrous Metal Materials and Electric Wires	化工原料类 Chemical Raw Materials	木材及纸浆类 Timber and Paper Pulp	建筑材料及非金属类 Construction Materials and Nonmetal Ores	其他工业原材料及半成品类 Other Industrial Materials and Semi-finished Products	农副产品类 Agricultural Products	纺织原料类 Textile Raw Materials
100.5	106.9	103.4	94.8	101.9	98.4	94.5	91.5
100.3	97.9	97.6	98.3	99.5	98.8	103.5	100.6
96.4	96.1	99.3	102.5	97.6	92.3	93.6	97.8
110.9	101.4	107.3	100.6	99.0	95.2	114.3	98.1
124.5	120.9	111.1	100.7	105.8	103.8	122.3	102.8
108.3	123.3	114.9	103.6	101.8	102.8	96.3	106.2
96.7	138.3	104.1	100.3	99.4	98.0	101.3	100.9
115.6	112.2	106.7	101.7	103.5	95.3	138.6	99.2
128.5	97.9	108.3	108.5	115.2	94.9	132.6	101.5
79.8	81.1	82.3	97.0	99.4	95.3	88.2	97.6
115.4	121.6	111.7	104.2	102.7	99.0	106.6	102.8
112.7	115.2	112.7	105.7	103.0	98.9	128.8	108.2
92.2	96.7	102.5	99.0	93.9	98.8	98.5	100.8
94.6	92.1	98.6	98.4	94.2	98.9	102.2	99.6
95.3	95.3	99.2	99.9	96.8	98.9	97.5	100.7
87.2	93.7	94.1	99.0	95.7	98.4	103.1	99.8
99.7	97.2	96.6	99.1	100.6	98.3	112.8	99.8
111.3	123.4	102.9	101.4	106.3	99.9	93.0	101.9
105.7	105.8	101.5	101.1	105.0	98.8	90.7	100.8
100.4	97.2	97.0	98.4	99.3	99.4	111.9	100.2
101.4	100.0	96.4	99.3	99.0	99.3	119.7	100.2
114.7	113.1	105.1	99.9	100.0	100.3	89.8	98.1
97.7	107.8	103.2	99.4	105.3	99.6	101.3	101.0

Note: According to the statistical system, the statistical survey on industrial producer price in China is subject to the alternation of base period once every five years, and the price indexes with 2020 as the base period were started to be compiled and published since January 2021. Compared with the previous base period, the survey classification catalogues, the representative specifications and the enterprises for survey have all been adjusted in the new base period, and the classification weights have been changed as well so as to reflect the latest changes in the industrial production structure.

4-7 工业生产者出厂价格指数
PRODUCER PRICE INDEX FOR INDUSTRIAL PRODUCTS

(上年=100) (preceding year=100)

项目	Item	2022	2021
总指数	**General Index**	**102.3**	**101.1**
按轻、重工业分	**By Light Industry and Heavy Industry**		
轻工业	Light Industry	99.2	99.9
以农产品为原料	Using Farming Products as Raw Materials	101.6	100.6
以非农产品为原料	Using Non-agricultural Products as Raw Materials	97.8	99.5
重工业	Heavy Industry	102.9	101.4
采掘	Excavation	94.9	117.6
原材料	Raw Materials	108.4	102.3
加工	Processing	99.1	100.2
按生产、生活资料分	**By Capital Goods and Consumer Goods**		
生产资料	Means of Production	104.3	102.1
采掘	Excavation	94.9	117.6
原材料	Raw Materials	108.5	102.3
加工	Processing	100.1	101.1
生活资料	Consumer Goods	98.1	99.1
食品	Foods	102.0	100.5
衣着	Clothing	94.7	96.6
一般日用品	Articles for Daily Use	96.7	99.6
耐用消费品	Durable Consumer Goods	97.5	98.6

4-8 工业生产者出厂价格指数(按行业分)
PRODUCER PRICE INDEX FOR INDUSTRIAL PRODUCTS (BY SECTOR)

(上年=100) (preceding year=100)

项　　目	Item	2022	2021
总 指 数	**General Index**	**102.3**	**101.1**
石油和天然气开采业	Extraction of Petroleum and Natural Gas	120.7	98.9
黑色金属矿采选业	Mining and Processing of Ferrous Metal Ores	82.0	153.8
开采专业及辅助性活动	Professional and Support Activities for Mining	101.2	96.4
农副食品加工业	Processing of Food from Agriculture Products	103.5	99.1
食品制造业	Manufacture of Foods	101.3	99.9
酒、饮料和精制茶制造业	Manufacture of Wines, Beverage and Refined Tea	102.3	101.7
烟草制品业	Manufacture of Cigarettes and Tobacco	102.5	109.7
纺织业	Manufacture of Textile	101.0	105.5
纺织服装、服饰业	Manufacture of Textile Wearing Apparel and Ornament	94.7	96.6
家具制造业	Manufacture of Furniture	101.3	102.6
造纸和纸制品业	Manufacture of Paper and Paper Products	100.4	100.7
印刷和记录媒介复制业	Printing, Reproduction of Recording Media	99.3	98.5
文教、工美、体育和娱乐用品制造业	Manufacture of Articles for Culture, Education, Artwork, Sports and Entertainment Activity	101.6	103.2
石油、煤炭及其他燃料加工业	Processing of Petroleum, Coal and Other Fuels	129.0	120.2
化学原料和化学制品制造业	Manufacture of Chemical Raw Material and Chemical Products	97.8	112.5
医药制造业	Manufacture of Medicines	96.4	99.6
橡胶和塑料制品业	Manufacture of Rubber and Plastics Products	97.8	95.3
非金属矿物制品业	Manufacture of Non-Metallic Mineral Products	104.7	102.8
黑色金属冶炼和压延加工业	Smelting and Pressing of Ferrous Metals	91.3	122.8
有色金属冶炼和压延加工业	Smelting and Processing of Non-ferrous Metals	117.7	126.4
金属制品业	Manufacture of Fabricated Metal Products	105.0	104.5
通用设备制造业	Manufacture of General-Purpose Machinery	101.1	100.6
专用设备制造业	Manufacture of Special-Purpose Machinery	99.6	99.1
汽车制造业	Manufacture of Motor Vehicles	100.0	100.4
铁路、船舶、航空航天和其他运输设备制造业	Manufacture of Railway, Ships, Aerospace and Other Transport Equipments	100.3	100.5
电气机械和器材制造业	Manufacture of Electrical Machinery and Equipment	100.5	102.1
计算机、通信和其他电子设备制造业	Manufacture of Computer, Communication Equipment and Other Electronic Equipment	95.5	97.4
仪器仪表制造业	Manufacture of Measuring Instrument and Meter	99.1	100.0
其他制造业	Other Manufacturing	109.0	99.7
废弃资源综合利用业	Waste Recycling and Recovery	105.2	93.1
金属制品、机械和设备修理业	Repair of Fabricated Metal Products, Machinery and Equipment	99.6	101.0
电力、热力生产和供应业	Production and Supply of Electricity and Heating Power	107.0	99.7
燃气生产和供应业	Production and Supply of Gas	102.0	105.2
水的生产和供应业	Production and Supply of Water	100.0	100.0

4-9 工业生产者购进价格指数 PURCHASING PRICE INDEX FOR INDUSTRIAL PRODUCERS

(上年=100) (preceding year=100)

项目	Item	2022	2021
总 指 数	**General Index**	**106.2**	**103.7**
燃料、动力类	Fuels and Power	115.7	106.1
黑色金属材料类	Ferrous Metal Materials	97.7	114.7
#钢 材	Steel Products	98.3	114.4
其 他	Others	93.7	116.8
有色金属材料和电线类	Nonferrous Metal Materials and Electric Wires	107.8	113.1
化工原料类	Chemical Raw Materials	103.2	105.1
木材及纸浆类	Timber and Paper Pulp	99.4	99.9
建筑材料及非金属类	Construction Materials and Non-metallic materials	105.3	100.0
其他工业原材料及半成品类	Other Industrial Materials and Semi-finished Products	99.6	100.3
农副产品类	Agricultural Products	101.3	89.8
纺织原料类	Textile Raw Materials	101.0	98.1

4-10 住宅销售价格指数(2022年各月) SELLING PRICE INDEX OF RESIDENTIAL HOUSES (EACH MONTH OF 2022)

(上年同月=100) (same month of previous year=100)

项目	Item	1月 Jan.	2月 Feb.	3月 Mar.	4月 Apr.	5月 May	6月 Jun.
新建商品住宅	**New Commercial Residential Houses**	**105.5**	**105.5**	**105.7**	**105.8**	**105.9**	**105.8**
90平方米及以下	90sq.m and below	105.7	105.6	105.5	105.6	105.2	104.8
90-144平方米	90-144sq.m	105.3	105.6	106.0	105.8	105.2	105.2
144平方米以上	Above 144sq.m	105.6	105.4	105.7	106.0	106.8	106.9
二手住宅	**Second-hand Residential Houses**	**108.0**	**107.4**	**107.2**	**106.5**	**105.3**	**104.5**
90平方米及以下	90sq.m and below	107.9	107.0	106.9	106.2	104.7	103.8
90-144平方米	90-144sq.m	107.9	107.5	107.2	106.6	105.7	104.7
144平方米以上	Above 144sq.m	108.2	108.2	107.9	107.1	106.1	106.0

4-10 续表 Continued

(上年同月=100) (same month of previous year=100)

项目	Item	7月 Jul.	8月 Aug.	9月 Sep.	10月 Oct.	11月 Nov.	12月 Dec.
新建商品住宅	**New Commercial Residential Houses**	**105.5**	**105.8**	**106.1**	**105.9**	**105.7**	**105.8**
90平方米及以下	90sq.m and below	104.1	104.8	105.2	105.0	104.8	105.2
90-144平方米	90-144sq.m	104.9	104.8	104.8	104.9	104.7	105.1
144平方米以上	Above 144sq.m	106.8	107.1	107.5	107.0	106.9	106.7
二手住宅	**Second-hand Residential Houses**	**104.1**	**103.9**	**104.6**	**105.2**	**105.2**	**103.9**
90平方米及以下	90sq.m and below	103.4	103.5	104.3	105.1	104.8	103.1
90-144平方米	90-144sq.m	104.2	104.1	104.8	104.9	105.0	104.0
144平方米以上	Above 144sq.m	105.6	104.6	105.1	106.0	106.4	105.9

主要统计指标解释

居民消费价格指数 是度量消费商品及服务项目价格水平随着时间而变动的相对数，反映一定时期内居民家庭购买的消费品及服务价格水平的变动趋势和变动程度。居民消费价格指数变动率通常被用来作为反映通货膨胀（或紧缩）程度的指标。

商品零售价格指数 是度量工业、商业、餐饮业和其他零售企业向城乡居民、机关团体出售生活消费品和办公用品价格水平随着时间而变动的相对数，反映市场商品零售价格的变动趋势和变动程度。

工业生产者出厂价格指数 是反映全部工业产品出厂价格总水平变动程度的相对数。其中包括工业企业售给商业、外贸、物资部门的产品，还包括售给工业和其他部门的生产资料以及直接售给居民的生活消费品。通过工业生产者价格指数能观察工业产品出厂价格变动对工业总产值的影响。

工业生产者购进价格指数 是反映全部工业原材料、燃料、动力购进价格总水平变动程度的相对数。用其可以观察和研究工业企业原材料价格变动对生产的影响，以及企业对原材料涨价的消化能力和承受能力，为制定价格政策提供依据。

固定资产投资价格指数 是反映固定资产投资额价格变动程度的相对数。固定资产投资额由建筑安装装饰工程投资完成额，设备、工器具购置投资完成额和其他费用投资完成额三部分组成。编制固定资产投资价格指数可以准确地反映固定资产投资中涉及的各类商品和取费项目价格变动幅度，消除按现价计算的固定资产投资指标中的价格变动因素，真实地反映固定资产投资的规模、速度、结构和效益，为国家科学地制定、检查固定资产投资计划，提高宏观调控水平，为完善国民经济核算体系提供科学、可靠的依据。

住宅销售价格指数 是反映住宅销售价格总水平变动趋势和程度的相对数。包括新建商品住宅销售价格指数和二手住宅销售价格指数。

农产品生产者价格指数 是指农产品生产者价格总水平变动程度的相对数。农产品生产者价格是指农产品生产者第一次出售其产品时的单位产品价格。

Explanatory Notes on Main Statistical Indicators

Consumer Price Index (CPI) is a relative number measuring the changes in prices of consumer goods and service over time, reflecting the trend and degree of changes in prices of consumer goods and service purchased by households over a period of time. The change rate of CPI is usually used for reflecting the level of inflation (or deflation).

Retail Price Index is a relative number measuring the changes in prices of consumer goods and office supplies provided by industry, commerce, restaurants and other retail businesses for urban and rural residents and government agencies and organizations over time. It reflects the trend and degree of changes in retail price of commodities in the market.

Producer Price Index for Industrial Products (PPI) is a relative number reflecting the degree of changes in general producer prices of all industrial products, including products sold by industrial enterprises to commercial, foreign trade and materials companies, as well as production materials sold to industrial and other enterprises, and consumer goods directly sold to consumers. It can be used to observe the impact of producer prices of industrial products on gross industrial output value.

Purchasing Price Index for Industrial Producers is a relative number reflecting the degree of changes in the overall level of prices of all industrial materials, fuels and power. It can be used to observe and study the impact of changes in prices of raw materials in industrial enterprises on their production, as well as the enterprises' capacity of digesting and bearing the rising prices of raw materials, thus providing basis for formulating price policies.

Price Index for Investment in Fixed Assets is a relative number reflecting the degree of changes in prices of investment in fixed assets. The investment in fixed assets consists of three components, i.e. the investment in construction and installation, the investment in purchasing equipment, tools and instruments, and the investment in other items. The compilation of the price index for investment in fixed assets can accurately reflect the range of changes in prices of various goods and charging items involved in the investment in fixed assets, can remove the factor of price change in the indicators for investment in fixed assets calculated at current price, can truly reflect the actual size, growth, structure, and efficiency of investment in fixed assets, can provide scientific and reliable basis for the state to scientifically formulate and inspect the plans for investment in fixed assets, improve the level of macro control and improve the national economic accounting system.

Selling Price Index of Residential Houses is a relative number reflecting the trend and degree of changes in the overall level of house selling prices, including newly built residential house selling price index and second-hand house selling price index.

Producer Price Index for Farm Products is a relative number reflecting the degree of changes in the overall producer prices of farm products. Producer price of farm products refers to the price of unit product at which the producers of farm products sell their products for the first time.

人民生活
PEOPLE'S LIVING CONDITIONS

简要说明

一、主要内容

本章资料反映北京市居民生活现状及变化情况，分为全市居民生活、城镇居民生活和农村居民生活三部分，主要包括家庭基本情况、家庭收入和消费支出情况、居住状况和耐用消费品拥有量等。

二、调查方法

城乡居民生活状况调查方法和方案由国家统计局统一制定，采用抽样调查的方法，按对全市及分区居民主要收支指标有代表性的原则在全市城乡住户中抽取样本，并按一定的周期对样本进行轮换以保证其代表性。对抽中的住户采用日记账和问卷相结合的方式采集数据。

三、本章资料的调查范围

城镇住户调查的口径范围：2000—2003 年为 1000 户城市居民，覆盖城八区；2004—2006 年为 2000 户城市居民，覆盖城八区；2007 年为 3000 户城镇居民，覆盖所有区县；2008—2012 年为 5000 户城镇居民，覆盖所有区县。

农村住户调查的口径范围：2000—2002 年为 2710 户，覆盖 14 个郊区县；2003 年为 2670 户（石景山区全部农民转居民，40 个样本取消），覆盖 13 个郊区县；2004—2012 年为 3000 户，覆盖 13 个郊区。

城乡住户调查一体化：2013 年，根据国家统计局实施城乡住户调查一体化改革的要求和《住户收支与生活状况调查方案》的有关规定，国家统计局北京调查总队对全市城乡住户进行了统一的样本抽取，城乡住户调查样本量共计 10000 户。

按照国家统计局要求，自 2015 年起，北京按照改革后的新口径发布全市和分城乡的居民收支数据。与老口径相比，新口径的差异主要体现在三个方面：一是对居民收支指标口径进行了调整，将反映居民收入的核心指标由原来的城镇居民人均可支配收入和农村居民人均纯收入统一为人均可支配收入；二是按照国家城乡划分标准，将城镇地区的村委会由原来的农村划入城镇进行统计；三是在分城乡的居民收支数据基础上，增加了全体居民的人均可支配收入、人均消费支出数据。

Brief Introduction

I. Main Content

Statistics in this chapter reflect the living conditions of residents in Beijing and their changes, consisting of three parts, including the living conditions of the residents of the whole city, urban residents and rural residents. Figures include the basic family situation, household income and consumption expenditure, housing conditions and number of durable consumer goods in possession.

II. Method of Survey

Methods and plans of survey for living conditions of urban and rural residents are designated by National Bureau of Statistics. The method of sampling survey is adopted to take samples across urban and rural residents of the whole city following the principle of selecting representative residents in terms of major income and expenditure indicators across the city and the districts. Samples are changed in certain periods to ensure their representativeness. For selected residents, statistics are gathered through journals and questionnaires.

III. Scope of Survey

Scope of survey for urban residents: In 2000-2003, the survey covered 1,000 urban households in 8 urban districts; in 2004-2006, covered 2,000 urban households in 8 urban districts; in 2007 covered 3,000 urban households in all districts and counties; in 2008-2012, covered 5,000 households in all districts and counties.

Scope of survey for rural residents: In 2000-2002, the survey covered 2,710 households in 14 suburban districts and counties; in 2003, covered 2,670 households (All rural residents became urban residents in Shijingshan District, so 40 samples were cancelled.) in 13 suburban districts and counties; in 2004-2012, covered 3,000 households in 13 suburban districts.

Integration of survey on urban and rural residents: in 2013, according to the requirements of the National Bureau of Statistics on carrying out integrated reforms of urban and rural resident survey, and *Survey Plan on Income and Expenditure, and Living Conditions of Households*, the NBS Survey Office in Beijing took a total of 10,000 samples of urban and rural residents in an integrated way.

According to requirements of National Bureau of Statistics, since 2015, Beijing has started to issue data on income and expenditure of residents in the city and residents in urban and rural areas according to new standards after the reform. As compared with former standards, the new standards mainly show differences in the following 3 aspects: first, standards on resident income and expenditure indicators are adjusted. Core indicators reflecting resident income are unified from original per capita disposable income of urban residents and per capita net income of rural residents to per capita disposable income; second, according to national standards on division of urban and rural areas, village committees in urban areas that were classified into rural areas are now classified into urban areas; third, based on data on resident income and expenditure in urban and rural areas, data on per capita disposable income and per capita consumption expenditure of residents in Beijing are added.

5-1 全市居民家庭生活基本情况(1978-2022年)
BASIC LIVING CONDITIONS OF HOUSEHOLDS OF THE WHOLE CITY (1978-2022)

年 份 Year	人均可支配收入(元) Per Capita Disposable Income (yuan)	人均可支配收入实际增长(%) Real Growth Rate of Per Capita Disposable Income (%)	人均消费支出(元) Per Capita Consumption Expenditure (yuan)	#食品烟酒 Food, Tobacco and Liquor	全市居民家庭恩格尔系数(%) Engel Coefficient of Households of the Whole City (%)
1978	302		281	169	60.1
1979	344	11.9	321	191	59.5
1980	412	13.0	390	214	55.0
1981	469	12.4	428	240	56.1
1982	507	6.2	463	264	57.1
1983	561	10.0	496	278	56.2
1984	682	18.9	572	315	55.1
1985	854	6.5	757	376	49.6
1986	971	6.4	900	444	49.3
1987	1078	2.2	974	502	51.5
1988	1292	-0.4	1234	614	49.7
1989	1457	-3.8	1312	705	53.7
1990	1741	13.4	1469	787	53.6
1991	1975	1.3	1578	846	53.6
1992	2303	6.1	1882	981	52.1
1993	3126	14.0	2514	1198	47.7
1994	4419	13.2	3502	1636	46.7
1995	5501	6.1	4366	2125	48.7
1996	6429	4.7	4972	2317	46.6
1997	6837	0.9	5629	2466	43.8
1998	7472	6.7	6099	2515	41.2
1999	8155	8.4	6670	2620	39.3
2000	9230	9.4	7644	2750	36.0
2001	10399	9.3	8150	2885	35.4
2002	11300	10.7	9480	3061	32.3
2003	12628	11.5	10451	3131	30.0
2004	14342	12.5	11672	3490	29.9
2005	16853	15.8	13289	3912	29.4
2006	19296	13.5	15123	4228	28.0
2007	21458	8.6	15933	4572	28.7
2008	24371	8.1	17447	5157	29.6
2009	26571	10.7	19381	5561	28.7
2010	29228	7.4	21834	5853	26.8
2011	33176	7.5	24298	6086	25.0
2012	36817	7.5	26562	6574	24.8
2013	40830	7.4	29176	7008	24.0
2014	44489	7.3	31103	7468	24.0
2015	48458	7.0	33803	7584	22.4
2016	52530	6.9	35416	7609	21.5
2017	57230	6.9	37425	7549	20.2
2018	62361	6.3	39843	8065	20.2
2019	67756	6.3	43038	8489	19.7
2020	69434	0.8	38903	8374	21.5
2021	75002	6.8	43640	9307	21.3
2022	77415	1.4	42683	9223	21.6

注：本表数据为城乡住户调查一体化改革后的可比口径数据，下同。

Note: Figures in this table are that of comparable standard after the reform to the integration of survey on urban and rural residents, the same below.

5-2 全市居民家庭生活基本情况(2015-2022年)
BASIC LIVING CONDITIONS OF HOUSEHOLDS OF THE WHOLE CITY (2015-2022)

单位：元 (yuan)

项　　目	Item	2015	2016	2017	2018	2019	2020	2021	2022	2022年为2021年% 2022 as % of 2021
全市居民家庭生活基本情况	**Basic Living Conditions of Households of the Whole City**									
人均可支配收入	Per Capita Disposable Income	48458	52530	57230	62361	67756	69434	75002	77415	103.2
人均消费支出	Per Capita Consumption Expenditure	33803	35416	37425	39843	43038	38903	43640	42683	97.8
居民家庭恩格尔系数(%)	Engel's Coefficient of Households (%)	22.4	21.5	20.2	20.2	19.7	21.5	21.3	21.6	
人均住房建筑面积(平方米)	Per Capita Floor Space of Houses (sq.m)	33.23	34.02	34.23	34.86	34.52	34.56	35.59	35.85	100.7
城镇居民家庭生活基本情况	**Basic Living Conditions of Urban Households**									
人均可支配收入	Per Capita Disposable Income	52859	57275	62406	67990	73849	75602	81518	84023	103.1
人均消费支出	Per Capita Consumption Expenditure	36642	38256	40346	42926	46358	41726	46776	45617	97.5
居民家庭恩格尔系数(%)	Engel's Coefficient of Households (%)	22.1	21.1	19.8	20.0	19.3	21.0	20.8	21.1	
人均住房建筑面积(平方米)	Per Capita Floor Space of Houses (sq.m)	31.69	32.38	32.56	33.08	32.54	32.60	33.40	33.63	100.7
农村居民家庭生活基本情况	**Basic Living Conditions of Rural Households**									
人均可支配收入	Per Capita Disposable Income	20569	22310	24240	26490	28928	30126	33303	34754	104.4
人均消费支出	Per Capita Consumption Expenditure	15811	17329	18810	20195	21881	20913	23574	23745	100.7
居民家庭恩格尔系数(%)	Engel's Coefficient of Households (%)	27.7	26.9	24.7	23.8	25.3	28.5	28.3	27.4	
人均住房建筑面积(平方米)	Per Capita Floor Space of Houses (sq.m)	43.03	44.50	44.89	46.26	47.19	47.08	49.61	50.16	101.1

5-3 全市居民家庭基本情况(2015-2022年)
BASIC DATA ON HOUSEHOLDS OF THE WHOLE CITY (2015-2022)

项　　目	Item	2015	2016	2017	2018	2019	2020	2021	2022
平均每户常住人口 (人)	Average Permanent Population Per Household (person)	2.8	2.7	2.7	2.8	2.8	2.8	2.8	2.8
平均每户就业人口数 (人)	Average Employee Per Household (person)	1.4	1.3	1.3	1.3	1.3	1.2	1.3	1.2
平均每一就业者负担人数 (人)	Average Dependents Per Employee (person)	1.6	1.6	1.6	1.6	1.7	1.7	1.7	1.7
人均可支配收入 (元)	Per Capita Disposable Income (yuan)	48458	52530	57230	62361	67756	69434	75002	77415
人均消费支出 (元)	Per Capita Consumption Expenditure (yuan)	33803	35416	37425	39843	43038	38903	43640	42683

5-4 全市居民家庭人均收支情况(2015-2022年)
PER CAPITA INCOME AND CONSUMPTION EXPENDITURE OF HOUSEHOLDS OF THE WHOLE CITY (2015-2022)

单位：元 (yuan)

项目	Item	2015	2016	2017	2018	2019	2020	2021	2022	2022年为2021年% 2022 as % of 2021
人均可支配收入	**Per Capita Disposable Income**	**48458**	**52530**	**57230**	**62361**	**67756**	**69434**	**75002**	**77415**	**103.2**
工资性收入	Wage Income	30241	33114	35217	37687	41214	41439	45675	47758	104.6
经营净收入	Net Business Income	1421	1396	1408	1201	1201	812	940	903	96.1
财产净收入	Net Property Income	7499	8230	9306	10612	11257	11789	12460	12418	99.7
转移净收入	Net Transfer Income	9297	9790	11299	12861	14084	15394	15927	16336	102.6
人均消费支出	**Per Capita Consumption Expenditure**	**33803**	**35416**	**37425**	**39843**	**43038**	**38903**	**43640**	**42683**	**97.8**
食品烟酒	Food, Tobacco and Liquor	7584	7609	7549	8065	8489	8374	9307	9223	99.1
衣着	Clothing	2426	2433	2238	2176	2230	1804	2104	1861	88.5
居住	Housing	10350	11188	12295	14110	15751	15711	16847	17170	101.9
生活用品及服务	Living Articles and Services	2098	2327	2492	2372	2387	2146	2560	2193	85.7
交通通信	Transportation and Communication	4490	4702	5034	4767	4979	3789	4227	4129	97.7
教育文化娱乐	Education, Cultural and Entertainment	3635	3687	3917	3999	4311	2766	3348	3008	89.8
医疗保健	Healthcare	2229	2456	2900	3275	3740	3513	4285	3982	92.9
其他用品及服务	Other Supplies and Services	991	1015	1000	1079	1151	800	962	1117	116.1

注：2022年全市居民人均可支配收入实际增长1.4%。
Note: Real growth rate of the per capita disposable income of residents of the whole city in 2022 is 1.4%.

5-5 全市居民人均可支配收入(按收入水平分)(2015-2022年)
PER CAPITA DISPOSABLE INCOME OF RESIDENTS OF THE WHOLE CITY (BY INCOME LEVEL)(2015-2022)

单位：元 (yuan)

组别	Group	2015	2016	2017	2018	2019	2020	2021	2022
低收入户 (20%)	Low income 20%	18343	20204	22170	23926	25723	25394	27057	27997
中低收入户 (20%)	Medium-low income 20%	32968	36277	38452	41886	44971	44855	50226	51844
中等收入户 (20%)	Medium income 20%	45239	49342	53023	57864	62596	63969	70453	72830
中高收入户 (20%)	Medium-high income 20%	60627	65555	71451	77910	85170	88026	94678	97129
高收入户 (20%)	High income 20%	99621	105425	116018	126970	139298	145915	157816	162630

5-6 全市居民家庭每百户主要耐用消费品拥有量(2022年)
NUMBER OF MAIN DURABLE CONSUMER GOODS PER 100 HOUSEHOLDS OF THE WHOLE CITY(2022)

项　　目		Item		全市居民 Residents	城镇居民 Urban Residents	农村居民 Rural Residents
家用汽车	(辆)	Household Cars	(unit)	60	60	57
摩托车	(辆)	Motorcycles	(unit)	5	4	10
助力车	(台)	Powered Bicycles	(unit)	30	22	87
洗衣机	(台)	Washing Machines	(unit)	102	101	108
电冰箱(柜)	(台)	Refrigerators	(unit)	105	103	118
微波炉	(台)	Microwave Ovens	(unit)	78	79	73
彩色电视机	(台)	Color TV Sets	(unit)	124	122	136
空调	(台)	Air Conditioners	(unit)	208	206	225
热水器	(台)	Water Heaters	(unit)	101	100	106
烤箱	(台)	Ovens	(unit)	19	19	18
洗碗机	(台)	Dishwashers	(unit)	5	5	1
排油烟机	(台)	Smoke Exhaust Ventilators	(unit)	97	97	96
固定电话	(线)	Fixed-line Telephones	(unit)	34	35	30
移动电话	(部)	Mobile Phones	(unit)	241	237	268
计算机	(台)	Computers	(unit)	86	90	62
照相机	(台)	Cameras	(unit)	34	37	13
乐器	(架)	Musical Instruments	(unit)	14	15	5
健身器材	(台)	Fitness Equipment	(unit)	10	9	12
空气净化器（含新风系统）	(台)	Air Purifiers (with Fresh Air System)	(unit)	39	43	12
地面清洁电器	(台)	Gound Cleaning Appliances	(unit)	34	36	19

5-7 全市居民家庭居住构成情况(2022年)
COMPOSITION OF HOUSING CONDITIONS FOR HOUSEHOLDS OF THE WHOLE CITY (2022)

单位：% (%)

项　　目	Item	全市居民 Residents	城镇居民 Urban Residents	农村居民 Rural Residents
居住空间样式	**Style of Living Space**	**100.0**	**100.0**	**100.0**
单栋楼房占比重	Individual Storied Buildings	3.8	2.7	11.5
单栋平房占比重	Individual Single-storey Buildings	16.5	7.8	81.6
四居室及以上单元房占比重	Four-bedroom and above Flat	1.6	1.8	
三居室单元房占比重	Three-bedroom Flat	19.2	21.6	1.1
二居室单元房占比重	Two-bedroom Flat	47.1	53.0	3.1
一居室单元房占比重	One-bedroom Flat	8.2	9.0	1.8
筒子楼或连片平房占比重	Tube-shaped Apartment or Closely Grouped Single-storey Buildings	3.7	4.1	0.8
其他占比重	Others			
房屋来源	**Housing Source**	**100.0**	**100.0**	**100.0**
租赁公房占比重	Public Houses Rented	6.0	6.8	
租赁私房占比重	Private Houses Rented	5.7	6.1	3.1
自建住房占比重	Self-built Houses	19.2	9.7	90.1
购买商品房占比重	Purchased Commercial Houses	28.3	32.1	0.3
购买房改住房占比重	Purchased Houses from Housing Reform	20.3	22.9	0.3
购买保障性住房占比重	Purchased Indemnificatory Housing	4.7	5.4	
拆迁安置房占比重	Resettlement Housing	12.4	13.5	4.2
继承或获赠住房占比重	Housing under Inheritance or Donation	0.8	0.9	0.3
免费借用房占比重	Free Borrowed Houses	1.4	1.4	0.9
雇主提供免费住房占比重	Free Housing Supplied by Employers	0.5	0.5	0.6
其他来源占比重	Others	0.7	0.8	0.1
取水位置	**Water-taking Location**	**100.0**	**100.0**	**100.0**
住宅内管道取水	Water-taking through Pipes in the House	96.8	97.8	88.7
住宅内其他方式取水	Water-taking by Other Means in the House	0.4	0.3	1.2
院内管道取水	Water-taking through Pipes in the Yard	2.2	1.3	9.1
院内其他方式取水	Water-taking by Other Means in the Yard	0.3	0.3	0.5
其他位置取水	Water-taking from Other Locations	0.3	0.3	0.6
饮用水来源情况	**Source of Drinking Water**	**100.0**	**100.0**	**100.0**
经过净化处理的自来水占比重	Tap Water via Purification Treatment	93.2	96.1	71.3
受保护的井水和泉水占比重	Protected Well Water and Spring Water	5.4	2.4	27.4
不受保护的井水和泉水占比重	Unprotected Well Water and Spring Water			

5-7 续表 continued

单位：% (%)

项　目	Item	全市居民 Residents	城镇居民 Urban Residents	农村居民 Rural Residents
江河湖泊水占比重	Water from Rivers and Lakes			
收集雨水占比重	Collecting Rainwater			
桶装水占比重	Barreled Water	1.4	1.5	1.1
其他占比重	Others	0.1		0.1
住户厕所类型	**Toilet Type of Households**	**100.0**	**100.0**	**100.0**
水冲式卫生厕所占比重	Water-flushing Sanitary Toilets	99.2	99.8	94.5
卫生旱厕占比重	Sanitary Pit Toilet	0.4	0.1	2.1
普通旱厕占比重	Common Pit Toilet	0.4	0.1	3.4
住户厕所使用情况	**Toilet Use Conditions of Households**	**100.0**	**100.0**	**100.0**
本住户独用占比重	Exclusive Use by One Household	96.4	96.3	97.2
几户合用占比重	One Toilet Shared by Several Households	1.4	1.3	2.1
公用厕所占比重	Communal Toilet	2.2	2.4	0.7
主要炊用能源状况	**Main Cooking Energy Conditions**	**100.0**	**100.0**	**100.0**
柴草占比重	Firewood			0.2
煤炭占比重	Coal			
罐装液化石油气占比重	Bottled LPG	18.6	12.0	67.7
管道液化石油气占比重	Pipeline LPG	0.2	0.2	0.1
管道煤气占比重	Pipeline Gas			
管道天然气占比重	Pipeline Natural Gas	79.4	86.2	28.4
电占比重	Electricity	1.7	1.5	3.0
燃料用油占比重	Oil Used in Fuel			
沼气占比重	Marsh Gas	0.1		0.5
其他占比重	Others			
无炊用行为占比重	Non-cooking Behaviors	0.1	0.1	0.2
住宅外道路路面状况	**Pavement Conditions of Roads Outside Houses**	**100.0**	**100.0**	**100.0**
水泥或柏油路面的户数占比重	Cement or Tar-coated Surface	98.7	98.8	97.6
沙石或石板等硬质路面的户数占比重	Hard Surface Paved with Sand and Stones or Slates	1.2	1.0	2.3
其他路面的户数占比重	Other Pavements	0.1	0.1	0.1

5-8 全市居民家庭主要食品人均消费量(2022年)
PER CAPITA CONSUMPTION OF MAJOR FOODS OF HOUSEHOLDS OF THE WHOLE CITY (2022)

单位：公斤 (kg)

项　目	Item	全市居民 Residents	城镇居民 Urban Residents	农村居民 Rural Residents
粮　食	Grain	94.5	91.3	114.5
豆　类	Beans	9.4	9.3	10.2
蔬菜及菜制品	Vegetables and Vegetable Products	109.9	110.5	106.0
植物油	Vegetable Oil	6.0	5.7	8.0
猪　肉	Pork	17.5	17.1	20.6
牛羊肉	Beef and Mutton	6.7	6.9	5.8
禽　类	Poultry	6.9	7.0	6.1
蛋类及其制品	Eggs and Egg Products	16.3	16.1	17.7
奶及奶制品	Milk and Dairy Products	22.0	23.3	13.9
水产品	Aquatic Products	9.4	9.7	7.7
食　糖	Sugar	0.9	0.9	1.0

5-9 城镇居民家庭生活基本情况(1978-2022年) BASIC LIVING CONDITIONS OF URBAN HOUSEHOLDS (1978-2022)

年份 Year	人均可支配收入(元) Per Capita Disposable Income (yuan)	人均可支配收入实际增长(%) Real Growth Rate of Per Capita Disposable Income (%)	人均消费支出(元) Per Capita Consumption Expenditure (yuan)	#食品烟酒 Food, Tobacco and Liquor	城镇居民家庭恩格尔系数(%) Engel Coefficient of Urban Households (%)	每一城镇就业者负担人数(人) Dependents Per Urban Employee (person)	城镇居民人均住房建筑面积(平方米) Per Capita Floor Space of Houses in Urban Areas (sq.m)
1978	365		360	211	58.7	1.86	6.70
1979	415	11.6	409	237	57.9	1.83	6.73
1980	501	14.0	490	271	55.3	1.80	7.06
1981	555	9.3	511	295	57.7	1.72	7.48
1982	561	-0.7	535	318	59.3	1.66	7.92
1983	591	4.7	574	338	58.8	1.65	8.37
1984	694	15.0	667	379	56.8	1.63	8.72
1985	908	11.2	923	467	50.6	1.66	9.09
1986	1068	10.1	1067	543	50.9	1.66	9.20
1987	1182	1.9	1148	605	52.7	1.65	9.75
1988	1437	1.0	1456	743	51.1	1.71	10.30
1989	1597	-5.2	1520	841	55.3	1.52	10.74
1990	1902	13.0	1646	892	54.2	1.52	11.17
1991	2170	2.0	1748	955	54.7	1.47	11.64
1992	2556	7.2	2135	1126	52.8	1.43	12.09
1993	3547	16.6	2940	1405	47.8	1.42	12.45
1994	5085	14.8	4134	1919	46.4	1.41	12.85
1995	6235	4.5	5020	2436	48.5	1.41	13.34
1996	7332	5.4	5730	2672	46.6	1.41	13.82
1997	7813	1.2	6532	2854	43.7	1.43	14.36
1998	8536	6.7	7069	2906	41.1	1.40	14.96
1999	9322	8.5	7712	3030	39.3	1.41	15.88
2000	10590	9.8	8866	3174	35.8	1.41	16.75
2001	11939	9.3	9443	3352	35.5	1.39	17.62
2002	12949	10.5	11050	3558	32.2	1.41	19.22
2003	14535	12.0	12122	3627	29.9	1.39	19.71
2004	16502	12.4	13487	4026	29.9	1.44	21.49
2005	18775	12.1	14851	4363	29.4	1.39	22.03
2006	21415	13.1	16869	4692	27.8	1.40	23.65
2007	23752	8.3	17682	5058	28.6	1.40	24.77
2008	26918	7.8	19253	5684	29.5	1.40	26.90
2009	29329	10.7	21230	6125	28.9	1.40	27.69
2010	32132	7.0	23999	6437	26.8	1.40	28.94
2011	36365	7.2	26467	6610	25.0	1.50	29.38
2012	40306	7.3	28949	7123	24.6	1.40	29.26
2013	44564	7.1	31632	7515	23.8	1.50	31.31
2014	48532	7.2	33717	8007	23.7	1.50	31.54
2015	52859	7.0	36642	8091	22.1	1.50	31.69
2016	57275	6.9	38256	8070	21.1	1.56	32.38
2017	62406	7.0	40346	8003	19.8	1.58	32.56
2018	67990	6.2	42926	8577	20.0	1.61	33.08
2019	73849	6.2	46358	8951	19.3	1.63	32.54
2020	75602	0.7	41726	8751	21.0	1.68	32.60
2021	81518	6.6	46776	9720	20.8	1.69	33.40
2022	84023	1.3	45617	9645	21.1	1.71	33.63

5-10 城镇居民家庭基本情况(2015-2022年)
BASIC DATA ON URBAN HOUSEHOLDS (2015-2022)

项 目	Item	2015	2016	2017	2018	2019	2020	2021	2022
平均每户常住人口 （人）	Average Permanent Population Per Household (person)	2.7	2.6	2.6	2.8	2.7	2.7	2.7	2.7
平均每户就业人口数 （人）	Average Employee Per Household (person)	1.3	1.3	1.2	1.2	1.2	1.1	1.2	1.1
平均每一就业者负担人数 （人）	Average Dependents Per Employee (person)	1.5	1.6	1.6	1.6	1.6	1.7	1.7	1.7
人均可支配收入 （元）	Per Capita Disposable Income (yuan)	52859	57275	62406	67990	73849	75602	81518	84023
人均消费支出 （元）	Per Capita Consumption Expenditure (yuan)	36642	38256	40346	42926	46358	41726	46776	45617

5-11 城镇居民家庭人均收支情况(2015-2022年)
PER CAPITA INCOME AND CONSUMPTION EXPENDITURE OF URBAN HOUSEHOLDS (2015-2022)

单位：元 (yuan)

项 目	Item	2015	2016	2017	2018	2019	2020	2021	2022	2022年为2021年% 2022 as % of 2021
人均可支配收入	**Per Capita Disposable Income**	**52859**	**57275**	**62406**	**67990**	**73849**	**75602**	**81518**	**84023**	**103.1**
工资性收入	Wage Income	32568	35701	37883	40489	44327	44620	49150	51295	104.4
经营净收入	Net Business Income	1337	1292	1293	1073	1034	685	795	756	95.1
财产净收入	Net Property Income	8492	9310	10520	11983	12690	13152	13869	13791	99.4
转移净收入	Net Transfer Income	10462	10972	12710	14445	15798	17145	17704	18181	102.7
人均消费支出	**Per Capita Consumption Expenditure**	**36642**	**38256**	**40346**	**42926**	**46358**	**41726**	**46776**	**45617**	**97.5**
食品烟酒	Food, Tobacco and Liquor	8091	8070	8003	8577	8951	8751	9720	9645	99.2
衣 着	Clothing	2651	2643	2429	2346	2391	1924	2235	1977	88.5
居 住	Housing	11252	12128	13347	15391	17235	17163	18382	18605	101.2
生活用品及服务	Living Articles and Services	2273	2511	2633	2496	2569	2307	2745	2322	84.6
交通通信	Transportation and Communication	4860	5078	5396	5033	5229	3925	4358	4261	97.8
教育文化娱乐	Education, Cultural and Entertainment	4028	4055	4325	4402	4738	3021	3665	3272	89.3
医疗保健	Healthcare	2370	2630	3088	3476	3974	3755	4610	4303	93.3
其他用品及服务	Other Supplies and Services	1117	1141	1125	1205	1271	880	1061	1232	116.1

注：2022年城镇居民人均可支配收入实际增长1.3%。
Note: Real growth rate of the per capita disposable income of urban residents in 2022 is 1.3%.

5-12 城镇居民家庭每百户主要耐用消费品拥有量(1978-2022年)
NUMBER OF MAIN DURABLE CONSUMER GOODS PER 100 URBAN HOUSEHOLDS (1978-2022)

年份 Year	热水器 (台) Water Heaters (unit)	洗衣机 (台) Washing Machines (unit)	彩色电视机 (台) Color TV Sets (unit)	电冰箱 (台) Refrige-rators (unit)	照相机 (台) Cameras (unit)	空调 (台) Air Conditioners (unit)	计算机 (台) Computers (unit)	移动电话 (部) Mobile Phones (unit)	家用汽车 (辆) Household Cars (unit)
1978					8				
1979		…			10				
1980		2		…	11				
1981		12	2	2	13				
1982		19	2	3	17				
1983		29	4	7	21				
1984		42	8	15	29				
1985		58	32	42	35				
1986		76	51	62	47				
1987		83	58	72	56				
1988		86	70	81	60				
1989		90	81	89	62				
1990		93	91	96	67				
1991		93	97	102	73	…			
1992	17	96	101	101	77	1			
1993	23	100	107	101	82	2			
1994	39	103	112	104	85	5			
1995	45	100	114	104	87	12			
1996	52	101	119	105	87	14			
1997	58	101	124	104	88	27	12	1	1
1998	65	102	133	105	95	34	15	3	1
1999	67	100	141	103	95	50	24	13	3
2000	74	103	146	107	96	70	32	28	3
2001	78	102	149	107	101	90	45	62	3
2002	84	99	148	102	100	107	56	94	4
2003	85	99	147	100	103	119	68	134	7
2004	94	102	151	103	100	136	79	165	13
2005	97	105	153	104	109	147	89	190	14
2006	98	107	155	105	113	157	96	206	18
2007	99	102	147	108	99	157	92	207	20
2008	95	99	134	103	82	152	86	191	23
2009	98	100	138	104	89	163	97	213	30
2010	98	100	140	103	92	169	104	221	34
2011	97	100	138	103	85	171	104	215	38
2012	99	101	141	103	90	179	112	226	42
2013	99	100	140	103	85	180	110	225	43
2014	99	101	141	104	88	186	114	229	45
2015	93	96	130	98	65	161	107	220	47
2016	93	95	127	97	58	166	103	223	49
2017	92	95	126	97	58	168	105	224	50
2018	99	100	124	103	46	179	100	226	52
2019	99	101	125	103	47	182	101	230	53
2020	100	101	125	104	47	187	96	232	54
2021	100	101	122	103	36	205	91	237	60
2022	100	101	122	103	37	206	90	237	60

5-13 农村居民家庭生活基本情况(1978-2022年)
BASIC LIVING CONDITIONS OF RURAL HOUSEHOLDS (1978-2022)

年份 Year	人均可支配收入(元) Per Capita Disposable Income (yuan)	人均可支配收入实际增长(%) Real Growth Rate of Per Capita Disposable Income (%)	人均消费支出(元) Per Capita Consumption Expenditure (yuan)	#食品烟酒 Food, Tobacco and Liquor	农村居民家庭恩格尔系数(%) Engel Coefficient of Rural Households (%)	每一农村劳动力负担人数(人) Dependents Per Rural Labor Force (person)	农村居民人均住房面积(平方米) Per Capita Living Space of Rural Residents (sq.m)
1978	225		185	117	63.2	2.15	9.20
1979	250	9.2	205	131	63.9	2.16	9.67
1980	290	9.6	253	138	54.5	2.13	10.09
1981	351	19.2	313	164	52.4	2.14	12.35
1982	433	21.2	362	190	52.5	1.97	13.01
1983	519	19.5	384	194	50.5	1.82	14.24
1984	664	25.2	435	223	51.3	1.79	14.22
1985	775	-0.8	510	240	47.1	1.64	16.48
1986	823	-0.6	644	292	45.3	1.66	17.41
1987	916	2.5	706	341	48.4	1.64	18.38
1988	1063	-3.7	883	408	46.2	1.63	19.23
1989	1231	-1.2	976	484	49.6	1.62	20.09
1990	1297	-0.04	981	497	50.7	1.61	20.62
1991	1422	-2.0	1100	537	48.8	1.59	21.92
1992	1572	0.6	1149	559	48.7	1.58	22.67
1993	1883	0.7	1255	587	46.8	1.51	23.70
1994	2401	2.1	1584	780	49.2	1.49	24.42
1995	3224	14.5	2336	1158	49.6	1.47	24.74
1996	3562	-1.0	2565	1191	46.4	1.45	25.74
1997	3662	-2.4	2693	1202	44.7	1.48	27.39
1998	3932	4.9	2873	1215	42.3	1.44	27.64
1999	4183	5.8	3123	1226	39.3	1.43	28.65
2000	4533	4.7	3426	1286	37.5	1.51	28.91
2001	4921	5.3	3553	1222	34.4	1.52	31.01
2002	5259	8.9	3733	1239	33.2	1.48	32.58
2003	5429	3.0	4149	1260	30.4	1.45	33.95
2004	5948	8.5	4619	1406	30.4	1.46	34.21
2005	7041	16.7	5318	1611	30.3	1.45	36.94
2006	7888	11.0	5728	1731	30.2	1.42	39.10
2007	8948	10.7	6403	1924	30.0	1.40	39.54
2008	10052	6.9	7289	2189	30.0	1.40	39.40
2009	10942	10.6	8904	2365	26.6	1.39	39.42
2010	12368	10.4	9262	2460	26.6	1.39	40.62
2011	13742	5.2	11086	2895	26.1	1.38	48.63
2012	15365	8.2	11888	3197	26.9	1.40	49.08
2013	17101	7.7	13564	3786	27.9	1.49	51.35
2014	18867	8.6	14535	4048	27.9	1.50	52.42
2015	20569	7.1	15811	4372	27.7	1.60	43.03
2016	22310	7.0	17329	4667	26.9	1.62	44.50
2017	24240	6.7	18810	4653	24.7	1.68	44.89
2018	26490	6.6	20195	4802	23.8	1.70	46.26
2019	28928	6.7	21881	5542	25.3	1.76	47.19
2020	30126	2.4	20913	5968	28.5	1.86	47.08
2021	33303	9.3	23574	6664	28.3	1.75	49.61
2022	34754	2.6	23745	6503	27.4	1.76	50.16

5-14　农村居民家庭基本情况(2015-2022年)
BASIC DATA ON RURAL HOUSEHOLDS (2015-2022)

项目	Item	2015	2016	2017	2018	2019	2020	2021	2022
平均每户常住人口 (人)	Average Permanent Population Per Household (person)	2.9	3.0	2.9	3.1	3.0	3.0	3.1	3.1
平均每户整半劳动力 (人)	Average Full/Semi Labor Force Per Household (person)	2.3	2.4	2.4	2.3	2.4	2.5	2.5	2.5
平均每一劳动力负担人口 (人)	Average Dependents Per Labor Force (person)	1.6	1.6	1.7	1.7	1.8	1.9	1.8	1.8
人均住房面积 (平方米)	Per Capita Living Space (sq.m)	43.03	44.50	44.89	46.26	47.19	47.08	49.61	50.16
人均可支配收入 (元)	Per Capita Disposable Income (yuan)	20569	22310	24240	26490	28928	30126	33303	34754
人均消费支出 (元)	Per Capita Consumption Expenditure (yuan)	15811	17329	18810	20195	21881	20913	23574	23745
农村居民家庭恩格尔系数 (%)	Engel Coefficient of Rural Households (%)	27.7	26.9	24.7	23.8	25.3	28.5	28.3	27.4

5-15　农村居民家庭人均收支情况(2015-2022年)
PER CAPITA INCOME AND CONSUMPTION EXPENDITURE OF RURAL HOUSEHOLDS (2015-2022)

单位：元　　(yuan)

项目	Item	2015	2016	2017	2018	2019	2020	2021	2022	2022年为2021年% 2022 as % of 2021
人均可支配收入	**Per Capita Disposable Income**	**20569**	**22310**	**24240**	**26490**	**28928**	**30126**	**33303**	**34754**	**104.4**
工资性收入	Wage Income	15491	16637	18223	19827	21376	21174	23434	24928	106.4
经营净收入	Net Business Income	1959	2062	2140	2021	2262	1613	1874	1850	98.7
财产净收入	Net Property Income	1204	1350	1570	1877	2127	3103	3443	3556	103.3
转移净收入	Net Transfer Income	1915	2260	2307	2765	3163	4236	4552	4420	97.1
人均消费支出	**Per Capita Consumption Expenditure**	**15811**	**17329**	**18810**	**20195**	**21881**	**20913**	**23574**	**23745**	**100.7**
食品烟酒	Food, Tobacco and Liquor	4372	4667	4653	4802	5542	5968	6664	6503	97.6
衣　着	Clothing	996	1095	1025	1088	1200	1036	1265	1108	87.6
居　住	Housing	4636	5199	5588	5951	6298	6453	7020	7910	112.7
生活用品及服务	Living Articles and Services	993	1157	1595	1580	1230	1121	1377	1360	98.8
交通通信	Transportation and Communication	2140	2306	2730	3078	3385	2924	3388	3282	96.9
教育文化娱乐	Education, Cultural and Entertainment	1145	1342	1314	1436	1587	1143	1317	1307	99.2
医疗保健	Healthcare	1336	1347	1699	1992	2247	1973	2212	1900	85.9
其他用品及服务	Other Supplies and Services	193	217	206	268	392	295	331	375	113.3

注：2022年农村居民人均可支配收入实际增长2.6%。
Note: Real growth rate of the per capita disposable income of rural residents in 2022 is 2.6%.

5-16 农村居民家庭每百户主要耐用消费品拥有量(1985-2022年)
NUMBER OF MAIN DURABLE CONSUMER GOODS PER 100 RURAL HOUSEHOLDS (1985-2022)

年份 Year	洗衣机 (台) Washing Machines (unit)	彩色电视机 (台) Color TV Sets (unit)	电冰箱 (台) Refrige-rators (unit)	照相机 (台) Cameras (unit)	空调 (台) Air Conditioners (unit)	计算机 (台) Computers (unit)	移动电话 (部) Mobile Phones (unit)	家用汽车 (辆) Household Cars (unit)
1985	23	7	2	2				
1986	39	12	5	4				
1987	48	15	9	5				
1988	56	20	14	7				
1989	61	25	19	8				
1990	63	29	23	8				
1991	69	42	36	11				
1992	73	46	40	14				
1993	76	56	47	15				
1994	80	65	53	17	1			
1995	81	74	63	21	2			
1996	83	79	67	21	2			
1997	84	85	72	25	3			
1998	85	92	75	26	5			
1999	86	101	81	29	9			
2000	85	107	84	26	20	7	14	3
2001	91	112	86	29	27	12	30	5
2002	94	116	91	32	35	16	52	6
2003	94	116	94	32	39	22	77	6
2004	96	119	96	35	47	27	102	8
2005	97	129	100	37	63	36	139	10
2006	97	131	100	38	72	41	161	10
2007	99	134	104	37	78	46	182	11
2008	101	137	104	39	89	52	201	12
2009	101	138	105	42	98	58	212	12
2010	103	139	107	42	107	64	224	16
2011	99	134	104	37	108	63	231	19
2012	99	136	103	37	113	67	235	21
2013	95	132	102	32	123	74	221	34
2014	97	132	103	32	127	75	222	35
2015	90	131	95	21	118	69	230	32
2016	94	138	101	20	135	74	243	38
2017	94	138	103	21	141	74	244	38
2018	100	136	111	13	168	66	248	45
2019	102	136	112	12	180	65	249	45
2020	103	137	113	12	185	67	251	47
2021	108	135	118	12	225	62	268	56
2022	108	136	118	13	225	62	268	57

5-17 农村居民家庭人均粮食收支情况(2015-2022年)
PER CAPITA GRAIN BALANCE OF RURAL HOUSEHOLDS(2015-2022)

单位：公斤 (kg)

项目	Item	2015	2016	2017	2018	2019	2020	2021	2022
年内粮食收入实物量	**Grain Collected in the Year**	**226.9**	**219.2**	**174.1**	**145.0**	**130.1**	**147.4**	**159.6**	**134.5**
家庭经营生产	Household-based Production	139.6	132.2	91.7	48.8	35.2	41.4	39.9	34.6
购买	Purchased	87.3	87.0	82.4	96.2	94.9	106.0	119.7	99.9
年内粮食消费量	**Grain Consumed in the Year**	**105.6**	**102.1**	**96.7**	**110.2**	**107.2**	**120.1**	**135.0**	**114.5**
#稻谷	Rice	33.4	32.0	29.3	34.0	28.8	32.1	37.5	30.9
小麦	Wheat	57.3	54.7	52.5	58.6	59.4	67.3	76.8	63.9
年内粮食出售量	**Grain Sold in the Year**	**99.6**	**102.8**	**92.3**	**79.2**	**43.0**	**33.8**	**54.5**	**45.5**
#出售谷物	Cereal Sold	99.1	102.6	92.3	79.1	42.9	33.7	54.5	45.5
#小麦	Wheat	19.8	20.0	9.6	3.6	2.2	0.5	8.2	2.2

主要统计指标解释

可支配收入 指调查户在调查期内获得的、可用于最终消费支出和储蓄的总和，即调查户可以用来自由支配的收入。可支配收入既包括现金，也包括实物收入。按照收入的来源，可支配收入包含四项，分别为：工资性收入、经营净收入、财产净收入和转移净收入。计算公式为：

可支配收入＝工资性收入+经营净收入+财产净收入+转移净收入

其中：经营净收入=经营收入-经营费用-生产性固定资产折旧-生产税

财产净收入=财产性收入-财产性支出

转移净收入=转移性收入-转移性支出

工资性收入 指就业人员通过各种途径得到的全部劳动报酬和各种福利，包括受雇于单位或个人、从事各种自由职业、兼职和零星劳动得到的全部劳动报酬和福利。

经营净收入 指住户或住户成员从事生产经营活动所获得的净收入，是全部经营收入中扣除经营费用、生产性固定资产折旧和生产税之后得到的净收入。计算公式为：

经营净收入=经营收入-经营费用-生产性固定资产折旧-生产税

财产净收入 指住户或住户成员将其所拥有的金融资产、住房等非金融资产和自然资源交由其他机构单位、住户或个人支配而获得的回报并扣除相关的费用之后得到的净收入。财产净收入不包括转让资产所有权的溢价所得，计入“非收入所得”。

转移净收入 指国家、单位、社会团体对住户的各种经常性转移支付和住户之间的经常性收入转移，在扣减调查户对国家、单位、住户或者个人的经常性或义务性转移支付后的净收入。

计算公式为：转移净收入=转移性收入-转移性支出

转移性收入 指国家、单位、社会团体对住户的各种经常性转移支付和住户之间的经常性收入转移。包括养老金或退休金、社会救济和补助、政策性生产补贴、政策性生活补贴、救灾款、经常性捐赠和赔偿、报销医疗费、住户之间的赡养收入，以及本住户非常住成员寄回带回的收入等。转移性收入不包括住户之间的实物馈赠。

转移性支出 指调查户对国家、单位、住户或个人的经常性或义务性转移支付。包括缴纳的税款、各项社会保障支出、赡养支出、经常性捐赠和赔偿支出以及其他经常转移支出等。

消费支出 指住户用于满足家庭日常生活消费需要的全部支出，包括用于消费品的支出和用于服务性消费的支出。根据用途不同，消费支出可划分为食品烟酒、衣着、居住、生活用品及服务、交通通信、教育文化娱乐、医疗保健、其他用品及服务八大类。根据来源不同，消费支出可划分为现金消费支出、实物消费支出（含自产自用、来自单位或雇主、来自政府和其他社会组织）。

农村居民家庭整半劳动力 指农村常住居民家庭成员中有劳动能力并经常参加实际劳动的人员，是生产的基本要素指标之一，是发展生产增加农民家庭收入的重要源泉。按规定，农村男18周岁至50周岁、女18周岁至45周岁为整劳动力；男16周岁至17周岁、51周岁至60周岁，女16周岁至17周岁、46周岁至55周岁为半劳动力。农民家庭整半劳动力既包括在上述规定劳动年龄内和在劳动年龄以外有劳动能力并经常参加实际劳动的男女整半劳动力，也包括农民家庭常住人员中属于职工的劳动力，但不包括在劳动年龄内已丧失劳动能力的人员。

现住房总建筑面积 指调查户现住房的总建筑面积。现住房计算总建筑面积时以房屋产权证或租赁证为准，建筑面积也可按使用面积×1.333计算得出，应扣除住房中专门用于出租的建筑面积。

恩格尔系数 随着家庭和个人收入增加，收入中用于食品方面的支出比例将逐渐减小，这一定律被称为恩格尔定律，反映这一定律的系数被称为恩格尔系数。计算公式为：

$$\text{恩格尔系数}=\frac{\text{食品支出总额}}{\text{家庭或个人消费支出总额}}\times 100\%$$

按收入水平分组 指将住户调查样本按人均可支配收入从低到高排队分成五等份，即低收入组、中低收入组、中等收入组、中高收入组和高收入组五部分，各组的户数均占总户数的 20%。

Explanatory Notes on Main Statistical Indicators

Disposable Income refers to the total income at the disposal of sampled households gained during the survey, which can be used for final consumption expenditure and savings. Disposable income includes cash and income in kind. By income source, disposable income can be divided into 4 types, namely wage income, net business income, net property income and net transfer income. The following formula is used:

Disposable Income = wage income + net business income + net property income + net transfer income

Of which: Net business income = business income - business expense - depreciation of productive fixed assets - production tax

Net property income = property income - property expenditure

Net transfer income = transfer income - transfer expenditure

Wage Income refers to all payments of labor and various welfares earned by employed persons through all channels, including all payments of labor and welfare gained from institutional or individual employers, various freelance work, part-time job, and scattered work.

Net Business Income refers to the net income of a family or family members from productive and operating activities. It is the net income of all operating income deducting business expense, depreciation of productive fixed assets and production tax. The following formula is used:

Net business income = business income - business expense - depreciation of productive fixed assets - production tax

Net Property Income refers to the net income of a family or family members earned by deducting relevant expenses from returns of their financial assets, non-financial assets (such as house) and natural resource delivered to other institutions, families or individuals for management. Net property income does not include income from premium of property ownership transfer and it shall be regarded as non-revenue proceeds.

Net Transfer Income refers to net income after deducting recurrent or compulsory transfer payment of sampled households to the nation, institutions, households or individuals from various recurrent transfer payments by the nation, institutions, social groups to households and recurrent income transfer among households.

The following formula is used: Net transfer income = transfer income - transfer expenditure

Transfer Income refers to various recurrent transfer payment from the nation, institutions and social groups to households, along with recurrent income transfer among households, including retirement pension, social relief and allowance, policy production subsidiary, policy living subsidiary, disaster relief fund, recurrent donation and compensations, medical expense reimbursement, alimony income among households and income mailed or brought by non-permanent members of such household, etc. Transfer income does not include physical donation among households.

Transfer Expenditure refers to the recurrent or compulsory transfer payment made by the sampled households to the nation, institutions, households or individuals, including tax payment, various social security expenditures, alimony expenditure, recurrent donation and compensation expenditure and other recurrent transfer expenditure, etc.

Consumption Expenditure refers to total expenditures of households for consumption in daily life, including expenditures on consumer goods and services. By usage, it includes 8 categories, i.e. expenditures on food, tobacco and liquor, clothing, housing, living articles and services, transportation and communication, educational, cultural and recreational services, healthcare and medical services, and other goods and services. By source, it includes cash consumption and physical consumption (including self-produced and self-used products and those from institutions or employers, government and other social organizations).

Full/Semi Labor Force in Rural Households refers to persons among permanent family members in rural households who are capable of working and work frequently. This is one of the indicators for basic production elements, and an important source for production development and increase of farmer's household income. As stated in regulations, rural males aged 18-50 and females aged 18-45 are full labor force. Males aged 16-17 and 51-60 and females aged 16-17 and 46-55 are semi labor force. Full/Semi Labor Force in Rural Households includes the male and female full/semi labor force within the above-mentioned range age as well as those beyond such range of ages who are capable of working and work frequently; also include labor force among permanent members in rural households who are employees. But it excludes persons who are within the range of labor age but incapable of working.

Total Building Area of Current Houses refers to the total building area of house resided by the surveyed households, which is calculated on the basis of the property ownership certificate or lease certificate. The building area can also be calculated as the usable floor space multiplied by 1.333, which shall deduct the building area of the house specially used for lease.

Engel Coefficient Along with the increase in household and personal income, a gradually smaller proportion of income is used for purchase of food. This law is called Engel's law, and the coefficient reflecting such law is called Engel's Coefficient. The following formula is used:

$$\text{Engel Coefficient} = \frac{\text{expenditure on food}}{\text{total household or individual consumption expenditure}} \times 100\%$$

Meaning of Income level Grouping Means that households are divided into five groups in a low-to-high order regarding the per capita disposable income. These five groups are the low income, medium-low income, medium income, medium-high income and high income groups. The number of households in each group accounts for 20% of the total.

财政与税收
GOVERNMENT FINANCE AND TAX REVENUES

简要说明

一、主要内容

本章资料包括北京市政府预算收支情况，北京市税收收入情况。

二、有关情况的说明

地方政府预算收支包括一般公共预算收支、政府性基金预算收支、国有资本经营预算收支和社会保险基金预算收支情况，相关数据为决算数。2015 年，财政部门对财政收支统计口径进行了调整，将 11 项政府性基金收入纳入一般公共预算收入。2016 年，根据财政部、国家税务总局《营业税改征增值税试点实施办法》，在全国全面推开营改增试点。因此，自 2019 年起，“营业税”无数据。

2017 年及以前，税收收入情况包括国税收入和地税（费）收入。自 2018 年起，根据机构改革要求，北京市地方税务局与北京市国家税务局合并为国家税务总局北京市税务局，取消“国税收入”和“地税（费）收入”，统一使用税收收入。

Brief Introduction

I. Main Content

Statistics in this chapter include budgetary revenue and expenditure of Beijing Municipal Government and the tax revenues of Beijing.

II. Condition Explanation

Local government budgetary revenue and expenditure includes general public budgetary revenue and expenditure, governmental fund budgetary revenue and expenditure, budgetary revenue and expenditure of state-owned capital operation, and social insurance fund budgetary revenue and expenditure; the relevant data are final accounts. In 2015, the financial department adjusted the statistical caliber of financial revenue and expenditure, and incorporated 11 governmental fund revenues into general public budgetary revenue. In 2016, the pilot program of replacing business tax with value-added tax was implemented in an all-round manner throughout the country in accordance with the *Measures for Implementation of the Pilot Program of Replacing Business Tax with Value-added Tax* issued by the Ministry of Finance and the State Taxation Administration. Therefore, there has been no data on business tax since 2019.

In and before 2017, the statistics for tax revenues included state tax revenues and local tax revenues. Since 2018, according to the institutional reform requirements, Beijing Local Taxation Bureau and Beijing Municipal Bureau of State Taxation have been merged into Beijing Municipal Tax Service of the State Taxation Administration; the state tax revenue and local tax revenue are cancelled and uniformly replaced with tax revenue.

6-1 地方政府预算收入(1978-2022年)

单位：亿元

年 份 Year	一般公共预算收入 General Public Budget Revenue	税收收入 Tax Revenue	#增值税 Value-added Tax	#房产税 Housing Property Tax	#土地增值税 Increment Tax On Land Value	#契税 Deed Tax	#营业税 Business Tax
1978		18.25					
1979		19.41					
1980		21.22					
1981		24.22					
1982		25.81	0.05				
1983		38.03	1.30				
1984		43.91	2.20				1.23
1985		59.99	4.79				10.23
1986		60.83	7.61				13.19
1987		67.77	9.09				15.42
1988		84.04	15.10				21.11
1989		91.09	16.75				25.33
1990		94.23	16.47				27.95
1991		100.58	19.53				30.78
1992		110.54	22.29				35.86
1993		148.19	42.30				52.07
1994		120.53	25.54				45.63
1995		163.40	27.22				64.46
1996		201.32	29.53				81.61
1997	182.32	235.82	32.67				97.54
1998	229.45	272.23	37.58				113.00
1999	281.37	315.10	39.72				128.86
2000	345.00	372.79	45.96				149.05
2001	454.17	475.00	59.00				181.35
2002	533.99	539.87	66.69				227.79
2003	592.54	588.96	75.26	30.79	3.07	20.40	263.69
2004	744.49	726.50	68.88	31.97	1.85	43.68	333.16
2005	919.21	886.13	97.60	35.21	2.38	60.68	383.76
2006	1117.15	1076.82	117.80	43.29	5.67	64.87	460.99
2007	1492.64	1435.67	134.84	51.75	24.34	80.30	601.06
2008	1837.32	1775.58	158.34	63.84	34.67	82.97	651.78
2009	2026.81	1913.97	179.73	73.98	54.16	103.16	752.60
2010	2353.93	2251.59	210.01	83.83	85.86	134.27	855.40
2011	3006.28	2854.63	237.76	99.40	121.29	136.17	1071.51
2012	3314.93	3124.75	314.00	110.72	132.07	126.58	1152.74
2013	3661.11	3514.52	574.89	122.54	187.24	177.49	1034.79
2014	4027.16	3861.29	646.69	140.22	214.33	192.52	1068.64
2015	4723.86	4263.91	716.12	152.06	174.86	210.23	1186.13
2016	5081.26	4452.97	1214.34	198.22	177.35	254.29	584.41
2017	5430.79	4676.68	1657.88	273.11	288.99	197.46	14.02
2018	5785.92	4988.83	1792.96	299.52	209.13	245.30	8.48
2019	5817.10	4822.98	1820.90	354.43	225.37	225.19	
2020	5483.89	4643.87	1653.11	308.47	259.30	231.20	
2021	5932.31	5164.64	1742.86	342.86	247.43	245.09	
2022	5714.36	4867.07	1315.00	336.63	335.09	219.91	

资料来源：北京市财政局。

LOCAL GOVERNMENT BUDGETARY REVENUE(1978-2022)

(100 million yuan)

#个人所得税 Individual Income Tax	#企业所得税 Corporate Income Tax	#城市维护建设税 Urban Maintenance and Construction Tax	非税收入 Non-tax Revenue	政府性基金预算收入 Governmental Fund Budgetary Revenue	国有资本经营预算收入 Budgetary Revenue of State-owned Capital Operation	社会保险基金预算收入 Social Insurance Fund Budgetary Revenue
0.02	1.76					
0.05	1.43					
0.07	11.70					
0.13	12.70					
0.34	16.18	2.16				
0.97	20.46	2.51				
1.54	21.87	2.70				
1.23	27.70	3.37				
1.53	24.31	3.74				
2.02	22.55	4.35				
2.56	20.59	4.77				
3.15	19.08	5.13				
4.30	14.20	6.57				
9.24	21.70	7.18				
16.21	29.67	10.42				
22.67	37.22	11.36				
28.76	41.05	12.74	-53.50	27.59		
36.49	41.42	14.12	-42.78	32.56		
45.88	45.99	15.27	-33.74	39.07		
56.38	58.03	17.35	-27.79	53.39		
79.52	86.07	20.53	-20.83	53.51		
61.29	100.00	24.91	-5.88	66.97		
57.21	93.70	28.85	3.58	73.40		
73.34	121.70	34.72	17.99	85.55		
84.52	164.76	38.83	33.08	88.14		
102.28	213.86	45.17	40.33	118.63		
135.20	309.34	56.63	56.97	389.40		
171.33	497.52	63.95	61.75	444.71		
177.84	430.42	71.28	112.84	651.96		
215.33	513.09	80.00	102.34	1456.98	46.26	1011.23
272.90	683.71	145.65	151.65	1352.82	52.74	1254.17
281.49	752.47	160.34	190.18	1197.92	60.87	1664.60
333.84	802.12	177.41	146.59	1841.76	63.21	1988.63
383.52	915.84	187.24	165.87	3122.91	64.46	2251.68
478.12	1024.73	204.36	459.95	2028.37	61.60	2667.13
571.26	1095.23	221.64	628.29	1316.47	64.75	3446.83
643.20	1229.80	225.41	754.11	3132.76	61.63	3587.41
728.46	1287.74	245.58	797.09	2009.26	65.41	4186.00
544.16	1228.53	234.98	994.12	2216.30	74.99	4734.44
611.91	1182.49	222.05	840.02	2317.35	80.81	4237.43
743.28	1395.07	245.61	767.66	2705.73	78.09	5545.52
784.59	1449.32	217.69	847.29	2227.46	89.22	5610.78

Source: Beijing Municipal Finance Bureau.

6-2 地方政府预算支出(1997-2022年)

单位：亿元

年 份 Year	一般公共预算支出 General Public Budget Expenditures	#一般公共服务 General Public Service	#教 育 Education	#科学技术 Science and Technology	#文化旅游体育与传媒 Culture, Tourism, Sports and Media	#社会保障和就业 Social Security and Employment	#卫生健康 Health
1997	236.39						
1998	280.68						
1999	355.19						
2000	443.00						
2001	559.11						
2002	628.35						
2003	734.80						
2004	898.28						
2005	1058.31						
2006	1296.84	159.95	209.21	70.14	40.51	149.22	100.95
2007	1649.50	179.56	263.00	90.74	53.62	179.28	118.95
2008	1959.29	196.27	316.30	112.19	61.11	209.33	145.05
2009	2319.37	212.21	365.67	126.31	74.75	234.29	166.63
2010	2717.32	239.57	450.22	178.92	79.36	275.90	186.82
2011	3245.23	261.38	520.08	183.07	87.01	354.88	225.49
2012	3685.31	286.57	628.65	199.94	141.37	424.31	256.06
2013	4173.66	297.12	681.18	234.67	154.71	469.13	276.13
2014	4524.67	272.23	742.05	282.71	163.90	509.01	322.29
2015	5737.70	300.12	855.67	287.80	188.50	700.48	370.52
2016	6406.77	367.20	887.38	285.78	198.35	716.21	397.95
2017	6824.53	493.24	964.62	361.76	208.96	795.38	427.87
2018	7471.43	512.40	1025.51	425.87	245.43	835.65	490.09
2019	7408.19	499.43	1137.18	433.42	279.32	972.98	534.41
2020	7116.18	527.10	1138.29	410.96	225.11	1055.86	605.64
2021	7205.12	532.65	1147.83	449.45	220.06	1054.19	632.67
2022	7469.15	589.25	1171.12	488.70	204.95	1067.80	775.82

注：自2019年起，原“文化体育与传媒”更名为“文化旅游体育与传媒”，原“医疗卫生与计划生育”更名为“卫生健康”，下同。
资料来源：北京市财政局。

LOCAL GOVERNMENT BUDGETARY EXPENDITURE(1997-2022)

(100 million yuan)

#节能环保 Energy Conservation and Environmental Protection	#交通运输 Transportation	#城乡社区 Urban and Rural Community	#农林水 Agriculture Forestry and Water Conservancy	政府性基金预算支出 Governmental Fund Budget Expenditure	国有资本经营预算支出 Budget Expenditure of State-owned Capital Operation	社会保障基金预算支出 Social Security Fund Budget Expenditure
20.14	7.05	153.26	88.62	114.74		
29.27	33.09	187.43	102.51	418.15		
35.47	80.35	199.84	121.77	441.64		
54.04	147.07	347.82	142.01	501.50		
60.85	154.99	294.30	158.64	1347.65	47.74	811.92
94.51	199.12	339.27	187.34	1329.71	67.46	986.99
113.54	243.76	430.76	222.69	1118.45	62.68	1268.73
138.17	231.79	510.67	297.62	1798.81	66.95	1490.34
213.36	214.55	567.40	343.67	2559.09	63.99	1672.32
303.26	295.63	995.39	424.78	2281.30	61.72	1896.03
363.38	353.48	1120.37	443.55	1432.09	45.63	2497.23
458.44	446.48	1034.14	518.35	2461.60	58.86	2594.95
399.45	462.99	1246.22	576.04	2560.27	52.80	3011.72
308.81	401.59	1074.61	584.62	2960.23	52.24	3755.05
236.90	327.97	872.94	497.33	3470.47	57.89	4124.84
249.24	362.70	860.00	497.87	3462.81	53.26	4675.51
222.90	395.25	808.60	462.79	2642.10	64.54	4285.02

Note: Since 2019, "the Culture, Sports and Media" has been changed to "Culture, Tourism, Sports and Media"; and "the Health Care and Family Planning" has been changed to "Health". The same below.
Source: Beijing Municipal Finance Bureau.

6–3 地方政府预算收入
LOCAL GOVERNMENT BUDGETARY REVENUE

单位：亿元 (100 million yuan)

项　　目	Item	2022	2021
一般公共预算收入	**General Public Budget Revenue**	**5714.36**	**5932.31**
#增值税	Value-added Tax	1315.00	1742.86
房产税	Housing Property Tax	336.63	342.86
土地增值税	Increment Tax on Land Value	335.09	247.43
契税	Deed Tax	219.91	245.09
个人所得税	Individual Income Tax	784.59	743.28
企业所得税	Company Income Tax	1449.32	1395.07
城市维护建设税	Urban Maintenance and Construction Tax	217.69	245.61
耕地占用税	Arable Land Occupation Tax	2.74	4.52
罚没收入	Income of Fines and Confiscations	60.75	69.98
行政事业性收费收入	Administrative Fees	58.81	68.74
政府性基金预算收入	**Governmental Fund Budget Revenue**	**2227.46**	**2705.73**
国有资本经营预算收入	**Budgetary Revenue of State-owned Capital Operation**	**89.22**	**78.09**
社会保险基金预算收入	**Social Insurance Fund Budget Revenue**	**5610.78**	**5545.52**

资料来源：北京市财政局。
Source: Beijing Municipal Finance Bureau.

6–4 地方政府预算支出
LOCAL GOVERNMENT BUDGETARY EXPENDITURE

单位：亿元 (100 million yuan)

项　　目	Item	2022	2021
一般公共预算支出	**General Public Budget Expenditures**	**7469.15**	**7205.12**
#一般公共服务	General Public Service	589.25	532.65
教　育	Education	1171.12	1147.83
科学技术	Science and Technology	488.70	449.45
文化旅游体育与传媒	Culture, Tourism, Sports and Media	204.95	220.06
社会保障和就业	Social Security and Employment	1067.80	1054.19
卫生健康	Health	775.82	632.67
节能环保	Energy Conservation and Environmental Protection	222.90	249.24
交通运输	Transportation	395.25	362.70
城乡社区	Urban and Rural Community	808.60	860.00
农林水	Agriculture, Forestry and Water Conservancy	462.79	497.87
政府性基金预算支出	**Governmental Fund Budget Expenditure**	**2642.10**	**3462.81**
国有资本经营预算支出	**Budget Expenditure of State-owned Capital Operation**	**64.54**	**53.26**
社会保险基金预算支出	**Social Security Fund Budget Expenditure**	**4285.02**	**4675.51**

资料来源：北京市财政局。
Source: Beijing Municipal Finance Bureau.

6–5 地税税费收入分税种、分行业完成情况(2010–2017年) LOCAL TAX REVENUE BY CATEGORY AND INDUSTRY (2010-2017)

单位：亿元 (100 million yuan)

项目	Item	2010	2011	2012	2013	2014	2015	2016	2017
地税税费收入	**Local Tax Revenue**	**2104.9**	**2666.6**	**2865.3**	**3061.6**	**3387.8**	**3868.2**	**3261.8**	**3683.1**
按税种分	**By Category**								
#增值税	Value-added Tax							44.6	41.5
营业税	Business Tax	855.4	1071.5	1152.7	1032.4	1067.9	1186.1		
企业所得税	Coporate Income Tax	173.2	210.5	221.0	258.1	333.9	374.1	479.8	555.9
个人所得税	Individual Income Tax	536.3	681.3	703.5	834.5	958.8	1195.3	1428.1	1608.0
按行业分	**By Sector**								
第一产业	Primary Industry	3.7	4.0	4.9	5.0	7.7	7.9	7.4	7.8
第二产业	Secondary Industry	235.2	303.1	326.2	348.5	388.5	408.7	345.5	386.4
#制造业	Manufacturing	101.8	138.4	150.4	160.7	179.4	206.3	219.5	235.8
电力、燃气及水的生产和供应业	Production and Distribution of Electricity, Gas and Water	15.7	19.4	21.2	25.2	28.9	29.2	35.1	37.5
建筑业	Construction	109.9	134.4	144.6	154.0	171.7	166.5	85.1	106.6
第三产业	Tertiary Industry	1866.0	2359.5	2534.1	2708.1	2991.6	3451.6	2908.9	3288.9
#交通运输、仓储和邮政业	Transport, Storage and Post	51.4	64.0	60.6	38.1	40.5	46.4	47.1	52.5
信息传输、计算机服务和软件业	Information Transmission, Computer Services and Software	98.0	125.5	132.8	123.7	141.8	147.1	171.1	192.0
批发和零售业	Wholesale and Retail Trade	111.4	159.4	169.3	188.8	206.2	230.1	244.2	283.9
金融业	Finance	276.4	366.4	446.7	478.0	599.5	763.0	411.2	429.4
房地产业	Real Estate	437.4	520.4	525.4	659.3	734.2	745.7	841.7	938.0

资料来源：国家税务总局北京市税务局。
Source: Beijing Municipal Tax Service of State Taxation Administration.

6-6 国税税收收入分税种、分行业完成情况(2010—2017年) STATE TAX REVENUE BY CATEGORY AND INDUSTRY (2010-2017)

单位：亿元 (100 million yuan)

项　　目	Item	2010	2011	2012	2013	2014	2015	2016	2017
国税税收收入	**State Tax Revenue**	**4346.8**	**5332.5**	**6339.4**	**7470.9**	**8325.2**	**8655.2**	**9378.5**	**9605.7**
按税种分	**By Category**								
#增值税	Value-added Tax	868.3	961.7	1096.0	1456.3	1659.8	1710.5	2486.2	3286.1
营业税	Business Tax	145.4	161.3	191.3	203.7	80.7	150.7		
企业所得税	Corporate Income Tax	2642.0	3506.5	4252.0	5024.4	5757.3	5937.2	5976.0	5373.9
按行业分	**By Sector**								
第一产业	Primary Industry	5.8	0.7	0.3	2.6	0.9	2.5	4.3	4.5
第二产业	Secondary Industry	779.1	881.1	843.8	1069.3	1159.4	1182.2	1198.0	1339.7
#制造业	Manufacturing	623.2	709.2	764.6	832.0	889.5	963.2	960.7	985.3
电力、燃气及水的生产和供应业	Production and Distribution of Electricity, Gas and Water	105.2	103.5	131.0	261.4	194.1	171.1	169.2	203.2
建筑业	Construction	30.1	45.3	54.8	57.0	50.9	63.9	170.2	260.3
第三产业	Tertiary Industry	3561.9	4450.8	5495.3	6399.0	7164.8	7470.5	8176.1	8261.5
#交通运输、仓储和邮政业	Transport, Storage and Post	157.9	209.2	212.1	245.1	242.6	242.6	189.4	239.3
信息传输、计算机服务和软件业	Information Transmission, Computer Services and Software	30.8	105.9	245.9	373.2	296.2	285.0	306.3	371.4
批发和零售业	Wholesale and Retail Trade	1081.6	1410.8	1314.6	1451.0	1474.0	1420.6	1468.5	1645.7
金融业	Finance	1831.2	2158.0	3034.0	3500.2	4153.2	4401.4	4828.6	4115.7
房地产业	Real Estate	107.6	122.3	111.6	157.0	156.9	104.3	274.9	380.9

资料来源：国家税务总局北京市税务局。
Source: Beijing Municipal Tax Service of State Taxation Administration.

6-7 税收收入情况(2017-2022年)
STATISTICS FOR TAX REVENUE(2017-2022)

单位：亿元 (100 million yuan)

项　目	Item	2017	2018	2019	2020	2021	2022
税收收入	**Tax Revenue**	**12403.9**	**12655.5**	**13098.1**	**12805.9**	**13990.9**	**13633.4**
按税种分	**By Category**						
#增值税	Value-added Tax	3327.6	3595.3	3629.9	3252.4	3541.3	2774.1
企业所得税	Corporate Income Tax	5929.8	5727.5	6501.1	6467.5	6922.2	7195.9
个人所得税	Individual Income Tax	1610.3	1824.2	1363.1	1553.1	1885.7	1994.2
按行业分	**By Sector**						
第一产业	Primary Industry	11.7	11.2	12.6	10.5	9.5	9.1
第二产业	Secondary Industry	1665.8	1808.3	1746.4	1601.6	1744.4	1768.2
#制造业	Manufacturing	1179.0	1202.5	1222.7	1189.8	1258.4	1204.2
电力、热力、燃气及水生产和供应业	Production and Distribution of Electricity, Heating Power, Gas and Water	235.9	213.6	186.0	127.6	121.4	124.2
建筑业	Construction	354.0	367.3	351.2	325.0	342.8	321.7
第三产业	Tertiary Industry	10726.4	10836.0	11339.1	11193.8	12237.0	11856.1
#交通运输、仓储和邮政业	Transport, Storage and Post	286.0	344.7	354.7	144.7	247.9	141.5
信息传输、软件和信息技术服务业	Information Transmission, Software and Information Technology Services	550.4	630.7	664.6	700.6	976.6	973.4
批发和零售业	Wholesale and Retail Trade	1324.5	1529.1	1243.9	1098.0	1470.5	1186.8
金融业	Finance	4515.4	4252.7	5217.0	5710.4	5669.6	5676.3
房地产业	Real Estate	1302.1	1175.8	1203.1	1122.3	1167.7	1136.5

注：本表税收收入不含各项非税收入，2017年为同口径数据。
资料来源：国家税务总局北京市税务局。
Note: Tax revenue in this table doesn't include the non-tax revenues. That of 2017 was the data of the same caliber.
Source: Beijing Municipal Tax Service of State Taxation Administration.

主要统计指标解释

财政部分

一般公共预算收入　是通过一定的形式和程序，由各级财政部门组织并纳入预算管理的各项收入。

政府性基金预算收入　是按规定收取，转入或通过当年财政安排，由财政管理并具有指定用途的政府性基金预算收入等。

国有资本经营预算收入　指国家以所有者身份依法取得国有资本收益，并对所得收益进行分配而发生的各项收支预算，是政府预算的重要组成部分。

社会保险基金预算收入　社会保险基金预算是指社会保险经办机构根据国家预算管理和社会保险相关法律法规编制的、经规定程序审批的具有法律效力的年度基金财务收支计划。

税收收入　包括增值税、营业税、企业所得税、个人所得税、资源税、城市维护建设税、房产税、印花税、城镇土地使用税、土地增值税、车船税、耕地占用税、契税等。

非税收收入　包括专项收入、行政事业性收费、罚没收入和其他收入。

一般公共预算支出　是各级财政部门对集中的一般预算收入有计划地分配和使用而安排的支出。

政府性基金预算支出　是各级财政部门用基金预算收入安排的支出。

一般公共服务支出　指政府提供基本公共管理与服务的支出，包括人大事务、政协事务、政府办公厅（室)及相关机构事务、发展与改革事务、统计信息事务、财政事务、税收事务、审计事务、海关事务、人力资源事务、纪检监察事务、人口与计划生育事务、商贸事务、知识产权事务、工商行政管理事务、国土资源事务、海洋管理事务、测绘事务、地震事务、气象事务、民族事务、宗教事务、港澳台侨事务、档案事务、共产党事务、民主党派事务及工商联事务、群众团体事务、彩票事务等。

教育支出　指政府教育事务支出，包括教育行政管理、学前教育、小学教育、初中教育、普通高中教育、普通高等教育、初等职业教育、中专教育、技校教育、职业高中教育、高等职业教育、广播电视教育、留学生教育、特殊教育、干部继续教育、教育机关服务等。

科学技术支出　指用于科学技术方面的支出，包括科学技术管理事务、基础研究、应用研究、技术研究与开发、科技条件与服务、社会科学、科学技术普及、科技交流与合作等。

文化旅游体育与传媒支出　指政府在文化、文物、体育、广播影视、新闻出版等方面的支出。

社会保障和就业支出　指政府在社会保障与就业方面的支出，包括社会保障和就业管理事务、民政管理事务、财政对社会保险基金的补助、补充全国社会保障基金、行政事业单位离退休、企业改革补助、就业补助、抚恤、退役安置、社会福利、残疾人事业、城市居民最低生活保障、其他城镇社会救济、农村社会救济、自然灾害生活救助、红十字事务等。

卫生健康支出　指政府医疗卫生与计划生育管理方面的支出。

节能环保支出　指政府环境保护支出，包括环境保护管理事务支出、环境监测与监察支出、污染治理支出、自然生态保护支出、天然林保护工程支出、退耕还林支出、风沙荒漠治理支出、退牧还草支出、已垦草原退耕还草、能源节约利用、污染减排、可再生能源和资源综合利用等支出。

交通运输支出　指政府交通运输和邮政业方面的支出，包括公路运输支出、水路运输支出、铁路运输支出、民用航空运输支出、邮政业支出等。

城乡社区支出　指政府城乡社区事务支出，包括城乡社区管理事务支出、城乡社区规划与管理支出、城乡社区公共设施支出、城乡社区住宅支出、城乡社区环境卫生支出、建设市场管理与监督支出等。

农林水支出　指政府农林水事务支出，包括农业支出、林业支出、水利支出、扶贫支出、农业综合开发支出等。

税收部分

税费收入　指由税务局征缴的各项税收收入和罚没收入。包括企业所得税、个人所得税、资源税、房产税、契税、城市维护建设税等。

税收收入　指由税务局征缴的各项税收收入。包括增值税、消费税、企业所得税、个人所得税、城市维护建设税等。

企业所得税　是对中国境内全部企业的生产经营所得和其他所得征收的一种税。

增值税　指以商品或劳务销售额为计税依据并实行扣除已征税款制度的一种流转税。

个人所得税　是对个人（自然人）取得的各项应税所得征收的一种税。

Explanatory Notes on Main Statistical Indicators

Finance

General Public Budgetary Revenue refers to the revenue organized by finance authorities at all levels in certain form and through certain procedures and involved in budgetary management.

Governmental Fund Budgetary Revenue refers to governmental fund budgetary revenues collected, transferred or allocated by government finance in the current year in accordance with regulations, and regulated by government finance and used for specific purpose.

Budgetary Revenue of State-owned Capital Operation refers to the state-owned capital income of the country as the owner and all kinds of income and expenditure budgets resulted from the allocation of the income. It is an important part of governmental budget.

Social Insurance Fund Budgetary Revenue refers to a legally effective annual financial revenue and expenditure plan of fund formulated by social insurance agencies in accordance with relevant laws and regulations of state budget management and social insurance as well as specified approval procedures.

Tax Revenue includes value-added tax, business tax, corporate income tax, individual income tax, resource tax, urban maintenance and construction tax, house property tax, stamp tax, urban land use tax, land appreciation tax, tax on vehicles and boat operation, farm land occupation tax, deed tax, etc.

Non-tax Revenue includes special program receipts, charge of administrative and institutional units, income of fines and confiscation, and other non-tax revenues.

General Public Budgetary Expenditure refers to the expenditure arranged by finance authorities at all levels from the general budgetary revenue according to the planned distribution.

Governmental Fund Budgetary Expenditure refers to the expenditure arranged by finance authorities at all levels according to the fund budget revenue.

Expenditure for General Public Services refers to the spending on the basic public management and services provided by the government, including the expenses on affairs of Beijing Municipal People's Congress, CPC Beijing Municipal Committee, General Office of Beijing Municipal Government and relative institutions, development and reform, statistical information, finance, taxation, audit, customs, human resources, discipline inspection and supervision, population and family planning, commerce and trade, intellectual property, administration for industry and commerce, land and resources, oceanic administration, surveying and mapping, earthquake, weather, ethnics, religions, Hong Kong, Macao, Taiwan, and Overseas Chinese, archive administration, Chinese Communist Party, democratic parties, federation of industry and commerce, mass organizations, and lottery, etc.

Expenditure for Education refers to the spending of government on education, including the expenses on the administration of education, pre-school education, primary education, junior high school education, senior high school education, general higher education, primary vocational education, secondary vocational education, technical school education, vocational senior high school education and higher vocational education, radio and television education, overseas student education, special education, continuing education for management personnel, and services for education authorities, etc.

Expenditure for Science and Technology refers to the spending on science and technology (S&T), including the expense on the administration of S&T, basic research, applied research, technology research and development, conditions and services of S&T, popularization of social science and S&T, exchanges and cooperation of S&T, etc.

Expenditure for Cultural, Tourism Sport and Media refers to the spending on culture, cultural relics, sports, radio, films, television, press and publication, etc.

Expenditure for Social Security and Employment refers to the spending on social security and employment, including the expenses on social security and employment administration affairs, civil affairs, budgetary subsidy on the social insurance funds, subsidy on National Social Security Fund, subsidy on retirees of administrative and institutional units, subsidy on enterprise reform, subsidy on employment, pension, reemployment of ex-serviceman, social welfare, the handicapped undertakings, subsistence allowances for urban residents, other urban social relief, rural social relief, relief for natural disasters, affairs of Red Cross, etc.

Expenditure for Health refers to the spending of government on health care and family planning.

Expenditure for Energy Conservation and Environmental Protection refers to the spending of government on environmental protection, including the expenses on administration of environmental protection, environment monitoring and supervision, pollution control, natural and ecological protection, projects of natural forest protection, reforestation, control of sand storms, returning pasture and grazing land to grassland, energy conservation and utilization, emission reduction, comprehensive utilization of renewable energy and resources, etc.

Expenditure for Transportation refers to the spending of government on transportation and postal services, including the expenses on highway transportation, waterway transportation, railway transportation, civil aviation transportation and postal services, etc.

Expenditure for Urban and Rural Community refers to the spending of government on urban and rural community affairs, including the expenses on administration of urban and rural communities, planning and management of urban and rural communities, public facilities in urban and rural communities, residential houses in urban and rural communities, sanitation in urban and rural communities, management and supervision of construction markets, etc.

Expenditure for Agriculture, Forestry and Water Conservancy refers to the spending of government on agriculture affairs, forestry affairs, water conservancy affairs, poverty alleviation and comprehensive agricultural development, etc.

Taxes

Local Tax Revenue refers to the revenue of taxes levied and collected by tax authorities at all levels, including corporate income tax, personal income tax, resource tax, house property tax, deed tax, urban maintenance and construction tax, etc.

State Tax Revenue refers to the revenue of taxes levied and collected by tax authorities at all levels, including value-added tax, excise tax, corporate income tax, individual income tax, urban maintenance and construction tax, etc.

Corporate Income Tax is a sort of tax levied against income of China domestic enterprises from their production and operation and other income.

Value-Added Tax is a sort of commodity turnover tax based on commodity and service sales, with a system of deduction of tax levied.

Personal Income Tax is a sort of tax levied against taxable income earned by individuals (natural persons).

北京统计年鉴2023　BEIJING STATISTICAL YEARBOOK 2023

能源、资源和环境
ENERGY, RESOURCES AND ENVIRONMENT

简要说明

一、主要内容

本章资料包括北京市能源生产与消费情况、万元地区生产总值能耗、能源平衡表、能源消费弹性系数和北京地区用电量情况、气象情况、水资源情况、排水及节水情况、园林绿化及森林情况、大气环境、固体废物处置情况等。

二、能源统计范围及测算方法

（一）关于统计范围。能源部分统计范围为全社会口径。

（二）关于测算方法。第二、三产业限额以上法人单位能源消费统计采取全面调查、限额以下法人单位能源消费情况根据普查年度数据资料推算、农林牧渔业、居民生活能源消费统计根据农林牧渔中间消耗和能源供应部门的能源供应资料核算。

三、关于历史数据调整的问题

2004年能源消费数据为北京市第一次全国经济普查数据，1995-2003年的能源消费数据根据第一次全国经济普查的数据结果进行了修订。

2008年能源消费数据为北京市第二次全国经济普查数据，1995-2007年的能源消费数据根据第二次全国经济普查的数据结果进行了修订。

2010年，根据北京市第六次全国人口普查的数据结果对2006-2010年的人均指标数据进行了修订。

2013年能源消费数据为北京市第三次全国经济普查数据。2005-2012年的能源生产量、能源消费总量、万元地区生产总值能耗及下降率，以及2010-2012年的能源消费构成、能源消费弹性系数、平均每万元地区生产总值能源消费量、人均生活用能源、主要能源日均消费量数据已根据第三次全国经济普查的数据结果进行了修订。

2018年能源消费数据为北京市第四次全国经济普查数据。2015-2017年的能源消费数据根据第四次全国经济普查的数据结果进行了修订。1992-2017年的万元地区生产总值能耗及下降率、万元地区生产总值水耗及下降率、能源消费弹性系数、平均每万元地区生产总值能源消费量中使用的地区生产总值数据，根据北京市第四次全国经济普查的数据结果进行了修订。

2020年，根据北京市第七次全国人口普查的数据结果对2011-2019年的人均指标数据进行了修订。

四、有关统计标准的变化说明

（一）关于行业划分。2012年以前，执行《国民经济行业分类》（GB/T 4754-2002）标准。2012-2017年执行《国民经济行业分类》（GB/T 4754-2011）标准。自2018年起，执行《国民经济行业分类》（GB/T 4754-2017）标准。

（二）关于三次产业划分。2003年，根据《国民经济行业分类》（GB/T 4754—2002），国家统计局印发了《国家统计局关于印发〈三次产业划分规定〉的通知》（国统字〔2003〕14号）。2012年，根据国家质检总局和国家标准委颁布的《国民经济行业分类》（GB/T 4754—2011），国家统计局对2003年《三次产业划分规定》进行了修订。主要在以下方面作出调整：一是将门类“农、林、牧、渔业”中的“农、林、牧、渔服务业”，“采矿业”中的“开采辅助活动”，“制造业”中的“金属制品、机械和设备修理业”等三个大类一并调整到第三产业。调整后，第一产业为4个大类；第二产业为2个门类和36个大类；第三产业为15个门类和3个大类。二是明确第三产业即为服务业。

本章2012年及以后三次产业的分类执行调整后的划分规定。

Brief Introduction

I. Main Content

Statistics in this chapter include the energy production and energy consumption in Beijing, energy consumption in regions with RMB 10,000 of GDP, energy balance sheet, energy consumption elasticity coefficient, electricity consumption in Beijing, meteorology, water resources, water drainage and water saving, landscaping and forest, atmospheric environment, solid waste disposal, etc.

II. Scope of Statistics and Calculation Method for Energy

(I) Scope of Statistics. Statistics on energy cover the entire society.

(II) Calculation Method. Comprehensive survey is adopted on energy consumption of legal entities above designated size in the secondary and tertiary industries, and energy consumption of legal entities below designated size are estimated and calculated on the basis of the annual census data; statistics on energy consumption in agriculture, forestry, animal production and hunting, fishing and statistics on household energy consumption are calculated based on the information on intermediate consumption in agriculture, forestry, animal production and hunting, fishing and based on the energy supply data of the energy supply departments.

III. Adjustment to Historical Data

Data on energy consumption for 2004 were collected from the first national economic census in Beijing; data on energy consumption for the period between 1995 and 2003 had been revised according to the data of the first national economic census.

Data on energy consumption for 2008 were collected from the second national economic census in Beijing; data on energy consumption for the period between 1995 and 2007 had been revised in accordance with the data of the second national economic census.

In 2010, the per-capita index data from 2006 to 2010 were revised in accordance with the results of the sixth national population census in Beijing.

Data on energy consumption for 2013 were collected from the third national economic census in Beijing. Data on energy production, total energy consumption, energy consumption per RMB 10,000 of GDP and the decrease rate for the period between 2005 and 2012, and the data on composition of energy consumption from 2010 to 2012, the data on energy consumption elasticity coefficient, average energy consumption per RMB 10,000 of GDP, per-capita energy consumption for living, daily average consumption of main energy, have been revised in accordance with the results of the third national economic census.

Data on energy consumption for 2018 were collected from the fourth national economic census in Beijing. Data on energy consumption for the period between 2015 and 2017 had been revised according to the results of the fourth national economic census. Data on energy consumption per RMB 10,000 of GDP and the decrease rate, water consumption per RMB 10,000 of GDP and the decrease rate, energy consumption elasticity coefficient, and the GDP data for energy consumption per RMB 10,000 of GDP, for the period between 1992 and 2017 have been revised in accordance with the results of the fourth national economic census in Beijing.

In 2020, the per-capita index data from 2011 to 2019 were revised in accordance with the results of the seventh national population census in Beijing.

IV. Changes in Relevant Statistical Standards

(I) Classification of Sectors. The standards in the *Classification of National Economic Sectors* (GB/T 4754-2002) were implemented before 2012. The standards in the *Classification of National Economic Sectors* (GB/T 4754-2011) were implemented from 2012 to 2017. The standards in the *Classification of National Economic Sectors* (GB/T 4754-2017) are implemented since 2018.

(II) Classification of Three Industries. According to the *Classification of National Economic Sectors* (GB/T 4754-2002), the National Bureau of Statistics issued the *Notice of the National Bureau of Statistics on the Issuance of the 'Regulations on Three Industries Classification'* (G.T.Z. [2003] No. 14) in 2003. According to the *Classification of National Economic Sectors* (GB/T 4754-2011) promulgated by the General Administration of Quality Supervision, Inspection and Quarantine of the People's Republic of China and the Standardization Administration of the People's Republic of China, the National Bureau of Statistics revised the *Regulations on Three Industries Classification* of 2003 version in 2012. Adjustments were mainly made in the following aspects: Firstly, the "service activities for agriculture, forestry, animal husbandry and fishing" in the category of "agriculture, forestry, animal production and hunting, fishing", the "mining support service activities" in the category of "mining and quarrying", and the "repair of fabricated metal products, machinery and equipment" in the category of "manufacturing" were adjusted to the Tertiary Industry. After adjustment, the Primary Industry fell into 4 categories; the secondary industry fell into 2 classes and 36 categories; and the Tertiary Industry fell into 15 classes and 3 categories. Secondly, the Tertiary Industry was defined as the service industry.

The classification of three industries since 2012 as mentioned in this chapter has all been subject to the classification provisions after adjustment.

7-1 能源生产量(2005-2022年) ENERGY PRODUCTION (2005-2022)

年 份 Year	一次能源合 计(万吨标准煤) Total Primary Energy (10000 tons of SCE)	#原 煤(万吨) Raw Coal (10000 tons)	#水 电(亿千瓦时) Hydropower (100 million kW·h)	#风 电(亿千瓦时) Wind Power (100 million kW·h)	#光伏发电(亿千瓦时) Photovoltaic Power (100 million kW·h)
2005	679.5	945.2	4.0		
2006	460.6	642.1	4.1		
2007	466.1	648.8	4.2		
2008	414.2	578.5	4.5	0.9	
2009	475.7	641.3	4.4	1.4	
2010	499.9	500.1	4.3	3.1	
2011	500.3	500.1	4.5	3.1	
2012	507.2	493.1	4.2	3.1	
2013	541.7	500.1	4.7	3.3	0.1
2014	514.0	457.5	6.8	2.8	0.1
2015	545.6	450.1	6.6	2.6	0.5
2016	445.8	317.6	12.2	3.3	1.1
2017	416.9	255.0	11.2	3.5	2.0
2018	611.5	176.2	9.9	3.5	3.1
2019	691.1	36.1	10.2	3.4	4.8
2020	576.8		11.5	3.7	6.2
2021	385.6		13.7	4.0	6.2
2022	440.2		9.4	5.0	9.1

7-1 续表 Continued

年 份 Year	二次能源合 计(万吨标准煤) Secondary Energy (10000 tons of SCE)	#汽 油(万吨) Gasoline (10000 tons)	#煤 油(万吨) Kerosene (10000 tons)	#柴 油(万吨) Diesel Oil (10000 tons)	#燃料油(万吨) Fuel Oil (10000 tons)	#液化石油气(万吨) Liquefied Petroleum Gas (10000 tons)	#热 力(万百万千焦) Heat Petroleum Gas (10000 million kilo-joule)	#电 力(亿千瓦时) Electricity (100 million kW·h)
2005	2772.6	142.2	12.4	154.7	64.5	47.3	11335.7	209.8
2006	2632.9	145.6	11.6	167.1	57.9	23.0	12181.6	209.7
2007	2767.9	160.4	36.4	244.7	36.7	41.0	12686.9	224.2
2008	3104.9	202.3	85.2	354.8	28.6	42.9	13650.5	244.7
2009	3146.9	242.1	111.6	314.8	28.0	28.8	14226.1	241.9
2010	3397.8	247.7	116.1	314.5	33.7	29.0	15345.0	262.0
2011	3080.9	245.3	126.4	309.3	21.3	27.2	14795.5	256.1
2012	3135.6	255.2	132.9	274.5	18.4	31.9	15400.5	283.3
2013	3000.2	223.9	99.4	194.7	16.9	28.1	14893.6	326.7
2014	3314.3	287.4	152.3	219.8	4.7	32.1	15055.4	351.6
2015	3460.4	296.3	160.0	180.4	1.4	34.0	15819.7	412.5
2016	3267.7	260.5	149.8	152.5	0.7	41.3	16091.9	419.0
2017	3316.6	271.0	190.8	156.6	3.6	41.6	16473.3	376.2
2018	3523.4	276.2	187.6	159.8	4.2	42.4	18380.0	432.1
2019	3601.5	285.5	191.3	173.1	0.7	46.1	18195.2	443.0
2020	3311.2	207.8	103.1	160.4	4.8	29.3	19774.0	436.1
2021	3392.0	227.3	106.3	140.0	3.6	52.7	19178.1	448.7
2022	3426.2	201.7	76.2	169.5	1.1	105.5	20563.7	443.6

7-2 能源消费总量及构成情况(2010-2022年)
TOTAL ENERGY CONSUMPTION AND ITS COMPOSITION(2010-2022)

年份 Year	能源消费总量(万吨标准煤) Total Energy Consumption (10000 tons of SCE)	占能源消费总量的比重(%) As Percentage of Total Energy Consumption (%)						非化石能源占能源消费总量的比重(%) Non-fossil Energy as Percentage of Total Energy Consumption
		煤炭 Coal	石油 Petroleum	天然气 Natural Gas	一次电力 Primary Electricity	电力净调入(+)调出(-)量 Net Amount of Electricity Transferred in/out	其他能源 Other Energy	
2010	6359.49	29.59	30.94	14.58	0.45	24.35	0.09	
2011	6397.30	26.66	32.92	14.02	0.45	25.62	0.33	
2012	6564.10	25.22	31.61	17.11	0.42	25.38	0.26	
2013	6723.90	23.31	32.19	18.20	0.35	24.99	0.96	
2014	6831.23	20.37	32.56	21.09	0.41	24.03	1.54	
2015	6802.79	13.05	33.79	29.18	0.40	21.71	1.88	
2016	6916.72	9.22	33.14	31.88	0.66	23.37	1.73	4.60
2017	7088.33	5.06	34.00	32.00	0.65	26.15	2.14	7.20
2018	7269.76	2.77	34.14	34.17	0.61	25.68	2.63	7.80
2019	7360.32	1.81	34.55	34.01	0.67	25.79	3.17	7.90
2020	6762.10	1.50	29.27	37.16	0.84	26.96	4.26	10.40
2021	7103.62	1.44	28.66	36.15	0.90	28.70	4.15	11.96
2022	6896.89	1.02	23.06	38.92	0.92	31.73	4.35	14.25

7-3 能源消费总量及万元地区生产总值能耗(1980-2022年)
TOTAL ENERGY CONSUMPTION AND ENERGY CONSUMPTION PER 10000 YUAN OF GDP (1980-2022)

单位：万吨标准煤 (10000 tons of SCE)

年份 Year	能源消费总量 Total Energy Consumption	第一产业 Primary Industry	第二产业 Secondary Industry	第三产业 Tertiary Industry	生活消费 Residential Consumption	万元地区生产总值能耗（吨标准煤） Energy Consumption per 10000 Yuan of GDP (ton of SCE)	万元地区生产总值能耗下降率(%) Decrease Rate of Energy Consumption per 10000 Yuan GDP(%)
1980	1907.7	66.8	1400.3	297.6	143.0	13.715	
1981	1902.6	53.3	1339.4	334.9	175.0	13.668	-0.23
1982	1920.4	55.7	1346.2	338.0	180.5	12.398	6.02
1983	1984.7	73.4	1379.4	313.6	218.3	10.839	11.22
1984	2144.1	85.8	1470.9	347.3	240.1	9.899	7.98
1985	2211.4	90.7	1488.3	351.6	280.8	8.601	5.12
1986	2400.0	95.7	1612.0	380.4	311.9	8.424	-0.49
1987	2475.8	89.0	1647.8	424.7	314.3	7.576	5.88
1988	2612.6	111.7	1748.1	412.2	340.6	6.369	6.45
1989	2653.2	114.4	1735.9	427.0	375.9	5.818	2.73
1990	2709.7	105.7	1720.1	515.3	368.6	5.411	2.92
1991	2872.0	126.7	1807.6	542.0	395.7	4.795	3.56
1992	2987.5	143.6	1888.1	552.4	403.4	4.877	6.54
1993	3264.6	133.6	2150.9	561.0	419.1	4.745	2.69
1994	3385.9	143.6	2234.1	574.8	433.4	4.329	8.78
1995	3533.3	120.4	2328.4	632.7	451.8	4.033	6.83
1996	3734.5	110.8	2477.0	698.1	448.6	3.882	3.76
1997	3719.2	95.7	2369.6	799.8	454.1	3.508	9.64
1998	3808.1	96.2	2400.5	856.4	455.0	3.277	6.58
1999	3906.6	86.9	2370.7	971.8	477.2	3.029	7.57
2000	4144.0	104.8	2424.8	1080.9	533.5	2.868 (1.264)	5.29
2001	4229.2	105.4	2366.6	1196.2	561.0	1.154	8.71
2002	4436.1	103.0	2414.6	1334.5	584.0	1.083	6.18
2003	4648.2	99.9	2476.7	1391.0	680.6	1.021	5.69
2004	5139.6	85.6	2664.2	1638.0	751.8	0.997	2.41
2005	5049.8	85.4	2363.7	1771.7	829.0	0.872 (0.706)	4.33
2006	5399.3	91.1	2421.2	1962.8	924.2	0.669	5.21
2007	5747.7	95.1	2434.6	2198.4	1019.6	0.623	6.96
2008	5786.2	95.2	2215.6	2394.3	1081.1	0.575	7.63
2009	6008.6	97.1	2206.5	2527.3	1177.7	0.543	5.63
2010	6359.5	98.5	2364.1	2654.4	1242.5	0.521 (0.425)	4.12
2011	6397.3	98.3	2160.1	2818.9	1320.0	0.396	6.94
2012	6564.1	98.1	2082.1	2967.0	1416.9	0.377	4.74
2013	6723.9	97.3	2079.2	3109.1	1438.3	0.358	4.93
2014	6831.2	91.7	1998.4	3236.5	1504.6	0.339	5.40
2015	6802.8	84.6	1902.7	3312.6	1502.9	0.316 (0.275)	6.18
2016	6916.7	80.4	1870.8	3414.4	1551.1	0.261	4.91
2017	7088.3	72.0	1844.2	3519.3	1652.8	0.251	4.04
2018	7269.8	60.7	1835.2	3681.4	1692.4	0.241	3.88
2019	7360.3	55.8	1850.7	3762.5	1691.4	0.230	4.53
2020	6762.1	50.9	1751.5	3246.9	1712.8	0.209 (0.188)	9.09
2021	7103.6	50.3	1690.1	3534.2	1829.0	0.182	3.46
2022	6896.9	48.1	1670.9	3314.8	1863.0	0.175	3.58

注：1.本表能源消费量指标按等价值计算,万元地区生产总值能耗下降率按可比价格计算。
2.1992年以前万元地区生产总值能耗按当年价格计算；自1992年起按可比价格计算。更换基期年份计算两个可比价格数据，括号内数据按新基期价格计算。
3.第一产业中包含农林牧渔专业及辅助性活动能源消费；2017年及以前，第二产业中包含开采专业及辅助性活动，金属制品、机械和设备修理业的能源消费，下同。
4.2022年万元地区生产总值能耗及其下降率为初步核算数据，下同。

Note: a) Energy consumption in this table is calculated at current prices. Decrease rate of energy consumption per 10000 yuan of GDP is calculated at comparable prices.
b) Energy consumption per 10000 yuan of GDP before 1992 was calculated at the price of that year; figures in and after 1992 were calculated at comparable prices. Two figures at comparable prices were calculated for the year in which the base period was changed. Figures in brackets were calculated at the price of new base period.
c) In the primary industry, the energy consumption of the professional and supporting activities of agricultare,forestry,animal husbandry and fishery were included; the energy consumption in the mining and support activities, repair of fabricated metal products, machinery and equipment were included in the secondary industry in and before 2017, the same below.
d) The data for 2022 on the energy consumption per 10000 yuan of GDP and its decrease rate were the preliminary accounting data, the same below.

7-4 按产业、行业分能源消费总量
TOTAL ENERGY CONSUMPTION BY INDUSTRIES AND BY SECTOR

单位：万吨标准煤 (10000 tons of SCE)

项　　目	Item	2022	2021
能源消费总量	**Total Energy Consumption**	**6896.9**	**7103.6**
按产业分	**By Three Industries**		
第一产业	Primary Industry	48.1	50.3
第二产业	Secondary Industry	1670.9	1690.1
第三产业	Tertiary Industry	3314.8	3534.2
生活消费	Residential Consumption	1863.0	1829.0
按行业分	**By Sector**		
#采矿业	Mining	1.2	2.5
制造业	Manufacturing	1129.3	1108.0
电力、热力、燃气及水生产和供应业	Production and Distribution of Electricity, Heating Power, Gas and Water	438.6	472.2
建筑业	Construction	106.7	111.8
批发和零售业	Wholesale and Retail Trade	241.9	236.1
交通运输、仓储和邮政业	Transport, Storage and Post	875.7	1147.5
住宿和餐饮业	Accommodation and Catering	197.8	199.4
信息传输、软件和信息技术服务业	Information Transmission, Software and Information Technology Services	335.1	315.7
金融业	Finance	77.2	69.6
房地产业	Real Estate	492.3	488.0
租赁和商务服务业	Leasing and Business Services	200.3	192.7
科学研究和技术服务业	Scientific Research and Development, Technical Services	208.3	197.0
水利、环境和公共设施管理业	Management of Water Conservancy, Environment and Public Facilities	85.3	83.1
居民服务、修理和其他服务业	Resident Services, Repair and Other Services	44.4	41.4
教　育	Education	247.2	243.9
卫生和社会工作	Health and Social Works	117.0	106.7
文化、体育和娱乐业	Culture, Sports and Entertainment	82.0	81.5
公共管理、社会保障和社会组织	Public Administration, Social Security and Social Organizations	93.0	114.5

7-5 按产业、行业分万元地区生产总值能耗(2000-2022年) ENERGY CONSUMPTION PER 10000 YUAN OF GDP BY INDUSTRIES AND BY SECTOR(2000-2022)

单位：吨标准煤 (ton of SCE)

年 份 Year	万元地区生产总值能耗 Energy Consumption per 10000 yuan of GDP	按产业分 By Three Industies			按行业分 By Sector	
		第一产业 Primary Industry	第二产业 Secondary Industry	第三产业 Tertiary Industry	#工 业 Industry	#交通运输、仓储和邮政业 Transport, Storage and Post
	地区生产总值按2000年可比价格计算 GDP calculated at the comparable prices of 2000					
2000	1.264	1.322	2.369	0.497	2.836	1.420
2001	1.154	1.284	2.121	0.485	2.525	1.653
2002	1.083	1.218	2.007	0.475	2.397	1.732
2003	1.021	1.199	1.868	0.443	2.202	1.798
2004	0.997	1.032	1.742	0.462	2.003	2.162
2005	0.872	1.046	1.409	0.439	1.619	2.091
	地区生产总值按2005年可比价格计算 GDP calculated at the comparable prices of 2005					
2005	0.706	0.983	1.239	0.344	1.422	1.502
2006	0.669	1.041	1.155	0.334	1.341	1.806
2007	0.623	1.065	1.037	0.324	1.201	1.968
2008	0.575	1.048	0.941	0.315	1.089	2.262
2009	0.543	1.022	0.852	0.302	0.989	2.294
2010	0.521	1.054	0.805	0.289	0.923	2.228
	地区生产总值按2010年可比价格计算 GDP calculated at the comparable prices of 2010					
2010	0.425	0.802	0.731	0.229	0.852	1.711
2011	0.396	0.793	0.627	0.224	0.724	1.723
2012	0.377	0.767	0.566	0.218	0.658	1.717
2013	0.358	0.738	0.525	0.212	0.611	1.725
2014	0.339	0.696	0.472	0.205	0.554	1.716
2015	0.316	0.720	0.437	0.194	0.527	1.733
	地区生产总值按2015年可比价格计算 GDP calculated at the comparable prices of 2015					
2015	0.275	0.603	0.430	0.164	0.516	1.689
2016	0.261	0.627	0.402	0.157	0.484	1.684
2017	0.251	0.590	0.380	0.151	0.454	1.605
2018	0.241	0.507	0.364	0.147	0.434	1.631
2019	0.230	0.491	0.353	0.141	0.425	1.664
2020	0.209	0.489	0.326	0.121	0.398	1.325
	地区生产总值按2020年可比价格计算 GDP calculated at the comparable prices of 2020					
2020	0.188	0.470	0.305	0.108	0.387	1.266
2021	0.182	0.452	0.239	0.111	0.283	1.320
2022	0.175	0.439	0.267	0.100	0.328	1.055

7-6 按产业、行业分万元地区生产总值能耗下降率(2001-2022年)
DECREASE RATE OF ENERGY CONSUMPTION PER 10000 YUAN GDP BY INDUSTRIES AND BY SECTOR(2001-2022)

单位：% (%)

年份 Year	万元地区生产总值能耗下降率 Decrease Rate of Energy Consumption per 10000 yuan GDP	按产业分 By Three Industies			按行业分 By Sector	
		第一产业 Primary Industry	第二产业 Secondary Industry	第三产业 Tertiary Industry	#工业 Industry	#交通运输、仓储和邮政业 Transport, Storage and Post
2001	8.71	2.92	10.45	2.43	10.94	-16.41
2002	6.18	5.12	5.39	2.04	5.07	-4.76
2003	5.69	1.53	6.91	6.83	8.15	-3.79
2004	2.41	13.97	6.77	-4.40	9.03	-20.27
2005	4.33	-2.46	7.52	-2.98	7.64	-4.09
2006	5.21	-5.87	6.83	2.87	5.66	-20.22
2007	6.96	-2.31	10.16	3.00	10.49	-8.99
2008	7.63	1.52	9.27	2.83	9.34	-14.92
2009	5.63	2.50	9.50	4.12	9.15	-1.43
2010	4.12	-3.10	5.51	4.16	6.63	2.89
2011	6.94	1.09	14.29	2.19	15.07	-0.73
2012	4.74	3.34	9.73	2.56	9.10	0.37
2013	4.93	3.69	7.29	2.78	7.13	-0.46
2014	5.40	5.73	10.01	3.28	9.32	0.50
2015	6.18	-3.44	7.37	5.38	4.96	-0.98
2016	4.91	-4.07	6.67	4.00	6.13	0.27
2017	4.04	5.94	5.38	4.06	6.32	4.70
2018	3.88	15.90	4.22	2.50	4.38	-1.61
2019	4.53	3.33	2.94	4.08	1.98	-2.04
2020	9.09	0.33	7.61	14.39	6.51	20.37
2021	3.46	3.83	21.69	-2.50	26.92	-4.26
2022	3.58	2.77	-11.59	9.22	-16.12	20.03

注：表内万元地区生产总值能耗下降率按可比价格计算。
Note: Decrease rate of energy consumption per 10000 yuan GDP in the table is calculated at comparable prices.

7-7 电力平衡表
ELECTRICITY BALANCE

单位：亿千瓦时 (100 million kW·h)

项　　目	Item	2022	2021
可供本地区消费的能源量	**Total Energy Available for Local Consumption**	**838.89**	**786.10**
加工转换投入(−)产出(+)量	**Input(-) or Output(+) in Processing and Conversion**	**443.38**	**448.49**
火力发电	Thermal Power	443.57	448.68
供　热	Heating	-0.19	-0.19
煤炭洗选	Washing of Coal		
炼　焦	Coking		
炼油及煤制油	Oil Refining and Coal to Liquid		
#油品再投入量(−)	Oil Product Re-input(-)		
制　气	Gas Production		
#再投入量(−)	Re-input(-)		
天然气液化	Natural Gas Liquefaction		
煤制品加工	Coal Product Processing		
回收能	Energy Recycled		
损失量	**Losses**	**46.47**	**44.61**
#运输和输配损失	Losses in Transportation and Transmission	46.47	44.61
终端消费量	**End-use Energy Consumption**	**1234.14**	**1188.11**
农、林、牧、渔业	Agriculture, Forestry, Animal Husbandry and Fishery	15.48	16.13
工　业	Industry	232.82	236.37
#用作原料、材料	Use as Materials		
建筑业	Construction	25.76	26.57
交通运输、仓储和邮政业	Transport, Storage and Post	59.92	61.47
批发和零售业、住宿和餐饮业	Wholesale and Retail Trade, Accommodation and Catering	107.81	106.72
其　他	Others	471.42	454.46
居民生活	Residential Consumption	320.92	286.39
平衡差额	**Balance**	**1.66**	**1.86**
消费量合计	**Total Energy Consumption**	**1280.80**	**1232.92**

7-8 综合能源平衡表(标准量)
COMPREHENSIVE ENERGY BALANCE (STANDARD VOLUME)

单位：万吨标准煤 (10000 tons of SCE)

项　目	Item	2022	2021
可供本地区消费的能源量	**Total Energy Available for Local Consumption**	**6899.82**	**7107.62**
加工转换投入(-)产出(+)量	**Input(-) or Output(+) in Processing and Conversion**	**-86.02**	**-101.33**
火力发电	Thermal Power		
供　热	Heating	-78.88	-79.08
煤炭洗选	Washing of Coal		
炼　焦	Coking		
炼油及煤制油	Oil Refining and Coal to Liquid	386.30	395.49
#油品再投入量(-)	Oil Product Re-input(-)	-409.65	-414.36
制　气	Gas Production	6.90	-1.91
#再投入量(-)	Re-input(-)	-20.33	-14.87
天然气液化	Natural Gas Liquefaction		
煤制品加工	Coal Product Processing		
回收能	Energy Recycled	29.65	13.39
损失量	**Losses**	**180.22**	**167.85**
#运输和输配损失	Losses in Transportation and Transmission	124.99	119.64
终端消费量	**End-use Energy Consumption**	**6630.65**	**6834.44**
农、林、牧、渔业	Agriculture, Forestry, Animal Husbandry and Fishery	48.12	50.29
工　业	Industry	1302.80	1313.59
#用作原料、材料	Use as Materials	205.83	174.21
建筑业	Construction	106.73	111.82
交通运输、仓储和邮政业	Transport, Storage and Post	875.74	1147.48
批发和零售业、住宿和餐饮业	Wholesale and Retail Trade, Accommodation and Catering	439.68	435.51
其　他	Others	1994.56	1946.73
居民生活	Residential Consumption	1863.01	1829.01
平衡差额	**Balance**	**2.94**	**4.00**
消费量合计	**Total Energy Consumption**	**6896.89**	**7103.62**

7-9 能源平衡表(实物量简表)(2022年)
ENERGY BALANCE (PHYSICAL VOLUME SIMPLE EDITION) (2022)

单位：万吨 (10000 tons)

项目	Item	原煤 Coal	洗精煤 Washed Coal	其他洗煤 Other Washed Coal	煤制品 Coal Products	焦炭 Coke	原油 Crude Oil	汽油 Gasoline	煤油 Kerosene
可供本地区消费的能源量	**Total Energy Available for Local Consumption**	**79.29**			**11.76**		**774.92**	**173.14**	**254.17**
加工转换投入(-)产出(+)量	**Input(-) or Output(+) in Processing and Conversion**	**-51.43**					**-773.99**	**201.68**	**76.15**
火力发电	Thermal Power	-21.35							
供热	Heating	-30.07							
煤炭洗选	Washing of Coal								
炼焦	Coking								
炼油及煤制油	Oil Refining and Coal to Liquid						-773.99	201.68	76.15
#油品再投入量(-)	Oil Product Re-input(-)								
制气	Gas Production								
#再投入量(-)	Re-input(-)								
天然气液化	Natural Gas Liquefaction								
煤制品加工	Coal Product Processing								
回收能	Energy Recycled								
损失量	**Losses**						**0.93**		
#运输和输配损失	In Transportation and Transmission								
终端消费量	**Final Consumption Industry**	**27.87**			**11.76**			**374.82**	**330.32**
农、林、牧、渔业	Agriculture, Forestry, Animal Production and Hunting, Fishing	1.28						1.83	
工业	Industry	26.56						5.88	0.05
#用作原料、材料	Use as Materials								
建筑业	Construction							6.62	
交通运输、仓储和邮政业	Transport, Storage and Post	0.02						20.00	329.73
批发和零售业、住宿和餐饮业	Wholesale and Retail Trade, Accommodation and Catering							15.18	
其他	Others							29.14	0.54
居民生活	Residential Consumption				11.76			296.17	
平衡差额	**Balance**								
消费量合计	**Total Energy Consumption**	**79.29**			**11.76**		**774.92**	**374.82**	**330.32**

7-9 续表 1 Continued 1

单位：万吨 (10000 tons)

项　　目	Item	柴　油 Diesel Oil	燃料油 Fuel Oil	石脑油 Naphtha	润滑油 Grease Oil	石　蜡 Oilfin	溶剂油 Solvent Oil	石油沥青 Oil Asphalt	石油焦 Petroleum Coal
可供本地区消费的能源量	**Total Energy Available for Local Consumption**	**-43.84**	**-0.86**	**15.06**	**0.42**	**0.03**		**19.81**	**-46.86**
加工转换投入(-)产出(+)量	**Input(-) or Output(+) in Processing and Conversion**	**169.23**	**0.90**	**-3.72**				**1.15**	**46.86**
火力发电	Thermal Power	-0.13							
供　热	Heating	-0.18	-0.16						
煤炭洗选	Washing of Coal								
炼　焦	Coking								
炼油及煤制油	Oil Refining and Coal to Liquid	169.55	1.06	129.91				1.15	46.86
#油品再投入量(-)	Oil Product Re-input(-)			-133.63					
制　气	Gas Production								
#再投入量(-)	Coke Re-input(-)								
天然气液化	Natural Gas Liquefaction								
煤制品加工	Coal Product Processing								
回收能	Energy Recycled								
损失量	**Losses**								
#运输和输配损失	Losses in Transportation and Transmission								
终端消费量	**End-use Energy Consumption**	**125.39**	**0.04**	**11.34**	**0.42**	**0.03**		**20.96**	
农、林、牧、渔业	Agriculture, Forestry, Animal Husbandry and Fishery	1.71							
工　业	Industry	11.32		11.34	0.42	0.03		20.96	
#用作原料、材料	Use as Materials			11.34	0.41	0.03		20.96	
建筑业	Construction	12.84	0.02						
交通运输、仓储和邮政业	Transport, Storage and Post	73.47							
批发和零售业、住宿和餐饮业	Wholesale and Retail Trade, Accommodation and Catering	4.61							
其　他	Others	21.43	0.01						
居民生活	Residential Consumption								
平衡差额	**Balance**								
消费量合计	**Total Energy Consumption**	**125.71**	**0.20**						

7-9 续表 2 Continued 2

单位：万吨 (10000 tons)

项　　目	Item	液化石油气 Liquefied Petroleum Gas	炼厂干气 Refinery Gas	其他石油制品 Other Petroleum Products	天然气（亿立方米） Natural Gas (100 million cu.m)	液化天然气 Liquefied Natural Gas	热力（万百万千焦） Heat (10000 million kilo-joule)	电力（亿千瓦时） Electricity (100 million kWh)	其他能源（万吨标准煤） Others (10000 tons of SCE)
可供本地区消费的能源量	**Total Energy Available for Local Consumption**	**-15.49**		**-41.77**	**197.95**	**17.14**	**849.40**	**838.89**	**269.73**
加工转换投入(－)产出(＋)量	**Input(-) or Output(+) in Processing and Conversion**	**32.32**	**66.07**	**189.75**	**-129.77**	**-0.37**	**20589.49**	**443.38**	**-144.57**
火力发电	Thermal Power	-0.05	-0.05	-0.28	-68.75		-346.86	443.57	-143.25
供　热	Heating	-0.67	-1.05	-9.46	-59.49	-0.37	20563.74	-0.19	
煤炭洗选	Washing of Coal								
炼　焦	Coking								
炼油及煤制油	Oil Refining and Coal to Liquid	105.48	75.28	271.99					-39.87
#油品再投入量(－)	Oil Product Re-input(-)	-71.29		-72.50					
制　气	Gas Production	-1.14	-8.11						21.61
#再投入量(－)	Re-input(-)				-1.53				
天然气液化	Natural Gas Liquefaction								
煤制品加工	Coal Product Processing								
回收能	Energy Recycled						372.61		16.94
损失量	**Losses**				**4.21**			**46.47**	
#运输和输配损失	Losses in Transportation and Transmission							46.47	
终端消费量	**Final Consumption Industry**	**16.83**	**66.07**	**147.98**	**63.98**	**16.77**	**21438.89**	**1234.14**	**126.68**
农、林、牧、渔业	Agriculture, Forestry, Animal Husbandry and Fishery	0.04			0.01			15.48	0.06
工　业	Industry	0.67	66.07	147.98	9.99	0.97	4933.88	232.82	4.28
#用作原料、材料	Use as Materials		4.06	128.48					0.05
建筑业	Construction	0.42			0.26		134.19	25.76	0.32
交通运输、仓储和邮政业	Transport, Storage and Post	1.52			2.59	15.80	675.50	59.92	6.32
批发和零售业、住宿和餐饮业	Wholesale and Retail Trade, Accommodation and Catering	1.43			5.55		1245.65	107.81	4.65
其　他	Others	0.75			25.04		8346.50	471.42	45.05
居民生活	Residential Consumption	12.01			20.54		6103.16	320.92	66.00
平衡差额	**Balance**							**1.66**	**-1.52**
消费量合计	**Total Energy Consumption**	**89.99**	**75.28**	**230.22**	**197.95**	**17.14**	**21785.75**	**1280.80**	**309.81**

7-10 能源平衡表(标准量简表)(2022年)
ENERGY BALANCE (STANDARD VOLUME SIMPLE EDITION) (2022)

单位：万吨标准煤 (10000 tons of SCE)

项目	Item	合计 Total	原煤 Coal	洗精煤 Washed Coal	其他洗煤 Other Washed Coal	煤制品 Coal Products	焦炭 Coke	原油 Crude Oil	汽油 Gasoline	煤油 Kerosene
可供本地区消费的能源量	**Total Energy Available for Local Consumption**	**6899.82**	**63.89**			**6.21**		**1107.05**	**254.75**	**373.99**
加工转换投入(−)产出(+)量	**Input(-) or Output(+) in Processing and Conversion**	**-86.02**	**-41.44**					**-1105.73**	**296.76**	**112.05**
火力发电	Thermal Power		-17.21							
供　热	Heating	-78.88	-24.23							
煤炭洗选	Washing of Coal									
炼　焦	Coking									
炼油及煤制油	Oil Refining and Coal to Liquid	386.30						-1105.73	296.76	112.05
#油品再投入量(−)	Oil Product Re-input(-)	-409.65								
制　气	Gas Production	6.90								
#再投入量(−)	Re-input(-)	-20.33								
天然气液化	Natural Gas Liquefaction									
煤制品加工	Coal Product Processing									
回收能	Energy Recycled	29.65								
损失量	**Losses**	**180.22**						**1.32**		
#运输和输配损失	Losses in Transportation and Transmission	124.99								
终端消费量	**Final Consumption Industry**	**6630.65**	**22.45**			**6.21**			**551.51**	**486.04**
农、林、牧、渔业	Agriculture, Forestry, Animal Husbandry and Fishery	48.12	1.03						2.70	
工　业	Industry	1302.80	21.40						8.66	0.07
#用作原料、材料	Use as Materials	205.83								
建筑业	Construction	106.73							9.73	
交通运输、仓储和邮政业	Transport, Storage and Post	875.74	0.02						29.43	485.17
批发和零售业、住宿和餐饮业	Wholesale and Retail Trade, Accommodation and Catering	439.68							22.33	
其　他	Others	1994.56							42.88	0.79
居民生活	Residential Consumption	1863.01				6.21			435.78	
平衡差额	**Balance**	**2.94**								
消费量合计	**Total Energy Consumption**	**6896.89**								

7-10 续表 1 Continued 1

单位：万吨标准煤 (10000 tons of SCE)

项　目	Item	柴　油 Diesel Oil	燃料油 Fuel Oil	石脑油 Naphtha	润滑油 Grease Oil	石　蜡 Oilfin	溶剂油 Solvent Oil	石油沥青 Oil Asphalt	石油焦 Petroleum Coal
可供本地区消费的能源量	**Total Energy Available for Local Consumption**	**-63.88**	**-1.23**	**22.59**	**0.60**	**0.04**		**26.36**	**-52.65**
加工转换投入(-)产出(+)量	**Input(-) or Output(+) in Processing and Conversion**	**246.59**	**1.28**	**-5.58**				**1.53**	**52.65**
火力发电	Thermal Power	-0.19							
供　热	Heating	-0.27	-0.22						
煤炭洗选	Washing of Coal								
炼　焦	Coking								
炼油及煤制油	Oil Refining and Coal to Liquid	247.05	1.51	194.87				1.53	52.65
#油品再投入量(-)	Oil Product Re-input(-)			-200.44					
制　气	Gas Production								
#再投入量(-)	Re-input(-)								
天然气液化	Natural Gas Liquefaction								
煤制品加工	Coal Product Processing								
回收能	Energy Recycled								
损失量	**Losses**								
#运输和输配损失	Losses in Transportation and Transmission								
终端消费量	**Final Consumption Industry**	**182.70**	**0.05**	**17.01**	**0.60**	**0.04**		**27.89**	
农、林、牧、渔业	Agriculture, Forestry,Animal Husbandry and Fishery	2.49							
工　业	Industry	16.50	0.01	17.01	0.60	0.04		27.89	
#用作原料、材料	Use as Materials			17.01	0.58	0.04		27.89	
建筑业	Construction	18.71	0.03						
交通运输、仓储和邮政业	Transport, Storage and Post	107.06							
批发和零售业、住宿和餐饮业	Wholesale and Retail Trade, Accommodation and Catering	6.72	0.01						
其　他	Others	31.23	0.01						
居民生活	Residential Consumption								
平衡差额	**Balance**								
消费量合计	**Total Energy Consumption**								

7-10 续表 2

单位：万吨标准煤

项　目	Item	液化石油气 Liquefied Petroleum Gas	炼厂干气 Refinery Gas
可供本地区消费的能源量	**Total Energy Available for Local Consumption**	**-26.56**	
加工转换投入(-)产出(+)量	**Input(-) or Output(+) in Processing and Conversion**	**55.41**	**103.82**
火力发电	Thermal Power	-0.09	-0.07
供　热	Heating	-1.15	-1.64
煤炭洗选	Washing of Coal		
炼　焦	Coking		
炼油及煤制油	Oil Refining and Coal to Liquid	180.82	118.29
#油品再投入量(-)	Oil Product Re-input(-)	-122.21	
制　气	Gas Production	-1.96	-12.75
#再投入量(-)	Re-input(-)		
天然气液化	Natural Gas Liquefaction		
煤制品加工	Coal Product Processing		
回收能	Energy Recycled		
损失量	**Losses**		
#运输和输配损失	Losses in Transportation and Transmission		
终端消费量	**Final Consumption Industry**	**28.85**	**103.82**
农、林、牧、渔业	Agriculture, Forestry, Animal Husbandry and Fishery	0.08	
工　业	Industry	1.14	103.82
#用作原料、材料	Use as Materials		6.39
建筑业	Construction	0.72	
交通运输、仓储和邮政业	Transport, Storage and Post	2.60	
批发和零售业、住宿和餐饮业	Wholesale and Retail Trade, Accommodation and Catering	2.44	
其　他	Others	1.28	
居民生活	Residential Consumption	20.59	
平衡差额	**Balance**		
消费量合计	**Total Energy Consumption**		

7-10 Continued 2

(10000 tons of SCE)

其他石油制品 Other Petroleum Products	天然气 Natural Gas	液化天然气 Liquefied Natural Gas	热力 Heat	电力 Electricity	其他能源 Others
-50.49	**2654.04**	**30.12**	**28.96**	**2256.29**	**269.73**
227.70	**-1780.46**	**-0.65**	**702.10**	**1192.52**	**-144.57**
-0.33	-1020.04		-11.83	1193.02	-143.25
-11.35	-740.09	-0.65	701.22	-0.50	
326.39					-39.87
-87.00					
					21.61
	-20.33				
			12.71		16.94
	53.91			**124.99**	
				124.99	
177.21	**819.67**	**29.47**	**731.07**	**3319.35**	**126.68**
	0.12			41.65	0.06
177.21	128.01	1.71	168.25	626.20	4.28
153.87					0.05
	3.33		4.58	69.30	0.32
	33.19	27.76	23.03	161.16	6.32
	71.09		42.48	289.96	4.65
	320.78		284.62	1267.94	45.05
	263.15		208.12	863.15	66.00
				4.46	**-1.52**

7-11 分行业能源消费总量和主要能源品种消费量(2022年)

单位：万吨

项目	Item	能源消费总量(万吨标准煤) Total Energy Consumption (10000 tons of SCE)	煤炭 Coal
合计	**Total**	**6896.89**	**91.05**
农、林、牧、渔业	Agriculture, Forestry,Animal Husbandry and Fishery	48.12	1.28
采矿业	Mining	1.16	
煤炭开采和洗选业	Mining and Washing of Coal		
石油和天然气开采业	Extraction of Petroleum and Natural Gas	0.01	
黑色金属矿采选业	Mining and Processing of Ferrous Metal Ores	0.80	
有色金属矿采选业	Mining and Processing of Non-Ferrous Metal Ores		
非金属矿采选业	Mining and Processing of Nonmetal Ores	0.01	
开采专业及辅助性活动	Professional and Support Activities for Mining	0.35	
其他采矿业	Mining of Other Ores n.e.c		
制造业	Manufacturing	1129.30	26.56
农副食品加工业	Processing of Food from Agricultural Products	17.28	
食品制造业	Manufacture of Foods	25.24	
酒、饮料和精制茶制造业	Manufacture of Wine, Beverage and Refined Tea	22.25	
烟草制品业	Manufacture of Cigarettes and Tobacco	1.05	
纺织业	Manufacture of Textile	0.77	
纺织服装、服饰业	Manufacture of Textile Wearing Apparel and Ornament	5.13	
皮革、毛皮、羽毛及其制品和制鞋业	Manufacture of Leather, Fur, Feather and Its Products, and Footwear	0.32	
木材加工和木、竹、藤、棕、草制品业	Processing of Timbers, Manufacture of Wood, Bamboo, Rattan, Palm, and Straw Products	0.38	
家具制造业	Manufacture of Furniture	3.44	
造纸和纸制品业	Manufacture of Paper and Paper Products	5.93	
印刷和记录媒介复制业	Printing, Reproduction of Recording Media	17.08	
文教、工美、体育和娱乐用品制造业	Manufacture of Articles for Culture, Education, Artwork, Sport and Entertainment Activities	1.67	
石油、煤炭及其他燃料加工业	Processing of Petroleum, Coal and Other Fuels of Nucleus Fuel	482.02	
化学原料和化学制品制造业	Manufacture of Chemical Raw Materials and Chemical Products	55.80	
医药制造业	Manufacture of Medicines	66.49	
化学纤维制造业	Manufacture of Chemical Fibers	1.05	
橡胶和塑料制品业	Manufacture of Rubber and Plastics Products	7.98	
非金属矿物制品业	Manufacture of Non-Metallic Mineral Products	93.60	26.56

注：各行业能源消费总量不等于各品种能源消费量(标准煤)的简单加总，应扣除能量重复计算部分。

CONSUMPTION OF TOTAL ENERGY AND MAIN ENERGY VARIETIES BY SECTOR (2022)

(10000 tons)

汽 油 Gasoline	煤 油 Kerosene	柴 油 Diesel Oil	燃料油 Fuel Oil	液 化 石油气 Liquefied Petroleum Gas	液 化 天然气 Liquefied Natural Gas	天然气 (亿立方米) Natural Gas (100 million cu.m)	热 力 (万百万千焦) Heat (10 billion kilo-joule)	电 力 (亿千瓦时) Electricity (100 million kW·h)
374.82	**330.32**	**125.71**	**0.20**	**89.99**	**17.14**	**197.95**	**21785.75**	**1280.80**
1.83		1.71		0.04		0.01		15.48
0.04		0.15				0.11	170.75	0.23
						0.11		
0.01							170.75	0.20
0.03		0.15						0.03
5.25	0.05	10.57		73.78	0.97	15.50	4891.65	169.53
0.17		0.35		0.01	0.25	0.33	67.31	3.50
0.14		0.27		0.02	0.14	0.60	88.39	5.07
0.12		0.12		0.01		0.89	41.62	3.39
						0.04		0.22
0.01							2.11	0.24
0.13		0.03			0.01	0.10	21.55	0.99
0.01							2.90	0.06
0.05		0.02						0.10
0.17		0.03		0.01		0.04	3.74	0.94
0.08		0.04			0.08	0.12	3.07	1.47
0.28		0.16				0.15	33.66	4.95
0.04		0.01		0.01		0.01	10.20	0.39
0.01		0.01		73.32		6.89	2905.27	22.36
0.23		0.30		0.18	0.17	0.23	349.06	11.31
0.31		0.09		0.01		1.25	379.83	13.76
0.01						0.03		0.24
0.12		0.11		0.02		0.04	7.53	2.54
0.29		6.98		0.01	0.28	1.08	114.36	8.24

Note: The data on total energy consumption of all sectors is not equal to the simplesum of consumption (SCE equivalent) of all sorts of energy,which should exclude the double-counted part of energy.

7-11 续表

单位：万吨

项目	Item	能源消费总量(万吨标准煤) Total Energy Consumption (10000 tons of SCE)	煤炭 Coal
黑色金属冶炼及压延加工业	Smelting and Pressing of Ferrous Metals	11.87	
有色金属冶炼及压延加工业	Smelting and Processing of Non-ferrous Metals	4.35	
金属制品业	Manufacture of Fabricated Metal Products	11.07	
通用设备制造业	Manufacture of General-purpose Machinery	20.24	
专用设备制造业	Manufacture of Special-purpose Machinery	21.57	
汽车制造业	Manufacture of Motor Vehicles	76.84	
铁路、船舶、航空航天和其他运输设备制造业	Manufacture of Railway, Ships, Aerospace and Other Transport Equipments	30.46	
电气机械和器材制造业	Manufacture of Electrical Machinery and Equipment	14.14	
计算机、通讯和其他电子设备制造业	Manufacture of Computer, Communication Equipment and Other Electronic Equipment	114.35	
仪器仪表制造业	Manufacture of Measuring Instruments and Meters	6.22	
其他制造业	Other Manufacturing	4.89	
废弃资源综合利用业	Waste Recycling and Recovery	1.38	
金属制品、机械和设备修理业	Repair of Fabricated Metal Products, Machinery and Equipment	4.44	
电力、燃气及水的生产和供应业	Production and Supply of Electricity, Gas and Water	438.58	51.43
电力、热力生产和供应业	Production and Supply of Electric Power and Heat Power	316.27	51.43
燃气生产和供应业	Production and Supply of Gas	56.12	
水的生产和供应业	Production and Supply of Water	66.19	
建筑业	Construction	106.73	
批发和零售业	Wholesale and Retail Trade	241.86	…
交通运输、仓储和邮政业	Transport, Storage and Post	875.74	0.02
住宿和餐饮业	Accommodation and Catering	197.82	
信息传输、软件和信息技术服务业	Information Transmission,Software and Information Technology Services	335.07	
金融业	Finance	77.19	
房地产业	Real Estate Trade	492.33	
租赁和商务服务业	Leasing and Business Services	200.33	
科学研究和技术服务业	Scientific Research and Development, Technical Services	208.34	
水利、环境和公共设施管理业	Management of Water Conservancy,Environment and Public Facilities	85.29	
居民服务、修理和其他服务业	Resident Services, Repair and Other Services	44.36	
教育	Education	247.17	
卫生和社会工作	Healthcare and Social Works	116.97	
文化、体育和娱乐业	Culture, Sports and Entertainment	81.95	
公共管理、社会保障和社会组织	Public Management, Social Security and Social Organizations	92.99	
居民生活	Residential Consumption	1863.01	11.76

7-11 Continued

(10000 tons)

汽 油 Gasoline	煤 油 Kerosene	柴 油 Diesel Oil	燃料油 Fuel Oil	液 化 石油气 Liquefied Petroleum Gas	液 化 天然气 Liquefied Natural Gas	天然气 (亿立方米) Natural Gas (100 million cu.m)	热 力 (万百万千焦) Heat (10 billion kilo-joule)	电 力 (亿千瓦时) Electricity (100 million kW·h)
0.01		...	...			0.82	2.16	2.74
0.02		...				0.03	4.71	1.39
0.40		0.09		0.01	0.01	0.15	43.22	2.54
0.41		0.06		0.08	0.01	0.15	87.34	5.27
0.58	0.05	0.22		0.02	...	0.12	122.58	5.40
0.24		0.81		0.02	...	1.65	72.45	19.02
0.15		0.10		...	0.01	0.16	103.36	9.10
0.40		0.08		0.02		0.11	45.77	3.68
0.31		0.03		...	...	0.37	282.09	36.90
0.23		0.01		0.01		0.02	41.64	1.55
0.04		0.42		0.01		0.01	37.13	1.02
0.02		0.05		...		0.01	0.07	0.40
0.25		0.15		0.01		0.09	18.53	0.76
0.59		0.92	0.16	0.04	0.38	128.36	218.34	109.72
0.34		0.80	0.16	0.02	0.37	123.97	178.84	86.01
0.13		0.02			...	4.29	6.66	0.36
0.12		0.11		0.02	0.01	0.09	32.84	23.35
6.62		12.84	0.02	0.42		0.26	134.19	25.76
14.28		4.51		0.24		0.92	629.51	67.01
20.00	329.73	73.47		1.52	15.80	2.59	675.50	59.92
0.90		0.10	...	1.19		4.63	616.14	40.80
3.40		0.55		0.02		0.35	378.67	115.34
0.95		0.02		0.01		0.20	409.06	21.97
2.38		0.33		0.07		10.93	1950.97	102.67
7.41		10.23		0.11		1.37	795.85	47.48
7.26	0.54	0.82	...	0.08		2.75	1029.20	46.15
1.67		7.69		0.09		0.45	110.93	22.72
2.25		0.83		0.03		1.74	52.67	5.20
1.18		0.56	...	0.13		4.69	1829.01	42.49
1.07		0.12		0.15		1.45	697.14	26.12
1.28		0.23		0.07		0.69	449.27	20.03
0.30		0.07				0.42	643.73	21.25
296.17				12.01		20.54	6103.16	320.92

7-12 能源消费弹性系数(2000-2022年)
ELASTICITY COEFFICIENT OF ENERGY CONSUMPTION (2000-2022)

年 份 Year	能源消费比上年增长(%) Growth of Energy Consumption over the Previous Year (%)	电力消费比上年增长(%) Growth of Electricity Consumption over the Previous Year (%)	能源消费弹性系数 Elasticity Coefficient of Energy Consumption	电力消费弹性系数 Elasticity Coefficient of Electricity Consumption
2000	6.08	9.53	0.51	0.79
2001	2.06	5.68	0.17	0.48
2002	4.89	9.54	0.41	0.81
2003	4.78	5.71	0.43	0.51
2004	10.57	10.60	0.79	0.80
2005	7.44	11.16	0.60	0.91
2006	6.92	9.16	0.54	0.72
2007	6.45	9.06	0.45	0.63
2008	0.67	4.90	0.07	0.55
2009	3.84	7.15	0.38	0.71
2010	5.84	9.49	0.56	0.91
2011	0.59	2.21	0.07	0.27
2012	2.61	5.91	0.34	0.77
2013	2.44	4.42	0.32	0.57
2014	1.60	2.72	0.22	0.37
2015	0.31	1.91	0.04	0.28
2016	1.67	7.25	0.24	1.05
2017	2.48	4.57	0.36	0.67
2018	2.56	7.08	0.38	1.06
2019	1.25	2.10	0.21	0.35
2020	-8.13	-2.24	0.00	0.00
2021	5.05	8.13	0.57	0.92
2022	-2.91	3.88	0.00	5.62

7-13 平均每万元地区生产总值能源消费量(2010-2022年)
ENERGY CONSUMPTION PER 10000 YUAN OF GROSS DOMESTIC PRODUCT (2010-2022)

年 份 Year	能源总消费量 (吨标准煤) Total Energy Consumption (ton of SCE)	煤 炭 (千克) Coal (kg)	电 力 (千瓦时) Electricity (kW·h)	石 油 (千克) Petroleum (kg)	天然气 (立方米) Natural Gas (cu.m)
	地区生产总值按2010年可比价格计算 GDP calculated at the comparable prices of 2010				
2010	0.425	169.07	537.23	90.59	49.98
2011	0.396	140.04	508.04	89.50	45.45
2012	0.377	125.10	499.50	82.02	52.85
2013	0.358	107.57	484.10	78.89	52.64
2014	0.339	86.14	463.00	76.30	56.40
2015	0.316	54.06	441.32	73.48	68.14
	地区生产总值按2015年可比价格计算 GDP calculated at the comparable prices of 2015				
2015	0.275	47.02	383.89	63.92	59.28
2016	0.261	31.99	385.10	59.58	61.26
2017	0.251	17.33	377.06	58.52	58.16
2018	0.241	9.15	378.40	56.55	62.23
2019	0.230	5.71	364.28	54.73	59.15
2020	0.209	4.17	352.41	42.16	59.26
	地区生产总值按2020年可比价格计算 GDP calculated at the comparable prices of 2020				
2020	0.188	3.76	317.23	37.95	53.35
2021	0.182	3.34	315.13	35.44	49.27
2022	0.175	2.01	325.13	27.64	50.85

7-14 人均生活用能源(2010-2022年)
PER CAPITA ENERGY CONSUMPTION FOR LIVING PURPOSE (2010-2022)

年份 Year	合计 (千克标准煤) Total (kg of SCE)	煤炭 (千克) Coal (kg)	电力 (千瓦时) Electricity (kW·h)	液化石油气 (千克) Liquefied Petroleum Gas(kg)	天然气 (立方米) Natural Gas (cu.m)	汽油 (升) Gasoline (liter)
2010	650.2	173.6	729.1	11.3	53.1	164.9
2011	662.4	166.9	726.3	10.6	52.6	167.4
2012	690.9	158.5	789.2	9.3	56.3	173.9
2013	684.4	147.0	747.3	9.8	56.8	179.9
2014	700.4	136.6	787.9	10.9	59.2	181.3
2015	689.5	125.3	801.8	11.5	63.1	192.7
2016	707.7	109.8	891.6	12.0	58.5	196.5
2017	753.0	82.4	993.4	11.8	74.7	205.1
2018	771.7	34.7	1168.9	10.9	64.3	223.1
2019	772.0	22.2	1148.4	8.6	66.6	231.5
2020	782.3	16.4	1277.9	4.9	72.4	206.8
2021	835.6	8.7	1308.4	4.8	80.2	237.3
2022	852.1	5.4	1467.8	5.5	93.9	185.6

注：本表人均生活用能源按常住人口年平均数计算。2011—2019年数据根据北京市第七次全国人口普查结果进行了修订。

Note: Data on per capita energy consumption for living purpose in the table is calculated by the annual average permanent population. Data for 2011-2019 have been revised in accordance with the results of the seventh national population census in Beijing.

7-15 全社会用电量情况(1978-2022年)
TOTAL ELECTRICITY CONSUMPTION IN BEIJING (1978-2022)

单位：万千瓦时 (10000 kW·h)

年 份 Year	全社会用电量 Electricity Consumption	第一产业 Primary Industry	第二产业 Secondary Industry	工 业 Industry	建筑业 Construction	第三产业 Tertiary Industry	城乡居民生活用电 Residential Electricity Consumption	城 市 Urban	乡 村 Rural
1978	735000	48993	570621	570621		94555	20831	11022	9809
1979	802317	52134	620262	620262		107437	22484	11495	10989
1980	854638	65283	648496	648496		116947	23912	12441	11471
1981	867153	80027	643976	643976		121883	21267	9452	11815
1982	925700	104842	657060	657060		139403	24395	10820	13575
1983	956293	92601	687937	687937		151290	24465	12320	12145
1984	1029420	105234	716653	716653		177455	30078	16025	14053
1985	1106255	111110	746324	746324		210622	38199	22479	15720
1986	1181155	105688	851519	835725	15794	175090	48858	31008	17850
1987	1285023	77909	923797	899760	24037	224747	58570	35063	23507
1988	1378574	83809	970885	943383	27502	248446	75434	48624	26810
1989	1421817	100151	979216	949629	29587	258067	84383	56120	28263
1990	1504785	93049	1014037	986356	27681	302775	94924	65262	29662
1991	1613977	93256	1061207	1032064	29143	348769	110745	77575	33170
1992	1759611	101985	1155514	1123835	31679	375874	126238	88621	37617
1993	1924978	107010	1243115	1206001	37114	429835	145018	103579	41439
1994	2054504	101134	1307898	1262961	44937	479679	165791	119025	46766
1995	2225922	102099	1403864	1341398	62466	538936	181022	130897	50125
1996	2443709	111904	1496968	1422590	74378	617286	217551	158474	59077
1997	2636078	120444	1529201	1449129	80072	721774	264659	196641	68018
1998	2762080	108267	1548485	1457149	91336	811283	294045	220543	73502
1999	2972629	121242	1581977	1478523	103454	912834	356576	276642	79934
2000	3844266	130865	2172604	2066892	105712	1064322	476475	385396	91079
2001	3999415	131811	2105819	1978673	127146	1222471	539314	439058	100256
2002	4399637	137370	2293735	2145292	148443	1342490	626042	517386	108656
2003	4676056	107372	2418419	2250525	167894	1447344	702921	574623	128298
2004	5131804	104234	2593504	2391414	202090	1628731	805335	647474	157861
2005	5705364	114308	2795753	2605832	189921	1906093	889210	706405	182805
2006	6115719	122550	2943550	2744127	199423	2090888	958731	768884	189847
2007	6670089	133557	3091374	2881807	209567	2378399	1066759	862604	204155
2008	6897189	136065	2943893	2763399	180494	2654140	1163091	949878	213213
2009	7391465	157310	3027974	2853018	174956	2918229	1287952	982720	305232
2010	8099029	168992	3278682	3081364	197319	3258009	1393346	951811	441535
2011	8217055	170368	3109174	2894464	214708	3490143	1447370	945588	501782
2012	8742835	181391	3209078	2980645	228430	3734022	1618344	1370932	247412
2013	9131113	185749	3345854	3110626	235229	4029145	1570365	1347401	222964
2014	9370485	185633	3352904	3129060	223846	4139319	1692629	1457398	235231
2015	9527169	185031	3238220	3030638	207583	4356332	1747586	1496078	251508
2016	10202704	196243	3343189	3129675	213514	4708959	1954313	1664539	289774
2017	10668904	112930	3323724	3105551	218276	5063019	2169231	1842219	327012
2018	11423809	106382	3316045	3073165	253012	5437818	2563564	2106181	457383
2019	11663964	98872	3254317	2990649	263949	5794810	2515964	2049447	466517
2020	11399700	90673	2944549	2696395	248451	5566552	2797925	2306966	490959
2021	12329152	94160	3077101	2811754	265681	6294023	2863869	2356386	507482
2022	12808016	91235	3051841	2794799	257647	6455725	3209216	2666550	542666

注：1.1985年以前农、林、牧、渔和水利业用电量中，只包含农业排灌、农副业和社队企业的用电量。
2.1980年以前的城市居民用电量以全市市政用电量的 1/10计算。
3.2000年以前工业用电量不包含输配损失和发电企业自产自用电量。
4.自2018年起，行业划分执行《国民经济行业分类》(GB/T 4754—2017)标准，为保证数据可比，对2017年数据进行了修订。

资料来源：国网北京市电力公司。

Note: a) Before 1985, electricity consumption by agriculture, forestry, animal husbandry and fishery and water conservancy only included the electricity consumption by farming irrigation, agricultural and sideline products, and village enterprises.
b) Before 1980, electricity consumption by urban residents was one-tenth of the total electricity consumption by municipal administration in Beijing.
c) Before 2000, electricity consumption by industry excluded transmission and distribution losses and electricity generated and consumed by power generating enterprises.
d) Sectors are classified in accordance with the standard in the *Classification of National Economic Sectors* (GB/T 4754-2017) since 2018. In order to keep the data comparable, the data of 2017 have been revised.

Source: State Grid Beijing Electric Power Corporation.

7-16 水资源情况(2001-2022年)

单位：亿立方米

项　　目	Item	2001	2002	2003	2004	2005	2006
全年水资源总量	**Total Volume of Water Resource in the Year**	**19.2**	**16.1**	**18.4**	**21.4**	**23.2**	**22.1**
地表水资源量	Volume of Surface Water Resource	7.8	5.3	6.1	8.2	7.6	6.7
地下水资源量	Volume of Underground Water Resource	15.7	14.7	14.8	16.5	15.6	15.4
人均水资源(立方米)	**Per-capita Water Resource(cu.m)**	**139.7**	**114.7**	**127.8**	**145.1**	**153.1**	**140.6**
水资源配置量	**Water Resource Allocation**	**38.9**	**34.6**	**35.8**	**34.6**	**34.5**	**34.3**
按来源分	By Source						
地表水	Surface Water	11.7	10.4	8.3	5.7	7.0	6.4
地下水	Underground Water	27.2	24.2	25.4	26.8	24.9	24.3
再生水	Recycled Water			2.1	2.0	2.6	3.6
南水北调水	Water Transit from South to North						
全年用水总量	**Total Volume of Water Consumed in the Year**	**38.9**	**34.6**	**35.8**	**34.6**	**34.5**	**34.3**
按用途分	By Purpose						
农业用水	Water Used by Agriculture	17.4	15.5	13.8	13.5	13.2	12.8
工业用水	Water Used by Industry	9.2	7.6	8.4	7.7	6.8	6.2
生活用水	Domestic Water	12.0	10.8	13.0	12.8	13.4	13.7
生态环境用水	Water for the Environment	0.3	0.8	0.6	0.6	1.1	1.6
万元地区生产总值水耗(立方米)	**Water Consumption per 10000 yuan GDP (cu.m)**	**100.81**	**76.50**	**67.97**	**55.26**	**48.25**	**40.90**
万元地区生产总值水耗下降率(%)	**Decrease Rate of Water Consumption per 10000 yuan GDP (%)**	**13.81**	**20.46**	**6.92**	**14.82**	**11.08**	**11.86**

注：1.本表人均水资源按常住人口年平均数计算。2011-2019年数据根据北京市第七次全国人口普查结果进行了修订。
2.自2020年起，原“全年供水总量”更名为“水资源配置量”。
3.万元地区生产总值水耗按当年价格计算，下降率按可比价格计算。如按可比价格计算，2022年万元地区生产总值水耗为10.16立方米。
4.2022年万元地区生产总值水耗及下降率为初步核算数。

资料来源：除人均数据、万元地区生产总值水耗及其下降率以外，其他数据来自北京市水务局。

STATISTICS FOR WATER RESOURCES(2001-2022)

(100 million cu.m)

2007	2008	2009	2010	2011	2012	2013	2014	2015	2016	2017	2018	2019	2020	2021	2022
23.8	**34.2**	**21.8**	**23.1**	**26.8**	**39.5**	**24.8**	**20.3**	**26.8**	**35.1**	**29.8**	**35.5**	**24.6**	**25.8**	**61.3**	**23.7**
7.6	12.8	6.8	7.2	9.2	18.0	9.4	6.5	9.3	14.0	12.0	14.3	8.6	8.3	31.6	7.4
16.2	21.4	15.1	15.9	17.6	21.6	15.4	13.8	17.4	21.1	17.7	21.1	16.0	17.5	29.7	16.4
145.3	**198.5**	**120.3**	**120.8**	**134.5**	**192.6**	**118.1**	**94.3**	**122.8**	**160.0**	**135.6**	**161.7**	**112.1**	**117.6**	**280.1**	**108.6**
34.8	**35.1**	**35.5**	**35.2**	**36.0**	**35.9**	**36.4**	**37.5**	**38.2**	**38.8**	**39.5**	**39.3**	**41.7**	**40.6**	40.8	**40.0**
5.7	5.5	4.6	4.6	5.5	5.2	4.8	8.5	2.9	2.9	3.6	3.0	6.6	8.5	4.4	5.9
24.2	22.9	21.8	21.2	20.9	20.4	20.1	19.6	18.2	17.5	16.6	16.3	15.5	13.5	13.9	12.2
5.0	6.0	6.5	6.8	7.0	7.5	8.0	8.6	9.5	10.0	10.5	10.8	11.5	12.0	12.0	12.1
	0.7	2.6	2.6	2.6	2.8	3.5	0.8	7.6	8.4	8.8	9.3	8.1	6.6	10.5	9.9
34.8	**35.1**	**35.5**	**35.2**	**36.0**	**35.9**	**36.4**	**37.5**	**38.2**	**38.8**	**39.5**	**39.3**	**41.7**	**40.6**	**40.8**	**40.0**
12.4	12.0	12.0	11.4	10.9	9.3	9.1	8.2	6.5	6.1	5.1	4.2	3.7	3.2	2.8	2.6
5.8	5.2	5.2	5.1	5.0	4.9	5.1	5.1	3.8	3.8	3.5	3.3	3.3	3.0	2.9	2.4
13.9	14.7	14.7	14.7	15.6	16.0	16.3	17.0	17.5	17.8	18.3	18.4	18.7	17.0	18.4	18.6
2.7	3.2	3.6	4.0	4.5	5.7	5.9	7.2	10.4	11.1	12.6	13.4	16.0	17.4	16.7	16.4
33.38	**29.71**	**27.52**	**23.50**	**20.92**	**18.86**	**17.21**	**16.35**	**15.42**	**14.35**	**13.22**	**11.87**	**11.76**	**11.30**	**9.95**	**9.62**
11.32	**7.45**	**8.08**	**10.28**	**5.38**	**7.37**	**5.89**	**4.05**	**4.70**	**4.98**	**4.70**	**6.75**	**0.02**	**3.58**	**7.62**	**2.64**

Note: a) Data on per capita water resource in the table are calculated by the annual average permanent population. Data for 2011-2019 have been revised in accordance with the results of the seventh national population census in Beijing.

b) Since 2020, the original Total Volume of Water Supplied in the Year has been changed to Water Resource Allocation.

c) Water consumption per 10000 yuan of GDP is at calculated current prices, and decrease rate is calculated at comparable prices. If calculated at comparable prices, the water consumption per 10000 yuan of GDP in 2022 was 10.16 cubic metres.

d) The data on water consumption per 10000 yuan of GDP and its decrease rate in 2022 were the preliminary accounting data.

Source: Except for the per capita data and the data on water consumption per 10000 yuan of GDP and its decrease rate, all the other data are from Beijing Water Authority.

7-17 分行业规模以上工业用水量情况
WATER CONSUMPTION OF INDUSTRIAL ENTERPRISES ABOVE DESIGNATED SIZE BY SECTOR

项目	Item	用水量（万立方米）Water Consumption (10000 cu.m)		重复用水率(%) Reuse Rate of Water (%)	
		2022	2022年为2021年% 2022 as % of 2021	2022	2021
合　计	**Total**	**23777.6**	**99.3**	**95.6**	**95.5**
采矿业	**Mining**	**1026.0**	**90.3**	**91.9**	**90.5**
煤炭开采和洗选业	Mining and Washing of Coal				
石油和天然气开采业	Extraction of Petroleum and Natural Gas	3.0	64.9		
黑色金属矿采选业	Mining and Processing of Ferrous Metal Ores	881.5	86.3	92.9	91.4
有色金属矿采选业	Mining and Processing of Non-Ferrous Metal Ores				
非金属矿采选业	Mining and Processing of Nonmetal Ores				
开采专业及辅助性活动	Professional and Support Activities for Mining	141.4	128.4		
其他采矿业	Mining of Other Ores				
制造业	**Manufacturing**	**12057.7**	**100.6**	**95.7**	**95.4**
农副食品加工业	Processing of Food from Agricultural Products	445.9	100.1	77.6	71.6
食品制造业	Manufacture of Foods	654.1	96.5	89.0	90.1
酒、饮料和精制茶制造业	Manufacture of Wine, Beverage and Refined Tea	1483.1	98.8	61.7	64.3
烟草制品业	Manufacture of Cigarettes and Tobacco	15.6	73.5	98.5	98.2
纺织业	Manufacture of Textile	2.7	93.3		
纺织服装、服饰业	Manufacture of Textile, Wearing Apparel and Ornament	50.6	92.2	0.4	
皮革、毛皮、羽毛及其制品和制鞋业	Manufacture of Leather, Fur, Feather and Its Products, and Footwear	0.8	80.1		
木材加工和木、竹、藤、棕、草制品业	Processing of Timbers, Manufacture of Wood, Bamboo, Rattan, Palm and Straw Products	0.3	110.3		
家具制造业	Manufacture of Furniture	33.1	94.1	3.5	0.8
造纸和纸制品业	Manufacture of Paper and Paper Products	52.4	98.8	70.5	71.9
印刷和记录媒介复制业	Printing, Reproduction of Recording Media	172.3	101.9	63.7	66.0
文教、工美、体育和娱乐用品制造业	Manufacture of Articles for Culture, Education, Artwork, Sport and Entertainment Activities	13.7	86.2		
石油、煤炭及其他燃料加工业	Processing of Petroleum, Coal and Other Fuels	1748.2	102.4	98.8	98.7
化学原料和化学制品制造业	Manufacture of Chemical Raw Materials and Chemical Products	294.7	95.6	98.6	98.6
医药制造业	Manufacture of Medicines	1518.3	106.4	80.9	86.6
化学纤维制造业	Manufacture of Chemical Fibres	9.8	96.4	97.5	97.4
橡胶和塑料制品业	Manufacture of Rubber and Plastics Products	37.0	92.1	96.5	93.9
非金属矿物制品业	Manufacture of Non-metallic Mineral Products	724.2	95.1	86.4	85.4
黑色金属冶炼和压延加工业	Smelting and Pressing of Ferrous Metals	175.4	89.3	97.8	97.6
有色金属冶炼和压延加工业	Smelting and Pressing of Ferrous Metals	49.9	123.6	95.4	96.6
金属制品业	Manufacture of Fabricated Metal Products	84.0	98.4	19.5	93.5
通用设备制造业	Manufacture of General-Purpose Machinery	186.2	92.0	90.9	90.3
专用设备制造业	Manufacture of Special-Purpose Machinery	250.7	102.0	55.3	49.8
汽车制造业	Manufacture of Motor Vehicles	755.4	94.0	93.3	93.0
铁路、船舶、航空航天和其他运输设备制造业	Manufacture of Railway, Ships, Aerospace and Other Transport Equipments	68.3	102.3	94.3	94.6
电气机械和器材制造业	Manufacture of Electrical Machinery and Equipment	141.1	97.0	14.9	14.4
计算机、通信和其他电子设备制造业	Manufacture of Computers, Communication Equipment and Other Electronic Equipment	2888.4	106.2	95.3	93.5
仪器仪表制造业	Manufacture of Measuring Instrument and Meter	71.1	100.2	0.5	45.8
其他制造业	Other Manufacturing	5.7	106.5		
废弃资源综合利用业	Waste Rrecycling and Recovery	2.7	80.2		93.2
金属制品、机械和设备修理业	Repair of Fabricated Metal Products, Machinery and Equipment	122.0	71.2		
电力、热力、燃气及水生产和供应业	**Production and Supply of Electricity, Heating Power, Gas and Water**	**10693.9**	**98.9**	**95.7**	**95.9**
电力、热力生产和供应业	Production and Supply of Electric Power and Heat Power	6475.1	94.8	97.1	97.2
燃气生产和供应业	Production and Supply of Gas	35.0	90.1		9.6
水的生产和供应业	Production and Supply of Water	4183.8	106.0	79.7	81.5

注：重复用水率=重复用水量/(用新水量+重复用水量)×100%。

Note: Reuse Rate of Water = Volume of Water Used Repeatedly / (Volume of New Water Used + Volume of Water Used Repeatedly)×100%.

7–18 气象情况(1978–2022年)
METEOROLOGY (1978-2022)

年份 Year	降水量(毫米) Precipitation (mm)	平均气温(℃) Average Temperature (℃)	最高 Highest	最低 Lowest	日照时数(时) Hours of Sunshine (hour)	平均风速(米/秒) Average Wind Speed (meter/second)	平均气压(百帕) Average Air Pressure (100 pa)	大风日数(日) Days of Strong Wind (day)	雨日数(日) Days of Rain (day)
1978	664.8	11.6	37.5	-14.4	2865.4	2.6	1012.8	35	64
1979	718.4	11.1	35.9	-15.4	2667.4	2.5	1012.2	33	63
1980	380.7	11.0	35.1	-15.4	2920.8	2.5	1012.7	29	83
1981	393.2	12.3	38.1	-14.0	2803.9	2.5	1010.8	15	92
1982	544.4	12.8	37.3	-14.3	2825.1	2.6	1010.5	26	92
1983	489.9	13.0	37.2	-15.0	2844.3	2.4	1010.3	29	100
1984	488.8	11.9	36.1	-14.9	2767.6	2.4	1010.6	18	90
1985	721.0	11.5	35.1	-15.2	2511.9	2.2	1010.4	12	104
1986	665.3	12.1	38.5	-15.4	2804.1	2.3	1010.7	21	96
1987	683.9	12.3	36.1	-15.5	2631.9	2.4	1010.3	23	102
1988	673.3	12.7	38.1	-13.2	2558.1	2.4	1010.8	17	96
1989	442.2	13.2	35.8	-11.0	2626.2	1.9	1011.1	3	78
1990	697.3	12.7	37.5	-14.8	2325.0	1.9	1010.6	12	113
1991	747.9	12.5	35.7	-12.6	2536.6	2.1	1010.8	8	98
1992	541.5	12.8	37.5	-8.7	2712.5	2.2	1011.0	6	100
1993	506.7	13.0	35.8	-13.0	2669.8	2.6	1010.8	12	91
1994	813.2	13.7	37.2	-11.5	2470.5	2.5	1010.1	9	92
1995	572.5	13.3	35.0	-9.2	2519.1	2.6	1010.3	16	89
1996	700.9	12.7	36.0	-10.0	2418.7	2.6	1011.0	16	103
1997	430.9	13.1	38.2	-14.0	2596.5	2.5	1012.9	11	76
1998	731.7	13.1	37.2	-14.2	2420.7	2.3	1012.5	10	93
1999	266.9	13.1	41.9	-12.2	2594.0	2.4	1012.5	7	86
2000	371.1	12.8	39.4	-15.0	2667.2	2.5	1012.7	10	83
2001	338.9	12.9	39.6	-17.0	2611.7	2.4	1012.9	10	78
2002	370.4	13.2	41.1	-12.8	2588.4	2.3	1012.7	15	84
2003	444.9	12.9	37.6	-15.0	2260.2	2.5	1013.3	6	93
2004	483.5	13.5	38.9	-12.9	2515.4	2.4	1012.6	12	94
2005	410.7	13.2	38.9	-11.5	2576.1	2.4	1012.8	5	79
2006	318.0	13.4	37.3	-14.7	2192.7	2.2	1012.5	5	86
2007	483.9	14.0	37.3	-11.7	2351.1	2.2	1012.6	5	78
2008	626.3	13.4	36.3	-13.5	2391.4	2.2	1012.6	8	100
2009	480.6	13.3	39.6	-12.2	2511.8	2.2	1011.9	15	86
2010	522.5	12.6	40.6	-16.7	2382.9	2.3	1012.2	14	88
2011	720.6	13.4	35.9	-11.6	2485.7	2.2	1013.2	3	82
2012	733.2	12.9	38.0	-13.7	2450.2	2.2	1012.2	3	85
2013	578.9	12.8	38.2	-14.1	2371.1	2.1	1012.2	3	71
2014	461.5	14.1	41.1	-11.2	2344.1	2.1	1013.0	8	77
2015	458.6	13.7	38.9	-9.2	2420.2	2.1	1013.2	7	99
2016	669.1	13.8	37.8	-15.2	2502.1	2.1	1013.1	2	86
2017	576.2	14.2	38.5	-10.1	2600.1	2.1	1013.1	4	78
2018	546.5	13.6	39.9	-13.9	2483.7	2.0	1013.2	3	73
2019	406.3	13.8	38.0	-14.4	2542.3	2.1	1013.1	8	65
2020	527.1	13.8	37.8	-12.8	2527.4	2.0	1013.1	4	96
2021	698.4	13.6	37.2	-19.6	2292.2	1.9	1012.4	8	109
2022	585.4	13.4	39.2	-11.3	2579.1	1.9	1012.8	5	77

资料来源：北京市气象局。
Source: Beijing Municipal Bureau of Meteorology.

7-19 气　象(2022年)
METEOROLOGY (2022)

月 份 Month	降水量 (毫米) Precipitation (mm)	平均气温(℃) Average Temperature (℃)	日照时数(时) Hours of Sunshine (hour)	平均风速(米/秒) Average Wind Speed (meter/second)	平均气压(百帕) Average Air Pressure (100 pa)	大风日数(日) Days of Strong Wind (day)	雨日数(日) Days of Rain (day)
全 年 Total	**585.4**	**13.4**	**2579.1**	**1.9**	**1012.8**	**5**	**77**
1	2.8	-2.2	177.6	1.7	1024.5		
2	3.0	-0.9	221.9	2.1	1024.6		
3	12.1	7.6	199.6	2.0	1014.1	1	7
4	13.4	16.3	245.8	2.4	1011.2		4
5	11.2	21.3	281.6	2.1	1005.4		6
6	87.6	25.7	185.0	2.0	998.8		14
7	302.3	27.4	211.7	1.7	999.8		13
8	108.7	25.9	196.7	1.7	1002.4		17
9	4.2	22.7	281.6	1.7	1009.5	2	4
10	6.7	13.2	187.6	1.6	1019.6		5
11	33.4	6.7	174.4	1.6	1018.7	1	7
12		-3.1	215.6	2.2	1024.8	1	

注：1.年极端最高气温39.2℃，出现日期6月25日。
　　2.年极端最低气温-11.3℃，出现日期2月14日。
资料来源：北京市气象局。
Note: a)Annual utmost highest air temperature is 39.2℃, seen on the 25th of June .
　　b)Annual utmost lowest air temperature is -11.3℃, seen on the 14th of Feburary.
Source: Beijing Municipal Bureau of Meteorology.

7-20 污水处理及环境卫生(1978-2022年)
SEWAGE DISPOSAL AND ENVIRONMENTAL SANITATION (1978-2022)

年份 Year	污水管道长度(公里) Length of Sewage Pipes (km)	污水处理能力(万立方米/日) Sewage Treatment Capacity (10000 cu.m/day)	污水处理率(%) Sewage Treatment Rate (%)	再生水利用量(万立方米) Volume of Recycled Water Used (10000 cu.m)	生活垃圾无害化处理能力(吨/日) Harmless Disposal Capacity of Domestic Waste (ton/day)	生活垃圾产生量(万吨) Output of Domestic Waste (10000 tons)	生活垃圾清运量(万吨) Domestic Waste Removed and Transported (10000 tons)	生活垃圾无害化处理率(%) Rate of Harmless Disposal of Domestic Waste (%)	粪便清运量(万吨) Volume of Excrement Removed and Transported (10000 tons)
1978	290	23.2	7.6				107.2		88.9
1979	309	23.2	10.2				128.0		89.4
1980	334	23.2	9.4				147.0		95.1
1981	347	25.2	10.8				174.0		97.6
1982	365	25.2	10.9				204.7		99.3
1983	411	25.2	10.2				221.4		99.5
1984	568	25.2	10.0				235.4		98.8
1985	706	25.2	10.0				248.1		142.2
1986	747	26.4	8.9				274.4		167.5
1987	805	26.4	7.7				298.3		181.0
1988	770	26.4	7.4				319.9		190.0
1989	860	26.4	6.6				337.0		196.0
1990	904	30.4	7.3				384.1		210.0
1991	968	30.4	6.6				397.1		210.3
1992	1036	4.5	1.2				430.9		216.0
1993	1064	4.5	3.1				446.3		220.6
1994	1122	24.5	9.6				467.2		238.1
1995	1065	58.5	19.4				483.9		258.4
1996	1597	58.5	21.2				483.0		268.0
1997	1635	58.5	22.0				490.0		279.0
1998	1712	58.5	22.5				495.1		295.6
1999	1754	58.5	25.0				505.0		298.0
2000	1852	128.5	39.4		6550		295.6	56.40	274.0
2001	2163	143.5	42.0		6750		309.3	82.15	301.0
2002	2658	180.6	45.0		8750		321.4	86.36	311.7
2003	2903	215.0	50.1		9400		361.4	91.31	268.0
2004	2909	255.0	53.9		10050	495.5	405.9	93.78	175.0
2005	2521	324.0	62.4	23816	10350	536.9	454.6	95.96	171.7
2006	3398	331.0	73.2	36088	10350	585.1	538.3	92.45	175.7
2007	4357	348.0	76.2	49501	10350	619.5	600.9	95.70	189.1
2008	4458	329.4	78.9	60000	12148	672.8	656.6	97.71	206.8
2009	4495	356.0	80.3	64999	13680	669.1	656.1	98.22	211.2
2010	4479	365.0	81.0	68014	16680	634.9	633.0	96.95	194.4
2011	4765	369.4	82.0	71012	16930	634.4	634.4	98.24	207.5
2012	5735	388.5	83.0	75003	17530	648.3	648.3	99.12	207.2
2013	6363	393.0	84.6	80108	21971	671.7	671.7	99.30	220.7
2014	6536	425.0	86.1	86620	21971	733.8	733.8	99.59	216.1
2015	7157	439.5	87.9	94826	27321	790.3	790.3	99.80	204.7
2016	7889	612.0	90.0	100398	24341	872.6	872.6	99.84	204.0
2017	10207	665.6	92.4	105085	24341	924.8	924.8	99.88	214.3
2018	12147	670.6	93.4	107633	28591	975.7	975.7	99.94	201.1
2019	13188	679.2	94.5	115152	32711	1011.2	1011.2	99.98	198.0
2020	14920	687.9	95.0	120133	33811	797.5	797.5	100.00	201.7
2021	16132	707.9	95.8	120315	33861	784.2	784.2	100.00	209.4
2022	18050	712.1	97.0	120540	31461	740.6	740.6	100.00	211.5

注：1.污水处理能力等指标自1992年起为污水无害化处理情况，1992年以前为污水简易处理情况。

2.生活垃圾无害化处理率按清运量计算。

资料来源：北京市水务局、北京市城市管理委员会。

Note: a) The sewage treatment capacity and other indicators in and after 1992 were about harmless disposal of sewage, and those before 1992 were about simple disposal of sewage.

b) The rate of harmless disposal of domestic waste is calculated in terms of the waste removed and transported.

Source: Beijing Water Authority,Beijing Municipal Commission of Urban Management.

7-21 排水及节水
WATER DRAINAGE AND SAVING

项 目	Item	2022	2021
排 水	**Water Drainage**		
污水处理能力 （万立方米/日）	Sewage Treatment Capacity (10000 cu.m/day)	712.1	707.9
污水年处理量 （万立方米）	Annual Treatment Volume of Sewage (10000 cu.m)	222087	216270
#污水厂	Treated by Sewage Treatment Plants	214661	213044
污水处理率 (%)	Sewage Treatment Rate (%)	97.0	95.8
污水排放总量 （万立方米）	Total Volume of Sewage Drainage (10000 cu.m)	228913	225737
排水管道长度 （公里）	Length of Drainage Pipelines (km)	28939	26852
污水管	Sewage Pipes	18050	16132
雨水管	Rain Pipes	9398	9212
雨污合流管	Rain-sewage Sewer	1491	1508
再生水利用量 （万立方米）	Volume of Recycled Water Used (10000 cu.m)	120540	120315
节 水	**Water Saving**		
节水量 （万立方米）	Volume Saved (10000 cu.m)	7373	10181
节水措施 （项）	Water Saving Measures Implemented (unit)	63	74

资料来源：北京市水务局。
Source: Beijing Water Authority.

7-22 环境卫生
MUNICIPAL ENVIRONMENT AND SANITATION

项　　目		Item		2022	2021
工作量		**Work Load**			
清扫街道面积	(万平方米／日)	Area of Cleaned Streets	(10000 sq.m/day)	17812	17439
生活垃圾无害化处理能力	(吨／日)	Harmless Disposal Capacity of Domestic Waste	(ton/day)	31461	33861
生活垃圾清运量	(万吨)	Domestic Waste Removed and Transported	(10000 tons)	740.6	784.2
生活垃圾无害化处理量	(万吨)	Volume of Harmless Disposal of Domestic Waste	(10000 tons)	740.6	784.2
生活垃圾无害化处理率		Rate of Harmless Disposal of Domestic Waste		100.0	100.0
(按清运量计算)	(%)	(Calculated by Volume of Waste Cleared and Transported)	(%)		
餐厨垃圾处理量	(万吨)	Volume of Kitchen Waste Removed and Transported	(10000 tons)	58.1	69.7
粪便清运量	(万吨)	Volume of Excrement Removed and Transported	(10000 tons)	211.5	209.4
环卫机械数量	**(辆)**	**Number of Environmental Sanitation Machinery**	**(unit)**	**12159**	**12215**
环卫设施		**Environmental Sanitation Facilities**			
公共厕所	(座)	Public Lavatories	(unit)	6435	6343

资料来源：北京市城市管理委员会。
Source: Beijing Municipal Commission of City Administration.

7−23 环境保护(2000−2022年)
ENVIRONMENTAL PROTECTION (2000-2022)

年 份 Year	可吸入颗粒物 (PM_{10}) 年平均浓度值 (微克/立方米) Annual Average Concentration of Inspiratory Particulate Matter (μg/cu.m)	细颗粒物 ($PM_{2.5}$) 年平均浓度值 (微克/立方米) Annual Average Concentration of $PM_{2.5}$ (μg/cu.m)	二氧化硫 (SO_2) 年平均浓度值 (微克/立方米) Annual Average Concentration of Dioxide (μg/cu.m)	二氧化氮 (NO_2) 年平均浓度值 (微克/立方米) Annual Average Concentration of Nitrogen Dioxide (μg/cu.m)	化学需氧量 (COD) 排放量 (万吨) COD Emission Volume (10000 tons)	二氧化硫 (SO_2) 排放量 (万吨) SO_2 Emission Volume (10000 tons)	区域环境噪声平均值 (分贝) Average Value of Noises in Regional Environment (db)	道路交通干线噪声平均值 (分贝) Average Value of Noises in Road Transportation (db)
2000	162		71	71	17.9	22.4	53.9	71.0
2001	165		64	71	17.0	20.1	53.9	69.6
2002	166		67	76	15.3	19.2	53.5	69.5
2003	141		61	72	13.4	18.3	53.6	69.7
2004	149		55	71	13.0	19.1	53.8	69.6
2005	142		50	66	11.6	19.1	53.2	69.5
2006	161		53	66	11.0	17.6	53.9	69.7
2007	148		47	66	10.7	15.2	54.0	69.9
2008	122		36	49	10.1	12.3	53.6	69.6
2009	121		34	53	9.9	11.9	54.1	69.7
2010	121		32	57	9.2	11.5	54.1	70.0
2011	114		28	55	19.3	9.8	53.7	69.6
2012	109		28	52	18.7	9.4	54.0	69.2
2013	108	89.5	27	56	17.8	8.7	53.9	69.1
2014	116	85.9	22	57	16.9	7.9	53.6	69.1
2015	102	80.6	14	50	16.2	7.1	53.3	69.2
2016	92	73.0	10	48	8.7	3.3	54.3	69.3
2017	84	58.0	8	46	8.2	2.0	53.2	69.3
2018	78	51.0	6	42	5.6	1.1	53.7	69.6
2019	68	42.0	4	37	5.1	0.6	53.7	69.6
2020	56	38.0	4	29	5.4	0.2	53.6	69.0
2021	55	33.0	3	26	4.9	0.1	53.7	69.0
2022	54	30.0	3	23	4.5	0.1	52.8	68.7

资料来源：北京市生态环境局。
Source: Beijing Municipal Ecology and Environment Bureau.

7-24 环境保护
ENVIRONMENTAL PROTECTION

项　目		Item		2022	2021
水环境		**Water Environment**			
废水排放		Discharge of Sewage			
#工业废水排放量	(万吨)	Industrial Waste Water Discharge Volume	(10000 tons)	8103.50	8006.90
化学需氧量(COD)排放量	(吨)	COD Emission Volume	(ton)	44534	48705
#工业废水中COD排放量		Emission of COD in Industrial Waster Water		1335	1414
氨氮排放量	(吨)	Ammonia Nitrogen Discharge	(ton)	2028	2192
#工业废水中氨氮排放量		Ammonia Nitrogen Discharge in Industrial Waster Water		23	26
大气环境		**Atmosphere Environment**			
二氧化硫(SO_2)排放量	(吨)	SO_2 Emission Volume	(ton)	1078	1422
#工业二氧化硫排放量		Emission of Industrial SO_2		799	1004
氮氧化物排放量	(吨)	Emission of Nitrogen Oxides	(ton)	74180	82050
#工业氮氧化物排放量		Emission of Industrial Nitrogen Oxides		9765	9590
颗粒物排放量	(吨)	Particulate Emissions	(ton)	4124	5418
#工业颗粒物排放量		Industrial Particulate Emissions		1622	2180
固体废物		**Solid Waste**			
一般工业固体废物产生量	(万吨)	General Industrial Solid Waste Generated	(10000 tons)	171.44	194.14
一般工业固体废物综合利用量	(万吨)	General Industrial Solid Waste Recycled	(10000 tons)	143.25	114.12
一般工业固体废物处置量	(万吨)	General Industrial Solid Waste Disposed	(10000 tons)	28.17	80.00
危险废物产生量	(吨)	Hazardous Wastes Generated	(ton)	271234	262271
生态环境		**Ecological Environment**			
自然保护区个数	(个)	Number of Nature Reserves	(unit)	21	21
#国家级自然保护区		State-level Nature Reserves		2	2
自然保护区面积	(万公顷)	Area of Nature Reserves	(10000 hectares)	13.8	13.8

注：自2020年起，原“烟(粉)尘排放量”更名为“颗粒物排放量”。
资料来源：北京市生态环境局、北京市园林绿化局。
Note: Since 2020,the original Smoke and Dust Emission has been changed to Particulate Emissions.
Source: Beijing Municipal Ecology and Environment Bureau, Beijing Gardening and Green Bureau.

7-25 园林绿化及森林情况(1978-2022年)

年　份 Year	年末公园绿地面积 (公顷) Park Green Area (year-end) (hectare)	人均公园绿地面积 (平方米) Per Capita Park Green Area (sq.m)	城市绿化覆盖率 (%) Urban Green Coverage (%)	绿地面积 (公顷) Green Area (hectare)
1978	2693	5.1	22.3	
1979	2693	5.1	22.3	
1980	2746	5.1	20.1	
1981	2751	5.1	20.1	
1982	2779	5.1	20.1	
1983	2823	5.1	20.1	
1984	2878	5.1	20.1	
1985	3263	4.9	22.1	
1986	3606	5.1	22.9	
1987	3570	5.1	22.9	
1988	4074	5.8	25.0	
1989	6910	6.0	26.0	
1990	7110	6.1	28.0	
1991	4279	6.4	28.4	
1992	4213	6.7	30.3	
1993	4452	7.8	31.3	
1994	5221	7.9	32.4	
1995	5017	7.5	32.7	
1996	5147	7.5	33.2	
1997	5408	7.8	34.2	
1998	6351	9.0	35.6	
1999	6457	9.1	36.3	
2000	7140	9.7	36.5	26680
2001	7554	10.1	38.8	30224
2002	7907	10.7	40.6	32572
2003	9115	11.4	40.9	38475
2004	10446	11.5	41.9	36755
2005	11365	12.0	42.0	38877
2006	11788	12.0	42.5	45495
2007	12101	12.6	43.0	46320
2008	12316	13.6	43.5	46993
2009	18070	14.5	44.4	61695
2010	19020	15.0	45.0	62672
2011	19728	15.3	45.6	63541
2012	21178	15.5	46.2	65540
2013	22215	15.7	46.8	67048
2014	28798	15.9	47.4	80223
2015	29503	16.0	48.4	81305
2016	30069	16.1	48.4	82113
2017	31019	16.2	48.4	83501
2018	32619	16.3	48.4	85286
2019	35157	16.4	48.5	88704
2020	35720	16.6	49.0	92683
2021	36397	16.6	49.3	93127
2022	36900	16.9	49.8	93558

资料来源：自2019年起，森林火灾数据来源于北京市应急管理局，其余年份及其他指标数据均来源于北京市园林绿化局。

STATISTICS FOR LANDSCAPING AND FORESTS (1978-2022)

森林面积 (公顷) Forest Area (hectare)	森林覆盖率 (%) Forest Coverage Rate (%)	活立木蓄积量 (万立方米) Total Stock of Standing Trees (10000 cu.m)	森林蓄积量 (万立方米) Forest Stock (10000 cu.m)	森林火灾次数 (次) Number of Forest Fires (times)
619243.2		1521.4	1295.3	9
626006.3	35.9	1521.4	1295.3	13
636565.7	36.5	1559.5	1368.9	8
641368.3	36.5	1574.0	1394.4	
658914.1	36.7	1810.3	1406.2	2
666050.7	37.0	1854.7	1435.4	4
673411.8	37.6	1899.4	1468.7	3
691341.1	38.6	1943.3	1499.0	1
716456.1	40.1	1993.4	1536.8	
734530.6	41.0	2109.1	1669.9	1
744956.1	41.6	2149.3	1701.1	3
756000.7	42.3	2180.0	1724.6	4
767665.1	43.0	2211.1	1749.8	3
777603.5	43.5	2246.8	1798.0	1
791972.0	44.0	2306.2	1850.0	8
848313.9	44.4	3064.2	2520.7	8
852720.9	44.6	3830.0	3164.6	
855655.3	44.8	3924.1	3373.8	1

Source: Since 2019, the data on forest fires have been provided by Beijing Emergency Management Bureau; the data for other years and other indicator data were provided by Beijing Gardening and Greening Bureau.

主要统计指标解释

能源生产量 能源生产量是反映能源生产规模、构成、生产成果的重要指标。按能源的成因分为一次能源（亦称天然能源）生产量和二次能源（亦称人工能源）生产量。

一次能源生产量 指报告期内企业将自然界现存的能源资源经过开采而产出的合格产品数量，主要包括原煤、原油、天然气、水电等。

二次能源生产量 指报告期内经过各种加工转换设备生产出的另一种形式的各种合格的能源产品数量。如火电、热力、洗煤、焦炭、各种石油制品、焦炉煤气、其他煤气等。

能源消费总量 指一定地域（行政或地理区域）内，国民经济各行业和居民家庭在一定时期所消费的各种能源的总和。能源消费总量包括终端能源消费量、能源加工转换损失量、能源运输和管理过程的损失量三部分。

能源消费总量（等价值） 是电力按等价热值计算的能源消费总量。等价热值是能源统计中经常使用的一个热值概念，是指加工转换产出的某种二次能源所投入的一次能源的量，即获得一个度量单位的某种二次能源所消耗的以热值表示的一次能源。

能源加工转换投入产出量 能源具有由一种能量形式转换为另一种能量形式及耗用过程中可用一种能源替代另一种能源的特征。为提高能源的利用价值和效率，对能源进行加工、转换，产出适合生产和生活需要的更高级的能源产品。在加工转换投入(-)产出(+)量中，“-”表示能源加工转换的投入量，“+”表示二次能源的产出量。

投入量 是指为生产二次能源产品，所投入到能源加工转换设备的各种能源数量。在表中以负数表示。

产出量 是指各种能源（一次能源或少量再投入的二次能源）经过加工转换后，产出的各种二次能源产品（包括不作为能源使用的副产品，联产品）数量。

加工转换损失量 是指在能源加工、转换过程中损失的能量（能源），即能源加工、转换过程中投入的能源和产出的二次能源之间的差额。

损失量 指能源在经营管理和生产、输送、分配、储存等过程中发生的损失以及由于自然因素等原因造成的损失数量。不包括加工转换损失量。

终端消费量 是指能源消费环节的最后一个环节的能源消费，包括直接用作燃料、原材料和动力的各种能源的消费。它们的消费过程体现了能源消费的终止，不会再重新作为能源投入使用。终端消费量不包括用于能源加工转换投入量、加工转换损失量和损失量。

能源消费弹性系数 指能源消费总量增长率与地区生产总值增长率的比值。

电力消费弹性系数 指电力消费量增长率与地区生产总值增长率的比值。

平均每万元地区生产总值能源消费量 能源总消费量或分品种能源消费量与地区生产总值之比。

人均生活用能量 指用于生活消费的各种能源数量与人口总数之比。

垃圾无害化处理能力 指垃圾无害化处理场（厂）按工艺设计每天所能处理生活垃圾的数量。垃圾无害化处理场（厂）必须是按照有关技术、环境、卫生标准和规范进行设计、建设、运行、维护和管理的各种生活垃圾处理设施，主要包括卫生填埋场、堆肥厂和焚烧厂等。

大风日数 指出现瞬时风速达到或超过 17.0m/s（或目测估计风力达到或超过 8 级）大风的天数。

水资源总量 指降水形成的地表和地下水总量，是当地自产水资源，不包括入境水量。

排水管道长度 指所有排水总管、干管、支管、检查井及连接井进出口等长度之和。计算时应按单管计算，即在同一条街道上如有两条或两条以上并排的排水管道时，应按每条排水管道的长度相加计算。

污水处理能力 指污水处理厂（或处理装置）每昼夜处理污水量的设计能力。

污水处理量 指污水处理厂（或污水处理装置）处理装置实际处理的污水量。包括物理处理量、生物处理量和化学处理量。

污水处理率 指污水处理量与污水排放总量的比率。计算公式：

$$\text{污水处理率}=\frac{\text{污水处理量}}{\text{污水排放总量}}\times 100\%$$

生活垃圾清运量 指报告期内收集和运送到各垃圾处理场（厂）的垃圾的数量。

粪便清运量 指报告期内收集和运送到各粪便处理场（厂）的粪便的数量。

生活垃圾无害化处理量 指报告期内简易处理场和各种垃圾无害化处理场（厂）处理垃圾的总量。垃圾简易处理量指垃圾简易填埋场所处理的垃圾总量。垃圾无害化处理量指垃圾无害化处理场（厂）所处理的垃圾总量。

生活垃圾无害化处理率 指报告期垃圾无害化处理量与垃圾产生量的比率。计算公式：

$$\text{垃圾无害化处理率}=\frac{\text{垃圾无害化处理量}}{\text{垃圾产生量}}\times 100\%$$

在统计时，如果生活垃圾产生量不易取得，可用清运量代替。

化学需氧量（COD）排放量 指工业 COD 排放量、农业 COD 排放量、生活 COD 排放量及集中式治理设施（不含污水厂）COD 排放量之和。

二氧化硫（SO_2）排放量 指报告期内工业 SO_2 排放量生活 SO_2 排放量及集中式治理设施（不含污水厂）SO_2 排放量之和。

工业固体废物综合利用量 指报告期内企业通过回收、加工、循环、交换等方式，从固体废物中提取或者使其转化为可以利用的资源、能源和其他原材料的固体废物量（包括当年利用的往年工业固体废物贮存量）。如用做农业肥料、生产建筑材料、筑路等。

公园绿地 指城市中向公众开放的，以游憩为主要功能，有一定的游憩设施和服务设施，同时兼有健全生态、美化景观、科普教育、应急避险等综合作用的绿化用地，包括：综合公园、社区公园、专类公园和游园四个种类。

绿化覆盖率 指报告期末区域内绿化覆盖面积与区域面积的比率。

计算公式：

$$绿化覆盖率=\frac{区域内绿化覆盖面积}{区域面积}\times 100\%$$

森林面积 指乔木林面积、竹林面积与特殊灌木林面积之和。

活立木蓄积量 指一定范围土地上全部树木蓄积的总量，包括森林蓄积、疏林蓄积、散生木蓄积和四旁树蓄积。

森林蓄积量 指一定森林面积上存在着的林木树干部分的总材积，以立方米为计量单位。

森林火灾次数 指发生在城市市区外的一切森林、林木和林地的火灾次数，包括森林火警、一般灾害、重大灾害和特大灾害。

Explanatory Notes on Main Statistical Indicators

Energy Production is an important indicator reflecting the size, composition and results of energy production. By the cause of formation, it consists of the production of primary energy (also known as natural energy) and that of secondary energy (also known as artificial energy).

Production of Primary Energy means up-to-grade products produced by primary energy producers in the reporting period through extraction of existing energy in the nature, mainly including raw coal, crude oil, natural gas, hydroelectricity, etc.

Production of Secondary Energy means various up-to-grade energy products in another form that are made from primary energy with various processing and converting equipment in the reporting period, including thermal power, heating power, washed coal, coke, various petroleum products, coke oven gas and other gases, etc.

Total Energy Consumption means the total consumption of various energies by national economic sectors and resident households in a specific region (administrative or geographic). Total energy consumption can be divided into three parts: end-use energy consumption, loss during energy processing and conversion and loss during energy transport and management.

Total Energy Consumption (in Equivalent Caloricity) means the total consumption of electric power calculated in equivalent caloricity. Equivalent caloricity is a caloricity concept frequently used in statistics of energy. It means the quantity of primary energy input for a secondary energy produced through processing and conversion, i.e. the primary energy in terms of caloricity which is consumed to produce one measuring unit of a secondary energy.

Input and Output of Energy Processing and Conversion One form of energy can be converted into another form of energy. And in consumption, one sort of energy can be replaced with another. In order to improve the energy use value and efficiency, energy is processed and converted to produce energy products at higher levels which are suitable for productive and living needs. In the processing and conversion input (-) and output (+), "-" means the input for energy processing and conversion. And "+" means the output from energy processing and conversion.

Input means the volume of energy put into the energy processing and converting equipment in order to produce secondary energy products. It is shown as a negative number in the table.

Output means the volume of secondary energy products (including byproducts and multi-products that cannot be used as energy) from processing and conversion of energy sources (primary energy or a small amount of secondary energy re-input).

Loss during Processing and Conversion means the energy lost in the processing and conversion of energy, namely the difference between the energy input and the secondary energy output during energy processing and conversion.

Energy Loss means the loss of energy during operation, management, production, transportation, distribution and storage, as well as the loss due to natural factors and other reasons. It excludes the loss during processing and conversion.

End-use Energy Consumption means the energy consumption in the last section of energy consumption, including the consumption of various energy sources used as fuel, raw materials and power. Such consumption represents the end of energy consumption, and the energy will not be put into use again as energy. End-use energy consumption does not include the input for energy processing and conversion, loss during the processing and conversion of energy, and energy loss.

Elasticity Coefficient of Energy Consumption means the ratio of growth rate of total energy consumption to the growth rate of GDP.

Elasticity Coefficient of Electric Power Consumption means the ratio of growth rate of electric power consumption to the growth rate of GDP.

Average Energy Consumption per RMB 10,000 of GDP means the ratio of total energy consumption or energy consumption by variety to GDP.

Per-capital Energy Consumption by Households means the ratio of quantity of energy consumed by households to the total population.

Harmless Disposal Capacity of Waste means the daily quantity of domestic waste that can be disposed at harmless disposal facilities (sites) according to the process designed. Harmless disposal facilities (sites) must be domestic waste disposal facilities, including landfills, manure yards, incineration facilities and so on, which are designed, built, operated and managed in accordance with relevant technological, environmental, and sanitary standards and criterion.

Total Water Resources means the total volume of surface water and underground water caused by rainfall, which is locally generated water resources and excludes inbound water.

Number of Windy Days means the number of days with an instantaneous wind speed of 17.0 m/s or more (or with visually estimated force 8 or above wind).

Length of Sewage Pipes means the total length of all main drainage pipes, trunk pipes, branch pipes, access manholes, and connector well entrances and exits, and so on. The length of single pipes shall be included, i.e. if there are two or more drainage pipes parallel on a street, the length of every pipe shall be included.

Sewage Treatment Capacity means the designed capacity

of sewage disposal day and night for a sewage disposal plant (or facility).

Volume of Sewage Treated means the volume of sewage actually disposed by sewage disposal plants (or sewage disposal facilities), consisting of physical volume, biological volume and chemical volume of waste water disposed.

Sewage Treatment Rate means the ratio of sewage disposed to the total discharge of sewage. The formula is:

Sewage Disposal Rate = Volume of Sewage Disposed / Total Discharge of Sewage × 100%

Domestic Waste Removed and Transported means the quantity of waste collected and transported to waste treatment sites (plants) in the reporting period.

Excrement Removed and Transported means the quantity of excrement collected and transported to waste treatment sites (plants) in the reporting period.

Volume of Harmless Disposal of Domestic Waste means the total volume of waste disposed by simple disposal sites and harmless waste disposal sits (plants) in the reporting period. Simple disposal of waste means the total volume of waste by simple landfills. Harmless waste disposal means the total volume of waste disposed by harmless waste disposal sites (plants).

Rate of Harmless Disposal of Domestic Waste means the ratio of harmless waste disposal to the waste produced in the reporting period. The formula is:

Rate of Harmless Disposal of Domestic Waste = Harmless Waste Disposal / Waste Produced × 100%

In practical statistics, if it is hard to get figures on the volume of domestic waste produced, the volume removed and transported may be used.

COD Emission Volume means the sum of industrial COD emission, agricultural COD emission, domestic COD emission, and COD emissions from centralized treatment facilities (excluding sewage disposal plants).

SO_2 Emission Volume means the sum of industrial SO_2 emission, domestic SO_2 emission, and SO_2 emissions from centralized treatment facilities (excluding sewage disposal plants) in the reporting period.

Industrial Solid Waste Utilized means the volume of solid wastes from which useful materials can be extracted or which can be converted into usable resources, energy or other materials by means of reclamation, processing, recycling and exchange (including utilizing in the year the stocks of industrial solid wastes of the previous year). Examples of such utilizations include fertilizers, building materials and road materials.

Green Land and Parks means the green land open to the public, with main function of recreation, having some recreational facilities and service facilities, and simultaneously exerting the synthetic action in ecosystem health, landscaping, science popularization education, emergency avoidance, etc. They can be classified into four types of parks: comprehensive parks, community parks, special use parks and recreational parks.

Green Land Coverage means the ratio of area of green land in a region to the total area of the region in the reporting period. The formula is:

Green Land Coverage = Area of Green Land in a Region / Total Area of the Region × 100%

Forest Area means the sum of high-forest area, bamboo forest area and special shrub area.

Total Stock of Standing Trees mean the total stock of all trees on specific area of land, including trees in forest, trees in sparse forest, scattered trees and trees planted by the side of villages, farm houses and along roads and rivers.

Forest Stock means the total volume of timber of forest tree trunks growing on specific area of forest, which are measured in cubic meters.

Number of Forest Fires means the number of all fires occurring in forests, woods, woodlands outside the urban districts, including forest fires, general fires, severe fires and fire disasters.

城市公用事业
PUBLIC UTILITIES

主要内容

本章资料反映北京市城市公用事业的综合水平，主要包括：公路、城市道路及桥梁情况，水、气、热等供应及消费情况，城市公共交通情况，市政主要设施情况。

Brief Introduction

Main Content

Statistics in this chapter show the overall level of urban public utilities in Beijing, which consist: Highways,urban roads and bridges Water, gas and heating supply and consumption, Urban public transport , Main public facilities.

8-1 公路、城市道路及桥梁(1978-2022年)
HIGHWAYS, URBAN ROADS AND BRIDGES (1978-2022)

年 份 Year	境内道路总里程(公里) Total Length of Highways and Roads (km)	公 路 里 程(公里) Total Length of Highways (km)	#高 速 公 路 Express-ways	城市道路里 程(公里) Length of Urban Roads (km)	#快速路 Rapid Roads	#主干路 Trunk Roads	城市道路面 积(万平方米) Area of Urban Roads (10000 sq.m)	城市道路桥 梁(座) Number of Bridges (unit)	#立交桥 Overpasses
1978		6562		2078			1611	351	2
1979		7278		2131			1618	348	2
1980		7487		2185			1664	351	6
1981		7566		2234			1742	342	8
1982		7683		2671			2098	408	9
1983		8058		2820			2265	431	10
1984		8271		2928			2393	440	11
1985		8482		2979			2485	460	16
1986		8995		3038			2559	479	16
1987		9103		3087			2631	510	22
1988		9124		3151			2701	522	23
1989		9371		3235			2815	552	27
1990		9648	35	3276			2905	562	33
1991		10259	63	3308			3134	569	40
1992		10827	71	3189			3212	595	55
1993		11260	99	3285			3398	596	64
1994		11532	112	3316			3470	616	75
1995		11811	113	3194			3494	582	84
1996		12084	114	3665			3807	646	133
1997		12306	144	3637			4061	693	140
1998		12498	190	3721			4214	715	138
1999		12825	230	3753			4353	787	141
2000		13600	268	4126			4921	834	149
2001		13891	335	4312			6062	891	160
2002		14359	463	5444			7645	1051	180
2003	18239	14453	499	3055			5345	848	119
2004	19010	14630	525	4067	219	834	6417	949	271
2005	19015	14696	548	4073	239	922	7437	964	304
2006	25377	20503	625	4380	232	955	7286	1079	376
2007	25765	20754	628	4421	236	960	7632	1230	377
2008	26921	20340	777	6143	242	755	8940	1738	381
2009	27436	20755	884	6204	242	805	9179	1765	393
2010	27907	21114	903	6312	263	855	9395	1855	411
2011	28446	21347	912	6258	263	861	9164	1885	418
2012	28585	21492	923	6271	263	865	9236	1950	413
2013	28808	21673	923	6295	269	953	9611	1998	414
2014	29209	21849	982	6426	383	965	10002	2042	422
2015	29069	21885	982	6423	383	969	10029	2069	427
2016	29282	22026	1013	6374	390	970	10275	2088	431
2017	29463	22226	1013	6359	390	984	10347	2094	435
2018	29429	22256	1115	6203	390	998	10328	2156	435
2019	29531	22366	1168	6156	390	1006	10459	2165	437
2020	29537	22264	1173	6147	390	1020	10654	2184	437
2021	29631	22320	1177	6168	397	1028	10741	2203	439
2022	29716	22363	1196	6209	397	1040	10892	2203	441

注：1.境内道路总里程为全市道路和公路里程之和(剔除道路、公路交叉重复部分)。
2.道路及桥梁1978—1981年统计范围为城八区及通县；1982—2002年统计范围为城八区及14个县城；2003—2009年统计范围为城八区和北京经济技术开发区。自2010年起城市道路及其附属设施统计范围为城六区。
3.自2008年起道路数据为北京市城市道路普查数据。

资料来源：北京市交通委员会。

Note: a) Total length of highways and roads means the sum of roads and highways across the city (excluding intersections of roads and highways).
b) Statistics for roads and bridges covered 8 urban districts and Tongzhou County in 1978-1981; the coverage was extended to 8 urban districts and 14 counties in 1982-2002; in 2003-2009, the coverage included 8 central urban districts and Beijing Economic-Technological Development Zone; since 2010, statistics for urban roads and the auxiliary facilities have been confined to 6 urban districts.
c) Since 2008,Statistics for roads and highways were from Beijing Urban Road Census.

Source: Beijing Municipal Commission of Transport.

8-2 城市公共交通(1978-2022年)

年 份 Year	公共交通运营线路条数(条) Number of Operating Public Transport Routes (line)	公共汽电车 Buses and Trolley Buses	城市轨道交通 Urban Rail Transit	公共交通运营线路长度(公里) Length of Operating Public Transport Lines (km)	公共汽电车 Buses and Trolley Buses	城市轨道交通 Urban Rail Transit	公共交通运营车辆(辆) Number of Operating Public Transport Vehicles in Operation (vehicle)
1978	119	118	1	1427	1403	24	2743
1979	121	120	1	1469	1446	24	2997
1980	123	122	1	1479	1455	24	3113
1981	127	126	1	1525	1501	24	3375
1982	139	138	1	1678	1654	24	3620
1983	151	150	1	1820	1797	24	3907
1984	164	162	2	1939	1899	40	4221
1985	191	189	2	2312	2272	40	4583
1986	200	198	2	2574	2534	40	4576
1987	194	192	2	2382	2342	40	4776
1988	199	197	2	2445	2405	40	4787
1989	207	205	2	2525	2485	40	4890
1990	216	214	2	2654	2614	40	5160
1991	223	221	2	2755	2715	40	5182
1992	262	260	2	3379	3338	42	5223
1993	268	266	2	3532	3491	42	5213
1994	284	282	2	4117	4075	42	5319
1995	300	298	2	4538	4497	42	5367
1996	399	397	2	7317	7276	42	6828
1997	667	665	2	14011	13969	42	10479
1998	690	688	2	14929	14888	42	10819
1999	750	748	2	16566	16513	54	12509
2000	682	680	2	15639	15585	54	14191
2001	555	553	2	13180	13126	54	15420
2002	592	589	3	15835	15760	75	17580
2003	620	616	4	16131	16017	114	17445
2004	621	617	4	15247	15133	114	19343
2005	626	622	4	18328	18214	114	19471
2006	624	620	4	18582	18468	114	20489
2007	649	644	5	17495	17353	142	20525
2008	679	671	8	18057	17857	200	23221
2009	701	692	9	18498	18270	228	23730
2010	727	713	14	19079	18743	336	24011
2011	764	749	15	19832	19460	372	24478
2012	795	779	16	19989	19547	442	25831
2013	830	813	17	20153	19688	465	27590
2014	895	877	18	20776	20249	527	28331
2015	894	876	18	20740	20186	554	28311
2016	895	876	19	20392	19818	574	27892
2017	908	886	22	19898	19290	608	30966
2018	910	888	22	19881	19245	637	29732
2019	1181	1158	23	28331	27632	699	29459
2020	1231	1207	24	29145	28417	727	30727
2021	1244	1217	27	29363	28580	783	30189
2022	1318	1291	27	30971	30174	797	30739

注：自2006年5月1日起，公共汽电车、城市轨道交通售票采取刷卡方式，并陆续进行了票制票价改革，客运量统计口径方法相应调整，因此与历史数据不可比。

资料来源：本表自2005年起数据来源于北京市交通委员会。

URBAN PUBLIC TRANSPORT (1978-2022)

		公共交通客运量(万人次) Passengers Traffic of Public Transport (10000 person-times)			出租小汽车 Taxis Service	
公共汽电车 Buses and Trolley Buses	城市轨道交通 Urban Rail Transit		公共汽电车 Buses and Trolley Buses	城市轨道交通 Urban Rail Transit	运营车辆(辆) Operating Vehicles (vehicle)	客运量(万人次) Passenger Traffic (10000 person-times)
2627	116	172559	169465	3094		
2889	108	205703	200918	4785		
3001	112	236998	231477	5521		
3259	116	263944	257478	6466		
3500	120	284175	276922	7253		
3753	154	302501	294301	8200		
4037	184	324437	314132	10305		
4398	185	335227	321264	13963		
4371	205	328770	312990	15780		
4524	252	330417	311190	19227		
4535	252	337094	306396	30698		
4587	303	306435	275383	31052		
4857	303	334673	296495	38178		
4877	305	344525	307438	37087		
4900	323	348770	305959	42811		
4890	323	335378	286268	49110		
4984	335	353289	299993	53296		
4984	383	371579	315777	55802		
6427	401	349847	305433	44414		
10044	435	391182	346676	44507		
10382	437	418825	372494	46331		
12018	491	426706	378483	48223		
13604	587	406691	363213	43478		
14803	617	449720	402850	46870		
16939	641	492122	443880	48242		
16753	692	426628	379380	47248		
18451	892	499830	439130	60700		
18503	968	517769	449793	67976	66000	65000
19522	967	468225	397919	70306	66646	64121
19395	1130	488138	422645	65493	66646	64111
21507	1714	592523	470863	121660	66646	69000
21716	2014	658785	516517	142268	66646	68000
21548	2463	689788	505144	184645	66646	69000
21628	2850	722552	503272	219280	66646	69600
22146	3685	761578	515416	246162	66646	69862
23592	3998	804775	484306	320469	67046	69946
23667	4664	815849	477180	338668	67546	66828
23287	5024	738384	406003	332381	68284	58750
22688	5204	734953	369019	365934	68484	47665
25624	5342	713396	335595	377801	68484	39378
24076	5656	703818	318975	384843	70035	34021
23010	6449	709604	313366	396238	71517	33110
23948	6779	411967	182567	229400	74875	17427
23079	7110	538626	229634	308992	79600	21451
23465	7274	398889	172558	226331	70230	18669

Note: Since May 1, 2006, buses, trolley buses and rail transit tickets were sold by card swiping. Ticket system and prices were also reformed successively. The statistical coverage and methods for passenger traffic were adjusted accordingly, so these figures were incomparable with historical data.

Source: Since 2005, data in this table were provided by Beijing Municipal Commission of Transport.

8-3 城市供水、供气及供热(1978-2022年)
URBAN WATER SUPPLY, GAS SUPPLY AND HEAT SUPPLY (1978-2022)

年份 Year	全市集中供热管道长度(公里) Total Length of Pipelines for Centralized Heating (km)	全市集中供热面积(万平方米) Centralized Heating Area in Beijing (10000 sq.m)	#住宅 Residence	煤气销售量(万立方米) Sales Volume of Coal Gas (10000 cu.m)	液化石油气销售量(吨) Sales Volume of Liquefied Petroleum Gas (ton)	天然气销售量(万立方米) Sales Volume of Natural Gas (10000 cu.m)
1978				32687	97255	
1979				32113	114350	
1980				34935	128990	
1981				36309	134771	
1982				36748	149805	
1983				37319	150058	
1984				38710	156421	
1985				41678	169720	
1986				44542	182239	
1987				47594	178205	
1988				49595	177112	287
1989				56056	175814	1805
1990		3702		59508	172688	3544
1991		4560		66111	174326	5062
1992		5281		73615	174694	6040
1993		5730		80163	177065	6702
1994		7056		80409	173105	7623
1995		7537		85201	177637	11003
1996		7838		88356	185304	13504
1997		8399		76429	172879	16565
1998		9102		68998	174464	32619
1999		9992		61846	188450	64833
2000		10860		46719	190571	95919
2001		14729		33960	182188	150585
2002		18172		21077	234680	176504
2003		25108		23991	311657	208837
2004		28150	18962	17714	431660	250326
2005	6272	31736	22218	16776	356551	294279
2006	7013	34977	23158	9763	415268	389202
2007	10424	37203	23697		319631	441327
2008	11948	42501	26738		289576	578626
2009	12156	44240	27694		332693	645356
2010	12224	46715	32305		299392	677009
2011	11734	50794	34563		394437	726229
2012	11031	52555	35104		379371	883385
2013	11192	54591	36806		453546	956852
2014	12038	56786	38085		531556	1088999
2015	12207	58465	39031		523391	1427808
2016	13545	61136	41084		489473	1538425
2017	60169	60751	42215		457024	1577065
2018	60549	62932	43460		448107	1807388
2019	60166	63928	44419		395029	1823476
2020	63740	65935	45486		292445	1779490
2021	65376	68378	46596		413474	1868398
2022	68277	71301	48400		156291	1946384

注：1.自2017年起，全市集中供热管道长度数据包含一级、二级管网数据，2016年及以前只包含一级管网数据。
2.自2006年6月起，全市煤气家庭用户已全部置换为天然气用户，因此自2007年起煤气销售量无数据。
3.2011-2021年，液化石油气销售量数据包含市内销售量数据和市外销售量数据，自2022年起，液化石油气销售量数据不包含市外销售量及作为化工原料的销售量数据，下同。
4.2019-2021年，天然气销售量数据包含市内销售量数据和市外销售量数据，自2022年起，天然气销售量数据不包含市外销售量数据，下同。

资料来源：北京市城市管理委员会、北京市水务局。

Note: a) Since 2017, the figures of total length of pipelines for centralized heating included that of the primary and secondary heating network; in and before 2016, the said figures included the primary network data only.
b) Since June 2006, all households using coal gas have started to use natural gas. Therefore, there are no data on sales volume of coal gas since 2007.
c)The sales volume data of liquefied petroleum gas (LPG) in 2011-2021 included both in-the-city and out-of-city sales. Starting from 2022, LPG sales volume data excluded out-of-city sales and sales as chemical raw material, the same below.
d)The natural gas sales volume data in 2019-2021 included both in-the-city and out-of-city sales. Starting from 2022, the natural gas sales volume data excluded out-of-city sales, the same below.

Source: Beijing Municipal Commission of Urban Administration, Beijing Water Authority.

8-3 续表 Continued

年 份 Year	居 民 燃气用户 (万户) Gas Using Households (10000 households)	自来水综合 生产能力 (万立方米/日) General Production Capacity of Tap Water (10000 cu.m/day)	自来水供水 管道长度 (公里) Length of Tap Water Supply Pipelines (km)	自 来 水 售 水 量 (万立方米) Sales Volume of Tap Water (10000 cu.m)
1978	65.2	134	2926	32664
1979	76.7	151	3083	36232
1980	80.3	163	3272	38933
1981	85.1	167	3435	41634
1982	88.0	164	4216	41136
1983	90.9	166	4452	42778
1984	96.9	167	4622	43716
1985	102.3	176	4927	45601
1986	153.6	188	5079	46695
1987	160.9	185	5257	47680
1988	165.4	189	5550	50059
1989	172.6	206	5647	50145
1990	176.1	215	5770	52718
1991	184.7	221	5947	56107
1992	192.4	226	6130	58704
1993	197.5	234	6367	60794
1994	210.3	242	6727	67977
1995	219.8	264	6907	67877
1996	188.1	266	6907	69684
1997	243.0	302	6339	79046
1998	254.4	330	6989	75969
1999	259.8	357	7179	78098
2000	291.9	367	7610	75364
2001	310.0	371	8146	69807
2002	336.4	428	8555	79322
2003	406.0	429	9278	71583
2004	438.6	399	9981	82986
2005	462.6	348	9831	71600
2006	540.2	373	11899	74970
2007	556.4	391	13133	77778
2008	591.0	404	14118	80792
2009	600.0	424	14791	86881
2010	634.2	445	16144	89185
2011	644.1	473	16963	94622
2012	713.5	411	14029	93826
2013	737.4	444	14495	98178
2014	846.0	503	14994	103402
2015	885.7	506	15421	103929
2016	886.5	504	15742	108386
2017	929.0	522	16105	110587
2018	926.4	527	16448	115852
2019	873.2	598	16735	119668
2020	902.2	606	17819	112279
2021	950.4	700	18432	121312
2022	973.6	702	18998	123267

注：自2012年起，自来水数据口径调整为城镇公共供水，下同。
Note:Since 2012, the statistical coverage of tap water data was adjusted to urban public water supply , the same below.

8-4 液化石油气及天然气
LIQUEFIED PETROLEUM GAS AND NATURAL GAS

项目	Item	2022	2021
液化石油气	**Liquefied Petroleum Gas**		
供气总量 (吨)	Gas Supply (ton)	156679	428603
销售气量 (吨)	Gas Sales (ton)	156291	413474
#家庭用量	Househlod Consumption	120088	104844
家庭用户 (万户)	Househlod Consumers (10000 households)	220.4	213.1
天然气	**Natural Gas**		
供气总量 (万立方米)	Gas Supply (10000 cu.m)	1991095	1906214
销售气量 (万立方米)	Gas Sales (10000 cu.m)	1946384	1868398
#家庭用量	Househlod Consumption	204687	175571
家庭用户 (万户)	Househlod Consumers (10000 households)	753.2	737.3
居民燃气用户 (万户)	**Household Gas Users (10000 households)**	**973.6**	**950.4**

注：本表液化石油气、天然气供气总量和销售气量数据均包含燕山石化数据。
资料来源：北京市城市管理委员会、中国石化集团北京燕山石化有限公司。
Note: Data on liquefied petroleum gas and natural gas supply and sales in this table include the data of Yanshan Petrochemical.
Source: Beijing Municipal Commission of City Administration, and SINOPEC Beijing Yanshan Petrochemical Co.Ltd.

8-5 自来水及城镇自建设施
TAP WATER AND URBAN SELF-BUILT FACILITIES

项目	Item	2022	2021
自来水	**Tap Water**		
综合生产能力 (万立方米/日)	General Production Capacity (10000 cu.m/day)	701.5	700.4
供水管道长度 (公里)	Length of Water Supply Pipelines (km)	18998	18432
售水量 (万立方米)	Sales Volume of Water (10000 cu.m)	123267	121312
生产用水	For Production Use	11083	10953
生活用水	For Domestic Use	109395	107954
环卫绿化	For Environmental Sanitation and Greening Use	2789	2405
城镇自建设施	**Urban Self-built Facilities**		
供水总量 (万立方米)	Total Water Supply (10000 cu.m)	5056	5622
生产用水	For Production Use	652	709
生活用水	For Domestic Use	4342	4688
环卫绿化	For Environmental Sanitation and Greening Use	61	225

注：城镇自建设施2020年口径为城镇范围的自备井用户，不含村级供水；自2021年起调整为自行建设的地下水取水设施、供水管道及其附属设施向本单位或者附带向周边单位、城镇居民提供生活、生产用水，不包括村域内的各类供水设施。
资料来源：北京市水务局。
Note: The data on urban self-built facilities for 2020 covered the users of self-supply wells within urban area and excluded the data on water supply in villages; since 2021, the data were adjusted to cover the self-built water intake facilities for underground water, water supply pipelines and their ancillary facilities providing themselves or surrounding entities and urban residents with water for domestic and production use, but excluding the water supply facilities in villages.
Source: Beijing Water Authority.

8-6 市政设施情况
BASIC STATISTICS FOR MUNICIPAL FACILITIES

项目		Item		2022	2021
境内道路总里程	（公里）	Total Length of Highways and Roads	(km)	29716	29631
高速公路里程	（公里）	Length of Expressways	(km)	1196	1177
城市道路里程	（公里）	Area of Urban Roads	(km)	6209	6168
#快速路		Rapid Roads		397	397
#主干路		Trunk Roads		1040	1028
城市道路面积	（万平方米）	Coverage of Urban Roads	(10000 sq.m)	10892	10741
#铺装步道		Paved Roads		1908	1872
城市道路立交桥数	（座）	Number of Overpasses in City	(unit)	441	439
城市过街天桥数	（座）	Number of Pedestrain Overpasses in City	(unit)	562	554
城市地下通道数	（座）	Number of Underpasses in City	(unit)	218	218
备案停车场个数	（个）	Number of Parking Lots Recorded	(unit)	3079	3103
备案停车场车位总数	（个）	Total Capacity of Parking Lots Recorded	(unit)	822731	786266
电视监视点位	（台）	TV Monitors	(unit)	6913	2910

注：本表统计范围为城六区。
资料来源：北京市交通委员会、北京市公安局公安交通管理局。
Note: Data in this table covers 6 urban districts .
Source: Beijing Municipal Communission of Transport,Beijing Traffic Management Bureau.

主要统计指标解释

自来水综合生产能力 指按供水设施取水、净化、送水、出厂输水干管等环节实际测定计算的综合生产能力。不包括供水高峰阶段，超负荷增加的生产能力。计算时，以四个环节中最薄弱的环节为主确定能力。

自来水供水管道长度 指从送水泵至用户水表之间所有管道的长度。不包括新安装尚未使用的管道。

生产用水 指在生产活动中取用的水量，包含农业用水量、工业用水量和建筑业用水量。

生活用水 指城乡居民家庭日常生活及商业、饮食业、宾馆业、服务业、机关团体、医院、学校、部队等服务业范围的用水。

公共交通运营车辆 指公交企业（单位）用于运营业务的全部车辆数。

运营线路长度 指全部运营线路长度之和。计算公式：

$$\text{运营线路长度} = \sum \text{各条运营线路长度}$$

$$= \sum\left[\begin{pmatrix}\text{上行起点至终点里程} + \text{下行起点至终点里程} \\ + \text{上下行终点掉头里程}\end{pmatrix}\right]$$

公路里程 指公路的长度，凡达到《公路工程技术标准（JTGB01-2003）》规定的技术等级的公路，均统计公路里程，包括大、中城市的郊区公路里程，公路通过城镇（指县城、集镇）街道的里程和公路桥梁长度、隧道长度、渡口的宽度以及分期修建的公路已验收交付使用的里程。国道、省道、县道、乡道和专用公路中新增的人工修建的、路基宽度在 4.5 米以上的等外路里程也纳入公路里程统计。按技术等级公路可分为高速公路、一级公路、二级公路、三级公路、四级公路和等外公路。

道路里程 指道路长度和与道路相通的桥梁、隧道的长度，按车行道中心线计算。城市道路由车行道和人行道两部分组成。在统计时只统计路面宽度在 3.5 米（含 3.5 米）以上的各种铺装道路，包括开放型工业区和住宅区道路在内。

道路面积 指道路面积和与道路相通的广场、桥梁、隧道的面积（统计时，将人行道面积单独统计）。人行道面积按道路两侧面积相加计算。包括步行街和广场，不含人车混行的道路。

Explanatory Notes on Main Statistical Indicators

General Production Capacity of Tap Water means the comprehensive production capacity of water facilities calculated by on-site measurement, including capacity of the water in-taking, treatment, transmission and delivery; while overloaded capacity during water supply peak hours are not included. Calculation of the capacity was mainly dependent upon the weakest link of the whole production process.

Length of Tap Water Supply Pipelines means the length of all pipes linking between the water outlet pumps and users' water meters, excluding the ones newly installed and not yet put into use.

Water for Production Use means the water used in production activities, including agricultural water, industrial water and construction water.

Water for Public Service Use means the water used in the daily life of urban and rural households and in the service industry including commerce, catering, hotels, government organizations, hospitals, schools, and troops.

Public Transport Vehicles in Operation means the number of all vehicles used for operational businesses in public transit enterprises (institutions).

Length of Public Transport Routes means the sum of all lines in operation. It is calculated with the formula:

Length of Public Transit Lines = ∑ Length of all lines in operation = ∑ [(mileage from the upward starting point to the end point + mileage from the downward starting point to the end point + mileage of double back from upward and downward end points)]

Total Length of Highways means the length of highways. Such statistics apply for any highway reaching the technical grade stated in *Highway Engineering Technical Standards* (JTGB01-2003), including the mileage of highways in suburbs of middle and large cities, mileage of highways passing through streets in towns (counties and townships), length of highway bridges, length of tunnels, width of ferries, and mileage of highways constructed in several phases and put into use. The mileage of non-graded new highways built manually onto national highways, provincial highways, county highways, township highways and special highways, with roadbed width of 4.5m and above, are also incorporated. In terms of technical grade, highways fall into expressways, first-grade highways, second-grade highways, third-grade highways, fourth-grade highways, and non-graded highways.

Length of Highways and Roads means the length of roads and bridges and tunnels connecting with roads, calculated by the central lines of carriage ways. Urban roads consist of carriageways and sidewalks. Statistics only cover paved roads with width of pavement above 3.5m (including 3.5m), roads in open industrial zones and residential zones included.

Area of Roads means the area of roads and the area of squares, bridges and tunnels connecting to the roads (the area of sidewalks is calculated separately). The area of sidewalks is the sum of area on both sides of roads, including pedestrian streets and squares, excluding roads passable for both pedestrians and vehicles.

北京统计年鉴2023　BEIJING STATISTICAL YEARBOOK 2023

固定资产投资和房地产开发

INVESTMENT IN FIXED ASSETS AND REAL ESTATE DEVELOPMENT

简要说明

一、主要内容

本章资料包括北京市固定资产投资、房地产开发情况等。

二、统计范围

1996 年及以前固定资产投资统计起点为 5 万元及以上，1996 年以后调整为 50 万元及以上，自 2011 年起调整为 500 万元及以上。

房地产开发的统计范围是有开发经营活动的全部房地产开发经营业法人单位。

三、有关统计标准的变化说明

（一）关于行业划分。自 2018 年起执行《国民经济行业分类》（GB/T 4754-2017）标准。

（二）关于三次产业划分。2003 年，根据《国民经济行业分类》（GB/T 4754-2002），国家统计局印发了《国家统计局关于印发〈三次产业划分规定〉的通知》（国统字〔2003〕14 号）。2012 年，根据国家质检总局和国家标准委颁布的《国民经济行业分类》（GB/T 4754-2011），国家统计局对 2003 年《三次产业划分规定》进行了修订。主要在以下方面作出调整：一是将门类“农、林、牧、渔业”中的“农、林、牧、渔服务业”，“采矿业”中的“开采辅助活动”，“制造业”中的“金属制品、机械和设备修理业”等三个大类一并调整到第三产业。调整后，第一产业为 4 个大类；第二产业为 2 个门类和 36 个大类；第三产业为 15 个门类和 3 个大类。二是明确第三产业即为服务业。

本章 2012 年及以后三次产业的分类执行调整后的划分规定。

Brief Introduction

I. Main Content

Statistics in this chapter include figures on investment in fixed assets and real estate development in Beijing, etc.

II. Scope of Statistics

Before and in 1996, the threshold of fixed assets investment statistics was RMB 50,000 and above; after 1996, it was adjusted to RMB 500,000 and above; since 2011, the figure has been adjusted to RMB 5 million and above.

The scope of statistics on real estate development covers all legal entities in real estate exploitation management that have development and business activities.

III. Changes in Relevant Statistical Standards

(I) Classification of Sectors. The standards in the *Classification of National Economic Sectors* (GB/T 4754-2017) *are implemented since 2018.*

(II) Classification of Three Industries. According to the *Classification of National Economic Sectors* (GB/T 4754-2002), the National Bureau of Statistics issued the *Notice of the National Bureau of Statistics on the Issuance of the 'Regulations on Three Industries Classification'* (G.T.Z. [2003] No. 14) in 2003. According to the *Classification of National Economic Sectors* (GB/T 4754-2011) promulgated by the General Administration of Quality Supervision, Inspection and Quarantine of the People's Republic of China and the Standardization Administration of the People's Republic of China, the National Bureau of Statistics revised the *Regulations on Three Industries Classification* of 2003 version in 2012. Adjustments were mainly made in the following aspects: Firstly, the "service activities for agriculture, forestry, animal husbandry and fishing" in the category of "agriculture, forestry, animal production and hunting, fishing", the "mining support service activities" in the category of "mining and quarrying", and the "repair of fabricated metal products, machinery and equipment" in the category of "manufacturing" were adjusted to the tertiary industry. After adjustment, the primary industry fell into 4 categories; the secondary industry fell into 2 classes and 36 categories; and the tertiary industry fell into 15 classes and 3 categories. Secondly, the tertiary industry was defined as the service industry.

The classification of three industries since 2012 as mentioned in this chapter has all been subject to the classification provisions after adjustment.

9-1 全社会固定资产投资和增长速度情况(1978—2018年)
TOTAL INVESTMENT IN FIXED ASSETS AND GROWTH RATE(1978-2018)

单位：亿元 (100 million yuan)

年 份 Year	全社会固定资产投资 Total Investment in Fixed Assets		#房地产开发投资 Investment in Real Estate Development		#基础设施投资 Infrastructure Investment		#建筑安装投资 Construction and Installation Investment	
	绝对量 Absolute Volume	比上年增长(%) Growth Rate (%)	绝对量 Absolute Volume	比上年增长(%) Growth Rate (%)	绝对量 Absolute Volume	比上年增长(%) Growth Rate (%)	绝对量 Absolute Volume	比上年增长(%) Growth Rate (%)
1978	22.6				5.4			
1979	26.5	17.3			5.8	7.4		
1980	33.2	25.3			6.0	3.4		
1981	36.6	10.2			5.8	-3.3		
1982	38.6	5.5			6.1	5.2		
1983	51.3	32.9			6.7	9.8		
1984	66.3	29.2			8.8	31.3		
1985	94.0	41.8			13.2	50.0		
1986	106.2	13.0			14.5	9.8		
1987	136.2	28.2			22.1	52.4		
1988	163.0	19.7			23.2	5.0		
1989	139.5	-14.4			26.5	14.2		
1990	179.2	28.5	22.5		31.6	19.2		
1991	192.0	7.1	24.0	6.7	35.2	11.4	107.3	
1992	266.0	38.5	33.7	40.4	58.8	67.0	136.2	26.9
1993	410.4	54.3	58.4	73.3	91.4	55.4	232.0	70.3
1994	648.8	58.1	99.5	70.4	153.4	67.8	362.6	56.3
1995	841.5	29.7	352.8	254.6	156.1	1.8	459.0	26.6
1996	876.9	4.2	328.2	-7.0	188.8	20.9	515.8	12.4
1997	961.2	9.6	330.3	0.6	218.3	15.6	546.2	5.9
1998	1155.6	20.2	377.4	14.3	320.4	46.8	626.9	14.8
1999	1170.6	1.3	421.5	11.7	302.7	-5.5	679.1	8.3
2000	1297.4	10.8	522.1	23.9	351.9	16.3	701.5	3.3
2001	1530.5	18.0	783.8	50.1	356.4	1.3	801.6	14.3
2002	1814.3	18.5	989.4	26.2	411.9	15.6	964.9	20.4
2003	2157.1	18.9	1202.5	21.5	417.8	1.4	1151.3	19.3
2004	2528.3	17.2	1473.3	22.5	463.2	10.9	1438.9	25.0
2005	2827.2	11.8	1525.0	3.5	610.7	31.8	1569.5	9.1
2006	3371.5	19.3	1719.9	12.8	935.3	53.2	1836.0	17.0
2007	3966.6	17.6	1995.8	16.0	1175.8	25.7	2117.9	15.4
2008	3848.5	-3.0	1908.7	-4.4	1160.7	-1.3	1798.8	-15.1
2009	4858.4	26.2	2337.7	22.5	1462.0	26.0	1983.0	10.2
2010	5493.5 (5218.3)	13.1	2901.1	24.1	1403.5	-4.0	2124.9	7.2
2011	5910.6	13.3	3036.3	10.1	1400.2	0.3	2585.3	22.4
2012	6462.8	9.3	3153.4	3.9	1789.2	27.8	3076.6	19.0
2013	7032.2	8.8	3483.4	10.5	1785.7	-0.2	3482.2	13.2
2014	7562.3	7.5	3911.3	12.3	2018.1	13.0	3468.1	-0.4
2015	7990.9	5.7	4226.3	8.1	2174.5	7.7	2996.5	-13.6
2016	8461.7	5.9	4045.4	-4.3	2399.5	10.3	3132.8	4.5
2017	8948.1	5.7	3745.9	-7.4	2984.2	24.4	3279.1	4.7
2018		-9.9		3.4		-10.7		3.6

注：1.自2004年起，全社会固定资产投资中不包括零星购置投资，下同。

2.自2011年起，固定资产投资统计起点由50万元调整至500万元。2010年未加括号的为原口径数，括号内为调整后的数据，固定资产投资增长速度按可比口径计算。

Note: a) Since 2004, total investment in fixed assets has not included investment in acquiring minor items, the same below.

b) Since 2011, the statistical threshold of investment in fixed assets has been adjusted from RMB 500,000 to RMB 5 million.Figures in 2010 with no brackets are based on the former standard.Figures in brackets are data after adjustment. The growth rates of fixed assets investment are calculated in comparable terms.

9-2 按产业分全社会固定资产投资和增长速度情况(1978-2018年)
INVESTMENT IN FIXED ASSETS AND GROWTH RATE BY INDUSTRY (1978-2018)

单位：亿元 (100 million yuan)

年 份 Year	全社会固定资产投资 Total Investment in Fixed Assets		第一产业 Primary Industry		第二产业 Secondary Industry		第三产业 Tertiary Industry	
	绝对量 Absolute Volume	比上年增长(%) Growth Rate (%)	绝对量 Absolute Volume	比上年增长(%) Growth Rate (%)	绝对量 Absolute Volume	比上年增长(%) Growth Rate (%)	绝对量 Absolute Volume	比上年增长(%) Growth Rate (%)
1978	22.6		1.4		10.8		10.4	
1979	26.5	17.3	1.0		12.0		13.5	
1980	33.2	25.3	0.7		15.7		16.8	
1981	36.6	10.2	0.6		13.6		17.2	
1982	38.6	5.5	1.2		15.4		17.9	
1983	51.3	32.9	1.2		16.4		20.9	
1984	66.3	29.2	1.3		20.3		30.6	
1985	94.0	41.8	1.6		32.4		43.8	
1986	106.2	13.0	1.5		41.4		51.6	
1987	136.2	28.2	1.6		46.9		72.9	
1988	163.0	19.7	2.0		48.8		87.9	
1989	139.5	-14.4	1.9		38.4		81.9	
1990	179.2	28.5	2.4		43.3		89.9	
1991	192.0	7.1	2.7		51.3		90.4	
1992	266.0	38.5	3.9		82.9		114.2	
1993	410.4	54.3	2.1		150.4		165.7	
1994	648.8	58.1	3.7		185.8		318.4	
1995	841.5	29.7	3.1		153.7		284.8	
1996	876.9	4.2	2.8		174.9		319.7	
1997	961.2	9.6	0.9		201.1		380.1	
1998	1155.6	20.2	1.5		201.7		479.7	
1999	1170.6	1.3	1.7		179.4		470.4	
2000	1297.4	10.8	3.0		157.2		510.3	
2001	1530.5	18.0	8.4		154.2		1367.9	
2002	1814.3	18.5	7.5		185.0		1621.8	
2003	2157.1	18.9	21.0		260.7		1875.4	
2004	2528.3	17.2	14.6		401.0		2112.7	
2005	2827.2	11.8	11.9		409.7		2405.6	
2006	3371.5	19.3	14.5	21.8	363.2	-11.4	2993.8	24.5
2007	3966.6	17.6	16.7	15.5	484.1	33.3	3465.8	15.8
2008	3848.5	-3.0	28.1	68.2	386.0	-20.3	3434.4	-0.9
2009	4858.4	26.2	57.4	104.6	411.4	6.6	4389.5	27.8
2010	5493.5	13.1	43.2	-24.8	528.1	28.4	4922.3	12.1
2011	5910.6	13.3	47.2	13.8	762.2	47.2	5101.3	9.5
2012	6462.8	9.3	145.4	208.4	719.8	-5.6	5597.5	9.7
2013	7032.2	8.8	175.5	20.6	755.0	4.9	6101.7	9.0
2014	7562.3	7.5	163.9	-6.6	716.8	-5.1	6681.6	9.5
2015	7990.9	5.7	111.0	-32.2	677.1	-5.5	7202.8	7.8
2016	8461.7	5.9	99.8	-10.1	722.9	6.8	7639.0	6.1
2017	8948.1	5.7	95.9	-3.9	893.8	23.6	7958.4	4.2
2018		-9.9		8.9		-43.2		-6.3

注：2000年及以前按产业划分中，不含房地产开发投资及农村投资。自2001年起含房地产开发投资及农村固定资产投资。

Note: Data of investment in fixed assets grouped by industry excluded investment in real estate development and rural investment in 2000 and before. Since 2001, data of investment in fixed assets included investment in real estate development and rural fixed assets.

9-3 固定资产投资增长速度情况(2019-2022年)
GROWTH RATE OF INVESTMENT IN FIXED ASSETS (2019-2022)

单位：% (%)

项　目	Item	2019	2020	2021	2022
固定资产投资(不含农户)	**Investment In Fixed Assets (Excluding Rural Households)**	**-2.4**	**2.2**	**4.9**	**3.6**
#建筑安装工程	Construction and Installation	5.9	-3.0	2.3	3.2
按产业分	**By Three Industies**				
第一产业	Primary Industry	20.6	-22.8	-59.5	11.6
第二产业	Secondary Industry	-9.0	28.0	38.2	20.5
第三产业	Tertiary Industry	-2.3	1.0	3.0	1.7
按行业分	**By Sector**				
农、林、牧、渔业	Agriculture, Forestry, Animal Husbandry and Fishery	20.9	-23.8	-59.7	14.6
采矿业	Mining	-9.5	26.5	-21.9	0.2
制造业	Manufacturing	0.8	66.6	68.3	18.4
电力、热力、燃气及水生产和供应业	Production and Distribution of Electricity, Heating Power, Gas and Water	-15.4	-10.3	-12.6	29.8
建筑业	Construction	-52.8	67.7	-36.8	-94.4
批发和零售业	Wholesale and Retail Trade	-46.1	-40.0	3.9	9.3
交通运输、仓储和邮政业	Transport, Storage and Post	-15.4	-9.4	-3.5	-7.6
住宿和餐饮业	Accommodation and Catering	116.2	45.0	10.5	-49.9
信息传输、软件和信息技术服务业	Information Transmission, Software and Information Technology Services	-13.3	0.2	20.0	36.0
金融业	Finance	6.9	-9.1	68.2	41.3
房地产业	Real Estate	-3.9	3.6	6.9	0.3
租赁和商务服务业	Scientific Research and Technical Services	157.7	-22.4	-8.0	31.0
科学研究和技术服务业	Scientific Research and Development, Technical Services	27.0	57.0	-25.7	60.7
水利、环境和公共设施管理业	Management of Water Conservancy, Environment and Public Facilities	1.8	-10.0	-18.2	-9.5
居民服务、修理和其他服务业	Resident Services, Repair and Other Services		173.3	-93.6	212.6
教　育	Education	-13.0	34.9	17.4	13.0
卫生和社会工作	Health and Social Works	49.0	22.7	22.8	10.9
文化、体育和娱乐业	Culture, Sports and Entertainment	77.0	1.1	-13.7	-34.9
公共管理、社会保障和社会组织	Public Management, Social Security and Social Organizations	-27.9	8.9	29.6	-6.7
国际组织	International Organizations				

9-4 固定资产投资资金来源情况(1978-2022年)
INVESTMENT IN FIXED ASSETS BY SOURCE OF FUNDS (1978-2022)

单位：亿元 (100 million yuan)

年份 Year	上年末结余资金 Surplus Funds by the End of the Previous Year	本年资金来源小计 Subtotal of Funds at Current Year	中央预算资金 Central Budgetary Fund	国内贷款 Domestic Loans	债券 Bonds	利用外资 Foreign Investment	自筹资金 Self-raised Funds	其他资金 Others
1978		22.5	16.9					
1979		26.5	19.2					
1980		33.2	18.5					
1981		31.4	15.4					
1982		34.5	14.1					
1983		38.5	16.0					
1984		52.2	22.5					
1985		77.8	30.4					
1986		94.5	33.0					
1987		126.2	43.1					
1988		149.4	37.4					
1989		123.1	35.0	12.8		18.2	44.5	12.6
1990		136.2	34.4	22.8		15.2	52.3	11.5
1991		151.1	35.5	28.2		13.9	65.5	8.0
1992		216.7	42.2	40.1		14.9	109.9	9.6
1993	54.3	425.2	47.1	79.2	1.6	28.0	205.2	64.1
1994	71.1	695.7	64.1	91.5	0.8	96.9	331.2	111.2
1995	200.8	915.8	70.3	122.7	1.1	187.3	339.8	194.6
1996	204.9	926.1	76.7	152.8	1.0	161.2	330.5	203.9
1997	183.1	1016.7	86.3	194.3		139.2	383.4	213.5
1998	207.1	1140.1	98.4	223.8	17.0	132.1	450.2	218.6
1999	212.1	1183.8	136.2	262.2	1.4	82.7	461.3	240.0
2000	293.1	1439.1	107.0	373.8	0.6	51.5	505.6	400.6
2001	325.5	1796.8	136.7	429.4	2.5	35.6	595.6	597.0
2002	433.2	2075.3	108.5	543.8	1.9	41.5	672.8	706.8
2003	542.7	2674.0	78.4	755.2		52.6	887.9	899.9
2004	654.6	3712.8	118.6	804.7		120.5	1245.7	1423.3
2005	924.4	4553.7	128.8	1055.8		70.9	1452.8	1845.4
2006	1043.8	4927.3	126.4	1347.5	32.7	76.2	1532.2	1812.3
2007	1202.2	6193.0	102.2	1513.3	22.4	82.8	2195.6	2276.7
2008	1469.5	5184.7	104.2	1394.2	35.5	80.0	2016.4	1554.5
2009	1321.7	8702.2	118.1	3038.5	17.5	39.3	2441.3	3047.4
2010	2109.1	8327.8	99.5	2218.7	4.3	43.8	3209.1	2752.4
2011	2341.4	8235.4	71.7	1853.6	85.4	29.8	3588.6	2606.3
2012	2830.7	9156.0	156.1	2186.3	12.7	24.9	3478.4	3297.6
2013	3133.1	10580.3	159.6	2554.1	0.8	23.5	4295.2	3547.2
2014	3586.5	10208.7	161.7	2841.0	8.0	33.3	4347.9	2816.8
2015	4238.6	10773.9	184.9	2390.1	10.6	13.2	4853.6	3321.5
2016	4585.2	12065.0	107.9	2677.3	9.2	13.1	5047.8	4209.6
2017	4780.5	11396.2	123.0	2729.7	29.6	21.6	4884.2	3608.1
2018	5229.3	9154.7	289.4	2116.1	27.3	24.6	3877.7	2819.6
2019	4571.7	8767.3	148.2	2021.2	12.5	3.5	2564.8	4017.1
2020	4781.3	9058.7	98.4	2010.8	…	10.0	2767.3	4172.1
2021	5013.7	10242.1	107.8	1513.8	21.9	16.3	3552.2	5030.1
2022	5667.9	9556.0	158.3	1624.0	0.9	7.5	3223.2	4542.1

注：1.本表1978—1992年不含房地产开发和农村投资，1993—2003年不含农村投资，2004—2018年为全社会口径，自2019年起为不含农户口径。
2.自2017年起，原“国家预算内资金”调整为“中央预算资金”。
3.2018—2020年固定资产投资资金来源中不含5000万元以下项目数据。

Note: a) In this table, figures from 1978 to 1992 did not include investment in real estate development and rural investment; figures from 1993 to 2003 did not include rural investment; figures from 2004 to 2018 were those of full coverage; since 2019, the figures were those that excluding rural households.
b) Since 2017, the original "State Budgets" was adjusted to "Central Budgetary Fund".
c) The data on the source of funds for investment in fixed assets from 2018 to 2020 didn't cover the projects of less than RMB 50 million.

9-5 基础设施投资情况(1978-2022年)
INVESTMENT IN INFRASTRUCTURE (1978-2022)

单位：亿元 (100 million yuan)

年 份 Year	基础设施投资 Infrastructure Investment		#能 源 Energy		#公共服务业 Public Services		#交通运输 Transportation		#邮政电信 Post & Telecommunications		基础设施投资占固定资产投资比重(%) Infrastructure Investment as Percentage of Investment in Fixed Assets (%)
	绝对量 Absolute Volume	比上年增长(%) Growth Rate (%)	绝对量 Absolute Volume	比上年增长(%) Growth Rate (%)	绝对量 Absolute Volume	比上年增长(%) Growth Rate (%)	绝对量 Absolute Volume	比上年增长(%) Growth Rate (%)	绝对量 Absolute Volume	比上年增长(%) Growth Rate (%)	
1978	5.4		1.4		0.6		1.7		0.4		23.9
1979	5.8		1.1		1.3		1.7		0.4		21.9
1980	6.0		0.9		2.3		2.3		0.5		17.9
1981	5.8		1.3		2.0		1.8		0.4		15.8
1982	6.1		1.4		1.9		1.9		0.4		15.8
1983	6.7		1.5		1.9		2.6		0.6		13.1
1984	8.8		1.4		3.0		2.3		1.1		13.3
1985	13.2		3.8		2.5		2.6		2.7		14.0
1986	14.5		4.8		2.1		3.1		3.5		13.7
1987	22.1		8.0		3.1		6.6		3.2		16.2
1988	23.2		8.8		5.3		4.7		3.0		14.2
1989	26.5		9.2		6.6		5.2		5.2		19.0
1990	31.6		9.0		8.3		8.7		5.4		17.6
1991	35.2		12.4		7.5		9.3		5.8		18.3
1992	58.8		17.7		8.2		20.1		12.3		22.1
1993	91.4		19.3		4.1		29.4		24.2		22.3
1994	153.4		38.0		27.2		30.0		48.6		23.6
1995	156.1		46.7		15.9		34.2		46.4		18.6
1996	188.8		59.2		29.1		54.0		44.1		21.5
1997	218.3		75.6		24.3		51.2		60.3		22.7
1998	320.4		85.1		38.0		104.6		77.5		27.7
1999	302.7		90.3		75.0		63.0		54.0		25.9
2000	351.9		53.2		154.6		64.6		63.7		27.1
2001	356.4		40.8		114.6		104.4		84.8		23.3
2002	411.9		49.5		101.6		159.7		78.7		22.7
2003	417.8		36.1		152.8		129.2		82.2		19.4
2004	463.2		73.0		139.3		148.8		68.5		18.3
2005	610.7		102.3		160.3		224.1		69.9		21.6
2006	935.3	53.2	113.4	10.9	265.3	65.4	439.6	96.2	72.3	3.5	27.7
2007	1175.8	25.7	200.2	76.5	289.5	9.2	548.0	24.7	84.8	17.2	29.6
2008	1160.7	-1.3	144.1	-28.0	291.6	0.7	604.2	10.3	86.7	2.3	30.2
2009	1462.0	26.0	165.4	14.8	434.5	49.0	698.6	15.6	124.9	44.1	30.1
2010	1403.5	-4.0	157.2	-5.0	359.1	-17.3	720.5	3.1	94.2	-24.5	25.5
2011	1400.2	0.3	171.1	10.7	379.4	6.4	680.7	-5.4	82.3	-12.6	23.7
2012	1789.2	27.8	231.9	35.5	508.1	33.9	712.0	4.6	122.0	48.2	27.7
2013	1785.7	-0.2	270.2	16.5	451.3	-11.2	664.5	-6.7	132.9	8.9	25.4
2014	2018.1	13.0	352.7	30.5	502.5	11.3	756.5	13.9	127.3	-4.2	26.7
2015	2174.5	7.7	297.3	-15.7	494.4	-1.6	827.0	9.3	172.3	35.3	27.2
2016	2399.5	10.3	332.0	11.7	643.8	30.2	973.0	17.7	147.5	-14.3	28.4
2017	2984.2	24.4	502.5	51.4	694.5	7.9	1327.0	36.4	194.4	31.8	33.4
2018		-10.7		-45.4		-6.8		1.1		2.3	32.7
2019		-3.8		-15.4		2.4		-9.2		17.8	33.1
2020		-12.3		-10.3		-14.0		-10.2		-17.2	26.3
2021		-8.9		-12.6		-22.8		-4.0		22.6	22.9
2022		5.2		29.8		-7.6		-7.2		62.5	23.2

注：1.自2004年起基础设施投资包括农村基础设施投资。
2.2018年及以前的基础设施投资占比为占全社会固定资产投资比重，自2019年起为占固定资产投资(不含农户)的比重。

Note: a) Investment in infrastructure in and after 2004 includes that in rural infrastructure investment.
b) The proportion of infrastructure investment in and before 2018 referred to the percentage for infrastructure investment of the total investment in fixed assets; since 2019, it refers to the percentage for infrastructure investment of the fixed assets investment (excluding peasant households).

9-6 房地产开发面积(1990-2022年)

单位：万平方米

年份 Year	房屋施工面积 Floor Space of Buildings under Construction	#本年新开工面积 Floor Space of Buildings Newly Started Construction in Current Year	住宅 Residential Houses	办公楼 Office Buildings	商业、营业用房及其他 Buildings for Commercial, Business Operation Use and Others	房屋竣工面积 Floor Space of Buildings Completed	住宅 Residential Houses
1990	774.0	249.1	643.4	17.4	41.2	271.6	226.5
1991	815.1	317.6	692.1	2.1	57.6	275.2	240.4
1992	1021.1	508.6	865.4	7.6	54.8	331.4	300.8
1993	1262.0	524.8	887.6			356.4	280.6
1994	1593.2	659.4	1107.6			445.7	385.6
1995	2810.2	1012.2	1728.7	462.7	252.6	653.0	506.3
1996	2824.6	578.7	1520.7	638.7	283.9	663.4	470.8
1997	2869.6	848.4	1541.1	637.7	260.8	682.3	478.3
1998	3499.1	1193.4	2107.2	590.7	297.7	842.8	588.7
1999	3784.0	1061.8	2447.9	484.4	281.3	1208.5	908.3
2000	4455.0	1676.9	2971.6	449.1	281.3	1365.6	1013.7
2001	5966.7	2789.8	4349.6	495.5	330.6	1707.4	1393.4
2002	7510.7	3206.0	5397.5	672.5	400.3	2384.4	1926.2
2003	9070.7	3433.8	6352.9	901.3	557.7	2593.7	2080.8
2004	9931.3	3054.3	6759.4	1122.4	641.8	3067.0	2343.9
2005	10748.5	2965.9	7283.4	1209.8	809.2	3770.9	2841.4
2006	10483.5	3179.4	6311.3	1245.8	1403.0	3193.9	2193.3
2007	10438.6	2557.4	5914.5	1364.6	1482.1	2891.7	1854.0
2008	10014.3	2337.2	5538.2	1287.2	1429.8	2558.0	1399.3
2009	9719.1	2246.6	5551.9	1132.2	1323.4	2678.6	1613.2
2010	10300.9	2974.2	6176.0	1054.8	1229.3	2386.7	1498.5
2011	12065.4	4246.1	7168.1	1422.7	1187.5	2245.2	1316.1
2012	13122.5	3224.2	7510.4	1711.9	1236.9	2390.9	1522.7
2013	13886.9	3577.5	7406.9	2114.1	4365.9	2666.4	1692.0
2014	13641.5	2502.8	6999.7	2277.1	4364.7	3054.1	1804.3
2015	13095.0	2790.2	6314.6	2426.8	4353.6	2631.5	1378.2
2016	13089.8	2813.7	5927.6	2447.3	4714.9	2383.1	1275.2
2017	12608.6	2475.7	5506.6	2428.4	4673.6	1466.7	604.0
2018	12962.6	2321.1	5877.1	2220.5	4865.0	1557.9	731.2
2019	12515.0	2073.2	5640.1	1951.0	4923.9	1343.3	583.2
2020	13918.6	3006.6	6715.3	1654.2	5549.2	1545.7	728.5
2021	14055.3	1895.9	6895.6	1461.4	5698.3	1983.9	981.1
2022	13333.1	1774.4	6713.6	1307.3	5312.3	1938.5	1096.2

注：1.2005年以前的商品房销售面积为竣工后的全部商品房销售面积，自2005年起为期房与现房销售面积之和。
2.自2010年起，商品房销售面积中包含定向安置房数据。
3.2012年及以前商业、营业用房及其他只包括商业及服务性等营业性用房，自2013年起统计范围包括：厂房、仓库、商业营业用房、服务业用房、教育用房、文化体育用房、医疗用房、科研用房及其他用房，下同。自2017年起，原“商业、非公益用房及其他”更名为“商业、营业用房及其他”。

STATISTICS FOR FLOOR SPACE OF REAL ESTATE DEVELOPMENT (1990–2022)

(10000 sq.m)

办公楼 Office Buildings	商业、营业用房及其他 Buildings for Commercial, Business Operation Use and Others	商品房销售面积 Floor Space of Commercial Buildings Sold	住宅 Residential Houses	办公楼 Office Buildings	商业、营业用房及其他 Buildings for Commercial, Business Operation Use and Others	年末商品房待售面积 Floor Space of Vacant Commercial Buildings at the Year End	住宅 Residential Houses	办公楼 Office Buildings	商业、营业用房及其他 Buildings for Commercial, Business Operation Use and Others
9.7	13.3	142.2							
0.9	10.9	154.0	152.5						
2.7	8.3	159.1	153.0						
		182.0	182.0						
		168.6	149.0	17.2	1.1				
27.9	43.5	191.9	180.0	4.0	4.5	81.5			
79.0	38.3	215.3	183.1	13.7	14.4	214.8	179.6		
80.9	42.4	290.9	256.2	18.8	8.0	298.3	258.9		
92.3	69.8	409.2	377.0	23.2	7.0	334.8	262.9		
108.8	43.1	544.4	484.7	48.0	6.8	624.3	529.1		
97.2	48.7	956.9	898.2	41.2	6.1	627.4	515.1		
98.0	48.2	1205.0	1127.5	49.8	17.4	774.0	634.1		
97.4	82.9	1708.3	1604.4	44.0	32.9	919.0	763.2		
94.0	117.5	1895.8	1771.1	38.1	50.8	1123.4	896.9		
153.9	225.3	2472.0	2285.8	92.5	60.2	1044.1	723.8		
287.8	180.9	2803.2	2566.0	131.2	66.9	1374.2	799.7		
304.4	289.2	2607.6	2205.0	260.3	108.6	1039.7	494.1		
314.8	315.1	2176.6	1731.5	265.7	134.8	1136.2	411.8		
364.6	313.1	1335.4	1031.4	139.4	112.4	1438.3	522.7		
316.6	322.4	2362.3	1880.5	255.8	157.1	1351.4	426.8		
198.4	271.9	1639.5	1201.4	208.1	142.1	1482.7	511.9		
245.2	232.4	1440.0	1035.0	211.4	108.7	1792.6	699.8		
226.8	240.1	1943.7	1483.4	253.5	114.0	1911.8	789.5		
273.1	701.3	1903.1	1363.7	317.9	221.5	1861.4	829.3	180.1	852.0
387.5	862.3	1459.0	1141.3	136.8	180.9	2065.7	864.8	307.2	893.7
385.4	867.8	1554.7	1127.3	243.0	184.4	2168.1	867.7	332.5	968.0
343.7	764.2	1675.1	993.5	415.4	266.2	2160.8	845.8	320.7	994.3
321.2	541.5	875.0	612.8	108.3	153.9	2092.1	811.2	336.1	944.8
249.9	576.8	696.2	526.8	75.8	93.6	2153.3	833.7	390.6	929.0
290.3	469.8	938.9	789.0	53.4	96.5	2489.5	893.1	569.0	1027.4
242.2	575.0	970.9	733.6	73.2	164.1	2454.2	881.9	530.5	1041.8
142.9	859.9	1107.1	877.1	55.3	174.7	2396.3	830.8	555.5	1010.0
177.8	664.5	1040.0	741.9	74.8	223.3	2617.0	854.4	567.9	1194.7

Note: a) Before 2005, the floor space of commercial buildings sold referred to the total floor space of completed commercial buildings sold,since 2005, the figure is the sum of floor space of completed commercial buildings sold and those under construction sold.

b) Since 2010, the floor space of commercial buildings sold has included figures of targeted resettlement buildings.

c) In and before 2012, buildings for commercial, business operation use and others only included business and commercial buildings.Since 2013,the statistical range has included: factory buildings, warehouses, buildings for commercial and business operation use,service industry buildings, education buildings, cultural and sports buildings, medical buildings, scientific research buildings and others, the same below. Since 2017, the original "Buildings for Commercial Use, Non-public Buildings and Others "was renamed "Buildings for Commercial, Business Operation Use and Others".

9-7 房地产开发投资情况(1990-2022年)
INVESTMENT IN REAL ESTATE DEVELOPMENT(1990-2022)

单位：亿元 (100 million yuan)

年 份	房地产开发投资 Investment in Real Estate Development		#住 宅 Residential Buildings		#办公楼 Office Buildings	
	绝对量 Absolute Volume	比上年增长(%) Growth Rate (%)	绝对量 Absolute Volume	比上年增长(%) Growth Rate (%)	绝对量 Absolute Volume	比上年增长(%) Growth Rate (%)
1990	22.5		12.3			
1991	24.0		14.0			
1992	33.7		20.0			
1993	58.4		38.1			
1994	99.5		50.3			
1995	352.8		142.4		71.5	
1996	328.2	-7.0	124.9	-12.3	84.2	17.8
1997	330.3	0.6	132.9	6.4	91.1	8.2
1998	377.4	14.3	168.0	26.4	78.5	-13.8
1999	421.5	11.7	236.6	40.8	52.5	-33.1
2000	522.1	23.9	288.3	21.9	45.2	-13.9
2001	783.8	50.1	464.2	61.0	72.0	59.3
2002	989.4	26.2	586.7	26.4	97.3	35.1
2003	1202.5	21.5	633.0	7.9	142.7	46.7
2004	1473.3	22.5	776.0	22.6	187.9	31.7
2005	1525.0	3.5	779.5	0.5	196.2	4.4
2006	1719.9	12.8	863.6	10.8	216.7	10.4
2007	1995.8	16.0	991.7	14.8	242.2	11.8
2008	1908.7	-4.4	940.6	-5.2	170.5	-29.6
2009	2337.7	22.5	906.6	-3.6	166.7	-2.2
2010	2901.1	24.1	1509.0	66.4	259.1	55.4
2011	3036.3	10.1	1778.3	17.8	363.8	40.4
2012	3153.4	3.9	1628.0	-8.5	384.8	5.8
2013	3483.4	10.5	1724.6	5.9	611.7	59.0
2014	3911.3	12.3	1962.0	13.8	750.2	22.6
2015	4226.3	8.1	1962.7	...	906.6	20.8
2016	4045.4	-4.3	1950.9	-0.6	699.1	-22.9
2017	3745.9	-7.4	1725.5	-11.6	742.9	6.3
2018		3.4		17.4		-29.7
2019		-0.9		0.7		-27.3
2020		2.6		13.6		-17.5
2021		5.1		8.9		-7.6
2022		1.0		5.8		-22.5

9-8 房地产开发企业经营情况(2022年)
REAL ESTATE DEVELOPMENT ENTERPRISES (2022)

项目	Item	企业单位个数(个) Number of Enterprises (unit)	实收资本合计(万元) Paid-in Capital (10000 yuan)	资产总计(万元) Total Assets (10000 yuan)	主营业务收入(万元) Main Business Income (10000 yuan)	利润总额(万元) Total Profits (10000 yuan)
合　计	**Total**	**1178**	**67012527**	**542702630**	**43780288**	**772184**
按企业登记注册类型分	**By Registration Type**					
内资企业	Domestically-Funded Enterprises	1106	60623642	505763442	42052162	861849
国有企业	State-owned Enterprises					
集体企业	Collectively-owned Enterprises	2	***	***	***	***
私营企业	Private Enterprises	78	530179	10149662	722572	90339
股份合作企业	Joint-equity Cooperative Enterprises	3	***	***	***	***
联营企业	Associated Enterprise					
股份有限公司	Companies Limited by Shares	10	1373445	43495867	420536	181039
有限责任公司	Limited Liability Corporationss	1013	58662371	450971993	40836136	561417
其他企业	Others					
港澳台商投资企业	Hong Kong, Macao and Taiwan-invested Enterprises	32	3540415	20077739	1130979	33992
#港澳台合资经营	Joint Ventures	10	951260	5777973	444801	2194
港澳台合作经营	Cooperative	9	439623	2184101	161876	38303
港澳台商独资企业	Solely-funded Enterprises	12	1199532	10825699	524302	-6047
外商投资企业	Foreign-invested Enterprises	40	2848470	16861449	597147	-123657
中外合资经营	Joint Ventures	20	1598633	5815122	228760	-21497
中外合作经营	Cooperative	8	317741	4685439	76820	-46762
外资(独资)企业	Solely-funded Enterprises	12	932096	6360888	291567	-55398
外商投资股份有限公司	Corporations Limited by Shares					
按资质等级分	**By Qualification Grade**					
一　级	First-grade	34	5177376	83227463	1823163	426800
二　级	Second-grade	263	25203969	152102891	11648929	444944
三　级	Third-grade	52	2950163	31714594	1006314	-21237
四　级	Fourth-grade	473	16352754	162057709	8679844	-1112177
暂　定	Provisional	275	13330393	90173968	18987874	1090446
其　他	Others	81	3997873	23426005	1634165	-56591
按营业状况分	**By Operating Condition**					
营　业	Operating	1177	67011527	542701630	43780288	772184
停　业	Closed	1	***	***	***	***
其　他	Others					

9-9 房地产开发企业开发建设情况(2022年)
DEVELOPMENT OF REAL ESTATE DEVELOPMENT ENTERPRISES (2022)

项目	Item	2022	2022年为2021年% 2022 as % of 2021
本年实际到位资金（亿元）	**Total Actual Funds in Place This Year (100 million yuan)**	**5631.7**	**86.3**
#国内贷款	Domestic Loans	1045.8	113.2
自筹资金	Self-raised Funds	1137.3	66.3
定金及预收款	Down Payment and Advance Payment	2768.7	88.9
个人按揭贷款	Personal Mortgage Loans	390.9	78.9
本年购置土地面积（万平方米）	**Land Space Purchased in Current Year (10000 sq.m)**	**188.8**	**81.9**

主要统计指标解释

全社会固定资产投资 是指以货币形式表现的在一定时期内全社会建造和购置固定资产的工作量以及与此有关的费用的总称。

固定资产投资（不含农户） 是指城镇和农村各种登记注册类型的企业、事业行政单位及城镇个体户进行的计划总投资 500 万元及以上的建设项目投资和房地产开发投资。

基础设施投资 是指能够为企业提供作为中间投入用于生产的基本需求；能够为消费者提供所需的基本消费服务；能够为社区提供用于改善不利的外部环境的服务等建设的投资，包括固定资产投资中用于市政工程、电信工程、公共设施和水利环保等建设的投资。

上年末结余资金 是指上年资金来源中没有形成固定资产投资额而结余的资金。包括尚未用到工程上去的材料价值、未开始安装的需要安装设备价值及结存的现金和银行存款等。

本年资金来源小计 是指固定资产投资单位在报告期收到的，用于固定资产投资的各种货币资金。包括中央预算内资金、国内贷款、债券、利用外资、自筹资金和其他资金。

中央预算资金 指来源于中央公共预算安排的用于项目建设的资金数额。

国内贷款 是指报告期固定资产投资项目单位向银行及非银行金融机构借入的用于固定资产投资的各种国内借款，包括银行利用自有资金及吸收存款发放的贷款、上级拨入的国内贷款、国家专项贷款，地方财政专项资金安排的贷款、国内储备贷款、周转贷款等。

利用外资 是指报告期收到的用于固定资产建造和购置投资的境外资金(包括设备、材料、技术在内)。包括外商直接投资、对外借款(外国政府贷款、国际金融组织贷款、出口信贷、外国银行商业贷款、对外发行债券和股票)及外商其他投资(包括利用外商投资收益在国内进行固定资产再投资活动的资金)。不包括我国自有外汇资金(包括国家外汇、地方外汇、留成外汇、调剂外汇和国内银行自有资金发行的外汇贷款等)。

自筹资金 指在报告期内筹集的用于项目建设和购置的资金。包括自有资金、股东投入资金和借入资金，但不包括各类财政性资金、从各类金融机构借入资金和国外资金。

其他资金来源 是指在报告期收到的除以上各种资金之外其他用于固定资产投资的资金。包括社会集资、个人资金、无偿捐赠的资金、其他单位拨入的资金、市级预算资金和区级预算资金等。

建筑安装投资 是指各种房屋、建筑物的建造工程，各种设备、装置的安装工程，又称建筑安装工作量。建筑工程投资必须经过兴工动料，通过施工活动才能实现。在安装工程中，不包括被安装设备本身价值。

房地产开发投资 指自本年 1 月 1 日起至本年最后一天止，房地产开发项目中全部用于房屋建筑物、配套的服务设施、土地开发工程和土地购置的投资；不包括单纯的土地开发和交易活动。

房屋施工面积 是指报告期内施工的全部房屋建筑面积。包括本期新开工的房屋建筑面积、上期跨入本期继续施工的房屋建筑面积、上期停缓建在本期恢复施工的房屋建筑面积、本期竣工的房屋建筑面积以及本期施工后又停缓建的房屋建筑面积。多层建筑应填各层建筑面积之和。

房屋竣工面积 是指报告期内房屋建筑按照设计要求已全部完工，达到住人和使用条件，经验收鉴定合格(或达到竣工验收标准)，可正式移交使用的各栋房屋建筑面积的总和。

待售面积 指报告期末已竣工的可供销售或出租的商品房屋建筑面积中，尚未销售或出租的商品房屋建筑面积，包括以前年度竣工和本期竣工的房屋面积，但不包括报告期已竣工的拆迁还建、统建代建、公共配套建筑、房地产公司自用及周转房等不可销售或出租的房屋面积。

Explanatory Notes on Main Statistical Indicators

Total Investment in Fixed Assets refers to the volume of activities in construction and purchases of fixed assets of the whole city and the related fees, expressed in monetary terms during the reference period.

Investment in Fixed Assets (Excluding Rural Households) refers to the investment in construction projects with a total planned investment of RMB 5 million and over by urban and rural enterprises of various registration types, public institutions and administrative units and by urban self-employed individuals as well as the real estate development investment.

Infrastructure Investment refers to the investment that can provide enterprises with the basic needs as intermediate inputs for production, the investment that can provide consumers with the basic consumer services they need, and the investment in construction that can provide communities with services to improve the unfavorable external environment, including the investment in fixed assets that are used in municipal engineering, telecommunications engineering, public facilities, water conservancy and environmental protection, etc.

Surplus Funds by the Year End of the Previous Year refers to the fund in the previous year that was not included in the investment in fixed assets, including the value of materials not yet used for projects, value of equipment to be installed, and balance of cash and bank deposits.

Subtotal of Funds at Current Year refers to various monetary funds received during the reporting period by investors that was used for investment in fixed assets, including funds from central budgetary funds, domestic loans, bonds, foreign investment, self-raised funds and other funds.

Central Budgetary Fund refers to the amount of fund that comes from the central public budget arrangement and is used for project construction.

Domestic Loans refer to loans of various forms borrowed by fixed assets investment project entities from banks and non-bank financial institutions for the purpose of investment in fixed assets during the reporting period, including loans issued by banks from their self-owned funds and deposits, domestic loans appropriated by higher authorities in charge, special loans allocated by the central government, loans arranged by local government from special funds, domestic reserve loans and revolving loans.

Foreign Investment refers to foreign funds received during the reporting period for the investment in construction and purchase of fixed assets (including equipment, materials and technologies), including foreign direct investment, foreign loans (loans from foreign governments and international financial institutions, export credit, commercial loans from foreign banks, issued bonds and stocks overseas), and other foreign investments (including funds for domestic re-investment in fixed assets by earnings from foreign investment). It does not include foreign exchanges owned by China (including foreign exchanges owned by the central and local governments, foreign exchanges retained, foreign exchange swap, loans in foreign exchanges issued by the domestic banks with their self-owned funds, etc.).

Self-raised Funds refer to non-budgetary funds received by fixed assets investors during the reporting period that are raised by different regions, departments, enterprises and public institutions for investment in fixed assets, including self-owned funds of central departments, local authorities at all levels, enterprises and public institutions.

Other Funds refer to funds for investment in fixed assets received during the reporting period from sources other than those listed above, including social funds, personal funds, donated funds and funds transferred from other institutions, municipal-level budgetary fund and district-level budgetary fund, etc.

Construction and Installation Investment refers to the investment in construction projects of various houses and buildings, and installation projects of various equipment and devices, also known as the workload of construction and installation. It can only be realized through construction work and consumption of materials. For installation projects, the value of equipment installed is not included.

Real Estate Development Investment refers to the investment in real estate development projects that is all used in houses and buildings, supporting service facilities, land development projects and land purchase from January 1st to the last day of the year, but excludes the simple land development and trading activities.

Floor Space of Buildings under Construction refers to the total floor space area of buildings under construction in the reference period. It includes buildings new started; buildings started earlier and continued during the reference period; buildings suspended earlier but restarted during the reference period; buildings completed during the reference period; and buildings under construction but suspended during the reference period. For multi-floor building, please fill in the sum of floor space of all floors.

Floor Space of Buildings Completed refers to the total floor space of all houses and buildings fully completed as required in the design plan during the reporting period, which have been examined as qualified for living and use (or have met the completion inspection standards), and can be handed over and put into use.

Floor Space for Sale refers to floor space of commercial buildings that has not been sold or rented out among the floor space of completed commercial buildings available for sale or renting by the end of the reporting period. It consists of the floor space of completed buildings in previous years and in the current year, but does not include relocated houses or buildings of unified construction or agent contract, as well as houses not for sale or renting such as public supporting buildings, owner-occupied and relocation housing of real estate companies.

对外经济贸易
FOREIGN ECONOMIC RELATIONS AND TRADE

简要说明

一、主要内容

本章资料主要反映北京市对外经济贸易的发展状况，包括对外贸易、利用外资、对外经济合作的历年概况。

二、统计范围

（一）货物进出口情况

货物进出口统计的范围是凡能引起北京市海关境内物质资源存量增加或减少的进出口货物，除制度另有规定者外，均列入该项统计，调查方法采用全面调查。主要内容包括北京地区进出口总值；主要产品进出口数量等。

（二）口岸运营情况

口岸运营的统计范围是北京首都国际机场空港口岸、北京大兴国际机场空港口岸、北京丰台货运口岸、北京朝阳口岸、北京西站铁路口岸、北京平谷国际陆港、北京天竺综合保税区。主要内容包括旅客吞吐量、货邮吞吐量、监管货物的数量、征收关税等。

（三）利用外资情况

利用外资情况的统计范围是凡经工商行政管理机关核准登记，在中华人民共和国北京地域内所有使用外资（包括港澳台地区投资）的单位和部门，经批准设立的中外合资经营企业、合作经营企业、外资企业、外商投资股份制企业、合作开发项目等具有法人资格的独立核算企业(包括港澳台地区投资企业)，在华从事经营活动的外国及港澳台地区企业及外国公司在中国境内设立的分支机构。主要内容包括实际利用外商直接投资，外商投资企业经营情况，调查方法采用全面调查。

（四）对外经济合作

对外经济合作的统计范围是经各级商务部门批准的从事对外承包、劳务合作和设计咨询业务并具有法人资格的对外承包劳务企业；调查方法采用全面调查。主要内容包括对外承包工程、劳务合作和设计咨询。

Brief Introduction

I. Main Content

Data in this chapter mainly show the development of foreign economic relations and trade in Beijing, including foreign trade, use of foreign capital, and foreign economic cooperation in Beijing over the years.

II. Scope of Statistics

(I) Statistics for Imports and Exports of Goods

The scope of statistics for imports and exports of goods covers all imports and exports that lead to increase or decrease in the stock of physical resources at Beijing customs, except for those otherwise stated in regulations, and the survey was conducted with comprehensive survey method. Data mainly include: total value of imports and exports in Beijing, and quantity of imports and exports of major products, and so on.

(II) Statistics for Port Operation

The statistical scope of port operation covers the Port of Beijing Capital International Airport, the Port of Daxing International Airport, Beijing Fengtai Cargo Transport Port, Beijing Chaoyang Transport Port, Railway Port at Beijing West Railway Station, Beijing Pinggu International Land Port, and Beijing Tianzhu Comprehensive Bonded Zone. Data mainly include: passenger throughput, cargos carried, quantity of cargos under regulation and duties levied.

(III) Use of Foreign Capital

The scope of statistics for the use of foreign capital covers all the units and departments which have used foreign capitals (including investment from Hong Kong, Macao and Taiwan) in the region of Beijing of the People's Republic of China, all the Sino-foreign joint ventures, Sino-foreign cooperative enterprises, ventures exclusively with foreign investment, foreign-funded stock companies, Sino-foreign cooperative development projects (including the enterprises funded by the entrepreneurs from Hong Kong, Macao and Taiwan) with independent accounting system and legal person status which have been approved to be set up, and all foreign enterprises or enterprises funded by the entrepreneurs from Hong Kong, Macao and Taiwan which engaged in business activities in China, and branches of foreign companies which engaged in business activities in China, after verification and registration through the administrative authorities for industry and commerce. Data mainly include the actual use of foreign direct investment and the operations of foreign invested enterprises. The survey was conducted with comprehensive survey method.

(IV) Foreign Economic Cooperation

Statistics cover foreign labor service enterprises with legal person statues that are engaged in foreign contracting, labor service cooperation and design consulting with approval from departments of commerce at different levels. The survey was conducted with comprehensive survey method. Data mainly include: foreign contracting projects, labor service cooperation and design consulting.

10-1 北京地区对外经济贸易(1983-2022年)
FOREIGN ECONOMIC RELATIONS AND TRADE IN BEIJING (1983-2022)

年 份 Year	货物进出口总值(亿美元) Total Value of Imports and Exports of Goods (USD 100 million)	出 口 Exports	#高新技术产品 High-tech Products	#机电产品 Mechanical and Electrical Products	进 口 Imports	#高新技术产品 High-tech Products	#机电产品 Mechanical and Electrical Products
1983	306.0	146.9			159.1		
1984	355.9	175.2			180.8		
1985	325.4	43.7			281.7		
1986	306.0	37.1			268.9		
1987	267.0	35.4			231.6		
1988	298.9	39.6			259.3		
1989	286.1	30.2			255.9		
1990	236.4	44.1			192.3		
1991	242.4	45.7			196.7		
1992	249.8	56.1		15.8	193.7	27.1	73.1
1993	279.2	67.0		15.1	212.2	30.3	88.5
1994	288.8	83.4		19.5	205.4	42.1	112.1
1995	370.4	102.5		28.2	267.9	40.7	122.5
1996	293.2	81.2		25.4	212.0	24.1	73.4
1997	303.9	96.1		27.1	207.8	34.6	76.6
1998	305.1	105.1		32.5	199.9	34.8	90.9
1999	343.6	99.0		32.1	244.6	56.8	121.4
2000	494.0	119.7	22.7	43.7	374.3	74.0	142.6
2001	515.0	117.7	26.3	47.8	397.3	99.3	188.3
2002	525.1	126.1	31.4	57.1	398.9	91.6	170.2
2003	685.0	168.9	39.6	71.5	516.1	99.0	194.9
2004	945.8	205.7	58.1	97.0	740.1	105.3	227.2
2005	1255.1	308.7	97.1	155.7	946.4	136.6	269.6
2006	1580.4	379.5	138.9	217.1	1200.8	170.5	378.7
2007	1930.0	489.3	179.8	286.2	1440.7	236.0	447.8
2008	2716.9	575.0	190.6	335.4	2141.9	241.8	498.8
2009	2147.9	483.6	175.2	308.0	1664.3	235.7	519.4
2010	3016.6	554.4	193.7	339.4	2462.2	274.9	666.1
2011	3895.8	590.0	181.2	352.3	3305.9	314.5	766.8
2012	4081.1	596.3	190.2	373.8	3484.8	298.8	721.8
2013	4299.4	631.0	203.6	389.5	3668.4	292.4	716.8
2014	4155.4	623.4	187.5	379.0	3532.0	293.7	778.5
2015	3194.2	546.7	140.3	314.4	2647.5	261.3	659.2
2016	2823.8	520.2	113.2	272.8	2303.6	255.0	655.3
2017	3237.2	585.0	112.8	284.1	2652.2	264.9	659.4
2018	4124.3	741.7	152.2	322.1	3382.6	278.3	691.1
2019	4160.8	749.8	157.5	314.5	3411.0	269.7	658.3
2020	3350.4	670.1	197.4	320.7	2680.3	279.6	666.2
2021	4710.2	946.4	403.6	416.6	3763.8	360.3	790.1
2022	5465.0	881.7	259.1	406.3	4583.3	403.1	781.0

注：货物进出口总值为海关统计的北京地区进出口数据(包括中央单位)。
资料来源：中华人民共和国北京海关、北京市商务局。
Note: Figures of total value of imports and exports of goods are imports and exports data of Beijing counted by Beijing Customs (including central government entities).
Source: Beijing Customs of the People's Republic of China and Beijing Municipal Commerce Bureau.

10-1 续表 Continued

年份 Year	货物进出口总值（亿元）Total Value of Imports and Exports of Goods (100 million yuan)	出口 Exports	进口 Imports	服务贸易进出口总额（亿美元）Total Export-Import Volume of Service Trade (USD 100 million)	出口 Exports	进口 Imports	新设企业数（个）Number of Newly Established Enterprises (unit)	实际利用外商直接投资额（万美元）Actal Use of Foreign Direct Investment (USD10000)
1983								
1984								
1985								
1986								
1987								
1988								
1989								
1990								
1991								
1992	1377.1	309.2	1067.9					
1993	1607.9	385.8	1222.1					
1994	2492.4	719.2	1773.1					
1995	3108.2	863.2	2244.9					
1996	2450.3	680.9	1769.4					
1997	2522.5	798.4	1724.0					
1998	2530.6	872.2	1658.4					
1999	2356.9	665.6	1691.3					
2000	4090.1	991.4	3098.7				1145	168368
2001	4262.2	974.3	3287.8				1146	176818
2002	4345.7	1043.9	3301.8				1370	172464
2003	5674.5	1398.6	4275.9	162.24		66.12	1539	219126
2004	7824.5	1702.1	6122.4	235.70		93.08	1806	255974
2005	10331.9	2540.4	7791.4	300.74		109.62	2138	352834
2006	12670.7	3039.9	9630.8	393.23		154.08	2110	457969
2007	14831.0	3764.7	11066.3	503.06	252.81	250.25	2177	507571
2008	19113.6	4044.2	15069.4	691.92	341.69	350.23	1896	491795
2009	14648.2	3301.9	11346.3	644.10	311.60	332.50	1422	524780
2010	20478.2	3766.1	16712.1	798.29	388.22	410.07	1629	533617
2011	25303.9	3835.4	21468.5	895.40	415.00	480.40	1638	590661
2012	25765.2	3766.8	21998.4	1000.20	445.11	555.09	1361	616463
2013	26691.0	3920.1	22770.9	1023.30	426.90	596.40	1190	684245
2014	25517.9	3829.4	21688.6	1106.10	435.00	671.10	1318	816911
2015	19827.7	3395.0	16432.6	1302.78	490.67	812.11	1386	1271540
2016	18652.2	3433.5	15218.6	1508.60	532.13	976.47	1079	1258555
2017	21923.9	3962.5	17961.4	1434.26	437.21	997.06	1301	2325755
2018	27182.5	4878.5	22303.9	1606.19	562.75	1043.43	1641	1673635
2019	28663.5	5167.8	23495.7				1636	1362385
2020	23215.9	4654.9	18561.0				1261	1339335
2021	30438.4	6118.5	24319.9				1924	1443424
2022	36445.5	5890.0	30555.5				1408	1740768

10-2 北京地区货物进出口贸易总值(按企业性质、贸易方式分)
TOTAL VALUE OF IMPORTS AND EXPORTS OF GOODS IN BEIJING (BY ENTERPRISE TYPE AND COMPOSITION)

项目	Item	金额(万美元) Value (USD 10000)		金额(万元) Value (10000 yuan)	
		2022	2021	2022	2021
进出口总值	**Total Value of Imports and Exports**	**54649912**	**47102424**	**364455076**	**304383662**
出　口	**Local Exports**	**8817061**	**9464147**	**58900240**	**61184689**
按企业性质分	**By Enterprise Type**				
#国有企业	State-owned Enterprises	4789086	4423657	32078500	28626735
外商投资企业	Foreign-invested Enterprises	2507669	3463653	16683359	22370601
民营企业	Private Enterprises	1439247	1395158	9589339	9012962
按贸易方式分	**By Trade method**				
#一般贸易	General Trade	7163899	7671393	47870997	49599871
来料加工贸易	Trade of Processing with Supplied Materials	81439	51936	542250	335648
进料加工贸易	Trade of Processing Imported Materials	303387	433838	2019946	2802656
对外承包工程出口货物	Export of Goods for Contracted Foreign Projects	478234	479441	3218983	3097847
出料加工贸易	Trade of Processing Exported Materials	871	1330	5737	8590
进　口	**Imports**	**45832851**	**37638277**	**305554835**	**243198973**
按企业性质分	**By Enterprise Type**				
#国有企业	State-owned Enterprises	36086743	27503763	240763002	177631790
外商投资企业	Foreign-invested Enterprises	6558929	6965530	43543047	45091943
民营企业	Private Enterprises	3113463	3098981	20744851	20018338
按贸易方式分	**By Composition**				
#一般贸易	General Trade	40692722	33161416	271331466	214285782
来料加工贸易	Trade of Processing with Supplied Materials	1651947	1081314	10988575	6987663
进料加工贸易	Trade of Processing Imported Materials	154714	180183	1030126	1164050
外商投资企业作为投资进口的设备、物品	Equipment and Goods Imported as Investment by Foreign-invested Enterprises	1045	3667	6765	23708
租赁贸易	Leasing Trade	17505	37065	118290	239485

资料来源：中华人民共和国北京海关。
Source: Beijing Customs of the People's Republic of China.

10-3 北京地区货物进出口贸易总值(按国别、地区分)
TOTAL VALUE OF IMPORTS AND EXPORTS OF GOODS IN BEIJING (BY COUNTRY AND REGION)

项目	Item	金额(万美元) Value (USD 10000)		金额(万元) Value (10000 yuan)	
		2022	2021	2022	2021
进出口总值	**Total Value of Imports and Exports**	**54649912**	**47102424**	**364455076**	**304383662**
出口	**Exports**	**8817061**	**9464147**	**58900240**	**61184689**
按国别(地区)分	**By Country (Region)**				
#中国香港	Hong Kong, China	931108	964504	6196912	6234856
中国澳门	Macao, China	22783	23181	151135	149750
中国台湾	Taiwan, China	164273	163916	1090407	1058741
日本	Japan	381896	355239	2553866	2297086
新加坡	Singapore	774920	517515	5192796	3353536
韩国	Korea	260129	260987	1728665	1690159
越南	Vietnam	224496	222161	1488445	1436139
伊朗	Iran	50986	54596	342741	353305
印度	India	159233	168766	1064139	1091856
印度尼西亚	Indonesia	191205	361446	1271954	2338537
英国	United Kingdom	87025	81609	574918	527544
德国	Germany	162511	223727	1076697	1447130
法国	France	87852	121351	581259	783157
意大利	Italy	106639	102939	705531	664267
匈牙利	Hungary	19236	28604	127733	185103
俄罗斯联邦	Russian Federation	301574	219027	2032179	1414286
美国	United States	513497	445096	3417566	2875426
澳大利亚	Australia	240185	205095	1627570	1329815
进口	**Imports**	**45832851**	**37638277**	**305554835**	**243198973**
按国别(地区)分	**By Country (Region)**				
#中国香港	Hong Kong, China	119299	141434	803496	914250
日本	Japan	1649322	1643389	10968949	10633020
新加坡	Singapore	238851	304477	1582557	1964926
韩国	Korea	347704	348368	2326836	2250635
沙特阿拉伯	Saudi Arabia	3179436	2340150	21151767	15119699
英国	United Kingdom	543820	657054	3588868	4245436
德国	Germany	2544799	2617538	16906470	16942923
法国	France	351275	361326	2348224	2334375
意大利	Italy	248367	300191	1656578	1940295
瑞士	Switzerland	1982120	737125	13401589	4760796
比利时	Belgium	101905	99366	670146	641862
俄罗斯联邦	Russian Federation	2548910	1847925	16936496	11929016
加拿大	Canada	1863034	432540	12739015	2792642
美国	United States	3587006	4211270	23748428	27223830
澳大利亚	Australia	2439288	2744309	16204968	17735300
阿曼	Oman	2411889	1461325	16095176	9431983
安哥拉	Angola	1791136	1435599	11891559	9269745

资料来源：中华人民共和国北京海关。
Source: Beijing Customs of the People's Republic of China.

10-4 北京地区海关主要商品进口量及金额(2022年) VOLUME & VALUE OF MAJOR COMMODITIES IMPORTED AT BEIJING CUSTOMS (2022)

项目		Item		进口数量 Import Volume	进口金额(万美元) Import Value (USD 10000)
粮　食	(吨)	Grain	(ton)	37187354	1591964
食用植物油	(吨)	Edible Vegetable Oil	(ton)	704467	101847
食　糖	(吨)	Sugar	(ton)	1275619	63358
酒类及饮料		Alcohol and Beverage			30434
天然及合成橡胶(包括胶乳)	(吨)	Natural and Synthetic Rubber(Including Latex)	(ton)	47692	8276
纸浆、纸及其制品	(吨)	Paper Pulp, Paper and Paper Products	(ton)	1542226	129542
#纸　浆	(吨)	Paper Pulp	(ton)	1149405	92228
羊毛及毛条	(吨)	Wool and Wool Top	(ton)	9693	6795
棉　花	(吨)	Cotton	(ton)	1137155	300812
纺织纱线、织物及其制品		Textile Yarn, Fabric and Products			42212
#合成纤维纱线	(吨)	Synthetic Fiber Yarn	(ton)	1466	1900
铁矿砂及其精矿	(吨)	Iron Sand and Iron Ore Concentrates	(ton)	105867819	1254234
原　油	(吨)	Crude Oil	(ton)	277419253	20400735
成品油	(吨)	Product Oil	(ton)	5395362	412700
医药材及药品	(吨)	Medicinal and Pharmaceutical Materials and Medicines	(ton)	28795	1321648
肥　料	(吨)	Fertilizers	(ton)	5635095	306652
塑料制品	(吨)	Plastic Products	(ton)	33746	76817
服装及衣着附件		Clothes and Clothing Accessories			26944
钢　材	(吨)	Steel Products	(ton)	159460	39909
印刷、装订机械及其零件		Printing and Binding Machinery and Parts Thereof			103239
自动数据处理设备及其零部件		Automatic Data Processing Equipment and Their Components and Parts			113080
变压器	(个)	Voltage Transformers	(unit)	948374	3377
电视摄像机、数字照相机及视频摄录一体机	(台)	Television Cameras, Digital Cameras and Integrated Video Cameras and Recorders	(set)	1352204	80472
印刷电路	(万块)	Printed Circuits	(10000 pieces)	159538	8310
集成电路	(万个)	Integrated Circuits	(10000 units)	1735124	635858
电线及电缆	(吨)	Wires and Cables	(ton)	3341	16297
汽车(包括底盘)		Automobiles (Including Chassis)			2809006
汽车零配件		Auto Spare Parts			559615
飞机及其他航空器	(架)	Aircrafts and Others	(unit)	21	42929
船　舶		Ships and Boats			18397
医疗仪器及器械		Medical Instruments and Devices			307938
计量检测分析自控仪器及器具		Automatically-controlled Measuring, Testing and Analyzing Instruments			601516

资料来源：中华人民共和国北京海关。
Source: Beijing Customs of the People's Republic of China.

10-5 北京地区海关主要商品出口量及金额(2022年)
VOLUME & VALUE OF MAJOR COMMODITIES EXPORTED AT BEIJING CUSTOMS (2022)

项 目		Item		出口数量 Export Volume	出口金额 Export Value (万美元) (USD 10000)
粮 食	(吨)	Grain	(ton)	2084385	90464
果蔬汁	(吨)	Fruit and Vegetable Juice	(ton)	102097	12571
肥 料	(吨)	Fertilizers	(ton)	938142	40765
煤及褐煤	(吨)	Coal and Lignite	(ton)	1646839	53703
焦炭、半焦炭	(吨)	Coke and Semi-coke	(ton)	1151117	58311
成品油	(吨)	Product Oil	(ton)	31641136	2896775
医药材及药品	(吨)	Medicinal and Pharmaceutical Materials and Medicines	(ton)	21293	137332
纺织纱线、织物及其制品		Textile Yarn, Fabric and Products			74912
铁合金	(吨)	Ferroalloy	(ton)	11826	10385
钢 材	(吨)	Steel Products	(ton)	2448205	283780
未锻轧铝及铝材	(吨)	Non-forged Aluminum and Aluminum Products	(ton)	76924	30518
纺织机械及其零件		Textile Machinery and Parts			21836
机 床	(台)	Machine Tools	(set)	47131	12347
自动数据处理设备及其零部件		Automatic Data Processing Equipment and Their Components			125331
液晶平板显示模组	(个)	LCD Flat-panel Display Module Groups	(unit)	18254150	93116
变压器	(个)	Voltage Transformers	(unit)	712026	19661
蓄电池	(个)	Storage Cells	(unit)	1575055	17410
手 机	(台)	Cell phones	(set)	74595917	1049592
二极管及类似半导体器件	(万个)	Diode and Similar Semiconductor Devices	(10000 units)	163004	87547
集成电路	(万个)	Integrated Circuits	(10000 units)	1179109	375613
电线及电缆	(吨)	Wires and Cables	(ton)	29680	27662
汽车(包括底盘)		Automobiles			154310
汽车零配件		Auto Spare Parts			213018
船 舶		Boats and Ships			32619
医疗仪器及器械		Medical Instruments and Devices			107258
家具及其零件		Furniture and Their Parts			15768
服装及衣着附件		Clothes and Clothing Accessories			89381
鞋 靴	(吨)	Shoes and Boots	(ton)	13074	16472
塑料制品	(吨)	Plastic Products	(ton)	104164	52741

资料来源：中华人民共和国北京海关。
Source: Beijing Customs of the People's Republic of China.

10-6 北京口岸运营情况
STATISTICS FOR PORT OPERATION IN BEIJING

项目		Item		2022	2021
北京首都国际机场空港口岸		**Port of Beijing Capital International Airport**			
旅客吞吐量	（万人次）	Passenger Throughput	(10000 person-times)	1270.7	3263.9
出入境人员	（万人次）	Inbound/Outbound Visitors	(10000 person-times)	58.4	53.1
#外籍人员出入境		Inbound/Outbound Foreign Visitors		10.0	4.5
货邮吞吐量	（万吨）	Cargos Carried	(10000 tons)	98.8	140.1
飞机起降	（架次）	Takeoff and Landing of Airplanes	(unit)	157662	298179
#出入境飞机起降		Takeoff and Landing of Airplanes Inbound/Outbound		25018	33960
海关监管货物	（万吨）	Cargos under Customs Regulation	(10000 tons)	4466.9	6228.7
北京大兴国际机场空港口岸		**Port of Daxing International Airport**			
旅客吞吐量	（万人次）	Passenger Throughput	(10000 person-times)	1027.8	2504.9
出入境人员	（万人次）	Inbound/Outbound Visitors	(10000 person-times)	…	0.1
#外籍人员出入境		Inbound/Outbound Foreign Visitors			…
货邮吞吐量	（万吨）	Cargos Carried	(10000 tons)	12.7	18.6
飞机起降	（架次）	Takeoff and Landing of Airplanes	(unit)	105922	211264
#出入境飞机起降		Takeoff and Landing of Airplanes Inbound/Outbound		8	90
海关监管货物	（万吨）	Cargos under Customs Regulation	(10000 tons)	0.2	0.4
北京丰台货运口岸		**Beijing Fengtai Cargo Transport Port**			
海关监管货物	（吨）	Cargos under Customs Regulation	(ton)	940	16400
北京朝阳口岸		**Beijing Chaoyang Transport Port**			
海关监管货物	（吨）	Cargos under Customs Regulation	(ton)	669451	658066
北京西站铁路口岸		**Railway Port at Beijing West Railway Station**			
进出境人员	（人次）	Inbound/Outbound Visitors	(person-times)		
#外籍人员进出境		Inbound/Outbound Foreign Visitors			
北京平谷国际陆港		**Beijing Pinggu International Land Port**			
海关监管货物	（吨）	Cargos under Customs Regulation	(ton)	35044	43150
北京天竺综合保税区		**Beijing Tianzhu Comprehensive Bonded Zone**			
实际进出货物	（吨）	Actual Import and Export Goods	(ton)	80471	77664
海关征收税款净入库税额	**（亿元）**	**Net Paid-in Duties Levied and Collected by Customs**	**(100 million yuan)**	**670.0**	**568.8**

资料来源：北京市人民政府口岸办公室。
Source: Port Administration Office of the People's Government of Beijing Municipality.

10－7 外商投资企业实际利用外资情况(2010－2022年)

单位：万美元

项 目	Item	2010	2011
实际利用外商直接投资额	**Actual Use of Foreign Direct Investment**	**533617**	**590661**
按产业分	**By Industry**		
第一产业	Primary Industry		
第二产业	Secondary Industry		
第三产业	Tertiary Industry		
按行业分	**By Sector**		
农、林、牧、渔业	Agriculture, Forestry, Animal Husbandry and Fishery	1250	144
采矿业	Mining	85	456
制造业	Maunfacturing	62774	46405
电力、热力、燃气及水生产和供应业	Production and Supply of Electricity, Heating, Gas and Water	2461	14712
建筑业	Construction	104	1920
批发和零售业	Wholesale and Retail Trade	57416	93712
交通运输、仓储和邮政业	Transport, Storage and Post	14930	13611
住宿和餐饮业	Accommodation and Catering	2352	1074
信息传输、软件和信息技术服务业	Information Transmission, Software and Information Technology Services	74504	93631
金融业	Finance	7899	23168
房地产业	Real Estate	110138	95333
租赁和商务服务业	Leasing and Business Services	153509	142154
科学研究和技术服务业	Scientific Research and Development, Technical Services	35345	38382
水利、环境和公共设施管理业	Management of Water Conservancy, Environment and Public Facilities		3164
居民服务、修理和其他服务业	Resident Services, Repair and Other Services	5441	21390
教 育	Education	211	4
卫生和社会工作	Health and Social Works	1390	
文化、体育和娱乐业	Culture, Sports and Entertainment	3808	1401
按外商国别(地区)分	**By Country (Region) of Foreign Investors**		
#中国香港	Hong Kong, China	263620	284755
新加坡	Singapore	20331	8784
日 本	Japan	35508	56704
英属维尔京群岛	British Virgin Islands	69101	98505
美 国	United States	20346	28760
韩 国	Korea	12269	20406
德 国	Germany	10406	17697
瑞 典	Sweden	3150	705
瑞 士	Switzerland	1600	3915
开曼群岛	Cayman Islands	38513	33340
中国台湾	Taiwan, China	966	622
比利时	Belgium	487	62
英 国	United Kingdom	770	6247
法 国	France	3476	6139
卢森堡	Luxembourg	4780	3216

资料来源：北京市商务局。

ACTUAL USE OF FOREIGN CAPITAL BY FOREIGN INVESTED ENTERPRISES (2010-2022)

(USD 10000)

2012	2013	2014	2015	2016	2017	2018	2019	2020	2021	2022
616463	**684245**	**816911**	**1271540**	**1258555**	**2325755**	**1673635**	**1362385**	**1339335**	**1443424**	**1740768**
						6725	63		11775	37
						224817	56931	14919	29552	52445
						1442093	1305391	1324416	1402097	1688286
632	1634	2224	7563	2303	838	6725	63		11775	37
260		81			247					
84150	81054	67471	50535	56402	35546	90166	19502	9923	27661	43662
25305	37563	12244		4347	69057	134634	36632	4957	1168	2341
383	108	688	131	113	451	15	813	35	724	6442
76789	69900	43601	241579	576878	167306	52009	52427	59648	61899	57485
6124	22304	4962	975	88655	126718	113176	11231	48573	2810	5580
2648	1807	2013	548	3009	1221	29448	1873	72	43842	5500
130829	101372	107632	44599	111176	1303210	446614	530902	446383	390513	394366
18748	14034	30570	729245	85230	20015	67749	152203	107293	37361	133554
87437	139250	131627	27296	66160	205690	193193	67825	44270	70137	17795
122680	155597	324028	66988	103902	202648	287787	107131	138320	177673	369097
52871	56774	83140	94146	152429	188879	243834	364897	466241	591825	698192
270		2635	4720	1754	490		1534		18582	
4497	390	331	83	16	176	2146	2227	964	80	5565
321	73		15				253			
554		1594			397	412	1455	8734	2044	
1965	2385	2070	3117	6181	2866	5727	11417	3922	5330	1152
296511	323419	518833	981380	546756	2087813	1250642	1063860	989852	1223722	1591663
26829	18314	35268	16218	54226	8924	10743	20045	21949	40241	31718
39679	42747	30706	11546	11921	18977	20290	14353	24446	33159	7544
27433	45405	20661	187185	205933	26056	29388	12837	30214	29108	2895
20279	14863	14421	2346	6273	12356	34892	25145	42569	25572	4230
69920	13180	18236	6906	38229	24227	57825	70562	26255	16470	24384
24314	68822	99654	35575	95643	11419	28588	20887	47475	16216	210
840	10687	100	381	8	48	2022	8253	3465	12770	26792
20271	1216	2804	313	204	68	7166	5652	474	11048	83
56378	37520	31535	5604	268307	34409	59455	54177	125859	8380	7599
903	673	1776	288	291	134	265	220	96	7465	51
18	3	510	69	109	24	11	13	1649	4727	490
3481	2216	1738	1952	1693	418	916	1430	3141	3115	9670
2286	1406	6261	15154	14346	5783	7437	2424	3535	2680	134
334	17139	123	250	7146		6461	860	1258	1997	62

Source: Beijing Municipal Commerce Bureau.

10-8 限额以上港澳台及外商投资法人企业基本情况(2022年) STATISTICS FOR HONGKONG, MACAO, TAIWAN AND FOREIGN-INVESTED CORPORATE ENTERPRISES ABOVE DESIGNATED SIZE(2022)

项目	Item	企业单位数(个) Number of Enterprises (unit)	平均用工人数(万人) Average Number of Employees (10000 persons)	营业收入(万元) Business Income (10000 yuan)	利润总额(万元) Total Profits (10000 yuan)	应交税金合计(万元) Total Taxes Payable (10000 yuan)
合计	**Total**	**4435**	**152.3**	**566822177**	**63103568**	**17870079**
按登记注册类型分	**By Registration Type**					
港澳台商投资企业	Hong Kong, Macao and Taiwan-invested Enterprises	1571	68.9	252819602	25320238	5518653
与港澳台商合资	Joint Ventures	378	12.7	13765826	1768428	681584
与港澳台商合作	Cooperatives	49	1.4	1011448	266758	201878
港澳台商独资	Solely-funded Enterprises	1071	46.8	220962771	25062042	3928826
港澳台商投资股份有限公司	Companies Limited by Shares	50	7.0	16233132	-1848340	674221
其他港澳台投资企业	Others	23	1.0	846425	71350	32144
外商投资企业	Foreign-invested Enterprises	2864	83.4	314002576	37783330	12351426
中外合资	Joint Ventures	768	22.7	84479326	8114167	5402438
中外合作	Cooperatives	59	1.0	900762	-30998	65904
外商独资	Solely-funded Enterprises	1924	53.4	219700776	27076156	6543039
外商投资股份有限公司	Companies Limited by Shares	101	6.1	8399577	2620873	280213
其他外商投资企业	Others	12	0.2	522136	3131	59832
按国民经济行业分	**By Sector**					
农、林、牧、渔业	Agriculture, Forestry, Animal Husbandry Fishery					
制造业	Manufacturing	624	23.4	98150508	9294805	5081578
建筑业	Construction	50	3.2	1840040	37443	44734
批发和零售业	Hong Kong, Macao and	862	18.5	275879192	11088723	3883217
住宿和餐饮业	Accommodation and Restaurants	219	15.0	3707384	-228347	129873
交通运输、仓储和邮政业	Transport, Storage and Post	93	11.3	22180845	-1150480	871656
信息传输、软件和信息技术服务业	Information Transmission, Software and Information Technology Services	675	39.8	94591551	27345294	3579579
房地产业	Real Estate	364	9.7	9006158	431572	1054027
租赁和商务服务业	Leasing and Business Services	691	12.3	20412125	7378095	778474
其他行业	Other Sectors	857	19.1	41054375	8906463	2446943
按三次产业分	**By Industry**					
第一产业	Primary Industry					
第二产业	Secondary Industry	697	27.8	106172369	9927074	5277515
第三产业	Tertiary Industry	3738	124.5	460649808	53176493	12592563

注：1.行业划分执行《国民经济行业分类》(GB/T 4754—2017)标准。
2.应交税金合计包括应交增值税、所得税费用和税金及附加。

Note: a) Sectors in this table are classified in accordance with the *Standard for Industrial Classification for National Economic Activities* (GB/T 4754-2017).
b) Total tax payable includes VAT payable, income tax expense, tax and surtax.

10-9 境外投资情况(2003-2022年)
STATISTICS FOR OVERSEAS INVESTMENT (2003-2022)

单位：万美元 (USD 10000)

年 份 Year	对外直接投资额 Amount of Outward Direct Investment	截至各年期末直接投资存量 Diret Investment Stock by the Year End
2003	30054	44844
2004	15739	70086
2005	11306	92940
2006	5612	91873
2007	15295	159195
2008	47299	251019
2009	45185	375865
2010	76614	480882
2011	117503	603380
2012	168900	757800
2013	413010	1276456
2014	727353	2848870
2015	1228033	3879895
2016	1557362	5438141
2017	665126	6484394
2018	647042	6995279
2019	826601	7368891
2020	598518	8527566
2021	704790	9588300
2022	599877	10153818

资料来源：北京市商务局。
Source: Beijing Municipal Commerce Bureau.

10-10 对外经济合作(1984-2022年)
STATISTICS FOR FOREIGN ECONOMIC COOPERATION (1984-2022)

年份 Year	对外承包工程 Foreign Contracted Works				对外劳务合作 Foreign Labor Service Cooperation		
	新签合同数(份) Number of Newly Signed Contracts (unit)	新签合同额(万美元) Newly Signed Contract Value (USD 10000)	完成营业额(万美元) Fulfilled Turnover (USD 10000)	年末在国外人数(人) Workers Staying Abroad by the End of Year (person)	新签劳务人员合同工资总额(万美元) Total Contract Wages of Newly Signed Labor Service Workers (USD 10000)	劳务人员实际收入总额(万美元) Total Actual Income of Labor Service Workers (USD 10000)	年末在国外人数(人) Workers Staying Abroad by the End of Year (person)
1984	2	2768	331	163		200	378
1985	2	736	355	18	100	1700	2383
1986	7	319	90	71	100	1400	766
1987	5	354	186	20	200	500	670
1988	5	344	281	104	500	500	715
1989	7	235	459	83	1500	500	517
1990	16	2253	625	25	1500	500	311
1991	9	1671	1469	306	1500	400	674
1992	16	7762	2543	264	1100	600	688
1993	48	27625	8871	532	1700	900	1023
1994	34	15089	17822	1694	600	1000	1026
1995	35	14014	12156	1297	1600	600	1307
1996	49	62945	38124	1559	4744	4933	957
1997	37	23374	17945	1993	12265	11684	1129
1998	48	19292	24930	2239	6233	6080	1408
1999	28	18715	19690	2199	6517	6477	1277
2000	54	9936	13543	1660	6346	6255	1545
2001	54	14758	11680	2141	6134	6591	1353
2002	42	19376	14453	1112	8779	9527	1022
2003	99	30761	17334	1270	18373	18558	827
2004	109	50788	29134	1583	30049	30389	923
2005	237	56596	35526	2854	37023	35727	1896
2006	143	158918	69227	6760	16424	13456	2202
2007	139	211493	71685	7059	25321	22350	4239
2008	190	520594	130849	6337	37741	36730	5056
2009	182	296851	184997	7057	39372	41876	5316
2010	170	251114	222514	17145	35065	37282	5354
2011	230	261088	248098	12414	1941	3805	5428
2012	344	404037	289909	12143	2434	5746	4616
2013	349	562440	335854	16549	1943	5192	4487
2014	283	429369	357432	21683	8094	7926	7774
2015	209	464840	354900	19287	7180	16012	14896
2016	229	514151	249642	13176	1519	10531	7260
2017	272	905968	402944	11806	2168	16138	12782
2018	230	730314	399820	12383	10400	19380	18744
2019	186	1173673	421872	11043	30274	66088	53899
2020	154	792162	364794	9575	15328	52136	32813
2021	181	476823	368370	8738	16080	51905	34959
2022	299	1011412	532290	8190	23054	50357	27511

注：1984—2008年，对外承包工程统计中含对外设计咨询统计数据。
资料来源：北京市商务局。
Note: In 1984-2008, statistics for foreign contracted works included statistics for consultation on foreign design.
Source: Beijing Municipal Commerce Bureau.

主要统计指标解释

货物进出口总值 指实际进、出我国海关并能引起我国境内物质资源增加或减少的进出口货物总金额。包括我国境内法人和其他组织以一般贸易、易货贸易、加工贸易、补偿贸易、寄售代销贸易等方式进出口的货物、租赁期一年及以上的租赁进出口货物、边境小额贸易货物、国际援助物资或捐赠品、保税区和保税仓库进出口货物等的金额合计。进出口总值用以观察一个国家在对外贸易方面的总规模。我国规定出口货物按离岸价格统计，进口货物按到岸价格统计。

一般贸易 指我国境内有进出口经营权的企业单边进口或单边出口的货物。

来料加工装配贸易 指由外商提供全部或部分原材料、辅料、零部件、元器件、配套件和包装物料，必要时提供设备，由我方按对方的要求进行加工装配，成品交对方销售，我方收取工缴费；或对方提供的作价设备价款，我方用工缴费偿还的交易形式。

进料加工贸易 指我方用外汇购买进口的原料、材料、辅料、元器件、零部件、配套件和包装物料，加工成品或半成品后再外销出口的交易形式。

旅客吞吐量 指经乘航班进出北京民用运输机场的中国公民、港澳台同胞、华侨及外国人等旅客数量的总和。

货邮吞吐量 指通过民用运输机场的航班运输的货物、邮寄物品和随身携带的行李物品重量总和。

飞机起降架次 指进出民用运输机场的正常航班架次，不包括包机和其他非正常航班。

海关征收税款净入库税额 指北京海关征收的税款合计，包含进出口关税和进口环节税。

实际利用外商直接投资额 指批准的合同外资金额的实际执行数，外国投资者根据批准外商投资企业的合同（章程）的规定实际缴付的出资额和企业投资总额内外国投资者以自己的境外自有资金实际直接向企业提供的贷款。

对外承包工程 指企业按照国际通行做法，在国（境）外承揽和实施各类工程项目的经济活动。企业承揽的我国对外经济援助项目、我国驻外使（领）馆等建设项目视同对外承包工程项目。

对外劳务合作 指企业按照与国（境）外政府有关机构、团体、企业、私人雇主所签合同规定，向国（境）外派遣各类劳务人员的经济活动。企业自带设备以提供技术服务的形式在国（境）外承揽的项目视同对外劳务合作项目。

Explanatory Notes on Main Statistical Indicators

Total Value of Imports and Exports refer to the total value of goods actually imported and exported at China's customs, which lead to increase or decrease in the physical resources in China, including goods imported/exported by China domestic legal persons and other organizations in such manners as general trade, barter trade, processing trade, compensation trade, commission-based sales trade, leasing imports/exports with a lease period of one year and more, small-sum border trade goods, international aid goods and donations, imports/exports in bonded zones and bonded warehouses. The indicator of the Total Value of Imports and Exports can be used to observe the total size of foreign trade in a country. In accordance with the stipulation of the Chinese government, imports are calculated at CIF, while exports are calculated at FOB.

General Trade means goods imported and exported unilaterally by domestic enterprises with import/export rights.

Trade of Processing and Assembling Supplied Materials is a form of transaction in which all or part of raw materials, auxiliary materials, parts and components, elements, fittings, and packaging materials, and equipment if necessary are provided by the foreign party, processed or assemble by Chinese party according to requirements of the foreign party, and the finished products are sold by the foreign party. The Chinese party charges processing fees and pays back the money of priced equipment provided by the foreign party with processing charges.

Trade of Processing Imported Materials is a form of transaction in which the Chinese party purchases raw materials, auxiliary materials, parts and components, elements, fittings, and packaging materials with foreign exchange, processing them into finished or semi-finished products and export them.

Passenger Throughput means the total number of Chinese citizens, compatriots form Hong Kong, Macao and Taiwan, oversea Chinese and foreigners that take off and land at civil airports in Beijing by flights.

Cargos Throughput means the sum of goods, mailed articles and luggage transported by flights taking off from and landing at civil airports in Beijing.

Takeoff and Landing of Airplanes means the number of regular flights taking off from and landing at civil airports in Beijing, excluding chartered flights and other non-regular flights.

Net Paid-in Duties Levied and Collected by Customs mean the sum of duties actually levied by customs in Beijing, including import and export duties and import linkage taxs.

Actual Use of Foreign Direct Investment means the value of approved contractual foreign investment actually used, the amount of actual capital contribution by foreign investors according to the contract (articles of incorporation) of the foreign-invested enterprise approved and, in the total investment of an enterprise, the amount of loans provided directly by foreign investor with its own overseas money for the enterprise.

Foreign Contracted Projects refer to economic activities in which enterprises undertake and implement various projects in foreign (overseas) countries in line with international practices. Foreign economic aid projects and construction projects of Chinese Embassies (Consulates) undertaken by enterprises are deemed as foreign contracted projects.

Foreign Labor Service Cooperation means any economic activity in which enterprises dispatch labors to foreign (overseas) countries as stated in contracts signed with foreign (overseas) government agencies, groups, enterprises, and private employers. Projects undertaken by enterprises in foreign (overseas) countries in a manner of providing technical service with their own equipment are deemed as foreign labor service cooperation projects.

农业及农村经济
AGRICULTURE AND RURAL ECONOMY

简 要 说 明

一、主要内容

本章资料反映北京市农业生产和农村经济基本情况，主要包括农村基本情况、农业生产条件、农林牧渔业产值及主要农产品生产情况、农作物播种面积、设施农业、农业观光园、乡村旅游等。

二、统计范围和调查方法

（一）统计范围

农林牧渔业统计范围包括辖区内全部农林牧渔业生产单位、非农行业单位附属的农林牧渔业生产活动单位以及农户的农业生产活动。军委系统的农林牧渔业生产（除军马外）也应包括在内，但不包括农业科学试验机构进行的农业生产。

1．农业：指各种农作物的种植活动。包括谷物、豆类、薯类、棉花、油料、糖料、麻类、烟叶、蔬菜、食用菌及花卉盆景园艺产品、水果、坚果、饲料和香料作物、药材及其它作物的种植。

2．林业：包括林木的栽培(不包括茶园、桑园和果园的栽培、管理和收获等活动)、木材和竹材的采运、林产品的采集。

3．牧业：包括牲畜饲养和放牧、家禽饲养以及野生动物的捕猎和饲养。

4．渔业：分为淡水养殖和海水养殖，包括水生动物和海藻类植物的养殖和捕捞。

农村社会经济统计范围包括所有乡镇辖区内的社会经济活动。

（二）调查方法

农林牧渔业生产统计采取全面调查方法，农业生产统计从行政村和农业生产单位起报。主要粮食播种面积数据通过卫星遥感测量方法取得,粮食产量数据通过抽样调查方法取得。

三、农林牧渔总产值的核算方法

（一）核算方法

根据农业生产特点，农林牧渔业总产值的核算采用“产品法”计算，即用产品产量乘以价格求出各种产品的产值，按产品产值类别分别汇总，计算出农林牧渔各业的产值，各业相加为农林牧渔业总产值。

1．农业：包括谷物和其他作物；蔬菜、食用菌及花卉盆景园艺产品；水果、坚果、饲料、香料；中药材。

2．林业：包括林木的培育和种植；木材、竹材采运；林产品的采集。

3．牧业：包括除渔业养殖以外的一切动物饲养和放牧以及野生动物的捕猎和饲养。

4．渔业：包括水生动物和海藻类植物的养殖和捕捞。

5．农林牧渔专业及辅助性活动：产值等于农林牧渔专业及辅助性活动营业收入。

（二）核算内容的变化情况。自 1958 年起林业产值中增加了村及村以下竹木采伐产值；牧业中取消了厩肥产值；副业中取消了农民自给性手工业产值；渔业中增加了海洋捕捞水产品产值。自 1980 年起农业总产值，在副业中增加了农民家庭兼营工业商品部分的产值。自 1984 年起村及村以下办工业产值划归工业。自 1993 年起，取消副业，将野生动物的捕猎划入牧业，野生植物采集和农民家庭兼营商品性工业划归农业。自 2003 年起按照新的《国民经济行业分类》标准取消了“其他农业”；将农林牧渔服务业产值纳入农林牧渔业总产值中；从农林牧渔业总产值中取消了“家庭兼营商品性工业”；将村以上木材和竹材的采运划入了林业。

（三）核算方法变化情况。自 2003 年起，计算农林牧渔业总产值使用的价格从农产品综合平均价调整为农产品生产价格。2004 年，国家统计局报表制度规定农林牧渔业总产值增加按可比价格计算的产值及发展速度（计算方法：用现价产值的中类数据除以中类缩减指数求得各中类的可比价产值，各中类相加得大类的可比价产值，最后用大类数据相加得农业可比价总产值，可比价产值除以上年现价产值得发展速度）。自 2005 年起，取消了按 1990 年价格计算的农业产值。由于 2006 年农业普查后对农业生产历史数据进行了修订，新修订的农业产值数据只到大类，如果按大类缩减计算农业可比价总产值不符合国家报表制度要求，故 2005 年及以前年度没有按可比价格计算的发展速度。

四、有关统计标准的变化说明

关于行业划分标准。2003 年至 2011 年执行《国民经济行业分类》(GB/T 4754—2002）标准；2012-2017 年执行《国民经济行业分类》(GB/T 4754-2011)标准；自 2018 年起，执行《国民经济行业分类》(GB/T 4754—2017) 标准。

五、关于历史数据调整

根据 2006 年北京市第二次全国农业普查结果，北京市统计局、国家统计局北京调查总队按照国务院农普办要求，依照国际通用做法，对 1997—2005 年的相关指标历史数据进行了修订；根据 2016 年北京市第三次全国农业普查结果，对 2016 年相关指标历史数据进行了修订。

自 2010 年起，根据新的《统计用产品分类目录》，将原林业产值中的核桃、栗子、白果、松子等干果产值调整至农业产值中，为同口径对比，将 2009 年数据也作了相应调整。

Brief Introduction

I. Main Content

Statistics in this chapter show the basic situation of agricultural production and rural economy in Beijing, mainly consisting of basic statistics on rural areas, agricultural production conditions, output of agriculture, forestry, animal production and hunting, fishing, and statistics on production of main agricultural products, sown area, facility agriculture, agricultural sightseeing gardens, and rural tourism, and so on.

II. Scope of Statistics and Method for Survey

(I) Scope of Statistics

Statistics on agriculture, forestry, animal production and hunting, fishing cover the agricultural production activities of all producing entities of agriculture, forestry, animal production and hunting, fishing within the jurisdiction, that of the production activity units of agriculture, forestry, animal production and hunting, fishing affiliated to non-agricultural industry units, and that of the farmers. Production by the military commission system shall also be included (except for army horse breeding), but the agricultural production carried out by agricultural scientific testing agencies is not included.

1. Agriculture: It refers to the growing of various agricultural crops, including grains, beans, tuber crops, cotton, oil-bearing crops, sugar plants, fiber plants, tobacco leaves, vegetables, edible fungus, flower bonsai and gardening products, fruits, nuts, feedstuff, and spice crops, herbs, and other crops.

2. Forestry: It includes tree planting (except for the cultivation, management and harvest of tea gardens, mulberry fields, and orchards), the logging of timber and bamboo, and the collection of forestry products.

3. Animal production and hunting: It includes the breeding and grazing of livestock, poultry agriculture, as well as hunting and breeding of wildlife.

4. Fishing: It falls into two parts: freshwater aquaculture and mariculture, including the cultivation and fishing for aquatic animals and algae.

Statistics for social and economic development in rural areas cover social and economic activities of all villages and towns within the jurisdiction.

(II) Method for Survey

The statistics for production of agriculture, forestry, animal production and hunting, fishing are made with the comprehensive survey method; data on agricultural production are collected from the administrative village and agricultural production unit level. Data on sown area of main grain crops are obtained by means of satellite remote sensing measurements; data on grain output are obtained by sampling survey method.

III. Accounting Method for the Gross Output Value of Agriculture, Forestry, Animal Production and Hunting, Fishing

(I) Accounting Method

Based on agricultural production characteristics, the gross output value of agriculture, forestry, animal production and hunting, fishing was calculated by the "Product Approach", that is to multiply production volume by the unit price, so as to get output value of each product, then sum it up by category, namely agriculture, forestry, animal production and hunting, fishing; and the sum total of these categories will be gross output value of the whole sector.

1. Agriculture: including cereal and other crops; vegetables, edible mushrooms, flower bonsai and gardening products; fruits, nuts, feedstuff, spices, and herbs.

2. Forestry: including the cultivation and planting of forest trees; logging of timber and bamboo; and collection of forestry products.

3. Animal production and hunting: including the breeding and grazing of animals other than fish breeding, as well as hunting and breeding of wildlife.

4. Fishing: including cultivation and catching of aquatic animals and seaweed plants.

5. Professional and supporting activities of agriculture, forestry, animal production and hunting, fishing: the output value equals the operating income of professional and supporting activities of agriculture, forestry, animal production and hunting, fishing.

(II) Changes in Accounting Content. Since 1958, output value of bamboo and timber logging by villages and units subordinated to villages has been included in the statistics of forestry; output value of barnyard manure has been excluded from animal production and hunting statistics; output value of subsistence handicrafts has been excluded from sideline products output value; and the output value of aquatic products by marine fishing has been added to fishing. Since 1980, among the gross output value of agriculture, the output value of industrial commodities operated by rural households has been included in the output value of sideline products. Since 1984, industrial output value produced by villages and units subordinated to villages has been added in the sector of industry. Since 1993, the group "sideline products" was cancelled; the hunting of wild animals has been classified as animal production and hunting, and the gathering of wild plants and commercial industrial businesses run by rural households have been included in agriculture. A new standard for the *Classification of National Economic Sectors* was introduced in 2003. According to the new *Classification*, the group "other agricultural activities" was cancelled; the output value of service activities for agriculture, forestry, animal husbandry and fishing is included in the gross output value of agriculture, forestry, animal production and hunting, fishing; the "commercial industrial businesses run by households" is excluded from the gross output value of agriculture, forestry, animal production and hunting, fishing; output value of wood and bamboo logging of units above village level is included in forestry statistics.

(III) Changes in Accounting Method. Since 2003, the price used for calculating the gross output value of agriculture, forestry, animal production and hunting, fishing has been adjusted from the overall average price of farm products into the producer price for farm products. In 2004, the Reporting System of the National Bureau of Statistics stated to add new statistical items in the gross output value of agriculture, forestry, animal production and hunting, fishing, namely the output value and the growth rate calculated at a comparable price (calculation method: use the output value of groups at present prices to divide the groups' deflator, so as to get the output value at comparable prices; then add up the groups' output value to get the whole subsector's output value at comparable prices; in the end, add up all subsectors' output value to get the gross output value at comparable prices for the agriculture sector and divide the output value at comparable prices by the output value at current prices in the previous year to get the growth rate). Since 2005, the practice of using prices of 1990 as reference numbers to calculate agricultural output value has been cancelled. As the historical data of agricultural production were revised after the Agricultural Census in 2006, revised agricultural production output value figures were presented only by subsectors; and it does not meet the requirements of the national reporting system to calculate the gross agricultural output value at comparable prices by subsectors' deflator. Therefore, there were no figures for growth rate at comparable prices in and prior to 2005.

IV. Changes in Relevant Statistical Standards

Standard for Classification of Sectors. The standards in the *Classification of National Economic Sectors* (GB/T 4754-2002) were implemented from 2003 to 2011. The standards in the *Classification of National Economic Sectors* (GB/T 4754-2011) were implemented from 2012 to 2017. The standards in the *Classification of National Economic Sectors* (GB/T 4754-2017) have been implemented since 2018.

V. Adjustments to Historical Statistics

Based on the results of the Second National Agricultural Census in 2006 in Beijing, Beijing Municipal Bureau of Statistics and Survey Office of the National Bureau of Statistics in Beijing revised the historical data of relevant indicators during 1997-2005 as required by the Agricultural Census Office of the State Council and in accordance with the international practice; and the historical data of relevant indicators for 2016 were revised based on the results of the Third National Agricultural Census in 2016 in Beijing.

Since 2010, the output value of nuts such as walnuts, chestnuts, gingkoes and pine nuts formerly included in forestry has been added in the output value of agriculture according to the new *Catalog on Statistical Product Classification*. In order to conduct same-caliber comparison, data in 2009 annual report have also been adjusted accordingly.

11−1 农村基本情况(1978−2022年)
BASIC STATISTICS FOR RURAL AREAS (1978-2022)

年 份 Year	乡政府 (个) Township Governments (unit)	镇政府 (个) Town Governments (unit)	村 民 委员会 (个) Villagers' Committees (unit)	行 政 村 常住户数 (万户) Number of Permanent Households in Administrative Villages (10000 households)	行 政 村 常住人口 (万人) Permanent Population in Administrative Villages (10000 persons)	行 政 村 从业人员 (万人) Employed Persons in Administrative Villages (10000 persons)
1978				91.9	382.1	165.3
1979				92.9	374.7	165.1
1980				95.0	374.3	167.4
1981				98.9	377.6	172.9
1982				103.2	381.8	179.4
1983				106.6	384.0	184.6
1984				108.9	385.6	188.9
1985	350	15	4394	111.8	387.2	190.0
1986	327	15	4400	113.1	386.9	189.5
1987	324	14	4326	115.7	388.9	189.8
1988	321	13	4111	118.6	389.6	189.2
1989	322	14	4483	121.5	390.0	186.1
1990	252	77	4481	124.5	392.0	184.3
1991	209	77	4480	125.5	390.7	182.1
1992	209	77	4229	126.2	387.6	178.7
1993	192	81	4476	126.5	382.4	176.0
1994	174	92	4464	124.9	376.0	171.6
1995	166	100	4355	125.0	371.5	163.6
1996	166	100	4357	124.6	368.9	164.2
1997	132	108	4348	124.6	365.3	161.2
1998	126	105	4032	125.9	364.4	161.0
1999	125	103	4040	125.9	363.9	165.3
2000	70	142	4039	126.8	363.7	165.8
2001	52	139	4010	127.6	361.6	165.3
2002	51	141	4005	128.0	357.6	165.6
2003	45	142	3985	131.1	360.6	169.6
2004	42	142	3985	132.8	359.9	171.4
2005	43	142	3953	142.2	381.8	184.0
2006	41	142	3957	143.6	501.6	316.9
2007	41	142	3955	176.9	510.0	313.4
2008	40	142	3951	189.8	547.4	321.3
2009	40	142	3950	203.8	572.5	338.7
2010	40	142	3943	216.0	589.4	347.8
2011	38	144	3941	212.4	574.8	338.3
2012	38	144	3940	215.2	582.5	341.7
2013	38	144	3938	221.9	599.5	353.5
2014	38	144	3937	225.2	606.9	357.0
2015	38	144	3936	221.4	593.5	348.0
2016	38	143	3941	232.6	612.6	385.9
2017	38	143	3920	216.7	566.6	352.2
2018	38	143	3915	211.9	558.0	337.5
2019	38	143	3891	211.7	555.7	333.7
2020	35	143	3887	224.6	577.9	344.3
2021	35	143	3784	221.5	569.0	340.3
2022	35	143	3783	217.7	559.6	333.3

资料来源：乡政府、镇政府和村民委员会个数由中共北京市委社会工作委员会北京市民政局提供。

Source: Numbers of township governments, town governments, villagers' committees are provided by Social Work Committee of Beijing Municipal Committee of the Communist Party of China Beijing Municipal Civil Affairs Bureau.

11-2 农业生产条件(1978-2022年)
CONDITIONS FOR AGRICULTURAL PRODUCTION (1978-2022)

年 份 Year	农业机械总动力(万千瓦) Total Power of Agricultural Machinery (10000 kW)	化肥施用量(万吨) Consumption of Chemical Fertilizers (10000 tons)
1978	189.4	11.6
1979	212.2	11.3
1980	234.6	12.3
1981	244.8	11.2
1982	242.2	12.0
1983	261.8	12.0
1984	290.8	10.7
1985	320.4	8.2
1986	345.5	9.1
1987	388.4	10.0
1988	399.7	10.6
1989	423.9	11.8
1990	416.2	14.4
1991	384.8	14.4
1992	399.8	14.4
1993	450.5	14.9
1994	459.2	19.8
1995	468.1	18.8
1996	468.4	18.9
1997	433.2	19.7
1998	415.5	19.3
1999	410.4	19.0
2000	399.2	17.9
2001	394.9	15.7
2002	381.8	14.9
2003	366.9	14.3
2004	340.3	14.5
2005	337.7	14.8
2006	325.5	14.8
2007	300.5	14.0
2008	267.0	13.6
2009	271.5	13.8
2010	276.0	13.7
2011	265.2	13.8
2012	241.1	13.7
2013	207.7	12.8
2014	195.8	11.6
2015	185.9	10.5
2016	144.4	9.7
2017	133.5	8.5
2018	125.6	7.3
2019	122.8	6.2
2020	120.2	6.1
2021	121.2	6.3
2022	116.4	6.6

注：1.化肥施用量为折纯量。
2.农业机械总动力数据由北京市农业农村局提供。

Note: a) Data on consumption of chemical fertilizers were net amount.
b) Figures of total power of agricultural machinery were provided by Beijing Municipal Bureau of Agriculture and Rural Affairs.

11-3 农作物播种面积和造林面积(1978-2022年)
SOWN AND AFFORESTATION AREA (1978-2022)

单位：万公顷 (10000 hectares)

年 份 Year	农作物播种面积 Sown Area	#粮食作物 Grain Crops	#玉米 Corn	#小麦 Wheat	#油料 Oil-bearing Crops	#蔬菜及食用菌 Vegetables and Edible Mushrooms	#瓜类及草莓 Melons & Strawberries	#饲料 Forage	造林面积 Afforestation Area
1978	69.1	56.1	16.9	19.2	3.3	5.6	0.2	2.0	1.4
1979	67.7	56.0	18.2	19.7	3.0	5.4	0.3	2.0	1.6
1980	65.7	54.9	19.7	18.8	2.8	5.1	0.4	1.8	2.4
1981	64.4	53.0	19.8	18.4	2.7	5.5	0.6	1.7	2.7
1982	64.2	52.7	19.7	18.1	2.4	5.9	0.8	1.6	2.8
1983	63.8	53.0	20.1	18.7	1.9	5.7	0.5	1.5	3.3
1984	63.3	52.3	20.6	19.5	1.8	5.8	0.7	1.5	3.2
1985	61.8	51.1	21.7	19.1	2.0	5.4	0.9	1.3	3.0
1986	60.5	49.9	21.6	18.5	2.0	5.8	1.1	1.0	1.5
1987	59.8	49.5	22.3	18.3	1.6	6.0	0.9	1.1	2.0
1988	59.5	48.8	22.2	18.6	1.5	6.3	1.0	1.2	1.6
1989	58.9	48.3	21.9	18.5	1.3	6.8	0.8	1.1	0.8
1990	59.0	48.4	22.4	18.8	1.2	7.0	0.6	1.1	1.3
1991	59.0	48.3	22.3	19.2	1.2	7.3	0.5	1.0	1.5
1992	58.5	47.7	22.4	19.2	1.2	7.5	0.5	0.8	1.5
1993	56.5	45.6	21.8	17.8	1.3	7.8	0.5	0.7	4.8
1994	55.1	43.0	20.6	16.4	1.2	9.1	0.6	0.6	5.5
1995	55.3	43.4	20.8	17.2	1.2	9.1	0.5		4.7
1996	53.8	42.7	20.8	17.1	1.1	8.8	0.5	0.5	4.0
1997	53.6	42.5	20.6	17.1	1.0	8.9	0.5	0.5	3.8
1998	53.5	42.3	20.8	17.1	1.0	9.0	0.5	0.5	3.7
1999	52.6	41.0	19.8	16.8	1.0	9.2	0.5	0.5	3.0
2000	45.4	30.8	13.6	12.2	1.5	10.4	0.8	1.2	2.6
2001	38.0	21.4	10.0	7.3	1.4	11.3	0.9	1.9	3.2
2002	33.5	16.9	8.7	4.7	1.6	11.5	0.9	1.8	4.8
2003	30.1	14.1	7.5	3.6	1.4	10.8	0.9	1.9	4.7
2004	30.4	15.4	9.4	3.9	1.1	9.1	0.8	2.8	3.2
2005	30.8	19.2	12.0	5.3	0.9	7.9	0.8	1.5	1.2
2006	32.0	22.0	13.6	6.3	0.7	7.1	0.9	0.6	1.3
2007	29.5	19.7	13.9	4.1	0.7	7.0	0.9	0.4	1.1
2008	32.2	22.6	14.6	6.4	0.7	6.8	0.8	0.4	0.9
2009	32.0	22.6	15.1	6.1	0.6	6.8	0.8	0.4	1.8
2010	31.7	22.3	15.0	6.2	0.5	6.8	0.8	0.5	1.4
2011	30.3	20.9	14.1	5.8	0.5	6.7	0.8	0.5	2.1
2012	28.3	19.4	13.2	5.2	0.5	6.4	0.8	0.3	3.6
2013	24.2	15.9	11.4	3.6	0.3	6.2	0.7	0.2	4.4
2014	20.0	12.0	8.9	2.4	0.3	5.7	0.6	0.3	2.3
2015	17.7	10.4	7.6	2.1	0.2	5.4	0.5	0.2	0.8
2016	15.0	8.6	6.4	1.6	0.2	4.7	0.4	0.3	1.0
2017	12.6	6.7	5.0	1.1	0.2	4.2	0.4	0.3	0.9
2018	10.6	5.6	4.0	1.0	0.2	3.6	0.4	0.2	2.0
2019	9.2	4.7	3.4	0.8	0.1	3.1	0.3	0.3	2.2
2020	10.2	4.9	3.6	0.8	0.1	3.8	0.3	0.4	1.8
2021	12.2	6.1	4.3	1.3	0.1	4.6	0.3	0.4	1.3
2022	14.7	7.7	5.1	1.8	0.3	5.3	0.3	0.6	1.0

注：1.2016年粮食作物、玉米播种面积为农业普查衔接数据。
2.造林面积2009年以前为人工造林面积，自2009年起调整为人工造林、无林地和疏林地新封面积之和。造林面积数据由北京市园林绿化局提供。

Note: a) The data on sown area of grain crops and corn for 2016 were linked up with the agricultural census.
b) Afforestation area before 2009 was artificial afforestation area, and since 2009 it became the sum of the area of artificial forests, non-forest land and newly enclosed forest land. The data on afforestation area are provided by Beijing Municipal Forestry and Parks Bureau.

11-4 农、林、牧、渔业总产值(1978-2022年)
GROSS OUTPUT VALUE OF AGRICULTURE, FORESTRY, ANIMAL HUSBANDRT AND FISHERY (1978-2022)

年份 Year	农林牧渔业总产值(亿元) Gross Output Value of Agriculture, Forestry,Animal Husbandry and Fishery (100 million yuan)	农业 Agriculture	林业 Forestry	牧业 Animal Husbandry	渔业 Fishery	农林牧渔专业及辅助性活动 Professional and Supporting Activities of Agricultare,Forestry, Animal Husbandry and Fishery	农林牧渔业总产值比上年增长(%) Growth Rate (%) 按当年价格计算 Calculated at Current Price	按可比价格计算 Calculate at Comparable Price
1978	11.5	8.9	0.2	2.4	0.01			
1979	12.3	8.8	0.2	3.3	0.02		7.0	
1980	14.3	9.8	0.5	3.9	0.05		16.3	
1981	14.9	10.1	0.7	4.1	0.05		4.2	
1982	16.8	11.3	0.7	4.7	0.05		12.8	
1983	19.6	12.7	0.8	6.0	0.1		16.7	
1984	22.2	14.4	0.9	6.7	0.2		13.3	
1985	25.9	16.1	0.8	8.6	0.4		16.7	
1986	28.1	17.2	0.8	9.4	0.7		8.5	
1987	34.4	20.3	0.8	12.3	1.0		22.4	
1988	52.6	31.4	0.9	18.6	1.7		52.9	
1989	60.4	34.2	0.7	23.3	2.2		14.8	
1990	70.2	39.0	0.9	28.0	2.3		16.2	
1991	76.5	39.6	1.5	32.8	2.6		9.0	
1992	84.5	43.2	1.6	36.3	3.4		10.5	
1993	100.4	51.1	2.3	42.7	4.3		18.8	
1994	144.3	72.5	3.1	64.0	4.7		43.7	
1995	164.4	86.8	2.7	68.8	6.1		13.9	
1996	168.9	89.2	2.8	71.1	5.8		2.7	
1997	170.5	86.8	2.9	74.6	6.2		0.9	
1998	174.8	88.3	3.2	75.8	7.5		2.5	
1999	180.6	89.4	4.1	79.5	7.6		3.3	
2000	188.6	88.1	5.2	87.5	7.8		4.4	
2001	202.2	84.7	9.0	99.3	9.2		7.2	
2002	213.5	83.5	11.9	108.6	9.5		5.6	
2003	224.7	80.9	12.3	114.3	9.3	7.9	5.2	
2004	234.9	83.1	11.4	124.3	8.9	7.2	4.5	
2005	239.3	91.0	12.4	120.8	8.7	6.4	1.9	
2006	240.2	104.5	14.8	105.1	9.8	6.0	0.4	0.9
2007	272.3	115.5	17.8	122.4	10.1	6.5	13.4	0.8
2008	303.9	128.1	20.5	140.5	9.8	5.0	11.6	0.8
2009	315.0	146.1	17.2	136.1	10.3	5.3	3.6	5.5
2010	328.0	154.2	16.8	139.6	11.5	5.9	4.1	-1.7
2011	363.1	163.4	18.9	162.7	11.5	6.6	10.7	0.9
2012	395.7	166.3	54.8	154.2	13.0	7.5	9.0	2.9
2013	421.8	170.4	75.9	154.8	12.8	8.0	6.6	2.1
2014	420.1	155.1	90.7	152.7	13.2	8.4	-0.4	…
2015	368.2	154.5	57.3	135.9	11.9	8.7	-12.3	-11.7
2016	338.1	145.2	52.2	122.7	9.2	8.7	-8.2	-9.9
2017	308.3	129.8	58.8	101.4	9.6	8.7	-8.8	-6.9
2018	296.8	114.7	95.1	72.0	6.1	8.8	-3.7	-6.0
2019	281.7	102.3	115.6	49.3	5.3	9.1	-5.1	-6.3
2020	263.4	107.6	97.7	45.2	4.1	8.8	-6.5	-6.7
2021	269.5	123.0	88.8	46.3	4.4	7.1	2.3	2.8
2022	268.2	129.8	86.5	42.3	3.9	5.8	-0.5	-2.0

11-5 主要农业产品产量(1978-2022年)
OUTPUT OF MAJOR AGRICULTURAL PRODUCTS (1978-2022)

单位：万吨 (10000 tons)

年 份 Year	粮 食 Grain	油 料 Oil-bearing Crops	蔬菜及食用菌 Vegetables and Edible Mushroom	干鲜果品 Nuts and Fresh Fruits	牛 奶 Milk	肉 类 Meat	#猪牛羊肉 Pork, Beef and Mutton	禽蛋产量 Poultry and Eggs	水产品 Aquatic Products
1978	186.0	2.6	164.5	17.5	5.4	11.9	11.9	2.1	0.2
1979	172.8	2.6	181.3	15.8	6.0	13.1	13.1	3.1	0.3
1980	186.0	3.1	175.9	15.9	6.8	15.1	15.1	3.4	0.4
1981	180.7	2.2	172.8	15.6	7.6	13.2	13.2	3.7	0.4
1982	185.5	2.3	208.3	13.8	8.9	13.9	13.9	5.4	0.4
1983	201.5	2.1	199.1	18.2	10.6	14.9	14.9	8.9	0.6
1984	217.4	2.6	218.0	20.2	12.6	13.4	13.4	12.2	1.0
1985	219.7	3.9	204.0	18.9	13.5	13.6	13.6	14.1	1.6
1986	216.5	3.0	222.7	18.7	14.6	13.3	13.3	14.7	2.2
1987	227.0	3.3	241.1	22.5	15.5	12.9	12.9	16.8	3.0
1988	234.6	3.0	271.3	23.8	18.0	14.5	14.5	21.8	3.9
1989	239.2	2.8	331.0	26.7	19.9	23.3	17.2	24.7	4.6
1990	264.6	3.1	356.1	27.6	21.7	26.8	20.4	25.8	5.1
1991	279.7	3.3	368.4	29.3	23.9	33.9	24.8	27.9	5.6
1992	281.9	3.4	381.4	34.0	24.5	35.9	27.3	30.0	6.4
1993	284.1	3.8	418.8	39.6	22.5	36.7	28.2	31.4	7.0
1994	249.2	3.8	350.0	48.8	22.2	34.4	24.8	31.2	7.6
1995	259.8	3.3	397.3	46.8	20.6	39.8	28.9	28.5	8.1
1996	237.4	2.9	403.2	51.3	21.0	38.2	27.3	24.7	7.8
1997	237.5	2.7	408.8	54.8	22.2	39.9	27.8	23.8	7.7
1998	239.3	2.8	403.8	59.5	22.7	43.4	30.3	17.9	7.6
1999	201.0	2.8	419.8	60.2	24.0	46.1	30.2	15.8	7.6
2000	144.2	3.8	466.3	66.0	30.3	50.5	30.9	16.0	7.5
2001	104.9	4.3	491.0	71.9	42.9	55.9	33.0	15.6	7.4
2002	82.3	4.6	507.4	78.7	55.1	60.9	35.2	15.2	7.4
2003	58.0	3.3	486.7	84.1	63.3	60.6	35.2	16.2	7.1
2004	70.2	2.9	444.1	90.9	70.0	57.4	34.0	15.9	6.7
2005	94.9	2.5	373.1	93.9	64.2	53.3	31.7	16.0	6.4
2006	109.2	2.2	341.2	88.7	61.9	45.3	26.9	15.2	5.4
2007	102.1	2.2	340.1	91.1	62.2	47.9	27.1	15.6	6.0
2008	125.5	2.2	321.3	89.8	66.4	45.1	25.9	15.2	6.1
2009	124.8	1.8	317.1	90.3	67.4	47.2	27.6	15.4	5.8
2010	115.7	1.6	303.0	85.4	64.1	46.3	27.5	15.1	6.3
2011	121.8	1.4	296.9	87.8	64.0	44.4	27.6	15.1	6.1
2012	113.8	1.3	279.9	84.3	65.1	43.2	27.3	15.2	6.4
2013	96.1	1.0	266.9	79.5	61.5	41.8	27.9	17.5	6.4
2014	63.9	0.7	236.2	74.5	59.5	39.3	26.9	19.6	6.8
2015	62.6	0.6	205.1	71.4	57.2	36.4	25.2	19.6	6.6
2016	52.8	0.6	183.6	66.1	45.7	30.4	24.4	18.3	5.4
2017	41.1	0.5	156.8	61.1	37.4	26.4	21.7	15.7	4.5
2018	34.1	0.4	130.6	49.9	31.1	17.5	15.1	11.2	3.0
2019	28.8	0.3	111.5	48.9	26.4	5.1	3.4	9.6	3.0
2020	30.5	0.3	137.9	43.0	24.2	3.5	2.1	9.7	2.3
2021	37.8	0.5	165.6	38.5	25.8	4.4	3.3	9.4	2.3
2022	45.4	0.9	198.9	29.4	26.2	4.3	3.4	8.7	1.7

注：1.1988年及以前肉类产量为猪牛羊肉产量。
2.2006年及以前水产品产量为淡水鱼产量，自2007年起含远洋捕捞量。水产品数据由北京市农业农村局提供。

Note: a) Output of meat in and before 1988 was the output of pork, beef and mutton.
b) Output of aquatic products was output of fresh water fish in and before 2006, and long-range fishing has been included since 2007. Figures of aquatic products were provided by Beijing Municipal Bureau of Agriculture and Rural Affairs.

11-6 农业观光园、乡村旅游、种业和设施农业(2005-2022年)

项目	Item	2005	2006	2007
农业观光园	**Agricultural Sightseeing Gardens**			
农业观光园个数 (个)	Number of Agricultural Sightseeing Gardens (unit)	1012	1230	1302
高峰期从业人员 (人)	Employed Persons in Peak Production Period (person)	40729	52828	51392
接待人次 (万人次)	Visits Received (10000 person-times)	892.5	1210.6	1446.8
经营总收入 (亿元)	Total Operating Income (100 million yuan)	7.9	10.5	13.1
乡村旅游	**Rural Tourism**			
实际经营的乡村旅游接待户和单位 (户、个)	Number of Actual Operating Households in Rural Tourism Reception (household、unit)	7268	8726	10323
高峰期从业人员 (人)	Employed Persons in Peak Production Period of the Term (person)	14070	18253	20750
乡村旅游接待人次 (万人次)	Number of Visits Received by Rural Tourism (10000 person-times)	758.9	982.5	1167.6
乡村旅游总收入 (亿元)	Total Income of Rural Tourism (100 million yuan)	3.1	3.7	5.0
种业	**Seed Industry**			
种业收入 (亿元)	Income (100 million yuan)	5.9	7.7	9.9
#销往外埠收入	Sales to Other Areas			4.0
#牧业收入	Income from Animal Production and Hunting			8.3
设施农业	**Facility Agriculture**			
设施农业实际利用占地面积 (公顷)	Actual Area Utilized by Facility Agriculture (hectare)	15645	17832	18022
设施农业播种面积 (公顷)	Sown Area of Facility Agriculture (hectare)			30331
设施农业产值 (亿元)	Output Value of Facility Agriculture (100 million yuan)	18.6	21.1	28.1

注：2018年及以前乡村旅游为民俗旅游口径；自2019年起，乡村旅游统计范围除包括民俗旅游农户外，还包括乡镇及乡镇以下范围内为乡村旅游服务的宾馆、饭店、旅游商品专卖店等。

AGRICULTURAL SIGHTSEEING GARDENS, RURAL TOURISM, BREEDING OF SEEDS AND FACILITY AGRICULTURE(2005-2022)

2008	2009	2010	2011	2012	2013	2014	2015	2016	2017	2018	2019	2020	2021	2022
1332	1294	1303	1300	1283	1299	1301	1328	1258	1216	1172	948	925	1009	1027
49366	49504	42561	46038	48906	50406	47088	42617	40349	39624	39726	33815	28706	29451	29441
1498.2	1597.4	1774.9	1842.9	1939.9	1944.4	1911.2	1903.3	2250.5	2105.3	1897.6	1538.0	867.2	1154.5	707.0
13.6	15.2	17.8	21.7	26.9	27.4	24.9	26.3	28.0	29.9	27.3	23.2	15.5	18.4	18.4
9151	8705	7979	8396	8367	8530	8863	8941	9026	8363	7783	7354	5832	6793	7105
19421	19790	16856	18232	18705	19578	21493	22313	22215	22455	21203	23720	19626	21607	21463
1205.6	1393.1	1553.6	1668.9	1695.8	1806.5	1914.2	2139.7	2297.4	2232.1	2042.3	1920.1	1010.3	1365.7	1080.9
5.3	6.1	7.3	8.7	9.1	10.2	11.3	12.9	14.4	14.2	13.0	14.4	9.5	14.1	13.7
10.9	12.8	14.6	18.1	16.1	14.0	14.0	12.7	14.0	12.7	12.4	15.1	12.1	11.9	8.9
5.8	7.3	8.1	11.7	9.7	8.2	8.0	6.6	7.7	6.7	7.4	10.6	8.5	8.4	5.5
9.3	10.6	12.1	15.1	13.6	12.6	12.5	11.2	12.9	11.1	10.8	13.3	10.7	10.1	7.1
17051	18762	18323	18616	19059	18852	18232	17397	15404	14941	13880	12900	13252	13026	13370
33889	36203	36811	38006	37797	38763	38115	41088	37666	35740	32324	27068	29010	31172	32496
28.2	33.9	40.7	45.6	52.0	57.3	51.3	55.5	54.4	54.5	51.7	47.1	50.1	57.9	59.8

Note: In and before 2018, rural tourism was uniformly called folk-custom tourism; since 2019, the scope of statistics of rural tourism covered not only the peasant households engaging in folk-custom tourism, but also the hotels, restaurants and tourists commodities stores, etc. at or below township level that served the rural tourism.

11-7 农业生产条件
PRODUCTIVE CONDITIONS OF AGRICULTURE

项目		Item		2022	2021
主要农业机械拥有量		**Possession of Major Agricultural Machinery**			
农业机械总动力	(万千瓦)	Total Power of Agricultural Machinery	(10000 kW)	116.4	121.2
大中型拖拉机	(混合台)	Large and Medium-sized Tractors	(unit)	4069	4163
小型拖拉机	(台)	Mini Tractors	(unit)	1816	1855
机引农具	(台)	Tractor-propelled Farm Tools	(unit)	13039	12580
机动喷雾器	(部)	Motorized Sprayers	(unit)	11597	11478
联合收割机	(台)	Combine Harvesters	(unit)	679	734
机动脱粒机	(台)	Motorized Shellers	(unit)	3545	3628
米面加工机	(台)	Processing Machines of Rice and Flour	(unit)	3154	3187
机动挤奶器	(台)	Motorized Milkers	(unit)	755	1378
饲料粉碎机	(台)	Fodder Grinders	(unit)	1925	1969
农业机械作业面积		**Operation Area of Agricultural Machinery**			
机耕面积	(公顷)	Cultivated Area by Machinery	(hectare)	90404	71470
占应机耕面积比重	(%)	Share in the Area Supposed to be Cultivated by Machinery	(%)	97.2	95.3
机播面积	(公顷)	Sown Area by Machinery	(hectare)	95943	59488
占播种面积比重	(%)	Share in the Total Sown Area	(%)	71.2	54.3
机收面积	(公顷)	Harvest Area by Machinery	(hectare)	71069	52114
占收获面积比重	(%)	Share in the Total Harvest Area	(%)	52.8	47.6
农田水利		**Irrigation and Water Conservancy**			
排灌用动力机械	(台)	Power Machinery for Drainage and Irrigation	(unit)	30456	30789
排灌用动力机械动力	(万千瓦)	Power of the Power Machinery for Drainage and Irrigation	(10000 kW)	37.5	37.8
机(电)井	(眼)	Motor-pumped (Electric) Wells	(unit)	38024	34972
化肥施用量(折纯)		**Consumption of Chemical Fertilizers (converted into net amount)**			
化肥施用量	(吨)	Consumption of Chemical Fertilizers	(ton)	66087.5	62971.5
#氮　肥	(吨)	Nitrogenous Fertilizers	(ton)	20413.0	20894.5
磷　肥	(吨)	Phosphate Fertilizers	(ton)	3271.9	3146.4
钾　肥	(吨)	Potash Fertilizers	(ton)	3274.8	3337.9

注：1.农业机械作业面积统计口径2020年为八大作物，2021年调整为全部粮、菜和设施农业。
2.主要农业机械拥有量、农业机械作业面积及排灌动力机械数据由北京市农业农村局提供。
3.机(电)井数据由北京市水务局提供。

Note: a) The statistical scope of operation area of agricultural machinery covered the eight major crops in 2020 and was adjusted to cover all grain, vegetables and facility agriculture in 2021.
b) Figures of possession of major agricultural machinery, operation area of agricultural machinery, and power machinery for drainage and irrigationare provided by Beijing Municipal Bureau of Agriculture and Rural Affairs.
c) Figures of motor-pumped (electric) wells are provided by Beijing Water Authority.

11-8 农、林、牧、渔业总产值
GROSS OUTPUT VALUE OF AGRICULTURE, FORESTRY, ANIMAL HUSBANDRY AND FISHERY

单位：万元 (10000 yuan)

项　目	Item	总产值 Gross Output Value		2022年为2021年% 2022 as % of 2021
		2022	2021	
合　计	**Total**	**2681755.8**	**2695138.5**	**99.5**
农　业	**Agriculture**	**1297652.4**	**1229825.9**	**105.5**
#谷　物	Cereal	121423.8	96392.4	126.0
豆　类	Beans	6357.7	2709.6	234.6
经济作物	Cash Crops	7032.8	4264.8	164.9
蔬菜、食用菌	Vegetables and Edible Mushromms	723650.3	652110.2	111.0
水果（含瓜果类）	Fruits (including melons)	344062.1	372279.7	92.4
林　业	**Forestry**	**865169.3**	**888021.3**	**97.4**
牧　业	**Animal Husbandry**	**422891.8**	**462669.3**	**91.4**
牲畜饲养	Animal Breeding	182685.2	181796.4	100.5
养　猪	Hogs	71327.8	88111.5	81.0
家禽饲养	Poultry	165116.0	188864.7	87.4
#禽　蛋	Poultry Eggs	122583.4	123660.8	99.1
其　他	Others	3762.8	3896.7	96.6
渔　业	**Fishery**	**38531.3**	**43740.1**	**88.1**
农林牧渔专业及辅助性活动	**Professional and Supporting Activities of Agricultare, Forestry,Animal Husbandry and Fishery**	**57511.0**	**70881.9**	**81.1**

11-9 主要农作物播种面积及产量
SOWN AREA AND OUTPUT OF MAJOR CROPS

项　　目	Item	2022			2021		
		播种面积 (公顷) Sown Areas (hectare)	单　产 (公斤／公顷) Output Per Unit (kg/hectare)	总产量 (吨) Total Output (ton)	播种面积 (公顷) Sown Areas (hectare)	单　产 (公斤／公顷) Output Per Unit (kg/hectare)	总产量 (吨) Total Output (ton)
粮　食	**Grain**	**76734.4**	**5910.9**	**453565.9**	**60922.6**	**6196.8**	**377527.9**
按季节分	By Season						
夏　粮	Summer Grain	18222.6	5251.9	95702.7	13099.9	5235.3	68581.6
秋　粮	Autumn Grain	58511.7	6116.1	357863.1	47822.8	6460.2	308946.3
按品种分	By Variety						
#稻　谷	Rice	416.6	5062.1	2108.9	308.6	5659.7	1746.4
冬小麦	Winter Wheat	17631.5	5292.6	93316.4	13003.6	5245.7	68212.5
玉　米	Corn	51149.4	6556.6	335368.5	42772.8	6789.3	290397.4
薯　类	Tubers	1251.2	5348.5	6691.9	1626.9	5566.6	9056.1
大　豆	Soybeans	3774.7	2289.7	8642.8	1404.2	2441.3	3428.0
棉　花	**Cotton**	**4.4**	**1120.4**	**4.9**	**5.6**	**1095.8**	**6.1**
油　料	**Oil-bearing Crops**	**3179.7**	**2795.1**	**8887.8**	**1470.7**	**3562.0**	**5238.7**
#花　生	Peanuts	2762.6	3020.0	8343.1	1252.7	3792.3	4750.5
中草药材	**Chinese Medicine Herbs**	**1537.7**	**502.0**	**771.9**	**1672.2**	**462.0**	**772.5**
蔬菜及食用菌	**Vegetables and Edible Mushrooms**	**53166.0**	**37404.4**	**1988641.1**	**46450.2**	**35651.5**	**1656020.3**
瓜类及草莓	**Melons & Strawberries**	**3001.8**	**38591.2**	**115842.4**	**3261.5**	**41144.2**	**134192.9**
#西　瓜	Watermelons	2086.5	45076.8	94051.5	2313.1	48314.4	111756.0
饲　料	**Forage**	**5507.3**	**38420.6**	**211591.8**	**4369.4**	**38125.6**	**166586.4**
#牧　草	Forage Grass	14.8	31385.1	464.5	22.3	24000.0	536.0
花　卉	**Flowers**	**1724.9**			**1998.8**		

11-10 林业及干鲜果品生产
FORESTRY, NUTS AND FRESH FRUIT PRODUCTION

项目	Item	2022	2021	2022年为2021年% 2022 as % of 2021
林业生产	**Forestry**			
营造林面积 (公顷)	Sulviculture and Afforestation Area (hectare)	100600	114879	87.6
#人工造林面积	Artificial Afforestation Area	10120	10674	94.8
育苗面积 (公顷)	Seedling Growing Area (hectare)	10542	13233	79.7
果类生产	**Fruits**			
干鲜果总产量 (吨)	Output of Nuts and Fresh Fruit (ton)	293514	384592	76.3
干　果	Nuts	26021	30337	85.8
#核　桃	Walnuts	6284	7574	83.0
板　栗	Chinese Chestnuts	18475	21513	85.9
鲜　果	Fresh Fruits	267493	354254	75.5
#苹　果	Apples	28832	34372	83.9
梨	Pears	43290	55291	78.3
葡　萄	Grapes	10111	14545	69.5
柿　子	Persimmons	4854	5166	93.9
桃	Peaches	149443	209114	71.5
年末实有果园面积 (公顷)	**Actual Orchard Area (year-end) (hectare)**	**32588**	**39552**	**82.4**

注：本表中营造林面积为人工造林、飞播造林、封山育林、退化林修复、人工更新、森林抚育面积之和。
资料来源：林业生产数据由北京市园林绿化局提供。
Note: The Silviculture and Afforestation Area in this table refers to the sum of the area of the artificial afforestation, air seeding and afforestation, closing hillsides for afforestation, restoration of degraded forest, artificial regeneration and forest tending.
Source: Figures of forestry are from Beijing Municipal Bureau of Landscape and Forestry.

11－11 牲畜饲养及畜产品产量
LIVESTOCK BREEDING AND OUTPUT

项　目		Item		2022	2021	2022年为2021年% 2022 as % of 2021
畜禽存栏		**Amount of Livestock and Poultry on Hand**				
大牲畜	(万头)	Large Animals	(10000 heads)	8.4	8.6	98.4
#牛		Cattle and Buffaloes		8.2	8.3	99.3
猪	(万头)	Hogs	(10000 heads)	36.8	59.0	62.3
羊	(万只)	Sheep	(10000 units)	19.5	18.0	108.1
山　羊		Goats		6.1	5.7	107.6
绵　羊		Sheep		13.3	12.3	108.3
家　禽	(万只)	Poultry	(10000 units)	774.0	847.5	91.3
#产蛋鸡		Hens		765.8	836.5	91.5
肉　鸡		Chickens		1.8	1.5	126.6
鸭		Ducks		5.7	8.8	64.9
兔	(万只)	Rabbits	(10000 units)	0.2	0.1	111.2
畜禽出栏		**Amount of Livestock and Poultry Marketed**				
牛	(万头)	Cattle	(10000 heads)	2.3	2.4	97.2
猪	(万头)	Hogs	(10000 heads)	32.2	30.9	104.3
羊	(万只)	Sheep	(10000 units)	10.9	11.4	96.0
畜禽产品产量		**Output of Livestock and Poultry Products**				
肉类产量	(万吨)	Output of Meat	(10000 tons)	4.3	4.4	97.9
#猪　肉		Pork		2.8	2.6	105.8
牛　肉		Beef		0.4	0.4	100.7
羊　肉		Mutton		0.2	0.2	95.7
牛奶产量	(万吨)	Output of Milk	(10000 tons)	26.2	25.8	101.4
禽　蛋	(万吨)	Poultry Eggs	(10000 tons)	8.7	9.4	93.4
#鸡　蛋		Eggs		8.7	9.2	94.2
蜂　蜜	(吨)	Honey	(ton)	882.1	1043.0	84.6

11-12 水产品生产
AQUATIC PRODUCTS

项　　目	Item	2022	2021
渔业水域面积　（公顷）	**Area of Fishery Waters　(hectare)**	**24832**	**33497**
#淡水养殖面积	Freshwater Aquaculture Area	1387	1891
#池　塘	Puddles and Ponds	1381	1890
水产品产量　（吨）	**Output of Aquatic Products　(ton)**	**17492**	**22779**
#淡水鱼产量	Output of Freshwater Fish	13240	15307
#大水库	Large Reservoirs	2801	2652
池　塘	Puddles and Ponds	10439	12655

资料来源：北京市农业农村局。
Source: Beijing Municipal Bureau of Agriculture and Rural Affairs.

11-13 种业生产
STATISTICS FOR PRODUCTION OF SEED INDUSTRY

项　　目	Item	产　量 Output			收　入(万元) Income (10000 yuan)		
		2022	2021	2022年为2021年% 2022 as % of 2021	2022	2021	2022年为2021年% 2022 as % of 2021
合　计	**Total**				**89448.2**	**119057.2**	**75.1**
农　业	**Agriculture**				**13080.5**	**13095.4**	**99.9**
#小麦种　（公斤）	Wheat Seeds　(kg)	500000	550000	90.9	140.0	134.2	104.3
玉米种　（公斤）	Corn Seeds　(kg)	68000	62775	108.3	54.9	45.1	121.7
蔬菜种　（公斤）	Vegetable Seeds　(kg)	9337	47991	19.5	688.0	2505.1	27.5
林　业	**Forestry**				**3598.3**	**2098.4**	**171.5**
#树　苗　（百株）	Saplings　(100 units)	2028.1	5140.6	39.5	3598.3	2098.4	171.5
牧　业	**Animal Husbandry**				**71225.2**	**100826.8**	**70.6**
#种　猪　（头）	Breeding Pig　(head)	34123	30255	112.8	8931.7	14716.1	60.7
种雏禽　（万只）	Brood Bird　(10000 units)	1433.2	1829.2	78.3	25709	40775.7	63.0
种　蛋　（万枚）	Breeding Eggs　(10000 units)	19203.7	23431.5	82.0	22424.4	29252.7	76.7
渔　业	**Fishery**				**1544.2**	**3036.6**	**50.9**
#种鱼苗　（万尾）	Breeding Fish Fry　(10000 units)	6431.8	10114.2	63.6	1544.2	3036.6	50.9

11-14 设施农业(2022年)
FACILITY AGRICULTURE (2022)

项　目	Item	设施农业播种面积(公顷) Sown Area of Facility Agriculture (hectare)	设施农业产量(吨) Output of Facility Agriculture (ton)	设施农业产值(万元) Output Value of Facility Agriculture (10000 yuan)
合　计	**Total**	**32496.0**		**598172.5**
温　室	**Greenhousse**	**14657.0**		**386596.8**
蔬菜及食用菌	Vegetables and Edible Mushrooms	12929.2	554653.2	267733.7
花卉苗木	Flowers and Saplings	507.7		18607.8
#切　花	Cut Flowers	31.2	30394.1	1251.0
盆　花	Potted Flowers	471.5	537047.0	17212.3
瓜果类	Melons	934.3	23250.4	90517.1
园林水果	Fruits	243.3	1209.5	5480.7
其　他	Others	42.5		4257.5
大　棚	**Greenhouse Garden**	**16485.0**		**196173.3**
蔬菜及食用菌	Vegetables and Edible Mushrooms	14493.8	501720.7	149950.9
花卉苗木	Flowers and Sapling	199.0		4565.0
#切　花	Cut Flowers	58.4	144420.0	1405.4
盆　花	Potted Flowers	140.6	170245.6	3159.6
瓜果类	Melons	1600.0	74324.9	37814.5
园林水果	Fruits	135.7	712.8	1661.3
其　他	Other	56.5		2181.6
中小棚	**Medium and Small Shed**	**1354.0**		**15402.5**
蔬菜及食用菌	Vegetables and Edible Mushrooms	1141.2	30759.5	11305.5
花卉苗木	Flowers and Sapling	22.7		525.9
#切　花	Cut Flowers	1.2	1350.0	18.1
盆　花	Potted Flowers	21.5	12862.3	507.8
瓜果类	Melons	189.4	7850.8	3567.0
园林水果	Fruits	0.8	2.0	4.0
其　他	Other			

注：切花产量的计量单位是百枝，盆花产量的计量单位是百盆。
Note: Cut flowers output are measured in 100 ones; and potted flowers output are measured in 100 pots.

11-15 农村双层经营主要指标情况(2022年) MAIN INDICATORS OF RURAL DOUBLE-LAYER MANAGEMENT SYSTEM (2022)

项目		Item		2022
集体经济组织情况		**Organizations of Collective Economy**		
乡镇级集体经济组织数	(个)	Number of Township-level Collective Economic Organizations	(unit)	188
村级集体经济组织数	(个)	Number of Village-level Collective Economic Organizations	(unit)	4000
汇总农户数	(户)	Total Number of Peasant Households	(household)	1337306
汇总人口数	(人)	Total Number of Population	(person)	3148568
劳动力总人数	(人)	Total Number of Labor Force	(person)	1833374
就业率	(%)	Employment Rate	(%)	93.1
集体经济经营情况		**Operation of Collective Economy**		
集体经济总收入	(亿元)	Gross Income of Collective Economy	(100 million yuan)	654.1
#主营业务收入		Main Business Income		394.4
利润总额	(亿元)	Total Profit	(100 million yuan)	-0.9
净利润	(亿元)	Net Profit	(100 million yuan)	-8.5
可供分配的利润	(亿元)	Profit Available for Distribution	(100 million yuan)	-153.8
未分配利润	(亿元)	Undistributed Profit	(100 million yuan)	-189.1
资产总计	(亿元)	Total Assets	(100 million yuan)	9342.9
乡镇级		Township Level		3287.4
村　级		Village Level		6055.5
所有者权益合计	(亿元)	Total Owner's Equity	(100 million yuan)	3207.3
乡镇级		Township Level		616.8
村　级		Village Level		2590.5
人均所有者权益	(元)	Per-capita Owner's Equity	(yuan)	101864
农户收入情况		**Income of Peasant Households**		
农户总收入	(亿元)	Total Income	(100 million yuan)	1458.5
农户所得总额	(亿元)	Total Earnings	(100 million yuan)	949.8
人均所得	(元)	Per-capita Earnings	(yuan)	30166
农户从集体经济获取的所得总额	(亿元)	Total Earnings of Peasant Household from Collective Economy	(100 million yuan)	219.6

注：双层经营指农民家庭分散经营和集体统一经营相结合。

资料来源：北京市农业农村局。

Note: Double-layer management system refers to a system with integration of decentralized management of peasant households and collective unified management.

Source: Beijing Municipal Bureau of Agriculture and Rural Affairs.

主要统计指标解释

农林牧渔业总产值　是以货币表现的农林牧渔业的全部产品总量和对农林牧渔业生产活动进行的各种支持性服务活动的价值。

农作物播种面积　指本年度内收获农作物在全部土地（耕地或非耕地）上的播种或移植面积。凡是本年内收获的农作物，无论是本年还是上年播种，都算为播种面积，但不包括本年播种、下年收获的农作物面积。在播种季节基本结束后，因遭灾而重新改种和补种的农作物面积，也包括在内。

设施农业　指以工厂化生产方式，建造人工设施，改变气候条件，提高农作物抵御自然灾害的能力，改良生物特性，使作物实现错季或反季节生产，达到农作物均衡生产的目的。

农业机械总动力　指主要用于农、林、牧、渔业的各种动力机械的动力总和。包括耕作机械、排灌机械、收获机械、农用运输机械、植物保护机械、牧业机械、渔业机械和其他农用机械[内燃机按引擎马力折成瓦（特）计算，电动机按功率折成瓦（特）计算]。不包括专门用于乡、镇、村、组办工业、基本建设、非农业运输、科学实验和教学等非农业生产方面用的动力机械与作业机械。

农用化肥施用量　指本年度内实际用于农业生产的化学肥料数量，包括氮肥、磷肥、钾肥和复合肥。施用量要求按折纯量计算数量，即各类化学肥料的实际施用数量按其含氮、含五氧化二磷、含氧化钾的比例折成百分之百计算。

折纯量＝实物量×某种化肥有效成份含量的百分比

行政村常住户数　指长期（一年以上）居住在行政村管理区域内的住户，户口不在本地而在本地居住一年及以上的住户也包括在本地农村住户内；有本地户口，但举家外出谋生一年以上的住户，无论是否保留承包耕地都不包括在本地农村住户范围内。不包括乡村地区内的国有经济的机关、团体、学校、企业、事业单位的集体户。

行政村常住人口　指行政村常住居民户数中的常住人口数，即经常在家或在家居住6个月以上，而且经济和生活与本户连成一体的人口。外出从业人员在外居住时间虽然在6个月以上，但收入主要带回家中，经济与本户连为一体，仍视为家庭常住人口；在家居住，生活和本户连成一体的国家职工、退休人员也为家庭常住人口。但是现役军人、中专及以上（走读生除外）的在校学生、以及常年在外（不包括探亲、看病等）且已有稳定的职业与居住场所的外出从业人员，不应当作家庭常住人口。

行政村从业人员　指全部行政村人口中16岁以上实际参加生产经营活动并取得实物或货币收入的人员，既包括劳动年龄内经常参加劳动的人员，也包括超过劳动年龄但经常参加劳动的人员。但不包括户口在家的在外学生、现役军人和丧失劳动能力的人，也不包括待业人员和家务劳动者。从业人员按从事主业时间最长（时间相同按收入）分为农业从业人员，工业从业人员，建筑业从业人员，交通运输仓储及邮政业从业人员，信息传输、计算机服务和软件业，批发与零售业从业人员，住宿和餐饮业从业人员，其他从业人员。

Explanatory Notes on Main Statistical Indicators

Gross Output Value of Agriculture, Forestry, Animal Production and Hunting, Fishing refers to the monetary value of all products of agriculture, forestry, animal production and hunting, fishing, as well as the monetary value of services provided in support of all the above-mentioned sectors.

Sown Area refers to the area of all lands actually sown or transplanted with crops, including both the cultivated and non-cultivated land. Area of lands re-planted after seedtime has passed due to natural disasters is also included.

Facility Agriculture means to produce in an industrialized manner, put in place facilities of manual intervention, change climate conditions, increase the crops' capability to resist natural disasters, and improve the crops' biological property, so as to stagger harvest seasons, create anti-season production, and achieve balanced production of crops.

Total Power of Agricultural Machinery refers to the total power of motive power machines used in agriculture, forestry, animal production and hunting, fishing sectors, including machinery for ploughing, irrigation and drainage, harvesting, agricultural transport, plant protection, animal production and hunting, fishing and other farm machinery (The horsepower of internal combustion engines is converted into watts, and the output of electric motors is also converted into watts). Motive power machines and operating machines exclusively used for non-agricultural production activities, such as industrial operations run by counties, towns, villages and teams, capital construction, non-agricultural transport, scientific experiments and teaching, are not included.

Rural Electricity Consumption refers to the total rural production and rural residents' electricity consumption in the whole year (unit of measurement: kilowatt-hour; the data representing accumulative usage of the year), deducting the consumption by entities like state-owned industry, transport, and infrastructure construction. The data cover both power supplies by the State Grid and by the rural self-run power stations.

Consumption of Chemical Fertilizers refers to the total quantity of chemical fertilizers applied in agricultural production within the year, including nitrogenous fertilizer, phosphate fertilizer, potash fertilizer, and compound fertilizer. The amount of chemical fertilizers applied is calculated in terms of net amount, that is, to use the gross weight of the respective fertilizers in calculating the quantity of effective ingredients (e.g. nitrogen content in nitrogenous fertilizer, phosphorous pent oxide content in phosphate fertilizer, and potassium oxide content in potash fertilizer).

Net Amount = Physical Quantity× Content (%) of Effective Ingredients in Certain Chemical Fertilizer

Number of Resident Households in Towns and Administrative Villages refers to households living in the administrative areas of towns and villages (excluding township government premises) on a long-term basis (more than one year), including those living in administrative villages within township government premises. Households with non-local household registration but having been living locally for more than one year are also counted as local rural households; while households with local household registration but left to make a living elsewhere for more than one year, with or without contract lands, are not counted as local rural households. Collective households of state-owned government agencies, organizations, schools, enterprises, and public institutions of the state-owned economy in rural areas are not included.

Permanent Population in Towns and Administrative Villages refers to the population of permanent households in rural areas, namely those who stay home regularly or live at home for more than 6 months with their economic life and livelihood incorporated into the household. Migrant workers who live away from home for more than 6 months but taking most of their earnings back home, with their economic life still incorporated into the household, are also counted as permanent population of the household; state employees and retirees who live locally with their life incorporated into the household are also considered permanent population. But soldiers in active service, enrolled students (externs excluded) in technical secondary schools or above, as well as migrant workers who lived away from home for years (excluding those who travel to visit their families or to seek medical care) with a stable job and residence elsewhere, are not regarded as permanent population.

Employed Persons in Towns and Administrative Villages refer to persons aged above 16 in all towns and administrative villages, who actually participate in productive and operating activities and earn incomes in kind or cash, including persons within the range of labor age and regularly participating in labor, and persons beyond the range of labor age but regularly participating in labor; while local registered students who left home for education, soldiers in active service, and people who lost the ability to work are not included, neither are the people waiting for employment or domestic workers. In terms of the length of employment period (or in terms of income if the employment periods are identical), employment falls into the following categories: agriculture, industry, construction, transportation, storage and post, information transmission, computer services and software industry, wholesale and retail trade, accommodation and restaurants, and other sectors.

工 业
INDUSTRY

简 要 说 明

一、主要内容

本章资料反映北京市工业基本情况，主要包括按登记注册类型、轻重工业、企业规模、行业大类等分组的主要经济指标数据。

具体指标包括单位数、工业总产值、资产总计、负债合计、营业收入、营业成本、税金及附加、利润总额、应交增值税、总资产贡献率、资产负债率、主要工业产品产量等。

二、统计范围

1984年以前农村的村及村以下办工业归属农业，自1984年起划归工业。

1999年及以前，工业的统计范围按隶属关系划分为乡及乡以上独立核算工业企业和非独立核算生产单位、村办工业、城镇合作工业、农村合作工业、城镇个体工业、农村个体工业六大部分（1984年以前村办工业不在工业统计范围内）。

自2000年起，工业统计调查范围由按隶属关系划分，改变为按企业规模划分。其中，2000-2006年规模以上工业统计范围为全部国有及年主营业务收入在500万元及以上非国有工业企业；2007-2010年为年主营业务收入在500万元及以上法人工业企业；自2011年起为年主营业务收入在2000万元及以上法人工业企业。

三、有关统计标准的变化说明

（一）关于行业划分。2002年及以前，工业行业分类执行《国民经济行业分类及代码》(GB/T 4754- 94)标准，2003-2011年执行《国民经济行业分类标准》(GB/T 4754- 2002)标准，2012-2017年执行《国民经济行业分类》(GB/T 4754-2011)标准，自2018年起执行《国民经济行业分类》(GB/T 4754-2017)标准。

与2002版相比，2011版《国民经济行业分类》标准中，将原“交通运输设备制造业”调整为“汽车制造业”，将原“通信设备、计算机及其他电子设备制造业”调整为“计算机、通信和其他电子设备制造业”，将原“石油加工业”与“炼焦、煤气及煤制品业”合并为“石油加工、炼焦和核燃料加工业”。

（二）关于企业标准划分。2010年以前企业大中小型划分执行2003年《统计上大中小型企业划分办法（暂行）》。2011年至2017年大中小微型企业划分标准执行国家统计局《关于统计上大中小微型企业划分办法》（国统字〔2011〕75号）；自2018年起，执行《统计上大中小微型企业划分办法（2017）》（国统字〔2017〕213号）。

四、关于历史数据调整

1993-2003年规模以上工业总产值历史资料根据北京市第一次全国经济普查的结果采用“趋势离差法”进行了修订，2004年为第一次全国经济普查数据，2008年为第二次全国经济普查数据，2013年为第三次全国经济普查数据，2018年为第四次全国经济普查数据。

Brief Introduction

I. Main Content

Data in this chapter show the basic situation of industry in Beijing, mainly including major economic indicators grouped by type of registration, light or heavy industry, enterprise scale, and industries.

Specific indicators include unit number, gross industrial output value, total assets, total liabilities, business income, business cost, business tax and surtax, total profits, payable VAT, contribution rate to total assets, asset-liability ratio, and output of main industrial products, etc.

II. Scope of Statistics

Prior to 1984, the rural industrial production run by villages and units subordinated to villages was classified as agriculture. Since 1984, it has been grouped into industry.

Before 1999, industrial statistics coverage was divided into six parts by administrative relationship, i.e. independent accounting industrial enterprises and non-independent accounting production units at the township-level and above, village-run industry, urban cooperative industry, rural cooperative industry, urban individual operated industry, and rural individual operated industry (village-run industry was not included in the industrial statistics before 1984).

Since 2000, the scope of industrial statistics was grouped by enterprise scale instead of administrative relationship. Specifically, from 2000 to 2006, the scope of statistics of industry above designated size covers all state-owned enterprises and non-state-owned industrial enterprises with annual main business income of RMB 5 million and above; from 2007 to 2010, the scope of statistics covers the corporate industrial enterprises with annual main business income of RMB 5 million and above; since 2011, the scope of statistics covers the corporate industrial enterprises with annual main business income of RMB 20 million and above.

III. Changes in Relevant Statistical Standards

(I) Classification of Sectors: The standards in the *Classification and Codes of National Economic Sectors* (GB/T 4754-94) were implemented in the classification of industrial sectors before 2002. The standards in the *Standard for Classification of National Economic Sectors* (GB/T 4754-2002) were implemented from 2003 to 2011. The standards in the *Classification of National Economic Sectors* (GB/T 4754-2011) were implemented from 2012 to 2017. The standards in the *Classification of National Economic Sectors* (GB/T 4754-2017) are implemented since 2018.

Contrary to the 2002 version, in the standards in the *Classification of National Economic Sectors* (2011), the original "manufacture of transport equipment" was adjusted to "manufacture of motor vehicles, the original "manufacture of communication equipment, computer and electronic equipment" was adjusted to "manufacture of computer, communication equipment and other electronic equipment, and the original "petroleum processing and coking, gas and coal products" were combined into "processing of petroleum ,coking, processing of nucleus fuel" .

(II) Before 2010, the classification of small, medium and large-sized enterprises should comply with the standards in the *Measures for Statistical Classification of Small, Medium and Large-sized Enterprises (Temporary)* (2003). The classification of micro, small, medium and large-sized enterprises should comply with the standards in the *Measures for Statistical Classification of Micro, Small, Medium and Large-sized Enterprises* (G.T.Z. [2011] No. 75) of the National Bureau of Statistics from 2011 to 2017. Since 2018, the classification has been in line with the standards in the *Measures for Statistical Classification of Micro, Small, Medium and Large-sized Enterprises (2017)* (G.T.Z. [2017] No. 213).

IV. Adjustment to Historical Data

The historical data on gross output value of industry above designated size for the period between 1993 and 2003 had been revised based on results from the first national economic census in Beijing by the trend deviation method. The data for 2004 were collected from the first national economic census, the data for 2008 were collected from the second national economic census, the data for 2013 were collected from the third national economic census, and the data for 2018 were collected from the fourth national economic census.

12-1 规模以上工业总产值(1984-2022年)

单位：亿元

年份 Year	合计 Total	轻工业 Light Industry	重工业 Heavy Industry	#大中型工业 Medium and Large-sized Industry	#制造业 Manufacturing	#计算机、通信和其他电子设备制造业 Manufacture of Computers, Communication Equipment and Other Electronic Equipment	#汽车制造业 Manufacture of Motor Vehicles	#电力、热力生产和供应业 Production and Supply of Electricity and Heating Power
1984	276.2	118.0	158.2	178.7				
1985	324.2	135.8	188.4	213.7				
1986	336.5	140.8	195.7	231.6		14.5	23.1	9.2
1987	387.6	160.1	227.5	272.1		19.5	28.6	9.4
1988	495.6	212.5	283.1	345.4		28.9	39.2	11.0
1989	602.7	264.1	338.6	408.3		33.6	44.0	13.7
1990	625.9	262.2	363.7	433.8		37.3	48.7	16.1
1991	730.2	298.1	432.1	507.4		45.7	69.6	18.7
1992	860.0	306.5	553.5	587.4		47.8	100.9	22.5
1993	1166.6	361.9	804.7	747.6		71.4	126.6	28.9
1994	1576.6	497.9	1078.7	990.7		120.3	162.1	39.9
1995	1493.3	472.2	1021.1	937.7		154.8	173.8	41.1
1996	1590.6	509.1	1081.5	962.3		199.2	166.6	17.5
1997	1819.7	577.8	1241.9	999.6		300.9	158.5	75.5
1998	1947.0	598.2	1348.8	1059.8		467.1	112.9	71.1
1999	2183.5	621.8	1561.7	1090.9		611.8	121.6	74.8
2000	2842.0	719.3	2122.7	1653.1		934.1	109.7	83.2
2001	3270.1	842.4	2427.7	2298.4		1066.0	180.9	83.8
2002	3620.2	882.4	2737.8	2434.7		1018.9	269.4	99.9
2003	4410.8	936.7	3474.1	3183.9		1091.1	528.0	118.3
2004	5733.3	1084.7	4648.6	3699.3		1235.6	748.9	492.8
2005	6946.2	1164.9	5781.3	5242.1	6159.3	1775.5	817.7	600.0
2006	8210.0	1258.2	6951.8	6237.9	7130.2	2234.2	1003.6	847.6
2007	9648.4	1505.5	8142.9	7365.9	8273.0	2663.1	1057.4	1068.0
2008	10413.1	1674.3	8738.8	7898.9	8654.5	2385.9	1153.3	1242.4
2009	11039.1	1766.7	9272.4	8349.3	8897.3	2095.5	1663.8	1435.6
2010	13699.8	2000.0	11699.8	10505.3	10793.4	2229.1	2177.7	2120.2
2011	14513.6	2227.2	12286.4	11289.3	10925.1	2026.2	2495.6	2283.4
2012	15596.2	2402.1	13194.1	12239.6	11103.1	2054.9	2521.5	3018.1
2013	17370.9	2541.5	14829.4	13941.3	12259.0	2217.0	3269.2	3739.1
2014	18452.9	2568.0	15884.9	15039.5	13103.8	2424.5	3647.6	4087.0
2015	17449.6	2610.8	14838.8	14250.3	12591.5	2110.2	3882.9	4085.6
2016	18087.3	2731.6	15355.7	15053.2	13291.9	2019.9	4771.6	4105.5
2017	18901.1	2924.1	15977.0	15747.2	13640.9	2199.5	4492.5	4496.7
2018	19669.0	2975.7	16693.3	16224.5	13769.2	2492.0	3945.3	5032.2
2019	20386.1	2964.1	17422.0	16541.0	13997.4	2600.5	3964.5	5474.9
2020	20879.3	2945.5	17933.8	17211.4	14394.4	2881.8	4139.4	5585.7
2021	24988.1	5649.6	19338.5	20896.4	17869.1	3744.4	3433.2	6176.7
2022	23870.0	3388.4	20481.7	19649.6	15597.0	3517.0	3398.6	7317.4

注：工业总产值按当年价格计算。

GROSS OUTPUT VALUE OF INDUSTRY ABOVE DESIGNATED SIZE (1984–2022)

(100 million yuan)

#铁路、船舶、航空航天和其他运输设备制造业 Manufacture of Railway Ships, Aerospace and Other Transport Equipments	#化学原料和化学制品制造业 Manufacture of Chemical Raw Materials and Chemical Products	#通用设备制造业 Manufacture of General-Purpose Machinery	#专用设备制造业 Manufacture of Special-Purpose Machinery	#电气机械和器材制造业 Manufacture of Electrical Machinery and Equipment	#仪器仪表制造业 Manufacture of Measuring Instruments and Meters	#医药制造业 Manufacture of Medicines	#非金属矿物制品业 Manufacture of Non-Metallic Mineral Products	#石油、煤炭及其他燃料加工业 Processing of Petroleum, Coal and Other Fuel
	48.1			15.7	3.7	5.4	15.9	4.8
	57.2			17.0	4.0	7.1	17.6	5.6
	69.4			22.2	5.3	9.8	20.1	7.0
	83.4			27.0	5.5	10.8	24.7	8.2
	87.1			22.1	4.9	11.4	24.1	9.7
	42.8			25.7	5.7	14.0	27.1	65.6
	62.0			30.5	7.4	15.8	31.8	67.4
	70.1	64.8	33.8	40.9	12.2	18.2	50.3	92.4
	90.6	76.1	62.1	53.4	15.4	21.8	81.1	117.3
	101.4	55.3	40.4	37.0	24.3	21.9	54.5	133.9
	104.3	54.3	41.4	44.8	32.1	26.4	71.4	133.3
	100.1	49.9	53.1	52.2	30.6	32.3	73.7	148.4
	100.1	53.5	81.0	69.2	33.2	38.9	92.6	111.8
	116.6	43.4	100.0	87.5	37.0	47.1	95.0	156.7
	144.2	49.1	123.4	97.7	42.4	58.5	102.8	289.2
	145.6	71.9	98.0	111.5	49.7	71.5	102.8	269.8
	168.0	81.4	130.2	119.1	74.8	98.6	132.9	318.0
	312.7	128.1	151.0	169.2	97.8	123.0	143.4	241.9
	399.0	186.7	189.8	197.5	124.4	119.7	184.5	274.6
	236.9	237.1	232.0	222.3	158.2	131.1	193.8	592.5
	257.5	292.5	300.9	260.7	183.9	150.1	234.6	540.4
	318.0	347.8	331.9	333.7	215.7	202.3	258.5	601.7
	306.7	409.2	434.4	387.2	211.4	263.9	296.5	753.2
	255.9	377.9	423.1	596.4	205.4	313.1	344.4	682.1
	358.3	547.7	502.4	699.1	227.9	372.8	392.5	825.2
	371.2	597.9	565.6	775.1	242.3	452.9	445.2	902.5
200.2	345.9	524.7	510.3	669.7	224.3	543.3	461.1	886.3
262.0	349.6	516.9	614.7	714.1	245.8	599.1	491.1	767.2
381.5	352.1	550.6	590.3	737.6	257.3	669.0	488.0	845.4
384.5	319.3	488.0	543.7	786.2	257.7	733.0	392.2	591.1
391.5	302.3	490.0	512.1	678.6	254.9	814.4	432.1	494.4
423.7	333.9	537.3	557.2	665.8	269.1	981.6	432.1	580.0
434.8	303.4	532.0	694.8	665.1	241.9	1142.7	464.5	638.5
457.3	270.1	507.7	789.0	686.0	294.0	1221.6	482.1	579.8
446.7	255.0	524.4	805.6	848.3	268.3	1313.9	471.0	455.9
497.1	290.4	596.9	872.3	794.6	307.3	3930.3	522.0	616.8
509.0	279.7	666.8	1010.4	795.6	323.1	1748.8	481.2	732.3

Note: Gross output value is calculated at current prices.

12-2 规模以上工业企业主要经济指标(1978-2022年)
MAIN ECONOMIC INDICATORS FOR INDUSTRIAL ENTERPRISES ABOVE DESIGNATED SIZE (1978-2022)

单位：亿元 (100 million yuan)

年份 Year	企业单位个数(个) Number of Enterprises (unit)	平均用工人数(万人) Average Number of Employed Persons (10000 persons)	资产总计 Total Assets	负债合计 Total Liabilities	固定资产原价 Original Value of Fixed Assets	营业收入 Business Income	营业成本 Business Cost	利润总额 Total Profits	利税总额 Total Taxes & Profits
1978	4225	114.8			130.5	109.8		37.1	50.2
1979	3746	116.8	141.7		137.1	118.6		41.4	55.5
1980	3733	140.9	154.7		149.5	198.8		45.3	60.4
1981	3778	152.9	165.1		162.2	205.5		44.1	59.9
1982	3867	158.7	174.9		175.1	218.3		44.0	60.4
1983	4011	162.0	184.7		188.7	240.9		46.9	64.2
1984	4291	165.5	200.4		204.5	272.9		50.5	70.7
1985	4458	165.6	233.8		233.7	317.6		54.9	82.9
1986	5461	169.9	272.0		262.7	338.5		52.4	81.4
1987	5746	170.5	314.7		300.9	393.5		57.1	88.5
1988	5932	170.5	360.7		341.3	503.2		70.2	108.1
1989	6175		434.3		389.0	559.8		63.8	108.7
1990	6272	173.5	498.3		438.2	610.5		48.9	95.7
1991	6344	172.4	567.3		505.2	727.2		58.3	110.6
1992	6205	175.5	640.9		575.4	852.7		74.8	134.7
1993	10320	167.9	1521.0		998.7	1282.2		109.5	181.2
1994	10889	179.5	1969.2		964.8	1320.7		96.2	185.7
1995	10712	176.2	2582.6	1528.8	1390.0	1590.4		85.3	193.0
1996	16905	166.6	2875.6	1722.1	1632.0	1580.1		33.1	122.5
1997	19387	157.5	3408.3	2049.7	1850.3	1707.1	1409.1	40.5	140.5
1998	18089	167.1	4012.9	2483.9	2221.3	2034.5	1669.7	48.4	161.7
1999	19682	161.1	4254.1	2586.3	2312.1	2218.6	1824.7	69.8	184.6
2000	16027	145.6	4612.7	2676.4	2531.6	2821.4	2338.0	127.1	256.1
2001	4356	108.0	4448.2	2459.6	2503.7	3006.9	2533.4	137.0	279.5
2002	4551	107.6	4742.9	2527.8	2655.4	3182.8	2612.9	165.5	322.0
2003	4019	100.8	5178.0	2751.2	2756.0	3885.7	3203.2	235.3	419.0
2004	6872	113.6	12049.5	4143.1	3922.2	5992.7	4288.5	397.4	641.8
2005	6301	117.1	12829.8	4706.7	4434.0	7279.1	6309.6	413.5	683.1
2006	6400	117.4	14244.4	5542.3	5030.6	8914.2	7779.9	531.1	847.9
2007	6398	119.3	16215.5	6508.3	5814.8	10440.2	9034.1	695.6	1055.2
2008	7206	123.4	16802.4	8085.0	6574.6	11275.8	9866.7	557.0	937.9
2009	6891	120.4	19540.7	9874.6	7083.6	12173.1	10406.4	742.9	1269.9
2010	6885	124.2	22750.6	11548.1	7936.1	14807.1	12611.2	1028.3	1649.0
2011	3740	117.9	25321.7	12648.6	8620.8	16105.8	13681.9	1129.5	1806.2
2012	3692	120.2	28613.2	14837.2	10277.2	17277.1	14595.8	1267.9	2010.4
2013	3641	116.1	30800.7	16208.0	10788.6	19058.7	16124.8	1282.9	2125.2
2014	3686	116.6	33557.0	17137.6	11532.9	20179.4	17012.1	1515.8	2407.9
2015	3548	110.4	38609.8	18102.4	12265.5	19256.1	15998.5	1597.7	2528.0
2016	3340	104.4	43093.7	19798.1	12978.0	20213.8	16750.7	1608.3	2521.6
2017	3231	99.5	45985.8	20671.0	13964.0	21181.0	17481.1	2023.7	2937.0
2018	3108	92.7	49321.5	22270.2	14651.0	22348.1	18482.2	1647.0	2594.9
2019	3121	86.8	52222.0	21974.5	15448.8	23419.1	19364.2	1710.3	2544.7
2020	3028	83.1	55167.0	24193.8	17105.1	23849.0	19709.9	1729.5	2429.7
2021	3073	81.0	61056.0	26371.6	18044.1	28745.1	22261.5	3684.4	4583.8
2022	3141	81.7	66052.5	29327.9	19093.5	27713.6	23090.6	1998.7	2970.5

注：2010年及以前，营业收入为主营业务收入数据，营业成本为主营业务成本数据。

Note: In and before 2010, the data of business income referred to the data of main business income, and the data of business cost referred to the data of main business cost.

12-3 规模以上工业产品产量(1978-2022年)
OUTPUT OF INDUSTRIAL PRODUCTS ABOVE DESIGNATED SIZE (1978-2022)

年 份 Year	布 (万米) Cloth (10000 m)	机制纸及纸板 (万吨) Machine-made Paper and Paperboard (10000 tons)	饮料酒 (万千升) Alcoholic Beverage (10000 kL)	乳制品 (万吨) Dairy Products (10000 tons)	家用电冰箱 (万台) Household Refrigerators (10000 units)	照相机 (万台) Camera (10000 units)	家具 (万件) Furniture (10000 pieces)	原煤 (万吨) Raw Coal (10000 tons)
1978	25436	12.1	8.4			0.5	137.8	818.7
1979	27297	13.9	9.9		2.0	0.7	171.3	711.1
1980	28940	14.0	11.6		2.6	1.0	200.2	791.0
1981	28635	14.5	13.4		3.1	4.2	217.7	788.7
1982	29758	15.8	14.9	0.2	4.5	0.9	243.5	811.3
1983	30068	17.1	17.4	0.3	6.4	2.8	254.2	840.5
1984	27621	18.9	20.3	0.6	10.3	5.3	297.9	884.3
1985	25998	20.6	21.3	0.9	17.3	12.5	335.1	944.3
1986	27503	21.9	21.5	0.7	18.1	15.9	303.8	917.2
1987	29738	24.1	22.7	0.8	19.4	16.5	283.0	899.8
1988	32262	23.3	23.9	1.0	23.6	15.8	347.1	906.0
1989	32271	25.8	28.7	1.0	24.7	13.5	572.1	1016.8
1990	31258	25.4	34.6	1.2	10.7	12.9	590.6	1005.5
1991	31497	27.2	43.8	1.3	7.1	5.4	602.0	996.5
1992	29717	22.6	56.6	1.2	9.1	4.2	570.0	1015.2
1993	26816	19.1	72.6	1.6	4.2	39.3	729.0	835.4
1994	21440	21.0	83.1	0.3	6.6	158.8	605.0	1008.5
1995	24524	26.6	91.2	1.5		243.1	755.0	995.4
1996	22585	15.3	102.2	1.2	6.3	234.3	510.6	1013.7
1997	25185	18.1	…	1.7	…	157.7	469.4	1011.7
1998	21299	13.1		0.9	0.3	177.7	348.5	989.5
1999	14753	13.0	148.8	1.4	5.8	81.6	386.2	792.1
2000	12183	10.6	185.6	2.1	3.6	55.2	272.1	553.0
2001	11353	8.8	135.8	3.7	5.9	61.3	370.6	690.2
2002	10314	6.2	138.7	1.4	16.2	220.7	368.3	880.9
2003	8393	7.9	132.8	1.3	22.8	238.3	323.8	822.6
2004	4081	19.6	148.0	56.4	63.1	116.8	567.7	1067.9
2005	4270	17.0	145.6	56.9	81.7	47.9	406.5	897.9
2006	930	14.0	170.8	63.5	74.1	49.2	893.4	629.2
2007	536	10.4	189.1	57.9	73.1	34.7	638.8	633.3
2008	1583	14.9	180.0	44.9	79.0	49.0	690.9	567.7
2009	965	14.1	181.1	52.2	128.7	27.1	719.4	641.3
2010	495	10.6	185.8	52.3	92.1	29.2	822.8	500.0
2011	339	10.0	187.0	58.6	73.5	26.6	750.2	500.1
2012	351	11.3	191.7	56.6	80.4	18.2	720.1	493.1
2013	361	10.0	198.0	58.5	83.7	17.9	995.9	500.1
2014	361	6.6	187.4	60.6		6.6	674.7	457.5
2015	174	5.0	167.1	62.1		1.6	700.5	450.1
2016		6.1	167.5	62.2		0.1	776.2	317.6
2017		5.9	164.9	59.7		0.1	686.3	255.0
2018		4.4	148.5	53.2			626.1	176.2
2019		4.2	128.2	55.4			463.1	36.1
2020		3.9	115.1	53.7			389.9	
2021		3.4	121.9	54.2			402.0	
2022		3.2	129.1	48.9			333.5	

12-3 续表 1 continued 1

年份 Year	原油加工量(万吨) Crude Oil Processed (10000 tons)	乙烯(万吨) Ethylene (10000 tons)	发电量(万千瓦时) Electricity Generated (10000 kW·h)	粗钢(万吨) Crude Steel (10000 tons)	钢材(万吨) Rolled Steel (10000 tons)	水泥(万吨) Cement (10000 tons)	交流电动机(万千瓦) Alternator (10000 kW)
1978			990750	191.0	116.8	191.5	152.5
1979			1042870	196.5	137.5	196.9	179.7
1980	591.1		1065060	200.9	152.1	217.4	142.7
1981	533.5	24.7	993071	190.3	149.5	225.7	104.0
1982	533.5	25.6	1003446	200.4	159.4	249.1	123.3
1983	563.8	27.3	1028826	214.1	177.9	270.8	148.3
1984	589.4	26.9	1038842	241.7	200.1	291.6	165.4
1985	591.1	27.8	1037171	267.7	221.0	318.5	172.0
1986	619.0	25.3	1043208	303.6	255.5	310.5	178.4
1987	640.2	27.0	1057493	335.5	283.4	319.6	196.4
1988	645.0	30.3	1110758	369.0	314.9	334.3	199.5
1989	651.9	29.1	1191269	386.0	327.9	345.9	163.8
1990	654.4	30.1	1253554	443.7	375.0	339.0	151.6
1991	653.4	31.1	1318000	499.7	402.9	377.6	156.7
1992	662.5	32.8	1423000	575.0	438.3	403.0	174.9
1993	664.0	27.2	1410900	702.7	525.3	477.9	162.3
1994	642.0	28.1	1298718	828.7	617.6	531.7	165.0
1995	648.0	53.0	1322114	804.9	629.8	574.2	165.4
1996	633.6	57.5	1415555	794.7	654.3	666.0	151.9
1997	657.0	58.0	1464302	801.7	652.4	700.9	148.7
1998	602.3	57.0	1566621	803.2	676.1	762.0	149.7
1999	701.9	68.0	1431772	734.5	663.8	803.0	142.0
2000	741.7	65.5	1452564	803.4	696.7	827.0	161.0
2001	647.9	54.3	1326588	824.9	727.3	809.0	175.1
2002	695.2	90.4	1419754	816.9	750.0	884.0	199.3
2003	701.1	88.8	1451197	816.4	785.0	882.0	253.1
2004	783.4	98.2	2038933	827.5	868.3	1204.5	279.4
2005	796.9	99.0	2133451	827.6	966.3	1183.8	262.9
2006	828.9	99.1	2136918	818.1	1016.3	1269.4	269.0
2007	915.0	90.9	2278658	810.8	1030.4	1167.3	281.9
2008	1114.6	85.4	2431255	466.8	656.8	880.8	259.7
2009	1161.3	84.1	2424839	464.9	769.6	1077.4	159.0
2010	1123.4	96.2	2688350	427.5	794.0	1049.0	191.1
2011	1103.1	89.6	2628331	2.9	287.0	911.5	146.0
2012	1075.0	84.0	2908214	2.6	253.8	874.5	117.1
2013	881.6	72.3	3312116	2.3	221.8	868.4	145.4
2014	1051.1	77.6	3385699	2.1	195.0	703.1	115.0
2015	1000.1	78.6	4173847	1.5	175.0	553.5	40.3
2016	844.8	69.6	4336690		162.8	510.3	46.1
2017	898.9	79.3	3878163		179.0	374.4	48.2
2018	911.3	79.4	4372998		179.1	397.0	35.4
2019	936.5	81.5	4311921		170.7	318.7	20.7
2020	779.6	81.7	4413422		184.4	286.9	7.4
2021	775.5	71.2	4589948		203.4	258.1	12.3
2022	774.0	71.1	4499192		184.3	203.4	13.0

12-3 续表 2 continued 2

年 份 Year	汽 车 (万辆) Motor Vehicles (10000 units)	#轿 车 Sedan Cars	移动通信手持机 (万台) Mobile Phones (10000 units)	微型计算机设备 (万台) Micro-Computers (10000 units)	数控金属切削机床 (台) CNC Metal Cutting Lathe (unit)	显示器 (万台) Display Devices (10000 units)	集成电路 (亿块) IC (100 million units)
1978	1.8						
1979	2.4						
1980	2.8						
1981	2.7						
1982	2.8						
1983	3.1			0.3			
1984	3.6			1.2			
1985	5.0			0.5			
1986	5.8			0.5			
1987	7.4			0.9			
1988	9.0			3.0			
1989	8.5			1.3			
1990	8.8			1.2			
1991	11.0			1.7			
1992	13.8			3.0			
1993	13.4			4.1			
1994	14.7			4.3			
1995	17.9			19.2			
1996	13.4			28.1	326		0.5
1997	11.0			59.8	433		0.6
1998	8.5			160.9	430		0.6
1999	12.3	1.0		180.0	481		1.3
2000	12.5	0.5	1549.6	257.8	568		2.4
2001	14.3	0.5	2163.4	339.7	1004		2.1
2002	18.1	0.7	2280.1	415.7	912		2.5
2003	34.7	7.3	3334.5	469.3	1188		4.7
2004	53.9	15.0	4172.1	532.7	1024		11.1
2005	58.6	22.2	9131.1	649.6	1655		12.6
2006	68.3	27.0	14068.0	736.1	1875	680.7	11.8
2007	70.7	20.3	22719.9	843.3	2382	513.6	15.7
2008	76.6	28.3	20725.5	691.7	3108	478.1	19.1
2009	127.1	53.8	21355.3	842.7	6125	655.6	18.3
2010	150.3	62.2	27388.0	938.6	9766	877.8	25.3
2011	150.5	67.1	25962.3	1083.7	12537	851.4	32.0
2012	167.0	78.5	19949.3	1074.5	13332	796.9	31.9
2013	203.8	94.5	18783.4	1106.9	6983	305.3	38.4
2014	216.7	118.6	17983.6	1015.6	13890	548.1	54.3
2015	221.9	118.9	9540.8	885.6	12471	519.0	62.7
2016	260.4	120.7	6923.9	684.1	12420	503.5	80.5
2017	225.0	107.6	7483.1	742.4	14877	360.8	93.1
2018	163.2	78.8	8448.0	555.5	11862	406.3	149.5
2019	164.0	77.8	8373.3	513.2	7611	470.1	154.5
2020	166.0	65.3	9928.5	552.4	8188	577.8	170.7
2021	135.5	52.2	11624.5	647.3	6184	518.2	207.7
2022	87.1	46.5	9429.5	858.6	5072	233.6	217.9

注：根据统计制度规定，自2022年起，汽车整车制造行业产业活动单位视同法人单位按经营地在地原则进行统计，北京在京外设立的汽车整车制造分厂按照制度规定在当地纳统。

Note:According to the statistical system, since 2022, the industrial activity units in the sector of manufacture of finished automobiles shall be deemed as legal entities and shall be subject to statistics in accordance with the principle of regional statistics of the business place,the finished automobile manufacturing branches set up outside of Beijing shall be included in local statistics according to the rules and regulations.

12-4 规模以上工业企业主要经济指标(2022年)

单位：万元

项目	Item	企业单位个数(个) Number of Enterprises (unit)	#亏损企业 Loss-Suffering Enterprises	工业总产值(当年价格) Gross Output Value of Industry (at current year's prices)	平均用工人数(人) Average Number of Employed Persons (person)	资产总计 Total Assets
合计	**Total**	**3141**	**789**	**238700122**	**817131**	**660524680**
按行业分	**By Sector**					
采矿业	Mining	9	3	3172536	27881	39362423
制造业	Manufacturing	2968	753	155970127	696735	318280667
电力、热力、燃气及水生产和供应业	Production and Supply of Electricity, Heating, Gas and Water	164	33	79557459	92515	302881590
按轻重工业分	**By Light and Heavy Industries**					
轻工业	Light Industry	1027	297	33883505	257579	72424624
重工业	Heavy Industry	2114	492	204816618	559552	588100056
按规模分	**By Size**					
大型	Large-sized	113	20	159391261	338400	479100979
中型	Medium-sized	412	87	37105110	213592	93898165
小型	Small-sized	2411	624	40229822	260877	85003870
微型	Micro-sized	205	58	1973931	4262	2521667
按登记注册类型分	**By Registration Type**					
内资企业	Domestially-Invested Enterprises	2494	592	156940081	571285	524403649
国有企业	State-owned Enterprises	15	2	2158858	8969	5718464
集体企业	Collectively-owned Enterprises	21	10	118505	2108	255169
股份合作企业	Joint-equity Cooperative Enterprises	31	8	198867	3039	243332
有限责任公司	Limited Liability Corporations	1094	288	118561446	324689	414306367
股份有限公司	Corporations Limited by Shares	190	36	20233203	100123	63282784
私营企业	Private Enterprises	1143	248	15669203	132357	40597534
港澳台商投资企业	Hong Kong, Macao and Taiwan-invested Enterprises	130	35	27558677	55019	50096518
港澳台合资经营	Joint Ventures	64	17	2518745	14921	6077037
港澳台合作经营	Cooperatives	1		***	***	***
港澳台商独资企业	Solely-funded Enterprises	48	15	22804186	34532	37501056
港澳台商投资股份有限公司	Companies Limited by Shares	16	3	2103781	5283	6251092
其他港澳台投资	Other Hong Kong, Macao and Taiwan-invested Enterprises	1		***	***	***
外商投资企业	Foreign-invested Enterprises	517	162	54201365	190827	86024513
#中外合资经营	Joint Ventures	195	60	34899123	86600	40019031
中外合作经营	Cooperatives	8	2	116936	3680	235773
外资(独资)企业	Solely-funded Enterprises	285	95	16939081	82020	38074224
外商投资股份有限公司	Companies Limited by Shares	28	5	2142735	18005	7523969
按控股类型分	**By Holding Types**					
#国有控股	State-holding Enterprises	664	124	148727303	346026	461811983
集体控股	Collectively-holding Enterprises	63	23	975326	11324	3104207
私人控股	Private-holding Enterprises	1917	491	36928800	282070	96388694
港澳台控股	Hong Kong, Macao, and Taiwan-holding Enterprises	103	26	25543262	49270	43771968
外商控股	Foreign-Investor-holding Enterprises	387	123	26433173	127332	52812009

注：应交税金合计包括应交增值税、所得税费用、税金及附加，下同。

MAIN ECONOMIC INDICATORS OF INDUSTRIAL ENTERPRISES ABOVE DESIGNATED SIZE (2022)

(10000 yuan)

资产负债						
#流动资产合计 Total Current Assets	#存货 Inventories	#产成品 Finished Products	#应收账款 Accounts Receivable	#固定资产原价 Original Value of Fixed Assets	负债合计 Total Liabilities	#流动负债合计 Total Current Liabilities
274129431	**39051962**	**13525274**	**60275776**	**190935351**	**293278656**	**219363193**
7359883	79386	16177	1466900	9882700	25245657	12731435
209136720	38454800	13450919	48193608	65075292	161572772	143592761
57632828	517776	58178	10615269	115977359	106460228	63038997
46374870	8376802	3766318	7673204	14667591	26426478	22582324
227754561	30675160	9758957	52602572	176267760	266852179	196780869
162576448	18001539	7149774	30990348	152855010	210813868	149932745
54243134	9244976	2199602	12785165	20523757	40363007	32264010
55685816	11568815	4080757	16070396	16848009	40492788	36189208
1624034	236633	95142	429868	708575	1608994	977231
180946487	23782762	7010423	39425769	154866716	218640487	152360642
4598511	1324804	1384	826450	881497	4791060	4665366
198818	28528	11982	32825	87913	124935	80095
209402	27275	13295	79011	53073	150316	110331
117647934	13965552	3910467	25216772	137716220	172467939	112353678
32551065	3851575	1375080	5772281	11017524	23800638	19337386
25740758	4585029	1698216	7498430	5110491	17305600	15813786
33761640	5689799	2098428	5891736	8530797	22617346	18975058
3139961	519037	258375	935529	3126524	2427870	1717968
***	***	***	***	***	***	***
26614314	4739950	1707237	3985271	4530265	17852013	15564605
3774039	398672	102322	831168	867966	2159083	1514770
***	***	***	***	***	***	***
59421304	9579401	4416423	14958271	27537838	52020823	48027494
26413946	4861593	2252545	10592599	17228808	24198388	21727775
214159	22053	3007	53433	57771	99780	97645
28932602	4295151	2043692	3855641	9358909	26082844	25072955
3706933	374044	101204	416969	873108	1615386	1104695
142190368	17209882	5481330	32771628	156044597	196593694	134525066
2124242	447413	113285	770038	511684	1558185	1123073
60941070	9945091	3345540	15500791	13374179	42509005	36235625
30403254	5328572	1990854	4957345	5591685	21226956	18141207
38049453	6096667	2591189	6262719	15369313	31028559	29056376

Note: Total tax payable includes VAT payable, income tax expense, tax and surtax, the same below.

12-4 续表

单位：万元

项目	Item	资产负债 Assets and Liabilities #应付账款 Accounts Payable	所有者权益合计 Total Owner's Equity	#实收资本 Paid-up Capital
合　计	**Total**	**63028280**	**367233753**	**232639982**
按行业分	**By Sector**			
采矿业	Mining and Quarrying	1440306	14116766	6398349
制造业	Manufacturing	50580884	156695624	54495211
电力、热力、燃气及水生产和供应业	Production and Distribution of Electricity, Heating Power, Gas and Water	11007090	196421363	171746422
按轻重工业分	**By Light and Heavy Industries**			
轻工业	Light Industry	5898692	45976265	10328234
重工业	Heavy Industry	57129588	321257488	222311748
按规模分	**By Size**			
大　型	Large-sized	37584342	268287111	194905355
中　型	Medium-sized	10537716	53535157	17866202
小　型	Small-sized	14572040	44511067	19245283
微　型	Micro-sized	334182	900418	623142
按登记注册类型分	**By Registration Type**			
内资企业	Domestially-Invested Enterprises	37406771	305743421	210972140
国有企业	State-owned Enterprises	867459	927404	142000
集体企业	Collectively-owned Enterprises	16741	127602	15297
股份合作企业	Joint-equity Cooperative Enterprises	52403	93015	55273
有限责任公司	Limited Liability Companies	26289287	241825961	195573166
股份有限公司	Companies Limited by Shares	4553418	39482144	9293943
私营企业	Private Enterprises	5627464	23287294	5892461
港澳台商投资企业	Hong Kong, Macao and Taiwan-invested Enterprises	7747209	27486848	5496997
港澳台合资经营	Joint Ventures	498550	3649167	2400717
港澳台合作经营	Cooperatives	***	***	***
港澳台商独资企业	Solely-funded Enterprises	6758822	19656720	2023569
港澳台商投资股份有限公司	Companies Limited by Shares	360518	4092009	1017711
其他港澳台投资	Other Hong Kong, Macao and Taiwan-invested Enterprises	***	***	***
外商投资企业	Foreign-invested Enterprises	17874299	34003485	16170845
#中外合资经营	Joint Ventures	13353237	15820642	10540341
中外合作经营	Cooperatives	56198	135993	114230
外资(独资)企业	Solely-funded Enterprises	4202238	11991177	4307868
外商投资股份有限公司	Companies Limited by Shares	251696	5908582	1198407
按控股类型分	**By Holding Types**			
#国有控股	State-holding Enterprises	37473812	265235247	202442689
集体控股	Collectively-holding Enterprises	397860	1543390	401578
私人控股	Private-holding Enterprises	11421330	53845620	16751974
港澳台控股	Hong Kong, Macao, and Taiwan-holding Enterprises	7315472	22552689	2893325
外商控股	Foreign-Investor-holding Enterprises	6309113	21783246	9727083

12-4 Continued

(10000 yuan)

损益 Profits and Losses							应交税金合计 Total Tax Payable	#税金及附加 Tax and Surtax	#应交增值税 Value Added Tax Payable
营业收入 Business Income	营业成本 Business Cost	销售费用 Sales Expenses	管理费用 Management Expenses	研发费用 R&D Expenses	财务费用 Financial Expenses	利润总额 Total Profits			
277135513	**230905876**	**12734374**	**9503811**	**7171881**	**1345417**	**19987243**	**12700521**	**3486348**	**6231790**
5929273	5625991	5644	260725	85458	593834	93493	236019	41697	104456
189011312	146612804	12621590	8301346	6803933	-1085573	15100002	9596454	3058742	4240722
82194928	78667081	107140	941740	282491	1837157	4793748	2868049	385910	1886612
39794253	24398453	6616981	3013440	1920631	-350233	4081213	2783784	778321	1430785
237341261	206507423	6117393	6490371	5251251	1695651	15906030	9916738	2708027	4801005
183044529	159085820	7239633	3953121	2905454	1054452	12661131	8283195	2628623	3895507
42823440	30942948	2984124	2574652	2165332	38272	4537274	2377266	599464	1064099
49128948	38896831	2472613	2903804	2076140	220250	2779759	1988487	251849	1236210
2138596	1980277	38004	72232	24955	32444	9080	51574	6412	35974
172803185	148741695	5280900	5984773	4901124	2377164	10097612	7467740	2173575	3974373
1681050	1545971	2666	80803	29106	-9066	35657	19895	2629	11583
138870	118740	4030	12082	1387	305	10582	8693	808	5495
214546	173563	14601	11985	7293	566	7038	7004	687	5733
128583452	115481236	2275535	3329739	2684509	2239163	7045083	4961478	1010406	2929523
24087270	18284244	1634598	1293512	1098015	75932	1663947	1794835	1074485	553849
18097996	13137941	1349470	1256651	1080813	70264	1335304	675835	84560	468191
42612903	36843995	2277948	1174812	1028739	-549929	2807617	526840	68536	259905
2813961	2076919	178044	153309	107983	11461	284875	147382	21549	76360
***	***	***	***	***	***	***	***	***	***
37266752	32876771	2022494	921162	804296	-545994	2120231	287085	30402	143965
2400692	1779501	75953	95626	111201	-15272	393747	86002	16140	34420
***	***	***	***	***	***	***	***	***	***
61719426	45320186	5175526	2344225	1242019	-481818	7082014	4705942	1244237	1997512
37350391	28075805	2436095	1081097	608688	-64026	4061030	3488195	1117568	1357473
321453	248090	32120	14828	2279	2282	21234	18103	1550	10865
21697231	15926240	2204113	1096761	372828	-411028	2529101	1059541	106932	538789
2253120	1030416	488451	148490	251041	-7403	438249	128461	17251	83724
160372871	141463940	3036264	3982158	2356123	2174849	10284777	9123384	3057938	4204601
1393170	1053680	121869	111725	78248	4765	77407	41524	9058	23953
41625773	28927729	4036438	2645151	3018266	78301	3399677	1552987	219214	979761
40424279	35132526	2299157	1077773	929548	-518187	2460593	447293	45920	229743
33149890	24177709	3234081	1673117	692681	-389864	3762564	1533979	153406	793483

12-5 分行业规模以上工业企业主要经济指标(2022年)

单位：万元

项目	Item	企业单位个数(个) Number of Enterprises (unit)	#亏损企业 Loss-Suffering Enterprises	工业总产值(当年价格) Gross Output Value of Industry (at current year's prices)
合　计	**Total**	**3141**	**789**	**238700122**
采矿业	**Mining**	**9**	**3**	**3172536**
石油和天然气开采业	Extraction of Petroleum and Natural Gas	2	2	***
黑色金属矿采选业	Mining and Processing of Ferrous Metal Ores	2		***
开采专业及辅助性活动	Mining and Support Service Activities	5	1	1762502
制造业	**Manufacturing**	**2968**	**753**	**155970127**
农副食品加工业	Processing of Agricultural and Sideline Products	101	41	2654579
食品制造业	Manufacture of Foods	115	41	2898075
酒、饮料和精制茶制造业	Manufacture of Wines, Beverage and Refined Tea	36	11	2170281
烟草制品业	Manufacture of Cigarettes and Tobacco	1		***
纺织业	Manufacture of Textile	10	2	192145
纺织服装、服饰业	Manufacture of Textile Wearing Apparel and Ornament	70	27	757553
皮革、毛皮、羽毛及其制品和制鞋业	Manufacture of Leather, Fur, Feather and Its Products, and Footwear	2	2	***
木材加工和木、竹、藤、棕、草制品业	Processing of Timbers, Manufacture of Wood, Bamboo, Rattan, Palm, and Straw Products	5	1	48668
家具制造业	Manufacture of Furniture	32	7	574403
造纸和纸制品业	Manufacture of Paper and Paper Products	27	2	581754
印刷和记录媒介复制业	Printing, Reproduction of Recording Media	91	27	1167523
文教、工美、体育和娱乐用品制造业	Manufacture of Articles for Culture, Education, Artwork, Sport and Entertainment Activities	21	2	254202
石油、煤炭及其他燃料加工业	Processing of Petroleum, Coal and Other Fuels	14	6	7322986
化学原料和化学制品制造业	Manufacture of Chemical Raw Materials and Chemical Products	136	31	2797323
医药制造业	Manufacture of Medicines	263	58	17487793
化学纤维制造业	Manufacture of Chemical Fibres	1		***
橡胶和塑料制品业	Manufacture of Rubber and Plastics Products	50	12	423014
非金属矿物制品业	Manufacture of Non-metallic Mineral Products	169	45	4812459
黑色金属冶炼和压延加工业	Smelting and Pressing of Ferrous Metals	5		1184806
有色金属冶炼和压延加工业	Smelting and Pressing of Non-ferrous Metals	21	2	1748038
金属制品业	Manufacture of Fabricated Metal Products	145	36	2435433
通用设备制造业	Manufacture of General-purpose Machinery	205	45	6667541
专用设备制造业	Manufacture of Special-purpose Machinery	372	85	10104349
汽车制造业	Manufacture of Motor Vehicles	192	86	33985865
铁路、船舶、航空航天和其他运输设备制造业	Manufacture of Railway, Ships, Aerospace and Other Transport Equipments	97	21	5089708
电气机械和器材制造业	Manufacture of Electrical Machinery and Equipment	215	43	7955894
计算机、通信和其他电子设备制造业	Manufacture of Computers, Communication Equipment and Other Electronic Equipment	329	84	35170374
仪器仪表制造业	Manufacture of Measuring Instruments and Meters	200	29	3231274
其他制造业	Other Manufacturing	11	2	2564336
废弃资源综合利用业	Waste Recycling and Recovery	11	2	129644
金属制品、机械和设备修理业	Repair of Fabricated Metal Products, Machinery and Equipment	21	3	876664
电力、热力、燃气及水生产和供应业	**Production and Supply of Electricity, Heating Power, Gas and Water**	**164**	**33**	**79557459**
电力、热力生产和供应业	Production and Supply of Electricity and Heating Power	109	20	73174140
燃气生产和供应业	Production and Supply of Gas	21	4	5051221
水的生产和供应业	Production and Supply of Water	34	9	1332098

MAIN ECONOMIC INDICATORS OF INDUSTRIAL ENTERPRISES ABOVE DESIGNATED SIZE BY SECTOR(2022)

(10000 yuan)

平均用工人数（人） Average Number of Employed Persons (person)	资产负债							
	资产总计 Total Assets	#流动资产合计 Total Current Assets	#存货 Inventories	#产成品 Finished Products	#应收账款 Accounts Receivable	#固定资产原价 Original Value of Fixed Assets	负债合计 Total Liabilities	#流动负债合计 Total Current Liabilities
817131	**660524680**	**274129431**	**39051962**	**13525274**	**60275776**	**190935351**	**293278656**	**219363193**
27881	**39362423**	**7359883**	**79386**	**16177**	**1466900**	**9882700**	**25245657**	**12731435**
***	***	***	***	***	***	***	***	***
***	***	***	***	***	***	***	***	***
15178	4587812	1896100	55970	4135	616825	2938524	1939743	1389678
696735	**318280667**	**209136720**	**38454800**	**13450919**	**48193608**	**65075292**	**161572772**	**143592761**
18763	5291594	2696524	795935	265690	345678	1056112	2720827	2159337
34312	5204201	3258713	355205	162212	726492	1599053	2687540	2389246
17838	6611707	4220104	420394	156852	352979	1820198	2941117	2582783
***	***	***	***	***	***	***	***	***
1131	278771	241271	72874	44565	52154	32170	151362	148785
18984	1458775	1171894	398893	263801	187852	288357	742005	691750
***	***	***	***	***	***	***	***	***
213	38875	34735	4223	1418	14260	4980	26664	26585
5521	1289312	845236	246945	198117	147365	229415	928705	683280
3096	480103	303990	124457	32844	108811	289426	240404	223399
16431	2220736	1421840	283808	87794	201778	1599286	748868	630254
2494	639480	449429	281997	141280	58406	138445	498158	399901
9381	5958751	2538970	1470356	131624	180605	4506221	3130654	2566458
16598	5521729	3626706	700712	349122	702639	1258656	1873939	1757830
93761	36183189	23050108	4086029	1949203	3922174	5736734	10216246	8637417
***	***	***	***	***	***	***	***	***
4951	617680	473586	110015	43816	153710	240881	271191	262557
28696	11062409	7490939	697310	301789	3388108	1673354	6705842	6265844
1024	701698	295983	89057	31621	62140	722198	763027	302784
2812	1037083	701279	170904	67064	135502	196200	472696	407747
16885	6546260	4493350	669497	154057	769548	992436	3718099	3351508
41743	12405346	9338289	2406291	874828	2192532	2087611	5546006	5158826
68624	30285737	18815098	3178843	977831	4408738	2187487	14817075	12397860
68227	44884063	29254778	4244581	2345071	11934207	15019561	30012242	27085445
33393	13507721	10496374	3095305	513218	2305134	2242006	7524021	7056332
37038	14884940	11623932	1470652	392265	3130281	1407675	8558501	7872469
105549	92544963	60348482	10320095	3493976	9953286	17436453	47331463	42434487
28013	7973216	5615707	1164300	232729	1526316	827200	3019204	2832395
4040	4693122	4241276	1185926	189824	867106	484700	3989547	3856579
970	412026	315884	13235	5075	92850	43914	166091	147467
14459	4881070	1234486	274059	9653	251040	629177	1590342	1094166
92515	**302881590**	**57632828**	**517776**	**58178**	**10615269**	**115977359**	**106460228**	**63038997**
67900	279239361	51690683	421077	53191	8648108	102344207	95921688	57942168
9982	9940204	2591231	73470	4005	243535	3707889	3701256	2355225
14633	13702024	3350915	23229	983	1723627	9925264	6837284	2741604

12-5 续表

单位：万元

项目	Item	资产负债 Assets and Liabilities		
		#应付账款 Accounts Payable	所有者权益合计 Total Owner's Equity	#实收资本 Paid-up Capital
合 计	**Total**	**63028280**	**367233753**	**232639982**
采矿业	**Mining**	**1440306**	**14116766**	**6398349**
石油和天然气开采业	Extraction of Petroleum and Natural Gas	***	***	***
黑色金属矿采选业	Mining and Processing of Ferrous Metal Ores	***	***	***
开采专业及辅助性活动	Mining and Support Service Activities	762756	2648069	3072962
制造业	**Manufacturing**	**50580884**	**156695624**	**54495211**
农副食品加工业	Processing of Agricultural and Sideline Products	285082	2570747	1207183
食品制造业	Manufacture of Foods	809040	2487918	968976
酒、饮料和精制茶制造业	Manufacture of Wines, Beverage and Refined Tea	388340	3678267	1093653
烟草制品业	Manufacture of Cigarettes and Tobacco	***	***	***
纺织业	Manufacture of Textile	48538	127409	46472
纺织服装、服饰业	Manufacture of Textile Wearing Apparel and Ornament	116504	716771	257212
皮革、毛皮、羽毛及其制品和制鞋业	Manufacture of Leather, Fur, Feather and Its Products, and Footwear	***	***	***
木材加工和木、竹、藤、棕、草制品业	Processing of Timbers, Manufacture of Wood, Bamboo, Rattan, Palm, and Straw Products	10285	12211	8400
家具制造业	Manufacture of Furniture	115797	360607	221582
造纸和纸制品业	Manufacture of Paper and Paper Products	81515	239699	99996
印刷和记录媒介复制业	Printing, Reproduction of Recording Media	234581	1471077	833872
文教、工美、体育和娱乐用品制造业	Manufacture of Articles for Culture, Education, Artwork, Sport and Entertainment Activities	154719	141322	175375
石油、煤炭及其他燃料加工业	Processing of Petroleum, Coal and Other Fuels	580403	2828097	1249313
化学原料和化学制品制造业	Manufacture of Chemical Raw Materials and Chemical Products	656460	3647788	1152275
医药制造业	Manufacture of Medicines	2459277	25966941	3669867
化学纤维制造业	Manufacture of Chemical Fibres	***	***	***
橡胶和塑料制品业	Manufacture of Rubber and Plastics Products	126312	346489	187756
非金属矿物制品业	Manufacture of Non-metallic Mineral Products	2883253	4356565	1683111
黑色金属冶炼和压延加工业	Smelting and Pressing of Ferrous Metals	180675	-61329	275429
有色金属冶炼和压延加工业	Smelting and Pressing of Non-ferrous Metals	136152	561755	113641
金属制品业	Manufacture of Fabricated Metal Products	851450	2820921	1260187
通用设备制造业	Manufacture of General-purpose Machinery	2070660	6859338	2041078
专用设备制造业	Manufacture of Special-purpose Machinery	3538302	15468660	4093890
汽车制造业	Manufacture of Motor Vehicles	14949799	14876511	9515779
铁路、船舶、航空航天和其他运输设备制造业	Manufacture of Railway, Ships, Aerospace and Other Transport Equipments	2592316	5999692	1820579
电气机械和器材制造业	Manufacture of Electrical Machinery and Equipment	2886788	6325248	2691002
计算机、通信和其他电子设备制造业	Manufacture of Computers, Communication Equipment and Other Electronic Equipment	12080678	45213498	17039815
仪器仪表制造业	Manufacture of Measuring Instruments and Meters	1007797	4954011	1334916
其他制造业	Other Manufacturing	1050541	703574	287562
废弃资源综合利用业	Waste Recycling and Recovery	50243	245935	64616
金属制品、机械和设备修理业	Repair of Fabricated Metal Products, Machinery and Equipment	221254	3290729	983233
电力、热力、燃气及水生产和供应业	**Production and Supply of Electricity, Heating Power, Gas and Water**	**11007090**	**196421363**	**171746422**
电力、热力生产和供应业	Production and Supply of Electricity and Heating Power	9821402	183317674	165198187
燃气生产和供应业	Production and Supply of Gas	552854	6238948	1471201
水的生产和供应业	Production and Supply of Water	632834	6864741	5077035

12-5 Continued

(10000 yuan)

损 益 Profits and Losses							应交税金合计 Total Tax Payable	#税金及附加 Tax and Surtax	#应交增值税 Value Added Tax Payable
营业收入 Business Income	营业成本 Business Cost	销售费用 Sales Expenses	管理费用 Management Expenses	研发费用 R&D Expenses	财务费用 Financial Expenses	利润总额 Total Profits			
277135513	**230905876**	**12734374**	**9503811**	**7171881**	**1345417**	**19987243**	**12700521**	**3486348**	**6231790**
5929273	**5625991**	**5644**	**260725**	**85458**	**593834**	**93493**	**236019**	**41697**	**104456**
***	***	***	***	***	***	***	***	***	***
***	***	***	***	***	***	***	***	***	***
1797956	1668917	4681	60948	47324	-20877	50637	25560	7534	3126
189011312	**146612804**	**12621590**	**8301346**	**6803933**	**-1085573**	**15100002**	**9596454**	**3058742**	**4240722**
4717839	4281326	188472	171849	39489	23769	94652	55270	8607	37386
5227888	3678126	1025025	286036	52381	-5935	221731	281235	29098	172201
2540448	1880416	248541	183788	29754	14791	210032	309296	207784	80877
***	***	***	***	***	***	***	***	***	***
249709	195049	7670	8356	8821	-1040	36990	7224	658	2391
1023332	685346	191797	89932	24647	3864	33140	49720	6620	36412
***	***	***	***	***	***	***	***	***	***
55254	47926	3278	3202		182	534	1130	96	928
652167	528838	33118	43586	18861	16950	19413	21378	3161	15407
683780	590064	18320	49619	6796	-80	18186	11347	2154	7253
1370153	1068058	35708	157081	37669	-402	72590	86770	12786	52813
388699	313684	38346	29047	4666	6326	1605	13194	2593	9061
7552635	6476381	20972	154023	19602	23802	101984	964598	776415	135838
3754685	2752109	241547	234661	111033	-1704	447396	226794	18329	125041
17112662	7941933	4171209	1423944	1338788	-389955	2624881	1214807	128512	782986
***	***	***	***	***	***	***	***	***	***
514152	421116	20020	41234	12205	571	19147	17915	2350	12217
5418507	4654603	148211	309248	179096	34795	125449	179135	23486	143534
1274614	1219417	1629	10040	4614	7189	22985	17655	3913	13380
1926519	1797092	8189	31792	26744	3227	65869	32521	3947	19976
3154664	2739813	76011	182486	87278	4059	82936	63059	12274	53354
7426509	5513208	367253	402040	315090	-3710	894149	375420	36301	187974
11299528	8202560	753658	820279	704458	40966	985646	411068	60728	222554
37979513	30451789	1662704	985798	548279	-6757	3120326	3401981	1154246	1295340
5174566	4035480	88565	341619	341210	4652	358795	211426	23048	146022
9432637	7542341	506857	427506	354560	4904	699592	343335	41321	210951
52463081	43987818	2447917	1368785	2193406	-906411	4226618	667749	124601	276703
3845631	2613765	287159	313328	268857	9553	403745	173180	23910	106749
1996357	1773472	3308	60669	44365	-3162	121537	38327	3167	13963
141151	105956	2073	14199	6957	731	15267	6680	753	5068
942182	920348	13029	120166	17107	42132	-19717	-10255	6382	13807
82194928	**78667081**	**107140**	**941740**	**282491**	**1837157**	**4793748**	**2868049**	**385910**	**1886612**
75482213	72848916	22095	684756	115808	1668761	4359069	2575306	151480	1865719
5137366	4619961	16851	156604	152939	31017	397043	36834	5610	-860
1575349	1198203	68195	100380	13744	137379	37636	255909	228820	21752

12-6 分行业规模以上国有控股工业企业主要经济指标(2022年)

单位：万元

项目	Item	企业单位个数（个）Number of Enterprises (unit)	#亏损企业 Loss-Suffering Enterprises	工业总产值（当年价格）Gross Output Value of Industry (at current year's prices)
合　计	**Total**	**664**	**124**	**148727303**
采矿业	**Mining**	**7**	**3**	**3044583**
石油和天然气开采业	Extraction of Petroleum and Natural Gas	2	2	***
黑色金属矿采选业	Mining and Processing of Ferrous Metal Ores	2		***
开采专业及辅助性活动	Mining and Support Service Activities	3	1	***
制造业	**Manufacturing**	**547**	**101**	**71313407**
农副食品加工业	Processing of Agricultural and Sideline Products	16	7	1068651
食品制造业	Manufacture of Foods	14	5	619524
酒、饮料和精制茶制造业	Manufacture of Wines, Beverage and Refined Tea	10	3	1297613
烟草制品业	Manufacture of Cigarettes and Tobacco	1		***
纺织业	Manufacture of Textile	2	1	***
纺织服装、服饰业	Manufacture of Textile Wearing Apparel and Ornament	5	2	49663
家具制造业	Manufacture of Furniture	2	1	***
造纸和纸制品业	Manufacture of Paper and Paper Products	3		***
印刷和记录媒介复制业	Printing, Reproduction of Recording Media	29	10	673333
文教、工美、体育和娱乐用品制造业	Manufacture of Articles for Culture, Education, Artwork, Sport and Entertainment Activities	4		45707
石油、煤炭及其他燃料加工业	Processing of Petroleum, Coal and Other Fuels	7	4	7254661
化学原料和化学制品制造业	Manufacture of Chemical Raw Materials and Chemical Products	24	1	1276132
医药制造业	Manufacture of Medicines	34	6	3627190
化学纤维制造业	Manufacture of Chemical Fibres	1		***
橡胶和塑料制品业	Manufacture of Rubber and Plastics Products	6		38424
非金属矿物制品业	Manufacture of Non-metallic Mineral Products	45	6	1950022
黑色金属冶炼和压延加工业	Smelting and Pressing of Ferrous Metals	3		***
有色金属冶炼和压延加工业	Smelting and Pressing of Non-ferrous Metals	6		1462910
金属制品业	Manufacture of Fabricated Metal Products	20	3	1254086
通用设备制造业	Manufacture of General-purpose Machinery	38	7	1251738
专用设备制造业	Manufacture of Special-purpose Machinery	48	7	2340889
汽车制造业	Manufacture of Motor Vehicles	39	9	26852986
铁路、船舶、航空航天和其他运输设备制造业	Manufacture of Railway, Ships, Aerospace and Other Transport Equipments	36	4	4324020
电气机械和器材制造业	Manufacture of Electrical Machinery and Equipment	20	6	1032828
计算机、通信和其他电子设备制造业	Manufacture of Computers, Communication Equipment and Other Electronic Equipment	80	13	8553024
仪器仪表制造业	Manufacture of Measuring Instruments and Meters	38	2	1143572
其他制造业	Other Manufacturing	5		2467699
废弃资源综合利用业	Waste Recycling and Recovery	5	1	68850
金属制品、机械和设备修理业	Repair of Fabricated Metal Products, Machinery and Equipment	6	3	763328
电力、热力、燃气及水生产和供应业	**Production and Supply of Electricity, Heating Power, Gas and Water**	**110**	**20**	**74369313**
电力、热力生产和供应业	Production and Supply of Electricity and Heating Power	72	12	72298827
燃气生产和供应业	Production and Supply of Gas	12	1	851544
水的生产和供应业	Production and Supply of Water	26	7	1218942

MAIN ECONOMIC INDICATORS OF STATE-HOLDING INDUSTRIAL ENTERPRISES ABOVE DESIGNATED SIZE BY SECTOR(2022)

(10000 yuan)

平均用工人数（人） Average Number of Employed Persons (person)	资产负债							
	资产总计 Total Assets	#流动资产合计 Total Current Assets	#存货 Inventories	#产成品 Finished Products	#应收账款 Accounts Receivable	#固定资产原价 Original Value of Fixed Assets	负债合计 Total Liabilities	#流动负债合计 Total Current Liabilities
346026	**461811983**	**142190368**	**17209882**	**5481330**	**32771628**	**156044597**	**196593694**	**134525066**
27310	**38471664**	**6988892**	**59889**	**12633**	**1163115**	**9843975**	**24720806**	**12574200**
***	***	***	***	***	***	***	***	***
***	***	***	***	***	***	***	***	***
***	***	***	***	***	***	***	***	***
239836	**131416375**	**81064681**	**16924658**	**5433630**	**21396948**	**34283516**	**70114501**	**61855446**
8030	2103931	1298303	539016	181966	108014	454151	1126360	760094
5813	1240577	455149	75066	44064	115716	272223	425032	304827
12002	4636374	3022104	303684	111366	37560	1111212	1543755	1243548
***	***	***	***	***	***	***	***	***
***	***	***	***	***	***	***	***	***
496	50971	39844	18378	8496	11705	11733	35348	33857
***	***	***	***	***	***	***	***	***
***	***	***	***	***	***	***	***	***
9317	1368693	904744	186279	62002	90752	1055466	397293	322616
554	231850	132959	73399	49075	14684	51756	158198	79865
9142	5779232	2454667	1446512	118764	166015	4498113	3112020	2547937
3653	2043005	1065143	276244	180746	279667	553704	780872	747881
16316	9982291	5162828	980327	281361	864744	1824411	1904695	1481804
***	***	***	***	***	***	***	***	***
738	109638	92242	17388	11783	10560	16307	21896	21105
11723	6065521	3575282	357827	194670	1174134	930286	3224724	2875138
***	***	***	***	***	***	***	***	***
1362	786244	524309	119888	41951	98701	92737	322066	284171
6367	2763551	2030698	356823	39418	123817	519582	1773343	1578087
9869	2842006	2035294	472746	80753	462572	500468	1796948	1699874
14083	8858968	5017640	1044544	345125	1354463	561171	4611259	4135483
39719	36259205	23510270	3168428	1871227	9869211	12103040	25068166	22760226
25260	10178251	7954131	2689503	384882	1588643	1866361	6344408	6001641
2854	1967508	1506704	163724	50052	469159	165943	1247954	1172504
34699	21214634	12615524	2662581	1066618	2979758	5343521	8655039	7424273
7353	2413186	1697828	363994	67856	446760	239822	1112313	1031418
3679	4581143	4144923	1179680	186556	850631	445584	3965584	3833662
443	100895	79085	2021	1083	39961	13130	80701	65201
13046	4436010	904412	231780	126	147860	584659	1465840	978826
78880	**291923943**	**54136795**	**225335**	**35066**	**10211564**	**111917107**	**101758386**	**60095421**
63139	277422003	50574507	216104	33203	8495999	101586025	94747077	56939601
1883	1347842	373872	2436	1493	35951	491674	557463	492970
13858	13154098	3188416	6796	371	1679615	9839408	6453846	2662850

12-6 续表

单位：万元

项 目	Item	资产负债 Assets and Liabilities #应付账款 Accounts Payable	所有者权益合计 Total Owner's Equity	#实收资本 Paid-up Capital
合 计	**Total**	**37473812**	**265235247**	**202442689**
采矿业	**Mining**	**1421055**	**13750858**	**6222845**
石油和天然气开采业	Extraction of Petroleum and Natural Gas	***	***	***
黑色金属矿采选业	Mining and Processing of Ferrous Metal Ores	***	***	***
开采专业及辅助性活动	Mining and Support Service Activities	***	***	***
制造业	**Manufacturing**	**25820776**	**61318832**	**25557997**
农副食品加工业	Processing of Agricultural and Sideline Products	69191	977551	439506
食品制造业	Manufacture of Foods	139680	815545	271220
酒、饮料和精制茶制造业	Manufacture of Wines, Beverage and Refined Tea	120167	3092619	540890
烟草制品业	Manufacture of Cigarettes and Tobacco	***	***	***
纺织业	Manufacture of Textile	***	***	***
纺织服装、服饰业	Manufacture of Textile Wearing Apparel and Ornament	12934	15623	49615
家具制造业	Manufacture of Furniture	***	***	***
造纸和纸制品业	Manufacture of Paper and Paper Products	***	***	***
印刷和记录媒介复制业	Printing, Reproduction of Recording Media	127997	971401	553100
文教、工美、体育和娱乐用品制造业	Manufacture of Articles for Culture, Education, Artwork, Sport and Entertainment Activities	49498	73651	137905
石油、煤炭及其他燃料加工业	Processing of Petroleum, Coal and Other Fuels	575424	2667213	1120281
化学原料和化学制品制造业	Manufacture of Chemical Raw Materials and Chemical Products	212599	1262133	489712
医药制造业	Manufacture of Medicines	368959	8077595	1020824
化学纤维制造业	Manufacture of Chemical Fibres	***	***	***
橡胶和塑料制品业	Manufacture of Rubber and Plastics Products	6820	87743	24556
非金属矿物制品业	Manufacture of Non-metallic Mineral Products	932990	2840797	998876
黑色金属冶炼和压延加工业	Smelting and Pressing of Ferrous Metals	***	***	***
有色金属冶炼和压延加工业	Smelting and Pressing of Non-ferrous Metals	107808	464178	82736
金属制品业	Manufacture of Fabricated Metal Products	372105	991196	521170
通用设备制造业	Manufacture of General-purpose Machinery	527020	1045058	631098
专用设备制造业	Manufacture of Special-purpose Machinery	1487806	4247708	1274098
汽车制造业	Manufacture of Motor Vehicles	12590147	11191039	7832081
铁路、船舶、航空航天和其他运输设备制造业	Manufacture of Railway, Ships, Aerospace and Other Transport Equipments	2202903	3849836	1327263
电气机械和器材制造业	Manufacture of Electrical Machinery and Equipment	518639	719554	447800
计算机、通信和其他电子设备制造业	Manufacture of Computers, Communication Equipment and Other Electronic Equipment	3563240	12559595	5853287
仪器仪表制造业	Manufacture of Measuring Instruments and Meters	393359	1300873	366012
其他制造业	Other Manufacturing	1046788	615559	267597
废弃资源综合利用业	Waste Recycling and Recovery	32044	20194	11222
金属制品、机械和设备修理业	Repair of Fabricated Metal Products, Machinery and Equipment	161321	2970170	878582
电力、热力、燃气及水生产和供应业	**Production and Supply of Electricity, Heating Power, Gas and Water**	**10231981**	**190165557**	**170661846**
电力、热力生产和供应业	Production and Supply of Electricity and Heating Power	9507426	182674926	164913195
燃气生产和供应业	Production and Supply of Gas	121278	790380	833606
水的生产和供应业	Production and Supply of Water	603277	6700251	4915045

12-6 Continued

(10000 yuan)

损益 Profits and Losses							应交税金合计 Total Tax Payable	#税金及附加 Tax and Surtax	#应交增值税 Value Added Tax Payable
营业收入 Business Income	营业成本 Business Cost	销售费用 Sales Expenses	管理费用 Management Expenses	研发费用 R&D Expenses	财务费用 Financial Expenses	利润总额 Total Profits			
160372871	**141463940**	**3036264**	**3982158**	**2356123**	**2174849**	**10284777**	**9123384**	**3057938**	**4204601**
5771582	**5494356**	**963**	**254090**	**82222**	**588315**	**87852**	**233590**	**41471**	**103371**
***	***	***	***	***	***	***	***	***	***
***	***	***	***	***	***	***	***	***	***
***	***	***	***	***	***	***	***	***	***
77724380	**62023423**	**2947556**	**2959409**	**2141759**	**-196435**	**5894119**	**6097709**	**2642621**	**2234367**
2778358	2585199	106042	53397	10210	13771	34965	29580	4571	18727
878699	710728	130542	35816	11481	1541	1131	26017	3797	15739
1336232	930662	99118	122393	20203	10915	150837	247891	196692	46955
***	***	***	***	***	***	***	***	***	***
***	***	***	***	***	***	***	***	***	***
86238	82403	1306	3712	615	669	-2790	1925	320	1600
***	***	***	***	***	***	***	***	***	***
***	***	***	***	***	***	***	***	***	***
791663	585306	12953	114315	22217	-2625	54363	63723	9923	37774
109841	87808	9434	10276	1354	1610	3956	6677	1298	4682
7470275	6402357	18153	150282	17708	23850	102398	963776	776235	135214
1547503	1197395	18574	102044	48462	625	181428	93958	7527	54610
2728349	1220094	481610	230968	191111	-177444	807080	298600	34798	165042
***	***	***	***	***	***	***	***	***	***
74559	52501	2716	9873	3417	-665	7384	3794	678	2616
2264977	1917806	44886	158096	92687	15988	74954	75878	12131	59969
***	***	***	***	***	***	***	***	***	***
1605972	1525444	4610	16294	14848	2162	47837	23113	2833	13766
1564789	1404463	9889	72518	49286	-5659	45802	27032	6524	19330
1473577	1245732	38137	105262	60633	6484	70811	69366	9993	50239
2508578	1992889	77533	166508	140239	26439	128300	70994	16506	40716
29843552	23264689	1479439	642446	367175	-38775	2964098	3155446	1127961	1141404
4331436	3542914	48021	230090	210668	-1928	299235	162908	17970	121044
1118728	999314	32098	37323	35066	2514	41260	39833	4414	33488
9208411	7294192	248782	381455	704138	-115492	627481	247638	47522	145033
1240465	913681	63402	96335	73674	807	118758	53725	7445	37351
1896707	1748949	2198	58160	38622	-3223	55732	11059	1902	3663
69520	48098	603	7267	3494	637	6792	3531	305	2681
793701	826794	4087	103915	11221	43117	-44866	-22179	5640	7942
76876910	**73946161**	**87745**	**768660**	**132141**	**1782969**	**4302807**	**2792085**	**373847**	**1866862**
74528183	72011444	12966	643820	109406	1658379	4269762	2515803	145768	1829418
882802	811305	8305	32239	11151	1187	1594	27122	1522	19438
1465925	1123413	66475	92600	11584	123403	31451	249160	226557	18006

12-7 分行业规模以上港澳台及外商投资工业企业主要经济指标(2022年)

单位：万元

项目	Item	企业单位个数(个) Number of Enterprises (unit)	#亏损企业 Loss-Suffering Enterprises	工业总产值(当年价格) Gross Output Value of Industry (at current year's prices)
合计	**Total**	**647**	**197**	**81760041**
采矿业	**Mining**	**1**		***
开采专业及辅助性活动	Mining and Support Service Activities	1		***
制造业	**Manufacturing**	**624**	**194**	**75769212**
农副食品加工业	Processing of Agricultural and Sideline Products	18	8	479354
食品制造业	Manufacture of Foods	47	17	2115236
酒、饮料和精制茶制造业	Manufacture of Wines, Beverage and Refined Tea	19	6	586235
纺织业	Manufacture of Textile	1	1	***
纺织服装、服饰业	Manufacture of Textile Wearing Apparel and Ornament	12	7	135809
家具制造业	Manufacture of Furniture	6	3	208549
造纸和纸制品业	Manufacture of Paper and Paper Products	8	1	482146
印刷和记录媒介复制业	Printing, Reproduction of Recording Media	11	2	133870
文教、工美、体育和娱乐用品制造业	Manufacture of Articles for Culture, Education, Artwork, Sport and Entertainment Activities	3		***
石油、煤炭及其他燃料加工业	Processing of Petroleum, Coal and Other Fuels	1	1	***
化学原料和化学制品制造业	Manufacture of Chemical Raw Materials and Chemical Products	29	7	834048
医药制造业	Manufacture of Medicines	47	11	7528678
橡胶和塑料制品业	Manufacture of Rubber and Plastics Products	13	5	163218
非金属矿物制品业	Manufacture of Non-metallic Mineral Products	7	2	103781
有色金属冶炼和压延加工业	Manufacture and Pressing of Non-ferrous Metals	2		***
金属制品业	Manufacture of Fabricated Metal Products	23	8	203210
通用设备制造业	Manufacture of General-purpose Machinery	53	12	4185164
专用设备制造业	Manufacture of Special-purpose Machinery	84	19	2589833
汽车制造业	Manufacture of Motor Vehicles	101	47	29809920
铁路、船舶、航空航天和其他运输设备制造业	Manufacture of Railway, Ships, Aerospace and Other Transport Equipments	2	1	***
电气机械和器材制造业	Manufacture of Electrical Machinery and Equipment	33	8	2337381
计算机、通信和其他电子设备制造业	Manufacture of Computers, Communication Equipment and Other Electronic Equipment	62	20	22287539
仪器仪表制造业	Manufacture of Measuring Instruments and Meters	32	5	607219
其他制造业	Other Manufacturing	2	1	***
废弃资源综合利用业	Waste Recycling and Recovery	2	1	***
金属制品、机械和设备修理业	Repair of Fabricated Metal Products, Machinery and Equipment	6	1	739564
电力、热力、燃气及水生产和供应业	**Production and Supply of Electricity, Heating Power, Gas and Water**	**22**	**3**	**5878882**
电力、热力生产和供应业	Production and Supply of Electricity and Heating Power	11		1544147
燃气生产和供应业	Production and Supply of Gas	5		4178624
水的生产和供应业	Production and Supply of Water	6	3	156111

MAIN ECONOMIC INDICATORS OF HONGKONG, MACAO, TAIWAN AND FOREIGN-INVESTED INDUSTRIAL ENTERPRISES ABOVE DESIGNATED SIZE BY SECTOR(2022)

(10000 yuan)

平均用工人数(人) Average Number of Employed Persons (person)	资产负债							
	资产总计 Total Assets	#流动资产合计 Total Current Assets	#存货 Inventories	#产成品 Finished Products	#应收账款 Accounts Receivable	#固定资产原价 Original Value of Fixed Assets	负债合计 Total Liabilities	#流动负债合计 Total Current Liabilities
245846	**136121031**	**93182945**	**15269200**	**6514851**	**20850007**	**36068635**	**74638170**	**67002552**
***	***	***	***	***	***	***	***	***
***	***	***	***	***	***	***	***	***
234394	**124082772**	**89837906**	**15141858**	**6483675**	**19977177**	**29961354**	**69679978**	**64378881**
3564	487833	324673	76909	12543	88867	194876	246850	185518
21616	3727416	2233808	197221	104013	559882	1171357	1868194	1653778
4653	906529	645095	76214	36374	229381	452161	748162	713557
***	***	***	***	***	***	***	***	***
3898	195159	163637	63651	18186	30915	41806	157645	156354
1202	541920	502010	180550	168753	39196	76836	606291	457592
1761	345914	217491	91864	16159	86516	238484	150131	145688
2158	208678	162101	26336	8092	21374	178189	55473	51882
***	***	***	***	***	***	***	***	***
***	***	***	***	***	***	***	***	***
6036	1841909	1492781	301839	114827	105406	453777	394224	362509
36542	15415046	11591327	2192723	1249655	1599302	1685812	4599785	3667314
1283	243769	201893	51945	15707	73603	99715	88179	86198
1927	146386	112763	26914	6542	34584	110282	70582	67480
***	***	***	***	***	***	***	***	***
2311	603681	373485	92250	27054	123307	104659	324094	231759
18498	5283224	4596851	1271887	509415	1061327	1187668	1892282	1735161
18097	7039245	4367577	578854	167208	838414	691704	3320217	2910863
45040	30397746	20826933	3516166	2026320	9469587	12291609	21064249	19467815
***	***	***	***	***	***	***	***	***
8704	2821255	2241845	375735	86242	497039	385746	1532111	1394005
39816	51441507	38057357	5543940	1877695	4630571	9942763	31216882	29856670
4160	1223039	913710	205676	21374	278013	120026	488994	481566
***	***	***	***	***	***	***	***	***
***	***	***	***	***	***	***	***	***
11715	818178	499927	228864	2622	124002	453653	631289	546500
11144	**11183273**	**2998357**	**110120**	**27632**	**585694**	**6087727**	**4438928**	**2471898**
2160	2106262	700537	40248	26723	341864	2790101	979016	592984
8031	8539333	2187034	69090	909	196923	3204679	3097996	1816178
953	537678	110787	782		46907	92947	361916	62737

12-7 续表

单位：万元

项　目	Item	资产负债 Assets and Liabilities #应付账款 Accounts Payable	所有者权益合计 Total Owner's Equity	#实收资本 Paid-up Capital
合 计	**Total**	**25621509**	**61490332**	**21667842**
采矿业	**Mining**	***	***	***
开采专业及辅助性活动	Mining and Support Service Activities	***	***	***
制造业	**Manufacturing**	**24839823**	**54410265**	**19997398**
农副食品加工业	Processing of Agricultural and Sideline Products	56020	240983	146410
食品制造业	Manufacture of Foods	645821	1859222	763871
酒、饮料和精制茶制造业	Manufacture of Wines, Beverage and Refined Tea	175578	166044	380728
纺织业	Manufacture of Textile	***	***	***
纺织服装、服饰业	Manufacture of Textile Wearing Apparel and Ornament	19774	37514	30079
家具制造业	Manufacture of Furniture	48635	-64371	32099
造纸和纸制品业	Manufacture of Paper and Paper Products	62585	195783	72921
印刷和记录媒介复制业	Printing, Reproduction of Recording Media	22764	153205	99832
文教、工美、体育和娱乐用品制造业	Manufacture of Articles for Culture, Education, Artwork, Sport and Entertainment Activities	***	***	***
石油、煤炭及其他燃料加工业	Processing of Petroleum, Coal and Other Fuels	***	***	***
化学原料和化学制品制造业	Manufacture of Chemical Raw Materials and Chemical Products	160425	1447685	319901
医药制造业	Manufacture of Medicines	1102602	10815261	1042583
橡胶和塑料制品业	Manufacture of Rubber and Plastics Products	65151	155590	65317
非金属矿物制品业	Manufacture of Non-metallic Mineral Products	36846	75804	53343
有色金属冶炼和压延加工业	Smelting and Pressing of Non-ferrous Metals	***	***	***
金属制品业	Manufacture of Fabricated Metal Products	53108	279587	165765
通用设备制造业	Manufacture of General-purpose Machinery	1083608	3390941	787044
专用设备制造业	Manufacture of Special-purpose Machinery	662899	3719028	818284
汽车制造业	Manufacture of Motor Vehicles	12621956	9334485	6204428
铁路、船舶、航空航天和其他运输设备制造业	Manufacture of Railway, Ships, Aerospace and Other Transport Equipments	***	***	***
电气机械和器材制造业	Manufacture of Electrical Machinery and Equipment	561118	1287954	905624
计算机、通信和其他电子设备制造业	Manufacture of Computers, Communication Equipment and Other Electronic Equipment	7071423	20224625	7609046
仪器仪表制造业	Manufacture of Measuring Instruments and Meters	180384	734045	177079
其他制造业	Other Manufacturing	***	***	***
废弃资源综合利用业	Waste Recycling and Recovery	***	***	***
金属制品、机械和设备修理业	Repair of Fabricated Metal Products, Machinery and Equipment	171730	186890	232484
电力、热力、燃气及水生产和供应业	**Production and Supply of Electricity, Heating Power, Gas and Water**	**765573**	**6744345**	**1501580**
电力、热力生产和供应业	Production and Supply of Electricity and Heating Power	328068	1127246	697668
燃气生产和供应业	Production and Supply of Gas	409242	5441337	633145
水的生产和供应业	Production and Supply of Water	28262	175762	170767

12-7 Continued

(10000 yuan)

损 益 Profits and Losses							应交税金合计 Total Tax Payable		
营业收入 Business Income	营业成本 Business Cost	销售费用 Sales Expenses	管理费用 Management Expenses	研发费用 R&D Expenses	财务费用 Financial Expenses	利润总额 Total Profits		#税金及附加 Tax and Surtax	#应交增值税 Value Added Tax Payable
104332329	**82164181**	**7453474**	**3519038**	**2270757**	**-1031747**	**9889631**	**5232782**	**1312773**	**2257417**
***	***	***	***	***	***	***	***	***	***
***	***	***	***	***	***	***	***	***	***
98150508	**76712314**	**7442250**	**3352259**	**2116458**	**-1092267**	**9294805**	**5081578**	**1290376**	**2193249**
629401	559207	34708	29721	1513	1534	1880	12769	1698	9067
4275867	2982026	904734	224337	25972	-8722	175531	232127	23288	139961
779214	562924	107296	46016	7511	390	61868	52108	9283	27805
***	***	***	***	***	***	***	***	***	***
188070	151903	20168	10430	4507	1814	-2187	2472	679	2902
216919	168168	6847	15720	8625	10184	6387	9558	1201	6533
558619	484124	15869	38671	3840	-1525	16308	8116	1507	4747
159292	125933	5784	15393	4540	-1514	7551	9011	1100	5978
***	***	***	***	***	***	***	***	***	***
***	***	***	***	***	***	***	***	***	***
1185363	733883	155095	67857	21199	-7839	234794	106013	6970	49002
8256860	4334462	2074139	817710	525508	-189954	613889	455984	49158	323881
189740	151533	7520	18329	2898	-1642	7091	6161	885	2915
121558	97943	4627	11003	2544	288	3865	7698	1087	5862
***	***	***	***	***	***	***	***	***	***
398814	337469	26994	24390	6787	3739	841	6856	1251	5372
4522453	3249100	212753	186805	147316	-23960	729883	254399	19508	98721
3102130	2105005	228905	278558	182456	16820	367945	139679	16923	69245
31145654	24257473	1570628	640382	321893	-78825	3158403	3198772	1082613	1198771
***	***	***	***	***	***	***	***	***	***
2692292	1958622	148603	149517	68521	-1169	380635	153626	12755	69038
37875605	32945004	1848621	611259	732726	-832576	3467808	369906	50297	138307
821882	572461	59359	63152	30831	6726	107929	39075	4023	17486
***	***	***	***	***	***	***	***	***	***
***	***	***	***	***	***	***	***	***	***
765611	784445	7903	87308	9073	12735	-133704	-23099	4249	3380
6040135	**5329433**	**7999**	**162084**	**152549**	**55067**	**590511**	**149287**	**22231**	**63421**
1647334	1423527	462	23338	10108	13348	183541	129089	15808	77272
4232954	3782124	7537	122348	142288	29560	403000	12345	4128	-18736
159847	123782		16399	153	12158	3970	7853	2295	4886

12-8 分行业规模以上大中型工业企业主要经济指标(2022年)

单位：万元

项目	Item	企业单位个数(个) Number of Enterprises (unit)	#亏损企业 Loss-Suffering Enterprises	工业总产值(当年价格) Gross Output Value of Industry (at current year's prices)
合计	**Total**	**525**	**107**	**196496370**
采矿业	**Mining**	**6**	**2**	**2994146**
石油和天然气开采业	Extraction of Petroleum and Natural Gas	1	1	***
黑色金属矿采选业	Mining and Processing of Ferrous Metal Ores	1		***
开采专业及辅助性活动	Mining and Support Service Activities	4	1	1746496
制造业	**Manufacturing**	**483**	**102**	**117487004**
农副食品加工业	Processing of Agricultural and Sideline Products	15	6	1248302
食品制造业	Manufacture of Foods	29	10	2066566
酒、饮料和精制茶制造业	Manufacture of Wines, Beverage and Refined Tea	8		1785587
烟草制品业	Manufacture of Cigarettes and Tobacco	1		***
纺织业	Manufacture of Textile	1		***
纺织服装、服饰业	Manufacture of Textile Wearing Apparel and Ornament	11	5	393848
家具制造业	Manufacture of Furniture	5	1	293228
造纸和纸制品业	Manufacture of Paper and Paper Products	3		***
印刷和记录媒介复制业	Printing, Reproduction of Recording Media	11	4	639840
文教、工美、体育和娱乐用品制造业	Manufacture of Articles for Culture, Education, Artwork, Sport and Entertainment Activities	1		***
石油、煤炭及其他燃料加工业	Processing of Petroleum, Coal and Other Fuels	3	2	***
化学原料和化学制品制造业	Manufacture of Chemical Raw Materials and Chemical Products	8	2	876829
医药制造业	Manufacture of Medicines	68	15	14291523
化学纤维制造业	Manufacture of Chemical Fibres	1		***
橡胶和塑料制品业	Manufacture of Rubber and Plastics Products	1		***
非金属矿物制品业	Manufacture of Non-metallic Mineral Products	18	3	2018328
黑色金属冶炼和压延加工业	Smelting and Pressing of Ferrous Metals	1		***
有色金属冶炼和压延加工业	Smelting and Pressing of Non-ferrous Metals	3		***
金属制品业	Manufacture of Fabricated Metal Products	6		1177670
通用设备制造业	Manufacture of General-purpose Machinery	29	4	4664600
专用设备制造业	Manufacture of Special-purpose Machinery	57	7	6217957
汽车制造业	Manufacture of Motor Vehicles	35	14	30400304
铁路、船舶、航空航天和其他运输设备制造业	Manufacture of Railway, Ships, Aerospace and Other Transport Equipments	23	2	3970097
电气机械和器材制造业	Manufacture of Electrical Machinery and Equipment	30	6	4795338
计算机、通信和其他电子设备制造业	Manufacture of Computers, Communication Equipment and Other Electronic Equipment	84	20	28408476
仪器仪表制造业	Manufacture of Measuring Instruments and Meters	23		1410802
其他制造业	Other Manufacturing	5		2467699
金属制品、机械和设备修理业	Repair of Fabricated Metal Products, Machinery and Equipment	3	1	***
电力、热力、燃气及水生产和供应业	**Production and Supply of Electricity, Heating Power, Gas and Water**	**36**	**3**	**76015220**
电力、热力生产和供应业	Production and Supply of Electricity and Heating Power	26	2	70583802
燃气生产和供应业	Production and Supply of Gas	2		***
水的生产和供应业	Production and Supply of Water	8	1	1093876

MAIN ECONOMIC INDICATORS OF LOCAL MEDIUM AND LARGE-SIZED INDUSTRIAL ENTERPRISES ABOVE DESIGNATED SIZE BY SECTOR(2022)

(10000 yuan)

平均用工人数（人） Average Number of Employed Persons (person)	资产负债 资产总计 Total Assets	#流动资产合计 Total Current Assets	#存货 Inventories	#产成品 Finished Products	#应收账款 Accounts Receivable	#固定资产原价 Original Value of Fixed Assets	负债合计 Total Liabilities	#流动负债合计 Total Current Liabilities
551992	**572999143**	**216819581**	**27246514**	**9349376**	**43775512**	**173378767**	**251176875**	**182196754**
27331	**38140331**	**6822585**	**77112**	**16177**	**1443071**	**9857664**	**24878530**	**12447087**
***	***	***	***	***	***	***	***	***
***	***	***	***	***	***	***	***	***
14915	4552039	1871791	53695	4135	600176	2919353	1934156	1384215
444646	**239838217**	**155290615**	**26925925**	**9330748**	**32284212**	**52088502**	**124428925**	**109638355**
9885	3654193	1640126	549035	163072	104720	610567	1750625	1287743
24820	3295733	1944602	197185	102598	540457	1113644	1796670	1627498
15033	5595995	3502896	300752	118648	124139	1374252	2171811	1845285
***	***	***	***	***	***	***	***	***
***	***	***	***	***	***	***	***	***
12365	930742	763272	223789	164001	100995	145889	376626	347017
2565	539967	201471	27507	5936	58600	126017	255626	165650
***	***	***	***	***	***	***	***	***
7553	1238097	765886	147923	43405	101360	923463	342691	295657
***	***	***	***	***	***	***	***	***
***	***	***	***	***	***	***	***	***
6654	2440907	1514225	168868	107807	306824	325438	775712	704571
70102	30950198	19647925	3351711	1599219	2999264	4381204	7808201	6397244
***	***	***	***	***	***	***	***	***
***	***	***	***	***	***	***	***	***
13107	5557011	3282866	210391	87721	1130481	751690	2832444	2538319
***	***	***	***	***	***	***	***	***
***	***	***	***	***	***	***	***	***
5490	3680255	2451461	300392	14939	137120	489101	2231856	2018612
25070	8192799	6038845	1573011	671286	1289867	1503221	3328985	3168700
35664	20172927	11470354	1636564	542988	2484759	1193209	9805243	7946398
52463	39946788	25920889	3680615	2177526	10667427	13276355	27295438	24574201
24424	9690814	7637017	2573188	333767	1480996	1785884	5906933	5627638
20668	8854383	6936262	736715	175595	1536650	778762	5307157	4889688
76352	74717755	50367005	7663251	2549868	7249875	16231868	41452363	36974445
10650	3607544	2410809	439969	87227	631320	316066	1195975	1124546
3679	4581143	4144923	1179680	186556	850631	445584	3965584	3833662
***	***	***	***	***	***	***	***	***
80015	**295020595**	**54706381**	**243478**	**2450**	**10048230**	**111432601**	**101869420**	**60111311**
59825	274079050	49546937	168555	1230	8208865	98687537	92652466	55731129
***	***	***	***	***	***	***	***	***
12046	12331386	2897998	6009	369	1635976	9550273	6001996	2446038

12-8 续表

单位：万元

项　目	Item	资产负债 Assets and Liabilities #应付账款 Accounts Payable	所有者权益合计 Total Owner's Equity	#实收资本 Paid-up Capital
合　计	**Total**	**48122058**	**321822268**	**212771558**
采矿业	**Mining**	**1301800**	**13261801**	**6258686**
石油和天然气开采业	Extraction of Petroleum and Natural Gas	***	***	***
黑色金属矿采选业	Mining and Processing of Ferrous Metal Ores	***	***	***
开采专业及辅助性活动	Mining and Support Service Activities	759618	2617883	3066322
制造业	**Manufacturing**	**36889811**	**115409291**	**37339854**
农副食品加工业	Processing of Agricultural and Sideline Products	94497	1903568	810181
食品制造业	Manufacture of Foods	648319	1499062	631575
酒、饮料和精制茶制造业	Manufacture of Wines, Beverage and Refined Tea	211131	3424183	609815
烟草制品业	Manufacture of Cigarettes and Tobacco	***	***	***
纺织业	Manufacture of Textile	***	***	***
纺织服装、服饰业	Manufacture of Textile Wearing Apparel and Ornament	46636	554116	75388
家具制造业	Manufacture of Furniture	59446	284340	71425
造纸和纸制品业	Manufacture of Paper and Paper Products	***	***	***
印刷和记录媒介复制业	Printing, Reproduction of Recording Media	112178	895405	451535
文教、工美、体育和娱乐用品制造业	Manufacture of Articles for Culture, Education, Artwork, Sport and Entertainment Activities	***	***	***
石油、煤炭及其他燃料加工业	Processing of Petroleum, Coal and Other Fuels	***	***	***
化学原料和化学制品制造业	Manufacture of Chemical Raw Materials and Chemical Products	189598	1665194	282206
医药制造业	Manufacture of Medicines	1715690	23141997	2572875
化学纤维制造业	Manufacture of Chemical Fibres	***	***	***
橡胶和塑料制品业	Manufacture of Rubber and Plastics Products	***	***	***
非金属矿物制品业	Manufacture of Non-metallic Mineral Products	891773	2724567	794660
黑色金属冶炼和压延加工业	Manufacture and Pressing of Ferrous Metals	***	***	***
有色金属冶炼和压延加工业	Manufacture and Pressing of Non-ferrous Metals	***	***	***
金属制品业	Manufacture of Fabricated Metal Products	359420	1448399	518190
通用设备制造业	Manufacture of General-purpose Machinery	1345150	4863815	1191003
专用设备制造业	Manufacture of Special-purpose Machinery	2054237	10367685	2439065
汽车制造业	Manufacture of Motor Vehicles	13617463	12651351	8309474
铁路、船舶、航空航天和其他运输设备制造业	Manufacture of Railway, Ships, Aerospace and Other Transport Equipments	1949513	3783881	1062870
电气机械和器材制造业	Manufacture of Electrical Machinery and Equipment	1526957	3547226	954209
计算机、通信和其他电子设备制造业	Manufacture of Computers, Communication Equipment and Other Electronic Equipment	9634896	33265391	13367948
仪器仪表制造业	Manufacture of Measuring Instruments and Meters	353551	2411569	537343
其他制造业	Other Manufacturing	1046788	615559	267597
金属制品、机械和设备修理业	Repair of Fabricated Metal Products, Machinery and Equipment	***	***	***
电力、热力、燃气及水生产和供应业	**Production and Supply of Electricity, Heating Power, Gas and Water**	**9930447**	**193151176**	**169173018**
电力、热力生产和供应业	Production and Supply of Electricity and Heating Power	8981114	181426585	163895344
燃气生产和供应业	Production and Supply of Gas	***	***	***
水的生产和供应业	Production and Supply of Water	505269	6329390	4668285

12-8 Continued

(10000 yuan)

损益 Profits and Losses							应交税金合计 Total Tax Payable		
营业收入 Business Income	营业成本 Business Cost	销售费用 Sales Expenses	管理费用 Management Expenses	研发费用 R&D Expenses	财务费用 Financial Expenses	利润总额 Total Profits		#税金及附加 Tax and Surtax	#应交增值税 Value Added Tax Payable
225867969	**190028767**	**10223757**	**6527774**	**5070787**	**1092723**	**17198404**	**10660461**	**3228087**	**4959605**
5852655	**5570404**	**3820**	**242833**	**78529**	**584646**	**107813**	**193091**	**37886**	**104147**
***	***	***	***	***	***	***	***	***	***
***	***	***	***	***	***	***	***	***	***
1781950	1659716	3226	59008	45839	-20943	49311	25048	7474	2787
141642116	**109139424**	**10143127**	**5507298**	**4732187**	**-1247968**	**12609694**	**7865781**	**2838522**	**3128347**
2812959	2556188	117882	103030	22531	14443	77474	27899	5133	16611
4182300	2953773	850288	194929	30478	-8305	173882	221951	21634	131012
2024061	1512789	211736	132606	23681	14916	153331	264347	193052	63926
***	***	***	***	***	***	***	***	***	***
***	***	***	***	***	***	***	***	***	***
558983	291560	152758	52893	19899	1232	39567	36694	4347	26154
320186	249957	12335	21484	13630	5612	23883	14447	2114	10218
***	***	***	***	***	***	***	***	***	***
739964	565296	14427	80463	20405	552	56368	54815	8455	32337
***	***	***	***	***	***	***	***	***	***
***	***	***	***	***	***	***	***	***	***
1097867	684741	123360	95503	39369	-3933	155328	82734	7747	53875
13800058	6208680	3557883	1128546	1117442	-400813	2168193	991273	106617	643660
***	***	***	***	***	***	***	***	***	***
***	***	***	***	***	***	***	***	***	***
2288925	1933670	36023	154804	83789	7274	105945	63144	9926	46669
***	***	***	***	***	***	***	***	***	***
***	***	***	***	***	***	***	***	***	***
1571077	1409362	22042	82945	39299	-4960	47749	25078	6663	17762
5082713	3722234	219589	216977	185207	-7541	779493	284715	25283	122901
6740179	4961071	445230	452067	358681	19745	684825	231236	36736	112537
33641075	26534100	1602133	785855	477344	-31531	3074508	3291863	1139023	1222268
3947451	3180815	47238	223523	233837	569	254661	140237	16533	102506
5770910	4526003	348358	248426	195393	-6423	537179	220932	26428	117909
42779688	35965787	2204420	1004833	1668880	-913151	3725405	437022	90694	135877
1673051	1133960	124381	127479	103993	5166	256639	72439	10128	45391
1896707	1748949	2198	58160	38622	-3223	55732	11059	1902	3663
***	***	***	***	***	***	***	***	***	***
78373198	**75318940**	**76810**	**777643**	**260070**	**1756046**	**4480897**	**2601589**	**351680**	**1727111**
72695627	70408342	6596	576553	103959	1614577	4054283	2347784	130476	1724252
***	***	***	***	***	***	***	***	***	***
1311968	997037	63468	79814	8764	111995	27186	238311	217104	17533

12-9 规模以上工业企业主要效益指标(2022年)

单位：%

项　目	Item	总资产贡献率 Contribution Rate of Total Assets	资产保值增值率 Rate of Assets Preservation and Appreciation
合　计	**Total**	**4.80**	**105.88**
按行业分	**By Sector**		
采矿业	Mining	2.10	102.55
制造业	Manufacturing	6.96	109.73
电力、热力、燃气及水生产和供应业	Production and Supply of Electricity, Heating, Gas and Water	2.89	103.23
按轻重工业分	**By light and heavy industries**		
轻工业	Light Industry	8.51	97.34
重工业	Heavy Industry	4.35	107.23
按规模分	**By Size**		
大　型	Large-sized	4.38	103.75
中　型	Medium-sized	6.60	111.87
小　型	Small-sized	5.23	112.98
微　型	Micro-sized	3.22	90.73
按登记注册类型分	**By Registration Type**		
内资企业	Domestially-Invested Enterprises	3.55	104.45
国有企业	State-owned Enterprises	0.71	82.50
集体企业	Collectively-owned Enterprises	6.54	101.18
股份合作企业	Joint-equity Cooperative Enterprises	5.74	106.79
有限责任公司	Limited Liability Corporations	3.19	103.23
股份有限公司	Corporations Limited by Shares	5.34	108.66
私营企业	Private Enterprises	4.82	112.16
港澳台商投资企业	Hong Kong, Macao and Taiwan-invested Enterprises	5.93	115.29
港澳台合资经营	Joint Ventures	6.46	130.75
港澳台合作经营	Cooperatives	***	***
港澳台商独资企业	Solely-funded Enterprises	5.65	169.44
港澳台商投资股份有限公司	Corporations Limited by Shares	7.15	155.99
其他港澳台投资	Other Hong Kong, Macao and Taiwan-invested Enterprises	***	***
外商投资企业	Foreign-invested Enterprises	11.79	112.23
#中外合资经营	Joint Ventures	16.26	104.30
中外合作经营	Cooperatives	13.80	69.71
外资(独资)企业	Solely-funded Enterprises	7.95	111.59
外商投资股份有限公司	Corporations Limited by Shares	7.12	141.07
按控股类型分	**By holding types**		
#国有控股	State-holding Enterprises	4.29	101.86

MAIN INDICATORS OF ECONOMIC BENEFITS OF INDUSTRIAL ENTERPRISES ABOVE DESIGNATED SIZE (2022)

(%)

资产负债率 Assets-Liabilities Ratio	流动资产周转率(次) Turnover of Current Assets (times)	收入利润率 Income-Profit Margin	每百元营业收入成本费用(元) Cost Expense of Per 100 Yuan of Main Business Income (yuan)	人均营业收入(元) Sales Revenue Per Capita (yuan)
44.40	**1.01**	**7.21**	**94.42**	**3391568**
64.14	0.81	1.58	110.83	2126636
50.76	0.90	7.99	91.66	2712815
35.15	1.43	5.83	99.56	8884497
36.49	0.86	10.26	89.46	1544934
45.38	1.04	6.70	95.25	4241630
44.00	1.13	6.92	95.19	5409117
42.99	0.79	10.60	90.38	2004918
47.64	0.88	5.66	94.79	1883223
63.81	1.32	0.42	100.44	5017822
41.69	0.95	5.84	96.81	3024816
83.78	0.37	2.12	98.12	1874289
48.96	0.70	7.62	98.33	658775
61.77	1.02	3.28	96.95	705977
41.63	1.09	5.48	98.00	3960204
37.61	0.74	6.91	92.94	2405768
42.63	0.70	7.38	93.35	1367362
45.15	1.26	6.59	95.69	7745125
39.95	0.90	10.12	89.83	1885906
***	***	***	***	***
47.60	1.40	5.69	96.81	10791947
34.54	0.64	16.40	85.27	4544183
***	***	***	***	***
60.47	1.04	11.47	86.84	3234313
60.47	1.41	10.87	86.04	4312978
42.32	1.50	6.61	93.20	873513
68.51	0.75	11.66	88.44	2645359
21.47	0.61	19.45	84.82	1251386
42.57	1.13	6.41	95.41	4634706

12-10 规模以上工业企业主要工业产品生产能力
PRODUCTION CAPACITY OF MAIN INDUSTRIAL PRODUCTS IN INDUSTRIAL ENTERPRISES ABOVE DESIGNATED SIZE

主要工业产品名称		Name of Main Industrial Products		2022	2021
原油加工能力	(万吨)	Crude Oil Processing Capacity	(10000 tons)	1100.0	1101.0
硅酸盐水泥熟料	(万吨)	Portland Cement Chamotte	(10000 tons)	305.0	305.0
发电设备容量总计	(万千瓦)	Total Capacity of Power Generation Equipment	(10000 kW)	1223.3	1225.5
#火电设备容量		Capacity of Thermal Power Equipment		1106.6	1109.8
水电设备容量		Capacity of Hydropower Equipment		80.0	80.0
风电设备容量		Capacity of Wind Power Equipment		0.4	0.4
卷　烟	(亿支)	Cigarette	(100 million units)	286.0	287.8
水　泥	(万吨)	Cement	(10000 tons)	400.0	400.0
钢　材	(万吨)	Rolled Steel	(10000 tons)	170.3	171.4
金属切削机床	(台)	Metal-Cutting Machine Tools	(unit)	12082	16878
汽　车	(万辆)	Motor Vehicles	(10000 units)	207.2	195.0
#基本型乘用车(轿车)		Basic-type Passenger Vehicles (Sedans)		190.2	181.2
移动通信手持机(手机)	(万台)	Mobile Communication Handsets (Mobile Phones)	(10000 units)	192.8	192.8
微型计算机设备	(万台)	Micro-computers	(10000 units)	1150.0	750.0

12-11 规模以上工业主要产品产量
OUTPUT OF MAIN INDUSTRIAL PRODUCTS ABOVE DESIGNATED SIZE

工业产品名称		Name of Main Industrial Product		2022	2021
鲜、冷藏肉	(万吨)	Fresh, Chilled Meat	(10000 tons)	46.2	54.5
乳制品	(万吨)	Dairy Products	(10000 tons)	48.9	54.2
饮料酒	(万千升)	Alcoholic Beverage	(10000 kl)	129.1	121.9
中成药	(万吨)	Finished Traditional Chinese Herbal Medicines	(10000 tons)	4.4	3.8
家 具	(万件)	Furniture	(10000 units)	333.5	402.0
沥青和改性沥青防水卷材	(万平方米)	Asphalt and Modified Asphalt Waterproof Roll Materials	(10000 sq.m)	3.3	6.1
纤维增强塑料制品	(万吨)	Fiber-reinforced Plastic Products	(10000 tons)	0.7	1.1
耐火材料制品	(万吨)	Products Made from Fire-resistant Materials	(10000 tons)	25.8	31.7
冷轧薄宽钢带	(万吨)	Cold-rolled Thin Broad Steel Bands	(10000 tons)	91.1	108.5
钢 材	(万吨)	Rolled Steel	(10000 tons)	184.3	203.4
单一稀土金属	(千克)	Single Rare Earth Metals	(kg)	915006	1122585
发动机	(万千瓦)	Engines	(10000 kW)	14261.5	18362.1
气动元件	(万件)	Pneumatic Components	(10000 units)	50403.4	36934.5
数控金属切削机床	(台)	Digital Metal Cutting Tools	(unit)	5072	6184
机床数控装置	(套)	CNC Units of Lathe	(unit)	11226	13674
工业电炉	(台)	Industrial Electric Cookers	(unit)	960	652
环境污染防治专用设备	(台套)	Special Equipment for Prevention and Control of Environmental Pollution	(set)	2139	3912
汽 车	(万辆)	Automobiles	(10000 units)	87.1	135.5
#基本型成用车(轿车)		Including: Basic-type Passenger Vehicles (Sedans)		46.5	52.2
运动型多用途乘用车(SUV)		Sport Utility Vehicles (SUV)		35.1	31.0
载货汽车		Freight Trucks		4.7	52.0
改装汽车	(万辆)	Refitted Automobiles	(10000 units)	1.2	1.1
风力发电机组	(万千瓦)	Wind Power Generator Units	(10000 kW)	643.3	441.9
锂离子电池	(万只)	Lithiums Ion Batteries	(10000 units)	1.0	0.6
移动通信手持机(手机)	(万台)	Mobile Communication Handsets (Mobile Phones)	(10000 units)	9429.5	11624.5
微型计算机设备	(万台)	Micro-computer Equipment	(10000 units)	858.6	647.3
服务器	(台)	Servers	(unit)	27848	20136
液晶显示模组	(万套)	Liquid Crystal Display Modules	(10000 sets)	14680.2	12034.2
显示器	(万台)	Display Devices	(10000 units)	233.6	518.2
集成电路	(亿块)	Integrated Circuits	(100 million pieces)	217.9	207.7
彩色电视机	(万台)	Color TV Sets	(10000 units)	391.9	410.2
交流电动机	(万千瓦)	Alternator	(10000 kW)	13.0	12.3

注：根据统计制度规定，自2022年起，汽车整车制造行业产业活动单位视同法人单位按经营地在地原则进行统计，北京在京外设立的汽车整车制造分厂按照制度规定在当地纳统。

Note:According to the statistical system, since 2022, the industrial activity units in the sector of manufacture of finished automobiles shall be deemed as legal entities and shall be subject to statistics in accordance with the principle of regional statistics of the business place,the finished automobile manufacturing branches set up outside of Beijing shall be included in local statistics according to the rules and regulations.

12-12 规模以上高技术制造业主要经济指标(2022年)
MAIN ECONOMIC INDICATORS OF HIGH-TECH MANUFACTURING ENTERPRISES ABOVE DESIGNATED SIZE (2022)

单位：亿元 (100 million yuan)

项　　目	Item	工业总产值 Gross Output Value of Industry	营业收入 Business Income	利润总额 Total Profits	应交税金 Tax Payable
合　　计	**Total**	**6386.7**	**8141.3**	**787.4**	**233.1**
按登记注册类型分	**By Registration Type**				
内资企业	Domestically-Invested Enterprises	3093.2	3170.5	354.5	138.4
国有企业	State-owned Enterprises	78.1	79.9	2.4	1.1
集体企业	Collectively-owned Enterprises	2.4	2.4	0.3	0.1
股份合作企业	Joint-equity Cooperative Enterprises	2.2	2.2	0.1	0.1
有限责任公司	Limited Liability Corporations	1865.6	1829.2	164.4	67.0
股份有限公司	Corporations Limited by Shares	581.5	625.4	112.0	41.3
私营企业	Private Enterprises	563.4	631.4	75.4	28.8
其他企业	Others				
港澳台商投资企业	Hong Kong, Macao and Taiwan-invested Enterprises	2030.2	3455.7	216.7	33.3
外商投资企业	Foreign-invested Enterprises	1263.3	1515.2	216.2	61.4
按高技术领域分	**By Field of High Technology**				
医药制造业	Manufacture of Medicines	1748.8	1711.3	262.5	121.5
航空、航天器及设备制造业	Manufacture of Aircrafts and Spacecrafts	417.6	405.9	1.8	6.4
电子及通信设备制造业	Manufacture of Electronic Equipment and Communication Equipment	3297.4	4805.1	394.1	55.6
计算机及办公设备制造业	Manufacture of Computers and Office Equipments	299.2	514.3	29.3	10.2
医疗仪器设备及仪器仪表制造业	Manufacture of Medical Equipments and Meters	623.6	704.6	99.8	39.4
信息化学品制造业	Information Chemical Product Manufacturing				

12-13 规模以上工业战略性新兴产业总产值
TOTAL OUTPUT VALUE OF STRATEGIC EMERGING INDUSTRIES AMONG INDUSTRIAL ENTERPRISES ABOVE DESIGNATED SIZE

单位：亿元 (100 million yuan)

项　　目	Item	2022	2021
合　　计	**Total**	**7612.7**	**9596.2**
节能环保产业	Energy Conservation and Environmental Protection Industry	442.3	410.9
新一代信息技术产业	New Generation IT Industry	3020.7	3204.1
生物产业	Bioindustry	2026.4	4189.0
高端装备制造业	High-end Equipment Manufacturing	1002.3	869.9
新能源产业	New Energy Industry	341.5	276.8
新材料产业	New Material Industry	502.2	459.0
新能源汽车产业	New Energy Automobiles	184.4	77.9
数字创意产业	Digital Creative Industry	92.9	108.5

主要统计指标解释

工业 指从事自然资源的开采，对采掘品和农产品进行加工和再加工的物质生产部门。具体包括：(1) 对自然资源的开采，如采矿、晒盐、森林采伐等（但不包括禽兽捕猎和水产捕捞）；(2) 对农副产品的加工、再加工，如粮油加工、食品加工、扎花、纺织、制革等；(3) 对采掘品的加工、再加工，如炼铁、炼钢、化工生产、石油加工、机器制造、木材加工等，以及电力、自来水、煤气的生产和供应等；(4) 对工业品的修理、翻新，如机器设备的修理。

轻工业 指主要提供生活消费品和制作手工工具的工业。按其所使用的原料不同，可分为两大类：(1) 以农业为原料的轻工业，是指直接或间接以农产品为基本原料的轻工业。主要包括食品制造、饮料制造、烟草加工、纺织、缝纫、皮革和毛皮制作、造纸以及印刷等工业；(2) 以非农产品为原料的轻工业，是指以工业品为原料的轻工业。主要包括文教体育用品、化学药品制造、合成纤维制造、日用化学制品、日用玻璃制品、日用金属制品、手工工具制造、医疗器械制造、文化和办公用机械制造等工业。

重工业 是指为国民经济各部门提供物质技术基础的主要生产资料的工业。按其生产性质和产品用途，可以分为下列三类：(1) 采掘（伐）工业，是指对自然资源的开采，包括石油开采、煤炭开采、金属矿开采、非金属矿开采和木材采伐等工业；(2) 原材料工业，指向国民经济各部门提供基本材料、动力和燃料的工业。包括金属冶炼及加工、炼焦及焦炭化学、化工原料、水泥、人造板以及电力、石油和煤炭加工等工业；(3) 加工工业，是指对工业原材料进行再加工制造的工业。包括装备国民经济各部门的机械设备制造工业、金属结构、水泥制品等工业，以及为农业提供的生产资料如化肥、农药等工业。

根据上述划分原则，修理业中以重工业产品为修理作业对象的划为重工业，反之划为轻工业。

工业总产值 指工业企业在报告期内生产的以货币形式表现的工业最终产品和提供工业劳务活动的总价值量。它包括：在本企业内不再进行加工，经检验、包装入库已经销售和准备销售的全部工业成品（包括半成品）价值，对外加工费收入，自制半成品、在制品期末期初差额价值。工业总产值采用“工厂法”计算，即以工业企业作为一个整体，按企业生产活动的最终成果来计算。

资产总计 指企业过去的交易或者事项形成的、由企业拥有或者控制的、预期会给企业带来经济利益的资源。资产一般按流动性分为流动资产和非流动资产。其中流动资产可分为货币资金、交易性金融资产、应收票据、应收账款、预付款项、其他应收款、存货等；非流动资产可分为长期股权投资、固定资产、无形资产及其他非流动资产等。

（1）流动资产合计 资产满足以下条件之一应归为流动资产：①预计在一个正常营业周期中变现、出售或耗用，主要包括存货、应收账款等；②主要为交易目的而持有；③预计在资产负债表日起一年内（含一年）变现；④自资产负债表日起一年内，交换其他资产或清偿负债的能力不受限制的现金或现金等价物。包括货币资金、应收票据、应收账款、存货等项目。

（2）固定资产原价 指固定资产的成本，包括企业在购置、自行建造、安装、改建、扩建、技术改造某项固定资产时所发生的全部支出总额。

负债合计 指企业过去的交易或者事项形成的，预期会导致经济利益流出企业的现时义务。负债一般按偿还期长短分为流动负债和非流动负债。

（1）流动负债合计 负债满足下列条件之一的应归为流动负债：①预计在一个正常营业周期中清偿；②主要为交易目的而持有；③自资产负债表日起一年内到期应予清偿；④企业无权自主地将清偿推迟至资产负债表日后一年以上。包括短期借款、应付票据、应付账款、应付职工薪酬、应交税费等项目。

（2）非流动负债合计 指流动负债之外的负债。包括长期借款、应付债券等。

所有者权益合计 指企业资产扣除负债后由所有者享有的剩余权益。公司的所有者权益又称股东权益。包括实收资本、资本公积、盈余公积、未分配利润等。

实收资本 指企业各投资者实际投入的资本（或股本）总额，包括货币、实物、无形资产等各种形式的投入。实收资本按投资主体可分为国家资本、集体资本、法人资本、个人资本、港澳台资本和外商资本。

营业收入 指企业从事销售商品、提供劳务和让渡资产使用权等生产经营活动形成的经济利益流入。

营业成本 指企业从事销售商品、提供劳务和让渡资产使用权等生产经营活动发生的实际成本。

税金及附加 指企业因从事生产经营活动按税法规定应缴纳的消费税、城市维护建设税、资源税、环境保护税、教育费附加及房产税、土地使用税、车船使用税、印花税等相关税费。

利润总额 指企业在一定会计期间的经营成果，是生产经营过程中各种收入扣除各种耗费后的盈余，反映企业在报告期内实现的亏盈总额。

应交增值税 指企业按税法规定，以销售货物、服务、无形资产或提供加工、修理修配劳务的增值额和货物进口金额为计税依据而课征的一种流转税。

应交增值税=销项税额−（进项税额−进项税额转出）−出口抵减内销产品应纳税额−减免税款+出口退税+简易计税

平均用工人数 指报告期企业平均实际拥有的、参与本企业生产经营活动的人员数。

流动资产周转率 指在一定时期内流动资产完成的周转次数，反映流动资产的周转速度。计算公式：

$$流动资产周转率(次)=\frac{营业收入}{流动资产平均余额}$$

资产负债率 反映在企业资产总额中有多少资产是通过借债而得的，也可以用于衡量企业利用债权人提供资金进行经营活动的能力以及企业在清算时保护债权人利益的程度。计算公式：

$$资产负债率=\frac{负债总额}{资产总额}\times100\%$$

总资产贡献率 反映企业全部资产的获利能力，是企业经营业绩和管理水平的集中体现，是评价和考核企业盈利能力的核心指标。计算公式为：

$$总资产贡献率=(利润总额+税金总额+利息支出)\div平均资产总额\times100\%$$

其中：税金总额为税金及附加与应交增值税之和；平均资产总额为期初期末资产总计的算术平均值。

资产保值增值率 反映企业净资产的变动状况，是企业发展能力的集中体现。计算公式为：

$$资产保值增值率=\frac{报告期期末所有者权益}{上年同期期末所有者权益}\times100\%$$

高技术制造业 是指国民经济行业中 R&D 投入强度相对较高的制造业行业，根据国家统计局《高技术产业（制造业）分类（2017）》标准界定。

Explanatory Notes on Main Statistical Indicators

Industry refers to the material production sector which is engaged in extraction of natural resources and processing and reprocessing of mining products and agricultural products, including (1) extraction of natural resources, such as mining, salt production, logging (but not including animal hunting and fishing); (2) processing and reprocessing of agricultural products, such as grain and oil processing, food processing, embroidery, textile manufacturing and leather making; (3) processing and reprocessing of mining products, such as iron making, steel making, chemical production, petroleum processing, machine building, timber processing; and production and supply of electric power, tap water and gas; (4) repair and refurbishment of industrial products, such as the repair of machinery equipment.

Light Industry refers to the industries that produce consumer goods and hand tools. It falls into two categories, based on different raw materials: (1) Light industries basing the raw materials on agriculture, which directly or indirectly use farm products as basic raw materials, mainly include the manufacture of foods and beverages, tobacco processing, textile manufacturing, tailoring, fur and leather manufacturing, paper making, printing, etc. (2) Light industries using non-agricultural products as raw materials, which means the manufactured goods are used as raw materials, mainly include the manufacture of cultural, educational articles and sports goods, chemical medicines, synthetic fiber, daily chemical products, glass products for daily use, metal products for daily use, hand tools, medical appliances and instruments, as well as stationery and office machinery.

Heavy Industry refers to the industries that provide material and technical foundation as key means of production for various sectors of the national economy. It falls into the following three categories according to the nature of its production and the use of its products: (1) Mining, quarrying and logging industry refers to the industry that extracts natural resources, including the extraction of petroleum, coal, metal and non-metal ores and logging. (2) Raw material industry refers to the industry that provides various sectors of the national economy with basic materials, power and fuels. It includes smelting and processing of metals, coking and coke chemistry, chemical materials, cement, artificial boards, as well as power generation, petroleum refining and coal processing. (3) Processing industry refers to the industry that reprocesses the industrial raw materials. It includes machine manufacturing, which equips various sectors of the national economy, metal structure, cement products, and chemical fertilizer and pesticide industry that provide means of production for agriculture.

According to the above principle of classification, the repair services for products of heavy industry are classified as heavy industry, while the repair services for products of light industry are classified as light industry.

Gross Output Value of Industry is the total value in monetary terms for final industrial products and industrial labor service provided by industrial enterprises during the reporting period. It includes the value of all the finished industrial products (including semi-finished products), which will not be further processed in the enterprises and have been sold or have been prepared for sales upon being inspected, packed and put in storage, the revenue from processing products for others, the difference value of self-made semi-finished products and the articles in process at the end and beginning of the period. The gross industrial output value is calculated with factory method; that is, to take an industrial enterprise as a whole. It calculates the final products created by the enterprise.

Total Assets refer to resources formed by previous transactions or matters of an enterprise, owned or controlled by the enterprise, and expected to bring economic benefits to the enterprise. Classified by the liquidity, assets fall into current assets and non-current assets. Current assets include monetary capital, tradable financial assets, notes receivable, accounts receivable, prepayment, other receivables, and inventory, etc.; while non-current assets include long-term equity investment, fixed assets, intangible assets, and other non-current assets, etc.

(1) Total Current Assets Assets that meet any of the following requirements are considered current assets: ①assets expected to be cashed in, sold or consumed in a normal operating cycle, which mainly includes inventory and accounts receivable, etc.; ②assets held mainly for transaction; ③assets expected to be cashed in within one year (including one year) from the balance sheet date; ④ cash or cash equivalents with unrestricted capacity of exchanging for other assets or paying off debts within one year from the balance sheet date, which include monetary capital, notes receivable, accounts receivable, inventory, etc.

(2) Original Value Fixed Assets refers to the cost of fixed assets, including the total amount of expenditure incurred to an enterprise in its acquisition, self-construction, installation, reconstruction, expansion or technological transformation of a certain fixed asset.

Total Liabilities refer to the present obligations formed by previous transactions or matters of an enterprise, expected to lead the flow of economic benefits out of the enterprise. By the term of payment, liabilities generally include current liabilities and non-current liabilities.

(1) Total Current liabilities Liabilities that meet any of the following requirements are considered current liabilities: ① assets expected to be paid off within one normal operating cycle; ② assets held mostly for the purpose of transaction; ③ assets expected to be due and paid off within one year from the balance sheet date; ④ liabilities for which the enterprise has no right to delay the payment to more than one year after the balance sheet date on its own. They include short-term loans, notes payable, accounts payable, wages payable, taxes and fees payable, etc.

(2) Total Non-current Liabilities refer to liabilities other than current liabilities, including long-term borrowings and bonds payable, etc.

Total Owner's Equity refers to the remaining equity of assets in an enterprise held by owners after deducting the liabilities. Owner's equity of a company is also called shareholders' equity, including paid-up capital, capital reserves, operating surplus reserves and non-distributed profits, etc.

Paid-up Capital refers to the total capital (or equity) actually contributed by investors to an enterprise, including input in various forms, such as monetary investment, physical investment and intangible assets. Categorized by investors, paid-up capital includes state capital, collective capital, legal person's capital, personal capital, capital from Hong Kong, Macao and Taiwan, and foreign capital.

Business Income refers to the inflow of economic benefits formed in an enterprise's production and operating activities such as sales of commodities, rendering of labor services and assignment of the right to use assets, etc.

Business Cost refers to the actual cost incurred by an enterprise in its production and operating activities such as sales of commodities, rendering of labor services and assignment of the right to use assets, etc.

Tax and Surtax refers to the consumption tax, urban maintenance and construction tax, resource tax, environmental protection tax, educational surcharge as well as the house property tax, land use tax, vehicle and vessel use tax, stamp tax and other relevant taxes and fees that are payable by an enterprise for engaging in production and operating activities in accordance with the tax law.

Total Profits refer to the operating results of an enterprise during certain accounting period, representing the surplus of various incomes from production and operation deducting various expenses, reflecting the total gains and losses realized by the enterprise during the reporting period.

VAT Payable refer to a kind of turnover tax that should be levied on an enterprise according to the provisions tax law, with the value added and the import amount of goods in its sales of goods, services, intangible assets or in its offering of processing, repair and replacement labor services.

VAT Payable = Output Tax – (Input Tax – Transfer-out of Input Tax) – Tax Payable Deducted by Export from Output Tax of Domestically Sold Products – Tax Concession + Export Rebate+Simple Taxation.

Average Number of Employees refers to the average number of employees actually in the enterprise and engaged in its production and operation activities during the reporting period.

Turnover of Current Assets refers to the number of times for current assets turnover within a period of time. It reflects the turnover velocity of current assets. Calculation formula is listed below:

Turnover of Current Assets (No. of times) = Business Income / Average Balance of Current Assets

Assets-liabilities Ratio reflects how many assets—out of the total assets of the enterprise, are obtained by borrowing. It can be used to evaluate the enterprise's capability of operating by using the funds provided by creditors, and to what extent the enterprise will be able to protect the creditors' interests in the case of liquidation. The following formula is used:

Assets-liabilities Ratio = Total Liabilities / Total Assets × 100%

Contribution Rate of Total Assets indicates the profitability of all assets in an enterprise, reflecting the operating performance and management of the enterprise. It serves as a core indicator evaluating the enterprise's profitability. The following formula is used:

Contribution Rate of Total Assets = (Total Profit + Total Tax + Total Interest Expenses) / Average Total Assets × 100%

Specifically, the total tax is the sum of tax and surtax, and VAT payable; average total assets are represented by the arithmetic average of total assets at the beginning and the end of the period.

Assets Maintenance and Appreciation Rate reflects the changes in the net assets of an enterprise. It embodies the development ability of the enterprise. Calculation formula is listed below:

Assets Maintenance and Appreciation Rate = Owner's Equity at the End of the Reporting Period / Owner's Equity at the End of the Same Period in the Previous Year × 100%

High-tech Manufacturing Sector refers to the manufacturing industry with relatively high R&D input intensity in national economic sectors, and is defined in accordance with the standards in the *High Technology Industry (Manufacturing Industry) Classification 2017* of the National Bureau of Statistics.

建筑业
CONSTRUCTION

简要说明

一、主要内容

本章资料主要反映北京市建筑业企业基本情况和生产经营情况。主要指标包括企业个数、从业人员、建筑业总产值、建筑业企业房屋建筑面积、利润、税金等。

二、统计范围

建筑业统计范围从 2004 年起，由原具有建筑业资质等级四级及四级以上的独立核算的建筑业企业调整为具有施工总承包、专业承包资质的所有法人建筑业企业。

三、调查方法

本章建筑业企业统计数据根据国家统计局制定的《建筑业统计报表制度》整理汇总。建筑业统计数据采取全面调查的方法。

四、有关统计标准的变化说明

2002-2011 年建筑业行业分类执行《国民经济行业分类》(GB/T 4754-2002)标准，2012-2017 年执行《国民经济行业分类》(GB/T 4754-2011)标准。自 2018 年起，执行《国民经济行业分类》(GB/T 4754-2017) 标准。

五、关于历史数据调整

2004 年开展了北京市第一次全国经济普查，按照国家统计局统一要求和统一方法，1993-2003 年建筑业总产值根据普查结果采用“趋势离差法”进行了修订，2004 年为北京市第一次全国经济普查数据，2008 年为北京市第二次全国经济普查数据，2013 年为北京市第三次全国经济普查数据，2018 年为北京市第四次全国经济普查数据。

Brief Introduction

I. Main Content

Statistics in this chapter mainly show the basic situation and operation of construction enterprises in Beijing. Main indicators include number of enterprises, employees, gross output value of the construction sector, as well as floor space, profits, and tax of construction enterprises.

II. Scope of Statistics

Since 2004, data on construction sector, which previously covered construction enterprises with independent accounting at or above Level-4 in construction qualifications, have been adjusted to cover all construction enterprises with qualifications of general and specialized contracting.

III. Methods of Survey

Data on construction enterprises in this chapter were gathered based on *Statistical Statement System for Construction Sector* developed by the National Bureau of Statistics. The figures were gained through complete survey.

IV. Changes in Relevant Statistical Standards

Classification of construction sectors during 2002-2011 was based on the standards in the *Classification of National Economic Sectors* (GB/T 4754-2002). The standards in the *Classification of National Economic Sectors* (GB/T 4754-2011) were implemented from 2012 to 2017. The standards in the *Classification of National Economic Sectors* (GB/T 4754-2017) are implemented since 2018.

V. Adjustment to Historical Data

As “the first national economic census in Beijing” was conducted in 2004, in accordance with the unified requirements and methods of the National Bureau of Statistics, the data on gross output value of construction sector during 1993-2003 were adjusted by “trend deviation method” based on the census results. The data for 2004 were collected from the first national economic census in Beijing, the data for 2008 were collected from the second national economic census in Beijing, the data for 2013 were collected from the third national economic census in Beijing, and the data for 2018 were collected from the fourth national economic census in Beijing.

13-1 建筑业企业基本情况(1978-2022年)
BASIC STATISTICS FOR ENTERPRISES IN THE CONSTRUCTION INDUSTRY (1978-2022)

年份 Year	企业单位数(个) Construction Enterprises (unit)	年末从业人员(万人) Employed Persons (year-end) (10000 persons)	建筑业总产值(亿元) Gross Output Value (100 million yuan)	企业利润总额(亿元) Total Profits (100 million yuan)	房屋建筑面积(万平方米) Floor Space of Buildings (10000 sq.m)	
					施工面积 Floor Space under Construction	竣工面积 Floor Space Completed
1978	64	25.4	10.5	0.7		
1979	70	26.4	12.7	0.9		
1980	71	27.8	14.7	1.5		
1981	71	27.0	14.5	1.6		
1982	91	30.7	17.3	1.7		
1983	116	37.2	22.6	2.5		
1984	2765	53.0	33.4	3.2		
1985	2549	63.9	43.9	3.9		
1986	2361	61.3	51.3	3.3		
1987	2292	64.4	67.0	4.1		
1988	1659	64.2	81.6	3.9		
1989	1545	60.0	89.0	3.8		
1990	994	60.2	94.7	3.4		
1991	922	60.3	99.6	2.8	2495	1172
1992	976	62.7	122.6	3.1	2774	1227
1993	1098	75.9	215.5	6.1	3499	1428
1994	1259	73.4	336.0	9.4	4035	1437
1995	1332	82.6	426.6	7.8	4602	1593
1996	1292	82.5	494.7	8.9	5328	1967
1997	1297	80.3	556.4	10.4	5801	2117
1998	1482	75.6	678.6	12.4	6525	2225
1999	1588	62.0	750.6	13.6	6824	2632
2000	1697	56.6	812.5	16.4	7247	2809
2001	1811	57.8	1055.4	18.7	8919	3198
2002	2122	57.0	1211.3	24.7	10241	3827
2003	2419	59.1	1521.2	31.5	12160	4486
2004	2623	51.2	1659.8	40.0	14424	5258
2005	2752	67.2	1894.0	67.3	15418	4862
2006	2800	66.9	2167.9	112.8	16202	4786
2007	2845	51.7	2576.8	115.7	18225	4946
2008	3527	47.0	3066.2	84.5	19537	4803
2009	3556	56.2	4059.7	217.4	22721	5225
2010	3594	59.9	5196.0	265.2	29440	5933
2011	3667	49.6	6046.3	219.6	36507	6456
2012	3572	49.2	6588.3	293.0	41660	8414
2013	3522	49.3	7459.6	385.8	49259	8950
2014	3426	51.0	8209.8	473.2	56477	9275
2015	3369	59.0	8436.7	520.1	59777	9886
2016	3218	59.2	8841.2	725.7	61098	10703
2017	2888	60.8	9736.7	773.5	65290	9844
2018	2854	53.4	10939.8	498.5	71969	9771
2019	2877	55.5	11999.4	822.7	80557	10937
2020	2625	52.7	12905.9	1072.1	88594	9592
2021	2658	56.8	13987.7	1011.9	91155	13255
2022	2770	58.3	13866.1	966.8	89888	13815

注：建筑业企业房屋建筑面积包括在本市和外省完成的施工、竣工面积。
Note: Data on floor space covers buildings under construction and completed in Beijing and other provinces.

13-2 建筑业企业基本情况(2022年) BASIC STATISTICS FOR ENTERPRISES IN THE CONSTRUCTION INDUSTRY (2022)

项 目	Item	建筑业总产值(亿元) Gross Output Value (100 million yuan)	年末从业人员(人) Employed Persons (year-end) (person)	签订合同额(亿元) Value of Contract Signed (100 million yuan)	竣工产值(亿元) Output Value of Completion (100 million yuan)
合 计	**Total**	**13866.1**	**583229**	**49320.4**	**6911.1**
按企业登记注册类型分	**By Registration Type**				
内资企业	Domestically-funded Enterprises	13740.5	570977	48874.3	6846.3
国有企业	State-owned Enterprises	0.2	83	0.4	0.2
集体企业	Collectively-owned Enterprises	51.9	3086	146.0	24.8
股份合作企业	Joint-equity Cooperative Enterprises	17.1	2657	21.2	5.2
有限责任公司	Limited Liability Corporations	12269.0	424601	44917.9	6114.3
股份有限公司	Corporations Limited by Shares	349.3	19229	2024.3	89.5
私营企业	Private Enterprises	1052.9	121321	1764.6	612.4
港澳台商投资企业	Hong Kong, Macao and Taiwan-invested Enterprises	73.6	8084	176.8	34.8
外商投资企业	Foreign-invested Enterprises	52.0	4168	269.3	30.0
按行业分	**By Sector**				
房屋建筑业	Construction of Buildings	7689.9	239189	27159.8	4610.2
土木工程建筑业	Civil Engineering Construction	4396.0	182486	19043.7	1268.6
建筑安装业	Construction Installation	879.3	66419	1698.0	527.5
建筑装饰、装修和其他建筑业	Building Decoration, Finishing and Other Construction	901.0	95135	1418.9	504.8

注：统计范围为施工总承包、专业承包的法人建筑业企业（下表同）。
Note: Statistics covers general contracting and specialized contracting corporate construction enterprises(same as the following table).

13-3 建筑业企业主要财务指标(2022年)

单位：亿元

项目	Item	企业单位数(个) Number of Enterprises (unit)	资产负债 Assets and Liabilities 资产总计 Total Assets	流动资产合计 Total Current Assets	固定资产原价 Original Value of Fixed Assets	负债合计 Total Liabilities	#流动负债合计 Total Current Liabilities	#应付账款 Accounts Payable
合　计	**Total**	**2770**	**38542.0**	**22237.0**	**1141.7**	**25386.6**	**22769.7**	**8341.7**
按企业登记注册类型分	**By Registration Type**							
内资企业	Domestically-funded Enterprises	2720	38308.4	22021.7	1129.7	25204.3	22595.3	8245.8
国有企业	State-owned Enterprises	4	0.8	0.7	0.4	0.3	0.3	0.2
集体企业	Collectively-owned Enterprises	26	94.3	86.6	5.9	80.2	80.0	22.4
股份合作企业	Joint-Equity Cooperative Enterprises	28	34.9	31.0	5.8	17.4	17.3	4.7
有限责任公司	Limited Liability Corporations	781	23854.5	17114.2	900.8	18279.5	16810.8	6813.6
股份有限公司	Corporations Limited by Shares	25	12278.6	2977.0	52.1	5333.0	4251.0	764.1
私营企业	Private Enterprises	1856	2045.3	1812.2	164.8	1493.8	1436.0	640.7
港、澳、台商投资企业	Hong Kong, Macao and Taiwan- invested Enterprises	25	98.8	95.1	2.9	69.2	63.9	36.1
外商投资企业	Foreign-invested Enterprises	25	134.9	120.2	9.1	113.1	110.5	59.8
按国民经济行业分	**By Sector**							
房屋建筑业	Construction of Buildings	517	14015.6	9504.9	424.6	10191.3	9159.0	3677.5
土木工程建筑业	Civil Engineering Construction	628	20730.8	9779.6	537.0	12599.8	11132.4	3460.9
建筑安装业	Construction Installation	623	2140.8	1531.4	87.9	1283.0	1218.7	666.5
建筑装饰、装修和其他建筑业	Building Decoration and Other Construction	1002	1654.8	1421.1	92.2	1312.4	1259.6	536.8

MAIN FINANCIAL INDICATORS OF ENTERPRISES IN THE CONSTRUCTION INDUSTRY (2022)

(100 million yuan)

		损益 Profits and Losses									
所有者权益合计 Total Owner's Equity	#实收资本 Paid-up Capital	营业收入 Business Income	营业成本 Business Cost	管理费用 Management Expenses	研发费用 R&D Expenses	财务费用 Financial Expenses	利润总额 Total Profits	应交税金合计 Total Taxes Payable	税金及附加 Tax and Surtax	所得税费用 Income Tax Expense	应交增值税（本期累计发生额） Value Added Tax Payable (Cumulative Amount Incurred in Current Period)
13155.4	**4274.0**	**18180.9**	**16807.7**	**504.6**	**450.9**	**105.1**	**996.8**	**345.5**	**42.5**	**75.6**	**227.4**
13104.1	4244.5	17996.9	16641.2	496.1	448.7	104.5	993.1	341.1	42.0	74.7	224.4
0.6	0.2	0.2	0.1	0.1		...	...	...	...	...	...
14.1	9.2	79.5	75.4	3.9		...	0.1	1.2	0.2	0.1	0.9
17.5	8.0	15.5	13.8	1.5		...	0.2	0.6	0.1	0.1	0.4
5574.9	2696.4	15294.4	14176.8	345.1	419.3	36.8	355.7	274.5	34.3	59.8	180.3
6945.6	1117.4	1087.8	1010.1	44.2	14.4	62.9	631.3	23.4	2.7	12.2	8.6
551.5	413.2	1519.5	1364.9	101.3	15.0	4.8	5.8	41.3	4.7	2.5	34.1
29.5	12.0	85.8	77.9	3.5	1.0	0.0	2.3	2.1	0.2	0.5	1.4
21.8	17.6	98.2	88.6	5.0	1.1	0.6	1.5	2.3	0.3	0.5	1.6
3824.3	1613.0	8623.2	8064.5	183.0	203.3	52.8	308.6	160.1	19.0	43.5	97.6
8131.0	2101.3	7131.8	6565.5	178.6	208.6	45.1	606.0	123.6	16.4	24.6	82.6
857.8	305.0	1292.6	1159.2	73.0	23.5	1.1	86.3	31.6	3.6	5.6	22.4
342.4	254.7	1133.4	1018.4	70.0	15.4	6.2	-4.1	30.2	3.5	2.0	24.7

13-3 续表 Continued

项目	Item	流动比率（倍）Current Ratio (times)	速动比率（倍）Quick Ratio (times)	资产负债率（%）Assets-Liabilities Ratio (%)	资本金利润率（%）Capital-Profit Ratio (%)
合计	**Total**	**0.98**	**0.94**	**65.9**	**23.3**
按企业登记注册类型分	**By Registration Type**				
内资企业	Domestically-funded Enterprises	0.97	0.94	65.8	23.4
国有企业	State-owned Enterprises	2.67	2.48	31.0	6.7
集体企业	Collectively-owned Enterprises	1.08	0.75	85.1	1.4
股份合作企业	Joint-Equity Cooperative Enterprises	1.79	1.32	49.8	2.7
有限责任公司	Limited Liability Companies	1.02	0.98	76.6	13.2
股份有限公司	Companies Limited by Shares	0.70	0.69	43.4	56.5
私营企业	Private Enterprises	1.26	1.14	73.0	1.4
港澳台商投资企业	Hong Kong, Macao and Taiwan-invested Enterprises	1.49	1.32	70.1	19.0
外商投资企业	Foreign-invested Enterprises	1.09	0.89	83.9	8.4
按国民经济行业分	**Grouped by Sector**				
房屋建筑业	Construction of Buildings	1.04	1.00	72.7	19.1
土木工程建筑业	Civil Engineering Construction	0.88	0.85	60.8	28.8
建筑安装业	Construction Installation	1.26	1.18	59.9	28.3
建筑装饰、装修和其他建筑业	Building Decoration, Finishing and Other Construction	1.13	1.05	79.3	-1.6

13-4 建筑业企业竣工率
PROJECT COMPLETION RATE OF ENTERPRISES IN THE CONSTRUCTION INDUSTRY

单位：% (%)

项目	Item	产值竣工率 Completion Rate by Output Value		面积竣工率 Completion Rate by Floor Space	
		2022	2021	2022	2021
合计	**Total**	**49.8**	**44.1**	**15.4**	**14.5**
按企业登记注册类型分	**By Registration Type**				
内资企业	Domestically-funded Enterprises	49.8	44.0	15.4	14.6
国有企业	State-owned Enterprises	83.4	75.1		36.4
集体企业	Collectively-owned Enterprises	47.7	112.1	13.7	29.9
股份合作企业	Joint-equity Cooperative Enterprises	30.5	54.3	9.6	26.9
有限责任公司	Limited Liability Corporations	49.8	42.6	15.4	14.6
股份有限公司	Corporations Limited by Shares	25.6	33.7		6.3
私营企业	Private Enterprises	58.2	58.7	21.7	11.8
港澳台商投资企业	Hong Kong, Macao and Taiwan-invested Enterprises	47.3	53.5	1.5	8.8
外商投资企业	Foreign-invested Enterprises	57.6	48.8	12.8	7.0
按国民经济行业分	**By Sector**				
房屋建筑业	Construction of Buildings	60.0	52.0	15.8	15.2
土木工程建筑业	Civil Engineering Construction	28.9	25.5	9.6	7.8
建筑安装业	Construction Installation	60.0	56.5	12.2	3.8
建筑装饰、装修和其他建筑业	Building Decoration, Finishing and Other Construction	56.0	56.0	34.4	26.9

主要统计指标解释

建筑业总产值 指以货币表现的建筑业企业在一定时期内生产的建筑产品和服务的总和。它包括建筑工程产值、安装工程产值、其他产值三部分内容。

（1）**建筑工程产值** 指列入建筑工程预（概）算内的各种工程价值。

（2）**安装工程产值** 指为设备安装而发生的安装工程费用，在设备安装产值中，不得包括被安装设备本身价值。

（3）**其他产值** 建筑业总产值中除建筑工程、安装工程以外的产值，包括房屋构筑物修理产值、非标准设备制造产值、总包企业向分包企业收取的管理费，以及不能明确划分的施工活动所完成的产值。

年末从业人员 指年末最后一日24小时在本单位工作并取得劳动报酬或收入的期末实有人员数。该指标为时点指标，不包括最后一日当天及以前与单位解除劳动合同关系的人员和建筑业整建制使用的人员。

房屋施工面积 指报告期内施工的全部房屋建筑面积，包括：本期新开工的房屋面积、上期施工跨入本期继续施工的房屋面积、上期停缓建本期复工的房屋面积、本期施工又停缓建和本期竣工的房屋面积。

房屋竣工面积 指在报告期内房屋建筑按照设计要求已全部完工，达到了住人和使用条件，经验收鉴定合格或达到竣工验收标准，可正式移交使用的各栋房屋建筑面积的总和。

签订合同额 指建筑业企业在报告期直接同建设单位签订的各种国内工程合同的总价款和以前年度同建设单位签订的各种国内工程合同的未完工程跨入本年度继续施工工程合同的总价款余额。

营业收入 指企业经营主要业务和其他业务所确认的收入总额。

营业成本 指企业从事销售商品、提供劳务和让渡资产使用权等生产经营活动发生的实际成本。

应交增值税（本期累计发生额） 指按照税法规定，以销售货物、服务、无形资产、不动产或提供加工、修理修配劳务的增值额和货物进口金额为计税依据而课征的一种流转税。

利润总额 指企业在一定会计期间的经营成果，是生产经营过程中各种收入扣除各种耗费后的盈余，反映企业在报告期内实现的亏盈总额。

Explanatory Notes on Main Statistical Indicators

Gross Output Value of Construction refers to total of construction products and services, expressed in money terms, completed by construction enterprises during a given period of time. It includes: output value of construction works, output value of installation works and other output value.

(1) Output Value of Construction Works means the value of works involved in project budgets.

(2) Output Value of Installation Works means the costs of installation works incurred for equipment installation. Output value of equipment installation does not include the value of installed equipment itself.

(3) Other Output Value means the total output value of construction other than that of construction and installations works. It includes the repair output value of houses and structures, manufacturing output value of non-standard equipment, management charges collected by general contracting enterprises from subcontracting enterprises, as well as the output value of construction activities falling in no specific categories.

Year-end Employed Persons refers to the year-end actual number of employed persons who still work during the 24 hours of the last day of a year and acquire labor compensation or income. This time-spot index does not include persons who terminate their labor contracts at or before the last day of the year or the persons used in the construction industry as a whole.

House Construction Area means the building area of all houses in the reporting period, including: the area of houses newly started in current period, area of houses built in the previous period and continued in current period, area of houses suspended in the previous period and restarted in current period, area of houses built and suspended in current period, and area of houses completed in current period.

Area of Houses Completed means the total area of all houses and buildings entirely completed in line with requirements of design, meeting conditions of living and use, being checked and accepted as qualified or reaching the acceptance standards of completed projects and officially delivered for use in the reporting period.

Value of Signed Contracts means total price of all kinds of domestic engineering contracts signed directly between construction enterprises and builders in the reporting period and the balance of total price of domestic engineering contracts signed with builders in previous year and continued for implementation in the current year.

Business Income means the income recognized by an enterprise from main business such as sale of commodities and rendering of service.

Business Cost means the total cost incurred in an enterprise for the operation of main business.

VAT Payable means a kind of turnover tax levied on the basis of the appreciation amount and amount of goods imported for sale of goods, services, intangible assets, real estate or for rendering of processing, repair and replacement services in accordance with the tax laws.

Total Profits mean the operating result of an enterprise in certain accounting period. It is the surplus of all revenues deducting all costs in its production and operation, reflecting its total profit and loss realized in the reporting period.

第三产业
TERTIARY INDUSTRY

简要说明

一、主要内容

本章资料包括第三产业主要指标及占全市比重、规模以上第三产业主要指标、规模以上第三产业企业财务状况以及会展活动情况等。

二、统计范围

（一）规模以上第三产业包括除公共管理和社会组织、国际组织以外的各行业限额以上的法人单位。具体为：批发业为年主营业务收入 2000 万元及以上的企业；零售业为年主营业务收入 500 万元及以上的企业；住宿业为星级饭店和星级以外年主营业务收入 200 万元及以上企业；餐饮业为年主营业务收入 200 万元及以上的企业；金融业为全部金融监管法人单位及下属产业活动单位、年营业收入（或收入合计）2000万元及以上或资产总计5亿元及以上的非金融监管的金融业法人单位；房地产开发业的全部法人单位。

交通运输、仓储和邮政业，信息传输、软件和信息技术服务业，水利、环境和公共设施管理业，卫生年营业收入 2000 万元及以上的企业；居民服务、修理和其他服务业，文化、体育和娱乐业,社会工作年营业收入 500 万元及以上的企业；其余行业为年营业收入 1000 万元及以上的企业；执行政府事业、民间非营利组织会计制度年收入合计 2000 万元及以上的卫生法人单位，其余行业为年收入合计 1000 万元以及上的法人单位。

（二）会展业统计对象涉及会展活动的举办服务单位和接待单位。具体包括限额以上住宿业法人单位和产业活动单位、从事各种会展活动的场馆、大型会展活动的举办单位（名单主要由北京市公安局提供）以及为会展活动提供各类专业服务的规模以上单位和旅行社。

三、有关统计标准的变化说明

（一）关于行业划分。行业划分执行《国民经济行业分类》（GB/T 4754-2017）标准。

（二）关于三次产业划分。2003 年，根据《国民经济行业分类》（GB/T 4754-2002），国家统计局印发了《国家统计局关于印发〈三次产业划分规定〉的通知》（国统字〔2003〕14 号）。2012 年，根据国家质检总局和国家标准委颁布的《国民经济行业分类》（GB/T 4754-2011），国家统计局对 2003 年《三次产业划分规定》进行了修订。主要在以下方面作出调整：一是将门类“农、林、牧、渔业”中的“农、林、牧、渔服务业”，“采矿业”中的“开采辅助活动”，“制造业”中的“金属制品、机械和设备修理业”等三个大类一并调整到第三产业。调整后，第一产业为 4 个大类；第二产业为 2 个门类和 36 个大类；第三产业为 15 个门类和 3 个大类。二是明确第三产业即为服务业。

本章自 2012 年及起三次产业的分类执行调整后的划分规定。

Brief Introduction

I. Main Content

Statistics in this chapter include: main indicators for the tertiary industry and their percentages of Beijing's total, main indicators for tertiary industry above designated size, financial status of tertiary industry enterprises above designated size and exhibition activities.

II. Scope of Statistics

(I) The tertiary industry above designated size includes legal entities above designated size in all sectors other than public management and social organization, and international organizations. Specifically, it includes enterprises in wholesale with annual main business income of RMB 20 million and above, enterprises in retail trade with annual main business income of RMB 5 million and above, star-rated hotels and non-star-rated enterprises with annual main business income of RMB 2 million and above in accommodation, enterprises in restaurants with annual main business income of RMB 2 million and above, all legal entities under financial regulation and the subordinate industrial activity units as well as the legal entities in finance that are not subject to financial regulation and with annual business income (or total income) of RMB 20 million and above or with total assets of RMB 500 million and above, all legal entities in real estate development sector.

Enterprises with annual business income of RMB 20 million and above in transport, storage and post, in information transmission, software and information technology services, in management of water conservancy, environment and public facilities, and in health care; enterprises with annual business income of RMB 5 million and above in resident services, repair and other services, and in culture, sports and entertainment as well as in social works; enterprises with annual business income of RMB 10 million and above in the rest of the sectors; legal entities in health care sector following the accounting system designed for government institutions and non-government non-profit organizations and with total annual income of RMB 20 million and above, and legal entities with total annual income of RMB 10 million and above in the rest of the sectors.

(II) Statistical scope of MICE industry covers service companies and reception companies holding the exhibitions, in details, including: legal entities and industrial activity units in accommodation sector above designated size, venues for exhibitions and sponsors of large exhibitions (with the list provided by Beijing Municipal Public Security Bureau), together with the above-designated-size units and travel agencies providing various professional services for exhibition activities.

III. Changes in Relevant Statistical Standards

(I) Classification of Sectors. The standards in the *Classification of National Economic Sectors* (GB/T 4754-2017) have been implemented in the classification of sectors.

(II) Classification of Three Industries. According to the *Classification of National Economic Sectors* (GB/T 4754-2002), the National Bureau of Statistics issued the *Notice of the National Bureau of Statistics on the Issuance of the 'Regulations on Three Industries Classification'* (G.T.Z. [2003] No. 14) in 2003. According to the *Classification of National Economic Sectors* (GB/T 4754-2011) promulgated by the General Administration of Quality Supervision, Inspection and Quarantine of the People's Republic of China and the Standardization Administration of the People's Republic of China, the National Bureau of Statistics revised the *Regulations on Three Industries Classification* of 2003 version. Adjustments were mainly made in the following aspects: Firstly, the "service activities for agriculture, forestry, animal husbandry and fishing" in the category of "agriculture, forestry, animal production and hunting, fishing", the "mining support service activities" in the category of "mining and quarrying", and the "repair of fabricated metal products, machinery and equipment" in the category of "manufacturing" were adjusted to the tertiary industry. After adjustment, the primary industry fell into 4 categories; the secondary industry fell into 2 classes and 36 categories; and the tertiary industry fell into 15 classes and 3 categories. Secondly, the tertiary industry was defined as the service industry.

The classification of three industries since 2012 as mentioned in this chapter has all been subject to the classification provisions after adjustment.

14-1 第三产业主要指标及占全市比重(2000—2022年)

项 目		Item		2000	2001	2002	2003	2004	2005	2006
增加值	(亿元)	Value Added	(100 million yuan)	2174.9	2653.6	3208.2	3726.7	4393.4	5155.5	6227.7
占全市比重	(%)	Percentage of the Total	(%)	66.4	68.7	70.9	70.8	70.3	72.1	74.3
劳动生产率	(元/人)	Overall Labor Productivity	(yuan/person)	65302	78046	89352	94215	90158	90091	102203
相当于全市比例	(%)	Percentage of the Total	(%)	123.3	126.1	129.1	123.6	112.3	109.1	109.5
常住就业人口	(万人)	Permanent Employed Population	(10000 persons)							
占全市比重	(%)	Percentage of the Total	(%)							
固定资产投资	(亿元)	Investment in Fixed Assets	(100 million yuan)	510.3	1367.9	1621.8	1875.4	2112.7	2405.6	2993.8
占全市比重	(%)	Percentage of the Total	(%)	39.3	89.3	89.4	86.9	83.6	85.1	88.8
实际利用外商直接		Actual Use of Foreign Direct								
投资金额	(亿美元)	Investment	(USD 100 million)							
占全市比重	(%)	Percentage of the Total	(%)							
能源消费总量	(万吨标准煤)	Energy Consumption	(10000 tons of SCE)	1080.9	1196.2	1334.5	1391.0	1638.0	1771.7	1962.8
占全市比重	(%)	Percentage of the Total	(%)	26.1	28.3	30.1	29.9	31.9	35.1	36.4

MAIN INDICATORS OF THE TERTIARY INDUSTRY AND THEIR PERCENTAGES OF BEIJING'S TOTAL(2000-2022)

2007	2008	2009	2010	2011	2012	2013	2014	2015	2016	2017	2018	2019	2020	2021	2022
7912.8	9175.1	10047.7	11608.1	13491.0	15020.3	16806.5	18333.9	20218.9	22245.7	24711.7	27508.1	29663.4	30095.9	33545.2	34894.3
75.9	77.7	77.9	77.6	78.5	79.0	79.5	80.0	81.6	82.3	82.7	83.1	83.7	83.7	81.7	83.9
122898	134512	138876	154363	175197	186426	199247	212038	228231	243228	264934	292888	315216	319642	356902	375410
109.8	109.5	106.5	104.7	109.9	108.1	106.2	105.4	106.2	105.8	105.5	105.3	105.5	104.4	100.9	103.3
			756.9	783.2	828.2	858.8	870.5	901.3	927.9	937.6	940.8	941.3	941.8	938.0	921.0
			70.9	71.9	74.3	75.5	76.2	77.4	78.1	78.7	79.1	79.5	80.9	81.0	81.4
3465.8	3434.4	4389.5	4922.3	5101.3	5597.5	6101.7	6681.6	7202.8	7639.0	7958.4					
87.4	89.2	90.3	89.6	86.3	86.6	86.8	88.4	90.1	90.3	88.9	92.4	92.3	91.3	89.5	87.9
											144.2	130.5	132.4	140.2	168.8
											86.2	95.8	98.9	97.1	97.0
2198.4	2394.3	2527.3	2654.4	2818.9	2967.0	3109.1	3236.5	3312.6	3414.4	3519.3	3681.4	3762.5	3246.9	3534.2	3314.8
38.2	41.4	42.1	41.7	44.1	45.2	46.2	47.4	48.7	49.4	49.6	50.6	51.1	48.0	49.8	48.1

14-2 规模以上第三产业法人单位主要经济指标(2004-2022年)
MAIN ECONOMIC INDICATORS FOR TERTIARY INDUSTRY LEGAL ENTITIES ABOVE DESIGNATED SIZE (2004-2022)

年份 Year	单位数 (个) Number of Enterprises (unit)	平均用工人数 (万人) Average Number of Employed Persons (10000 persons)	资产总计 (亿元) Total Assets (100 million yuan)	收入合计 (亿元) Total Income (100 million yuan)	应交税金合计 (亿元) Total Tax Payable (100 million yuan)	企业利润总额 (亿元) Total Profits (100 million yuan)
2004	25725	301.4	184985.5	21467.2	908.1	1544.8
2005	23661	323.3	274180.3	24444.6	1004.0	2696.1
2006	24921	340.4	336485.9	29468.7	1376.0	2967.2
2007	25651	373.5	422458.7	38361.8	2360.9	4511.2
2008	34820	443.6	579095.5	47524.3	1855.2	4577.6
2009	36177	472.1	712313.4	55390.3	2560.8	10540.8
2010	36064	487.9	798485.4	69106.8	3122.4	10236.3
2011	36102	509.9	909953.5	79246.0	4018.9	11413.1
2012	36616	545.0	1022849.7	92138.2	4652.8	14248.4
2013	36504	565.2	1093973.1	103398.8	5415.4	18410.6
2014	36361	586.6	1242344.8	110308.2	5998.0	20601.7
2015	32698	616.9	1397969.4	110154.4	6725.2	24752.9
2016	33308	635.5	1583118.8	116751.1	5928.1	23973.9
2017	34055	665.6	1716653.2	131866.5	6239.9	26742.6
2018	32747	664.4	1781671.1	134677.6		23006.8
2019	39736	680.3	1859323.9	151615.5	6211.7	28815.1
2020	39640	673.9	2094323.2	151919.5	5978.4	26152.4
2021	40322	680.6	2234249.5	178861.8	6513.9	30015.1
2022	41042	664.8	2414790.1	179653.5	5902.1	30420.9

注：1.自2020年起，表中数据不包括公共管理、社会保障和社会组织，下同。
2.应交税金合计主要包括应交增值税、所得税费用、税金及附加等，下同。
3.2018年金融业相关指标数据为北京市第四次全国经济普查数据，统计范围和方法与年度调查有所差异，平均用工人数、企业利润总额、应交税金合计汇总数据不可比。
4.自2021年起，平均用工人数中，除批发和零售业、住宿和餐饮业、金融业、房地产开发以外行业为期末用工人数。

Note: a) Since 2020, the data in this table have excluded that of public management, social security and social organization, the same below.
b) Total tax payable mainly includes VAT payable, income tax expense, tax and surtax, etc, the same below.
c) The finance related indicators and data for 2018 were collected from the fourth national economic census in Beijing, with the scope of statistics and method being different from that of the annual survey, so the aggregate data of average number of employed persons, total profitsare, total tax payable are not comparable.
d) Since 2021, the average number of employed persons in the sectors other than wholesale and retail trade, accommodation and catering, finance and real estate development referred to the period-end number of employed persons.

14－3 规模以上第三产业法人单位主要经济指标(2022年)

MAIN ECONOMIC INDICATORS FOR TERTIARY INDUSTRY LEGAL ENTITIES ABOVE DESIGNATED SIZE (2022)

项目	Item	单位数 (个) Number of Enterprises (unit)	平均用工人数 (万人) Average Number of Employed Persons (10000 persons)	资产总计 (亿元) Total Assets (100 million yuan)	收入合计 (亿元) Total Incomes (100 million yuan)	应交税金合计 (亿元) Total Tax payable (100 million yuan)	利润总额 (亿元) Total Profits (100 million yuan)
合　计	**Total**	**41042**	**664.8**	**2414790.1**	**179653.5**	**5902.1**	**30420.9**
按行业分	**By Sector**						
批发和零售业	Wholesale and Retail Trade	10727	65.8	62123.3	78731.9	1072.4	2464.0
交通运输、仓储和邮政业	Transport, Storage and Post	833	52.5	31349.4	8364.5	265.2	276.0
住宿和餐饮业	Accommodation and Catering	3302	34.5	2784.2	1020.5	46.5	-30.7
信息传输、软件和信息技术服务业	Information Transmission,Software and Information Technology Services	4288	117.0	76914.1	25366.9	766.8	4172.0
金融业	Financial Intermediation	2491	60.2	1975298.0	31212.2	2161.5	15797.0
房地产业	Real Estate	4088	47.7	77662.4	7245.9	695.5	275.5
租赁和商务服务业	Leasing and Business Services	5387	103.8	135721.9	9820.7	426.2	6439.0
科学研究和技术服务业	Scientific Research and Technical Services	3867	64.1	29149.3	8903.4	306.3	885.0
水利、环境和公共设施管理业	Management of Water Conservancy, Environment and Public Facilities	514	11.0	6517.0	803.9	31.2	28.4
居民服务、修理和其他服务业	Resident Services, Repair and Other Services	695	11.1	373.1	253.2	10.8	4.9
教　育	Education	1888	46.5	5777.1	2866.7	22.9	27.2
卫生和社会工作	Health and Social Works	893	32.0	3109.2	2927.3	6.7	-7.1
文化、体育和娱乐业	Culture, Sports and Entertainment	2069	18.7	8011.0	2136.5	90.1	89.7
按登记注册类型分	**By Registration Type**						
内　资	Domestic Investment Economy	37304	540.2	2269998.0	133588.5	4642.8	25103.3
国　有	State-owned Units	3415	95.3	262139.0	8256.2	139.4	4053.9
集　体	Collective-owned Units	291	2.8	2019.0	168.5	14.4	15.0
股份合作	Share Holding	272	2.0	1040.8	140.5	6.5	-7.9
联　营	Joint Ownership Units	16	0.1	48.2	17.9	0.9	0.8
有限责任公司	Limited-Liability Corporations	14890	229.3	806786.0	85001.6	2869.1	14090.1
股份有限公司	Share Holding Corporations Ltd.	877	66.5	1170602.7	22775.6	1174.6	6348.4
私　营	Private Units	17285	138.9	26390.7	16824.0	431.1	586.3
其　他	Others	258	5.3	971.5	404.2	6.8	16.7
港澳台商投资	Hong Kong, Macao and Taiwan-invested Enterprises	1416	61.4	63000.5	20934.9	497.0	2249.0
外商投资	Foreign Funded Units	2322	63.1	81791.5	25130.1	762.2	3068.7

注：本表平均用工人数中，除批发和零售业、住宿和餐饮业、金融业、房地产开发以外行业为期末用工人数。

Note: The average number of employed persons in the sectors other than wholesale and retail trade, accommodation and catering, finance and real estate development in this table referred to the period-end number of employed persons.

14-4 按登记注册类型分规模以上第三产业企业财务状况(2022年)

单位：亿元

项　　目	Item	企业单位个数(个) Number of Enterprises (unit)	资产总计 Total Assets
合　　计	**Total**	**37742**	**2163592.9**
按登记注册类型分	**By Registration Type**		
内资企业	Domestically-invested Enterprises	34006	2018802.5
国有企业	State-owned Enterprises	343	11397.1
集体企业	Collectively-owned Enterprises	271	1979.5
股份合作企业	Joint-equity Cooperative Enterprises	272	1040.8
联营企业	Associated Enterprises	16	48.2
有限责任公司	Limited-Liability Corporations	14888	806785.6
股份有限公司	Corporations Limited by Shares	877	1170602.7
私营企业	Private Enterprises	17275	26387.4
其他企业	Others	64	561.1
港澳台商投资企业	Hong Kong, Macao and Taiwan-invested Enterprises	1416	63000.5
外商投资企业	Foreign-invested Enterprises	2320	81789.9

FINANCIAL STATUS OF TERTIARY INDUSTRY ENTERPRISES ABOVE DESIGNATED SIZE BY REGISTRATION TYPE(2022)

(100 million yuan)

资产负债 Assets and Liabilites					
流动资产 合计 Total Current Assets	#应收账款 Accounts Receivable	固定资产原价 Original Value of Fixed Assets	负债合计 Total Liabilities	所有者权益合计 Total Owner's Equity	#实收资本 Paid-up Capital
227878.2	**30668.1**	**43316.7**	**1632858.2**	**530724.9**	**192897.0**
178287.1	23469.6	31777.3	1535201.8	483584.2	173271.9
3824.4	70.5	954.4	1463.4	9933.8	1464.6
1276.4	45.7	396.6	1295.3	684.1	52.4
668.0	18.2	280.2	618.1	422.7	51.9
21.5	4.3	34.1	29.7	18.5	58.7
132164.7	12348.6	21654.6	534796.2	271995.4	128381.5
22964.4	7835.3	6806.0	980005.3	190575.8	36761.8
17224.0	3130.4	1638.1	16638.0	9748.5	6361.1
143.6	16.7	13.4	355.7	205.4	140.0
27662.9	3141.3	7677.5	43567.2	19437.7	11920.7
21928.2	4057.2	3862.0	54089.2	27703.0	7704.4

14-4 续表

单位：亿元

项　　目	Item	营业收入 Businesses Income	营业成本 Business Cost	销售费用 Sales Expenses
合　　计	**Total**	**172556.0**	**118765.3**	**7624.5**
按登记注册类型分	**By Registration Type**			
内资企业	Domestically-invested Enterprises	126492.2	84963.0	4191.2
国有企业	State-owned Enterprises	1473.2	1161.3	44.7
集体企业	Collectively-owned Enterprises	147.1	92.2	11.5
股份合作企业	Joint-equity Cooperative Enterprises	140.5	93.5	13.0
联营企业	Associated Enterprises	17.9	13.9	0.9
有限责任公司	Limited-Liability Corporations	85000.9	63843.8	2583.1
股份有限公司	Corporations Limited by Shares	22775.6	6508.2	301.3
私营企业	Private Enterprises	16818.8	13208.9	1228.8
其他企业	Others	118.1	41.2	7.7
港澳台商投资企业	Hong Kong, Macao and Taiwan-invested Enterprises	20934.9	14079.4	2062.0
外商投资企业	Foreign-invested Enterprises	25128.9	19722.9	1371.3

14-4 continued

(100 million yuan)

损益及分配 Profits and Losses				应交		
管理费用 Management Expenses	研发费用 R&D Expenses	财务费用 Financial Expenses	利润总额 Total Profits	税金合计 Total Tax Payable	#税金及附加 Tax and Surtax	#所得税费用 Income Tax Expense
8100.0	**4067.9**	**1948.3**	**30420.9**	**5888.6**	**791.5**	**2087.4**
5295.0	2314.5	1744.8	25103.3	4629.3	634.1	1607.4
166.6	1.3	-68.8	4053.9	126.6	46.6	43.2
39.8	0.2	5.4	15.0	14.3	6.5	3.0
41.2	1.0	1.7	-7.9	6.5	2.9	1.0
2.2	0.1	...	0.8	0.9	0.2	0.5
3277.5	1427.4	1391.3	14090.1	2869.1	409.1	1179.7
484.9	404.1	306.1	6348.4	1174.6	119.0	287.5
1269.0	478.1	113.3	586.3	431.1	49.4	89.7
13.8	2.3	-4.1	16.7	6.3	0.3	2.7
1428.8	1417.9	105.7	2249.0	497.0	80.5	134.8
1376.2	335.4	97.8	3068.7	762.2	76.9	345.2

14-5 分行业规模以上第三产业企业财务状况(2022年)

单位：亿元

项目	Item	企业单位个数(个) Number of Enterprises (unit)	资产负债	
			资产总计 Total Assets	流动资产合计 Total Current Assets
合　　计	**Total**	**37742**	**2163592.9**	**227878.2**
批发和零售业	**Wholesale and Retail Trade**	**10727**	**62123.3**	**42701.1**
批发业	Wholesale	8163	56948.4	38791.5
零售业	Retail Trade	2564	5174.9	3909.5
交通运输、仓储和邮政业	**Transport, Storage and Post**	**833**	**31349.4**	**7429.2**
铁路运输业	Railway Transport	17	8736.0	912.6
道路运输业	Road Transport	336	4714.4	1928.8
水上运输业	Water Transport	4	6.7	3.0
航空运输业	Air Transport	33	3357.8	428.7
管道运输业	Transport Via Pipelines	3	11151.1	1605.3
多式联运和运输代理业	Multimodal Transport and Transport Agent Service	295	1964.8	1523.7
装卸搬运和仓储业	Loading, Unloading, Portage and Storage	107	668.9	496.1
邮政业	Post	38	749.7	531.1
住宿和餐饮业	**Accommodation and Catering**	**3302**	**2784.2**	**1272.3**
住宿业	Accommodation	1141	2198.5	923.7
餐饮业	Catering	2161	585.7	348.6
信息传输、软件和信息技术服务业	**Information Transmission, Software and Information Technology Services**	**4240**	**76572.9**	**40718.6**
电信、广播电视和卫星传输服务	Telecommunications, Broadcasting, Television and Satellite Transmission Services	242	32053.2	9760.3
互联网和相关服务	Internet and Related Services	781	12259.7	9048.9
软件和信息技术服务业	Software and Information Technology Services	3217	32260.0	21909.4
金融业	**Finance**	**2467**	**1738803.1**	**14911.1**
货币金融服务	Monetary Financial Services	722	1422639.4	1859.5
资本市场服务	Capital Market Services	926	91096.2	6348.7
保险业	Insurance	570	90377.8	316.7
其他金融业	Other Financial Services	249	134689.6	6386.2

FINANCIAL STATUS OF TERTIARY INDUSTRY ENTERPRISES ABOVE DESIGNATED SIZE BY SECTOR(2022)

(100 million yuan)

Assets and Liabilites				
#应收账款 Accounts Receivable	固定资产原价 Original Value of Fixed Assets	负债合计 Total Liabilities	所有者权益合计 Total Owner's Equity	#实收资本 Paid-up Capital
30668.1	**43316.7**	**1632858.2**	**530724.9**	**192897.0**
7777.3	**2255.3**	**41602.6**	**20502.8**	**9987.8**
7061.1	1695.9	37662.5	19281.9	9215.2
716.2	559.4	3940.0	1221.0	772.6
981.1	**14697.4**	**14447.4**	**16902.0**	**12475.4**
168.4	6487.5	3174.5	5561.5	4551.7
177.4	2303.8	2739.0	1975.3	743.9
0.7	8.2	3.8	2.8	1.6
94.7	2104.5	2665.9	691.9	531.2
192.7	3423.6	3470.0	7681.1	6014.1
197.2	57.6	1316.9	647.8	214.5
22.0	110.9	484.1	184.8	118.1
127.9	201.3	593.0	156.7	300.3
62.3	**1092.4**	**1820.3**	**972.1**	**810.5**
22.1	964.9	1303.2	898.4	709.0
40.2	127.5	517.1	73.7	101.5
7268.1	**7101.6**	**38275.5**	**38297.3**	**19099.5**
688.2	2885.0	12567.7	19485.4	12403.0
1236.8	1363.3	8179.6	4080.1	1697.4
5343.0	2853.3	17528.2	14731.8	4999.1
7807.9	**4189.9**	**1394235.5**	**344567.7**	**101123.4**
5137.3	3174.9	1263610.1	159029.4	28944.8
557.8	266.6	38026.0	53070.2	17471.1
1348.6	537.7	57775.0	32602.8	6855.3
764.2	210.7	34824.3	99865.3	47852.2

14-5 续表 1

单位：亿元

项目	Item	损益及分配 营业收入 Business Income	 营业成本 Business Cost	 销售费用 Sales Expenses
合计	**Total**	**172556.0**	**118765.3**	**7624.5**
批发和零售业	**Wholesale and Retail Trade**	**78731.9**	**73240.3**	**2639.8**
批发业	Wholesale	69007.0	64651.9	1819.9
零售业	Retail Trade	9724.9	8588.4	819.9
交通运输、仓储和邮政业	**Transport, Storage and Post**	**8364.5**	**7598.7**	**365.3**
铁路运输业	Railway Transport	1407.3	1327.8	0.6
道路运输业	Road Transport	2147.0	2123.8	29.1
水上运输业	Water Transport	8.1	7.1	0.1
航空运输业	Air Transport	772.2	1001.3	41.7
管道运输业	Transport Via Pipelines	709.0	403.4	0.5
多式联运和运输代理业	Multimodal Transport and Transport Agent Service	1908.4	1721.5	25.7
装卸搬运和仓储业	Loading, Unloading, Portage and Storage	234.1	207.4	4.0
邮政业	Post	1178.4	806.5	263.6
住宿和餐饮业	**Accommodation and Catering**	**1020.5**	**509.1**	**384.9**
住宿业	Accommodation	260.1	116.3	81.6
餐饮业	Catering	760.5	392.8	303.3
信息传输、软件和信息技术服务业	**Information Transmission, Software and Information Technology Services**	**25277.6**	**15055.8**	**2752.9**
电信、广播电视和卫星传输服务	Telecommunications, Broadcasting, Television and Satellite Transmission Services	1518.0	1184.3	118.1
互联网和相关服务	Internet and Related Services	7948.9	5374.4	1137.6
软件和信息技术服务业	Software and Information Technology Services	15810.8	8497.1	1497.2
金融业	**Finance**	**31130.8**	**848.8**	**144.5**
货币金融服务	Monetary Financial Services	11612.6	119.9	9.0
资本市场服务	Capital Market Services	-73.6	80.9	26.5
保险业	Insurance	9875.0	204.7	30.7
其他金融业	Other Financial Services	9716.7	443.3	78.3

14-5 continued 1

(100 million yuan)

Profits and Losses				应交税金合计 Total Tax Payable		
管理费用 Management Expenses	研发费用 R&D Expenses	财务费用 Financial Expenses	利润总额 Total Profits		#税金及附加 Tax and Surtax	#所得税费用 Income Tax Expense
8100.0	**4067.9**	**1948.3**	**30420.9**	**5888.6**	**791.5**	**2087.4**
1591.4	**159.7**	**263.3**	**2464.0**	**1072.4**	**148.0**	**329.9**
1338.0	147.4	235.6	2440.2	921.2	117.8	297.9
253.3	12.3	27.7	23.8	151.2	30.1	31.9
455.5	**30.5**	**190.8**	**276.0**	**265.2**	**20.1**	**140.6**
42.0	7.1	56.0	-13.2	48.3	3.0	30.4
184.2	10.6	16.4	21.2	33.8	2.9	8.4
0.5		...	0.4	0.2	...	0.2
41.8	1.3	103.4	-405.1	5.4	4.2	-11.6
22.3	5.8	12.9	500.6	116.3	5.7	68.9
78.7	4.2	-1.2	125.0	28.9	1.0	23.4
13.0	0.6	-0.6	12.6	5.9	1.1	2.8
73.0	0.8	4.0	34.5	26.3	2.2	18.0
206.9	**0.2**	**24.1**	**-30.7**	**46.5**	**11.0**	**17.5**
105.9	0.1	18.2	6.3	31.5	10.0	15.6
101.0	0.1	5.9	-37.0	15.0	1.0	1.9
2225.7	**3002.5**	**6.6**	**4172.0**	**766.6**	**89.4**	**179.4**
158.4	120.3	18.9	1711.1	55.7	7.8	20.7
479.2	734.7	-8.0	204.4	179.5	28.9	48.0
1588.1	2147.4	-4.2	2256.4	531.4	52.8	110.7
370.8	**155.0**	**63.8**	**15797.0**	**2161.5**	**134.1**	**949.7**
31.5	71.6	27.5	3847.5	1437.0	91.0	576.4
176.7	9.5	27.4	-777.6	410.4	14.7	268.2
60.7	9.7	-1.6	3991.9	121.2	18.5	-11.7
101.9	64.2	10.4	8735.2	192.8	9.9	116.8

14-5 续表 2

单位：亿元

项 目	Item	企业单位个数(个) Number of Enterprises (unit)	资产负债 资产总计 Total Assets
房地产业	**Real Estate**	**4083**	**77619.4**
租赁和商务服务业	**Leasing and Business Services**	**5176**	**134896.7**
租赁业	Leasing	199	1318.5
商务服务业	Business Services	4977	133578.3
科学研究和技术服务业	**Scientific Research and Development, Technical Services**	**3399**	**25476.4**
研究和试验发展	Research and Experimental Development	369	4534.3
专业技术服务业	Professional Technical Services	1841	15670.4
科技推广和应用服务业	Technique Generalization and Application Services	1189	5271.8
水利、环境和公共设施管理业	**Management of Water Conservancy, Environment and Public Facilities**	**339**	**5295.8**
水利管理业	Management of Water Conservancy	9	1788.8
生态保护和环境治理业	Ecological Protection and Environmental Control	91	712.5
公共设施管理业	Management of Public Facilities	230	1992.3
土地管理业	Management of Land	9	802.2
居民服务、修理和其他服务业	**Resident Services, Repair and Other Services**	**678**	**343.6**
居民服务业	Resident Services	183	176.4
机动车、电子产品和日用产品修理业	Repair of Motor Vehicles, Electronics and Household Appliances	204	91.7
其他服务业	Other Services	291	75.5
教 育	**Education**	**348**	**969.8**
卫生和社会工作	**Health and Social Works**	**337**	**646.5**
卫 生	Health	309	530.4
社会工作	Social Works	28	116.2
文化、体育和娱乐业	**Culture, Sports and Entertainment**	**1813**	**6711.7**
新闻和出版业	Journalism and Publishing	452	1982.4
广播、电视、电影和影视录音制作业	Radio Broadcasting, Television, Movies, Videos and Sound Recording	648	3158.9
文化艺术业	Culture and Arts	168	254.1
体 育	Sports Activities	151	424.2
娱乐业	Entertainment	394	892.1

14-5 Continued 2

(100 million yuan)

Assets and Liabilites					
流动资产合计 Total Current Assets	#应收账款 Accounts Receivable	固定资产原价 Original Value of Fixed Assets	负债合计 Total Liabilities	所有者权益合计 Total Owner's Equity	#实收资本 Paid-up Capital
54392.0	**862.4**	**4211.5**	**58530.5**	**19088.9**	**11309.6**
45500.5	**2646.4**	**3952.5**	**63678.1**	**71218.7**	**29348.6**
630.8	106.1	856.0	657.7	660.8	390.4
44869.7	2540.2	3096.5	63020.4	70557.9	28958.2
13764.6	**2480.1**	**2045.0**	**12908.4**	**12568.0**	**5178.2**
2265.3	239.0	558.8	1934.2	2600.0	989.7
8928.6	1673.7	976.3	8381.3	7289.1	2673.4
2570.8	567.4	510.0	2592.9	2678.9	1515.1
1849.4	**375.7**	**2204.6**	**2722.3**	**2573.4**	**1722.2**
189.8	103.1	1574.8	384.3	1404.5	1336.6
466.3	137.6	67.7	384.5	328.0	148.4
647.0	129.3	548.8	1310.8	681.5	189.1
546.2	5.8	13.3	642.7	159.4	48.2
267.1	**42.7**	**55.2**	**285.9**	**57.7**	**61.6**
135.7	7.8	27.5	173.8	2.6	16.7
71.6	16.0	16.6	70.8	20.9	24.0
59.8	19.0	11.1	41.2	34.2	20.9
725.3	**35.7**	**81.4**	**1030.3**	**-60.5**	**66.5**
410.3	**57.9**	**150.8**	**609.2**	**37.4**	**142.4**
328.8	51.5	136.0	514.3	16.1	107.1
81.5	6.4	14.8	94.9	21.3	35.2
3936.9	**270.6**	**1279.2**	**2712.3**	**3999.4**	**1571.4**
1444.9	82.0	256.6	570.2	1412.2	374.7
1950.3	122.0	409.8	920.4	2238.5	835.4
157.0	10.8	52.9	121.6	132.5	47.1
123.8	17.5	137.1	359.0	65.2	104.8
260.9	38.3	422.8	741.1	151.0	209.3

14-5 续表 3

单位：亿元

项　目	Item	损益及分配 营业收入 Business Income	营业成本 Business Cost
房地产业	**Real Estate**	**7241.2**	**5490.0**
租赁和商务服务业	**Leasing and Business Services**	**9609.9**	**7685.5**
租赁业	Leasing	288.3	220.2
商务服务业	Business Services	9321.5	7465.3
科学研究和技术服务业	**Scientific Research and Development, Technical Services**	**7457.7**	**5734.6**
研究和试验发展	Research and Experimental Development	1223.0	817.6
专业技术服务业	Professional Technical Services	4802.0	3905.4
科技推广和应用服务业	Technique Generalization and Application Services	1432.7	1011.6
水利、环境和公共设施管理业	**Management of Water Conservancy, Environment and Public Facilities**	**622.1**	**512.8**
水利管理业	Management of Water Conservancy	91.1	83.8
生态保护和环境治理业	Ecological Protection and Environmental Control	163.1	122.8
公共设施管理业	Management of Public Facilities	326.9	270.9
土地管理业	Management of Land	40.9	35.3
居民服务、修理和其他服务业	**Resident Services, Repair and Other Services**	**238.0**	**157.4**
居民服务业	Resident Services	72.0	40.6
机动车、电子产品和日用产品修理业	Repair of Motor Vehicles, Electronics and Household Appliances	67.6	45.7
其他服务业	Other Services	98.4	71.1
教　育	**Education**	**626.0**	**311.1**
卫生和社会工作	**Health and Social Works**	**465.7**	**343.4**
卫　生	Health	454.0	335.3
社会工作	Social Works	11.7	8.1
文化、体育和娱乐业	**Culture, Sports and Entertainment**	**1770.1**	**1277.7**
新闻和出版业	Journalism and Publishing	687.7	408.1
广播、电视、电影和影视录音制作业	Radio Broadcasting, Television, Movies, Videos and Sound Recording	689.0	557.4
文化艺术业	Culture and Arts	55.7	43.8
体　育	Sports Activities	95.5	77.3
娱乐业	Entertainment	242.2	191.1

14-5 continued 3

(100 million yuan)

Profits and Losses					应交税金合计 Total Tax Payable		
销售费用 Sales Expenses	管理费用 Management Expenses	研发费用 R&D Expenses	财务费用 Financial Expenses	利润总额 Total Profits		#税金及附加 Tax and Surtax	#所得税费用 Income Tax Expense
263.5	**600.3**	**5.4**	**442.0**	**275.5**	**695.4**	**272.6**	**179.0**
457.2	**1376.0**	**186.8**	**954.6**	**6439.0**	**424.5**	**58.1**	**170.6**
13.2	22.3	7.5	4.8	20.6	18.7	1.6	7.5
444.0	1353.7	179.3	949.8	6418.4	405.8	56.4	163.1
246.3	**676.9**	**438.9**	**-7.8**	**885.0**	**302.6**	**34.7**	**89.8**
54.4	107.7	189.1	-5.2	295.0	63.4	7.4	25.2
109.1	402.5	154.8	-15.1	443.6	175.5	20.8	44.3
82.7	166.6	95.0	12.5	146.3	63.7	6.5	20.2
15.3	**61.3**	**13.3**	**17.2**	**28.4**	**30.6**	**4.8**	**5.4**
0.3	7.3	0.6	9.7	-11.4	7.2	1.1	0.1
4.9	14.6	8.3	3.3	12.3	6.1	0.6	1.3
9.9	34.8	4.4	3.0	22.1	15.7	2.3	3.3
0.1	4.7		1.1	5.4	1.6	0.8	0.6
35.2	**41.3**	**0.9**	**1.2**	**4.9**	**10.7**	**1.0**	**2.5**
13.3	14.0	0.3	0.8	4.4	3.5	0.3	1.8
12.6	9.0	0.4	0.3	-0.5	2.8	0.3	0.3
9.3	18.3	0.2	0.1	1.0	4.3	0.4	0.4
127.1	**99.6**	**56.7**	**0.6**	**27.2**	**18.1**	**1.6**	**2.6**
52.6	**68.9**	**6.2**	**4.4**	**-7.1**	**5.8**	**1.2**	**3.3**
51.8	65.8	6.2	3.6	-5.4	4.5	0.3	3.2
0.8	3.1	…	0.9	-1.7	1.3	0.9	0.1
139.9	**325.3**	**11.8**	**-12.5**	**89.7**	**88.7**	**14.9**	**17.2**
71.6	127.0	2.0	-15.8	142.0	42.0	5.5	9.7
27.2	114.7	5.7	-20.0	3.7	22.1	5.6	2.0
4.0	12.3	0.6	-0.3	2.2	2.7	0.9	0.3
13.3	22.8	1.1	1.7	-19.8	4.0	1.0	0.6
23.7	48.4	2.3	21.8	-38.4	17.9	1.9	4.4

14-6　会展业活动情况(2022年)
STATISTICS FOR MICE INDUSTRY (2022)

项　目		Item		2022	2022年为2021年% 2022 as % of 2021
人员情况		**Employed Persons**			
从业人员平均人数	(万人)	Average Number of Employed Persons	(10000 persons)	2.1	93.4
接待设施情况		**Facilities**			
接待场所会议室个数	(个)	Number of Meeting Rooms in Reception Venue	(unit)	5193	99.6
#座位数超过500座的会议室		Number of Meeting Rooms with More Than 500 Seats		245	100.8
接待场所会议室使用面积	(万平方米)	Usable Area of Meeting Rooms in Reception Venue	(10000 sq.m)	84.6	100.9
接待场所会议室可容纳人数	(万人)	Capacity of Meeting Rooms in Reception Venue	(10000 persons)	52.1	100.5
会议情况		**Meetings**			
接待会议个数	(万个)	Number of Meetings Held in Beijing	(10000 units)	8.9	61.4
#国际会议		International Meetings		0.01	38.5
接待会议人数	(万人次)	Number of Meeting Participants	(10000 person-times)	388.5	44.5
#国际会议		International Meeting Participants		0.6	32.7
展览情况		**Exhibitions**			
接待展览个数	(个)	Number of Exhibitions Held in Beijing	(unit)	48	18.5
#国际展览		International Exhibitions		5	7.5
接待展览累计面积(含室外展览面积)	(万平方米)	Total Exhibition Area (including outdoor exhibition area)	(10000 sq.m)	42.8	6.0
#国际展览累计面积		International Exhibition Area		28.7	12.2
接待展览观众人数	(万人次)	Number of Exhibition Visitors	(10000 person-times)	61.6	40.3
#国际展览观众人数		International Exhibition Visitors		3.7	6.0
收入情况		**Revenues**			
会展收入	(亿元)	Total Revenues from MICE Industry	(100 million yuan)	126.8	67.0
#会议收入	(亿元)	Revenues from Meetings	(100 million yuan)	69.2	70.8
#国际会议收入		Revenues from International Meetings		4.0	94.1
展览收入	(亿元)	Revenues from Exhibitions	(100 million yuan)	56.1	62.8
#国际展览收入		Revenues from International Exhibitions		5.1	59.5

注：1.人员情况和收入情况包括会展场馆、限额以上住宿业法人单位和产业活动单位、会展举办单位以及规模以上会议及展览服务业法人单位等。
2.接待设施情况、会议情况和展览情况包括会展场馆、限额以上住宿业法人单位和产业活动单位。
3.表中发展速度按可比口径计算。

Note: a) Data on employed persons and revenues cover the MICE venues, legal entities above designated size and industrial activity units in accommodation industry, organizers of MICE, together with the legal entities above designated size in conference and exhibition services industry, etc.
b) Data on facilities, meetings and exhibitions cover the MICE venues, legal entities above designated size and industrial activity units in accommodation industry.
c) Indicators of development rate in the table are calculated in terms of comparable caliber.

主要统计指标解释

接待会议个数 指报告期内，接待的各种类型会议的个数。

接待国际会议个数 指报告期内，接待的国际会议的个数。国际会议是指在我国境内举办的，与会者来自 3 个或 3 个以上中国大陆以外国家和地区（含港、澳、台地区）的会议、论坛、研讨会、报告会、交流会等。

接待展览个数 指报告期内，接待的各种类型展览的个数。

接待国际展览个数 指报告期内，接待的国际展览的个数。国际展览指中国大陆以外国家和地区（含港、澳、台地区）的参展商参展面积达到该次展出面积 20%以上的展览个数。

Explanatory Notes on Main Statistical Indicators

Number of Meeting Held in Beijing refers to the number of various types of conference held in Beijing in the reporting period.

Number of International Meeting refers to the number of international conferences held in Beijing in the reporting period. International conference means any conference, forum, seminar, report conference, and workshops, etc. held in our country, with participants coming from 3 or more countries and regions (including Hong Kong, Macao and Taiwan) outside Chinese mainland.

Number of Exhibitions Held in Beijing refers to the number of various types of exhibitions held in Beijing in the reporting period.

Number of International Exhibitions Received refers to the number of international exhibitions received in the reporting period. International exhibition means any exhibition with participants from countries and regions (including Hong Kong, Macao and Taiwan) outside Chinese mainland whose exhibition floorage accounts for more than 20% of the exhibition.

北京统计年鉴2023　　BEIJING STATISTICAL YEARBOOK 2023

交通运输邮电业

TRANSPORT, POST AND TELECOMMUNICATION SERVICES

简要说明

一、主要内容

本章资料主要反映北京市交通运输业和邮政电信业发展的基本情况。包括客货运输、机动车保有量、邮政电信业务等数据。

二、统计调查范围和口径说明

铁路数据统计范围为国家铁路运营情况，不含地方铁路、合资铁路和军用铁路及由厂矿企事业单位自建的铁路专用线和专用铁道；公路里程口径为年末通车里程数，不含在建和未正式投入使用的公路里程；公路运输统计范围包括在北京市注册从事公路货运的全部企事业单位和私人(包括个体联户)的车辆；管道运输资料包括输送原油、成品油、天然气以及其他气体的管线长度、输送能力及完成的运输量；民航运输资料统计范围为各航空公司从事国内运输、港澳台运输、国际运输的定期航班航线条数及里程、运输量，不包括在京运输飞行的外省市及外国航空公司。

邮政电信资料包括邮政和基础电信运营企业为社会公众提供的各类邮政和电信服务，不含专用网业务资料；民用汽车包括在公安交通管理部门已注册登记领有民用车辆牌照的全部汽车。

Brief Introduction

I. Main Content

Statistics in this chapter mainly show the basic situation of development of transport, post and telecommunication in Beijing, including passenger and freight traffic, number of motor vehicles possessed, and business volume of post and telecommunication services, and so on.

II. Scope of Statistics and Survey and Explanations on Statistical Standards

Scope of statistics for data on railways covers the operation of national railways, excluding local railways, railways built by joint ventures, military railways, and dedicated lines and railways built by factories, mines, enterprises and public institutions. Data on the length of highways refer to the length open to traffic at the year end, excluding those under construction and not put into use. Highway transport statistics cover the vehicles of all enterprises and public institutions as well as individuals (including self-employed) registered in Beijing for highway freight transport. Data on pipeline transport include the length, capacity and completed traffic of pipelines for transport of crude oil, refined oil, natural gas, and other gases. Scope of statistics for data on civil aviation covers the number, mileage, and traffic volume of regular flight lines for domestic transport, transport from and to Hong Kong, Macao and Taiwan, and international transport of different airline companies, excluding non-local and foreign airlines which operate flights in Beijing.

Data on post and telecommunication include those on postal and telecom services offered by post and basic telecom operators to the public, excluding data on services of dedicated networks. Data on civil automobiles include all vehicles registered with public security traffic administration and granted with the license plates for civil automobiles.

15-1 交通运输邮电业基本情况(1978-2022年)
TRANSPORT, POST AND TELECOMMUNICATION SERVICES (1978-2022)

年份 Year	铁路里程(公里) Railway Mileage (km)	公路里程(公里) Highway Mileage (km)	客运量(万人) Passenger Traffic (10000 persons)	铁路 Railway	公路 Highway	民航 Civil Aviation	货运量(万吨) Freight Traffic (10000 tons)	铁路 Railway	公路 Highway	民航 Civil Aviation	管道 Pipeline
1978	699	6562	4431	2264	2120	47	7394	3370	4023	1	
1979	700	7278	4777	2504	2220	53	7764	3485	4277	2	
1980	707	7487	5285	2762	2465	58	7571	3356	4213	2	
1981	858	7566	5877	2982	2824	71	8546	3046	5498	2	
1982	858	7683	6215	3205	2931	79	9097	3065	5812	2	218
1983	860	8058	6662	3546	3038	78	9403	3152	6016	3	232
1984	864	8271	7273	3877	3287	109	9671	3133	6301	3	234
1985	876	8482	7203	4078	2978	147	8739	3029	5436	4	270
1986	876	8995	7337	4106	3059	172	22121	3030	18794	6	291
1987	876	9103	7763	4418	3117	228	23068	3125	19734	8	201
1988	876	9124	8491	4782	3460	249	24749	3168	21308	9	264
1989	876	9371	7434	4214	3034	186	25184	3144	21767	8	265
1990	876	9648	7480	3770	3490	220	26648	3051	23326	10	262
1991	876	10259	7704	4036	3378	289	26804	2983	23739	11	71
1992	875	10827	8158	4196	3593	369	27707	2912	24700	14	80
1993	875	11260	7607	4374	2781	452	29865	3048	26730	17	70
1994	875	11532	8537	3992	4008	537	30825	3006	27700	19	99
1995	875	11811	8913	4017	4250	646	32184	2974	29087	17	106
1996	922	12084	8801	3650	4395	756	32907	2851	29960	18	78
1997	924	12306	9263	3613	4902	748	32351	2883	29360	20	87
1998	924	12498	11228	3762	6704	762	30127	2563	27490	22	52
1999	997	12825	14866	4201	9878	788	28275	2583	25635	30	27
2000	997	13600	18396	4458	13009	929	30717	2612	28010	35	60
2001	987	13891	22469	4750	16630	1090	30607	2505	28007	38	57
2002	987	14359	28384	5032	22103	1249	30961	2348	28375	44	194
2003	964	14453	30520	4352	24940	1228	30925	2265	28361	45	254
2004	964	14630	49750	5437	41463	2850	31700	1959	29256	73	412
2005	966	14696	60841	5779	51925	3137	32509	1976	30050	77	406
2006	962	20503	12276	6269	2482	3525	33547	1956	30953	89	549
2007	962	20754	20040	6915	9275	3850	20770	1925	17872	98	875
2008	956	20340	128525	7644	117118	3763	21885	1733	18689	93	1369
2009	956	20755	133872	8161	121373	4339	22017	1635	18753	98	1531
2010	956	21114	140663	8903	126130	5630	23712	1572	20184	130	1827
2011	1067	21347	145773	9755	129918	6100	26849	1380	23276	132	2061
2012	1115	21492	149037	10315	132333	6389	28650	1232	24925	134	2359
2013	1116	21673	71056	11588	52481	6988	28294	1078	24651	136	2429
2014	1124	21849	71715	12609	52354	6752	29518	1132	25416	149	2821
2015	1124	21885	69924	12821	49931	7172	23236	1004	19044	158	3030
2016	1103	22026	69292	13380	48040	7872	24099	725	19972	163	3239
2017	1103	22226	67420	13873	44940	8607	23879	704	19374	175	3627
2018	1103	22256	67571	14273	44175	9123	25244	569	20278	177	4221
2019	1205	22366	72148	14755	48151	9241	27338	449	22325	166	4398
2020	1242	22264	36270	6383	24548	5339	26346	360	21789	147	4049
2021	1340	22320	42308	8550	28059	5699	28127	311	23075	162	4580
2022	1354	22363	28010	3907	21105	2998	24030	346	18549	128	5008

注：1.铁路数据为北京市市辖范围，2005年以前来源于北京铁路分局，自2005年起来源于北京铁路局，公路里程数据来源于北京市交通委员会。

2.自2006年起，公路里程包括村道数据。

3.2006-2007年公路客运量为持有道路运输经营许可证的客运车辆发生的旅客运输量；自2008年起，调整为旅游客运、省际客运企业、郊区客运和市郊公交的运输量。2013年公路客运量、公路旅客周转量范围调整为省际客运、旅游客运和郊区客运，市郊公交不再纳入客运量统计。

4.自2007年起，公路货物运输为营业性运量。2019年开展了道路货物运输量专项调查，公路货运量和公路货物周转量为当年调查数据，下同。

5.民航统计范围为北京地区的民航运输法人单位，不包括在京运输飞行的外省市及外国航空公司。

Note: a) Railway figures are statistics within Beijing's jurisdiction. Figures for years before 2005 were from Beijing Railway Branch, those in and after 2005 were from Beijing Railway Bureau. Highway mileage figures were from Beijing Municipal Commission of Transport.

b) Since 2006, highway mileage includes figures of rural roads.

c) In 2006 and 2007, highway passenger traffic referred to passenger traffic of passenger vehicles with road transport operation permit; since 2008, highway passenger traffic has been adjusted to refer to the transportation volume of tourist passenger transport, inter-provincial passenger transport enterprises, suburban passenger transport and suburban public transport. In 2013, the statistical scope of highway passenger traffic and highway passenger turnover was changed to inter-provincial, tourist and suburban passenger transport, and suburban public transport was no longer included in the statistics on passenger traffic.

d) From 2007, highway freight traffic refers to freight for operational purpose. Specific survey on road freight traffic was carried out in 2019; data on highway freight traffic and highway turnover in the table were the survey data of the year, the same below.

e) Civil aviation covers legal entities of civil aviation registered in Beijing, excluding airlines of other provinces and other countries with transport and flight in Beijing.

15-1 续表 1 Continued 1

年 份 Year	旅 客 周转量 (万人公里) Total Passenger Turnover (10000 passengers-km)	铁 路 Railway	公 路 Highway	民 航 Civil Aviation	货 物 周转量 (万吨公里) Total Freight Turnover (10000 tons-km)	铁 路 Railway	公 路 Highway	民 航 Civil Aviation	管 道 Pipeline
1978			59367				92247		
1979			64033				97616		
1980			73692				93899		
1981			81879				93254		
1982	755815	641550	90092	24173	3451037	3329450	106767	13530	1290
1983	853655	723200	103742	26713	3794223	3666600	110118	16099	1406
1984	968481	821431	113871	33179	4309798	4171789	115740	20896	1373
1985	1089919	936300	109184	44435	4719663	4576400	114156	27437	1670
1986	1133620	496288	119065	518267	2569579	2133836	405645	28281	1817
1987	1281763	534720	133735	613308	2792589	2282106	471393	37966	1124
1988	1503508	588947	141625	772936	2887270	2344684	498391	42612	1583
1989	1216981	521263	122435	573283	2765660	2179878	546022	38194	1566
1990	1198022	467332	132350	598339	2688246	2067402	574635	44662	1547
1991	1383465	506431	139041	737993	2799731	2153176	591187	54929	439
1992	1666810	531574	161735	973501	2938746	2230406	642200	65614	527
1993	1656130	551392	127461	977277	3143512	2301941	767790	73216	565
1994	1906718	547488	180030	1179200	3107722	2303265	725740	78142	575
1995	2076879	508995	234540	1333344	3231034	2393403	762027	74940	663
1996	2219196	459514	250488	1509194	3176234	2311011	784888	79983	352
1997	2272177	477538	261204	1533435	3129097	2263274	769190	96202	431
1998	2419787	505554	304592	1609641	2846652	1952602	783237	110470	343
1999	2701471	579759	400597	1721115	2838857	1929269	754264	155171	153
2000	3139918	627222	527645	1985051	2996414	2001875	826438	167691	410
2001	3462571	677146	529776	2255649	3159848	2167201	826437	165832	378
2002	3961623	642676	603510	2715437	3405498	2213728	835873	195792	160105
2003	3933077	619631	693100	2620346	3620777	2409620	789952	208058	213147
2004	7580057	738956	1582441	5258660	4022791	2571459	822992	270182	358158
2005	8380778	776028	1873754	5730996	4577370	3108137	854944	281672	332617
2006	8254536	890691	791947	6571898	4231243	2625719	885991	335693	383840
2007	9603464	908438	1474249	7220776	4490390	2684862	792883	376074	636572
2008	10419977	902281	2409604	7108091	4542168	2535249	840878	356744	809297
2009	11464758	935596	2677144	7852018	4412317	2293902	878887	355257	884271
2010	13995404	995507	2906492	10093405	5136580	2574567	1015944	482467	1063602
2011	15286501	1086609	3036655	11163237	6169272	3113203	1323259	474856	1257955
2012	15957877	1163833	3047757	11746287	6383052	3076143	1397736	489845	1419328
2013	14987719	1179555	1360831	12447333	6809063	3231824	1561929	491861	1523448
2014	16027249	1356313	1382967	13287969	6728238	2843623	1651938	553661	1679016
2015	17476775	1493106	1301210	14682459	6236947	2247538	1563562	637018	1788829
2016	18893132	1508200	1176740	16208192	6713288	2290438	1613192	671413	2138246
2017	20558450	1537625	993965	18026860	7000530	2464289	1592419	743891	2199932
2018	22199810	1545658	993699	19660453	7806542	2668681	1674068	784179	2679614
2019	22918448	1589007	1047823	20281618	9007714	2575184	2756801	727190	2948539
2020	10149918	706947	436697	9006274	8427606	2443443	2656831	660195	2667136
2021	10471705	954820	541106	8975779	8803872	2488089	2744131	756980	2814673
2022	5733035	435780	450311	4846944	8812490	2745242	2254273	668125	3144850

15-1 续表 2 Continued 2

年份 Year	机动车保有量(万辆) Possession of Motor Vehicles (10000 units)	#民用汽车 Civil Motor Vehicles	#私人汽车 Private Vehicles	邮电业务总量(亿元) Business Volume of Post and Telecommunication Services (100 million yuan)	年末固定电话用户数(万户) Year-end Number of Fixed Telephone Subscribers (10000 subscribers)	年末移动电话用户数(万户) Year-end Number of Mobile Phone Subscribers (10000 subscribers)	固定电话主线普及率(线/百人) Popularization Rate of Main Line of Fixed Telephones (line/100 persons)	移动电话普及率(户/百人) Popularization Rate of Mobile Phones (subscriber/100 persons)	固定互联网宽带接入用户数(万户) Subscribers of Broad Band Internet (10000 subscribers)
1978		6.1		2.4	7.3		0.8		
1979		7.0		2.7	7.8		0.9		
1980		8.1		3.0	8.4		0.9		
1981		8.9		3.2	9.2		1.0		
1982		9.3		3.5	9.8		1.1		
1983		9.8		3.9	10.9		1.2		
1984		12.1		4.6	12.1		1.3		
1985		16.0		5.4	13.6		1.4		
1986		18.6		6.2	16.5		1.6		
1987		19.3	0.7	7.1	19.5		1.9		
1988		22.2	1.3	8.4	23.8		2.2		
1989		24.8	2.4	9.8	27.8		2.6		
1990		27.1	2.8	11.9	33.3	0.3	3.1	0.03	
1991		29.7	3.5	15.7	39.5	0.7	3.6	0.1	
1992		34.1	4.9	21.6	48.0	1.2	4.4	0.1	
1993		41.6	6.7	31.1	66.5	3.2	6.0	0.3	
1994		48.1	8.5	41.9	100.4	7.7	8.9	0.7	
1995		58.9	12.8	56.1	150.5	16.9	12.0	1.4	
1996		62.2	17.4	72.9	195.7	31.0	15.5	2.5	
1997		78.4	29.8	93.0	251.2	62.0	20.3	5.0	
1998		89.8	40.7	129.1	313.3	104.2	25.1	8.4	
1999		95.1	44.7	165.9	376.3	186.2	29.9	14.8	
2000	157.8	104.1	49.4	214.7	451.2	347.2	33.1	25.5	
2001	169.9	114.5	62.4	218.3	525.7	629.4	38.0	45.4	
2002	189.9	133.9	81.1	254.0	585.5	919.5	41.1	64.6	
2003	212.4	163.1	107.1	304.0	682.7	1109.0	46.9	76.1	
2004	229.6	187.1	129.8	343.8	847.8	1340.9	56.8	89.8	
2005	258.3	214.6	154.0	413.0	943.5	1459.8	61.3	94.9	228.9
2006	287.6	244.1	181.0	504.6	905.2	1571.1	56.5	98.1	281.2
2007	312.8	277.8	212.1	705.0	914.5	1598.3	54.6	95.4	347.2
2008	350.4	318.1	248.3	841.6	884.9	1616.2	50.0	91.3	382.7
2009	401.9	372.1	300.3	955.6	893.1	1825.4	48.0	98.1	451.7
2010	480.9	452.9	374.4	1174.2	885.6	2129.8	45.1	108.6	545.6
2011	498.3	473.2	389.7	566.4	883.9	2575.9	43.7	127.3	523.4
2012	520.0	495.7	407.5	630.3	883.1	3168.0	42.5	152.5	572.0
2013	543.7	518.9	426.5	757.0	867.6	3373.8	40.8	158.7	534.7
2014	559.1	532.4	437.2	890.6	831.1	4076.2	38.3	187.7	552.7
2015	561.9	535.0	440.3	1181.9	784.7	4051.6	35.9	185.1	491.7
2016	571.7	548.4	452.8	1782.4	694.4	3868.7	31.6	176.2	475.5
2017	590.9	563.8	467.2	1294.8	649.0	3752.1	29.6	171.0	541.6
2018	608.4	574.6	479.0	2169.0	614.5	4008.8	28.0	182.9	634.7
2019	636.5	590.8	497.4	3142.1	555.4	4019.7	25.4	183.5	688.5
2020	657.0	600.3	507.9	3727.9	480.6	3906.4	22.5	178.5	747.8
2021	685.0	614.3	521.1	796.0	485.2	3972.0	22.2	181.5	806.3
2022	712.8	625.6	532.6	840.0	474.2	3926.9	21.7	179.8	877.3

注：1.邮电业务总量2000年及以前按1990年不变价格计算，2001—2010年按2000年不变价格计算，2011—2016年按2010年不变价格计算。2017—2020年，邮政行业业务总量按2010年不变价格计算，电信业务总量按2015年不变价格计算。自2021年起，邮政行业业务总量按2020年不变价格计算，电信业务总量按上年不变价格计算(按2020年不变价格计算，2020年邮电业务总量为668.7亿元，2021年同比增长18.6%)。

2.表内“邮电业务总量”中，2006年及以前邮政行业业务总量统计范围为中国邮政集团公司北京分公司和中国邮政快递物流股份有限公司北京分公司。自2007年起，邮政业务总量统计范围为邮政企业、取得快递业务经营许可的企业及其备案分支机构，下同。

3.表中主线普及率和移动电话普及率2006—2009年数据根据北京市第六次全国人口普查结果进行了修订，2011—2019年数据根据北京市第七次全国人口普查结果进行了修订。

Note: a)The business volume of post and telecommunication services in and before 2000 was calculated at 1990's constant prices; that of 2001-2010 was calculated at 2000's constant prices; that of 2011-2016 was calculated at 2010's constant prices; since 2017 until 2020, the business volume of post services was calculated at 2010's constant prices, and that of telecommunication services was calculated at 2015's constant prices. Since 2021, The business volume of post service was calculated at 2020's constant prices, and that of telecommunication services was calculated at constant prices of last year. (Calculated at 2020's constant prices, the business volume of post and telecommunication services in 2020 totaled RMB 66.87 billion, and that in 2021 increased by 18.6% year on year).

b) Among the "business volume of post and telecommunication services" in this table, the statistical range of the business volume of post services in and before 2006 was China Post Group Beijing Branch and China Postal Express & Logistics Co., Ltd. Beijing Branch.Since 2007, the statistical range of the business volume of post services covered the post enterprises, the enterprises permitted to conduct express delivery businesses and their filed branches, the same below.

c) Data of popularization rate of main line and mobile phones for 2006-2009 in this table were adjusted according to the results of the sixth national population census in Beijing, and the results for 2011-2019 were adjusted on the basis of the seventh national population census in Beijing.

15-2　社会客货运总量(换算周转量)
PASSENGER AND FREIGHT TRAFFIC (CONVERTED TURNOVER)

单位：万吨公里　　(10000 tons-km)

项　目	Item	2022	2021	2022年为2021年% 2022 as % of 2021	构　成(%) Composition(%)	
					2022	2021
运输总量	**Total**	**9720041.3**	**10608664.4**	**91.6**	**100.0**	**100.0**
铁　路	Railway	3181022.1	3444869.0	92.3	32.7	32.5
公　路	Highway	2299304.3	2798241.4	82.2	23.7	26.4
民　航	Civil Aviation	1094865.2	1550881.2	70.6	11.3	14.6
管　道	Pipeline	3144849.7	2814672.9	111.7	32.4	26.5

15-3　运输线路
TRANSPORTATION ROUTES

项　目	Item	条　数（条） Number (line)		长　度（公里） Length (km)	
		2022	2021	2022	2021
铁　路	Railway	72	67	1353.7	1340.0
公　路	Highway	10191	10161	22362.8	22319.9
民　航	Civil Aviation				
#中国国际航空公司	Air China	403	379		
中国新华航空有限责任公司	China Xinhua Airlines	408	529		
管　道	Pipeline	18	18	5715.4	5624.8

注：铁路长度为营业里程，管道长度为管输里程。
Note: Railway length refers to operating mileage, and pipeline length refers to transportation mileage.

15-4 铁路、民航主要技术经济指标
MAIN TECHNICAL AND ECONOMIC INDICATORS OF RAILWAY AND CIVIL AVIATION

项目	Item	2022	2021	2022年为2021年% 2022 as % of 2021
铁路	**Railway**			
内燃机车每万吨公里耗柴油（千克）	Diesel Consumption of Diesel Locomotives per 10 000 Ton-km (kg)	34.7	37.2	93.3
电力机车每万吨公里耗电（千瓦时）	Electricity Consumption of Electric Locomotives per 10000 Ton-km (kW·h)	96.5	101.8	94.8
民航	**Civil Aviation**			
每吨公里耗航空油（千克）	Aviation-oil Consumption per Ton-km (kg)	0.33	0.31	106.5

15-5 机动车保有量
POSSESSION OF MOTOR VEHICLES

单位：万辆 (10000 units)

项目	Item	2022	2021
机动车	**Motor Vehicles**	**712.8**	**685.0**
#民用汽车	Civil Automobiles	625.6	614.3
#载货汽车	Trucks	54.7	53.7
载客汽车	Passanger Vehicles	561.2	551.9
#私人汽车	Private Cars	532.6	521.1
#轿车	Sedans	290.6	294.1

资料来源：北京市公安局公安交通管理局。
Source: Beijing Traffic Management Bureau.

15-6 邮电业务主要指标(2022年)
MAIN INDICATORS OF POST AND TELECOMMUNICATION SERVICES(2022)

项　目	Item	2022	2022年为2021年% 2022 as % of 2021
邮电业务总量 (亿元)	**Business Volume of Post and Telecommunication Services (100 million yuan)**	**840.0**	**113.4**
邮政行业业务总量	Business Volume of Post Services	281.4	99.5
电信业务总量	Business Volume of Telecommunication Services	558.6	122.0
邮电业务	**Post and Telecommunication Services**		
函　件 (万件)	Letters (10000 pcs)	10738.3	81.8
包　裹 (万件)	Packages (10000 pcs)	109.1	86.6
特快专递业务量 (万件)	Express Mail Services (10000 pcs)	195628.5	88.5
汇　兑 (万笔)	Postal Remittance Transactions (10000 pcs)	18.3	66.5
订销报纸(累计) (万份)	Newspapers Subscribed and Sold (Accumulative) (10000 copies)	62192.6	95.8
订销杂志(累计) (万份)	Magazines Subscribed and Sold (Accumulative) (10000 copies)	2213.1	100.2
邮政代理储蓄期末余额 (亿元)	Ending Balance of Postal Agency Savings (100 million yuan)	1463.9	114.2
移动电话通话量 (亿分钟)	Calls of Mobile Phones (100 million minutes)	867.8	95.8
移动短信业务量 (亿条)	Short Message Services (100 million messages)	1632.3	142.7
年末移动电话用户 (万户)	Year-end Mobile Phone Subscribers (10000 subscribers)	3926.9	98.9
年末固定电话用户 (万户)	Year-end Fixed Telephone Subscribers (10000 subscribers)	474.2	97.7
移动电话交换机容量 (万户)	Capacity of Mobile Phone Exchanges (10000 subscribers)	10750	100.0
固定电话主线普及率 (线/百人)	Popularization Rate of Main Line of Fixed Telephones (line/100 persons)	21.7	97.7
移动电话普及率 (户/百人)	Popularization Rate of Mobile Phones (subscriber/100 persons)	179.8	99.1
固定互联网宽带接入用户数 (万户)	Subscribers of Broad Band Internet (10000 subscribers)	877.3	108.8

注：1.邮政行业业务总量按2020年不变价格计算，电信业务总量按上年不变价格计算。
2.特快专递业务量范围为取得快递业务经营许可企业及其备案分支机构。
3.表中发展速度按可比口径计算。

Note: a) The business volume of post services was calculated at 2020's constant prices,and that of telecommunication services was calculated at constant prices of last year.
b) Enterprises permitted to conduct express delivery businesses and their filed branches are required to submit the business volume of express mail services.
c) Indicators of development rate in the table are calculated in terms of comparable caliber.

主要统计指标解释

货（客）运量 指在一定时期内，各种运输工具实际运送的货物重量（旅客数量）。是反映运输业为国民经济和人民生活服务的数量指标，也是制定和检查运输生产计划，研究运输发展规模和速度的重要指标。货运按吨计算，客运按人计算。货物不论运输距离长短，货物类别，均按实际重量统计；旅客不论行程远近或票价多少，均按一人一次作为客运量统计。半价票、小孩票也按一人统计。

货物（旅客）周转量 指在一定时期内，由各种运输工具运送的货物（旅客）数量与其相应运输距离的乘积之总和，是反映运输业生产总成果的重要指标，也是编制和检查运输生产计划、计算运输效率、劳动生产率以及核算运输单位的主要基础资料。计算货物周转量通常按发出站与到达站之间的最短距离，也就是计费距离计算。

邮电业务总量 指以货币形式表示的邮政、电信通信企业为社会提供各类邮政、电信通信服务的总数量。计算方法为各类业务的实物量分别乘以相应的不变单价，求出各类业务的货币量加总求得。没有不变单价的业务按其业务收入直接相加。

函件 是指邮政部门为用户传递以书面信息为主的邮件，包括信件、印刷品和邮送广告。

包裹 指符合包裹准寄范围，通过邮政渠道寄递的物品。包括国内普通包裹、国内快递包裹、国际及港澳台包裹。

移动电话用户 指报告期末通过移动电话交换机进入移动电话网的全部电话用户。包括各类签约用户、智能网预付费用户、无线上网卡用户等。

固定电话用户 指在电信企业登记注册，且在报告期末实际已经接入电信企业固定电话网上的全部电话用户（包括局用电话交换机、接入网设备、软交换用户接入设备、无线市话设备）上的全部电话用户。

移动电话交换机容量 指移动电话交换机根据一定话务模型和交换机处理能力计算出来的最大同时服务用户的数量。

固定电话主线普及率 是指报告期行政区域常住人口中，平均每百人拥有的固定电话主线数。计算公式为：

$$\text{固定电话主线普及率}=\frac{\text{电话主线数}\left(\text{本地电话用户}\right)}{\text{行政区域常住人口数}}$$

移动电话普及率 是指报告期行政区域常住人口中，平均每百人拥有的移动电话的用户数。计算公式为：

$$\text{移动电话普及率}=\frac{\text{移动电话用户总数}}{\text{行政区域常住人口数}}$$

固定互联网宽带接入用户数 指报告期末在电信企业登记注册，通过 xDSL、FTTx+LAN 以及其他宽带接入方式和普通专线接入公众互联网的用户。

Explanatory Notes on Main Statistical Indicators

Freight (Passenger) Traffic refers to the weight of freight (number of passenger) transported with various means within a specific period of time It is a quantitative measure to show how the transport industry serves the national economy and people's life, and is also an important indicator for preparing and reviewing transport plan and studying the development scale and speed of the transport industry. Freight transport is calculated in tons and passenger traffic is calculated in the number of persons. Regardless of the types or traveling distance of freight, freight transport is calculated in terms of the actual weight of goods; and regardless of the traveling distance or ticket price, passenger traffic is calculated following the principle that one person can be counted only once in one trip. The passenger who travels with a half-price ticket or a child ticket is also calculated as one person.

Freight (Passenger) Turnover refers to the sum of the product of the volume of transported cargo (passengers) multiplied by the transport distance during a certain period of time. This is an important indicator to show the total results of the transport industry, and also serves as main basic data for preparing and reviewing transport plans and measuring transport efficiency, labor productivity and the transport unit. Freight turnover is usually calculated by the shortest distance between the departure station and the arrival station, namely the charging distance.

Business Volume of Post and Telecommunication Services refers to the total amount of post and telecommunication services, expressed in monetary terms, provided by the post and telecommunication enterprises for the society. Business volume of post and telecommunication is the sum of each service in kind multiplying with its correspondent unit price (constant price). For business without constant price, add their business revenue directly.

Letters mean mails mainly in the form of written information delivered by postal authorities, including letters, prints and delivered advertisements.

Package means articles permitted for mailing, and mailed through postal channels, including domestic regular parcels, domestic express parcels, international parcels, and parcels from and to Hong Kong, Macao and Taiwan.

Mobile Phone Subscribers refer to all users who have been connected with the mobile telephone communication network through the mobile telephone switchboards at the end of the reporting period. Included are various types of subscriber, prepaid users for intelligent network and wireless network card users.

Fixed-line Telephone Subscribers refer to all subscribers who have gone through registration procedures in the telecom companies and have actually been connected to the fixed-line telephone network of telecom companies at the end of the reporting period. Included are all subscribers of office telephone exchanges, access network equipment, soft switch user access equipment, and wireless local telephone equipment.

Capacity of Mobile Phone Exchanges means the maximum number of users receiving services simultaneously from mobile phone exchangers, calculated from certain traffic model and exchanger processing capacity.

Popularization Rate of Fixed-line Telephones means the average number of main lines of fixed-line telephones owned per one hundred persons of permanent population in administrative areas in the reporting period. It is calculated with the following formula:

Popularization Rate of Fixed-line Telephones = Number of Main Lines of Telephone (Local Phone Users) / Number of Permanent Population in Administrative Areas

Popularization Rate of Mobile Phones means the average number of mobile phones owned per 100 persons among permanent population in administrative areas in the reporting period. It is calculated with the following formula:

Popularization Rate of Mobile Phones = Total Number of Mobile Phone Users / Permanent Population in Administrative Areas

Subscribers of Broadband Internet means subscribers registered at telecom companies to connect with public Internet through xDSL, FTTx+LAN as well as other broadband connections and general special lines at the end of reporting period.

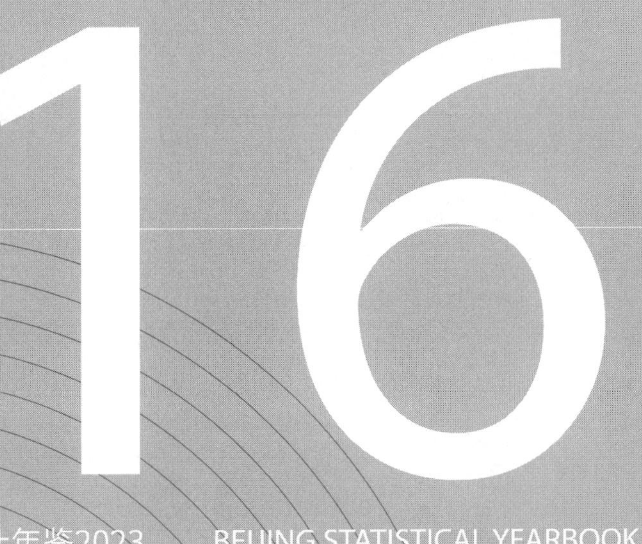

批发和零售业、住宿和餐饮业

WHOLESALE AND RETAIL TRADE, ACCOMMODATION AND CATERING

简要说明

一、主要内容

本章资料反映北京市商品流通市场发展及批发和零售业、住宿和餐饮业经营情况。包括社会消费品零售总额，批发和零售业商品购进、销售、库存、商品分类销售情况，住宿和餐饮业经营情况，限额以上批发和零售业、住宿和餐饮业财务状况，连锁企业基本情况，商品交易市场基本情况、成交额，北京消费者信心指数。

二、统计范围

社会消费品零售总额指标于1993年、1997年和2003年进行了调整。1993年起不再包括对农民的农业生产资料；1997年起不再包括居民购买住房；2003年起不再包括由各种经济类型的制造业法人企业、产业活动单位直接售给城乡居民（包括本企业职工）和社会集团的商品以及农民对非农业居民的零售额。

限额以上批发和零售业、住宿和餐饮业统计限额标准：2008 年以前，批发业为年销售额 2000 万元及以上；零售业为年销售额 500 万元及以上；住宿业为星级饭店和星级以外年营业收入 500 万元及以上；餐饮业为年营业额 200 万元及以上。自 2008 年起，批发业为年主营业务收入 2000 万元及以上；零售业为年主营收入 500 万元及以上；住宿业为星级饭店和星级以外年主营业务收入 200 万元及以上；餐饮业为年主营业务收入 200 万元及以上。2020 年调整后，住宿业为年主营业务收入 200 万元及以上。

北京消费者信心指数调查范围覆盖全市 16 个区。

三、调查方法

限额以上批发和零售业、住宿和餐饮业单位采用全面调查；连锁企业、商品交易市场采取全数调查。

北京消费者信心指数调查采用计算机辅助电话方式调查，调查对象为居住在北京市半年以上 18-65 周岁的城乡居民。

四、有关统计标准的变化说明

2010 年及以前，企业大中小型划分执行 2003 年《统计上大中小型企业划分办法（暂行）》。2011 年至 2017 年大中小微型企业划分标准执行国家统计局《关于统计上大中小微型企业划分办法》（国统字〔2011〕75 号）；自 2018 年起，执行《统计上大中小微型企业划分办法（2017）》（国统字〔2017〕213 号）。

五、本章中关于历史数据调整的问题

按照国家统计局统一要求和统一方法，本章中 1978 年至 2003 年的社会消费品零售总额数据，根据北京市第一次全国经济普查结果，采用“速度推算法”进行了修订，2004 年数据为北京市第一次全国经济普查数据；2005-2007 年数据根据北京市第二次全国经济普查结果，采用“趋势离差法”进行了修订，2008 年数据为北京市第二次全国经济普查数据；2009-2012 年数据根据北京市第三次全国经济普查结果进行了修订，2013 年数据为北京市第三次全国经济普查数据；在前三次普查数据修订基础上，1992-2019 年社会消费品零售总额数据根据北京市第四次全国经济普查结果，采用“趋势离差法”进行了修订，2018 年数据为北京市第四次全国经济普查数据。

Brief Introduction

I. Main Content

Statistics in this chapter show the development of commodity circulation market and the operations of wholesale and retail trades, accommodation and catering. Including: total retail sales of consumer goods, commodity purchase, sales and inventory in wholesale and retail trades, and sales of commodities by category, operation situation of accommodation and catering, financial status of wholesale, retail, accommodation and restaurants enterprises above designated size, basic situation of chain businesses, basic situation and turnover of commodity transaction markets, and Beijing consumer confidence index.

II. Scope of Statistics

Adjustments were made to the indicators of total retail sales of consumer goods in 1993, 1997 and 2003. From 1993, the indicator did not cover agricultural means of production for farmers any longer; from 1997, it did not cover houses bought by residents any longer; from 2003, it did not cover goods sold by corporate manufacturing enterprises and industrial activity entities of various economic types to urban and rural residents (including enterprises' own employees) and social groups as well as retail sales by farmers to non-agricultural residents any longer.

As for standards for wholesale and retail trades, accommodation and catering above designated size, before 2008, for wholesale trades, the standard was annual sales of RMB 20 million and above; for retail trades, annual sales of RMB 5 million and above; for accommodation, star-rated hotels and non-star-rated hotels with annual business income of RMB 5 million and above; for restaurants, annual turnover of RMB 2 million and above. Since 2008, the designated size is, for wholesale trades, annual main business income of RMB 20 million and above; for retail trades, annual main business income of RMB 5 million and above; for accommodation, star-rated hotels and non-star-rated hotels with annual main business income of RMB 2 million and above; for restaurants, annual main business income of RMB 2 million and above. After adjustments were made in 2020, for accommodation, annual main business income of RMB 2 million and above.

Survey of Beijing consumer confidence index covers 16 districts in the City.

III. Methods of Survey

The method of comprehensive survey was used for statistics of wholesale and retail trades, accommodation and catering service enterprises above designated size; complete enumeration was used for chain businesses, and commodity transaction markets.

Statistics on Beijing consumer confidence index were obtained through computer-aided phone calls to urban and rural residents aged 18-65 who have been living in Beijing for more than half a year.

IV. Changes in Relevant Statistical Standards

2010 and before, the classification of small, medium and large-sized enterprises should comply with the standards in the *Measures for Statistical Classification of Small, Medium and Large-sized Enterprises (Temporary)* 2003. The classification of micro, small, medium and large-sized enterprises should comply with the standards in the *Measures for Statistical Classification of Micro, Small, Medium and Large-sized Enterprises* (G.T.Z. [2011] No. 75) of the National Bureau of Statistics from 2011 to 2017. Since 2018, the classification has been in line with the standards in the *Measures for Statistical Classification of Micro, Small, Medium and Large-sized Enterprises (2017)* (G.T.Z. [2017] No. 213).

V. Adjustment to Historical Data

In accordance with the unified requirements and methods put forward by the National Bureau of Statistics, data for 1978-2003 on total retail sales of consumer goods were revised with the "speed calculation method" according to the results of the first national economic census in Beijing. Data for 2004 were gathered from the first national economic census in Beijing. Data for 2005-2007 were revised with the "trend deviation method" in accordance with the second national economic census in Beijing results in Beijing Data for 2008 were gathered from the second national economic census. Data for 2009-2012 were revised in accordance with the third national economic census in Beijing results. Data for 2013 were gathered from the third national economic census. in Beijing On the basis of the previous three revisions of the census data, data for 1992 – 2019 on total retail sales of consumer goods were revised with the "trend deviation method" in accordance with the fourth national economic census in Beijing results; and data for 2018 were gathered from the fourth national economic census in Beijing.

16-1 社会消费品零售总额(1978-2022年)
TOTAL RETAIL SALES OF CONSUMER GOODS (1978-2022)

单位：亿元 (100 million yuan)

年 份 Year	社会消费品零售总额 Total Retail Sales of Consumer Goods	#限额以上批发零售业、住宿餐饮业网上零售额 Online Retail Sales of Wholesale, Retail, Accommodation and Catering Enterprises above Designated Size	按商品类别分 By Category of Commodity 吃类商品 Food	穿类商品 Clothing	用类商品 Daily use Articles	烧类商品 Fuels
1978	44.2		18.0	8.9	16.0	1.3
1979	53.3		20.8	11.3	19.7	1.5
1980	62.8		24.9	13.4	22.9	1.6
1981	70.7		28.0	14.5	26.5	1.7
1982	75.4		29.7	13.7	30.3	1.7
1983	86.4		34.0	15.7	34.8	1.9
1984	105.8		39.6	18.7	45.2	2.3
1985	134.4		49.6	22.5	59.4	2.9
1986	155.0		60.7	22.8	68.0	3.5
1987	188.9		77.4	27.4	80.2	3.9
1988	256.0		100.6	36.0	114.9	4.5
1989	294.8		119.4	34.9	134.1	6.4
1990	345.1		136.8	45.6	154.6	8.1
1991	408.3		158.2	53.7	187.6	8.8
1992	503.0		193.6	66.9	230.5	12.0
1993	615.8		220.8	96.6	281.8	16.5
1994	778.1		283.5	125.6	349.3	19.7
1995	971.8		406.4	139.4	407.9	18.2
1996	1093.6		428.4	153.2	491.8	20.2
1997	1254.3		449.1	162.5	608.3	34.3
1998	1436.2		401.1	168.4	823.1	43.7
1999	1589.9		419.4	145.4	951.7	73.4
2000	1760.3		459.6	161.8	1050.5	88.4
2001	1958.1		515.7	180.8	1161.1	100.5
2002	2159.9		527.3	179.4	1330.2	123.0
2003	2492.6		563.0	200.8	1587.2	141.7
2004	2883.6		691.1	231.2	1748.7	212.6
2005	3221.4		802.8	269.1	1901.1	248.3
2006	3673.3		873.2	299.4	2172.8	328.0
2007	4307.4		1000.3	341.1	2614.9	351.1
2008	5257.5		1223.0	413.2	3233.4	387.8
2009	6140.0		1344.9	476.9	3928.0	390.2
2010	7273.0		1517.8	552.7	4718.9	483.5
2011	8334.8		1781.6	671.2	5262.8	619.3
2012	9440.2		1916.9	725.3	6140.2	657.8
2013	10382.5		1965.9	733.4	7039.2	644.0
2014	11354.0	1456.9	2027.7	740.1	7937.2	649.0
2015	12271.9	2016.9	2215.5	747.6	8758.8	549.9
2016	13134.9	2049.0	2336.4	764.2	9457.2	577.1
2017	13933.7	2458.0	2468.6	794.9	10069.9	600.4
2018	14422.3	2757.2	2623.1	817.3	10339.9	642.1
2019	15063.7	3507.6	2822.8	811.2	10829.1	600.6
2020	13716.4	4423.3	2795.7	697.7	9766.2	456.9
2021	14867.7	5392.7	2966.3	827.3	10472.5	601.7
2022	13794.2	5485.6	2832.4	657.0	9723.6	581.2

注：2014-2016年，限额以上批发零售业、住宿餐饮业网上零售额不含住宿和餐饮业。
Note: The data on the online retail sales of wholesale, retail, accommodation and catering enterprises above designated size from 2014 to 2016 didn't cover the accommodation and catering.

16-2 社会消费品零售总额(2022年)
TOTAL RETAIL SALES OF CONSUMER GOODS(2022)

单位：亿元 (100 million yuan)

项 目	Item	2022	2022年为2021年% 2022 as % of 2021
社会消费品零售总额	**Total Retail Sales of Consumer Goods**	**13794.2**	**92.8**
按商品类别分	**By Category of Commodity**		
吃类商品	Food	2832.4	95.6
穿类商品	Clothing	657.0	81.4
用类商品	Daily Use Articles	9723.6	92.6
烧类商品	Fuels	581.2	97.7
按消费品形态分	**By Form of Consumer Goods**		
餐饮收入	Food and Beverage Income	961.6	84.8
商品零售	Retail Sales of Commodities	12832.6	93.4

注：表中发展速度按可比口径计算。
Note: Indicators of development rate in the table are calculated in terms of comparable caliber.

16-3 按登记注册类型分限额以上批发和零售业商品零售额(2022年)
RETAIL SALES OF GOODS IN WHOLESALE AND RETAIL TRADE ABOVE DESIGNATED SIZE BY REGISTRATION TYPE (2022)

单位：亿元 (100 million yuan)

项　　目	Item	商品零售额 Retail Sales of Goods	批发业 Wholesale	零售业 Retail Trade
合　计	**Total**	**9255.4**	**773.2**	**8482.2**
内资企业	Domestic Funded Enterprises	5142.5	554.2	4588.3
#国　有	State-owned Enterprises	17.1	0.2	16.9
集　体	Collectively-owned Enterprises	19.9	0.3	19.6
股份合作	Joint-equity Cooperative Enterprises	17.3	5.4	11.9
有限责任公司	Limited Liability Corporations	3394.0	327.3	3066.7
股份有限公司	Corporationss Limited by Shares	552.6	89.6	462.9
私　营	Private Enterprises	1139.5	131.2	1008.3
港澳台商投资企业	Hong Kong, Macao and Taiwan-invested Enterprises	656.0	57.2	598.8
外商投资企业	Foreign-invested Enterprises	3456.9	161.8	3295.1

注：本表统计范围为限额以上批发和零售业法人单位(16-4至16-5表同)。
Note: This table covers legal entities in wholesale and retail trade above designated size (same as the table from 16-4 to 16-5).

16-4 限额以上批发和零售业商品购进、销售、库存情况(2022年)
TOTAL VALUE OF PURCHASES, SALES AND INVENTORY IN WHOLESALE AND RETAIL TRADE ABOVE DESIGNATED SIZE (2022)

单位：亿元 (100 million yuan)

项　　目	Item	合计 Total Sales	批发业 Wholesale	零售业 Retail Trade
商品购进额	**Total Purchases of Commodities**	**86296.6**	**76477.1**	**9819.5**
商品销售额	**Total Sales of Commodities**	**90690.8**	**80012.6**	**10678.2**
批发额	Wholesale Sales	81435.4	79239.5	2196.0
零售额	Retail Sales	9255.4	773.2	8482.2
期末商品库存额	**Inventory (Year-end)**	**7197.1**	**6349.9**	**847.2**

16-5 限额以上批发和零售业商品销售类值(2022年)
SALES BY CATEGORY FOR WHOLESALE AND RETAIL TRADE ABOVE DESIGNATED SIZE (2022)

单位：亿元 (100 million yuan)

项目	Item	商品销售额 Total Sales	批发额 Wholesale Sales	零售额 Retail Sales
合计	**Total**	**90690.8**	**81435.4**	**9255.4**
粮油、食品类	Cereal, Oil and Food	5915.1	5037.9	877.2
#粮油类	Cereal and Oil	3499.0	3410.4	88.6
肉禽蛋类	Meat, Poultry and Eggs	538.5	413.0	125.5
饮料类	Beverages	703.0	439.0	264.0
烟酒类	Tobacco and Liquor	1536.2	1274.2	261.9
服装、鞋帽、针纺织品类	Clothing, Shoes, Hats and Textiles	958.5	495.4	463.2
#服装类	Clothing	591.4	230.1	361.4
鞋帽类	Shoes and Hats	223.1	148.9	74.1
针纺织品类	Knitwear and Textiles	144.0	116.3	27.7
化妆品类	Cosmetics	356.4	187.7	168.7
金银珠宝类	Gold, Silver and Jewelry	1156.0	800.7	355.3
日用品类	Articles for Daily Use	2249.4	1529.4	720.0
#儿童玩具类	Children's Toys	157.5	74.4	83.1
五金、电料类	Hardware and Electrical Materials	302.4	291.5	10.9
体育、娱乐用品类	Sports and Recreation Goods	1563.5	1389.9	173.6
书报杂志类	Newspapers and Magazines	330.3	198.7	131.7
电子出版物及音像制品类	E-Journals and Video Products	79.4	40.5	38.9
家用电器和音像器材类	Household Appliances and Audiovisual Products	3550.4	3049.2	501.1
中西药品类	Traditional Chinese and Western Medicines	2525.7	2418.7	106.9
#西药类	Western Medicines	1626.6	1556.1	70.4
中草药及中成药类	Chinese Herbal Medicines and Chinese Patent Medicines	337.9	319.6	18.3
文化办公用品类	Cultural and Office Goods	6575.5	5591.2	984.3
家具类	Furniture	140.4	46.2	94.2
通讯器材类	Communication Devices	8871.7	7052.5	1819.2
煤炭及制品类	Coal and Coal Products	6286.6	6286.4	0.2
木材及制品类	Wood and Wooden Products	1020.1	1020.1	
石油及制品类	Petroleum and Its Products	10688.2	10228.1	460.1
化工材料及制品类	Raw Chemical Materials	8139.0	8139.0	
#化肥类	Fertilizer	1263.8	1263.8	
金属材料类	Metal Materials	10489.4	10489.4	
建筑及装潢材料类	Building and Decoration Materials	621.6	585.1	36.5
机电产品及设备类	Electric-mechanic Products and Equipment	3635.6	3554.5	81.1
#农机类	Agricultural Machinery	123.5	123.5	
汽车类	Automobiles	8982.4	7430.2	1552.2
种子饲料类	Seed and Feedstuff	725.6	725.6	
棉麻类	Cotton and Hemp	651.9	651.9	
其他类	Others	2636.5	2482.5	154.0

16–6 限额以上住宿和餐饮业经营情况(2022年)
STATISTICS FOR ACCOMMODATION AND CATERING ABOVE DESIGNATED SIZE (2022)

项目	Item	合计 Total	住宿业 Accommodation Industry	餐饮业 Catering Industry
客房数（间）	**Number of Rooms (room)**	**223148**	**218015**	**5133**
床位数（个）	**Number of Beds (unit)**	**341575**	**332439**	**9136**
餐位数（位）	**Number of Tables (table)**	**1791073**	**242458**	**1548615**
营业额（万元）	**Turnover (10000 yuan)**	**10739347**	**2727341**	**8012006**
客房收入	Income from Rooms	1424945	1395390	29555
餐费收入	Income from Meals	7819417	491268	7328149
商品销售额	Sales of Commodities	313317	37621	275695
其他收入	Other Incomes	1181669	803063	378606

注：本表统计范围为限额以上住宿和餐饮业法人单位。
Note:This table covers legal entities in accommodation and catering above designated size.

16-7 限额以上批发和零售业企业财务状况(2022年)

单位：亿元

项目	Item	企业单位个数(个) Number of Enterprises (unit)	资产总计 Total Assets	流动资产合计 Total Current Assets
合计	**Total**	**10727**	**62123.3**	**42701.1**
按企业登记注册类型分	**By Registration Type**			
内资	Domestically-invested Enterprises	9865	44994.5	29611.8
国有	State-owned Enterprises	41	398.1	364.5
集体	Collectively-owned Enterprises	52	21.0	14.9
股份合作	Joint-equity Cooperative Enterprises	71	31.0	27.3
联营	Associated Enterprises	5	14.3	8.8
有限责任公司	Limited Liability Corporations	2966	34385.1	22245.9
股份有限公司	Corporations Limited by Shares	110	5070.0	2521.1
私营	Private Enterprises	6612	5073.4	4428.2
其他	Other	8	1.5	1.0
港澳台商投资	Hong Kong, Macao and Taiwan-invested Enterprises	258	6635.9	5378.5
外商投资	Foreign-invested Enterprises	604	10493.0	7710.7
按国民经济行业分	**By Sector**			
批发业	Wholesale	8163	56948.4	38791.5
农、林、牧、渔产品批发	Wholesale of Agriculture, Forestry, Animal Husbandry and Fishery Products	170	3947.8	2608.3
食品、饮料及烟草制品批发	Wholesale of Foods, Beverage and Tobaccos	1028	3795.9	3098.4
纺织、服装及家庭用品批发	Wholesale of Textile, Clothes and Household Commodities	665	4781.3	3883.2
文化、体育用品及器材批发	Wholesale of Cultural and Sports Goods and Equipment	427	1670.6	1206.8
医药及医疗器材批发	Wholesale of Medicine and Medical Devices	1050	3392.4	2691.2
矿产品、建材及化工产品批发	Wholesale of Mineral Products, Building Materials, and Chemical Products	1854	23179.1	12672.8
机械设备、五金交电及电子产品批发	Wholesale of Mechanical Equipment, Hardware and Electronic Products	2790	13214.3	10104.8
贸易经纪与代理	Trade Broker and Agent	44	2171.1	1956.6
其他批发业	Others	135	796.0	569.4
零售业	Retail	2564	5174.9	3909.5
综合零售	Integrated Retail	249	1420.7	760.5
食品、饮料及烟草制品专门零售	Special Retails of Foods, Beverage and Tobacoos	234	264.4	229.7
纺织、服装及日用品专门零售	Special Retail of Textile, Clothing and Domestic Commodities	242	198.6	164.1
文化、体育用品及器材专门零售	Special Retail of Cultural and Sports Goods and Equipment	209	451.4	364.7
医药及医疗器材专门零售	Special Retail of Medicine and Medical Devices	121	64.6	55.0
汽车、摩托车、零配件和燃料及其他动力销售	Sales of Automobiles, Motorcycles, Accessories, Fuels and Other Power	877	997.0	744.4
家用电器及电子产品专门零售	Special Retail of Household Electrical Appliances and Electronic Products	217	585.4	510.1
五金、家具及室内装饰材料专门零售	Special Retail of Hardware, Furniture and Indoor Decoration Materials	86	103.7	56.5
货摊、无店铺及其他零售业	Stand Retail, Retail Without Shops and Other Retail	329	1089.1	1024.5
按规模划分	**By Size**			
#大中型企业	Medium and Large-sized Enterprises	3695	53632.0	35764.0

FINANCIAL STATUS OF ENTERPRISES ABOVE DESIGNATED SIZE IN WHOLESALE AND RETAIL TRADE (2022)

(100 million yuan)

资产负债 Assets and Liabilities						
#应收账款 Accounts Receivable	固定资产原价 Original Value of Fixed Assets	负债合计 Total Liabilities	#流动负债合计 Total Current Liabilities	#应付账款 Accounts Payable	所有者权益合计 Total Owner's Equity	#实收资本 Paid-up Capital
7777.3	**2255.3**	**41602.6**	**37359.9**	**10129.1**	**20502.8**	**9987.8**
5926.5	1786.3	29988.4	26633.3	6752.2	14982.0	8142.7
1.1	29.9	200.2	199.2	7.0	198.0	5.0
1.8	7.7	17.3	16.8	2.7	3.7	3.2
5.4	3.2	23.0	22.6	5.5	8.0	6.1
0.3	2.1	3.7	3.7	0.2	10.6	9.3
4589.2	1326.9	23342.2	20681.6	5506.2	11043.9	6975.0
282.1	162.1	2618.8	2048.3	279.4	2429.6	524.2
1046.1	253.7	3782.3	3660.4	950.9	1287.5	619.7
0.5	0.7	0.8	0.8	0.3	0.7	0.2
388.3	160.8	5376.3	5150.5	1406.4	1262.7	669.8
1462.6	308.1	6237.9	5576.0	1970.5	4258.2	1175.4
7061.1	1695.9	37662.5	33830.9	9023.7	19281.9	9215.2
363.8	51.6	2700.8	2314.6	217.9	1247.0	476.0
267.3	147.0	2936.7	2783.2	304.9	856.6	500.2
172.7	84.5	3613.8	3556.1	931.1	1165.9	455.6
114.3	77.9	1020.0	841.2	154.2	650.7	343.1
742.2	95.8	2210.7	2104.8	863.6	1181.6	451.0
2608.5	857.2	14266.0	12122.7	2868.5	8906.0	5127.0
1798.4	332.8	8456.1	7782.7	2449.0	4766.1	1617.9
908.2	30.6	1811.5	1790.4	1108.9	359.5	159.8
85.6	18.5	646.9	535.3	125.6	148.4	84.6
716.2	559.4	3940.0	3529.0	1105.4	1221.0	772.6
66.4	232.5	920.8	744.8	208.3	478.2	228.7
28.3	30.3	171.2	167.7	45.5	93.2	32.9
42.3	18.3	189.0	173.6	93.1	9.0	82.8
34.7	30.4	291.6	241.2	61.7	161.4	59.2
7.2	2.9	57.3	53.5	21.4	7.8	7.5
60.2	184.4	778.3	700.6	93.3	218.5	164.1
211.6	17.3	336.2	308.0	132.6	249.0	45.0
9.3	13.1	81.8	66.2	13.7	22.0	22.9
256.2	30.2	1113.8	1073.3	435.9	-18.2	129.5
6387.9	1690.3	35016.1	31680.9	8621.6	18615.9	8251.0

16-7 续表

单位：亿元

项目	Item	损益 营业收入 Business Income	 营业成本 Business Cost	 销售费用 Sales Expenses
合计	**Total**	**78731.9**	**73240.3**	**2639.8**
按企业登记注册类型分	**By Registration Type**			
内资	Domestically-invested Enterprises	51144.0	48317.5	1353.4
国有	State-owned Enterprises	724.9	631.9	16.1
集体	Collectively-owned Enterprises	28.4	24.3	2.3
股份合作	Joint-equity Cooperative Enterprises	52.5	47.5	2.2
联营	Associate Enterprises	1.8	1.6	0.1
有限责任公司	Limited Liability Corporations	38538.6	36857.1	827.3
股份有限公司	Corporations Limited by Shares	3622.7	3418.4	104.7
私营	Private Enterprises	8172.1	7333.9	400.7
其他	Other	2.9	2.7	0.0
港澳台商投资	Hong Kong, Macao and Taiwan-invested Enterprises	10540.0	9544.1	480.0
外商投资	Foreign-invested Enterprises	17047.9	15378.7	806.4
按国民经济行业分	**By Sector**			
批发业	Wholesale	69007.0	64651.9	1819.9
农、林、牧、渔产品批发	Wholesale of Agriculture, Forestry,Animal Husbandry and Fishery Products	3754.4	3604.4	17.7
食品、饮料及烟草制品批发	Wholesale of Foods, Beverage and Tobaccos	4157.0	3682.2	257.8
纺织、服装及家庭用品批发	Wholesale of Textile, Clothes and Household Commodities	8685.9	7862.7	370.5
文化、体育用品及器材批发	Wholesale of Cultural and Sports Goods and Equipment	1504.6	1325.8	80.6
医药及医疗器材批发	Wholesale of Medicine and Medical Devices	3513.8	2987.5	248.6
矿产品、建材及化工产品批发	Wholesale of Mineral Products, Building Materials, and Chemical Products	30143.3	29504.7	230.8
机械设备、五金交电及电子产品批发	Wholesale of Mechanical Equipment, Hardware and Electronic Products	16175.4	14732.2	579.2
贸易经纪与代理	Trade Broker and Agent	302.6	261.5	9.0
其他批发业	Others	770.0	691.1	25.8
零售业	Retail	9724.9	8588.4	819.9
综合零售	Integrated Retail	1189.8	930.2	187.6
食品、饮料及烟草制品专门零售	Special Retails of Foods, Beverage and Tobacoos	237.5	177.8	35.0
纺织、服装及日用品专门零售	Special Retail of Textile, Clothing and Domestic Commodities	261.6	147.6	101.6
文化、体育用品及器材专门零售	Special Retail of Cultural and Sports Goods and Equipment	439.5	346.8	45.7
医药及医疗器材专门零售	Special Retail of Medicine and Medical Devices	99.5	74.3	19.8
汽车、摩托车、零配件和燃料及其他动力销售	Sales of Automobiles, Motorcycles, Accessories, Fuels and Other Power	2081.3	1901.9	109.2
家用电器及电子产品专门零售	Special Retail of Household Electrical Appliances and Electronic Products	1452.3	1340.0	73.8
五金、家具及室内装修材料专门零售	Special Retail of Hardware, Furniture and Indoor Decoration Materials	89.9	57.2	25.4
货摊、无店铺及其他零售业	Stand Retail, Retail Without Shops and Other Retail	3873.5	3612.6	221.7
按规模划分	**By Size**			
#大中型企业	Medium and Large-sized Enterprises	68375.1	63599.8	2288.6

16-7 Continued

(100 million yuan)

Profits and Losses				应交税金合计 Total Tax Payable			
管理费用 Management Expenses	研发费用 R&D Expenses	财务费用 Financial Expenses	利润总额 Total Profits		税金及附加 Tax and Surtax	所得税费用 Income Tax Expense	应交增值税 Value Added Tax Payable
1591.4	**159.7**	**263.3**	**2464.0**	**1072.4**	**148.0**	**329.9**	**594.6**
791.8	97.6	262.5	1355.1	684.1	108.1	161.0	415.0
10.3	0.1	-7.7	55.7	59.9	36.6	11.2	12.1
1.7	0.0	0.2	0.0	0.5	0.1	0.0	0.4
2.0	0.3	0.2	-0.1	0.7	0.1	0.1	0.5
0.4		-0.3	0.2	0.1	0.0	0.0	0.0
448.7	60.4	216.6	1023.7	460.3	53.5	111.6	295.2
51.4	7.1	27.7	137.0	42.5	7.5	14.0	20.9
277.2	29.9	25.7	138.5	120.1	10.2	24.1	85.8
0.1		0.0	0.0	0.0	0.0	0.0	0.0
479.9	43.6	-3.5	293.9	73.7	12.5	16.1	45.0
319.7	18.5	4.3	814.9	314.6	27.3	152.7	134.6
1338.0	147.4	235.6	2440.2	921.2	117.8	297.9	505.4
28.8	2.8	44.7	107.4	26.9	3.8	14.3	8.9
83.0	4.2	9.5	143.5	130.0	44.1	27.7	58.2
422.1	12.0	-23.5	322.3	49.5	6.9	11.2	31.5
47.8	10.1	4.7	46.3	22.5	2.6	7.7	12.2
134.8	5.3	4.9	203.7	107.1	8.3	36.8	62.0
246.5	16.9	195.6	854.2	269.8	28.6	53.0	188.2
340.1	91.2	10.2	701.0	296.6	22.0	137.1	137.5
14.7	0.0	-10.2	47.5	10.7	1.0	7.0	2.7
20.3	4.8	-0.3	14.4	7.9	0.7	3.1	4.1
253.3	12.3	27.7	23.8	151.2	30.1	31.9	89.2
63.5	0.4	12.1	1.2	26.1	6.5	6.7	12.9
12.9	0.6	0.2	13.1	9.4	0.7	3.7	5.1
20.5	1.0	1.3	-8.0	12.6	1.2	1.3	10.1
29.3	1.1	1.8	12.7	16.7	4.9	4.9	6.8
5.0	0.3	0.2	0.2	2.6	0.2	0.4	2.0
58.4	1.7	10.7	-3.2	33.8	11.0	4.7	18.1
21.0	1.3	-0.2	16.2	20.9	2.0	6.5	12.4
9.1	0.2	0.5	-2.2	3.3	0.6	0.2	2.6
33.5	5.6	1.2	-6.2	25.8	3.0	3.5	19.3
1368.5	142.6	212.4	2380.4	852.7	131.8	294.4	426.5

16-8 限额以上住宿和餐饮业企业财务状况(2022年)

单位：万元

项目	Item	企业单位个数(个) Number of Enterprises (unit)	资产总计 Total Assets	流动资产合计 Total Current Assets
合　计	**Total**	**3302**	**27842414**	**12723023**
按登记注册类型分	**By Registration Type**			
内　资	Domestically-invested Enterprises	3083	20645055	9799668
#国　有	State-owned Enterprises	70	1001084	339739
集　体	Collectively-owned Enterprises	39	188984	48470
股份合作	Joint-equity Cooperative Enterprises	47	98616	42749
有限责任公司	Limited Liability Corporations	1068	16385409	7370580
股份有限公司	Corporations Limited by Shares	4	183216	40299
私　营	Private Enterprises	1852	2776274	1949897
港澳台商投资	Hong Kong, Macao and Taiwan-invested Enterprises	98	4400939	1987350
外商投资	Foreign-invested Enterprises	121	2796420	936005
按行业类别分	**By Sector Type**			
住宿业	Accommodation Enterprises	1141	21985034	9237043
#旅游饭店	Tourism Hotels	522	19377156	7940717
一般旅馆	General Hotels	562	2455263	1225873
餐饮业	Catering Enterprises	2161	5857380	3485980
正餐服务	Dinner Services	1709	2935723	1836685
快餐服务	Fast Food Services	125	1450332	523221
饮料及冷饮服务	Beverage and Cold Drink Services	50	675077	450322
餐饮配送及外卖送餐服务	Catering Distribution and Delivery Services	91	266930	225628
其他餐饮业	Other Catering Enterprises	186	529320	450124

FINANCIAL STATUS OF ENTERPRISES IN ACCOMMODATION AND CATERING ABOVE DESIGNATED SIZE (2022)

(10000 yuan)

资产负债 Assets and Liabilities						
#应收账款 Accounts Receivable	固定资产原价 Original Value of Fixed Assets	负债合计 Total Liabilities	#流动负债合计 Total Current Liabilities	#应付账款 Accounts Payable	所有者权益合计 Total Owner's Equity	#实收资本 Paid-up Capital
622561	**10923947**	**18202901**	**14025391**	**1325295**	**9721165**	**8104720**
455842	7899650	13176579	10848188	1051473	7544783	6429935
15553	1051775	576033	429987	19365	425051	317904
1285	234099	131579	339957	6520	56462	19605
3166	53498	83847	69679	21129	14769	9997
228425	5757179	9361189	7436780	553624	7074168	5602757
1774	67931	64142	56231	7407	119413	33306
205583	731707	2949404	2505730	442623	-146168	442372
40415	2026465	3036136	1749769	117155	1376710	1131689
126304	997832	1990186	1427434	156667	799672	543096
220567	9649267	13032084	9833528	510485	8984152	7089971
162919	8478860	11094340	8031186	394306	8315737	6211507
53137	1064940	1855647	1721641	105108	597897	844150
401994	1274680	5170817	4191863	814809	737014	1014749
192860	709413	3000222	2543981	435810	-9056	583240
33305	376514	1014763	565895	104746	430452	157109
9919	108634	591095	537075	56794	84168	120387
63995	30777	156551	155190	72083	110368	48330
101914	49342	408185	389721	145376	121082	105683

16-8 续表

单位：万元

项目	Item	损益 营业收入 Business Income	损益 营业成本 Business Cost	损益 销售费用 Sales Expenses	损益 管理费用 Management Expenses
合计	**Total**	**10205240**	**5091430**	**3848620**	**2069126**
按登记注册类型分	**By Registration Type**				
内资	Domestically-invested Enterprises	6497856	3451948	2120916	1547507
#国有	State-owned Enterprises	224464	49244	95980	130471
集体	Collectively-owned Enterprises	67283	18480	31202	23500
股份合作	Joint-equity Cooperative Enterprises	50102	23973	18376	11572
有限责任公司	Limited Liability Corporations	3512507	1907849	1116325	851107
股份有限公司	Corporations Limited by Shares	21671	26982	2040	9500
私营	Private Enterprises	2617536	1424491	854433	520158
港澳台商投资	Hong Kong, Macao and Taiwan-invested Enterprises	1917661	692514	1071409	272302
外商投资	Foreign-invested Enterprises	1789723	946968	656294	249316
按行业类别分	**By Sector Type**				
住宿业	Accommodation Enterprises	2600621	1163355	815658	1059496
#旅游饭店	Tourism Hotels	1892298	820144	569186	831758
一般旅馆	General Hotels	643316	307249	232546	206566
餐饮业	Catering Enterprises	7604618	3928075	3032962	1009629
正餐服务	Dinner Services	3661314	1773850	1559016	598823
快餐服务	Fast Food Services	1725966	744477	871446	145081
饮料及冷饮服务	Beverage and Cold Drink Services	590243	237746	342633	69430
餐饮配送及外卖送餐服务	Catering Distribution and Delivery Services	511177	399644	65557	46531
其他餐饮业	Other Catering Enterprises	1115917	772358	194309	149765

16-8 continued

(10000 yuan)

Profits and Losses			应交			
研发费用 R&D Expenses	财务费用 Financial Expenses	利润总额 Total Profits	税金合计 Total Tax Payable	税金及附加 Tax and Surtax	所得税费用 Income Tax Expense	应交增值税 Value Added Tax Payable
1522	**240857**	**-307491**	**465478**	**110475**	**174517**	**180486**
1422	150928	-79144	335605	73654	163752	98199
	-4639	-51270	17513	10074	1334	6106
	-233	-5788	2994	346	781	1867
	240	-4171	1924	616	303	1005
1035	127924	195931	265638	56488	157921	51229
277	355	-15131	728	635		93
110	27274	-198317	46708	5442	3404	37863
72	53199	-127771	71983	24742	5080	42161
28	36731	-100576	57890	12078	5685	40126
739	182071	62934	315396	100312	155999	59085
669	163415	187553	289389	91020	152627	45742
71	18876	-118991	24610	8774	3179	12657
783	58786	-370425	150082	10163	18518	121401
370	35886	-284366	72809	6149	6530	60130
334	25156	-35468	42420	1153	6072	35196
7	-3545	-60282	3693	515	-1402	4580
20	718	3744	6432	464	2279	3689
51	571	5947	24728	1882	5039	17807

16-9 连锁企业基本情况(2001-2022年)
STATISTICS FOR CHAIN ENTERPRISES (2001-2022)

年 份 Year	连锁总店(个) Number of General Chain Stores (unit)	门店总数(个) Number of Stores (unit)	从业人员年末人数(人) Year-end Number of Employed Persons (person)	营业面积(平方米) Operating Area (sq.m)	商品销售额(营业额)(万元) Sales of Commodities (Turnover) (10000 yuan)	#零售额 Retail Sales
2001	129	2123	139470	1605808	4831168	2186540
2002	146	3523	109089	2356266	6621975	6487185
2003	153	4519	132030	3405562	8404232	7601221
2004	196	5432	153942	3783507	8603560	8337829
2005	188	5973	166598	4376383	10612658	9507168
2006	205	6730	170007	5546003	11229026	9514297
2007	210	7645	185114	6677266	13890913	11573838
2008	240	8611	223954	6745802	15720473	12954839
2009	240	8928	218024	6995047	17366414	13816796
2010	234	9299	228292	7268786	21329783	16255496
2011	233	9845	280798	7953891	25742536	19507890
2012	220	10014	287975	8339674	26758403	20140433
2013	241	11111	299445	9026207	27834646	21495798
2014	243	11433	279567	9252645	28173728	21100845
2015	238	11942	279596	9238023	30453838	24508274
2016	245	12604	303319	11519137	32375249	27797369
2017	252	13450	316141	11121572	35574270	29557163
2018	277	15603	331018	11394589	38230004	31093369
2019	291	16126	326133	11183441	38223984	32566351
2020	295	16560	288096	11012622	36839402	32666424
2021	292	17974	290447	10059135	40485087	35526775
2022	288	17706	252537	9805062	38849911	33548258

16−10 连锁企业基本情况(按登记注册类型、经营业态分)(2022年)
STATISTICS FOR CHAIN ENTERPRISES (BY REGISTRATION TYPE OF ENTERPRISES AND OPERATION FORMS) (2022)

项 目	Item	门店总数 (个) Number of Stores (unit)	从业人员年末人数 (人) Year-end Number of Employed Persons (person)	营业面积 (平方米) Operating Area (sq.m)	商品销售额(营业额) (万元) Sales of Commodities (10000 yuan)	#零售额 Retail Sales
合 计	**Total**	**17706**	**252537**	**9805062**	**38849911**	**33548258**
按登记注册类型分	**By Registration Type**					
内 资	Domestically-invested Enterprises	10041	108532	7233553	20145347	15949288
国 有	State-owned Enterprises	143	2672	91786	350751	303336
集 体	Collectively-owned Enterprises	16	422	50584	46954	41475
股份合作	Joint-equity Cooperative Enterprises	3	20	630	278	278
联 营	Associated Enterprises					
国有独资公司	State-owned Solely-funded Corporations					
有限责任公司	Limited Liability Corporations	6093	55179	2892224	8837541	7042286
股份有限公司	Corporations Limited by Shares	1632	29130	3520847	9481447	7210340
私 营	Private Enterprises	2154	21109	677482	1428376	1351573
港澳台商投资	Hong Kong, Macao and Taiwan-invested Enterprises	4145	64471	1143176	2655801	2413873
外商投资	Foreign-invested Enterprises	3520	79534	1428333	16048764	15185097
按经营业态分	**By Operation Form**					
零售业态	Retail	10298	105020	7573012	34897030	29834550
便利店	Convenient Stores	2955	3223	263322	797108	713251
折扣店	Discount Stores	175	688	96997	157231	122680
超市及大型超市	Supermarkets and Large Supermarkets	1622	40827	2519605	7496347	6327065
仓储会员店	Warehouse Club Stores	5	1176	45192	367141	367141
百货店	Department Stores	95	12001	2979419	3033365	3023097
专业店	Specialty Stores	2260	16825	958472	4537672	3926007
加油站	Gas Stations	598	5424	283701	4646303	2832088
专卖店	Exclusive Stores	2588	24856	426304	13861863	12523221
餐饮业态	Catering Enterprises	7260	144829	2225567	3837693	3712512
中式正餐	Chinese Dinner	1118	32163	863091	1146349	1116332
中式快餐	Chinese Fast Food	1539	20468	340453	602183	559283
外国风味正餐	Exotic Dinner	934	35111	202552	495105	482364
外国风味快餐	Exotic Fast Food	1799	42142	466112	1079863	1045548
茶 馆	Teahouses					
咖啡店	Cafés	1765	13684	338106	454170	449191
其 他	Others	105	1261	15253	60024	59793
住宿业态	Accommodation Enterprises	148	2688	6483	115188	1197
旅游饭店	Tourism Hotels	20	435		18230	19
一般旅馆	General Hotels	128	2253	6483	96958	1177

16-11 商品交易市场基本情况(2022年)
STATISTICS FOR COMMODITY TRANSACTION MARKETS (2022)

项目	Item	市场数量(个) Number of Markets (unit)	总摊位数(个) Number of Booths (unit)	成交额(亿元) Turnover (100 million yuan)
合计	**Total**	**422**	**126837**	**2891.2**
按经营方式分	**By Business Practice**			
批发市场	Wholesale Market	44	37215	2171.6
零售市场	Retail Market	378	89622	719.6
按经营环境分	**By Business Environment**			
露天式	Open-air	77	32843	1589.0
封闭式	Closed	327	86448	1214.6
其他	Others	18	7546	87.6

16-12 亿元及以上商品交易市场基本情况(2022年)
STATISTICS FOR COMMODITY TRANSACTION MARKETS OVER RMB 100 MILLION (2022)

项目	Item	市场数量(个) Number of Markets (unit)	总摊位数(个) Number of Booths (unit)	#出租摊位数 Number of Booths on Lease	成交额(亿元) Turnover (100 million yuan)
合计	**Total**	**74**	**56711**	**45077**	**2836.5**
按经营方式分	**By Business Practice**				
批发市场	Wholesale Market	27	31757	24766	2167.8
零售市场	Retail Market	47	24954	20311	668.7
按经营环境分	**By Business Environment**				
露天式	Open-air	10	11070	7842	1583.9
封闭式	Closed	61	43741	35824	1169.2
其他	Others	3	1900	1411	83.4

16−13 商品交易市场经营情况(2022年)
STATISTICS FOR COMMODITY TRANSACTION MARKETS (2022)

项　　目	Item	市场数量(个) Number of Markets (unit)	出租摊位数(个) Number of Rental Booths (unit)	营业面积(万平方米) Operating Area (10000 sq.m)	成交额(亿元) Turnover (100 million yuan)
合　　计	**Total**	**422**	**87727**	**837.8**	**2891.2**
综合市场	**Comprehensive Markets**	**226**	**40637**	**364.4**	**1797.7**
生产资料综合市场	Comprehensive Market of Capital Goods				
工业消费品综合市场	Comprehensive Market of Industrial Consumer Goods	18	3239	16.7	10.2
农产品综合市场	Comprehensive Market of Agricultural Products	142	29254	273.0	1780.0
其他综合市场	Other Comprehensive Markets	66	8144	74.7	7.5
专业市场	**Specialized Markets**	**196**	**47090**	**473.4**	**1093.5**
生产资料市场	**Market of Capital Goods**	**22**	**4545**	**40.4**	**22.9**
木材市场	Timber Market				
建材市场	Building Material Market	20	3977	36.3	20.9
化工材料及制品市场	Chemical Material and Product Market				
金属材料市场	Metal Material Market	1	278	2.4	0.3
机械设备市场	Mechanical Equipment Market				
其他生产资料市场	Other Markets of Capital Goods	1	290	1.7	1.8
农产品市场	**Agricultural Product Market**	**33**	**6227**	**76.4**	**368.6**
粮油市场	Foodstuff and Oil Market	1	52	0.1	0.1
肉禽蛋市场	Meat, Poultry and Egg Market	7	1510	4.0	8.8
水产品市场	Aquatic Product Market	5	1614	16.5	131.9
蔬菜市场	Vegetable Market	12	2321	36.1	220.1
干鲜果品市场	Dried and Fresh Fruit Market	2	189	18.1	7.0
其他农产品市场	Other Agricultural Product Markets	6	541	1.6	0.8
食品、饮料及烟酒市场	**Food, Beverage, Tobacco and Wine Market**	**11**	**1268**	**8.1**	**4.2**
食品饮料市场	Food and Beverage Market				
茶叶市场	Tea Market	9	1197	7.7	3.9
其他食品饮料及烟酒市场	Other Food, Beverage, Tobacco and Wine Markets	2	71	0.5	0.3
纺织、服装、鞋帽市场	**Textile, Costume, Shoe and Hat Market**	**24**	**7221**	**39.1**	**16.7**
布料及纺织品市场	Cloth and Textile Market	1	125	0.4	0.3
服装市场	Clothing Market	16	1473	12.2	2.7
鞋帽市场	Shoe and Hat Market	1	20	0.1	...
其他纺织服装鞋帽市场	Other Textile, Costume, Shoe and Cap Markets	6	5603	26.5	13.7
日用品及文化用品市场	**Domestic Commodity and Cultural Article Market**	**12**	**2086**	**9.3**	**3.5**
小商品市场	Small Commodity Market				

16-13 续表 Continued

项　目	Item	市场数量(个) Number of Markets (unit)	出租摊位数(个) Number of rental Booths (unit)	营业面积(万平方米) Operating Area (10000 sq.m)	成交额(亿元) Turnover (100 million yuan)
箱包市场	Case and Bag Market				
玩具市场	Toy Market				
文具市场	Stationary Market				
图书、报刊杂志市场	Book, Newspaper and Magazine Market	2	181	1.6	1.5
音像制品及电子出版物市场	Audiovisual Product and E-journal Market				
体育用品市场	Sports Good Market				
其他日用品及文化用品市场	Other Domestic Commodity and Cultural Article Market	10	1905	7.8	2.0
黄金、珠宝、玉器等首饰市场	**Market of Gold, Jewelry and Jade**	**12**	**2109**	**11.0**	**4.4**
电器、通讯器材、电子设备市场	**Market of Electrical Appliances, Communication Devices and Electronic Equipment**	**6**	**2135**	**7.4**	**41.7**
家电市场	Household Appliance Market	1	54	0.6	0.1
通讯器材市场	Communication Device Market	1	157	0.8	0.2
照相、摄像器材市场	Photographic and Camera Shooting Equipment Market	1	157	0.9	1.0
计算机及辅助设备市场	Computer and Supporting Equipment Market	2	1167	2.9	27.8
其他电器、通讯器材、电子设备市场	Other Electrical Appliance, Communication Device and Electronic Equipment Market	1	600	2.2	12.6
医药、医疗用品及器材市场	**Medicine, Medical Article and Equipment Market**				
中药材市场	Chinese Herb Market				
其他医药、医疗用品及器材市场	Other Medicine, Medical Article and Equipment Market				
家具、五金及装饰材料市场	**Furniture, Hardware and Decoration Material Market**	**44**	**11436**	**181.8**	**195.3**
家具市场	Furniture Market	19	4626	101.5	40.5
装饰材料市场	Decoration Materials Market	14	4495	51.9	133.5
灯具市场	Lamp and Lantern Market	3	557	8.6	2.9
厨具、盥洗设备市场	Kitchen and Washroom Equipment Market				
五金材料市场	Hardware Market	1	23	0.3	0.1
其他装修市场	Other Decoration Market	7	1735	19.6	18.2
汽车、摩托车及零配件市场	**Automobile, Autobike and Part and Fitting Market**	**14**	**3431**	**78.1**	**431.7**
汽车市场	Automobile Market	8	1198	49.3	395.1
摩托车市场	Autobike Market				
机动车零配件市场	Automobile Part and Fitting Market	6	2233	28.8	36.7
花、鸟、鱼、虫市场	**Flower, Bird, Fish and Insect Market**	**6**	**1192**	**2.9**	**0.6**
花卉市场	Flower Market	5	751	1.7	0.5
鸟市场	Bird Market				
观赏鱼市场	Fish Market				
其他花鸟鱼虫市场	Other Flower, Bird, Fish and Insect Market	1	441	1.1	0.2
旧货市场	**Secondhand Goods Market**	**9**	**5382**	**10.6**	**2.1**
古玩、古董、字画市场	Curio, Antique, Calligraphy and Painting Market	6	1125	5.8	0.6
邮票、硬币市场	Stamp and Coin Market	1	887	0.8	0.5
其他旧货市场	Other Secondhand Goods Market	2	3370	4.1	1.0
其他专业市场	**Other Specialized Markets**	**3**	**58**	**8.2**	**1.8**

16-14 北京消费者信心指数(2022年各季度)
BEIJING CONSUMER CONFIDENCE INDEX(EACH QUARTER OF 2022)

项 目	Item	一季度 First Quarter	二季度 Second Quarter	三季度 Third Quarter	四季度 Fourth Quarter
消费者信心指数	**Consumer Confidence Index**	**118.7**	**108.9**	**111.5**	**106.3**
消费者满意指数	**Consumer Satisfaction Index**	**117.5**	**107.9**	**109.7**	**104.5**
就业状况满意指数	Index of Satisfaction with Employment Status	128.9	110.3	103.5	102.9
家庭收入状况满意指数	Index of Satisfaction with Household Income Status	113.2	108.3	118.3	109.7
消费意愿满意指数	Index of Satisfaction with Consumption Intention	110.5	105.2	107.5	100.8
消费者预期指数	**Consumer Expectation Index**	**119.4**	**109.5**	**112.7**	**107.6**
就业状况预期指数	Index of Expectation for Employment Status	121.5	108.7	105.3	104.9
家庭收入状况预期指数	Index of Expectation for Household Income Status	117.3	110.3	120.2	110.2

主要统计指标解释

社会消费品零售总额　指企业（单位、个体户）通过交易直接售给个人、社会集团用于非生产、非经营用的实物商品金额，以及提供餐饮服务所取得的收入金额。个人包括城乡居民和入境人员，社会集团包括机关、社会团体、部队、学校、企事业单位、居委会或村委会等。

批发和零售业单位　指在流通环节主要从事商品批发活动和零售活动的单位（含法人单位、产业活动单位、个体经营户）。

商品购进额　指从企业以外的单位和个人购进（包括从国外直接进口）作为转卖或加工后转卖的商品金额（含增值税）。本指标反映批发和零售业从国内外市场上购进商品的总价。

商品销售额　指对本单位以外的单位和个人出售的商品金额（包括售给本单位消费用的商品，含增值税）。本指标反映批发和零售业在国内市场上销售商品以及出口商品的总价。

期末商品库存额　对于批发和零售业法人单位和个体经营户，是指报告期末取得所有权的全部商品金额（含增值税）；对于批发和零售业产业活动单位，是指报告期末实际在库且归属法人具有所有权的全部商品金额（含增值税）。本指标反映批发和零售业的商品库存情况，以及对市场商品供应的保证程度。

连锁总店（总部）　负责连锁企业资源（商号、商誉、经营模式、服务标准、管理模式等）的开发、配置、控制或使用等功能的企业核心管理机构。连锁经营是指经营同类商品或服务，使用统一商号的若干店铺，在同一总店（总部）的管理下，采取统一采购或特许经营等方式，实现规模效益的组织形式，包括直营连锁、特许连锁和自愿连锁三种形式。直营连锁是指连锁店铺由连锁公司全资或控股开设，在总部的直接控制下，开展统一经营的连锁经营形式；特许连锁是指拥有注册商标、企业标志、专利、专有技术等经营资源的企业（特许人），以合同形式将其拥有的经营资源许可其他经营者（被特许人）使用，被特许人按合同约定在统一的经营模式下开展经营，并向特许人支付特许经营费用的连锁经营形式；自愿连锁是指若干个店铺或企业自愿组合起来，在不改变各自资产所有权关系的情况下，以同一个品牌形象面对消费者，以共同进货为纽带开展的连锁经营形式。

连锁门店　在连锁企业经营管理的基础上，按照总店（总部）的指示和服务规范要求，承担日常销售业务的店铺，称连锁门店，包括直营店（控股店）和加盟店。

（1）直营店（控股店）是指由连锁企业总部投资开设，按连锁经营管理模式，由总部统一管理的店铺。

（2）加盟店是指在特许连锁中，被特许人获得特许人授权后，使用其商标、商号、经营模式、专利和专有技术等经营资源建立的店铺，也包括自愿连锁的成员店。

门店总数　指该连锁企业所拥有的全部门店（包括直营店和加盟店）数量。其中，总店（如果总公司有门店的话）作为一个直营店处理。此外，有的地区分出控股店，控股店按直营店统计。

餐饮业单位　指在一定场所，专门从事对食物进行现场烹饪、调制，并出售给顾客主要供现场消费服务活动的单位（含法人单位、产业活动单位、个体经营户）。如各种饭馆、中西餐厅、酒馆、茶馆和火车餐车、车站食堂、飞机场餐厅等。

住宿业单位　指有偿为顾客提供临时住宿服务活动的单位（含法人单位、产业活动单位、个体经营户）。如旅游饭店、宾馆、酒店和旅馆、旅店等。

商品交易市场　指经有关部门和组织批准设立，有固定场所、设施，有经营管理部门和监管人员，若干市场经营者入内，常年或实际开业三个月以上，集中、公开、独立地进行生活消费品、生产资料等现货商品交易以及提供相关服务的交易场所，包括各类消费品市场、生产资料市场等。

消费者信心指数　消费者信心指数是反映消费者信心强弱的指标；它通过调查获取消费者对当前及未来一段时期就业状况、收入水平和消费意愿的主观判断和心理感受，以数学方法对其量化编制而成；是预测经济走势和消费趋向的一个先行指标，是监测经济周期变化的重要依据。消费者信心指数由消费者满意指数和消费者预期指数构成。其中消费者满意指数反映了消费者对当前经济生活的评价；消费者预期指数反映了消费者对未来一段时期经济前景发展变化的预期。

指数取值介于 0 和 200 之间，100 为指数强弱临界点，指数超过 100，表明消费者信心处于强信心区，数值由 100 趋近 200，表明消费者信心逐渐增强；反之，指数小于 100 时，表示消费者信心处于弱信心区，数值由 100 趋近 0，表明消费者信心逐渐减弱。

Explanatory Notes on Main Statistical Indicators

Total Retail Sales of Consumer Goods refer to the total prices of physical commodities sold by enterprises (entities or self-employed businesses) through transaction directly to individuals and social groups to be used for non-productive and non-operating purposes, combined with the amount of income from provision of food and beverage services. Individuals include urban and rural residents and persons entering China. Social groups include government agencies, social organizations, armies, schools, enterprises and public institutions, residents' committee or villagers' committee, and so on.

Wholesale and Retail Entities refer to entities engaged in commodity wholesale and retail activities in circulation (including legal entities, activity entities and individual entities).

Total Purchases of Commodities refer to the total value (VAT included) of purchases (including direct imports from foreign countries) of commodities by the enterprises from other entities or individuals for the purpose of re-selling, either with or without further processing of the commodities purchased. This indicator is used to show the total price of purchases of retail and wholesale commodities from domestic and overseas markets.

Total Sales of Commodities refer to value of commodities sold by the entities to other entities and individuals (including the commodities consumed by the enterprises themselves, VAT included). This indicator is used to show the total price of wholesale and retail commodities sold in domestic markets and exported.

Inventory (year-end) refers to, for legal entities and self-employed businesses in wholesale and retail trades, the value of all commodities with ownership gained (VAT included) at the end of the reference period; for industrial activity entities in wholesale and retail trades, it refers to the value of all commodities actually in storage and owned by their legal person at the end of the reference period (VAT included). This indicator shows the commodity inventory in wholesale and retail trades, and to what extent the commodities will be supplied to the market.

General Chain Store (Headquarters) means the core management organization in an enterprise, responsible for the development, deployment, control or use of resources (trade name, goodwill, operating model, service standards and management model, etc.) of the chain enterprise. Chain operation means an organization form in which several stores using unified trade name dealing in the same commodities or providing the same services through uniform purchase or franchise operation under the management of the same general store (headquarters) to achieve benefits of scale. Chain operation falls into direct-sale chain, franchised chain and voluntary chain. Direct-sale chain is a form of chain operation that chain stores are wholly funded or controlled by chain companies, carrying out uniform operation under the direct control of headquarters; franchised chain is a form of chain operation that any enterprise (the franchiser) owning operating resources, such as trademarks, logos, patents and proprietary technologies, authorize such operating resources to any other operator (the franchisee) by contract, and the franchisee operates under uniform operating model as stated in the contract, and pays franchise fees to the franchiser; voluntary chain is a form of chain operation that several stores or enterprises combine together voluntarily to face consumers with the same brand image without changing their own asset ownership relations, and link together through joint purchase.

Chain Stores Based on the operation and management of chain enterprises, stores carrying out daily sales business by following the general store's (headquarters') instruction and required service standards are called chained stores. They include direct-sale stores (controlled stores) and franchised stores.

(1) Direct-sale Stores (Controlled Stores) refer to stores opened with funds from the headquarters of chain enterprises, using the chain operation and management model, and under the uniform management of the headquarters.

(2) Franchised Stores refer to, in franchise chains, stores established after the franchisee is authorized by the franchiser to use its trademark, trade name, operating model, patent and proprietary technologies and other operating resources. Voluntary chain members are also included.

Total Number of Stores refers to the number of all stores owned by the chain enterprises (including direct-sale stores and franchised stores). The general store (if the parent company has stores) is regarded as a direct-sale store. In addition, controlled stores are considered separately in some areas, which are regarded as direct-sale stores.

Restaurants Entities refer to entities (including legal entities, industrial activity entities and self-employed businesses) specialized in cooking and seasoning food which is sold to clients for on-site consumption at a specific site, such as various restaurants, Chinese food and Western food restaurants, pubs, teahouses, dining compartments on trains, canteens at railway stations, and restaurants at airports.

Accommodation Entities refer to entities (including legal entities, industrial activity entities and self-employed businesses) providing clients with temporary accommodation services, such as tourist hotels, guesthouses, hotels, rest houses and inns, for a fee.

Commodity Transaction Markets refer to transaction sites approved by competent authorities and organizations, with fixed places and facilities. There are operation management departments and regulating personnel in the markets, where several operators stay over years or open for over three months, conducting transactions of on-hand commodities such as living consumables and capital goods, and offering relevant services in a concentrated, open and independent manner. Commodity transaction markets include various markets of consumer goods and capital goods markets, etc.

Consumer Confidence Index is an indicator reflecting and quantifying the consumers' evaluation on current economic situation, and their personal feeling about the economic prospects, income level, income expectation, and psychological state of consumption. It serves as a leading indicator predicting the trend of economy and tendency of consumption, and an essential basis for monitoring the changes in economic cycle. Consumer Confidence Index consists of consumer satisfaction index and consumer expectation index, and the former one reflects consumers' evaluation on current economic life; consumer expectation index reflects consumers' expectation on the development and changes in the economic prospect in the future.

The index ranges from 0 to 200. 100 represents a critical point between strong and weak confidence. An index greater than 100 indicates the consumers' confidence is strong. An index going toward 200 from 100 shows the consumers' confidence is becoming gradually strong; in contrary, an index smaller than 100 means the consumers' confidence is weak. When the index goes toward 0 from 100, it means the consumers' confidence is weakening gradually.

17

北京统计年鉴2023　BEIJING STATISTICAL YEARBOOK 2023

旅游业
TOURISM

简要说明

一、主要内容

本章资料主要反映北京市国际旅游和国内旅游情况。包括旅游人数及其在京花费情况、重点住宿业经营及接待住宿者情况、旅行社接待及出境旅游情况、旅游区（点）活动情况等。

二、调查方法

重点住宿业、旅行社、旅游区（点）有关数据通过全面调查取得。

三、调查范围

重点住宿业统计范围为有经营活动的星级及非星级重点住宿业法人单位、产业活动单位和个体经营户。

旅行社统计范围为有经营活动的全部旅行社（其中出境旅游情况统计范围为有特许经营出境旅游业务权的旅行社）。

旅游区（点）统计范围为有经营活动的 A 级及以上旅游区（点）和其他主要旅游区（点）。

Brief Introduction

I. Main Content

Statistics in this chapter mainly show the situation of tourism and international tourism in Beijing. Including: statistics for the number and spending of tourists to Beijing, operation and reception of key accommodation services, reception and outbound tourism made through travel agencies, activities of tourist attractions (sightseeing spots), and so on.

II. Methods of Survey

Data concerning key accommodation services, travel agencies, tourist attractions (sightseeing spots) were obtained through comprehensive survey.

III. Scope of Survey

The scope of statistics on key accommodation services covers the star-rated and non-star-rated key accommodation industry legal person units, industrial activity units and self-employed households that engage in business activities.

The scope of statistics on travel agencies covers all travel agencies that engage in business activities (of which, the scope of statistics for outbound tourism covers the travel agencies that have the franchise to engage in outbound tourism business).

The scope of statistics on tourist attractions (sightseeing spots) covers the Level A-or-above tourist attractions (sightseeing spots) and other major tourist attractions (sightseeing spots) that engage in business activities.

17－1 国际、国内旅游情况(1978－2022年)
STATISTICS FOR INTERNATIONAL AND DOMESTIC TOURISM (1978-2022)

年 份 Year	来京游客人数 (万人次) Number of Tourists to Beijing (10000 person-times)	入境游客 Inbound Tourists	国内游客 Domestic Tourists	国际旅游收入 (亿美元) Revenue from Inbound Tourism (USD 100 million)	国内旅游收入 (亿元) Revenue from Domestic Tourism (100 million yuan)
1978		18.7		1.0	
1979		25.2		0.9	
1980		28.6		1.2	
1981		39.4		1.2	
1982		45.7		1.3	
1983		50.9		1.4	
1984		65.7		2.3	
1985		93.7		3.2	
1986		99.0		4.6	
1987		108.1		5.5	
1988		120.4		6.7	
1989		64.5		4.7	
1990		100.0		6.6	
1991		132.0		8.5	
1992		174.8		10.7	
1993		202.8		12.4	
1994	6913.0	203.0	6710.0	20.1	298.0
1995	6527.0	207.0	6320.0	21.8	352.6
1996	7901.9	218.9	7683.0	22.5	359.6
1997	8450.8	229.8	8221.0	22.5	391.3
1998	8951.5	220.1	8731.4	23.8	424.5
1999	9512.4	252.4	9260.0	25.0	530.0
2000	10468.1	282.1	10186.0	27.7	683.0
2001	11292.8	285.8	11007.0	29.5	887.7
2002	11810.4	310.4	11500.0	31.1	930.0
2003	8885.1	185.1	8700.0	19.0	706.0
2004	12265.5	315.5	11950.0	31.7	1145.0
2005	12862.9	362.9	12500.0	36.2	1300.0
2006	13590.3	390.3	13200.0	40.3	1482.7
2007	14715.5	435.5	14280.0	45.8	1753.6
2008	14560.0	379.0	14181.0	44.6	1907.0
2009	16669.5	412.5	16257.0	43.6	2144.5
2010	18390.1	490.1	17900.0	50.4	2425.1
2011	21404.4	520.4	20884.0	54.2	2864.3
2012	23134.6	500.9	22633.7	51.5	3301.3
2013	25189.0	450.1	24738.8	47.9	3666.3
2014	26149.7	427.5	25722.2	46.1	3997.0
2015	27279.0	420.0	26859.0	46.1	4320.0
2016	28531.5	416.5	28115.0	50.7	4683.0
2017	29746.2	392.6	29353.6	51.3	5122.4
2018	31093.6	400.4	30693.2	55.2	5556.2
2019	32209.9	376.9	31833.0	51.9	5866.2
2020	18386.5	34.1	18352.4	4.8	2880.9
2021	25512.8	24.5	25488.3	4.3	4138.5
2022	18230.8	24.1	18206.7	4.4	2490.9

资料来源：本表除2019年以前入境游客数据外，其他数据均来源于北京市文化和旅游局。

Source: Except for the data on inbound tourists in and before 2019, all other data in this table were provided by Beijing Municipal Bureau of Culture and Tourism.

17−2 按客源地分入境游客人数(1978−2022年)
NUMBER OF INBOUND TOURISTS BY COUNTRY/REGION (1978-2022)

单位：万人次 (10000 person-times)

年 份 Year	入境游客人数 Number of Inbound Tourists	港澳台同胞 Hong Kong, Macao and Taiwan Tourists	#中国香港 Hong Kong, China	外国人 Foreigner	#日 本 Japan	#韩 国 Korea	#美 国 United States	#英 国 United Kingdom	#法 国 France	#德 国 Germany	#俄罗斯 Russia
1978	18.7	3.3		15.4							
1979	25.2	4.1		21.1							
1980	28.6	5.8		21.7	6.0		3.7	1.3	0.9	0.9	
1981	39.4	6.8		31.3	5.3		3.8	1.1	1.1	1.0	
1982	45.7	8.2		35.9	8.2		6.6	1.3	1.3	1.4	
1983	50.9	8.9		39.7	10.0		9.4	1.5	1.5	1.7	0.1
1984	65.7	10.0		52.1	17.2		12.5	2.3	2.1	2.5	0.1
1985	93.7	13.6		74.0	27.6		14.8	3.9	3.2	4.0	0.2
1986	99.0	15.8		79.0	25.5		14.7	4.1	3.1	4.6	0.3
1987	108.1	21.8		81.7	26.3		16.5	4.5	4.3	5.1	0.3
1988	120.4	28.8		86.5	27.8		16.7	4.2	4.2	5.4	0.7
1989	64.5	16.6		46.0	12.2		7.3	2.4	2.1	3.3	1.0
1990	100.0	34.7	11.4	63.8	18.2		8.6	2.9	2.0	4.0	1.5
1991	132.0	38.2	17.6	91.4	27.6	4.3	9.5	4.3	3.7	6.0	3.5
1992	174.8	51.2	24.6	120.5	37.6	5.6	12.3	4.4	6.6	9.4	5.1
1993	202.8	52.8	29.4	145.0	39.3	7.3	14.3	5.3	6.9	12.0	7.7
1994	203.0	39.4	25.7	160.0	41.1	12.7	15.4	5.4	6.7	9.7	4.9
1995	207.0	36.3	25.4	166.5	42.4	17.3	17.4	5.8	6.2	8.8	6.2
1996	218.9	38.6	25.5	176.2	43.0	18.0	18.5	7.5	6.6	10.0	6.9
1997	229.8	40.3	26.3	186.9	43.0	19.4	21.7	9.0	6.5	9.1	6.5
1998	220.1	39.1	25.0	178.2	43.5	8.2	23.2	8.8	6.9	11.3	6.2
1999	252.4	44.1	26.5	205.0	45.6	19.2	24.1	8.8	7.9	10.5	4.6
2000	282.1	44.1	25.0	238.0	54.3	27.8	31.1	9.7	9.6	12.1	3.9
2001	285.8	45.9	26.9	239.9	50.7	32.7	33.1	11.1	10.2	12.3	4.9
2002	310.4	43.9	25.5	266.5	56.5	38.0	37.4	12.9	11.3	12.2	5.2
2003	185.1	32.4	21.7	152.7	29.2	24.5	19.4	8.1	5.5	6.3	5.2
2004	315.5	47.4	27.7	268.1	52.3	42.4	37.4	11.8	11.1	11.5	8.2
2005	362.9	51.3	31.4	311.6	45.0	45.3	46.5	13.9	13.6	14.6	9.7
2006	390.3	52.0	30.3	338.3	50.6	42.4	49.8	14.8	14.2	15.3	15.0
2007	435.5	52.9	31.3	382.6	58.8	44.4	60.3	17.0	16.4	17.5	18.3
2008	379.0	43.3	28.1	335.7	40.0	35.3	53.8	17.5	14.5	16.0	17.9
2009	412.5	69.6	44.4	342.9	46.2	35.2	57.9	16.3	12.9	16.8	15.0
2010	490.1	68.4	40.3	421.6	52.6	50.6	70.0	16.8	14.3	20.1	19.0
2011	520.4	73.0	43.4	447.4	51.0	53.4	78.9	18.8	15.0	22.2	20.5
2012	500.9	66.5	37.6	434.4	43.7	44.2	75.1	18.5	15.1	24.5	20.0
2013	450.1	62.5	35.4	387.6	24.9	37.7	74.7	17.5	13.4	23.0	16.7
2014	427.5	62.0	34.2	365.5	24.9	38.7	71.5	16.9	13.4	22.6	13.7
2015	420.0	62.4	34.9	357.6	25.8	41.6	69.4	17.2	15.3	21.2	10.3
2016	416.5	61.8	35.3	354.8	24.8	37.9	70.3	18.3	13.2	20.6	9.5
2017	392.6	60.6	34.4	332.0	24.2	23.5	67.3	16.5	12.3	19.4	9.3
2018	400.4	60.6	34.8	339.8	24.9	24.8	72.0	15.9	12.7	19.4	8.7
2019	376.9	56.2	32.2	320.7	24.7	24.2	62.9	15.3	12.0	19.8	9.6
2020	34.1	7.7	4.8	26.4	1.9	2.5	5.8	1.1	0.9	1.7	0.9
2021	24.5	7.0	4.4	17.5	1.5	2.3	3.4	0.7	0.5	1.2	0.7
2022	24.1	5.2	3.2	18.9	3.2	1.6	3.0	0.9	0.4	1.2	0.6

注：1.1980—1999年的入境游客人数由外国游客、港澳台游客、华侨三部分组成，自2000年起华侨包括在外国游客内。

2.1990—1999年香港游客人数为香港、澳门合计。

资料来源：自2019年起，本表数据来源于北京市文化和旅游局。

Note: a) Number of inbound tourists in 1980-1999 consisted of foreign visitors, visitors from Hong Kong, Macao and Taiwan, and overseas Chinese. Overseas Chinese were included in the number of foreign visitors since 2000.

b) Tourists from Hong Kong in 1990-1999 were the total number of tourists from Hong Kong and Macao.

Source: Since 2019, all data in this table were from Beijing Municipal Bureau of Culture and Tourism.

17-3 来京游客人数
NUMBER OF TOURISTS TO BEIJING

单位：万人次 (10000 person-times)

项　　目	Item	2022	2021
合　　计	**Total**	**18230.8**	**25512.8**
国内游客人数	**Number of Domestic Tourists**	**18206.7**	**25488.3**
外地来京游客	Tourists to Beijing from Outside Beijing	8295.0	12881.1
本市游客	Local Tourists	9911.7	12607.2
入境游客人数	**Number of Inbound Tourists**	**24.1**	**24.5**
港澳台同胞	Hong Kong, Macao and Taiwan Tourists	5.2	7.0
中国香港	Hong Kong, China	3.2	4.4
中国澳门	Macao, China	0.2	0.3
中国台湾	Taiwan, China	1.7	2.4
外国人	Foreigners	18.9	17.5
亚　洲	Asia	7.8	6.2
#日　本	Japan	3.2	1.5
韩　国	Korea	1.6	2.3
菲律宾	Philippines	…	0.1
印度尼西亚	Indonesia	0.1	...
马来西亚	Malaysia	0.2	0.3
新加坡	Singapore	0.5	0.6
泰　国	Thailand	0.7	0.3
印　度	India	0.2	0.2
蒙　古	Mongolia	…	…
美　洲	America	3.7	4.4
#美　国	United States	3.0	3.4
加拿大	Canada	0.7	1.0
欧　洲	Europe	5.6	5.2
#英　国	United Kingdom	0.9	0.7
法　国	France	0.4	0.5
德　国	Germany	1.2	1.2
意大利	Italy	0.4	0.4
西班牙	Spain	0.2	0.1
瑞　典	Sweden	0.1	0.2
瑞　士	Switzerland	0.3	0.2
俄罗斯	Russia	0.6	0.7
大洋洲	Oceania	0.5	0.6
#澳大利亚	Australia	0.4	0.5
新西兰	New Zealand	0.1	0.1
非　洲	Africa	0.9	0.6
其　他	Others	0.4	0.4

资料来源：北京市文化和旅游局。
Source: Beijing Municipal Bureau of Culture and Tourism.

17-4 在京旅游花费构成情况(2005-2022年)

单位：%

项 目	Item	2005	2006	2007	2008	2009	2010
入境游客花费构成	**Composition of Expenditures for Inbound Tourists**	**100.0**	**100.0**	**100.0**	**100.0**	**100.0**	**100.0**
长途交通费	Long-distance Transportation Expenses	35.3	30.0	29.0	31.1	37.4	28.1
民 航	Civil Aviation	30.9	29.6	24.4	25.3	27.1	19.8
铁 路	Railway	1.1	0.3	3.0	3.6	5.5	5.3
公 路	Highway	3.3	0.1	1.6	2.2	4.8	3.0
市内交通费	Local Transportation Expenses	1.1	1.7	2.6	2.4	2.7	3.4
住 宿	Accommodation	17.3	32.0	16.9	16.4	14.5	14.4
餐 饮	Catering	9.2	11.7	8.7	8.7	7.5	8.7
购 物	Shopping	19.9	15.9	22.5	19.1	20.4	25.1
邮电通讯	Post and Telecommunications	3.4	0.8	2.7	3.8	2.7	3.2
景区游览	Scenic Spot Sightseeing	4.7	2.3	4.2	4.8	3.9	4.7
文化娱乐	Culture and Entertainment	4.6	3.2	5.0	4.5	4.6	5.0
其 他	Others	4.5	2.4	8.4	9.2	6.3	7.4
外地来京游客花费构成	**Composition of Expenditures for Tourists from Outside Beijing**	**100.0**	**100.0**	**100.0**	**100.0**	**100.0**	**100.0**
长途交通费	Long-distance Transportation Expenses	12.8	15.1	16.3	15.4	12.9	12.8
民 航	Civil Aviation		8.0	9.2	9.1	6.6	6.0
铁 路	Railway		6.1	6.4	4.5	1.3	5.8
公 路	Highway		1.1	0.7	1.8	5.0	1.0
市内交通费	Local Transportation Expenses	5.7	5.1	5.5	5.6	4.9	5.0
住 宿	Accommodation	17.2	14.9	17.3	15.1	17.7	19.6
餐 饮	Catering	19.8	18.7	20.5	23.2	21.8	20.2
购 物	Shopping	24.1	22.2	25.8	32.7	34.5	34.5
邮电通讯	Post and Telecommunications	1.0	1.2	1.8	1.0	0.6	0.5
景区游览	Scenic Spot Sightseeing	9.1	9.5	7.2	4.5	6.1	6.2
文化娱乐	Culture and Entertainment	3.1	2.5	1.9	1.6	1.2	1.0
其 他	Others	7.1	10.8	3.7	0.9	0.3	0.2

资料来源：北京市文化和旅游局。

COMPOSITION OF EXPENDITURES FOR TOURISM IN BEIJING (2005-2022)

(%)

2011	2012	2013	2014	2015	2016	2017	2018	2019	2020	2021	2022
100.0	**100.0**	**100.0**	**100.0**	**100.0**	**100.0**	**100.0**	**100.0**	**100.0**	**100.0**	**100.0**	**100.0**
26.4	28.0	26.9	27.0	36.8	38.3	37.7	27.2	28.4	31.5	32.6	32.6
20.5	22.3	21.2	21.4	30.8	38.0	37.1	26.2	27.6	30.5	31.6	31.6
3.4	3.3	3.7	3.6	3.2	0.2	0.4	0.6	0.6	0.7	0.7	0.7
2.5	2.4	2.0	2.0	2.7	0.1	0.2	0.3	0.2	0.3	0.3	0.3
3.5	3.5	2.5	2.6	2.4	2.5	1.4	3.0	4.0	1.8	4.3	4.3
15.5	16.5	16.9	16.7	12.8	18.3	14.4	19.0	19.0	34.6	27.1	27.1
6.8	7.4	7.3	7.4	6.2	11.4	6.8	8.2	9.4	17.1	13.4	13.4
25.3	23.5	27.6	26.7	19.9	18.5	27.6	26.0	24.5	5.4	13.0	13.0
2.0	2.2	1.7	1.7	2.4	0.2	0.6	0.7	0.4	0.8	0.6	0.6
4.2	5.0	4.2	4.3	3.3	4.2	2.4	3.9	4.5	1.0	2.4	2.4
6.0	5.4	3.8	4.0	4.2	4.6	2.1	2.3	1.4	0.3	0.7	0.7
10.3	8.5	9.1	9.6	12.1	2.0	7.0	9.7	8.3	7.6	6.0	5.9
100.0	**100.0**	**100.0**	**100.0**	**100.0**	**100.0**	**100.0**	**100.0**	**100.0**	**100.0**	**100.0**	**100.0**
13.5	15.5	17.0	17.6	17.0	15.8	14.3	12.4	11.8	14.6	17.9	16.1
6.2	7.7	7.5	7.1	7.4	7.5	6.2	4.7	4.8	6.9	10.0	8.5
6.9	7.5	9.1	10.2	9.3	8.0	7.3	6.4	5.8	6.3	6.4	6.1
0.3	0.3	0.4	0.3	0.3	0.3	0.8	1.4	1.2	1.4	1.6	1.6
4.5	4.0	3.8	3.8	4.0	3.9	4.1	3.9	4.2	4.3	2.4	2.4
20.0	19.8	19.5	20.2	18.7	17.8	19.0	18.8	19.1	20.1	17.3	17.4
20.9	21.4	21.4	22.1	22.1	22.8	22.2	21.6	21.1	20.0	18.7	19.7
34.3	32.1	30.9	28.2	30.2	31.3	31.2	32.4	31.8	25.6	24.5	23.6
0.3	0.2	0.2	0.3	0.3	0.2	0.2	0.2	0.2	0.2	0.1	0.1
5.7	6.1	6.6	6.5	6.2	6.6	7.3	8.0	9.2	10.0	10.8	13.2
0.8	0.7	0.5	0.6	0.7	0.9	1.2	1.9	2.0	2.4	6.7	6.2
0.1	0.1	0.1	0.7	0.8	0.7	0.6	0.8	0.8	2.8	1.6	1.3

Source: Beijing Municipal Bureau of Culture and Tourism.

17－5 重点住宿业出租率和平均房价
RENTING RATE AND AVERAGE PRICES OF KEY ACCOMMODATION

项 目	Item	出租率(%) Renting Rate (%)		平均房价(元/间夜) Average Prices (yuan/room.day)	
		2022	2021	2022	2021
合 计	**Total**	**38.7**	**47.8**	**442**	**453**
按住宿业等级分	**By the Rating of Accommodation**				
五 星	5-Star	28.9	44.8	712	761
四 星	4-Star	33.2	42.1	504	540
三 星	3-Star	36.8	42.8	372	399
二星及一星级	2-Star and 1-Star	42.7	44.0	307	289
非星级	Non-star-rated	42.3	51.5	409	394

资料来源：北京市文化和旅游局。
Source:Beijing Municipal Bureau of Culture and Tourism.

17－6 重点住宿业经营情况
OPERATION OF KEY ACCOMMODATION

项 目	Item	企业个数(个) Number of Enterprises (unit)		营业收入(万元) Business Income (10000 yuan)		利润总额(万元) Total Profits (10000 yuan)		从业人员平均人数(人) Average Number of Employed Persons (person)	
		2022	2021	2022	2021	2022	2021	2022	2021
合 计	**Total**	**1177**	**1177**	**2683764**	**3344062**	**-655298**	**-638674**	**92398**	**102690**
按住宿业等级分	**By the Rating of Accommodation**								
五星级	5-Star	64	64	532913	756499	-188045	-100646	19135	21371
四星级	4-Star	100	100	470845	568002	-121782	-60453	18427	20702
三星级	3-Star	132	132	292419	335186	-52745	-19765	10408	11270
二星及一星级	2-Star and 1-Star	54	54	40537	45206	-179	5413	1486	1691
非星级	Non-star-rated	827	827	1347050	1639169	-292547	-463223	42942	47656

资料来源：北京市文化和旅游局。
Source: Beijing Municipal Bureau of Culture and Tourism.

17-7 重点住宿业接待情况
RECEPTION OF KEY ACCOMMODATION

项　目	Item	接待住宿者人数（万人次）Guests Received (10000 person-times)		接待住宿者人天数（万人天）Person-days of Guests Received (10000 person-days)	
		2022	2021	2022	2021
合　计	**Total**	**1833.3**	**2669.0**	**3772.4**	**4790.0**
按住宿业等级分	**By the Rating of Accommodation**				
五星级	5-Star	188.7	324.9	369.0	576.2
四星级	4-Star	143.9	278.7	442.7	697.8
三星级	3-Star	147.0	199.4	415.2	493.6
二星及一星级	2-Star and 1-Star	44.8	60.0	117.4	118.6
非星级	Non-star-rated	1308.9	1805.8	2428.0	2903.7
按住宿者类别分	**By the Category of Guests**				
国内过夜游客	Domestic Overnight Tourists	1811.6	2644.6	3702.2	4734.7
入境过夜游客	Inbound Overnight Tourists	21.7	24.2	70.2	55.3
外国人	Foreigners	17.1	17.2	53.5	40.4
中国香港	Hong Kong, China	2.9	4.4	10.8	8.6
中国澳门	Macao, China	0.2	0.3	0.4	0.7
中国台湾	Taiwan, China	1.6	2.3	5.5	5.4

资料来源：北京市文化和旅游局。
Source: Beijing Municipal Bureau of Culture and Tourism.

17-8 旅行社接待及经营情况(1990-2022年)
RECEPTION AND OPERATION OF TRAVEL AGENCIES (1990-2022)

年份 Year	企业个数(个) Number of Enterprises (unit)	外联(组团)人数(万人次) Number of Inbound Tourists (Organized) (10000 person-times)	接待人数(万人次) Tourists Received (10000 person-times)	国内居民出境人数(万人次) Number of Outbound Chinese Tourists (10000 person-times)	营业收入(万元) Business Income (10000 yuan)	利润总额(万元) Total Profits (10000 yuan)	从业人员平均人数(人) Average Number of Employed Persons (person)
1990		32.5	54.7				
1991		53.3	69.1				
1992		61.2	100.7				
1993		71.3	103.6				
1994		84.1	91.0	1.0			
1995	100	85.7	87.4	1.2	290987.9	107654.6	
1996	105	88.0	78.6	2.7	351634.7	13520.8	
1997	110	87.3	76.0	3.8	386254.1	16009.6	
1998	131	85.0	69.0	6.6	387562.7	21319.9	
1999	120	103.1	92.9	11.1	485678.8	26572.0	
2000	127	123.7	101.0	13.7	576244.6	28744.7	6280
2001	140	143.4	130.1	21.9	700529.0	18682.5	8259
2002	151	179.4	176.3	28.5	823551.0	23362.0	9350
2003	147	80.2	82.4	31.9	553787.0	-11829.0	8382
2004	147	274.8	252.6	51.4	1059989.0	11444.0	7760
2005	147	308.4	278.2	51.7	1316063.0	10240.0	8752
2006	147	343.9	315.7	79.2	1610265.0	7012.0	8659
2007	189	424.1	377.9	100.2	2101874.5	28409.2	11597
2008	245	359.6	310.1	102.0	2166898.1	18121.6	14369
2009	265	370.6	306.6	84.9	2134058.8	5904.6	15262
2010	819	538.1	542.2	149.6	3517099.4	22636.2	21454
2011	919	593.9	552.3	184.3	4436713.3	20879.2	23871
2012	1021	684.5	519.1	272.5	5415692.9	35274.4	28022
2013	1147	661.3	441.6	331.0	6103603.4	64177.5	31694
2014	1243	628.0	427.0	410.2	6989125.4	27881.7	33591
2015	1238	655.5	468.0	533.1	8355826.3	-17132.1	37780
2016	1162	667.9	466.8	571.3	8788779.0	-29589.9	40812
2017	1139	573.0	422.3	511.5	8819738.7	122815.9	37952
2018	1192	544.5	377.8	510.9	9439120.6	590.2	37660
2019	1440	635.8	455.7	484.5	10394925.9	-6714.6	39779
2020	1413	168.1	91.1	47.2	1994239.0	-289717.0	26155
2021	1239	300.0	153.2		2265107.1	-147166.4	17125
2022	1225	177.9	31.8		2007777.4	-152663.4	13852

注：本表2009年及以前为国际旅行社口径，自2010年起调整为全部旅行社口径。

资料来源：自2020年起，表中数据均来自北京市文化和旅游局。

Note: Figures in this table refer to international travel agencies in and before 2009, and all travel agencies Since 2010.

Source: Since 2020, the data in the table were provided by Beijing Municipal Bureau of Culture and Tourism.

17-9 旅行社外联(组团)及接待情况
TOURISTS GROUPED (ORGANIZED) AND RECEIVED BY TRAVEL AGENCIES

项 目	Item	2022	2021
外联(组团)人数 （万人次）	**Tourists Grouped (Organized) (10000 person-times)**	**177.9**	**300.0**
国内旅游者	Domestic Tourists	177.9	299.8
港澳同胞	Compatriots from Hong Kong and Macao, China		
台湾同胞	Compatriots from Taiwan, China	…	0.1
外国人	Foreigners		0.1
接待人数 （万人次）	**Tourists Received (10000 person-times)**	**31.8**	**153.2**
国内旅游者	Domestic Tourists	31.8	153.1
港澳同胞	Compatriots from Hong Kong and Macao, China		…
台湾同胞	Compatriots from Taiwan, China	…	…
外国人	Foreigners		…
外联(组团)人天数(万人天)	**Persons-day of Tourists Grouped (Organized) (10000 persons-day)**	**534.6**	**896.9**
国内旅游者	Domestic Tourists	534.5	896.1
港澳同胞	Compatriots from Hong Kong and Macao, China		
台湾同胞	Compatriots from Taiwan, China	…	0.4
外国人	Foreigners		0.3
接待人天数 （万人天）	**Persons-day of Tourists Received (10000 persons-day)**	**64.8**	**433.5**
国内旅游者	Domestic Tourists	64.8	433.3
港澳同胞	Compatriots from Hong Kong and Macao, China		…
台湾同胞	Compatriots from Taiwan, China	…	…
外国人	Foreigners		0.2

资料来源：北京市文化和旅游局。
Source: Beijing Municipal Bureau of Culture and Tourism.

17-10 旅行社经营情况
OPERATION OF TRAVEL AGENCIES

单位：万元 (10000 yuan)

项　　目	Item	2022	2021
企业个数 （个）	Number of Enterprises (unit)	1225	1239
营业收入	Business Income	2007777	2265107
营业成本	Business Cost	2023566	2046556
营业利润	Business Profits	-152663	-146754
利润总额	Total Profits	-116757	-147166
从业人员平均人数 （人）	Average Number of Employed Persons (person)	13852	17125

资料来源：北京市文化和旅游局。
Source: Beijing Municipal Bureau of Culture and Tourism.

17-11 旅游区(点)活动情况
STATISTICS FOR ACTIVITIES OF TOURIST ATTRACTIONS (SIGHT SPOTS)

项　　目	Item	2022	2021
旅游区(点)个数 （个）	Number of Tourist Attractions (Sight Spots) (unit)	240	243
收入合计 （万元）	Total Income (10000 yuan)	673984	786606
门票收入	Ticket Income	244295	293076
商品销售收入	Commodity Sales	53728	82488
其他收入	Other Income	375960	411041
接待人数 （万人次）	Tourists Received (10000 person-times)	19064	21648

资料来源：北京市文化和旅游局。
Source: Beijing Municipal Bureau of Culture and Tourism.

主要统计指标解释

入境游客 指来中国（大陆）观光、度假、探亲访友、就医疗养、购物、参加会议或从事经济、文化、体育、宗教活动，且在中国（大陆）的旅游住宿设施内至少停留一夜的外国人、港澳台同胞等游客。入境游客不包括以下人员：(1) 应邀来华访问的政府部长以上官员及其随行人员；(2) 外国驻华使领馆官员、外交人员以及随行的家庭服务人员和受赡养者；(3) 常住中国（大陆）一年以上的外国专家、留学生、记者、商务机构人员等；(4) 乘坐国际航班过境不需要通过护照检查进入中国（大陆）口岸的中转旅客；(5) 边境地区往来的边民；(6) 回大陆定居的港澳台同胞；(7) 已在中国（大陆）定居的外国人和原已出境又返回在中国（大陆）定居的外国侨民；(8) 归国的中国（大陆）出国人员。

国内游客 指中国（大陆）居民离开惯常居住地在境内其他地方的旅游住宿设施内至少停留一夜，最长不超过 12 个月的国内游客。

国际旅游收入 指入境游客在中国（大陆）境内旅行、游览过程中用于交通、参观游览、住宿、餐饮、购物、娱乐等全部花费。

国内旅游收入 指国内游客在国内旅行、游览过程中用于交通、参观游览、住宿、餐饮、购物、娱乐等全部花费。

外联（组团）入境旅游者人数 指报告期内旅行社自组外联的入境旅游者人数，反映旅行社对外招徕的能力。旅行社按以下要求统计外联人数：入境游客不论其停留时间多少、旅游线路长短，只统计一次；旅行社只统计本社自组外联团的实到人数，不包括非本社外联，仅由本社接受委托办理签证的人数。

接待入境旅游者人数 指报告期内本旅行社派地陪接待的入境人数。

国内居民出境人数 指旅行社组织的中国（大陆）公民因公或因私出境前往其他国家、中国香港特别行政区、澳门特别行政区和台湾省观光、度假、探亲访友、就医疗养、购物、参加会议或从事经济、文化、体育、宗教活动的人数。统计时，出境游客按每出境一次统计 1 人次。

Explanatory Notes on Main Statistical Indicators

Inbound Tourists refer to tourists from foreign countries, Hong Kong, Macao and Taiwan to (mainland of) China for sightseeing, holidays, visiting relatives and friends, medical service and rehabilitation, shopping, conferences, or economic, cultural, sports and religious activities, and staying in a tour accommodation facility in (the mainland of) China for at least one night. They do not include: (1) officials above the rank of governmental ministers, and their accompanying persons who visit China upon invitation; (2) officials in foreign embassies and consulates in China, diplomatic personnel, and their accompanying family service personnel and dependents; (3) foreign experts, students, reporters, and personnel in business institutions who have been in (the mainland of) China for more than one year; (4) transit passengers via (the mainland of) China by international flights without passport checking; (5) people living on the frontiers who pass through borders; (6) compatriots from Hong Kong, Macao and Taiwan who settle down in the mainland of China; (7) Foreigners that have settled down in China and foreign nationals that have left the country and then come back to settle down in (the mainland of) China; (8) Chinese (mainland) people who have gone abroad and returned to China.

Domestic Tourists refer to domestic visitors as residents in (the mainland of) China who leave their regular dwelling places to stay at least one night and at most 12 months in a travel accommodation facility of other domestic places.

Revenue from Inbound Tourism means the total spending of inbound tourists on traffic, tour, accommodation, restaurants, shopping, entertainment and so on during their tour and travel in (the mainland of) China.

Revenue from Domestic Tourism means the total spending of domestic tourists on traffic, tour, accommodation, restaurants, shopping and entertainment, and so on during their tour and travel in China.

Number of Inbound Tourists Organized by Travel Agencies means the number of inbound tourists organized by travel agencies in the reporting period. It shows the capacity of travel agencies in attracting inbound tourists; travel agencies shall count the tourists organized as follows: an inbound tourist is regarded as one visit regardless of the duration and distance of the tour; only the actual tourists organized by travel agencies are included. Those organized by other travel agencies or those who have visa submitted by the travel agencies are not included.

Number of Inbound Tourists Received means the number of inbound tourists received by local guides dispatched by travel agencies in the reporting period.

Number of Chinese Residents Going Abroad means the number of citizens from (the mainland of) China who are organized by travel agencies to visit other countries, Hong Kong Special Administrative Region of PRC, Macao Special Administrative Region of PRC, and Taiwan for sightseeing, holiday, visiting relatives and friends, medical service and rehabilitation, shopping, conferences, or economic, cultural, sport and religious activities for official or private purpose. In compiling statistics, each time of leaving is counted as one person-time.

金融业
FINANCE

主要内容

本章资料主要包括北京市金融机构信贷收支情况、证券市场交易情况、保险业务情况、上市公司基本情况。

Brief Introduction

Main Content

Statistics in this chapter mainly consist of the balance of credit for financial institutions, transactions in securities market, insurance business, and basic information of listed companies in Beijing.

18-1 金融机构(含外资)存贷款余额(1978-2022年)
DEPOSIT AND LOAN BALANCE OF FINANCIAL INSTITUTIONS (INCLUDING FOREIGN BANKS) (1978-2022)

单位：亿元 (100 million yuan)

年份 Year	金融机构本外币存款余额 Balance of Savings Deposit in Domestic and Foreign Currencies in Financial Institutions	金融机构本外币存款 Deposits in Domestic and Foreign Currencies in Financial Institutions						
		#人民币存款 RMB Deposits	中资金融机构存款合计 Total Deposits in Chinese Financial Institutions	#人民币存款 RMB Deposits	#外汇(亿美元) Foreign Exchange (USD 100 million)	外资银行存款合计 Total Deposits in Foreign-funded Financial Bank	#人民币存款 RMB Deposits	#外汇(亿美元) Foreign Exchange (USD 100 million)
1978				114.7				
1979				139.1				
1980				168.0				
1981				220.5				
1982				279.2				
1983				321.3				
1984				375.5				
1985				411.0				
1986				508.8				
1987				610.8				
1988				609.9				
1989				717.6				
1990				893.9				
1991				1244.1				
1992				1528.3				
1993				1873.1				
1994				2677.3				
1995				3527.2				
1996				4378.9				
1997				5228.0				
1998				6666.8				
1999				8267.2				
2000	11526.0		11461.8	9759.8	205.6			
2001	14109.2		14042.1	12223.4	219.8			7.3
2002	17438.4		17369.9	15392.7	238.9			8.3
2003	20476.0		20398.2	18321.9	250.9			9.4
2004	23781.3	21625.9	23679.3	21625.9	248.1			12.3
2005	28969.9	26785.9	28800.9	26731.3	256.4		54.6	14.2
2006	33793.3	31313.8	33484.1	31179.2	295.2		134.5	22.4
2007	37700.3	35369.7	37087.5	35014.1	283.8		355.6	35.2
2008	43980.7	42107.6	43094.4	41500.0	233.3	886.3	607.5	40.8
2009	56960.1	54275.5	55804.8	53428.8	348.0	1155.3	846.6	45.2
2010	66584.6	64453.9	64897.6	63025.2	282.7	1687.0	1428.7	39.0
2011	75001.9	72655.4	73018.9	70985.1	322.8	1983.1	1670.3	49.6
2012	84837.3	81389.6	82615.9	79620.6	476.5	2221.4	1769.1	72.0
2013	91660.5	87990.6	89187.4	85897.2	539.6	2473.1	2093.4	62.3
2014	100095.5	95370.5	97645.9	93326.0	706.0	2449.6	2044.5	66.2
2015	128573.0	123767.4	126164.8	121878.9	660.0	2461.0	1941.3	80.0
2016	138408.9	132791.9	135510.3	130648.0	700.9	2933.1	2178.5	108.8
2017	144086.0	137952.1	141013.6	135501.4	843.6	3155.7	2534.0	95.1
2018	157092.2	150430.4	154237.3	148136.3	888.9	2960.6	2399.8	81.7
2019	171062.3	164349.5	168238.8	162063.9	885.1	2931.3	2393.4	77.1
2020	188081.6	181105.6	185026.8	178754.8	961.2	3069.8	2365.8	107.9
2021	199741.5	192104.3	196670.8	189717.8	1090.5	3112.7	2428.5	107.3
2022	218628.8	212446.7	215708.2	210025.3	816.0	2954.1	2454.9	71.7

资料来源：中国人民银行北京市分行。
Source: Beijing Municipal Branch of The People's Bank of China.

18-1 续表 Continued

单位：亿元 (100 million yuan)

年 份 Year	金融机构本外币贷款余额 Balance of Loans in Domestic and Foreign Currencies in Financial Institutions	#人民币贷款 RMB Loans	#中长期贷款 Medium-term &Long-term Loans	金融机构本外币贷款 Loans in Domestic and Foreign Currencies in Financial Institutions					
				中资金融机构贷款合计 Total Loans in Chinese Financial Institutions	#人民币贷款 RMB Loans	#外汇（亿美元） Foreign Exchange (USD 100 million)	外资银行贷款合计 Total Loans in Foreign-funded Financial Bank	#人民币贷款 RMB Loans	#外汇（亿美元） Foreign Exchange (USD 100 million)
1978					53.9				
1979					74.2				
1980					87.3				
1981					91.3				
1982					109.1				
1983					149.5				
1984					174.3				
1985					249.8				
1986					299.2				
1987					346.1				
1988					415.7				
1989					487.1				
1990					573.1				
1991					735.8				
1992					894.7				
1993					1128.1				
1994					1429.0				
1995					1779.1				
1996					2082.8				
1997					2720.7				
1998					3326.6				
1999					4007.8				
2000	6407.9		3106.7	6306.3	6008.2	27.7			9.0
2001	7612.2		3797.3	7514.9	7202.9	37.4			10.8
2002	9704.3		5026.9	9602.6	9230.8	44.9			12.1
2003	12057.7		6352.0	11884.4	11314.7	68.8			20.9
2004	13577.7		7506.4	13312.3	12600.2	86.0			32.0
2005	15335.5		8632.4	14996.6	13792.2	149.2		42.3	36.8
2006	18131.6	15632.7	11142.8	17631.7	15486.9	274.7		145.8	45.4
2007	19861.5	17812.5	12217.6	19053.9	17360.2	231.9	807.5	452.3	48.6
2008	23010.7	19985.0	14688.9	22160.5	19431.1	399.4	850.2	554.0	43.3
2009	31052.9	25421.8	21163.8	30151.6	24805.1	783.0	901.3	616.7	41.7
2010	36479.6	29563.8	26180.2	35352.0	28748.1	997.2	1127.6	815.6	47.1
2011	39660.5	33367.0	24886.3	38410.3	32434.6	948.4	1250.2	932.5	50.4
2012	43189.5	36441.3	26333.5	41839.8	35441.7	1017.9	1349.7	999.6	55.7
2013	47880.9	40506.7	28171.7	46539.5	39557.5	1145.2	1341.4	949.2	64.3
2014	53650.6	45458.7	30882.3	52254.3	44438.8	1277.3	1396.2	1019.9	61.5
2015	58559.4	50559.5	33671.3	57281.2	49530.8	1193.6	1994.3	1676.9	48.9
2016	63739.4	56618.9	37471.3	62492.2	55553.2	1000.3	2005.9	1725.8	40.4
2017	69556.2	63382.5	42001.7	68091.3	62132.4	911.9	2275.3	1945.2	50.5
2018	70483.7	66767.0	42948.9	69071.1	65520.3	517.4	1865.9	1641.2	32.7
2019	76875.6	73575.9	42861.7	75336.5	72177.0	452.9	1744.6	1589.7	22.2
2020	84308.8	81035.2	47507.1	82942.0	79808.6	480.2	1548.0	1402.7	22.3
2021	89032.9	86077.5	56189.6	87559.1	84741.4	441.9	1560.3	1414.7	22.8
2022	97819.9	95496.9	61514.6	96416.0	94201.9	317.9	1514.4	1388.9	18.0

18-2 金融机构(含外资)本外币信贷收支情况(2022年)
BALANCE OF CREDIT IN DOMESTIC AND FOREIGN CURRENCIES FOR FINANCIAL INSTITUTIONS (INCLUDING FOREIGN BANKS)(2022)

单位：亿元，汇率：6.9646 (100 million yuan ,at an exchange rate of 6.9646)

项目	Item	余额 Balance	比年初增减额(+、-) Increase or Decrease than the Beginning of the Year
各项存款	**Total Deposits**	**218628.8**	**18899.2**
#人民币存款	RMB Deposits	212446.7	20354.4
境内存款	Domestic Deposits	216495.2	20110.4
住户存款	Resident Deposits	58621.4	9877.0
非金融企业存款	Non-financial Corporate Deposits	70888.4	2100.7
机关团体存款	General Government Deposits	46456.1	3447.2
财政性存款	Fiscal Deposits	1625.7	-342.3
非银行业金融机构存款	Deposits of Non-banking Financial Institutions	38903.5	5027.8
境外存款	Overseas Deposits	2133.6	-1211.2
各项贷款	**Total Loans**	**97819.9**	**8786.9**
#人民币贷款	RMB Loans	95496.9	9419.4
境内贷款	Domestic Loans	96187.0	8960.8
住户贷款	Resident Loans	23753.8	1811.1
企(事)业单位贷款	Loans of Enterprises and Public Institutions	71877.2	6743.3
非银行业金融机构贷款	Loans of Non-banking Financial Institutions	556.0	406.5
境外贷款	Overseas Loans	1632.9	-173.9

资料来源：中国人民银行北京市分行。
Source: Beijing Municipal Branch of The People's Bank of China.

18-3 中资金融机构本外币信贷收支情况(2022年)
BALANCE OF CREDIT IN DOMESTIC AND FOREIGN CURRENCIES FOR DOMESTICALLY-FUNDED FINANCIAL INSTITUTIONS(2022)

单位：亿元，汇率：6.9646 (100 million yuan ,at an exchange rate of 6.9646)

项目	Item	余额 Balance	比年初增减额(+、-) Increase or Decrease than Year-beginning
各项存款	**Total Deposits**	**215708.2**	**19049.5**
#人民币存款	RMB Deposits	210025.3	20319.6
境内存款	Domestic Deposits	213852.6	20210.8
住户存款	Resident Deposits	58286.2	9833.8
非金融企业存款	Non-financial Corporate Deposits	68646.5	2248.1
机关团体存款	General Government Deposits	46455.9	3447.2
财政性存款	Fiscal Deposits	1625.7	-342.2
非银行业金融机构存款	Deposits of Non-banking Financial Institutions	38838.2	5023.9
境外存款	Overseas Deposits	1855.6	-1161.4
各项贷款	**Total Loans**	**96416.0**	**8857.0**
#人民币贷款	RMB Loans	94201.9	9460.5
境内贷款	Domestic Loans	94863.8	9017.4
住户贷款	Resident Loans	23559.5	1828.3
企(事)业单位贷款	Loans of Enterprises and Public Institutions	70748.3	6782.6
非银行业金融机构贷款	Loans of Non-banking Financial Institutions	556.0	406.5
境外贷款	Overseas Loans	1552.2	-160.4

资料来源：中国人民银行北京市分行。
Source: Beijing Municipal Branch of The People's Bank of China.

18-4 银行、保险系统机构及人员(2022年) INSTITUTIONS AND PERSONNEL OF BANKING AND INSURANCE SYSTEMS (2022)

项目	Item	银行系统 Banking System		保险系统 Insurance System	
		机构(个) Institutions (unit)	人员(人) Personnel (person)	机构(个) Institutions (unit)	人员(人) Personnel (person)
合计	**Total**	**3737**	**219394**	**701**	**149938**
东城区	Dongcheng District	261	15293	60	17770
西城区	Xicheng District	384	89093	85	25868
朝阳区	Chaoyang District	837	32049	168	59243
丰台区	Fengtai District	308	7316	36	7993
石景山区	Shijingshan District	95	9548	26	3643
海淀区	Haidian District	643	34251	57	9255
门头沟区	Mentougou District	52	1005	11	229
房山区	Fangshan District	120	2201	30	3590
通州区	Tongzhou District	171	3425	43	4599
顺义区	Shunyi District	168	12292	35	2504
昌平区	Changping District	171	3175	34	5519
大兴区	Daxing District	155	3048	25	2466
怀柔区	Huairou District	85	1328	18	1170
平谷区	Pinggu District	81	1273	27	3330
密云区	Miyun District	81	1421	26	1634
延庆区	Yanqing District	51	995	15	754
北京经济技术开发区	Beijing Economic-Technological Development Area	74	1681	5	371

注：1.本表口径为在北京地区经营的银行、保险公司的总行(总公司)、分行(分公司)及所属分支机构。
2.保险系统人员构成中含营销员。

Note: a) Figures in this table cover the headquarters (head offices), branches banks (branches companies) and subsidiaries of banks and insurance companies operating in Beijing.
b) Personnel of insurance system includes marketing personnel.

18-5 上市公司基本情况(1993-2022年)
LISTED COMPANIES (1993-2022)

年 份 Year	年 末 上市公司 (家) Companies Listed by Year-end (unit)	上市公司 总 股 本 (万股) Total Equity of Listed Companies (10000 Shares)	股 票 首发数量 (万股) Initial Public Offering Shares (10000 Shares)	首 发 募集资金 (亿元) Funds Raised Through IPO (100 million yuan)	增 发 募集资金 (亿元) Funds Raised Through Additional Issue (100 million yuan)	配 股 募集资金 (亿元) Funds Raised Through Allotment of Shares (100 million yuan)
1993	3	24592	3924	58.0		28.8
1994	7	124038	20300	11.7		0.5
1995	7	133309				3.8
1996	13	198956	29763	12.8		1.9
1997	26	470026	80200	52.2		7.0
1998	33	723561	52750	32.9		20.2
1999	43	1439894	121242	63.0	10.8	10.7
2000	54	2015049	156000	143.5	22.2	46.0
2001	63	9764783	345500	191.6		17.0
2002	68	11929954	23800	16.8	14.9	
2003	74	11493598	373600	188.7	2.8	2.2
2004	83	12553074	21300	16.7	28.4	7.1
2005	83	13159721			3.1	
2006	92	58156652	2667911	1073.4	79.4	
2007	104	86151941	2428976	2433.3	304.7	12.1
2008	109	90486962	698853	546.9	502.0	63.8
2009	126	97911881	2179290	1154.2	430.7	
2010	165	137726461	3481552	1298.3	348.7	777.0
2011	194	143088054	420483	462.0	661.7	175.6
2012	217	146788089	211752	191.4	436.2	69.1
2013	219	151694399			183.9	32.5
2014	235	214359521	67787	74.9	1319.0	4.9
2015	264	225020500	532142	312.5	1423.3	
2016	281	232028500	149046	130.3	1859.3	49.4
2017	306	240045300	224743	127.0	1281.4	7.7
2018	316	255999835	266223	127.3	1963.8	10.7
2019	346	269765900	1222741	686.7	924.0	
2020	381	276090100	804755	969.1	624.6	37.9
2021	424	295643400	1955335	988.0	1712.1	
2022	460	306071824	650555	1434.4	692.8	51.8

注：1.本表数据按注册地统计。
　　2.1995年、2005年和2013年无新股发行。
资料来源：中国证券监督管理委员会北京监管局。
Note: a) Statistics in this table are counted in terms of registered area.
　　b) There were no shares issued in 1995, 2005 and 2013.
Source: Beijing Office of The China Securities Regulatory Commission.

18-6 证券市场交易情况(2000-2022年)
STATISTICS FOR TRADING IN SECURITIES MARKETS (2000-2022)

单位：亿元 (100 million yuan)

年 份 Year	证券市场交易额 Trading Volume of Securities Market	#股票交易 Stock Trading	#基金交易 Fund Trading
2000	14727.2	9546.2	376.2
2001	12734.2	6473.1	401.2
2002	12827.0	4504.4	269.4
2003	24703.7	5492.9	152.3
2004	22169.4	7290.1	100.2
2005	12930.0	5352.1	69.1
2006	22639.7	15233.3	353.4
2007	92468.8	76476.3	1512.4
2008	71281.5	49581.7	734.0
2009	119975.9	95815.6	1229.3
2010	129495.2	100366.0	1649.5
2011	148956.4	80737.8	2188.2
2012	190779.0	62644.5	2413.6
2013	318274.3	92020.5	3732.5
2014	450773.4	138493.4	10557.4
2015	918064.8	453359.2	32363.6
2016	859649.2	208613.3	31085.7
2017	1000257.0	194744.7	22105.7
2018	911465.7	149887.0	25144.4
2019	946425.6	185027.5	25041.5
2020	1259914.7	318941.8	35120.9
2021	1800772.3	429319.5	46239.9
2022	1846185.7	402066.4	69664.1

注：2021年及以前，数据来源于上海证券交易所和深圳证券交易所；自2022年起，数据来源于北京证券交易所、上海证券交易所和深圳证券交易所。

Note: Data for 2021 and before were derived from Shanghai Stock Exchange and Shenzhen Stock Exchange; since 2022, data are derived from Beijing Stock Exchange,shanghai Stock Exchange and Shenzhen Stock Exchange.

18-7 保险业务情况(1997-2022年)
STATISTICS FOR INSURANCE BUSINESS (1997-2022)

单位：亿元 (100 million yuan)

年份 Year	原保险保费收入 Premium Income of Original Insurance	人身险 Life Insurance	财产险 Property Insurance	赔付支出 Compensation Expenses	人身险 Life Insurance	财产险 Property Insurance
1997	102.5					
1998	88.6					
1999	91.8			29.9		
2000	93.4			28.4		
2001	141.3			32.0		
2002	234.1			46.9		
2003	282.5			48.0		
2004	279.3			55.3		
2005	498.2			75.4		
2006	411.5	327.2	84.4	84.0	45.1	38.9
2007	498.1	386.3	111.8	135.4	85.7	49.7
2008	585.9	451.8	134.1	188.9	121.0	67.9
2009	697.6	533.2	164.4	196.0	110.6	85.4
2010	966.5	754.2	212.3	199.7	105.9	93.7
2011	820.9	588.4	232.6	232.8	113.8	119.0
2012	923.1	656.1	267.0	286.2	133.9	152.3
2013	994.4	706.4	288.0	318.2	152.9	165.3
2014	1207.2	892.5	314.8	407.2	224.6	182.7
2015	1403.9	1059.2	344.7	506.6	300.0	206.6
2016	1839.0	1469.7	369.2	596.6	367.3	229.3
2017	1973.2	1568.8	404.4	577.7	365.3	212.5
2018	1793.3	1370.7	422.7	629.4	383.5	245.9
2019	2076.5	1621.6	454.8	719.0	449.6	269.3
2020	2302.9	1861.6	441.4	750.6	488.1	262.5
2021	2526.9	2083.4	443.5	838.5	567.8	270.7
2022	2758.5	2279.4	479.1	776.0	495.9	280.1

资料来源：国家金融监督管理总局北京监管局。
Source: Beijing Office of The National Administration of Financial Regulation.

18-8 保险业务情况
STATISTICS FOR INSURANCE BUSINESS

单位：亿元 (100 million yuan)

项　　目	Item	原保险保费收入 Premium Income of Original Insurance		赔付支出 Compensation Expenses	
		2022	2021	2022	2021
合　计	**Total**	**2758.5**	**2526.9**	**776.0**	**838.5**
人身险业务小计	**Subtotal of Life Insurance**	**2279.4**	**2083.4**	**495.9**	**567.8**
人寿保险	Life Insurance	1724.2	1498.7	283.6	265.0
非分红产品	Non-participating Products	1202.1	925.7	91.5	102.7
分红产品	Participating Products	516.6	568.4	190.8	160.0
投资连接产品	Investment-linked Products	0.4	0.4	0.4	1.2
万能产品	Universal Products	5.1	4.2	0.9	1.0
意外伤害保险	Accident Insurance	48.5	62.4	22.1	25.8
健康保险	Health Insurance	506.7	522.3	190.3	277.0
财产险业务小计	**Subtotal of Property Insurance**	**479.1**	**443.5**	**280.1**	**270.7**
#企业财产保险	Enterprise Property Insurance	51.0	45.9	21.5	19.2
家庭财产保险	Household Property Insurance	4.8	2.7	1.0	1.3
机动车辆及第三者责任保险	Motor Vehicle and Third Party Liability Insurance	231.9	227.7	142.7	163.8
货物运输保险	Freight Transport Insurance	20.0	16.3	7.9	6.1
责任保险	Liability Insurance	79.0	70.2	45.0	35.7
工程险	Construction Insurance	13.3	13.1	6.2	6.8

资料来源：国家金融监督管理总局北京监管局。
Source: Beijing Office of The National Administration of Financial Regulation.

主要统计指标解释

存款 企业、机关、团体或居民根据可以收回的原则，把货币资金存入银行或其他信用机构保管并取得一定利息的一种信用活动形式。根据存款对象的不同可划分为非金融企业存款、财政性存款、机关团体存款、住户存款、非银行金融机构存款等科目。它是银行信贷资金的主要来源。

贷款 银行或其他信用机构根据必须归还的原则，按一定利率，为企业、个人等提供资金的一种信用活动形式。我国银行贷款分为短期贷款、中长期贷款、委托及信托类贷款、其他类贷款等。

原保险保费收入 是指保险企业确认的原保险合同保费收入。是投保人根据保险合同的有关规定，为被保险人取得因约定危险事故发生所造成的经济损失补偿（或给付）权利，付给保险人的代价。包括财产险和人身险收入。

保险赔付支出 公司按保险合同约定支付给被保险人（或受益人）的赔款、保险金、给付等。包括赔款支出、死伤医疗给付、满期给付和年金给付。

股票交易额 统计期末北京地区证券营业部在北京证券交易所、上海证券交易所和深圳证券交易所的股票交易金额。

基金交易额 统计期末北京地区证券营业部在北京证券交易所、上海证券交易所和深圳证券交易所的基金交易金额。

Explanatory Notes on Main Statistical Indicators

Deposit is a form of credit activity that enterprises, public institutions, groups or residents save their money, on a reclaimable basis, in banks or other credit institutions and receive certain interest. In terms of depositors, there are non-financial enterprise deposit, fiscal deposit, government agency deposit, household deposit, non-bank financial institution deposit and so on, which constitute a main source of bank funds for extending credit.

Loan is a form of credit activity that banks or other credit institutions provide funds which must be repaid for enterprise and individuals at a given interest rate. In China, bank loans are classified as short-, medium-, and long-term loans, entrusted and trust loans, and others.

Premium Income means the income of insurance premium of original insurance contracts confirmed by insurance companies. It is the price paid by policy holders to the insurer for the right to receive compensation (claim settlement) for any economic loss caused by agreed dangerous accidents pursuant to relevant provisions in the insurance contract. There are property insurance and life insurance incomes.

Insurance Indemnity Payments refer to indemnity, insurance money, and claim settlement, etc. paid by the insurance company to the insurant (or beneficiary) as agreed in the insurance contract, including indemnity payment, claim settlement for medical costs of death and injury, maturity payment and annuity payment.

Stock Market Turnover means the transaction amount of stocks traded by Beijing securities sales departments in Beijing Stock Exchange, Shanghai Stock Exchange and Shenzhen Stock Exchange, by the end of the statistical period.

Funds Turnover means the transaction amount of funds traded by Beijing securities sales departments in Beijing Stock Exchange, Shanghai Stock Exchange and Shenzhen Stock Exchange, by the end of the statistical period.

北京统计年鉴2023 BEIJING STATISTICAL YEARBOOK 2023

科技
SCIENCE AND TECHNOLOGY

简要说明

一、主要内容

本章资料主要包括研究与试验发展（R&D）人员情况，研究与试验发展（R&D）经费情况，研究与试验发展（R&D）项目（课题）情况，研究机构情况，规模以上工业企业 R&D 活动基本情况，限额以上信息传输、软件和信息技术服务业企业研究与试验发展(R&D)活动基本情况，规模以上高技术制造业主要科技指标，高等学校科技活动情况，研究与开发机构研发活动、专利申请及授权情况等。

二、统计范围

国民经济中研究与试验发展（R&D）活动相对密集行业的法人单位，主要数据包括：农、林、牧、渔业，采矿业，制造业，电力、热力、燃气及水的生产和供应业，建筑业，交通运输、仓储和邮政业，信息传输、软件和信息技术服务业，金融业，租赁和商务服务业，科学研究和技术服务业，水利、环境和公共设施管理业，教育，卫生和社会工作，文化、体育和娱乐业，公共管理、社会保障和社会组织等。

三、有关统计标准的变化说明

（一）关于行业划分。2017 年及以前执行《国民经济行业分类》（GB/T 4754-2011）标准，自 2018 年起执行《国民经济行业分类》（GB/T 4754-2017）标准。

（二）关于三次产业划分。2003 年，根据《国民经济行业分类》（GB/T 4754-2002），国家统计局印发了《国家统计局关于印发〈三次产业划分规定〉的通知》（国统字〔2003〕14 号）。2012 年，根据《国民经济行业分类》（GB/T 4754-2011），国家统计局对 2003 年《三次产业划分规定》进行了修订。主要在以下方面作出调整：一是将门类“农、林、牧、渔业”中的“农、林、牧、渔服务业”，“采矿业”中的“开采辅助活动”，“制造业”中的“金属制品、机械和设备修理业”等三个大类一并调整到第三产业。调整后，第一产业为 4 个大类；第二产业为 2 个门类和 36 个大类；第三产业为 15 个门类和 3 个大类。二是明确第三产业即为服务业。

本章自 2012 年起三次产业的分类执行调整后的划分规定。

（三）关于高技术制造业。根据国家统计局《关于印发高技术产业（制造业）分类（2017）的通知》（国统字〔2017〕200 号），自 2018 年开始执行此标准。

Brief Introduction

I. Main Content

Statistics in this chapter mainly consist of the situation of R&D personnel, R&D funds, R&D projects (tasks), research institutions, basic information on R&D activities of industrial enterprises above designated size, basic information on R&D activities of information transmission, software and information technology service enterprises above designated size, major science and technology indicators of high-tech manufacturing above designated size, scientific and technological activities of colleges and universities, R&D activities of research and development institutions, patent application and licensing, etc.

II. Scope of Statistics

Included in this chapter are the corporate entities in sectors with relatively intensive R&D activities in national economy, such as agriculture, forestry, animal production and hunting, fishing, mining, manufacturing, generation and distribution of electricity, heating, gas and water, construction, transport, storage and post, scientific research and development, technology services, information transmission, software and information technology services, finance, renting and leasing activities and business services, management of water conservancy, environment and public facilities, education, health and social works, culture, sports and entertainment, public administration, social security and social organizations, etc.

III. Changes in Relevant Statistical Standards

(I) Classification of Sectors. The standards in the *Classification of National Economic Sectors* (GB/T 4754-2011) were implemented before 2017. The standards in the *Classification of National Economic Sectors* (GB/T 4754-2017) *are implemented since 2018.*

(II) Classification of Three Industries. According to the *Classification of National Economic Sectors* (GB/T 4754-2002), the National Bureau of Statistics issued the *Notice of the National Bureau of Statistics on the Issuance of the 'Regulations on Three Industries Classification'* (G.T.Z. [2003] No. 14) in 2003. According to the *Classification of National Economic Sectors* (GB/T 4754-2011) the National Bureau of Statistics revised the *Regulations on Three Industries Classification* of 2003 version in 2012. Adjustments were mainly made in the following aspects: Firstly, the "service activities for agriculture, forestry, animal husbandry and fishing" in the category of "agriculture, forestry, animal production and hunting, fishing", the "mining support service activities" in the category of "mining and quarrying", and the "repair of fabricated metal products, machinery and equipment" in the category of "manufacturing" were adjusted to the tertiary industry. After adjustment, the primary industry fell into 4 categories; the secondary industry fell into 2 classes and 36 categories; and the tertiary industry fell into 15 classes and 3 categories. Secondly, the tertiary industry was defined as the service industry.

The classification of three industries since 2012 as mentioned in this chapter has all been subject to the classification provisions after adjustment.

(III) High-tech Manufacturing. According to the *Circular of National Bureau of Statistics on Printing and Issuing the Classification of High-tech Industry (Manufacturing) 2017* (G.T.Z. [2017] No.200). The standard has been put in place since 2018.

19−1 科技活动及专利情况(1986−2022年)
SCIENCE AND TECHNOLOGY ACTIVITIES AND PATENTS (1986-2022)

年 份 Year	科技活动人员(人) Personnel Engaged in Science and Technology Activities (person)	研究与试验发展(R&D)人员折合全时当量(人年) Full-time Equivalent of R&D Professionals (person-year)	研究与试验发展(R&D)经费内部支出(万元) Internal R&D Expenditures (10000 yuan)	研究与试验发展(R&D)经费内部支出相当于地区生产总值比例(%) Internal R&D Expenditures as Percentage of GDP (%)
1986				
1987				
1988				
1989				
1990				
1991	228167			
1992	247525			
1993	252811			
1994	240386			
1995	252232			
1996	265552	84793	418614	2.32
1997	273161	84913	532257	2.54
1998	237127	86602	861138	3.58
1999	229584	85740	938437	3.46
2000	261113	98723	1557011	4.85
2001	240609	95255	1711696	4.54
2002	257326	114919	2195402	4.99
2003	270921	110358	2562518	5.02
2004	301202	152132	3169064	5.14
2005	383153	177765	3795450	5.31
2006	382756	168875	4329878	5.21
2007	450331	204668	5270591	5.23
2008	450147	200080	6200983	5.44
2009	529985	191779	6686351	5.38
2010	529811	193718	8218234	5.69
2011	605980	217255	9366440	5.63
2012	651003	235493	10633640	5.59
2013	681346	242175	11850469	5.61
2014	726792	245384	12687953	5.53
2015	747461	245728	13840231	5.59
2016	810195	253337	14845762	5.49
2017		269835	15796512	5.29
2018		267338	18707701	5.65
2019		313986	22335870	6.30
2020		336280	23265793	6.47
2021		338297	26293208	6.41
2022		373235	28433394	6.83

资料来源：北京市统计局、北京市科学技术委员会、中关村科技园区管理委员会、北京市教育委员会、北京市经济和信息化局、北京市知识产权局。

Source: Beijing Municipal Bureau of Statistics, Beijing Municipal Science & Technology Commission, Administrative Commission of Zhongguancun Science Park, Beijing Municipal Commission of Education, Beijing Municipal Bureau of Economy and Information Technology, Beijing Municipal Intellectual Property Office.

19-1 续表 Continued

年份 Year	PCT国际专利申请量（件） PCT International Patent Applications (unit)	专利授权量（件） Patents Granted (unit)	发明 Inventions	实用新型 Utility Models	外观设计 Industrial Designs	国内专利有效量（件） Domestic Patents in Force (unit)	#发明专利 Invention Patents	万人发明专利拥有量（件） Invention Patent Ownership per 10000 Persons (unit)	万人高价值发明专利拥有量（件） High-value Invention Patent Ownership per 10000 Persons (unit)
1986		491	43	408	40				
1987		776	102	630	44				
1988		1376	169	1147	60				
1989		1789	207	1497	85				
1990		2268	216	1932	120				
1991		2369	263	1917	189				
1992		3265	312	2724	229				
1993		5806	530	4780	496				
1994		3914	368	3245	301				
1995		4025	328	3169	528				
1996		3295	246	2563	486				
1997		3327	281	2340	706				
1998		3800	309	2522	969				
1999		5829	573	3948	1308				
2000		5905	1074	3463	1368				
2001		6246	946	3600	1700				
2002		6345	1061	3721	1563				
2003		8248	2261	4244	1743				
2004		9005	3216	3956	1833				
2005		10100	3476	4498	2126		12102	8.0	
2006		11238	3864	5490	1884	36645	13319	8.5	
2007		14954	4824	7364	2766	43584	18421	11.2	
2008		17747	6478	8776	2493	55771	20329	11.8	
2009		22921	9157	10141	3623	71076	28774	15.8	
2010	1272	33511	11209	16579	5723	100623	38996	20.4	
2011	1862	40888	15880	19628	5380	131255	52522	26.4	
2012	2705	50511	20140	24672	5699	170516	69554	34.0	
2013	2981	62671	20695	36301	5675	219243	85434	40.8	
2014	3606	74661	23237	44071	7353	274667	103638	48.6	23.6
2015	4490	94031	35308	45773	12950	344916	133040	61.6	29.4
2016	6651	102323	41425	45376	15522	417666	166722	76.8	36.6
2017	5069	106948	46091	46011	14846	494941	205320	94.5	47.5
2018	6527	123496	46978	59219	17299	569929	241282	112.0	57.2
2019	7165	131716	53127	58393	20196	653053	284288	132.0	67.4
2020	8283	162824	63266	75336	24222	768090	335575	155.8	79.3
2021	10358	198778	79210	96078	23490	913616	405037	185.0	94.2
2022	11463	202722	88127	91947	22648	1046715	477790	218.0	112.0

注：自2016年起，对专利相关数据的统计范围进行了调整，下同。
Note: The statistical range of patent-related data was adjusted since 2016, the same below.

19-2 研究与试验发展(R&D)人员情况

项 目	Item	研究与试验发展(R&D)人员(人) R&D Personnel (person)	
		2022	2021
合 计	**Total**	**546747**	**472860**
按执行部门分	**By Executive Department**		
企 业	Enterprises	237479	190478
工业企业	Industrial Enterprises	79152	61490
非工业企业	Non-industrial Enterprises	158327	128988
科研机构	Scientific Research Institutions	150908	138829
高等学校	Institutions of Higher Education	146363	132061
事业单位	Public Institutions	11997	11492
按行业门类分	**By Sector**		
#制造业	Manufacturing	73478	59124
信息传输、软件和信息技术服务业	Information Transmission, Software and Information Technology Services	78603	85919
科学研究和技术服务业	Scientific Research and Technical Services	212556	175858
教 育	Education	146363	132061

资料来源：北京市统计局，北京市科学技术委员会、中关村科技园区管理委员会，北京市教育委员会，北京市经济和信息化局。

STATISTICS FOR RESEARCH AND EXPERIMENTAL DEVELOPMENT PERSONNEL

研究与试验发展(R&D)人员折合全时当量(人年) Full-time Equivalent of R&D Professionals (person-year)		基础研究 Basic Research		应用研究 Applied Research		试验发展 Experimental Development	
2022	2021	2022	2021	2022	2021	2022	2021
373235	**338297**	**84525**	**75525**	**110283**	**97159**	**178429**	**165615**
154507	137146	1751	977	14249	9528	138508	126641
53459	41496	256	80	3875	2188	49328	39228
101048	95650	1495	897	10374	7341	89180	87413
127513	119846	46540	42291	47763	44100	33210	33455
83037	73760	34031	30867	44034	39195	4973	3698
8178	7546	2203	1390	4237	4335	1738	1821
49707	39709	256	65	3082	1551	46370	38092
51730	67417	122	290	3007	3557	48600	63570
167132	145457	49492	44053	58160	51066	59480	50338
83037	73760	34031	30866	44034	39195	4973	3698

Source: Beijing Municipal Bureau of Statistics, Beijing Municipal Science & Technology Commission, Administrative Commission of Zhongguancun Science Park, Beijing Municipal Commission of Education, Beijing Municipal Bureau of Economy and Information Technology.

19-3 研究与试验发展(R&D)经费情况

单位：万元

项 目	Item	研究与试验发展(R&D)经费内部支出 Internal R&D Expenditures		基础研究 Basic Research	
		2022	2021	2022	2021
合 计	**Total**	**28433394**	**26293208**	**4706662**	**4225134**
按执行部门分	**By Executive Department**				
企 业	Enterprises	12400254	11366531	124982	99800
工业企业	Industrial Enterprises	3489973	3135144	32863	8968
非工业企业	Non-industrial Enterprises	8910281	8231387	92120	90832
科研机构	Scientific Research Institutions	12332269	11462361	3470484	3036019
高等学校	Institutions of Higher Education	3116342	2922095	1035284	1021150
事业单位	Public Institutions	584530	542220	75912	68164
按行业门类分	**By Sector**				
#制造业	Manufacturing	3341972	3040257	32817	8763
信息传输、软件和信息技术服务业	Information Transmission, Software and Information Technology Services	6067299	6115927	14732	33099
科学研究和技术服务业	Scientific Research and Technical Services	14769399	13299596	3592153	3144895
教 育	Education	3116342	2922095	1035284	1021150

资料来源：北京市统计局，北京市科学技术委员会、中关村科技园区管理委员会，北京市教育委员会，北京市经济和信息化局。

RESEARCH AND EXPERIMENTAL DEVELOPMENT FUNDS

(10000 yuan)

按活动类型分 Group by Type of Activity				按支出用途分 Group by Purpose of Payment			
应用研究 Applied Research		试验发展 Experimental Development		日常性支出 Routine Expenses		#人员劳务费 Labor Cost	
2022	2021	2022	2021	2022	2021	2022	2021
7311006	**6570210**	**16415727**	**15497865**	**25324198**	**23059539**	**10582789**	**10133491**
802923	641768	11472349	10624963	11345318	10206284	6521372	6320133
141996	84697	3315114	3041479	3313750	3027431	1394239	1144838
660927	557071	8157234	7583484	8031568	7178853	5127132	5175295
4281885	3887676	4579901	4538666	10915229	9875406	3184248	3011482
1833435	1654693	247623	246252	2731135	2613882	697238	629428
392764	386073	115855	87983	332515	363967	179931	172448
112256	52202	3196900	2979292	3180728	2938358	1330927	1100407
330509	295563	5722057	5787265	5223312	5162765	4183735	4028874
4918904	4468540	6258341	5686161	12980677	11469192	4304700	3863583
1833435	1654693	247623	246252	2731135	2613882	697238	629428

Source: Beijing Municipal Bureau of Statistics, Beijing Municipal Science & Technology Commission, Administrative Commission of Zhongguancun Science Park, Beijing Municipal Commission of Education, Beijing Municipal Bureau of Economy and Information Technology.

19-3 续表

单位：万元

项目	Item	资产性支出 Expenditures for Assets		#仪器和设备 Instruments and Equipment	
		2022	2021	2022	2021
合计	**Total**	**3109196**	**3233669**	**2510375**	**2632285**
按执行部门分	**By Executive Department**				
企业	Enterprises	1054935	1160247	1048934	1151199
工业企业	Industrial Enterprises	176223	107713	172896	101735
非工业企业	Non-industrial Enterprises	878713	1052535	876037	1049463
科研机构	Scientific Research Institutions	1417040	1586955	904831	1048920
高等学校	Institutions of Higher Education	385206	308214	336989	278038
事业单位	Public Institutions	252015	178253	219621	154129
按行业门类分	**By Sector**				
#制造业	Manufacturing	161244	101899	158602	96269
信息传输、软件和信息技术服务业	Information Transmission, Software and Information Technology Services	843987	953163	842703	952198
科学研究和技术服务业	Scientific Research and Technical Services	1788721	1830405	1244129	1267468
教育	Education	385206	308214	336989	278038

19—3　continued

(10000 yuan)

按资金来源分 Group by Fund Source							
政府资金 Governmental Funds		企业资金 Enterprise Funds		国外资金 Foreign Funds		其他资金 Others	
2022	2021	2022	2021	2022	2021	2022	2021
12896678	**11864952**	**13422113**	**12477196**	**146522**	**132322**	**1968082**	**1818738**
409771	371091	11917787	10911556	61742	65618	10954	18267
262553	211273	3208071	2888863	12093	28142	7256	6866
147217	159818	8709716	8022693	49649	37476	3699	11401
10109344	9309740	647991	682908	40472	26263	1534463	1443450
1889977	1714640	844654	849372	43655	40238	338055	317845
487586	469481	11682	33360	652	204	84610	39176
262137	205640	3060486	2799610	12093	28142	7256	6866
64867	57905	5996720	6049958	3655	357	2056	7708
10656765	9823602	2417899	1932849	74443	57108	1620292	1486038
1889977	1714640	844654	849372	43655	40238	338055	317845

19-4 规模以上工业企业研究与试验发展(R&D)活动基本情况(2022年)

项 目	Item	有研究与试验发展(R&D)活动的企业数(个) Enterprises with R&D Activities (unit)	研究与试验发展(R&D)人员(人) R&D Personnel (person)	研究与试验发展(R&D)人员折合全时当量(人年) Full-time Equivalent of R&D Personnel (person-year)	研究与试验发展(R&D)经费内部支出(万元) Internal R&D Expenditures (10000 yuan)
合 计	**Total**	**1325**	**79152**	**53459**	**3489973**
#大中型企业	Medium and Large-sized	331	56485	38640	2721706
按登记注册类型分	**By Registration Type**				
内资企业	Domestically-invested Enterprises	1107	58578	38552	2424738
#国有企业	State-owned Enterprises	4	385	199	12338
港澳台商投资企业	Hong Kong, Macao and Taiwan-invested Enterprises	61	8784	6994	598233
外商投资企业	Foreign-invested Enterprises	157	11790	7913	467002

BASIC INFORMATION ON RESEARCH AND EXPERIMENTAL DEVELOPMENT ACTIVITIES OF INDUSTRIAL ENTERPRISES ABOVE DESIGNATED SIZE (2022)

				专　利		新产品	
政府资金 Governmental Funds	企业资金 Enterprise Funds	国外资金 Foreign Funds	其他资金 Others	申请数（件） Patent Applications (unit)	#发明专利 Invention Pateuts	销售收入（万元） Sales Income of New Products (10000 yuan)	#出口 Exports
262553	**3208071**	**12093**	**7256**	**32594**	**19310**	**56037315**	**9631096**
224543	2482519	7929	6715	20968	14432	44716652	8780043
215294	2199703	2505	7236	25728	15227	28009474	1777197
11101	1237			260	251	412834	
17111	581114		8	3810	2409	21775678	6970158
30148	427253	9588	12	3056	1674	6252163	883741

19-5 规模以上工业企业研究与试验发展(R&D)及相关活动情况(按行业分)(2022年)

项目	Item	有研究与试验发展(R&D)活动的企业数(个) Enterprises with R&D Activities (unit)	研究与试验发展(R&D)人员(人) R&D Personnel (person)
合计	**Total**	**1325**	**79152**
采矿业	**Mining**	**7**	**3468**
煤炭开采和洗选业	Mining and Washing of Coal		
石油和天然气开采业	Extraction of Petroleum and Natural Gas	2	566
黑色金属矿采选业	Mining and Processing of Ferrous Metal Ores	1	***
有色金属矿采选业	Mining and Processing of Non-Ferrous Metal Ores		
非金属矿采选业	Mining and Processing of Nonmetal Ores		
开采专业及辅助性活动	Mining Support Service Activities	4	2491
其他采矿业	Mining of Other Ores		
制造业	**Manufacturing**	**1298**	**73478**
农副食品加工业	Processing of Food from Agriculture Products	22	757
食品制造业	Manufacture of Foods	27	1008
酒、饮料和精制茶制造业	Manufacture of Wine, Beverage and Refined Tea	7	1139
烟草制品业	Manufacture of Cigarettes and Tobacco	1	***
纺织业	Manufacture of Textile	4	113
纺织服装、服饰业	Manufacture of Textile Wearing Apparel and Ornament	7	210
皮革、毛皮、羽毛及其制品和制鞋业	Manufacture of Leather, Fur, Feather and Its Products, and Footwear		
木材加工和木、竹、藤、棕、草制品业	Processing of Timbers, Manufacture of Wood, Bamboo, Rattan, Palm, and Straw Products		
家具制造业	Manufacture of Furniture	6	160
造纸和纸制品业	Manufacture of Paper and Paper Products	7	93
印刷和记录媒介复制业	Printing, Reproduction of Recording Media	22	739
文教、工美、体育和娱乐用品制造业	Manufacture of Articles for Culture, Education, Artwork, Sport and Entertainment Activities	7	107
石油、煤炭及其他燃料加工业	Processing of Petroleum, Coal and Other Fuels	8	262
化学原料和化学制品制造业	Manufacture of Raw Chemical Materials and Chemical Products	57	1748
医药制造业	Manufacture of Medicines	151	9262
化学纤维制造业	Manufacture of Chemical Fibers	1	***
橡胶和塑料制品业	Manufacture of Rubber and Plastics Products	14	275
非金属矿物制品业	Manufacture of Non-Metallic Mineral Products	57	1928
黑色金属冶炼和压延加工业	Smelting and Pressing of Ferrous Metals	2	86
有色金属冶炼和压延加工业	Smelting and Pressing of Non-Ferrous Metals	10	445
金属制品业	Manufacture of Fabricated Metal Products	44	1224
通用设备制造业	Manufacture of General-Purpose Machinery	105	4779
专用设备制造业	Manufacture of Special-Purpose Machinery	226	9129
汽车制造业	Manufacture of Motor Vehicles	45	5966
铁路、船舶、航空航天和其他运输设备制造业	Manufacture of Railway, Ships, Aerospace and Other Transport Equipments	52	3690
电气机械和器材制造业	Manufacture of Electrical Machinery and Equipment	96	4031
计算机、通信和其他电子设备制造业	Manufacture of Computers, Communication Equipment and Other Electronic Equipment	187	21605
仪器仪表制造业	Manufacture of Measuring Instruments and Meters	117	3595
其他制造业	Other Manufacturing	5	399
废弃资源综合利用业	Recycling and Disposal of Waste	3	46
金属制品、机械和设备修理业	Repair of Fabricated Metal Products, Machinery and Equipment	8	590
电力、热力、燃气及水的生产和供应业	**Production and Supply of Electricity, Heating, Gas and Water**	**20**	**2206**
电力、热力生产和供应业	Production and Supply of Electricity and Heating Power	12	1111
燃气生产和供应业	Production and Supply of Gas	2	949
水的生产和供应业	Production and Supply of Water	6	146

STATISTICS FOR RESEARCH AND EXPERIMENTAL DEVELOPMENT AND RELATED ACTIVITIES OF INDUSTRIAL ENTERPRISES ABOVE DESIGNATED SIZE (BY SECTOR) (2022)

研究与试验发展(R&D)人员折合全时当量(人年) Full-time Equivalent of R&D Personnel (person-year)	研究与试验发展(R&D)经费内部支出(万元) Internal R&D Expenditures (10000 yuan)	政府资金 Governmental Funds	企业资金 Enterprise Funds	国外资金 Foreign Funds	其他资金 Others	专利申请数(件) Patent Applications (unit)	#发明专利 Invention Patents	新产品销售收入(万元) Sales Income of New Products (10000 yuan)	#出口 Exports
53459	**3489973**	**262553**	**3208071**	**12093**	**7256**	**32594**	**19310**	**56037315**	**9631096**
1934	**68903**	**225**	**68678**			**338**	**295**	**111947**	
375	17158	14	17144			34	26		
***	***	***	***			***	***		
1192	35771	78	35693			25	13	111947	
49707	**3341972**	**262137**	**3060486**	**12093**	**7256**	**30304**	**17719**	**51348206**	**9631096**
443	19070	1884	17185			218	106	450810	11177
558	28614	1065	27482	67		183	49	346400	10763
597	16573		16573			176	24	600728	1062
***	***		***					***	***
71	5483		5483			24	9	76178	7020
169	2199		2199			75	9	252263	59606
92	2561		2561			278	26	166466	348
48	1102		1102			76	13	57593	36905
373	13874	50	13824			170	62	542840	1811
69	1769		1769			25	6	55784	863
140	14328	6	14322			49	20	199833	
1410	49511	136	49376			375	250	603878	32392
5981	577976	17470	560491	15		1474	1039	3995466	316491
***	***		***			***	***	***	***
180	5856		5856			88	14	118167	108
1134	81675	2413	79209		53	972	446	1887894	59627
75	6428		6428			40	17	203310	
207	19007	7989	11018			194	163	677938	99005
668	50661	20174	30488			536	284	585941	70412
3326	164792	7568	157162		62	1639	571	2457020	364223
5783	370001	29648	338431	1843	80	4860	2284	3888162	442595
3850	228973	3460	225487		25	2115	806	3957027	171744
2372	153008	15153	135595		2261	1195	716	1698102	260
2501	161788	1191	159573	1024		2620	1255	5051471	68505
16863	1227298	145287	1072753	4484	4775	10761	8507	21914257	7816662
2449	121447	7185	109603	4660		1885	900	1409697	44169
149	9609	1459	8150			93	81	21865	
17	509		509			104	53	31585	
116	4412		4412			75	8	25186	
1818	**79098**	**191**	**78906**			**1952**	**1296**	**4577162**	
804	30566	65	30501			1704	1181	485639	
911	43028		43028			138	58	4085316	
103	5504	126	5377			110	57	6207	

19-6 规模以上高技术制造业研究与试验发展(R&D)及相关活动情况

项　目	Item	R&D人员折合全时当量（人年）Full-time Equivalent of R&D Personnel (person-year)	
		2022	2021
高技术制造业	**High-tech Manufacturing**	**30279**	**23104**
医药制造业	**Manufacture of Medicines**	**5981**	**5108**
#化学药品制造	Manufacture of Chemical Medicine	1610	1684
生物药品制造	Manufacture of Biological Medicine and Biochemical Chemical Products	2453	2053
航空、航天器及设备制造业	**Manufacture of Aircrafts and Spacecrafts**	**1754**	**2535**
#航空航天器修理	Repair of Air and Spacecrafts	87	38
电子及通信设备制造业	**Manufacture of Electronic Equipment and Communication Equipment**	**15148**	**10049**
#通信设备制造、雷达及配套设备制造	Manufacture of Communication Equipment	6260	3739
电子器件制造	Manufacture of Electronic Appliances	3856	3260
电子元件及电子专用设备制造	Manufacture of Electronic Components	1219	727
其他电子设备制造	Manufacture of Other Electronic Equipment	2179	1477
计算机及办公设备制造业	**Manufacture of Computers and Office Equipments**	**2336**	**1697**
#计算机整机制造	Manufacture of Entired Computer	239	94
医疗仪器设备及仪器仪表制造业	**Manufacture of Medical Equipments and Meters**	**5059**	**3715**
#医疗仪器设备及器械制造	Manufacture of Medical Equipment and Appliances	2619	1857
通用仪器仪表制造	Manufacture of Measuring Instrument and Meter	1610	1077

STATISTICS FOR RESEARCH AND EXPERIMENTAL DEVELOPMENT AND RELATED ACTIVITIES OF HIGH-TECH MANUFACTURING ABOVE DESIGNATED SIZE

R&D经费支出 (万元) R&D Expenditures (10000 yuan)		新产品销售收入 (万元) Sales Income of New Products (10000 yuan)		专利申请数 (件) Patent Applications (unit)		#发明专利 Inventions Pactents	
2022	2021	2022	2021	2022	2021	2022	2021
2209862	**2119085**	**29261987**	**53881022**	**17170**	**14457**	**12039**	**9231**
577976	**654060**	**3995466**	**25119293**	**1474**	**1045**	**1039**	**693**
113573	146760	1227820	994034	454	375	268	282
1664425	161831	157159	1683230	469	294	383	185
95628	**304261**	**771596**	**886115**	**770**	**1044**	**472**	**660**
3550	989	2934		54	112	3	12
1144715	**827931**	**19897283**	**22738362**	**8825**	**7038**	**7100**	**5081**
367567	229150	13738552	16857298	2538	2342	2314	1802
355259	281237	2258690	2624091	3351	2302	2779	1842
56929	45565	1185967	1020259	774	658	581	338
274239	222508	1073627	735697	914	829	696	597
126655	**100011**	**2419032**	**3067364**	**2287**	**2218**	**1697**	**1332**
18514	7807	1608441	2147255	1855	1874	1484	1180
264887	**232822**	**2178611**	**2068393**	**3814**	**3112**	**1731**	**1465**
143723	145935	785572	843320	1929	1544	831	692
78681	51925	1021489	840087	1154	916	489	431

19－7 限额以上信息传输、软件和信息技术服务业企业研究与试验发展(R&D)及相关活动情况(2022年)

项 目	Item	有研究与试验发展(R&D)活动的企业数(个) Enterprises with R&D Activities (unit)	研究与试验发展(R&D)人员(人) R&D Personnel (person)	研究与试验发展(R&D)人员折合全时当量(人年) Full-time Equivalent of R&D Personnel (person-year)
合 计	**Total**	**709**	**78603**	**51730**
按登记注册类型分	**By Registration Type**			
内资企业	Domestically-invested Enterprises	635	46053	30506
#国有企业	State-owned Enterprises	2	65	11
港澳台商投资企业	Hong Kong, Macao and Taiwan-invested Enterprises	42	23927	14644
外商投资企业	Foreign-invested Enterprises	32	8623	6580
按行业分	**By Sector**			
电信、广播电视和卫星传输服务	Telecommunications, Broadcasting, Television and Satellite Transmission Services	45	5485	3013
互联网和相关服务	Internet and Related Services	132	35090	24040
软件和信息技术服务业	Software and Information Technology Services	532	38028	24677

STATISTICS FOR RESEARCH AND EXPERIMENTAL DEVELOPMENT AND RELATED ACTIVITIES OF INFORMATION TRANSMISSIOM, SOFTWARE AND INFORMATION TECHNICIAL SERVICE ENTERPRISES ABOVE DESIGNATED SIZE (2022)

研究与试验发展(R&D)经费内部支出(万元) Internal R&D Expenditures (10000 yuan)	政府资金 Govern-mental Funds	企业资金 Enterprise Funds	境外资金 Overseas Funds	其他资金 Others	专利申请数(件) Patent Applications (unit)	#发明专利 Inventions Patents
6067299	**64867**	**5996720**	**3655**	**2056**	**73628**	**58913**
2808901	61157	2745704		2039	58089	45753
595	519	76			57	54
2168097	2316	2165781			11080	9068
1090301	1393	1085235	3655	17	4459	4092
333457	6199	326647		611	8484	7673
3635600	15315	3620150		135	13451	11174
2098242	43353	2049924	3655	1310	51693	40066

19－8 研究与开发机构研究与试验发展(R&D)及相关活动情况(2007－2022年)

项目		Item		2007
研究与开发机构基本情况		**Basic Information on R&D Institutions**		
机构数	(个)	Number	(unit)	265
中　央		Central		221
地　方		Local		44
研究与试验发展(R&D)投入情况		**R&D Input**		
R&D人员	(万人)	R&D Personnel	(10000 persons)	4.6
按隶属关系分		By Affiliation		
中　央		Central		4.4
地　方		Local		0.2
R&D人员折合全时当量	(万人年)	Full-time Equivalent of R&D Personnel	(10000 person-year)	3.8
基础研究		Basic Research		1.2
应用研究		Applied Research		1.6
试验发展		Experimental Development		1.0
R&D经费内部支出	(亿元)	Internal R&D Expenditures	(100 million yuan)	103.1
按隶属关系分		By Affiliation		
中　央		Central		99.0
地　方		Local		4.1
按活动类型分		By Type of Activity		
基础研究		Basic Research		26.4
应用研究		Applied Research		45.2
试验发展		Experimental Development		31.5
按资金来源分		By Source of Funds		
政府资金		Governmental Funds		88.6
企业资金		Enterprise Funds		3.2
境外资金		Foreign Funds		1.3
其他资金		Others		10.0
研究与试验发展(R&D)项目(课题)情况		**R&D Projects (Tasks)**		
R&D项目(课题)数	(项)	Number of R&D Projects (Tasks)	(unit)	15079
R&D项目(课题)人员折合全时当量	(万人年)	Full-time Equivalent of R&D Projects (Tasks) Personnel	(10000 person-year)	2.2
R&D项目(课题)经费内部支出	(亿元)	Internal R&D Projects (Tasks) Expenditures	(100 million yuan)	57.1
科技产出及成果情况		**Science & Technology Output and Achievement**		
发表科技论文	(篇)	Published Articles on Science and Technology	(unit)	37232
#国外发表		Published Abroad		9005
出版科技著作	(种)	Published Writings on Science and Technology	(sort)	1489
专利申请数	(件)	Number of Patents Applications	(unit)	1993
#发明专利		Invention Patents		1784
专利授权数	(件)	Number of Patents Granted	(unit)	985
#发明专利		Invention Patents		752

注：表中2018年及以前研究与开发机构统计范围为北京市政府部门属的科学研究与技术开发机构、科技信息与文献机构，自2019年起，调整为北京市科学研究和技术服务业事业单位。

资料来源：北京市科学技术委员会。

STATISTICS FOR RESEARCH AND EXPERIMENTAL DEVELOPMENT AND RELATED ACTIVITIES IN RESEARCH AND DEVELOPMENT INSTITUTIONS (2007-2022)

2008	2009	2010	2011	2012	2013	2014	2015	2016	2017	2018	2019	2020	2021	2022
266	275	281	280	288	287	299	296	303	300	292	432	445	417	405
225	228	231	231	238	237	248	245	254	250	242	334	345	344	328
41	47	50	49	50	50	51	51	49	50	50	98	100	73	77
4.8	5.2	5.7	5.9	6.3	6.6	6.6	6.8	6.9	7.4	7.3	8.7	9.6	9.9	10.7
4.5	4.9	5.4	5.6	5.9	6.2	6.2	6.3	6.4	6.9	6.8	8.1	9.0	9.2	9.0
0.3	0.3	0.3	0.3	0.4	0.4	0.4	0.5	0.5	0.5	0.5	0.6	0.6	0.7	1.7
3.9	4.2	4.6	4.7	5.3	5.5	5.5	5.6	5.6	5.9	6.0	6.8	7.6	7.8	8.2
1.3	1.4	1.5	1.6	1.8	1.9	2.0	2.1	2.5	2.4	2.6	2.8	3.4	3.4	3.8
1.6	1.7	2.0	2.1	2.2	2.3	2.3	2.2	2.2	2.7	2.6	2.9	3.1	3.1	3.4
1.0	1.1	1.1	1.0	1.3	1.3	1.2	1.3	0.9	0.8	0.8	1.1	1.1	1.3	1.0
123.8	150.3	187.0	195.1	222.0	246.8	271.2	295.6	301.5	329.1	373.0	505.2	509.2	572.6	597.1
117.4	143.9	178.9	185.1	211.5	236.3	253.6	277.0	280.4	309.2	351.3	480.7	481.3	543.2	551.0
6.4	6.4	8.1	10.0	10.5	10.5	17.6	18.6	21.1	19.9	21.7	24.5	27.9	29.4	46.1
28.3	39.2	49.9	58.5	65.1	73.6	86.5	96.8	109.1	130.2	156.9	200.4	206.1	226.9	252.3
49.0	61.5	78.0	84.0	92.0	102.2	108.9	120.5	131.3	146.4	157.8	222.6	228.1	259.5	282.7
46.5	49.6	59.1	52.6	64.9	71.0	75.8	78.3	61.1	52.5	58.3	82.2	75.0	86.2	62.1
106.6	126.3	164.4	168.0	192.6	220.0	244.6	266.3	262.1	289.6	317.9	440.5	442.5	496.2	507.0
4.0	4.4	3.6	6.6	6.5	8.2	8.2	12.1	16.1	16.7	22.7	24.6	34.0	45.2	47.1
1.8	2.0	1.5	2.5	1.5	1.9	1.8	2.0	1.7	2.2	2.1	2.6	1.7	2.6	4.1
11.4	17.6	17.5	18.0	21.4	16.7	16.6	15.2	21.6	20.6	30.3	37.5	30.9	28.6	38.9
16383	17816	19545	20333	22842	23949	25550	26762	26998	31749	32133	36994	40066	41018	43320
2.3	3.8	4.1	4.3	4.9	5.0	5.0	5.0	4.7	5.0	5.1	5.7	6.0	6.4	6.7
70.9	87.1	107.2	115.0	142.7	156.8	161.0	173.5	162.0	189.3	215.3	250.1	269.7	256.1	279.4
37149	39380	39384	41442	44218	45509	48040	48734	49517	49346	50178	59406	64425	65200	68417
9184	12011	11696	13361	14003	17216	17905	18915	19800	21687	23176	27628	31316	29902	36740
1636	1873	1601	1828	1670	1921	2058	2261	2453	2164	2461	2410	2445	2372	2273
2488	3182	3879	4880	5456	6192	6004	6464	6657	7141	7574	9693	10630	11716	12344
2119	2772	3450	4373	4798	5144	5115	5164	5543	5779	6059	7561	8436	9487	10055
1146	1574	1879	2260	3251	3646	3932	4702	5522	5449	5319	6733	8922	9995	10794
922	1299	1455	1756	2635	2763	3001	3529	4184	4246	3767	4670	6350	7115	7964

Note: The scope of statistics of R&D institutions in and before 2018 covered the scientific research and technological development institutions, and the scientific and technological information and literature institutions subordinate to government authorities of Beijing. Since 2019, the scope of statistics has been adjusted to the public institutions of scientific research and development, technical services of Beijing.

Source: Beijing Municipal Science & Technology Commission.

19-9 高等学校研究与试验发展(R&D)及相关活动情况
STATISTICS FOR RESEARCH AND EXPERIMENTAL DEVELOPMENT AND RELATED ACTIVITIES IN COLLEGES & UNIVERSITIES

项目	Item	2022	2021
高等学校基本情况	**Basic Information of Colleges & Universities**		
学校数 (个)	Number of Colleges and Universities (unit)	168	167
研究与试验发展(R&D)机构数 (个)	Number of R&D Institutions (unit)	1475	1327
研究与试验发展(R&D)投入情况	**R&D Input**		
R&D人员 (万人)	R&D Personnel (10000 person)	14.64	13.21
R&D人员折合全时当量 (万人年)	Full-time Equivalent of R&D Personnel (10000 person-year)	8.30	7.37
基础研究	Basic Research	3.40	3.08
应用研究	Applied Research	4.40	3.92
试验发展	Experimental Development	0.50	0.37
R&D经费内部支出 (亿元)	Internal R&D Expenditures (100 million yuan)	311.63	292.21
按活动类型分	By Type of Activity		
基础研究	Basic Research	103.53	102.12
应用研究	Applied Research	183.34	165.46
试验发展	Experimental Development	24.76	24.62
按资金来源分	By Source of Funds		
#政府资金	Governmental Funds	189.00	171.46
企业资金	Enterprise Funds	84.47	84.94
研究与试验发展(R&D)项目(课题)情况	**R&D Projects (Tasks)**		
R&D项目(课题)数 (项)	Number of R&D Projects (Tasks) (unit)	133210	130853
R&D项目(课题)人员折合全时当量 (万人年)	Full-time Equivalent of R&D Personnel (10000 person-year)	8.30	7.37
R&D项目(课题)经费内部支出 (亿元)	Internal R&D Expenditures (100 million yuan)	242.13	349.74
科技产出及成果情况	**Science & Technology Output and Achievement**		
发表科技论文 (篇)	Published Articles on Science and Technology (unit)	140824	132144
#国外发表	Published Abroad	76330	63262
出版科技著作 (种)	Published Writings on Science and Technology (sort)	4345	4502
专利申请数 (件)	Number of Patent Applications (unit)	23874	24390
#发明专利	Invention Patents	20926	20512
专利授权数 (件)	Number of Patents Granted (unit)	22278	20976
#发明专利	Invention Patents	17205	15071

资料来源：北京市教育委员会。
Source: Beijing Municipal Commission of Education.

19-10　技术合同成交情况(1990-2022年)
STATISTICS FOR CONCLUSION OF TECHNOLOGICAL CONTRACTS (1990-2022)

年　份 Year	合同数 (项) Number of Contracts (unit)	技术合同成交总额 (亿元) Total Volume of Transaction of Technological Contracts (100 million yuan)	#技术交易额 Total Volume of Transaction of Technology	#流向外省市 Flowing to Other Provinces and Municipalities	#流向天津和河北 Flowing to Tianjin and Hebei	实现合同总金额 (亿元) Total Volume of Transaction Achieved in Contracts (100 million yuan)	#技术交易实现金额 Amount of Technological Transactions Achieved
1990	18588	20.3	10.5			15.4	8.4
1991	18547	22.4	13.1			15.3	9.1
1992	23395	31.3	22.2			20.0	14.4
1993	20461	35.6	25.6			24.9	17.6
1994	15220	37.2	26.9			26.9	20.4
1995	16347	41.2	32.2			28.4	22.3
1996	14850	45.8	39.2			29.6	25.4
1997	13866	54.3	48.1			31.1	27.8
1998	20724	81.6	73.9			42.1	37.6
1999	20711	92.2	88.5			43.6	41.0
2000	21270	140.3	126.3	65.5		60.3	56.3
2001	23921	191.0	164.8	85.4		97.6	93.0
2002	27037	221.1	181.0	100.4		101.9	97.2
2003	32173	265.5	226.8	132.4		119.9	113.9
2004	35478	331.8	294.3	165.8		148.7	143.4
2005	37505	434.4	350.4	204.9		201.4	180.6
2006	51575	697.3	572.6	325.3		349.5	319.7
2007	50972	882.6	660.3	407.4		418.1	353.5
2008	52742	1027.2	778.1	487.0		406.2	375.0
2009	49938	1236.2	906.9	498.2		516.8	452.9
2010	50847	1579.5	1066.7	654.8		536.0	505.6
2011	53552	1890.3	1268.3	635.9		580.4	563.3
2012	59969	2458.5	2048.6	1385.0		739.8	707.0
2013	62743	2851.2	2252.4	1615.9		684.0	659.3
2014	67278	3136.0	2531.5	1722.0		708.2	675.1
2015	72272	3452.6	2767.8	1878.7	111.5	1229.7	1206.9
2016	74965	3940.8	2919.3	1997.2	154.7	749.2	717.0
2017	81266	4485.3	3703.9	2327.3	203.5	889.0	853.0
2018	82486	4957.8	4069.5	3014.9	227.4	986.2	889.5
2019	83171	5695.3	4389.0	2866.9	282.8	1075.7	1006.1
2020	84451	6316.2	4816.3	3718.5	347.0	938.6	898.5
2021	93563	7005.7	5347.8	4347.7	350.4	788.5	760.1
2022	95061	7947.5	6135.3	4555.7	356.9	942.4	910.8

资料来源：北京技术市场管理办公室。
Source: Beijing Technical Market Management Office.

19—11 技术合同成交情况
CONCLUSION OF TECHNICAL CONTRACTS

项目	Item	合同数(项) Number of Contracts (unit)		成交额(亿元) Volume of Transaction (100 million yuan)	
		2022	2021	2022	2021
合计	**Total**	**95061**	**93563**	**7947.5**	**7005.7**
按合同类别分类	**By Type of Contract**				
技术开发合同	Technological Development	26669	27171	1661.1	1306.5
技术转让合同	Technology Transfer	2422	2442	411.4	214.8
技术咨询合同	Technical Consultation	10096	5948	101.3	56.3
技术服务合同	Technical Service	55874	58002	5773.7	5428.1
按合同卖方类别分类	**By Type of Seller**				
机关法人	Government Organisations				
事业法人	Public Institutions	23308	19779	493.7	276.1
社团法人	Mass Organisations	37	14	0.4	0.1
企业法人	Enterprises	71457	73517	7438.6	6716.4
自然人	Natural Persons	44	26	0.9	0.4
其他组织	Other Organizations	215	227	13.9	12.5
按合同买方类别分类	**By Type of Buyer**				
机关法人	Government Organisations	7181	6682	223.4	282.5
事业法人	Public Institutions	16720	17635	413.7	416.7
社团法人	Mass Organisations	246	269	2.5	3.4
企业法人	Enterprises	69711	67594	6668.6	5946.4
自然人	Natural Persons	147	157	1.2	1.6
其他组织	Other Organizations	1056	1226	638.1	355.0
按服务社会经济目标分类	**By Social and Economic Service Objectives**				
环境保护、生态建设及污染防治	Environmental Protection, Ecological Development and Pollution Control	4358	4107	357.9	723.1
能源生产、分配和合理利用	Energy Production, Allocation and Reasonable Utilization	8656	6560	864.4	549.0
卫生事业发展	Health Services	3401	4762	289.7	144.3
教育事业发展	Education Development	4537	4908	30.2	39.7
基础设施以及城市和农村规划	Infrastructure and Rural and Urban Planning	5602	3574	2071.1	2056.1
社会发展和社会服务	Social Development and Social Services	33655	35235	2553.1	2103.6
地球和大气层的探索与利用	Exploration and Utilization Of The Earth and Atmosphere	175	194	1.8	1.4
民用空间探测及开发	Private Space Exploration and Development	167	261	7.9	4.7
农林牧渔业发展	Development in Agriculture, Forestry, Animal Production and Hunting, Fishing	3921	3413	31.8	27.7
工商业发展	Industrial and Commercial Development	5012	4656	499.0	227.4
非定向研究	Non-Directional Research	2866	2716	167.1	102.9
其他民用目标	Other Civilian Target	19436	18773	874.3	810.9
国防	National Defense	3275	4404	199.0	214.9
按技术流向分类	**By Spread Area of Technology**				
流向本市	To Beijing	33049	32948	1931.5	1814.2
#天津流入	From Tianjin	1607	1928	98.7	75.1
河北流入	From Hebei	1325	1341	98.7	71.0
流向外省市	To Other Provinces and Municipalities	60968	59492	4555.7	4347.7
#流向天津	To Tianjin	2256	1880	82.1	110.2
流向河北	To Hebei	3625	3554	274.8	240.2
技术出口	Exports	1044	1123	1460.3	843.8

资料来源：北京技术市场管理办公室。
Source: Beijing Technical Market Management Office.

19-12　科技成果及获奖情况(2001-2019年)
STATISTICS FOR SCIENTIFIC AND TECHNOLOGICAL ACHIEVEMENTS AND AWARDS (2001-2019)

单位：项　　(unit)

年　份 Year	科技成果登记数 Registered Number of Scientific and Technological Achievements	#国家技术发明奖 National Awards of Technical Invention	#国家科学技术进步奖 National Awards of Scientific and Technological Advancement
2001	326	1	38
2002	275	5	48
2003	468	5	52
2004	976	6	43
2005	1018	8	52
2006	1002	12	64
2007	1010	9	44
2008	1016	13	42
2009	1023	11	54
2010	1030	11	53
2011	1035	5	56
2012	1040	22	53
2013	1043	19	38
2014	1042	15	49
2015	1045	17	42
2016	728	10	47
2017	844	23	40
2018	863	16	40
2019	766	11	42

资料来源：北京市科学技术委员会。
Source: Beijing Municipal Science & Technology Commission.

19−13 专利授权情况
GRANTING OF PATENTS

单位：件 (unit)

项　目	Item	2022	2021
合　计	**Total**	**202722**	**198778**
按种类分	**By Type**		
发　明	Inventions	88127	79210
实用新型	Utility Models	91947	96078
外观设计	Industrial Designs	22648	23490
按对象分	**By Applicant**		
工矿企业	Industrial and Mining Enterprises	151168	144716
大专院校	Universities & Colleges	20962	20333
科研单位	Scientific Research Institutes	17392	17298
机关团体	Government Organizations	6014	5402
个　人	Individuals	7186	11029

资料来源：北京市知识产权局。
Source: Beijing Intellectual Property Office.

19−14 有效发明和高价值发明专利情况
STATISTICS FOR VALID INVENTION AND HIGH-VALUE INVENTION PATENTS

单位：件 (unit)

项　目	Item	有效发明 Valid Invention		高价值发明专利拥有量 High-value Invention Patent Ownership	
		2022	2021	2022	2021
合　计	**Total**	**477790**	**405037**	**245074**	**206246**
按对象分	**By Applicant**				
工矿企业	Industrial and Mininig Enterprises	315792	264717		
大专院校	Universities & Colleges	78439	67709		
科研单位	Scientific Research Institutes	70521	60397		
机关团体	Government Organizations	5474	4320		
个　人	Individuals	7564	7894		

资料来源：北京市知识产权局。
Source: Beijing Intellectual Property Office.

主要统计指标解释

科技活动人员　指报告年度调查单位直接从事科技活动、以及从事科技活动管理和为科技活动提供直接服务的人员。直接从事科技活动人员包括：在单位办的研究室、实验室、技术开发中心及中试车间（基地）等机构中从事科技活动的人员；虽不在上述机构工作，但编入科技活动项目（课题）组的人员等。从事科技活动管理和为科技活动提供直接服务的人员，包括：与科技活动相关的行政管理人员，以及直接为科技活动提供资料文献、材料供应、设备维护等服务的人员。

研究与试验发展（R&D）　指在科学技术领域，为增加知识总量、以及运用这些知识去创造新的应用而进行的系统的创造性的活动，包括基础研究、应用研究、试验发展三类活动。

研究与试验发展（R&D）人员　指单位内部从事基础研究、应用研究和试验发展三类活动的人员。包括直接参加上述三类项目活动的人员以及这三类项目的管理人员和直接服务人员。为研发活动提供直接服务的人员包括直接为研发活动提供资料文献、材料供应、设备维护等服务的人员。

研究与试验发展（R&D）人员折合全时当量　是国际上通用的、用于比较科技人力投入的指标。指 R&D 全时人员（全年从事 R&D 活动累积工作时间占全部工作时间的 90%及以上人员）工作量与非全时人员按实际工作时间折算的工作量之和。

研究与试验发展（R&D）内部支出　指调查单位在报告年度用于内部开展 R&D 活动（基础研究、应用研究和试验发展）的实际支出。包括用于 R&D 项目（课题）活动的直接支出，以及间接用于 R&D 活动的管理费、服务费、与 R&D 有关的基本建设支出以及外协加工费等，不包括生产性活动支出、归还贷款支出以及与外单位合作或委托外单位进行 R&D 活动而转拨给对方的经费支出。

专利　是专利权的简称，是对发明人的发明创造经审查合格后，由专利局依据专利法授予发明人和设计人对该项发明创造享有的专有权。包括发明、实用新型和外观设计。

发明专利　指专利法及其实施细则所称的发明，指对产品、方法或者改进所提出的新的技术方案。

实用新型专利　指专利法及其实施细则所称的实用新型，指对产品的形状、构造或者其结合所提出的适于实用的新的技术方案。

外观设计专利　指专利法及其实施细则所称的外观设计，指对产品的形状、图案、色彩或者其结合所做出的富有美感并适于工业上应用的新设计。

Explanatory Notes on Main Statistical Indicators

Personnel Engaged in Science and Technology Activities refer to persons directly engaged in science and technology activities as well as persons engaged in science and technology management and persons offering direct services to science and technology activities in the surveyed entities in the reporting year. Persons directly engaged in science and technology activities include: persons engaged in science and technology activities in such institutions as research labs of entities, laboratories, technical development centers and middle-stage test workshops (bases); persons not working in the above-mentioned institutions but included in the science and technology activity project (task) team, etc. Persons engaged in science and technology management and persons offering direct services for science and technology activities include administrative staff related to science and technology activities, as well as persons directly providing information and literature, supply of materials, equipment maintenance and other services.

R&D refers to systematic and creative activities in the field of science and technology to increase the total knowledge, and apply such knowledge to create new applications, including three kinds of activities, i.e. basic research, applied research, and experimental development.

R&D Personnel refer to persons in the surveyed entities who are engaged in three kinds of activities, i.e. basic research, applied research and experimental development. They include those who participate in the above-mentioned three kinds of activities directly, research management personnel and persons directly serving these activities. Persons providing direct services include those who provide information and literature, supply of materials, equipment maintenance and other services.

Full-Time Equivalent of R&D Personnel is an indicator globally used to compare input of scientific talents. It refers to the sum of workload of full-time R&D personnel (the personnel whose accumulative annual working time involved in R&D activities takes 90% and above of the whole working time) plus the workload of non-full time personnel that is equivalent of the actual working time.

Internal R&D Expenditure means the actual disbursement of investigated entities on internal R&D activities (basic research, applied research, and experimental development) in the reporting year, including direct spending on R&D project (task) activities, and management expenses and service fees indirectly spent on R&D activities, R&D related basic construction expense and external assisting processing charges, etc., excluding production-based activity expense, loan repayment expense and fund transferred to external institution cooperated or entrusted to conduct R&D activities.

Patent is the abbreviation of patent right, referring to the exclusive right granted by patent authorities upon examination and approval of inventions and creations to the inventors and designers with regard to the invention, including inventions, utility models and industrial designs.

Invention Patents means the invention mentioned in the Patent Law and its detailed rules for implementation, i.e. the new technological solutions presented for the product, methodology, or improvement.

Utility Model means the utility model mentioned in the Patent Law and its detailed rules for implementation, i.e. the new practical technological solutions presented for the product shape, structure, color or combination.

Industrial Design means the industrial design mentioned in the Patent Law and its detailed rules for implementation, i.e. new designs of product shape, pattern, color or combination which are aesthetic and suitable for industrial applications.

教育
EDUCATION

简要说明

主要内容

本章资料包括高等教育（研究生教育、普通本专科教育、成人本专科教育、其他各类高等学历教育）、中等教育(高中阶段、初中阶段)、小学教育、学前教育、特殊教育、专门学校等资料。主要指标包括学校数、在校生数、招生数、毕业生数、教职工数、专任教师数等内容。

Brief Introduction

Main Content

Statistics in this chapter include those for higher education (postgraduate education, undergraduate and junior college education, undergraduate and junior college education for adults, and other kinds of higher education for diplomas); secondary education (senior high school, junior high school); primary education; preschool education; special education; special schools for delinquent children. Main indicators include the number of schools, number of student enrollment, number of new enrollment, number of graduates, number of teachers and staff, and number of full-time teachers, etc.

20-1 教育基本情况(1978-2022年)

年份 Year	全市各类学校数(个) Total Number of Various Schools (unit)	#普通高等学校 General Institutions of Higher Education	#中等教育 Secondary Education	#普通高中 Regular Senior Secondary Schools	#小学教育 Primary Schools	全市各类学校在校生数(人) Enrolled Students in Various Schools (person)	#普通本专科 Regular Undergraduates and College Students
1978		35			4666		48618
1979		48			4534		55073
1980		50			4485		83032
1981		51			4445		98044
1982		51			4381		93878
1983		54			4269		90894
1984		57			4168		102962
1985		61			4059		122791
1986		66			3995		129647
1987		67			3875		136694
1988		67			3793		145134
1989		67			3703		141625
1990		67			3611		139646
1991	8496	67	1168	282	3482	2142085	136940
1992	8052	67	1150	279	3306	2194268	139978
1993	7789	66	1145	280	3190	2266932	158906
1994	7574	67	1150	280	3035	2348406	175203
1995	7158	65	1170	286	2867	2380096	182173
1996	7121	65	1189	296	2780	2388002	189953
1997	6858	65	1181	288	2696	2361438	195842
1998	6456	63	1190	282	2511	2325043	212984
1999	5807	64	1182	275	2352	2297673	234033
2000	5458	59	1159	302	2169	2299433	282585
2001	4873	61	1111	289	1960	2297107	340284
2002	4447	62	998	325	1824	2294947	398573
2003	4158	74	977	329	1652	2299416	458898
2004	3971	77	945	338	1504	2291594	500245
2005	3782	79	917	335	1403	2264004	536724
2006	3751	82	888	335	1310	2910228	554702
2007	3593	83	863	328	1235	3195763	567875
2008	3508	82	838	325	1202	3208704	575639
2009	3425	88	804	305	1160	3214354	577154
2010	3330	89	779	289	1104	3299555	577828
2011	3367	89	769	290	1090	3426025	578633
2012	3314	91	760	289	1081	3568273	581844
2013	3439	89	757	291	1093	3736003	589234
2014	3437	89	766	306	1040	3774868	594614
2015	3454	90	768	306	996	3734245	593448
2016	3524	91	767	305	984	3733544	588389
2017	3556	92	766	304	984	3861492	580663
2018	3585	92	757	309	970	4083211	581133
2019	3640	93	765	318	941	4124862	585971
2020	3799	92	766	321	934	4038504	590335
2021	3723	92	750	332	837	3970617	595776
2022	3605	92	761	351	719	4023949	602512

注：1.自2007年起，小学、中学、特殊教育和学前教育在校生数、招生数、毕业生数包括非本市户籍学生数。

2.小学初中在校生数包括小学、初中附设特教班、随班就读和送教上门学生数，高中包括随班就读特教学生数。

3.1991—2005年，中等教育为普通中等学校口径，包括普通中学、普通中专、职业中学、技工学校和专门学校；2006—2020年，中等教育包括普通中学、普通中专、成人中专、职业高中和技工学校，其中，技工学校数据由市人力资源和社会保障局提供；自2021年起，中等教育不包括技工学校。

4.自2021年起，全市各类学校数不含民办的其他高等教育机构，在校生数不含在职人员攻读硕士学位人数。

5.全市各类学校在校生数、全市各类学校招生数和全市各类学校毕业生数不包括国家开放大学附设中职班北京校区在校生数、招生数和毕业生数。

6.在校生数、招生数、毕业生数不含国际学生数。

资料来源：北京市教育委员会、北京市人力资源和社会保障局。

BASIC STATISTICS FOR EDUCATION (1978-2022)

			全　市 各类学校 招生数 (人) New Enrollment in Various Schools (person)				
#中　等 教　育 Secondary Education	#普通高中 Regular Senior Secondary Schools	#小　学 教　育 Primary Schools		#普　通 本专科 Regular Undergraduates and College Students	#中　等 教　育 Secondary Education	#普　通 高　中 Regular Senior Secondary Schools	#小　学 教　育 Primary Schools
	415612	937336		17445		161288	199076
	299974	968723		15848		160340	154809
	312188	951763		17972		131961	138751
	175180	900350		17921		54296	121744
	92401	854516		21936		35212	104357
	88657	838078		27988		40282	96028
	110916	763204		31805		47068	103482
	119876	733605		40670		35265	135048
	109862	749101		35390		27863	160513
	109023	777982		41163		41186	156954
	108106	850577		42187		35429	184516
	110745	934696		33557		33254	184609
	100669	995831		36275		30596	161742
565357	93728	1013268	571685	37700	205107	28589	148300
617847	82894	1001762	622142	41517	232765	25790	157145
679821	78261	1022166	651729	52205	242274	26275	175853
758310	86584	1024503	704933	51884	287642	34704	186315
834903	102522	1007301	691972	52868	308786	40803	168903
881912	118476	999740	628772	55269	289612	42603	156898
887644	133461	977323	581091	56884	289719	49566	124231
895042	145966	919531	581786	62264	308157	52956	100415
931029	161473	836655	603332	78354	320731	56998	94358
972930	179002	743109	635328	99397	324862	65890	92002
988985	194283	664443	641432	116344	313257	69195	91230
984117	220667	594241	671956	128320	326835	84679	86406
968035	250959	546530	662877	143483	302071	94894	82631
919178	274803	516042	635842	147298	271396	93519	73577
859132	278358	494482	630515	156124	259133	88605	71020
799074	259414	473275	851808	154969	234524	76375	73138
839038	243818	666617	927144	156222	252709	71590	109203
782866	219163	659500	938891	157238	236714	68397	110440
740396	203477	647101	962648	158992	240937	65983	102414
727741	198415	653255	1002141	155228	238954	65649	113728
711130	195072	680457	1050131	157543	243754	64146	132719
732224	193505	718655	1108574	162042	254790	63381	141738
706713	187586	789276	1182301	163081	239010	59983	165807
651443	177554	821152	1113688	160056	202434	55184	153249
587112	169412	850321	1091756	152741	186517	56743	145876
552468	163130	868417	1115515	154715	180881	53544	145274
522658	163977	875849	1248003	153028	181936	53755	157559
525434	155478	913216	1286509	155784	172981	47355	184339
538096	152857	941614	1196902	156820	190366	51403	182873
563743	160152	995046	1169955	159301	209327	61071	202157
573734	176095	1036584	1091101	160417	199189	62263	186440
609344	198928	1083813	1175320	165860	215522	74681	189935

Note: a) Since 2007, the number of enrolled students, new enrollments and graduates in primary schools, middle schools, special education schools and pre-school education has included the number of students from other provinces, municipalities and autonomous regions.

b) The number of enrolled students in primary schools and junior secondary schools includes the number of students in special classes attached to primary schools and junior secondary schools, students studying in primary schools and junior secondary schools,and students receiving home-based primary school and junior secondary education; the number of enrolled students in senior secondary schools includes the number of students in special classes studying in senior secondary schools.

c) Since 1991 until 2005, secondary education covered the general schools for secondary education, including general middle schools,general technical secondary schools, vocational secondary schools, technician training schools, and special schools. Since 2006 until 2020, secondary education covered general middle schools, general technical secondary schools, technical secondary schools for adults, vocational senior high schools, and technician training schools. Specifically, the data of technician training schools is provided by Beijing Municipal Human Resources and Social Security Bureau.Since 2021, secondary education has not covered technician training schools.

d) Since 2021, the number of schools has not included the number of other privately-funded institutions of higher education, and the number of enrolled students has not included the number of employees enrolled in graduate programs leading to master degrees.

e) The number of enrolled students in various schools, number of new enrollments in various schools and number of graduates in various schools do not include the number of enrolled students, new enrollments and graduates in Beijing campus for secondary vocational education classes attached to the Open University of China.

f) The number of enrolled students, new enrollments and graduates do not include the number of international students.

Source: Beijing Municipal Education Commission,Beijing Municipal Human Resources and Social Security Bureau.

20-1 续表 Continued

年 份 Year	全 市 各类学校 毕业生数 (人) Number of Graduates in Various Schools (person)	#普 通 本专科 Regular Undergraduates and College Students	#中 等 教 育 Secondary Education	#普 通 高 中 Regular Senior Secondary Schools	#小 学 教 育 Primary Schools	专 任 教师数 (人) Full-time Teachers (person)	平均每一专任教师负担学生数(人) Average Number of Students Instructed by a Full-time Teacher(person) 普通中学 General Middle Schools	小 学 Primary Schools
1978		10881		174899	151950		19.9	20.7
1979		8585		239813	114047		16.1	21.3
1980		8233		145501	144025		14.8	21.7
1981		2289		170992	162306		13.4	19.7
1982		25753		111153	135562		12.3	19.5
1983		31009			95919		11.5	19.6
1984		20110		24498	169251		13.2	18.2
1985		21442		24720	156035		13.9	17.4
1986		26953		36942	138350		14.1	17.3
1987		34894		43589	121599		12.8	16.8
1988		33066		36127	105948		11.4	17.6
1989		35863		29267	97208		11.0	19.1
1990		36171		40369	102782		10.1	18.6
1991	487740	37702		34428	132544	168485	10.5	18.0
1992	520787	37075		32471	156306	169249	11.3	17.4
1993	526982	32888		27428	157838	170361	12.1	17.4
1994	528199	34855		24112	184566	175025	13.1	16.9
1995	554690	45094		23353	183894	176591	13.6	16.5
1996	575969	46471		25170	162030	178006	13.7	16.1
1997	584120	49973		33010	146023	179080	13.2	15.7
1998	600662	49322		39683	156194	178210	12.8	14.9
1999	603027	49936		40660	175656	175496	13.2	13.7
2000	604900	51556		47569	185059	167040	14.1	12.8
2001	617889	55831		51263	167076	168080	14.3	12.1
2002	624329	67621		51180	156683	166490	14.2	11.2
2003	610826	83816		56601	123580	166510	13.7	11.0
2004	614137	99637		66556	100139	172055	12.9	10.6
2005	622974	117367		73260	93486	174589	11.8	10.3
2006	787596	132488	290047	78037	90799	191365	10.8	9.8
2007	851126	138834	272651	78408	112332	195568	11.5	13.8
2008	832585	149459	262871	78468	112268	199114	10.9	13.5
2009	865025	152336	253067	70132	110730	203825	10.0	13.0
2010	834340	150156	233837	62305	102971	206602	10.2	13.2
2011	838521	151277	223955	58275	101678	199789	9.8	13.4
2012	881804	152980	224938	55657	109492	204812	9.7	13.7
2013	923050	148689	240225	58072	111839	216463	9.5	14.4
2014	937209	147023	229640	57773	112819	225165	9.0	14.4
2015	961180	152118	205795	57738	103893	226043	8.4	14.3
2016	924267	153005	182511	52841	111481	231251	7.9	14.0
2017	939184	152990	168125	49685	125938	236346	7.7	13.6
2018	940336	146654	158863	51065	124610	241719	7.9	13.9
2019	1018835	144645	157545	50390	138968	248239	8.2	13.8
2020	1082842	147556	167817	52094	136671	256594	8.3	14.0
2021	1028294	147346	147102	45077	134051	264551	8.6	13.9
2022	1033042	154382	165804	49775	133331	272543	8.8	14.1

20-2 幼儿园基本情况(1978-2022年)
BASIC STATISTICS FOR KINDERGARTENS (1978-2022)

单位：人 (person)

年 份 Year	园数(所) Number of Kindergartens (unit)	班数(个) Number of Classes (unit)	离园人数 Children Leaving	入园人数 Children Entering	在园人数 Children Enrollment	教职工数 Teachers and Staff	#专任教师 Full-time Teachers
1978	5074				235923	39982	8369
1979	4623				237037	40424	8777
1980	3991				219407	38475	7765
1981	3888				233089	38832	8814
1982	3849				254458	42663	9271
1983	1999				306975	48666	8234
1984	3682				295427	47721	9499
1985	2955				316024	47033	10523
1986	3503				342824	52654	12690
1987	3732				364011	54211	14449
1988	3563				354367	52105	14705
1989	3509				344394	50280	17208
1990	3798				372555	49587	17972
1991	3761		133788	172884	402699	49472	18788
1992	3510		158740	181299	404779	48007	18513
1993	3369		165963	170580	372368	44741	18114
1994	3301		113652	167267	352979	42118	17413
1995	3024		103355	148272	315277	38549	16084
1996	3056		135376	112449	271752	33586	14792
1997	2892		110345	95140	253478	32811	14596
1998	2662		99279	93819	245046	30362	13841
1999	2180		91996	89463	237055	29367	13216
2000	2047		85301	91724	229012	27257	12595
2001	1719	8259	85842	87892	217521	26106	12479
2002	1540	8494	79447	91092	213794	25402	12127
2003	1430	7733	76879	86465	199390	26324	13056
2004	1422	8087	71677	86672	205532	28326	14208
2005	1358	8148	71926	83485	202301	28026	14813
2006	1361	8051	70400	68299	197546	28958	15632
2007	1306	8132	70681	83969	214423	30465	17013
2008	1266	8382	72119	85938	226681	32535	18176
2009	1253	9036	65684	89761	247778	34973	17952
2010	1245	9883	68135	105048	276994	37227	21677
2011	1305	11213	76790	115539	311417	44458	24170
2012	1266	11882	79131	115248	331524	48080	26330
2013	1384	12580	88322	128106	348681	53049	28806
2014	1426	13245	96478	133977	364954	57950	31692
2015	1487	14098	101928	149042	394121	61903	34040
2016	1570	14913	99626	152769	416982	65806	36071
2017	1604	15810	105651	177354	445535	69100	37903
2018	1657	16176	117102	165130	450645	71686	38867
2019	1733	16934	118178	168166	467595	79777	41187
2020	1899	18770	132884	221767	525878	88467	44740
2021	2000	20067	136077	190211	566735	98322	47973
2022	1989	20662	162717	178620	574235	99987	48774

资料来源：北京市教育委员会。
Source: Beijing Municipal Education Commission.

20-3 各类学校基本情况
BASIC STATISTICS FOR VARIOUS SCHOOLS

单位：人 (person)

项目	Item	校数(所) Number of Schools (unit) 2022	2021	教职工数 Teachers and Staff 2022	2021	#专任教师 Full-time Teachers 2022	2021
合计	**Total**	**3605**	**3723**	**437816**	**427968**	**272543**	**264551**
高等教育	**Higher Education**	**110**	**110**	**161304**	**157587**	**76730**	**73887**
研究生培养机构(不计校数)	Institutions Providing Postgraduate Programs (Number of Schools Not Counted)	(146)	(145)			(75067)	(66389)
高等学校(不计校数)	Institutions of Higer Education (Number of Schools Not Counted)	(59)	(59)			(61309)	(55382)
科研机构(不计校数)	Research Institutes (Number of Schools Not Counted)	(87)	(86)			(13758)	(11007)
普通高等学校	General Institutions of Higher Education	92	92	158136	154395	75381	72573
成人高等学校	Adult Institutions of Higher Education	18	18	3168	3192	1349	1314
中等教育	**Secondary Education**	**761**	**750**	**108169**	**105204**	**85230**	**82401**
高中阶段教育	Senior Secondary Education	428	415	108169	105204	59773	57619
普通高中	General Middle Schools	351	332	99779	96583	54382	52021
中等职业教育	Secondary Vocational Schools	77	83	8390	8621	5391	5598
普通中专	General Technical Secondary Schools	28	29	3193	3176	1630	1707
成人中专	Technical Secondary Schools for Adults	10	10	357	410	193	203
职业高中	Vocational Senior High Schools	39	44	4840	5035	3568	3688
初中阶段教育	Junior Secondary Education	333	335			25457	24782
小学教育	**Primary Schools**	**719**	**837**	**66748**	**65269**	**60484**	**59013**
专门学校	**Special Schools**	**6**	**6**	**253**	**295**	**204**	**220**
特殊教育	**Special Education**	**20**	**20**	**1355**	**1291**	**1121**	**1057**
学前教育	**Pre-school Education**	**1989**	**2000**	**99987**	**98322**	**48774**	**47973**

注：1.小学、初中在校生数包括小学、初中附设特教班、随班就读和送教上门学生数，高中包括随班就读特教学生数。
2.自2021年起，中等教育不包括技工学校。
3.自2021年起，全市各类学校数不含民办的其他高等教育机构，在校生数不含在职人员攻读硕士学位人数。
4.毕业生数、招生数和在校生数不包括国家开放大学附设中职班北京校区毕业生数、招生数和在校生数。
5.毕业生数、招生数和在校生数不含国际学生数。
6.表中带( )数据不计入"校数"的合计数据中。

资料来源：北京市教育委员会。

Note: a)The number of enrolled students in primary schools and junior secondary schools includes the number of students in special classes attached to primary schools and junior secondary schools, students studying in primary schools and junior secondary schools, and students receiving home-based primary school and junior secondary education; the number of enrolled students in senior secondary schools includes the number of students in special classes studying in senior secondary schools.
b)Since 2021, secondary education has not covered technician training schools.
c)Since 2021, the number of schools has not included the number of other privately-funded institutions of higher education, and the number of enrolled students has not included the number of employees enrolled in graduate programs leading to master degrees.
d)The number of graduates, new enrollments and enrolled students does not include the number of graduates, new enrollments and enrolled students in Beijing campus for secondary vocational education classes attached to the Open University of China.
e)The number of graduates, new enrollments and enrolled students does not include the number of international students.
f)The data with ( ) in this table are not included in the total number of schools.

Source: Beijing Municipal Education Commission.

20-3 续表 Continued

单位：人 (person)

项 目	Item	毕业生数 Graduates 2022	2021	招生数 New Enrollment 2022	2021	在校生数 Total Enrollment 2022	2021
合 计	**Total**	**1033042**	**1028294**	**1175320**	**1091101**	**4023949**	**3970617**
高等教育	**Higher Education**	**569297**	**609174**	**589955**	**513923**	**1748388**	**1785277**
研究生	Postgraduates	114422	103714	145894	139295	435035	413124
高等学校	Institutions of Higher Education	108694	98374	138245	132341	412030	391854
科研机构	Scientific Research Institutions	5728	5340	7649	6954	23005	21270
普通本专科	General Undergraduates and College Students	154382	147346	165860	160417	602512	595776
中央部委属高校	Under Central Ministries and Commissions	78131	75589	87348	85027	338754	332115
市属高校	Under Municipal Government	76251	71757	78512	75390	263758	263661
公办高校	Public Colleges and Universities	61667	57493	63240	60739	210493	210523
民办高校	Privately-funded Colleges and Universities	14584	14264	15272	14651	53265	53138
成人本专科	Adult Undergraduates and College Students	39448	45733	29620	26272	78225	93620
成人高等学校	Adult Institutions of Higher Education	3437	4871	1613	1502	3652	5942
普通高等学校	General Institutions of Higher Education	36011	40862	28007	24770	74573	87678
网络本专科生	Students Enrolled in Internet-based Courses	261045	312381	248581	187939	632616	682757
中等教育	**Secondary Education**	**165804**	**147102**	**215522**	**199189**	**609344**	**573734**
高中阶段教育	Senior Secondary	62290	59246	94252	78758	253524	224123
普通高中	General Middle Schools	49775	45077	74681	62263	198928	176095
中等职业教育	Secondary Vocational Schools	12515	14169	19571	16495	54596	48028
普通中专	General Technical Secondary Schools	8166	7945	11822	10028	34471	31064
成人中专	Technical Secondary Schools for Adults	1483	3933	1404	1384	4152	4293
职业高中	Vocational High Schools	2866	2291	6345	5083	15973	12671
初中阶段教育	Junior Secondary Education	103514	87856	121270	120431	355820	349611
小学教育	**Primary Education**	**133331**	**134051**	**189935**	**186440**	**1083813**	**1036584**
专门学校	**Special Schools**	**227**	**217**	**178**	**204**	**447**	**479**
特殊教育	**Special Education**	**1666**	**1673**	**1110**	**1134**	**7722**	**7808**
学前教育	**Pre-school Education**	**162717**	**136077**	**178620**	**190211**	**574235**	**566735**

20-4 高等教育学生情况(2022年)
STATISTICS FOR STUDENTS IN INSTITUTIONS OF HIGHER EDUCATION (2022)

单位：人 (person)

项 目	Item	毕(结)业生人数 Number of Graduates	招生数 New Enrollment	在校学生数 Total Enrollment
普通本科、专科生	General Undergraduates and Junior College Students	154382	165860	602512
专 科	Enrolled in Specialized Courses Education	26989	26166	67399
本 科	Enrolled in Full Undergraduate Courses	127393	139694	535113
成人本科、专科生	Adult Undergraduates and Junior College Students	39448	29620	78225
专 科	Enrolled in Specialized Courses Education	8566	4192	8668
本 科	Enrolled in Full Undergraduate Courses	30882	25428	69557
网络本科、专科生	Students Enrolled in Internet-based Courses	261045	248581	632616
专 科	Enrolled in Specialized Courses	100941	81955	197430
本 科	Enrolled in Full Undergraduate Courses	160104	166626	435186
研究生	Postgraduates	114422	145894	435035
硕 士	Master Degree	93900	114903	310065
博 士	Doctor Degree	20522	30991	124970
国际学生	International Students	16700	16471	34272

资料来源：北京市教育委员会。
Source: Beijing Municipal Education Commission.

20-5 普通高等学校本专科基本情况(2022年)
BASIC STATISTICS FOR GENERAL INSTITUTIONS OF HIGHER EDUCATION (2022)

单位：人 (person)

项 目	Item	校 数(所) Number of Schools (unit)	毕业生数 Graduates	招生数 New Enrollment	在校生数 Total Enrollment	教职工数 Teachers and Staff	#专任教师 Full-time Teachers
合 计	**Total**	**92**	**154382**	**165860**	**602512**	**158136**	**75381**
#女 生	Females		79449	81235	296545	82542	35019
按性质类别分	**By Nature and Category**						
综合大学	Comprehensive Universities	5	18688	19859	71312	25662	11865
理工院校	Science and Engineering	30	60511	65358	239622	61432	29924
农业院校	Agriculture	3	7304	7591	26360	4634	2928
林业院校	Forestry	1	3374	3498	13730	2011	1412
医药院校	Medicine	4	5402	5612	21443	19036	3597
师范院校	Teacher Training	2	5623	5669	22042	8982	3870
语文院校	Literature	10	11072	12175	44964	10144	6215
财经院校	Finance and Economics	16	21464	22032	76626	11550	6753
政法院校	Politics and Law	8	9625	10576	36642	5347	3112
体育院校	Physical Culture	3	3233	3450	13801	1888	1282
艺术院校	Art	9	5230	5432	22241	5529	3305
民族院校	Minorities Colleges	1	2856	4608	13729	1921	1118

资料来源：北京市教育委员会。
Source: Beijing Municipal Education Commission.

20-6 全市分学科研究生情况(2022年)
STATISTICS FOR POSTGRADUATES BY SUBJECT OF STUDY OF THE WHOLE CITY (2022)

单位：人 (person)

项　目	Item	毕业生数 Graduates			招生数 New Enrollment			在校生数 Student Enrollment		
		合计 Total	硕士 Master Degree	博士 Doctor Degree	合计 Total	硕士 Master Degree	博士 Doctor Degree	合计 Total	硕士 Master Degree	博士 Doctor Degree
合　计	**Total**	**114422**	**93900**	**20522**	**145894**	**114903**	**30991**	**435035**	**310065**	**124970**
#女　生	Females	60465	51567	8898	74565	61510	13055	214334	162407	51927
按学科分	**By Subject**									
哲　学	Philosophy	612	401	211	778	479	299	2689	1399	1290
经济学	Economics	8480	7668	812	9456	8317	1139	23878	18440	5438
法　学	Law	9648	8433	1215	11219	9449	1770	32986	25365	7621
教育学	Education	5507	5067	440	6291	5511	780	19005	15603	3402
文　学	Literature	6120	5432	688	6947	5979	968	19493	15211	4282
历史学	History	768	555	213	1037	745	292	3382	2095	1287
理　学	Science	8825	4307	4518	12568	6684	5884	42868	18435	24433
工　学	Engineering	39544	32110	7434	54450	41835	12615	168285	116335	51950
农　学	Agriculture	4245	3443	802	5553	4464	1089	15458	11348	4110
医　学	Medicine	6700	4114	2586	9693	5773	3920	27686	15977	11709
军事学	Military	3		3				8	8	
管理学	Management	19540	18387	1153	22429	20986	1443	63006	56116	6890
艺术学	Art	4413	3966	447	5247	4577	670	16047	13611	2436
交叉学科	Interdiscipline	17	17		226	104	122	244	122	122
按学位类型分	**By Degree Type**									
学术型学位	Academic Degree	57482	38171	19311	74161	47262	26899	246689	132478	114211
专业学位	Professional Degree	56940	55729	1211	71733	67641	4092	188346	177587	10759

资料来源：北京市教育委员会。
Source: Beijing Municipal Education Commission.

20-7 高等教育国际学生情况(2022年)
STATISTICS FOR INTERNATIONAL STUDENTS FOR HIGHER EDUCATION (2022)

单位：人 (person)

项　　目	Item	毕(结)业生数 Graduates	授予学位人数 Number of Students Conferred with Degree	招生数 New Enrollment	在校生数 Total Enrollment
合　计	**Total**	**16700**	**5325**	**16471**	**34272**
学历教育	**Academic-degree Education**	**5816**	**5325**	**7393**	**27652**
按学历划分	**By Educational Background**				
专　科	Enrolled in Specialized Courses	129		285	619
本　科	Enrolled in Full Undergraduate Courses	2793	2666	3176	13723
硕　士	Master Degree	2330	2173	2994	8382
博　士	Doctor Degree	564	486	938	4928
按地区划分	**By Region**				
亚　洲	Asia	3349	3088	4408	17412
非　洲	Africa	1092	935	1468	4845
欧　洲	Europe	709	664	799	2531
北美洲	North America	441	425	455	1702
南美洲	South America	121	114	127	655
大洋洲	Oceania	104	99	136	507
非学历教育(培训)	**Non-academic-degree Education (Training)**	**10884**		**9078**	**6620**

资料来源：北京市教育委员会。
Source: Beijing Municipal Education Commission.

20−8 幼儿园基本情况(2022年)
BASIC STATISTICS FOR KINDERGARTENS (2022)

项 目	Item	总 计 Total	#女 Females	城 区 In City	镇 区 In Counties and Towns	乡 村 In Villages
园 数 (所)	Number of Kindergartens (unit)	1989		1578	182	229
班 数 (个)	Number of Classes (unit)	20662		17379	1776	1507
在园幼儿数 (人)	Children Enrollment (person)	574235	277589	485308	49162	39765
教职工数 (人)	Teachers and Staff (person)	99987	89958	85876	7817	6294
#园 长	Headmasters	3288	3092	2705	295	288
专任教师	Full-time Teachers	48774	47798	41797	3950	3027
卫生保健人员	Health Workers	5192	5125	4529	378	285

资料来源：北京市教育委员会。
Source: Beijing Municipal Education Commission.

20−9 高等教育自学考试情况
STATISTICS FOR HIGHER EDUCATION SELF-STUDY EXAMINATION

项 目	Item	2022	2021
报考人次 (人次)	Number of Registered Person-times (person-time)	42028	101378
报考科次 (科次)	Number of Registered Subject-times (subject-time)	111059	291006
发出专科毕业证书 (个)	Number of Junior College Diplomas Issued (unit)	1828	2572
发出本科毕业证书 (个)	Number of General College Diplomas Issued (unit)	2685	2823
开考专业 (个)	Number of Majors Examined (unit)	48	48

资料来源：北京教育考试院。
Source: Beijing Education Examinations Authority.

20−10 特殊教育情况(2022年)
STATISTICS FOR SPECIAL EDUCATION (2022)

单位：人 (person)

项 目	Item	毕业生数 Graduates	招生数 New Enrollment	在校生数 Total Enrollment
合 计	**Total**	**1666**	**1110**	**7722**
#女 生	Females	604	365	2548
#特殊教育学校	Special Education Schools	490	528	3140
小学附设特教班	Special Classes Attached to Primary Schools	9	12	94
小学随班就读	Studying in Primary Schools	399	166	2743
普通(职业)初中随班就读	Studying in General Junior Secondary (Vocational) Classes	762	397	1721

资料来源：北京市教育委员会。
Source: Beijing Municipal Education Commission.

20-11 职业技术培训机构基本情况(2022年)
BASIC STATISTICS FOR VOCATIONAL AND TECHNICAL TRAINING INSTITUTIONS(2022)

项目	Item	学校数（所） Schools (unit)	教学班（点、个） Teaching Classes (site,unit)	结业生数（人次） Students Completing Courses (person-time)	#女性 Females
合计	**Total**	**1102**	**26036**	**1126840**	**601723**
#少数民族	National Miniorities			4274	2479
按培训机构分	**By Training Institution**				
职工技术培训学校(机构)	**Technical Training Schools (Institutions) for Employees**	**22**	**267**	**30223**	**18247**
#教育部门和集体办	Run by Education Authorities and Collectively-run	3	193	21029	14527
其他部门办	Run by Other Authorities				
民办	Privately-funded	19	74	9194	3720
农村成人文化技术培训学校(机构)	**Cultural and Technical Training Schools (Institutions) for Rural Adults**	**372**	**5322**	**320178**	**217936**
#教育部门和集体办	Run by Education Authorities and Collectively-run	372	5322	320178	217936
县办	Run by Counties	14	164	92195	67691
乡办	Run by Townships	29	3604	165847	110671
村办	Run by Villages	329	1554	62136	39574
其他培训机构(含社会培训机构)	**Other Training Institutions (Including Social Training Institutions)**	**708**	**20447**	**776439**	**365540**
教育部门和集体办	Run by Education Authorities and Collectively-run	51	186	68631	15719
其他部门办	Run by Other Authorities	141	6	222101	95498
民办	Privately-funded	516	20255	485707	254323
中外合作办	Jointly Run with Sino-foreign Investment				
按培训形式分	**Group by Form of Training**				
#资格证书培训	Qualification Certificate Training			128750	76030
岗位证书培训	Job Post Certificate Training			81808	48929

资料来源：北京市教育委员会。
Source: Beijing Municipal Education Commission.

20-11　续表　Continued

单位：人　(person)

项　目	Item	注册学生数 Student Enrollment	#女性 Females	教职工数 Teachers and Staff	#专任教师 Full-time Teachers	聘请校外教师 External Teachers Retained
合　计	**Total**	**1503404**	**801905**	**13227**	**5778**	**3866**
#少数民族	National Miniorities	3534	1989	133	63	29
按培训机构分	**By Training Institution**					
职工技术培训学校(机构)	**Technical Training Schools (Institutions) for Employees**	**22092**	**10681**	**437**	**319**	**202**
#教育部门和集体办	Run by Education Authorities and Collectively-run	7943	5657	242	198	117
其他部门办	Run by Other Authorities					
民　办	Privately-funded	14149	5024	195	121	85
农村成人文化技术培训学校(机构)	**Cultural and Technical Training Schools (Institutions) for Rural Adults**	**316681**	**222598**	**487**	**297**	**723**
#教育部门和集体办	Run by Education Authorities and Collectively-run	316681	222598	487	297	723
县　办	Run by Counties	100132	77511	230	167	427
乡　办	Run by Townships	151584	103077	189	108	165
村　办	Run by Villages	64965	42010	68	22	131
其他培训机构（含社会培训机构）	**Other Training Institutions (Including Social Training Institutions)**	**1164631**	**568626**	**12303**	**5162**	**2941**
教育部门和集体办	Run by Education Authorities and Collectively-run	59084	7225	956	177	139
其他部门办	Run by Other Authorities	238075	128063	4147	1922	883
民　办	Privately-funded	867472	433338	7200	3063	1919
中外合作办	Jointly Run with Sino-foreign Investment					
按培训形式分	**Group by Form of Training**					
#资格证书培训	Qualification Certificate Training					
岗位证书培训	Job Post Certificate Training					

20—12 民办教育基本情况(2022年)
BASIC STATSTICS FOR PRIVATELY-FUNDED EDUCATION (2022)

单位：人 (person)

项目	Item	校数(所) Number of Schools (unit)	毕业生数 Graduates	招生数 New Enrollment	在校生数 Total Enrollment	教职工数 Teachers and Staff	#专任教师 Full-time Teachers	校外教师数 Number of External Teachers
合计	**Total**	**1217**	**95554**	**105503**	**362790**	**68386**	**31379**	
民办高等教育	**Privately-funded Higher Education**	**15**	**14786**	**15537**	**53933**	**5477**	**2968**	
普通高校	General Institutions of Higher Education	15	14786	15537	53933	5477	2968	
民办中等教育	**Privately-funded Secondary Education**	**124**	**7286**	**10300**	**26182**	**14597**	**8189**	**52**
高中阶段教育	Senior High School Education	99	1466	4276	9767	14597	8189	52
民办普通高中	Privately-funded Senior High Schools	82	1218	3843	8678	14101	7949	52
民办中等职业教育	Privately-funded Secondary Vocational Education	17	248	433	1089	496	240	
初中阶段教育	Junior High School Education	25	5820	6024	16415			
民办小学	**Privately-funded Primary Schools**	**41**	**5136**	**5399**	**37753**	**1275**	**877**	**8**
民办幼儿园	**Privately-funded Kindergartens**	**1037**	**68346**	**74267**	**244922**	**47037**	**19345**	**30**

注：民办普通高中的教职工数、专任教师数、校外教师数中包含初中阶段教育的教职工数、专任教师数、校外教师数。
资料来源：北京市教育委员会。
Note: The number of teachers and staff, full-time teachers, and external teachers in privately-funded general senior high schools includes the number of teachers and staff, full-time teachers, and external teachers for junior high school education.
Source: Beijing Municipal Education Commission.

20—13 高校办学条件(2022年)
SCHOOL CONDITIONS OF HIGHER EDUCATION INSTITUTIONS (2022)

项目	Item	合计 Total	中央 Central	市属市管 Municipal
普通高校	**General Institutions of Higher Education**			
校舍建筑面积 (平方米)	Building Area (sq.m)	43082498	30728161	12354337
占地面积 (平方米)	Floor Space (sq.m)	53399765	37146784	16252981
图书 (万册)	Books (10000 volumes)	12029	7617	4413
固定资产总值 (万元)	Total Value of Fixed Assets (10000 yuan)	23636031	17211641	6424390
#科学科研仪器设备值	Value of Scientific Research Instruments and Equipment	7626931	5282600	2344330
成人高校	**Institutions of Higher Education for Adults**			
校舍建筑面积 (平方米)	Building Area (sq.m)	634927	354301	280626
占地面积 (平方米)	Floor Space (sq.m)	722527	516405	206123
图书 (万册)	Books (10000 volumes)	200	60	140
固定资产总值 (万元)	Total Value of Fixed Assets (10000 yuan)	378259	285048	93211
#科学科研仪器设备值	Value of Scientific Research Instruments and Equipment	28831	7181	21650

资料来源：北京市教育委员会。
Source: Beijing Municipal Education Commission.

20-14　基础教育办学条件(2022年)
SCHOOL CONDITIONS OF BASIC EDUCATION (2022)

单位：平方米　　(sq.m)

项　　目	Item	普通中学 General Middle Schools	小　学 Primary Schools
学校占地面积	Floor Space	28343317	14322096
校舍建筑面积	Building Area	18576293	8187150
#当年新增	Newly Added in the Year	1948768	1024128
#危房面积	Area of Dangerous Buildings		7944
教学及辅助用房面积	Area of Teaching and Auxiliary Houses	8432323	4664317
普通教室	Regular Classrooms	3073867	2293540
专用教室	Classrooms for Special Purposes	2225743	969876
理化生实验室	Physics, Chemistry, Biology Laboratories	823145	240
其他	Others	1402598	969636
公共教学用房	Public Teaching Houses	3132713	1400900
图书室	Libraries	494377	196903
室内体育用房	Indoor Sports Houses	974754	292420
心理辅导室	Psychological Counseling Room	69643	51698
其他	Others	1593939	859880
行政办公用房	Administrative Houses	2278828	1144604
生活用房	Houses for Life	7249843	2249334
其他用房	Houses for Other Purposes	615298	128895
数字终端数(台)	Number of Digital Terminals (set)	390592	258037
图书藏量(册)	Books Collections (volume)	32902893	28097147

资料来源：北京市教育委员会。
Source: Beijing Municipal Education Commission.

20–15 基础教育国际学生情况(2022年) STATISTICS FOR INTERNATIONAL STUDENTS FOR BASIC EDUCATION(2022)

单位：人 (person)

项　目	Item	国际学生数 International Students	#民办学校 Privately-funded Education
合　计	**Total**	**3441**	**1240**
普通中学	General Middle Schools	825	192
初　中	Junior Secondary Schools	538	177
高　中	Senior Secondary Schools	287	15
中等职业教育	Vocational Secondary Schools	90	
小　学	Primary Schools	1751	460
幼儿园	Kindergartens	775	588

资料来源：北京市教育委员会。
Source: Beijing Municipal Education Commission.

20–16 教育经费情况(2014–2021年) STATISTICS FOR EDUCATIONAL FUNDS (2014-2021)

单位：万元 (10000 yuan)

年 份 Year	合 计 Total	国家财政性教育经费 Government Appropriation for Education	#一般公共预算教育经费 General Public Budget for Education	民办学校中举办者投入 Funds from Runners of Private Schools	社会捐赠经费 Funds from Social Donations	事业收入 Income from Undertakings	#学费 Tuition Fees	其他教育经费 Other Educational Funds
2014	10937374	9683641	7584873	10529	10431	1048953	833849	183820
2015	11171250	9810774	8474342	10685	9624	1177133	925848	163034
2016	11934724	10491718	8822890	9261	10879	1299205	1034188	123662
2017	12512746	10863394	9557007	6368	9341	1478756	1201615	154888
2018	13525400	11661674	10207229	8711	6503	1651516	1331358	196996
2019	14794780	12791460	11253649	8906	5505	1876698	1536289	112212
2020	15085043	13130881	11279953	11903	5732	1531203	1251681	405325
2021	15325981	13130243	11351611	13689	5027	2056343	1689286	120679

资料来源：北京市教育委员会。
Source: Beijing Municipal Education Commission.

20—17　生均一般公共预算教育事业费支出和公用经费支出情况
AVERAGE GENERAL PUBLIC BUDGET FOR EDUCATIONAL EXPENSES AND PUBLIC EXPENDITURE

单位：元　(yuan)

项　目	Item	2021	2020	2021年为2020年% 2021 as % of 2020
生均一般公共预算	**Average General Public Budget**			
教育事业费支出	**Educational Expenses**			
幼儿园	Kindergartens	38540.98	39094.01	98.6
普通小学	Regular Primary Schools	33633.65	33546.46	100.3
普通初中	Regular Junior Secondary Schools	57156.75	58686.11	97.4
普通高中	Regular Senior Secondary Schools	66433.98	70295.87	94.5
中等职业学校	Secondary Vocational Schools	70514.69	68451.66	103.0
普通高等学校	General Institutions of Higher Education	65957.02	56861.41	116.0
生均一般公共预算	**Average General Public Budget**			
公用经费支出	**Public Expenditure**			
幼儿园	Kindergartens	14642.97	12966.63	112.9
普通小学	Regular Primary Schools	9791.18	8472.08	115.6
普通初中	Regular Junior Secondary Schools	17717.04	15479.42	114.5
普通高中	Regular Senior Secondary Schools	19545.35	18998.99	102.9
中等职业学校	Secondary Vocational Schools	24652.56	22601.06	109.1
普通高等学校	General Institutions of Higher Education	29133.45	21588.60	135.0

资料来源：北京市教育委员会。
Source: Beijing Municipal Education Commission.

主要统计指标解释

研究生培养机构 指经国家批准按国家计划招收和培养硕士、博士和其他研究生的高等学校和科学研究机构。

普通高等学校 指按国家规定的设置标准和审批程序批准举办的，通过国家统一招生考试，招收高中毕业生为主要培养对象，实施高等教育的全日制大学、独立设置的学院和高等专科学校、短期职业大学。

成人高等学校 指按国家规定的设置标准和审批程序批准举办的，通过全国成人高等教育统一招生考试，招收具有高中毕业或同等学历的人员为主要培养对象，利用函授、业余、脱产等多种形式对其实施高等学历教育的学校。包括：职工高等学校、农民高等学校、管理干部学院、教育学院、独立函授学院、广播电视大学和其他机构。

高等教育机构 指经省、自治区、直辖市教育行政部门审批并颁发办学许可证，不具有颁发学历文凭资格的实施高等教育的单位。

民办学校 指经有关主管部门批准，公民个人、社会团体及其他社会组织等利用非国家财政性教育经费，面向社会举办的学校及其他教育机构。

专科教育 应当使学生掌握本专业必备的基础理论、专门应用技术知识，具有从事本专业实际工作的基本技能和技术应用能力。全日制专科教育的基本修业年限为二至三年。

本科教育 应当使学生比较系统地掌握本学科、专业必需的基础理论、基本知识，掌握本专业必要的基本技能、方法和相关知识，具有从事本专业实际工作和研究工作的初步能力。全日制本科教育的基本修业年限为四至五年。

硕士研究生教育 应当使学生掌握本学科坚实的基础理论、系统的专业知识，掌握相应的技能、方法和相关知识，具有从事本专业实际工作和科学研究工作的能力。硕士研究生教育的基本修业年限为二至三年。

博士研究生教育 应当使学生掌握本学科坚实宽广的基础理论、系统深入的专业知识、相应的技能和方法，具有独立从事本学科创造性科学研究工作和实际工作的能力。博士研究生教育的基本修业年限为三至四年。

网络学生 指经教育部批准的现代远程教育试点学校设立的网络教育学院，基于互联网上实施高等学历教育所招收的普通和成人本科、专科学生。

国际学生 指根据《学校招收和培养国际学生管理办法》，不具有中国国籍在学校接受教育的外国学生。

毕业生数 指上学年度内具有学籍的学生完成教学计划规定课程，考试合格并且取得毕业证书的学生数。

招生数 是指实际招收入学并完成学籍注册的新生数。

在校生数 是指有学籍并在本学年初进行学籍注册的学生数。

结业生数 指具有学籍的学生学习期满，有一门以上主要课程(包括毕业论文或毕业设计)不及格或其他方面不合格，未予毕业而发给结业证书的学生数。不包括短训班和单科结业学生。

教职工数 指各级各类学校（机构）根据岗位聘用的全职为学校工作的人员（含在编人员和签订一年以上聘用合同人员）。

专任教师 指具有《中华人民共和国教师法》《教师资格条例》规定的教师资格，学校根据相关岗位设置管理指导意见，聘用的专职从事教学工作的教师岗位人员。

特殊教育学校 指具备适应残疾儿童少年学习、康复、生活特点的场所和设施，招收盲聋哑、智力残疾及其他有特殊需要的儿童少年实施普通初等、普通中等或中等职业教育的独立设置学校。包括盲人学校、聋人学校、弱智学校、其他特殊教育学校。

学校占地面积 指学校校园内的土地面积，不包括校园外学校拥有的农场、林场及校办工厂等的土地面积。

校舍建筑面积 指学校用于办学并可长期（一年以上）占有使用或拥有产权校舍的建筑面积。

危房面积 指年久失修、结构构件受到严重损坏，有倒塌危险，经房管部门鉴定属于危房的面积。

Explanatory Notes on Main Statistical Indicators

Institutions Providing Postgraduate Programs refer to institutions of higher education and scientific research institutions recruiting and educating postgraduates of master's degree, doctor's degree and other degree upon approval by the State and under the State plan.

Regular Institutions of Higher Education refer to full-time universities, independent colleges and higher professional schools, short-term vocational colleges that are set up according to the State's establishment standards and examination and approval procedures, recruiting graduates from senior secondary schools as the main target through national unified entrance examination, and providing higher education.

Adult Institutions of Higher Education refer to educational establishments, set up in line with the State's establishment standards and examination and approval procedures, recruiting personnel with senior high school or equivalent educational diploma as the main target through national unified entrance examination for adult higher education, and providing higher education courses in many forms including correspondence, spare-time, or full-time teaching for adults. Adult institutions of higher education include schools of higher education for staff and workers, schools of higher education for farmers, colleges for management cadres, pedagogical colleges, independent correspondence colleges, Radio and TV universities and other educational establishments.

Higher Education Institutions refer to institutions offering higher education upon examination and approval by administrative departments in charge of education in provinces, autonomous regions and municipalities, with an education license, which are not eligible for conferring diploma.

Privately-funded Schools refer to schools and other educational institutions run by individuals, social groups and other social organizations upon approval by relevant competent authorities, by using educational funds not from state revenues.

Secondary Technical Education shall enable students to understand necessary basic theories and special knowledge on applied technologies of a specialty, have basic skills and technical application ability for practice of the specialty. Full-time secondary technical education offers a basic study term of 2-3 years.

Undergraduate Education shall enable students to understand necessary basic theories and knowledge of a subject or specialty, have necessary basic skills, methodology and relevant knowledge of the specialty, and have preliminary skills for practical work and research of the specialty. Full-time undergraduate education offers a basic study term of 4-5 years.

Master's-degree Postgraduate Education shall enable students to understand solid basic theories, systematic professional knowledge of a subject, have relevant skills, methodology and relevant knowledge of the specialty, and have the ability for practical work and research of the specialty. Master's-degree postgraduate education offers a basic study term of 2-3 years.

Doctor's-degree Postgraduate Education shall enable students to understand solid and extensive basic theories, systematic and in-depth professional knowledge, relevant skills and methodology of a subject, have the ability for independent creative scientific research and practical work of the specialty. Doctor's-degree postgraduate education offers a basic study term of 3-4 years.

Online Students refer to students for Internet-based higher education for diplomas for general undergraduate courses, undergraduate courses for adults, and secondary technical courses, recruited in online education colleges opened in schools as modern remote education pilots approved by the Ministry of Education.

International Students refers to foreign students without Chinese nationality who are educated in schools in accordance with the *Administrative Measures for Schools in Recruiting and Educating International Students*.

Number of Graduates means the number of enrolled students who have completed all courses stated in the teaching plan within the last academic year, passed all exams and obtained a diploma.

Number of New Enrollments refers to the number of new students who have actually been recruited and completed their student status registration.

Number of Enrolled Students means the number of enrolled students who registered their student status at the beginning of this academic year.

Number of Students Completing Courses means the number of enrolled students completing their schooling with one and more courses not passed (including the graduation paper or graduation design) or other aspects not passed, who are not granted for graduation and awarded a certificate of completion, excluding the number of students completing short-term training courses and single-subject programs.

Number of Teachers and Staff means the number of full-time staff (including the permanent staff and those who have signed the employment contract for one year or more) employed by schools (institutions) of all levels and all kinds according to the position.

Full-time Teachers refer to the staff in teacher position engaged in full-time teaching work who have the teaching qualification under the *Teachers Law of the People's Republic of China* and the *Regulations on the Qualification of Teachers* and have been employed by schools according to the guidance on the management of setting of relevant positions.

Schools for Special Education refer to the independently set up schools with places and facilities with such characteristics as being suitable for learning, rehabilitation and life of disabled children and adolescents that enroll the blind, deaf and mute children and adolescents as well as those with mentally disabilities or other special needs to offer general primary, general secondary or secondary vocational education. They include schools for the blind, schools for the deaf, schools for the mentally disabled and other special education schools.

Area of Land Occupied by School means the area of land within campus, excluding the area of land occupied by farms, forest farms and school-run factories that are owned by the school but are outside the schoolyard.

Floor Space of Schoolhouse refers to the floor space of schoolhouses that are used by the school for school running and can be occupied and used for a long time (more than one year) or in which the school has property right.

Area of Dilapidated Houses refers to the area of those houses that have not been repaired for many years, have seriously damaged components, are at the risk of collapse, and are identified by the house administration authority as dilapidated houses.

北京统计年鉴2023　　BEIJING STATISTICAL YEARBOOK 2023

卫生及社会服务
HEALTH AND SOCIAL SERVICES

简 要 说 明

主要内容

本章资料主要反映卫生、社会服务、残疾人事业的发展情况。

卫生部分统计资料主要包括卫生事业基本情况、卫生总费用、医疗卫生机构、卫生技术人员、床位数、医院工作情况、全市主要健康指标等情况。

社会服务部分统计资料主要包括基层社会工作、收养性单位、社会救助、婚姻登记情况。

残疾人统计资料主要包括残疾人康复、培训、就业、扶贫、社会保障和维权援助情况。

Brief Introduction

Main Content

Statistics in this chapter mainly show the development of health, social services and undertakings for disabled people.

Statistics for health mainly include basic statistics on health, the total health expenditures, the number of medical and health institutions, number of medical technical personnel, number of ward beds, works of hospitals, main health indicators of Beijing, and so on.

Statistics for social services mainly consist of grass-roots social work, adoption institutions, social relief, and marriage registration.

Statistics for disabled persons mainly include information on rehabilitation, training, employment, proverty alleviation, social security and aid for right protection of disabled persons.

21-1 卫生事业基本情况(1978-2022年)

年份 Year	医疗卫生机构(个) Medical and Health Institutions (unit)	#医院 Hospitals	#疾病预防控制中心(防疫站) Disease Prevention and Control Centers (Epidemic Prevention Stations)	#妇幼保健院(所、站) Maternity and Child Care Centers (Stations)	#社区卫生服务中心(站) Community Health Services Centers (Stations)
1978	3263	125	22	15	
1979	3614	124	22	17	
1980	3818	129	22	19	
1981	4135	139	22	19	
1982	4389	149	22	18	
1983	4312	149	22	19	
1984	4173	160	22	18	
1985	4248	188	22	18	
1986	4483	198	22	20	
1987	4744	222	22	19	
1988	4342	266	22	17	
1989	4398	284	22	17	
1990	4953	325	22	17	
1991	4970	337	22	17	
1992	4868	345	22	16	
1993	4962	364	32	16	
1994	4958	387	33	16	
1995	4955	387	33	15	
1996	6470	405	33	13	
1997	6577	435	33	13	
1998	5723	449	32	11	
1999	5990	460	32	8	
2000	6176	458	30	8	
2001	5969	458	30	9	
2002	4998	461	24	19	35
2003	5075	459	29	19	36
2004	7236	503	29	19	43
2005	7536	519	28	18	93
2006	7640	541	28	18	90
2007	9023	535	31	18	1126
2008	9647	537	31	19	1282
2009	9717	522	31	19	1395
2010	9511	550	31	19	1587
2011	9699	569	32	19	1744
2012	9974	608	32	19	1897
2013	10141	647	32	19	1926
2014	10265	672	32	19	1958
2015	10425	701	30	19	1979
2016	10637	713	29	20	1997
2017	10986	732	28	20	2066
2018	11100	736	29	21	2079
2019	11340	745	29	19	2075
2020	11211	733	29	19	2069
2021	11727	733	25	19	2111
2022	12211	741	27	18	2123

注：1.2010年及以前，本表中所有数据都不包含村卫生室及驻京部队医院情况。自2011年起，包含村卫生室情况。自2012年起，除床位数外均包含驻京部队医院数据，下同。

2.自2010年起，原卫生院数据并入到社区卫生服务中心(站)等其他卫生机构。

资料来源：北京市卫生健康委员会。

BASIC STATISTICS ON HEALTH(1978-2022)

医疗卫生机构人员(人) Employed Persons in Medical and Health Institutions (person)	#卫生技术人员 Medical Technical Personnel	#执业(助理)医师 Certified (Assistant) Doctors	#注册护士 Registered Nurses
90174	65943	28435	16085
97942	72131	31842	17398
102601	74753	34365	17492
110774	81183	37886	20025
114420	83843	39385	20389
119222	86593	41216	21181
124664	89362	42112	22286
127771	90831	42216	23782
132865	94433	43403	25383
142556	101829	46007	27786
145362	105237	48216	30250
150062	108108	49361	32056
156304	111614	50934	34565
161103	114342	52309	35714
164213	115825	53254	36768
165170	116173	53906	36687
164867	116818	53865	36608
164436	115967	54114	36719
164981	116849	54091	37712
167090	119256	54909	38630
162609	115976	51902	38883
161823	116597	52646	39625
160258	115510	51570	39900
158185	115935	52100	40537
144021	109564	47236	38879
148406	112212	47887	39912
157157	116905	49283	41547
161432	120170	50913	42897
170586	127193	53084	45647
186290	139478	55156	50926
197765	150134	58904	55348
212086	160695	62578	61634
223694	171328	66165	67308
235708	181938	69749	72812
276654	219714	82192	95202
294012	229720	85819	100652
304990	242923	89590	106167
321151	256531	96445	114294
330777	264850	100878	117760
346255	276969	105732	123158
351765	281686	109376	123589
369139	297259	115771	131314
375673	303699	118541	134656
389779	317659	123503	141685
395381	322187	124916	142711

Note: a) In and before 2010, figures in this table did not include village health clinics and hospitals of troops stationed in Beijing. Since 2011, figures included village health clinics. Since 2012, figures in this table include troops stationed in Beijing with the bed number excluded. the same below.

b)From 2010, data on health centers were incorporated into other health institutions such as community health service centers (stations).

Source: Beijing Municipal Health Commission.

21-1 续表 Continued

年份 Year	医疗机构实有床位数(张) Beds in Medical Institutions (unit)	#医院 Hospitals	每千户籍人口执业(助理)医师数(人) Certified (Assistant) Doctors per 1000 Registered Population (person)	每千户籍人口注册护士数(人) Registered Nurses per 1000 Registered Population (person)	每千户籍人口医院床位数(张) Ward Beds per 1000 Registered Population (unit)	每千常住人口执业(助理)医师数(人) Certified (Assistant) Doctors per 1000 Permanent Population (person)	每千常住人口注册护士数(人) Registered Nurses per 1000 Permanent Population (person)	每千常住人口医院床位数(张) Ward Beds per 1000 Permanent Population (unit)
1978	29767	23668	3.35	1.89	2.79			
1979	30231	24092	3.66	1.87	2.77			
1980	32453	25770	3.88	1.97	2.91			
1981	33666	26934	4.20	2.20	2.99			
1982	34574	28209	4.30	2.23	3.07			
1983	35987	29612	4.40	2.26	3.17			
1984	38580	31933	4.40	2.33	3.38			
1985	41603	35166	4.44	2.48	3.67			
1986	43956	38133	4.47	3.72	3.93			
1987	47538	41178	4.66	2.81	4.17			
1988	53078	45334	4.82	3.02	4.53			
1989	55623	48558	4.83	3.14	4.76			
1990	59036	51860	4.93	3.35	5.02			
1991	61744	54888	5.03	3.44	5.28			
1992	63230	55858	5.10	3.52	5.35			
1993	65621	58605	5.13	3.49	5.58			
1994	67112	60661	5.07	3.45	5.71			
1995	66925	60337	5.06	3.43	5.64			
1996	66760	60997	5.02	3.50	5.66			
1997	67946	61865	5.06	3.56	5.70			
1998	69095	63144	4.76	3.56	5.79			
1999	69465	63660	4.79	3.60	5.79			
2000	71245	65138	4.66	3.60	5.88			
2001	73053	66537	4.64	3.61	5.93			
2002	75188	67750	4.18	3.44	5.96			
2003	74298	66990	4.21	3.51	5.83			
2004	77359	69850	4.25	3.60	6.01	3.30	2.78	
2005	79067	72329	4.32	3.66	6.13	3.31	2.79	
2006	81440	74762	4.41	3.84	6.24	3.36	2.89	6.77
2007	83736	76915	4.53	4.19	6.34	3.38	3.12	4.71
2008	86196	79089	4.78	4.50	6.43	3.48	3.27	4.67
2009	90100	82471	5.00	4.94	6.62	3.57	3.51	4.70
2010	92871	85935	5.24	5.35	6.83	3.37	3.43	4.38
2011	94735	87596	5.46	5.70	6.85	3.46	3.61	4.34
2012	100167	92610	6.33	7.34	7.14	3.97	4.60	4.48
2013	104034	96558	6.52	7.65	7.34	4.06	4.76	4.57
2014	109789	102851	6.72	7.96	7.71	4.16	4.93	4.78
2015	111555	104644	7.17	8.50	7.78	4.44	5.27	4.82
2016	116963	110021	7.40	8.64	8.07	4.64	5.42	5.06
2017	120530	113576	7.78	9.06	8.36	4.87	5.67	5.23
2018	123508	116279	7.95	8.98	8.45	5.08	5.74	5.40
2019	127111	119574	8.28	9.40	8.56	5.38	6.10	5.55
2020	127143	119310	8.46	9.61	8.52	5.41	6.15	5.45
2021	130259	122287	8.74	10.02	8.65	5.64	6.47	5.59
2022	133932	126309	8.75	10.00	8.85	5.72	6.53	5.78

21-2 卫生总费用(2000-2021年)
TOTAL HEALTH EXPENDITURES (2000-2021)

年份 Year	卫生总费用(亿元) Total Health Expenditures (100 million yuan)	政府卫生支出 Health Expenditures by Governments		社会卫生支出 Social Health Expenditures		个人现金卫生支出 Health Expenditures in Cash by Individuals	
		绝对数(亿元) Absolute Number (100 million yuan)	占卫生总费用比重(%) As % of Total (%)	绝对数(亿元) Absolute Number (100 million yuan)	占卫生总费用比重(%) As % of Total (%)	绝对数(亿元) Absolute Number (100 million yuan)	占卫生总费用比重(%) As % of Total (%)
2000	166.7	34.7	20.8	61.8	37.1	70.3	42.1
2001	201.1	45.3	22.5	73.2	36.4	82.7	41.1
2002	262.4	48.5	18.5	99.6	38.0	114.2	43.5
2003	314.2	65.8	20.9	132.0	42.0	116.3	37.0
2004	357.2	69.4	19.4	150.7	42.2	137.1	38.4
2005	432.8	85.7	19.8	187.8	43.4	159.2	36.8
2006	497.4	115.9	23.3	208.0	41.8	173.5	34.9
2007	523.2	142.0	27.2	212.0	40.5	169.2	32.3
2008	668.5	180.0	26.9	271.3	40.6	217.3	32.5
2009	689.6	201.1	29.2	296.3	43.0	192.2	27.9
2010	814.7	226.8	27.8	385.1	47.3	202.8	24.9
2011	977.3	275.5	28.2	453.2	46.4	248.6	25.4
2012	1190.0	320.4	26.9	601.0	50.5	268.7	22.6
2013	1349.6	356.4	26.4	717.8	53.2	275.5	20.4
2014	1594.6	394.4	24.7	890.6	55.9	309.7	19.4
2015	1834.8	445.8	24.3	1069.9	58.3	319.1	17.4
2016	2049.0	468.0	22.8	1247.2	60.9	333.8	16.3
2017	2193.8	507.4	23.1	1327.4	60.5	359.0	16.4
2018	2500.8	580.0	23.2	1530.0	61.2	390.9	15.6
2019	2964.8	703.2	23.7	1850.5	62.4	411.1	13.9
2020	3028.3	809.8	26.7	1812.8	59.9	405.6	13.4
2021	3351.9	784.0	23.4	2127.2	63.5	440.7	13.2

资料来源：北京市卫生健康委员会。
Source: Beijing Municipal Health Commission.

21-3 医疗卫生机构基本情况
BASIC STATISTICS FOR MEDICAL AND HEALTH INSTITUTIONS

项目	Item	2022	2021	构成(%) Composition (%) 2022	构成(%) Composition (%) 2021
机构数（个）	**Number of Institutions (unit)**	**12211**	**11727**	**100.0**	**100.0**
#医院	Hospitals	741	733	6.1	6.3
社区卫生服务中心(站)	Health Service Centers (Stations) for Community	2123	2111	17.4	18.0
门诊部	Outpatient Departments	1568	1490	12.8	12.7
妇幼保健院(所、站)	Maternity and Child Care Hospitals	18	19	0.1	0.2
疾病预防控制中心(防疫站)	Disease Prevention and Control Centers (Epidemic Prevention Stations)	27	25	0.2	0.2
专科疾病防治院(所、站)	Specific Disease Prevention and Cure Centers	21	22	0.2	0.2
诊所、卫生所、医务室、护理站	Clinics, Health Centers, Infirmaries, Nursing Stations	4565	4441	37.4	37.9
床位数（张）	**Number of Beds (unit)**	**133932**	**130259**	**100.0**	**100.0**
#医院	Hospitals	126309	122287	94.3	93.9
社区卫生服务中心(站)	Health Service Centers (Stations) for Community	5229	5243	3.9	4.0
妇幼保健院(所、站)	Maternity and Child Care Hospitals	1830	2090	1.4	1.6
专科疾病防治院(所、站)	Specific Disease Prevention and Cure Centers	564	639	0.4	0.5
卫生技术人员数（人）	**Number of Medical Technical Personnel (person)**	**322187**	**317659**	**100.0**	**100.0**
#医院	Hospitals	230090	227606	71.4	71.7
社区卫生服务中心(站)	Health Service Centers (Stations) for Community	35885	34792	11.1	11.0
妇幼保健院(所、站)	Maternity and Child Care Hospitals	5991	6042	1.9	1.9
专科疾病防治院(所、站)	Specific Disease Prevention and Cure Centers	641	733	0.2	0.2
#执业(助理)医师	Certified Doctors	124916	123503	38.8	38.9
注册护士	Registered Nurses	142711	141685	44.3	44.6

注：本表数据除床位数外均包含驻京部队医院数据。
资料来源：北京市卫生健康委员会。
Note: Figures in this table include troops stationed in Beijing with the bed number excluded.
Source: Beijing Municipal Health Commission.

21–4 医院基本情况(2022年)
BASIC STATISTICS ON HOSPITALS (2022)

项　目	Item	医院数 (个) Hospitals (unit)	床位数 (张) Beds (unit)	职工人数 (人) Employed Persons (person)	#卫生技术人员 Medical Technical Personnel	#执业医师 Certified Doctors	#中医 Doctors of Traditional Chinese Medicine
合　计	**Total**	**741**	**126309**	**276717**	**230090**	**82220**	**13943**
按隶属关系分	**By Affiliation**						
#市　属	Municipal	30	24874	56495	47474	16391	979
区　属	Districts	92	33701	59343	49661	18098	4462
按专业分	**By Specialty**						
#综合医院	General Hospitals	252	66905	165847	142559	50430	2324
中医医院	Hospitals Specialized in Traditional Chinese Medicine	193	16251	34118	27629	11483	8010
中西医结合医院	Hospitals Combining Western Medicine with Traditional Chinese Medicine	54	12589	19327	16005	6070	2713
民族医院	Nationality Hospitals	5	347	366	242	109	88
口腔医院	Stomatology Hospitals	44	833	7097	5533	2208	13
眼科医院	Ophthalmology Hospitals	17	537	1225	739	241	18
肿瘤医院	Tumor Hospitals	12	4571	7468	5882	1783	44
心血管病医院	Hospitals for Cardiovascular Diseases	2	1453	3849	3331	864	16
胸科医院	Thorax Hospitals	1	631	961	783	219	4
妇(产)科医院	Hospitals for Gynecology and Obstetrics	18	1379	4922	3458	1152	43
儿童医院	Children's Hospitals	11	2186	5880	4887	1820	87
精神病医院	Psychiatric Hospital	24	8411	6452	4848	1202	79
传染病医院	Infectious Disease Hospitals	3	1491	3314	2760	915	49
骨科医院	Hospitals of Orthopedics	8	779	1248	984	369	71
整形外科医院	Orthopaedics Hospitals	1	419	1039	721	309	1
其他专科医院	Other Specialized Hospitals	26	2461	3962	2781	864	114
护理院	Nursing Hospitals	9	640	452	194	47	7

注：本表数据除床位数外均包括驻京部队数据。
资料来源：北京市卫生健康委员会。
Note: Figures in this table include troops stationed in Beijing with the bed number excluded.
Source: Beijing Municipal Health Commission.

21-4 续表 Continued

单位：人 (person)

项目	Item	#执业助理医师 Certified Assistant Doctors	#中医 Doctors of Traditional Chinese Medicine	#注册护士 Registered Nurses	#药师(士) Pharmacists (Assistant Pharmacists)	#影像技师(士) Image Technicians (Assistant Technicians)	#检验师(士) Laboratorians (Assistant Laboratorians)
合计	**Total**	**1776**	**549**	**111841**	**9924**	**3907**	**6478**
按隶属关系分	**By Affiliation**						
#市级	Municipal	121	3	22933	2016	957	1453
区级	Districts	278	40	23260	2698	886	1812
按专业分	**By Specialty**						
#综合医院	General Hospitals	551	97	72982	4786	2310	3530
中医医院	Hospitals Specialized in Traditional Chinese Medicine	501	327	10421	2486	490	943
中西医结合医院	Hospitals Combining Western Medicine with Traditional Chinese Medicine	200	83	7208	977	247	533
民族医院	Nationality Hospitals	12	7	87	21	4	9
口腔医院	Stomatology Hospitals	125	1	2560	62	102	40
眼科医院	Ophthalmology Hospitals	14	2	358	36	6	24
肿瘤医院	Tumor Hospitals	32	4	2789	232	261	168
心血管病医院	Hospitals for Cardiovascular Diseases	1		1818	67	55	59
胸科医院	Thorax Hospitals			443	30	28	25
妇(产)科医院	Hospitals for Gynecology and Obstetrics	29		1773	128	32	208
儿童医院	Children's Hospitals	21	1	2057	228	98	268
精神病医院	Psychiatric Hospitals	54	4	2734	243	38	147
传染病医院	Infectious Disease Hospitals	1		1342	146	46	137
骨科医院	Hospitals of Orthopedics	20	5	442	45	26	36
整形外科医院	Orthopaedics Hospitals			305	14	5	12
其他专科医院	Other Specialized Hospitals	115	6	1250	126	67	99
护理院	Nursing Hospitals	1	1	113	10	2	4

21-5 医院工作情况(2022年)
WORKS OF HOSPITALS (2022)

项目	Item	诊疗人次数(千人次) Patients Treated (1000 person-times)	#门诊 Out-patients	健康检查人数(千人次) Health Check (1000 person-times)	平均开放病床数(张) Beds in Use (unit)	入院人数(千人次) In-patients (1000 person-times)	出院人数(千人次) Discharged Patients (1000 person-times)
合　计	**Total**	**148549.9**	**125972.4**	**3895.8**	**121156**	**3284.6**	**3700.5**
#综合医院	General Hospitals	91923.5	71792.6	2901.8	65720	2214.4	2633.4
中医医院	Hospitals Specialized in Traditional Chinese Medicine	26887.3	26010.8	334.0	15211	266.3	263.8
中西医结合医院	Hospitals Combining Western Medicine with Traditional Chinese Medicine	9769.1	9216.9	340.0	12227	189.3	187.4
民族医院	Nationality Hospitals	90.7	90.2		174	1.0	1.0
口腔医院	Stomatology Hospitals	3643.6	3513.7	4.7	503	8.7	8.8
眼科医院	Ophthalmology Hospitals	400.2	400.2	20.6	445	7.9	7.9
肿瘤医院	Tumor Hospitals	1645.7	1602.0	79.5	3705	208.9	209.8
心血管病医院	Hospitals for Cardiovascular Diseases	695.6	666.6	4.3	1438	59.3	59.8
胸科医院	Thorax Hospitals	221.7	215.0		631	20.0	19.9
妇(产)科医院	Hospitals for Gynecology and Obstetrics	2030.4	1977.8	4.4	1309	54.6	54.7
儿童医院	Children's Hospitals	4733.9	4226.9	4.9	2058	87.7	86.7
精神病医院	Psychiatric Hospitals	1594.3	1569.2	5.4	8358	27.1	27.6
传染病医院	Infectious Disease Hospitals	1004.1	958.4	1.3	1619	32.9	33.2
骨科医院	Hospitals of Orthopedics	553.0	509.6	17.4	779	13.5	13.4
整形外科医院	Orthopaedics Hospitals	250.9	238.4	0.1	293	8.3	8.3
其他专科医院	Other Specialized Hospitals	634.1	592.6	22.9	2307	26.8	26.6
护理院	Nursing Hospitals	4.1	4.0		428	1.0	1.0

资料来源：北京市卫生健康委员会。
Source: Beijing Municipal Health Commission.

21-5 续表 Continued

项目	Item	病死率 (%) Case Fatality Rate (%)	病床周转次数 (次) Turnover Beds (time)	病床使用率 (%) Utilization Rate of Beds (%)	出院者平均住院日 (日) Average Hospitalization Period (day)
合计	**Total**	**1.4**	**27.0**	**67.9**	**8.2**
#综合医院	General Hospitals	1.3	33.6	70.1	7.5
中医医院	Hospitals Specialized in Traditional Chinese Medicine	1.7	17.3	54.1	11.1
中西医结合医院	Hospitals Combining Western Medicine with Traditional Chinese Medicine	4.1	15.3	66.0	15.0
民族医院	Nationality Hospitals	1.1	5.9	34.5	20.0
口腔医院	Stomatology Hospitals		17.4	30.3	6.4
眼科医院	Ophthalmology Hospitals		17.8	25.3	5.1
肿瘤医院	Tumor Hospitals	0.3	56.6	72.9	4.7
心血管病医院	Hospitals for Cardiovascular Diseases	0.2	41.6	74.8	6.6
胸科医院	Thorax Hospitals	0.5	31.6	73.9	8.5
妇(产)科医院	Hospitals for Gynecology and Obstetrics		41.8	50.0	4.3
儿童医院	Children's Hospitals	0.2	42.1	68.4	5.9
精神病医院	Psychiatric Hospitals	0.8	3.3	92.9	84.1
传染病医院	Infectious Disease Hospitals	1.9	20.5	49.7	9.0
骨科医院	Hospitals of Orthopedics	3.8	17.2	64.2	13.4
整形外科医院	Orthopaedics Hospitals		28.2	41.8	5.2
其他专科医院	Other Specialized Hospitals	4.4	11.5	63.1	17.3
护理院	Nursing Hospitals	5.4	2.4	65.4	43.2

21-6 主要健康指标情况(1978-2022年)
MAJOR HEALTH INDICATIONS(1978-2022)

年 份 Year	婴 儿 死亡率 (‰) Infant Mortality (‰)	新生儿 死亡率 (‰) Newborn Baby Mortality (‰)	孕产妇 死亡率 (1/10万) Pregnant & Lying-in Women Mortality (1/100 thousand)	甲乙类传染 病发病率 (1/10万) Incidence Rate of Catogory A and B Epidemics (1/100 thousand)
1978	17.11	12.21	31.00	
1979	16.97	10.08	34.70	1584.25
1980	14.79	10.24	26.30	2165.23
1981	13.84	9.22	48.50	2225.71
1982	12.97	8.02	24.50	2193.16
1983	13.79	8.78	28.10	1904.55
1984	10.98	7.78	16.80	1666.68
1985	13.94	10.41	22.90	1335.23
1986	16.05	12.13	30.50	1120.19
1987	15.56	11.08	26.60	826.51
1988	14.98	10.48	24.80	640.98
1989	14.96	10.53	34.50	547.61
1990	11.66	8.49	25.00	509.55
1991	12.46	8.56	24.00	448.23
1992	12.12	8.93	30.10	385.98
1993	10.38	7.21	16.50	356.66
1994	10.93	7.29	18.94	374.31
1995	11.45	7.52	22.27	309.99
1996	10.05	6.97	15.32	340.24
1997	9.45	6.36	23.69	294.41
1998	7.58	5.53	10.46	306.37
1999	7.95	5.94	17.53	308.10
2000	5.36	3.70	9.70	301.19
2001	6.01	4.05	11.71	276.85
2002	5.56	3.70	15.12	282.95
2003	5.89	3.83	15.60	228.00
2004	4.61	3.49	15.19	408.03
2005	4.35	3.29	15.91	445.91
2006	4.66	3.42	7.87	448.70
2007	3.89	2.65	16.74	421.02
2008	3.70	2.45	18.52	312.99
2009	3.49	2.47	14.55	339.89
2010	3.29	2.06	12.14	268.99
2011	2.84	1.88	9.09	226.76
2012	2.87	1.91	6.05	174.45
2013	2.33	1.52	9.45	155.87
2014	2.33	1.46	7.19	165.49
2015	2.42	1.52	8.69	150.86
2016	2.21	1.48	10.83	138.00
2017	2.29	1.45	8.17	139.60
2018	2.15	1.26	10.64	131.50
2019	1.99	1.21	2.96	139.80
2020	1.98	1.06	4.98	80.80
2021	1.44	0.90	2.22	94.57
2022	1.26	0.67	3.73	265.40

资料来源：北京市卫生健康委员会。
Source: Beijing Municipal Health Commission.

21-7 基层社会工作情况
STATISTICS FOR GRASSROOT SOCIAL WORK

单位：个 (unit)

项 目	Item	2022	2021	2022年为2021年% 2022 as % of 2021
社区服务机构数	Number of Service Facilities in Urban Communities	10062	9799	102.7
#社区服务中心	Community Service Centers	131	183	71.6
城市便民利民服务网点数	Number of Urban Convenient Service Outlets	6383	6416	99.5

资料来源：中共北京市委社会工作委员会北京市民政局。
Source: Social Work Committee of Beijing Municipal Committee of the Communist Party of China Beijing Municipal Civil Affairs Bureau.

21-8 提供住宿机构情况(2022年)
STATISTICS FOR AGENCIES WITH ACCOMMODATIONS (2022)

项 目	Item	合 计 Total	社 会 福利院 Social Welfare Institutions	儿 童 福利院 Children's Welfare Institutions	福利类精神病院和医院 Welfare Mental Hospitals and Hospitals	养老公寓机 构 Urban Elderly Care Agencies	其他收养服务机构 Other Adopting Service Agencies
单位数 (个)	Institutions (unit)	617	8	10	1	576	22
职工人数 (人)	Employed Persons (person)	19957	899	503	96	17845	614
床位数 (张)	Beds (unit)	115356	3977	2791	52	106247	2289
年末在院人数 (人)	Persons Received (person)	43210	1754	1124	4	39890	438
#自 费	Self-supported	35443	963		4	34476	

资料来源：中共北京市委社会工作委员会北京市民政局。
Source: Social Work Committee of Beijing Municipal Committee of the Communist Party of China Beijing Municipal Civil Affairs Bureau.

21-9 婚姻登记(1981-2022年)
BASIC STATISTICS FOR MARRIAGE AND DIVORCE REGISTRATIONS (1981-2022)

年份 Year	结婚对数(对) Registered Marriages (couple)	#涉外及华侨、港澳台居民登记结婚对数 Registered Marriages with Foreigners and Overseas Chinese and Citizens of Hong Kong, Macao and Taiwan	初婚人数(人) Number of First Marriage (person)	离婚对数(对) Registered Divorces (couple)	#民政部门登记离婚对数 Divorces Registered in the Civil Affair Department
1981	200352		389936	5170	1780
1982	141253		261851	5359	1581
1983	117976		227676	5322	1465
1984	113362		217649	5654	1387
1985	134462		258255	5874	1746
1986	143105		274634	7541	2474
1987	149952		267424	8916	3218
1988	113333		212544	10664	4198
1989	103829		188287	12515	5174
1990	92988		169510	14748	5791
1991	91979		165752	15287	6483
1992	89095		158241	15567	6477
1993	89938		160127	17829	7589
1994	90379		160793	19928	8327
1995	85511		148722	20160	8096
1996	86803		146666	20716	8225
1997	84208		144040	22257	8628
1998	85534		146750	23708	9381
1999	83312		141740	23922	8502
2000	80212		136500	26616	6384
2001	79385	873	133259	27683	5425
2002	76136	606	126371	27691	5810
2003	93526	761	158729	30637	10142
2004	126436	974	214443	32657	21013
2005	96956	937	158736	34244	23991
2006	171286	1172	294223	35505	24954
2007	117926	991	193387	36622	26432
2008	147516	1165	246309	37619	27277
2009	181771	1176	305803	41299	29998
2010	138104	1085	222269	43970	32595
2011	173238	1260	288406	43521	32999
2012	174114	1242	287436	48575	38243
2013	163676	1070	251636	65018	54536
2014	170027	1149	253774	65627	56192
2015	166018	1018	229546	82195	73000
2016	166207	1012	200750	105806	97583
2017	151454	916	179316	80697	72964
2018	137818	847	169157	74349	66616
2019	128959	754	141528	83792	76358
2020	113790	376	124281	81949	76134
2021	103360	430	136303	52664	44582
2022	91300	435	118125	44320	36858

注：离婚对数包括在民政部门登记的对数以及经法院调离和判离的对数。
资料来源：中共北京市委社会工作委员会北京市民政局、北京市高级人民法院。
Note: Registered divorces include those registered in the civil affair department and those mediated and judged in courts.
Source: Social Work Committee of Beijing Municipal Committee of the Communist Party of China Beijing Municipal Civil Affairs Bureau, and The People's High Court of Beijing.

21－10 婚姻登记情况
BASIC STATISTICS ON MARRIAGE AND DIVORCE REGISTRATIONS

项　目		Item		2022	2021	2022年为2021年% 2022 as % of 2021
登记结婚对数	**(对)**	**Registered Marriages**	**(couple)**	**91300**	**103360**	**88.3**
按婚前状况分		**By Pre-marriage Status**				
初婚人数	(人)	First Marriages	(person)	118125	136303	86.7
再婚人数	(人)	Remarriages	(person)	64475	70417	91.6
#女　性		Females		31161	34428	90.5
按居住地分		**By Place of Residence**				
内地居民登记结婚对数	(对)	Registered Marriages in Mainland	(couple)	90865	102930	88.3
涉外及华侨、港澳台居民登记结婚对数	(对)	Registered Marriages with Foreigners and Overseas Chinese and Citizens of Hong Kong, Macao and Taiwan	(couple)	435	430	101.2
内地居民	(人)	Mainland Residents	(person)	435	429	101.4
#女　性		Females		281	279	100.7
香港居民	(人)	Hong Kong Residents	(person)	48	39	123.1
澳门居民	(人)	Macao Residents	(person)	9	12	75.0
台湾居民	(人)	Taiwan Residents	(person)	70	76	92.1
华　侨	(人)	Overseas Chinese	(person)	1	2	50.0
外国人	(人)	Foreigners	(person)	307	302	101.7
离婚登记对数	**(对)**	**Registered Divorces**	**(couple)**	**36858**	**44582**	**82.7**
内地居民登记离婚对数	(对)	Registered Divorces in Mainland	(couple)	36758	44491	82.6
涉外及华侨、港澳台居民登记离婚对数	(对)	Registered Divorces with Foreigners and Overseas Chinese and Citizens of Hong Kong, Macao and Taiwan	(couple)	100	91	109.9

注：离婚登记对数不含法院调离和判离数。
资料来源：中共北京市委社会工作委员会北京市民政局。
Note: Number of registered divorces excludes the divorces mediated and ruled by courts.
Source: Social Work Committee of Beijing Municipal Committee of the Communist Party of China Beijing Municipal Civil Affairs Bureau.

21-11 残疾人事业基本情况
BASIC INFORMATION OF UNDERTAKINGS FOR DISABLED PERSONS

项目	Item	2022	2021
康复	**Rehabilitation**		
0－6岁残疾儿童享受康复政策人数 (人)	Number of Disabled Children of 0 to 6 Years Old Enjoying Rehabilitation Policies (person)	3077	2739
7－15岁残疾儿童少年享受康复政策人数 (人)	Number of Disabled Children and Teenagers of 7 to15 Years Old Enjoying Rehabilitation Policies (person)	1646	1395
残疾人接受辅助器具服务人数 (人)	Number of Disabled Persons With Assistive Devices (person)	82568	73319
精神残疾人接受免费服药人数 (人)	Number of Mentally Disabled Persons Receiving Free (person)	34352	40491
培训	**Training**		
职业教育与培训机构数(残联认定) (个)	Number of Vocational Education and Training Institutions (recognized by China Disabled Persons' Federation) (unit)	93	93
职业技能培训人数 (人次)	Number of Persons Receiving Vocational Skill Training (person-time)	4123	8768
就业	**Employment**		
盲人按摩	Massage by Persons with Visual Disability		
医疗按摩机构 (家)	Medical Massage Institutions (unit)	3	2
医疗按摩员培训人次 (人次)	Keep-fit Massager Training (person-time)	200	63
扶贫	**Poverty Alleviation**		
扶持农村残疾人数 (人)	Number of Disabled Persons Supported in Rural Areas (person)	800	461
社会保障	**Social Security**		
已纳入最低生活保障范围人数 (人)	Covered by the Basic Living System (person)	33322	34368
参加城乡居民养老保险残疾人数 (人)	Number of Disabled Persons Covered by Pension Insurance for Urban and Rural Residents (person)	45455	61316
参加城乡居民医疗保险残疾人数 (人)	Number of Disabled Persons Covered by Medical Insurance for Urban and Rural Residents (person)	216000	210350
残联组织建设	**Organization Building of Disabled Persons' Federation**		
残疾人工作者数 (人)	Workers for Disabled Persons (person)	1229	1322
维权援助	**Aid for Right Protection**		
维权信访咨询件数 (件)	Right Protection Letters, Visits and Consulting (case)	8086	22126
维权法律服务件数 (件)	Right Protection Legal Aid (case)	2024	2749

资料来源：北京市残疾人联合会。
Source: Beijing Disabled Person's Federation.

21-12 救助情况
STATISTICS ON ASSISTANCE

单位：人 (person)

项目	Item	人数 Number of Persons		2022年为2021年% 2022 as % of 2021
		2022	2021	
社会救助对象总人数	**Total Number of Persons Receiving Social Relief**	**113169**	**116364**	**97.3**
城市居民最低生活保障人数	Number of Persons Receiving Subsistence Allowances in Urban Areas	69899	70828	98.7
农村居民最低生活保障人数	Number of Persons Receiving Subsistence Allowances in Rural Areas	36696	38851	94.5
农村特困供养人数	Number of Rural Poor Residents Enjoying Special Subsidies for Livelihood Guaranteed	5140	5307	96.9
#农村特困集中供养人数	Number of Rural Poor Residents Enjoying Centralized Special Subsidies for Livelihood Guaranteed	1611	1699	94.8
城市特困供养人数	Number of Urban Poor Residents Enjoying Special Subsidies for Livelihood Guaranteed	1434	1378	104.1
#城市特困集中供养人数	Number of Urban Poor Residents Enjoying Centralized Special Subsidies for Livelihood Guaranteed	759	764	99.3

资料来源：中共北京市委社会工作委员会北京市民政局。
Source: Social Work Committee of Beijing Municipal Committee of the Communist Party of China Beijing Municipal Civil Affairs Bureau.

主要统计指标解释

卫　生

医疗卫生机构　指从卫生行政部门取得《医疗机构执业许可证》，或从民政、工商行政、机构编制管理部门取得法人单位登记证书，为社会提供医疗保健、疾病控制、卫生监督服务或从事医学科研和医学在职培训等工作的单位。

卫生技术人员　包括执业医师、执业助理医师、注册护士、药师（士）、检验及影像技师（士）、卫生监督员和见习医（药、护、技）师（士）等卫生专业人员，包括从事临床或监督工作并同时从事管理工作的人员（如院长、书记等）。

执业（助理）医师和注册护士　指取得医师、护士执业证书且实际从事临床工作的人员，包括从事临床工作并同时从事管理工作的人员（如院长、书记等）。

死亡率（死因死亡率）　是指某种原因（如疾病）所致的死亡人数占户籍人口比重。

婴儿死亡率　指某地区一年内每 1000 名活产婴儿与未满 1 岁的婴儿死亡人数之比。婴儿死亡率可以衡量一个国家或地区经济文化、居民健康状况和卫生保健事业发展情况，同时也是人口平均期望寿命研究的重要内容。

新生儿死亡率　指年内新生儿死亡数与活产数之比，一般以千分率表示。新生儿死亡指出生至 28 天以内（即 0-27 天）死亡人数。

孕产妇死亡率　指某年某地每十万活产中的孕产妇死亡比例。同婴儿死亡率一样，孕产妇死亡率是评价某一地区社会发展状况的重要指标，它的高低与社会经济状况、孕产妇社会环境及卫生保健服务有直接的联系。

社会服务

社会救助对象总人数　指在报告期末生活在当地规定的最低生活保障线以下的家庭人员及国家规定由民政部门救济的特殊人员和 60 年代精简退职老职工救济人员等。

社区服务机构数　指报告期末社区服务站、社区服务中心、其它社区服务设施的总和。

Explanatory Notes on Main Statistical Indicators

Health

Medical and Health Institutions refer to institutions granted with *License for Medical Institution* by the health administration authority, or granted with certificate of corporate unit by the civil affair, administration for industry and commerce, management authority of institutional organization, and providing medical service and healthcare, disease control, health supervision service or carrying out medical research and education, and so on.

Medical Technical Personnel refer to all fixed employees and of contract-based employees, professional personnel in health technology, who receive pays from medical and health institutions, excluding personnel engaged in management.

Certified（Assistant） Doctors and Registered Nurses refer to personnel who have received a physician practicing certificate（Assistant） and certified nurse certificate, excluding physicians and nurses engaged in management.

Mortality (Cause-specific Death Rate) means the proportion of persons dead due to certain cause (such as disease) in the permanent population.

Infant Mortality means the rate of dead infants under 1 year old to 1,000 live infants in an area in a year. Infant death rate measures the development of economy, culture, citizen health and health care in a country or region. It is also an important component of study on average life expectancy of population.

Neonatal Mortality Rate refers to the rate of dead newborn babies to live births in a year, generally expressed in permillage. Death toll of newborns refers to the number of newborns that died within 28 days after birth (i.e. 0-27 days).

Pregnant and Lying-in Women Mortality refers to the rate of dead pregnant and lying-in women to 100,000 live pregnant and lying-in women in an area in a year. This is an important indicator to evaluate the social development status in an area. The figure of this indicator is directly related to the social and economic status, social environment and health care service for pregnant and lying-in women.

Social Services

Total Number of Persons Receiving Social Relief refer to the number of family members living under the minimum living standard provided by local governments, special persons receiving relief by civil affair authorities in line with national regulations, as well as employed persons retired because of streamlining in the 1960s, at the end of the reporting period.

Number of Service Facilities in Urban Communities refers to the total number of community service stations, service centers, and other service facilities, by the end of reporting period.

文化和体育
CULTURE AND SPORTS

简要说明

一、主要内容

本章资料主要反映文化、体育发展情况。

文化部分主要包括公共图书馆、文化馆、档案馆、博物馆、广播、电影、电视、新闻出版以及文化产业发展等情况。

体育部分主要包括体育场地情况、运动员和裁判员情况、运动员获奖情况以及体育彩票等。

二、有关统计标准的变化说明

关于文化产业。执行国家统计局印发的《文化及相关产业分类（2018)》。

关于体育产业。执行国家统计局印发的《体育产业统计分类（2019)》。

Brief Introduction

I. Main Content

Statistics in this chapter mainly show the development of culture and sports.

Cultural statistics mainly include the situation of public libraries, cultural centers, archives, museums, broadcast, films, television and press, and the development of cultural industry, etc.

Sports statistics mainly include sports venues, athletes and referees, awards received by athletes and sports lottery tickets, etc.

II. Changes in Relevant Statistical Standards

Cultural Industry. The *Classification of Cultural and Related Industries (2018)* issued by the National Bureau of Statistics is implemented.

Sports Industry. The *Classification of Sports Industry (2019)* issued by the National Bureau of Statistics is implemented.

22-1 图书馆、文化馆、档案馆情况(1978-2022年)
STATISTICS FOR LIBRARIES, CULTURAL CENTERS AND ARCHIVES (1978-2022)

年份 Year	公共图书馆 Public Libraries				群众艺术馆、文化馆 Mass Art Centers, Cultural Centers		档案馆 Archiving Institutions			
	个数(个) Number (unit)	总藏数(万册、万件) Total Collections (10000 volumes)	建筑面积(万平方米) Building Area (10000 sq.m)	书刊文献外借人次(万人次) Person-times Borrowing Books, Magazines, and Documents (10000 person-times)	个数(个) Number (unit)	组织文艺活动(次) Art Activities Organized (times)	个数(个) Number (unit)	建筑面积(平方米) Building Area (sq.m)	馆藏纸质档案(万卷件) Paper Archives in Collections (10000 rolls)	利用档案资料人次(万人次) Person-times of Using Files (10000 person-times)
1978	18	1423		169	19	516				
1979	21	1502		174	19	1033				
1980	20	1606	1.8	210	19	778				
1981	21	1614	1.9	211	19	1131				
1982	21	1676	2.0	228	20	1334				
1983	21	1733	1.9	243	20	1015				
1984	22	1824	2.3	224	22	489				
1985	22	1860	3.0	220	23	469				
1986	23	1874	6.0	220	23	883				
1987	23	1959	20.6	170	23	1067	20	10695	86.1	1.30
1988	23	2050	23.4	300	23	647	20	21472	116.0	1.46
1989	23	2128	24.5		23	1411	20	31280	156.3	1.48
1990	23	2205	25.0		23	1429	20	23618	167.4	2.51
1991	23	2281	25.3		23	1128	20	33491	177.5	3.24
1992	23	2397	25.4	147	23	978	20	35950	181.3	2.64
1993	23	2461	25.5	212	23	764	20	37650	192.4	1.73
1994	23	2548	23.8	384	23	1034	20	42641	192.4	1.50
1995	23	2629	24.1	139	23	1127	20	65489	204.1	1.42
1996	22	2652	25.3	146	23	2277	20	62994	223.7	3.03
1997	23	2789	25.7	188	23	1875	20	64147	227.4	2.69
1998	24	2848	25.6	189	23	2554	20	67759	240.8	2.71
1999	24	2934	26.4	607	23	1490	20	72597	259.5	2.52
2000	26	3020	27.0	283	23	1809	20	72596	278.3	3.01
2001	26	3133	31.4	288	23	1822	20	72730	297.0	4.17
2002	26	3248	30.7	338	20	1817	20	72946	328.4	4.53
2003	26	3355	30.9	335	20	2023	20	81519	359.0	6.27
2004	26	3451	30.9	405	22	1826	20	83162	379.1	7.03
2005	26	3626	31.7	480	22	3697	20	84656	404.7	6.97
2006	25	3776	31.0	515	21	2200	20	93773	436.7	10.59
2007	25	3940	31.5	479	21	4752	20	93463	461.7	9.51
2008	25	4100	33.4	450	20	3007	20	97605	495.7	9.00
2009	25	4368	41.9	471	20	3470	20	97605	523.8	9.88
2010	25	4613	42.4	441	20	3564	18	97611	558.0	13.45
2011	25	5049	42.1	333	20	3401	18	97976	582.9	12.30
2012	25	5556	47.6	317	20	3848	18	98879	602.5	12.37
2013	25	5316	48.4	325	20	4769	18	101896	636.1	23.85
2014	25	5601	52.7	407	20	2158	18	98220	697.9	22.18
2015	25	5943	52.4	438	20	2587	18	96256	733.2	14.90
2016	25	6229	55.3	549	21	3417	18	119930	764.7	21.95
2017	24	6528	57.8	431	20	3431	18	123401	827.7	19.99
2018	24	6777	57.6	503	20	3278	18	122722	867.5	15.04
2019	24	7048	57.6	480	20	3182	18	212864	910.0	14.83
2020	24	7241	57.7	88	20	1210	18	212864	980.3	11.53
2021	21	7548	62.1	171	19	2942	18	210076	1049.5	13.83
2022	21	7819	62.2	143	18	1774	18	227658	1093.8	10.13

注：1978—1981年，群众艺术馆、文化馆数据不包括群众艺术馆。
资料来源：北京市文化和旅游局、国家图书馆、中共北京市委办公厅(北京市档案局)。
Note: In 1978-1981, the data of mass art centers and cultural centers didn't include those of mass art centers.
Source: Beijing Municipal Bureau of Culture and Tourism, National Library of China, General Office of the CPC Beijing Municipal Committee (Beijing Municipal Archives Bureau).

22-2 博物馆情况(1982-2022年)
STATISTICS FOR MUSEUMS (1982-2022)

年份 Year	全市按行业管理登记的博物馆 Museums Registered by Industry Administration		文物局系统内博物馆及文物保护机构 Museums and Other Cultural Relic Protection and Administration Organizations under the Municipal Administration of Cultural Heritage				
	个数 (个) Number (unit)	文物藏品数 (万件) Cultural Relic Collections (10000 units)	个数 (个) Number (unit)	#博物馆 Museums	文物藏品数 (万件) Cultural Relic Collections (10000 units)	#一级品 (件) Grade-I Collections (unit)	参观人次 (万人次) Visitors (10000 person-times)
1982			28		8.4	294	9.7
1983			29		4.0		58.0
1984							
1985			32		9.0		20.0
1986			39	7	21.0		905.0
1987							
1988			42	11	21.0		1098.0
1989			46	12	14.0		992.0
1990							
1991			46	12	11.7	2901	6629.1
1992							
1993			50	16	17.4	479	2423.4
1994			51	17	16.7	447	955.0
1995			51	17	16.7	447	2100.3
1996			51	17	18.0	443	2009.3
1997			54	24	18.2	443	935.8
1998			56	26	18.3	387	697.8
1999			54	26	18.5	374	5641.8
2000			53	25	18.2	367	702.7
2001			58	26	17.3	366	99.1
2002			48	27	20.1	716	170.8
2003			55	27	112.4	716	119.2
2004			66	31	370.4	656	599.9
2005			73	34	115.1	620	1370.9
2006			70	33	115.5	643	1416.7
2007			69	34	113.5	439	1493.0
2008	148	331	71	37	116.0	678	1368.4
2009	151	331	76	40	117.0	722	1647.9
2010	156	332	79	41	117.0	725	1712.1
2011	162	430	78	41	117.0	852	1373.4
2012	165	430	78	41	117.0	903	1887.9
2013	167	430	78	41	117.0	903	1760.0
2014	171	430	78	41	128.0	891	1848.0
2015	173	430	77	40	126.0	931	2069.1
2016	178	430	79	43	128.0	960	1994.3
2017	179	430	78	43	128.0	1160	2362.7
2018	179	463	78	43	128.0	1144	2383.5
2019	183	463	78	43	129.0	1167	2530.8
2020	197	1625	80	45	130.0	1139	562.9
2021	204	1629	80	45	131.0	1093	1019.0
2022	215	1784	58	33	130.0	1098	413.3

注：自2020年起，全市按行业管理登记的博物馆文物藏品数中包含中央属及非国有博物馆数据，下同。
资料来源：北京市文物局。
Note: Since 2020, the data on cultural relic collections of the museums registered by industry administration have included the data of museums directly under the CPC Central Committee and the non-state-owned museums, the same below.
Source: Beijing Municipal Administration of Cultural Heritage.

22-3 博物馆及其他文物保护管理机构情况(2022年)
STATISTICS FOR MUSEUMS AND OTHER CULTURAL RELIC PROTECTION AND ADMINISTRATION ORGANIZATIONS (2022)

项目		Item		合计 Total	市属 Under the Jurisdiction of the City	区属 Under the Jurisdiction of the District
全市按行业管理登记的博物馆		**Museums Registered by Industry Administration**				
博物馆数	(个)	Museums	(unit)	215	51	47
#正常开放的博物馆数		Museums Normally Open		186	46	45
#免费开放的博物馆数		Museums Open for Free		102	27	28
文物藏品数	(万件)	Cultural Relic Collections	(10000 units)	1784.1		
参观人次	(万人次)	Visitors	(10000 person-times)	2622.9		
文物古迹个数	(处)	Cultural Relics and Historical Sites	(unit)	3840		
文物拍卖机构数	(个)	Organizations of Cultural Relic Auctions	(unit)	285		
举办文物艺术品拍卖场次	(场)	Cultural Relic Auctions	(time)	3317		
文物拍卖标的数	(件、套)	Auction Targets	(unit)	183432		
文物拍卖标的成交金额	(亿元)	Turnover of Cultural Relic Auctions	(100 million yuan)	92.5		
文物局系统内博物馆及文物保护管理机构		**Museums and Cultural Relic Protection and Administration Organizations under the Municipal Administration of Cultural Heritage**				
个数	(个)	Number	(unit)	58	15	43
#博物馆		Museums		33	10	23
博物馆按类别分		Grouped by Category				
综合性		Comprehensive		14	3	11
历史性		Historical		11	5	6
艺术性		Art		2	2	
自然科技类		Natural Science		2		2
其他类		Others		4		4
从业人员	(人)	Employment	(person)	3054	1246	1808
文物藏品数	(万件)	Cultural Relic Collections	(10000 units)	130	118	12
#一级品	(件)	Grade-I Collections	(unit)	1098	651	447
参观人次	(万人次)	Visitors	(10000 person-times)	413.3	116.8	296.5
本年收入	(万元)	Revenues in the Year	(10000 yuan)	183381	99627	83754
#财政收入		Fiscal Revenue		164273	96530	67743
门票收入		Ticket Revenue		5308	700	4608
本年支出	(万元)	Expenditures in the Year	(10000 yuan)	177204	87371	89833

注：全市按行业管理登记的博物馆合计数中包含中央属及非国有博物馆数据。
资料来源：北京市文物局。
Note: The total number of museums registered by industry administration includes the museums directly under the CPC Central Committee and the privately-funded museums.
Source: Beijing Municipal Administration of Cultural Heritage.

22-4 公共图书馆情况(2022年)
STATISTICS FOR PUBLIC LIBRARIES (2022)

项目		Item		合计 Total	中央属 Under Central Jurisdiction	市属 Under the Jurisdiction of the City	区属 Under the Jurisdiction of the District
个数	(个)	Number	(unit)	21	1	1	19
从业人员	(人)	Employed Persons	(person)	2643	1337	372	934
总藏数	(万册、万件)	Total Collections	(10000 volumes)	7819	4327	968	2524
#图书		Books		4996	1741	814	2440
建筑面积	(万平方米)	Building Area	(10000 sq.m)	62.2	27.8	9.4	25.0
阅览座席	(个)	Seating Capacity of Reading Roo	(unit)	23359	5339	3525	14495
总流通人次	(万人次)	Total Number of Visitors	(10000 person-times)	854	177	150	528
#书刊文献外借人次		Person-times Borrowing Books, Magazines and Documents		143	18	10	115
书刊文献外借册次	(万册次)	Volume-times of Borrowed Books, Magazines and Documents	(10000 volume-times)	610	31	50	529

资料来源：北京市文化和旅游局、国家图书馆。
Source: Beijing Municipal Bureau of Culture and Tourism, and National Library of China.

22-5 群众艺术馆、文化馆和文化站情况(2022年)
STATISTICS FOR MASS ART CENTERS, CULTURAL CENTERS AND CULTURAL STATIONS(2022)

项目		Item		合计 Total	群众艺术馆 Mass Art Centers	文化馆 Cultural Centers	文化站 Cultural Stations
个数	(个)	Number	(unit)	357	1	17	339
从业人员	(人)	Employed Persons	(person)	4273	62	920	3291
举办展览个数	(个)	Exhibitions Held	(unit)	1224	3	178	1043
组织文艺活动	(次)	Art Activities Organized	(time)	30971	22	1752	29197

资料来源：北京市文化和旅游局。
Source: Beijing Municipal Bureau of Culture and Tourism.

22-6 档案事业基本情况(2022年)
STATISTICS FOR ARCHIVING INSTITUTIONS (2022)

项目		Item		合计 Total	市属 Under the Jurisdiction of the City	区属 Under the Jurisdiction of the District
档案馆个数	**(个)**	**Number of Archives**	**(unit)**	**18**	**2**	**16**
建筑面积	**(平方米)**	**Building Areas**	**(sq.m)**	**227658**	**125650**	**102008**
馆藏档案情况		**Files Colllected in Archives**				
全宗	(个)	Full Archives	(unit)	3743	1059	2684
纸质档案	(万卷件)	Paper archives	(10000 rolls)	1093.8	386.0	707.9
新中国成立前档案		Files Prior to the Foundation of PRC		100.7	98.8	1.9
新中国成立后档案		Files After the Foundation of PRC		993.1	287.1	706.0
录音、录像、影片档案	(盘)	Tape, Video, and Film Files	(piece)	49839	35642	14197
照片档案	(张)	Photo Files	(disc)	792668	358103	434565
缩微胶片	(万幅)	Microfiches	(10000 rolls)	5621.1	5571.0	50.1
馆藏电子档案	(GB)	Electronic archives in collections	(GB)	52619.8	24530.8	28089.0
#文书类电子档案		Administrative instruments electronic archives		11305.1	41.0	11264.1
数码照片		Digital photo		3604.8	1425.6	2179.2
数字录音录像		Digital audio and video recording		37483.6	23064.2	14419.4
档案利用情况		**File Utilization**				
本年利用档案人次	(人次)	Person-times Using Files in the Year	(person-times)	101320	3654	97666
本年利用档案	(万卷件次)	Files Used in the Year	(10000 roll.times)	31.0	14.5	16.4
本年利用现行文件和资料人次	(人次)	Person-times Using Existing Documents and Data in the Year	(person-times)	437	84	353
本年利用现行文件和资料册次	(件册次)	Existing Documents and Data Books Used in the Year	(roll/volume-times)	898	354	544

资料来源：中共北京市委办公厅(北京市档案局)。
Source: General Office of the CPC Beijing Municipal Committee (Beijing Municipal Archives Bureau).

22-7 电影、电视、广播电台情况(1978-2022年)

年份 Year	电影 Films			电视 TVs		
	放映场次 (万场次) Show Times (10000 times)	观影人次 (万人次) Person-times Watching Film (10000 person-times)	票房收入 (亿元) Ticket Revenue (100 million yuan)	公共电视节目套数 (套) Number of Public TV Programs (unit)	平均每日电视节目播出时间 (小时) Average Daily Hours of TV Programs (hour)	电视综合覆盖率 (%) Comprehensive Coverage Rate of TVs (%)
1978	31.9	29924.1				
1979	35.5	34626.0				
1980	33.1	31189.5		1	4.3	
1981	31.9	30067.0		1	5.5	100.00
1982	32.8	28743.5		1	6.9	91.00
1983	30.1	27345.5		1	7.1	90.00
1984	27.8	23966.7		1	7.2	98.00
1985	23.0	18875.0		1	7.5	98.00
1986	20.6	15904.4		2	19.1	98.00
1987	19.0	13517.7		2	13.6	98.00
1988	19.2	13269.4		2	19.4	98.00
1989	21.5	14492.6		4	25.4	98.00
1990	20.7	12771.2		4	29.4	98.00
1991	21.3	12558.3		4	27.8	98.00
1992	22.1	11587.4		6	45.0	98.00
1993	11.9	5369.8		7	58.2	98.00
1994	10.6	2166.5	0.5	9	77.8	98.30
1995	9.2	1598.6	0.9	12	98.4	98.30
1996	11.5	1644.1	1.1	12	101.0	98.81
1997	12.6	1742.3	1.2	12	111.0	99.12
1998	12.3	1443.5	1.3	12	110.7	99.60
1999	11.7	964.7		12	118.4	99.80
2000	12.2	873.2		12	122.5	99.80
2001	12.6	804.7	0.9	16	200.2	99.91
2002	12.3	827.4	1.1	18	329.4	99.82
2003	11.8	683.0	1.4	19	259.3	99.90
2004	18.1	814.4	1.9	24	244.2	99.50
2005	22.6	873.8	2.3	25	329.8	99.99
2006	28.0	1221.0	3.0	25	294.2	99.99
2007	38.0	1711.0	3.7	25	309.1	99.99
2008	46.8	1767.3	5.4	24	309.1	99.99
2009	62.4	2451.5	8.2	26	319.1	99.99
2010	74.3	2923.3	11.8	26	319.2	99.99
2011	97.4	3235.9	13.5	25	334.2	100.00
2012	120.0	3954.6	16.2	26	343.7	100.00
2013	137.8	4288.5	18.6	26	347.9	100.00
2014	162.8	5281.3	22.9	26	344.0	100.00
2015	198.1	7212.7	31.6	26	351.1	100.00
2016	228.5	6926.7	30.3	26	360.3	100.00
2017	273.9	7701.7	34.0	26	360.5	100.00
2018	309.6	7645.3	35.0	26	375.7	100.00
2019	356.2	7634.1	36.1	26	353.5	100.00
2020	146.0	2117.5	10.3	26	370.2	100.00
2021	335.4	4224.3	22.3	26	446.4	100.00
2022	262.9	2575.4	14.2	27	482.9	100.00

注：1.自2019年起，原“电视节目套数”更名为“公共电视节目套数”，原“广播节目套数”更名为“公共广播节目套数”。
2.自2020年起，原“有线电视用户数”更名为“有线电视实际用户数”。

资料来源：北京市电影局、北京市广播电视局。

STATISTICS FOR FILMS, TELEVISIONS, AND BROADCASTING STATIONS (1978-2022)

电视 TVs			广播电台 Broadcasting Stations		
无线电视综合覆盖率 (%) Comprehensive Coverage Rate of Wireless TVs (%)	有线电视实际用户数 (万户) Actual Number of Cable TV Subscribers (10000 households)	有线电视入户率 (%) Access Rate of Cable TVs (%)	公共广播节目套数 (套) Number of Public Radio Programs (set)	平均每日广播节目播出时间 (小时) Average Daily Show Hours of Radio Programs (hour)	广播综合覆盖率 (%) Comprehensive Coverage Rate of Broadcast (%)
			4	56.1	
			4	57.2	100.00
			4	59.4	98.00
			5	62.0	98.00
			5	73.7	98.00
			5	65.9	98.00
			5	66.2	98.00
			6	68.8	98.00
			6	76.3	98.00
			7	78.7	98.00
			7	77.9	98.00
			7	77.9	98.00
			10	94.8	98.00
			12	134.8	98.00
	52.71		12	134.9	98.00
	82.21		13	148.3	91.00
	182.97		13	150.3	96.97
	202.75		15	156.1	98.44
	230.97		16	174.7	99.98
	165.78	43.24	16	178.2	99.96
	175.71	45.80	16	188.9	97.70
	205.95	51.76	16	192.4	99.91
	231.24	57.05	16	197.4	99.88
	243.00	58.39	16	197.9	99.91
97.57	265.50	62.09	16	229.6	100.00
99.99	282.00	64.12	17	281.9	100.00
94.90	319.58	70.75	17	282.9	100.00
93.13	345.06	74.43	17	288.9	99.98
93.19	383.13	81.00	17	297.4	99.98
94.38	413.50	85.90	18	316.6	99.99
98.72	448.12	91.68	18	324.8	99.99
99.74	475.92	95.90	18	329.6	100.00
99.75	495.70	99.13	25	471.7	100.00
99.75	524.59	103.00	25	473.6	100.00
99.75	551.57	106.85	25	472.6	100.00
99.75	569.13	108.88	25	470.4	100.00
99.75	580.42	109.66	26	493.6	100.00
99.81	586.83	109.04	26	496.3	100.00
99.81	594.55	109.48	26	496.2	100.00
100.00	598.92	109.12	26	499.6	100.00
100.00	606.24	109.35	26	476.7	100.00
100.00	614.67	110.24	19	339.0	100.00
100.00	612.54	109.24	19	340.0	100.00

Note: a) Since 2019, the original Number of TV Programs has been changed to Number of Public TV Programs, and the original Number of Radio Programs has been changed to Number of Public Radio Programs.

b) Since 2020,the original Number of Cable TV Subscribers has been changed to Actual Number of Cable TV Subscribers.

Source: Beijing Municipal Bureau of Film, Beijing Municipal Radio and Television Bureau.

22-8 电影、电视剧制作情况
STATISTICS FOR PRODUCTION OF FILMS AND TV PLAYS

项 目		Item		2022			2021		
				全国 National Total	北京 Beijing	占全国比重(%) As % of National Total	全国 National Total	北京 Beijing	占全国比重(%) As % of National Total
生产电影	(部)	Feature Films	(piece)		135		740	186	25.1
制作电视剧	(部)	TV Plays	(piece)	160	38	23.8	194	41	21.1
	(集)		(episode)	5283	1326	25.1	6736	1580	23.5

资料来源：北京市电影局、北京市广播电视局。
Source: Beijing Municipal Bureau of Film, Beijing Municipal Radio and Television Bureau.

22-9 电影放映单位情况
STATISTICS FOR MOVIE PROJECTION ORGANIZATIONS

项 目		Item		2022	2021
放映单位数	(个)	Number of Projection Organizations	(unit)	292	281
总银幕数	(块)	Total Screens	(piece)	2118	2052
放映场次	(万场次)	Show Times	(10000 times)	262.9	335.4
观影人次	(万人次)	Audience	(10000 person-times)	2575.4	4224.3
票房收入	(亿元)	Ticket Revenues	(100 million yuan)	14.2	22.3

资料来源：北京市电影局。
Source: Beijing Municipal Bureau of Film.

22-10 电视台情况
STATISTICS FOR TELEVISION STATIONS

项 目		Item		2022		2021	
				中 央 Central	地 方 Local	中 央 Central	地 方 Local
基本情况		**Basic Statistics**					
公共电视节目套数	(套)	Number of Public Programs	(set)	36	27	35	26
全年公共电视节目播出时间	(小时)	Annual Broadcast Time of Public Programs	(hour)	299369	176266	296543	162951
播放节目情况		**Shows of TV Programs**					
新闻咨询类节目	(小时)	News and Consulting Programs	(hour)	80985	26783	71044	26162
专题服务类节目	(小时)	Special Service Programs	(hour)	86589	48233	82712	47018
综艺益智类节目	(小时)	Entertainment and Education Programs	(hour)	49338	7831	48731	7779
影视剧类节目	(小时)	Movie and TV Play Programs	(hour)	62710	44211	64398	39355
广告类节目	(小时)	Commercial Programs	(hour)	11131	16857	10997	15151
其他类节目	(小时)	Other Programs	(hour)	8615	32351	8661	27484

资料来源：北京市广播电视局、国家广播电视总局。
Source:Beijing Municipal Radio and Television Bureau, National Radio and Television Administration.

22-11 广播电台情况
STATISTICS FOR BROADCASTING STATIONS

项目	Item	2022 中央 Central	2022 地方 Local	2021 中央 Central	2021 地方 Local
基本情况	**Basic Statistics**				
公共广播节目套数 (套)	Number of Public Programs (set)	23	19	23	19
全年公共广播节目播出时间 (小时)	Annual Broadcast Time of Public Programs (hour)	172127	124049	180127	123731
播放节目情况	**Shows of Radio Programs**				
新闻咨询类节目 (小时)	News and Consulting Programs (hour)	36331	17673	36119	21994
专题服务类节目 (小时)	Special Service Programs (hour)	56512	41092	67049	34079
综艺类节目 (小时)	Entertainment and Education Programs (hour)	68070	37748	65173	43614
广播剧类节目 (小时)	Radio Plays (hour)	3329	5017	3182	5655
广告类节目 (小时)	Commercial Programs (hour)	7238	10613	8149	11029
其他类节目 (小时)	Other Programs (hour)	647	11906	455	7359

注：公共节目套数中含区级广播电视台的广播节目套数。
资料来源：北京市广播电视局、国家广播电视总局。
Note: Public programs included broadcast programs of radio stations at district levels.
Source: Beijing Municipal Radio and Television Bureau, National Radio and Television Administration.

22-12 广播电视综合覆盖率(2022年)
COMPREHENSIVE COVERAGE RATE OF BROADCASTS AND TELEVISIONS (2022)

项目	Item	2022
广播综合覆盖率 (%)	Comprehensive Coverage Rate of Broadcasts (%)	100.00
无线广播综合覆盖率 (%)	Comprehensive Coverage Rate of Radios (%)	100.00
电视综合覆盖率 (%)	Comprehensive Coverage Rate of Televisions (%)	100.00
无线电视综合覆盖率 (%)	Comprehensive Coverage Rate of Wireless Televisions (%)	100.00
有线电视入户率 (%)	Access Rate of Cable TVs (%)	109.24
有线电视实际用户数 (万户)	Actual Number of Cable TV Subscribers (10000 households)	612.54
#高清电视实际用户数	Actual Number of High-definition Interactive Digital Television Subscribers	345.48
#农村有线广播电视实际用户数	Number of Wire Broadcasting and Cable TV Subscribers in Rural Areas	97.79
增值业务用户数 (万户)	Number of Value-added Services Subscribers (10000 households)	80.74

资料来源：北京市广播电视局。
Source: Beijing Municipal Radio and Television Bureau.

22-13 报纸、期刊、图书出版情况(1978-2021年)
STATISTICS FOR NEWSPAPER, JOURNAL AND BOOK PUBLICATIONS (1978-2021)

年份 Year	报纸出版 Newspaper Publications				期刊出版 Journal Publications				图书出版 Book Publications		
	种数(种) Types (kind)	平均期印数(万份) Average Printed Copies Per Issue (10000 copies)	总印数(亿份) Total Printed Copies (100 million copies)	总印张(亿印张) Total Sheets Printed (100 million pieces)	种数(种) Types (kind)	平均期印数(万册) Average Printed Copies Per Issue (10000 copies)	总印数(亿册) Total Printed Copies (100 million copies)	总印张(亿印张) Total Sheets Printed (100 million pieces)	种数(种) Types (kind)	总印数(亿册、亿张) Total Sheets Printed (100 million copies)	总印张(亿印张) Total Sheets Printed (100 million pieces)
1978	11		68.5		468		4.5		5253	5.1	
1979	16		81.6		697		5.9		6723	5.9	
1980	41		84.5		839		5.8		9534	6.3	
1981	55		83.1		886		6.7		11139	7.8	
1982	57		78.3		882		6.7		13862	8.7	
1983	61		79.9		940		6.8		14384	8.5	
1984	73		83.0		987		7.9		15636	8.4	
1985	99		86.0		1098		8.2		17178	9.0	
1986	126		82.0		1206		8.0		19362	5.8	
1987	129		86.0		1409		8.2		21843	6.9	
1988	151		87.0		1514		8.2		23689	7.3	
1989	161		66.0		1580		6.2		25980	6.3	
1990	148		68.0		1415		5.9		27345	6.2	
1991	157		76.7		1499		6.8		29609	7.1	
1992	164	3886	81.4	88.4	1594	6043	7.8	22.3	31320	7.8	58.7
1993	170	3965	81.7	87.7	1597	6037	7.8	22.4	34393	8.6	71.0
1994	233	3759	70.0	92.6	1854	5328	6.3	19.1	38498	8.3	71.7
1995	240	3823	72.9	108.3	1884	5018	6.4	19.6	38819	8.3	70.2
1996	242		70.5		2129		6.1		41572	9.5	
1997	242	3624	71.8	122.2	2162	5396	6.6	22.9	45775	9.9	78.6
1998	247	3561	71.7	130.0	2274	5797	7.3	26.5	50155	11.0	86.1
1999	247	3520	71.7	144.7	2273	6116	8.0	35.2	54783	11.3	93.4
2000	240	3343	68.7	149.6	2352	5909	7.9	33.0	57821	9.6	93.0
2001	243	3339	69.4	153.2	2374	5761	8.1	32.6	63928	10.3	105.1
2002	247	3364	71.0	169.9	2377	5708	8.2	34.3	73836	12.2	127.5
2003	250	3393	72.5	190.4	2382	5702	8.2	34.3	85244	13.8	140.8
2004	253	3405	70.4	206.5	2791	5233	8.0	35.5	98312	15.2	157.2
2005	255	3169	66.2	227.2	2809	4957	7.7	40.8	108152	17.1	180.5
2006	256	3651	74.0	240.4	2809	5077	8.3	47.4	113232	17.2	186.1
2007	256	3454	73.1	218.6	2809	5340	9.2	54.2	125412	18.7	195.3
2008	259	3328	73.2	241.3	2898	5392	9.4	55.4	136284	20.8	220.0
2009	260	3232	71.6	232.5	3030	5373	9.7	59.4	144211	21.0	220.2
2010	262	3406	77.5	275.6	3063	5519	10.0	69.6	155209	21.5	251.2
2011	254	3453	83.1	293.7	3044	5991	10.2	76.7	167942	22.6	243.1
2012	257	3725	89.5	300.2	3064	5940	10.3	76.7	179634	22.5	250.7
2013	254	3737	91.7	298.2	3053	6094	10.4	78.0	192137	24.0	269.5
2014	256	3550	89.9	289.3	3123	5867	10.0	74.0	194259	23.6	258.7
2015	253	3389	87.4	267.5	3168	5539	9.3	68.0	205992	24.5	271.0
2016	252	3297	86.0	259.3	3221	5471	9.1	63.2	213413	26.9	292.0
2017	249	3215	83.9	249.7	3242	5325	8.6	57.1	217765	26.7	294.3
2018	247	3120	83.1	239.9	3244	5299	8.1	55.1	220632	29.7	327.1
2019	246	2981	81.3	219.7	3266	5326	7.9	53.7	216994	31.2	342.2
2020	241	2857	77.7	196.8	3279	5143	7.5	54.3	211863	30.0	327.0
2021	30	111	2.7	8.4	171	129	0.2	1.5	14775	4.0	33.3

注：1.1991年及以前，报纸、期刊、图书为出版数；自1992年起均为总印数。
2.自2021年起，本表统计范围不含中央在京单位，下同。
资料来源：北京市新闻出版局。
Note: a)Figures on newspaper, journals and books in and before 1991 were figures of publications; since 1992, they were total sheet printed.
b)Since 2021, the statistical scope of the sheet does not include central units in Beijing,the same below.
Source: Beijing Municipal Press and Publication Bureau.

22-14 报纸出版情况(2021年)
STATISTICS FOR NEWSPAPER PUBLICATION (2021)

项 目	Item	种 数 (种) Types of Publications (kind)	平均期印数 (万册) Average Printed Copies Per Issue (10000 copies)	总印数 (万册) Total Printed Copies (10000 copies)	总印张 (万印张) Total Sheets Printed (10000 pieces)
合 计	**Total**	**30**	**111.3**	**26900**	**84313.4**
#综合报	Comprehensive	12	66.7	22737	76319.2
专业报	Professional	11	29.4	3435	7051.6

资料来源：北京市新闻出版局。
Source: Beijing Municipal Press and Publication Bureau.

22-15 期刊出版情况(2021年)
STATISTICS FOR JOURNAL PUBLICATION (2021)

项 目	Item	种 数 (种) Types of Publications (kind)	平均期印数 (万册) Average Printed Copies Per Issue (10000 copies)	总印数 (万册) Total Printed Copies (10000 copies)	总印张 (万印张) Total Sheets Printed (10000 pieces)
合 计	**Total**	**171**	**128.6**	**2273**	**14865.6**
综 合	Comprehensive	2	0.1	0.3	7.4
哲学、社会科学	Philosophy and Social Sciences	49	50.6	960	5359.2
自然科学技术	Natural Sciences and Technology	75	20.8	282	2321.3
文化、教育	Culture and Education	33	40.8	821	5131.0
文学、艺术	Literature and Art	12	16.3	209	2046.8

资料来源：北京市新闻出版局。
Source: Beijing Municipal Press and Publication Bureau.

22-16 图书出版情况(2021年)
STATISTICS FOR BOOK PUBLICATION(2021)

项　目	Item	出版图书种数合计(种) Types of Publications (kind)	#新　书 New Publications	总印数(万册、万张) Total Printed Copies (10000 volumes, 10000 pieces)	总印张(万印张) Total Sheets Printed (10000 print sheets)
合　计	**Total**	**14775**	**6242**	**40002**	**333463.7**
使用"中国标准书号"部分合计	**Publications with "China Standard Book Numbering"**	**14775**	**6242**	**40002**	**333463.7**
马列主义、毛泽东思想	Maxism, Leninism, Mao Zedong Thought	12	9	4	90.0
哲　学	Philosophy	341	175	519	7514.6
社会科学总论	General Social Sciences	121	68	118	1312.5
政治、法律	Politics and Law	183	134	265	3756.5
军　事	Military Science	23	12	83	635.1
经　济	Economics	660	339	406	5208.0
文化、科学、教育、体育	Culture, Science, Education and Sports	7161	2279	26408	195096.7
语言、文字	Languages	359	126	687	6529.8
文　学	Literature	3140	1434	7973	71495.4
艺　术	Art	670	468	655	7222.9
历史、地理	History and Geography	677	393	1112	14965.5
自然科学总论	General Natural Sciences	51	28	81	877.4
数学科学、化学	Mathematics and Chemistry	93	41	261	1865.0
天文学、物理科学	Astronomy and Physics	93	48	117	1301.8
生物科学	Biology	175	73	300	2849.5
医药、卫生	Medicine and Healthcare	343	216	316	4486.8
农业科学	Agricultural Sciences	33	12	52	520.8
工业技术	Industrial Technologies	361	216	229	3111.3
交通运输	Transportation	63	41	34	324.2
航空、航天	Aeronautics and Aerospace	27	13	54	255.1
环境科学	Environmental Sciences	27	12	22	237.3
综合性图书	General Books	162	105	306	3807.5
不使用"中国标准书号"部分合计	**Publications without "China Standard Book Numbering"**				

资料来源：北京市新闻出版局。
Source: Beijing Municipal Press and Publication Bureau.

22－17 录音制品出版情况(2021年)
STATISTICS FOR PUBLICATION OF AUDIO PRODUCTS (2021)

项 目	Item	录音带 Audio-tapes		激光唱盘 CDs		高密度激光唱盘及其他 DVDs-A and Others	
		种数(种) Types (kind)	数量(万盒) Number (10000 cassettes)	种数(种) Types (kind)	数量(万张) Number (10000 pieces)	种数(种) Types (kind)	数量(万张) Number (10000 pieces)
合 计	**Total**	**345**	**1599.9**	**1412**	**8347.5**	**210**	**109.1**
#市 属	Municipal	9	3.45	141	63.7	73	67.3

资料来源：北京市新闻出版局。
Source: Beijing Municipal Press and Publication Bureau.

22－18 录像制品出版情况(2021年)
STATISTICS FOR PUBLICATION OF VIDEO PRODUCTS (2021)

项 目	Item	录像带 Videotapes		激光视盘 VCDs		高密度激光视盘 DVD-Vs	
		种数(种) Types (kind)	数量(万盒) Number (10000 cassettes)	种数(种) Kind (kind)	数量(万张) Number (10000 pieces)	种数(种) Types (kind)	数量(万张) Number (10000 pieces)
合 计	**Total**	**363**	**39.1**	**63**	**117.0**	**1216**	**2931.9**
#市 属	Municipal	29	6.4			86	16.0

资料来源：北京市新闻出版局。
Source: Beijing Municipal Press and Publication Bureau.

22－19 电子出版物出版情况(2021年)
STATISTICS FOR PUBLICATION OF E-PUBLICATIONS (2021)

项 目	Item	只读光盘 CD-ROMs		高密度只读光盘 DVD-ROMs		交互式光盘及其他 CD-Is and Others	
		种数(种) Types (kind)	数量(万盒) Number (10000 cassettes)	种数(种) Types (kind)	数量(万张) Number (10000 pieces)	种数(种) Types (kind)	数量(万张) Number (10000 pieces)
合 计	**Total**	**2516**	**21232.3**	**935**	**3947.3**	**543**	**436.9**
#市 属	Municipal	17	0.9	16	22.7	3	0.3

资料来源：北京市新闻出版局。
Source: Beijing Municipal Press and Publication Bureau.

22-20 引进版权量情况
NUMBER OF IMPORTED COPYRIGHTS

单位：件 (set)

项　目	Item	2021	2020
引进版权量	**Number of Imported Copyrights**	**7526**	**7792**
软件和电子出版物	Softwares and E-Publications	15	31
录像制品	Video recordings	12	
图　书	Books	7499	7761

资料来源：北京市新闻出版局。
Source: Beijing Municipal Press and Publication Bureau.

22-21 主要年份文化产业增加值情况
ADDED VALUE OF CULTURAL INDUSTRY IN MAIN YEARS

年　份 Year	增加值 (亿元) Added Value (100 million yuan)	占地区生产总值比重 (%) As % of GDP (%)
2004	398.3	6.4
2008	681.6	5.8
2011	1358.7	7.9
2012	1569.4	8.2
2013	1754.2	8.3
2014	1937.2	8.5
2015	2081.4	8.4
2016	2217.4	8.2
2017	2723.5	9.1
2018	3075.1	9.3
2019	3318.4	9.4
2020	3770.2	10.5
2021	4509.2	11.0

注：2004—2012年文化产业增加值仅包括法人单位数据，自2013年起为包括个体经营户在内的全口径数据。
Note: The figures on the added value of cultural industry for 2004 to 2012 included the data of legal entities only; and figures for and after 2013 were those of full coverage including data of self-employed businesses.

22-22 规模以上文化产业企业经营情况(2013-2022年) OPERATION OF CULTURAL INDUSTRY ENTERPRISES ABOVE DESIGNATED SIZE (2013-2022)

年 份 Year	企业单位数 (个) Number of Enterprises (unit)	年末从业人员 (万人) Employed Persons at Year-end (10000 persons)	资产总计 (亿元) Total Assets (100 million yuan)	营业收入 (亿元) Business Income (100 million yuan)	利润总额 (亿元) Total Profits (100 million yuan)
2013	3981	41.6	5731.0	5155.2	390.2
2014	3820	47.8	7937.9	6876.9	495.6
2015	3418	47.4	9419.6	7548.1	550.8
2016	3539	48.1	10870.2	8195.4	530.5
2017	3994	54.1	13887.9	9586.0	802.9
2018	3887	53.7	16579.0	10963.0	852.7
2019	4831	54.2	19020.3	12997.3	739.1
2020	5119	56.0	23738.4	14944.0	1324.4
2021	5309	59.9	28067.4	17628.6	1458.0
2022	5450	54.9	29934.9	17797.3	1949.1

22-23 规模以上文化产业法人单位基本情况(2022年) BASIC STATISTICS OF LEGAL ENTITIES OF CULTURAL INDUSTRY ABOVE DESIGNATED SIZE (2022)

项 目	Item	资产总计 (亿元) Total Assets (100 million yuan)	收入合计 (亿元) Total Income (100 million yuan)	年末从业人员 (万人) Employed Persons at Year-end (10000 persons)
合 计	**Total**	**31153.3**	**18259.5**	**61.2**
文化核心领域	**Core Fields of Culture**	**29235.4**	**16508.4**	**52.0**
新闻信息服务	News and Information Service	8099.4	5065.3	11.9
内容创作生产	Content Creation and Production	10701.0	4904.7	18.4
创意设计服务	Creative Design Service	3377.4	3636.5	10.7
文化传播渠道	Culture Transmission Channel	4268.6	2726.8	7.7
文化投资运营	Cultural Investment and Operation	1856.3	48.2	0.3
文化娱乐休闲服务	Cultural, Entertainment and Recreational Service	932.7	126.8	3.0
文化相关领域	**Culture-related Fields**	**1917.9**	**1751.1**	**9.3**
文化辅助生产和中介服务	Cultural Auxiliary Production and Intermediary Service	1242.0	751.5	7.6
文化装备生产	Cultural Equipment Production	228.1	97.4	0.7
文化消费终端生产	Cultural Consumption Terminal Production	447.8	902.1	1.0

注:规模以上文化产业法人单位包括企业法人单位和事业单位。
Note: Legal entities of cultural industry above designated size include the legal bodies of enterprise and the public institutions.

22-24 主要年份体育场地情况
SITUATION OF THE GYMNASIUMS AND STADIUMS IN MAIN YEARS

单位：个 (unit)

年份 Year	合计 Total	#体育场 Stadiums	#体育馆 Gymnasiums	#游泳场馆 Natatoriums		#各种训练房 Exercise Rooms
					#室内 Indoor	
1950	19	1				2
1955	61	1		2	2	10
1960	124	2		4	3	19
1970	188	2	2	8	3	24
1975	234	3	2	11	4	28
1980	293	3	2	12	4	32
1985	405	4	2	20	8	54
1990	780	12	12	49	26	153
1995	1381	18	18	88	56	291
2000	2815	35	24	214	161	863
2001	3500	42	27	283	216	1101
2002	4176	57	33	334	263	1358
2003	6100	93	36	443	371	1729
2004	6104	93	36	443	371	1729
2005	6112	93	36	446	374	1731
2006	6122	93	36	446	374	1734
2007	6146	94	37	446	374	1736
2008	6149	94	37	446	374	1739
2009	6149	94	37	446	374	1739
2010	6151	94	37	446	374	1741
2011	6151	94	37	446	374	1741
2012	6156	94	37	447	375	1742
2013	20075	131	70	590	548	2836

注：自2013年起，体育场地数据不再按年度进行统计，年度数据可参考第六次全国体育场地普查数据(普查时点为2013年12月31日)，最新数据将于第七次体育场地普查结束后更新。

资料来源：北京市体育局。

Note: The data on gymnasiums and stadiums were not analyzed by year since 2013; for annual data, please refer to the data of the six thnational census on gymnasiums and stadiums (date of census: December 31st, 2013). The latest data shall be updated after the end of the seventh national census on gymnasiums and stadiums.

Source: Beijing Municipal Bureau of Sports.

22-25 体育场地情况(2018-2022年)
SITUATION OF THE GYMNASIUMS AND STADIUMS (2018-2022)

项目	Item	2018	2019	2020	2021	2022
综合指标	**Comprehensive Indicators**					
人均体育场地面积 (平方米)	Per capita Area of Gymnasiums and Stadiums (sq.m)	2.32	2.45	2.57	2.69	2.90
体育场地数量 (万个)	Number of Gymnasiums and Stadiums (10000 units)	3.16	3.57	3.86	4.24	4.28
基础运动场地 (个)	**Gymnasiums and Stadiums for Basic Sports (unit)**					
田径场地	Track-and-Field Ground	1771	1772	1878	1914	2015
游泳场地	Natatorium	904	912	925	903	941
球类运动场地 (个)	**Gymnasiums and Stadiums for Ball Games (unit)**					
足球场地	Football Pitch	1785	1915	2356	2467	2518
篮球场地	Basketball Court	6087	6150	7033	7273	7447
排球场地	Volleyball Court	280	296	401	415	431
乒乓球场地	Table Tennis Court	4358	6199	6295	6536	6587
羽毛球场地	Badminton Court	949	1152	1242	1448	1403
冰雪运动场地 (个)	**Gymnasiums and Stadiums for Ice & Snow Sports (unit)**					
滑冰场地	Skating Ground	65	72	82	112	124
滑雪场地	Skiing Field	22	28	35	35	33
体育健身场地	**Gymnasiums and Stadiums for Physical Fitness and Exercise**					
全民健身路径 (个)	Public Fitness Path (unit)	9064	9984	11382	12626	12306
健身房 (个)	Gym (unit)	2773	2789	2886	4067	4112
健身步道 (公里)	Fitness Footpath (km)	635.0	1001.9	1106.9	1289.6	2517.8

注：本表为北京市全国体育场地统计调查数据。
资料来源：北京市体育局。
Note: Data in this table are the statistical survey data of the national gymnasiums and stadiums of Beijing.
Source: Beijing Municipal Bureau of Sports.

22-26 运动员、裁判员情况
ATHLETES AND REFEREES

单位：人 (person)

项目	Item	2022	#女性 Females	2021	#女性 Females
分等级运动员发展人数	**Number of Graded Athletes**	**2524**	**1045**	**2272**	**893**
一级	First Grade Athletes	764	342	811	351
二级	Second Grade Athletes	1760	703	1461	542
分等级裁判员发展人数	**Number of Graded Referees**	**933**	**301**	**1390**	**504**
一级	First Grade Referees	183	76	384	144
二级	Second Grade Referees	750	225	1006	360

资料来源：北京市体育局。
Source: Beijing Municipal Bureau of Sports.

22-27 运动员获奖牌情况(2022年)
STATISTICS FOR MEDALS WON (2022)

单位：块 (piece)

项目	Item	金牌 Gold	银牌 Silver	铜牌 Copper
合计	**Total**	**78**	**71**	**79**
国际比赛	International Competitions	10	8	2
国内比赛	Domestic Competitions	68	63	77

资料来源：北京市体育局。
Source: Beijing Municipal Bureau of Sports.

22–28 体育彩票
SPORTS LOTTERY

项　　目	Item	2022	2021
电脑体育彩票销售点数 （个）	Number of Computer Sports Lottery Tickets Sold (unit)	3016	2661
体育彩票发行额 （万元）	Circulation of Sports Lottery (10000 yuan)	728816	660749
体育彩票公益金提取额 （万元）	Public Welfare Funds Drawn from Sports Lottery (10000 yuan)	180139	169014

资料来源：北京市体育局。
Source: Beijing Municipal Bureau of Sports.

22–29 体育产业增加值情况(2015–2021年)
ADDED VALUE OF SPORT INDUSTRY(2015-2021)

年　份 Year	增加值 (亿元) Added Value (100 million yuan)	占地区生产总值比重 (%) As % of GDP (%)
2015	225.2	0.91
2016	251.3	0.93
2017	289.7	0.97
2018	326.3	0.99
2019	345.4	0.97
2020	309.3	0.86
2021	340.1	0.83

主要统计指标解释

文　化

文化及相关产业（文化产业）　是指为社会公众提供文化产品和文化相关产品的生产活动的集合。

公共图书馆藏书　指各级文化部门举办的面向社会服务的独立的图书馆（不包括文化馆的图书室，也不包括文化系统以外的图书馆）藏书数量。

广播综合覆盖率　根据国家广电总局制定的《广播电视人口覆盖率统计技术标准和方法》进行统计调查的，在对象区内能接收到广播节目的覆盖人口数占本行政区域内人口总数的比率。

无线广播综合覆盖率　根据国家广电总局制定的《广播电视人口覆盖率统计技术标准和方法》进行统计调查的，在对象区内能接收到用中、短波、调频等无线传输技术发射转播的广播节目的人口数占本行政区域内人口总数的比率。包括中央、省、地市、县四级无线广播综合覆盖人口。

电视综合覆盖率　根据国家广电总局制定的《广播电视人口覆盖率统计技术标准和方法》进行统计调查的，在对象区内能接收到电视节目的人口数占本行政区域内人口总数的比率，包括中央、省、地市、县电视节目综合覆盖人口。

无线电视综合覆盖率　根据国家广电总局制定的《广播电视人口覆盖率统计技术标准和方法》进行统计调查的，在对象区内能接收到用中、短波、调频等无线传输技术发射转播的电视节目的人口数占本行政区域内人口总数的比率。包括中央、省、地市、县四级无线电视综合覆盖人口。

有线电视入户率　指通过广播电视有线传输网收看电视节目的家庭用户数（包括接收模拟信号和接收数字信号的有线电视用户数，不包括宾馆、单位、写字楼等集体用户）与本行政区域内总户数的比率。

有线电视实际用户数　指通过广播电视有线传输网收看电视节目的用户数。

体　育

体育产业　是指为社会提供各种体育产品（货物和服务）和体育相关产品的生产活动的集合。

体育场地　指专门用于体育训练、比赛和健身活动的，有一定投资的公益性或经营性体育建筑设施，包括必要的附属功能用房。

等级运动员人数　指经考核正式批准授予等级运动员称号的人数。运动员等级分为国际级运动健将、国家级运动健将、一级运动员、二级运动员、三级运动员、少年级运动员。

等级裁判员人数　指经考核正式批准授予等级裁判员称号的人数。裁判员等级分为国际级裁判、国家级裁判、一级裁判、二级裁判、三级裁判。

运动员获奖牌情况　指当年北京市运动员在世界比赛、亚洲比赛、全国比赛中获得金、银、铜牌的数量。

Explanatory Notes on Main Statistical Indicators

Culture

Cultural and Related Industries (Cultural Industry) means the collection of production activities that provide the public with cultural products and culture related products.

Collection of Books in Public Libraries means the number of books collected in independent libraries open to the public and run by all-level cultural bodies (excluding book rooms in cultural centers, and libraries not included in the cultural system).

Comprehensive Coverage Rate of Broadcast means the share of population who can receive broadcasting programs in the target area, calculated in line with the *Statistical Standard and Method on Television and Radio Coverage of Population* established by the National Radio and Television Administration, of the total population in the administrative area.

Comprehensive Coverage Rate of Radio means the share of population who can receive broadcasting programs transmitted with short-wave, medium-wave, FM and other radio transmission technologies in the target area, calculated in line with the *Statistical Standard and Method on Television and Radio Coverage of Population* established by the National Radio and Television Administration, of the total population in the administrative area, including the population covered by broadcasting programs from central, provincial, prefectural cities and county radio stations.

Comprehensive Coverage Rate of TV means the share of population who can receive TV programs in the target area, calculated in line with the *Statistical Standard and Method on Television and Radio Coverage of Population* established by the National Radio and Television Administration, of the total population in the administrative area, including the population covered by TV programs from central, provincial, prefectural cities and county TV stations.

Comprehensive Coverage Rate of Wireless TV means the share of population who can receive TV programs transmitted with short-wave, medium-wave, FM and other radio transmission technologies in the target area, calculated in line with the *Statistical Standard and Method on Television and Radio Coverage of Population* established by the National Radio and Television Administration, of the total population in the administrative area, including the population covered by wireless television programs from central, provincial, prefectural cities and county TV stations.

Access Rate of Cable TVs refers to the percentage of households which can watch television programs through the cable broadcasting and television transmission network (including cable TV households receiving analog signals and digital signals, excluding collective subscribers such as hotels, companies and entities, office buildings), to the total households in the administrative area.

Actual Number of Cable TV Subscribers means the number of subscribers watching television programs through the cable broadcasting and television transmission network.

Sports

Sports Industry refers to the collection of production activities that provide the society with various sports products (goods and services) and sports related products.

Sports Venues refer to sports building facilities, including necessary ancillary functional rooms, for public welfare or operating purpose, specially used for sports training, games and fitness activities, and with certain investment.

Number of Graded Athletes means the number of athletes formally granted with the title of graded athlete upon examination. Grades of athletes include international master sportsman, national maser sportsman, grade-I athlete, grade-II athlete, grade-III athlete and juvenile athlete.

Number of Graded Referees means the number of referees formally granted with the title of graded referees upon examination. Grades of referees include international referee, national referee, grade-I referee, grade-II referee and grade-III referee.

Medals Won by Athletes mean the number of gold, silver and copper medals won by athletes of Beijing in world games, Asian games and national games.

公共管理、社会保障和社会组织

PUBLIC MANAGEMENT, SOCIAL SECURITY AND SOCIAL ORGANIZATION

简要说明

主要内容

本章资料主要包括社会活动参与、公检法司、社会保障、妇女及儿童发展规划监测情况等。

1.社会活动参与部分主要包括历届北京市人大代表和政协委员人数及议案情况、妇联组织和工会组织等情况。

2.公检法司部分主要包括公安机关、法院、检察院的收案、结案情况，交通事故、安全生产情况，以及司法局提供的律师、公证、调解工作等情况。

3.社会保障部分主要包括社会保障相关待遇标准和参加社会保障情况。

4.妇女与儿童发展规划监测资料主要包括妇女的社会保障、妇女参与决策和管理、教育、健康、家庭建设、法律保护等情况及儿童的健康、教育、环境、法律保护等情况。

Brief Introduction

Main Content

Statistics in this chapter mainly consist of statistics for social activity participation, public security institutions, procuratorates, courts, judicial authorities, social security, women and children development planning and monitoring.

1. Statistics for social activity participation mainly consist of the numbers of deputies and proposals at people's congress and political consulting conferences of Beijing in previous years, women's federation organizations and labor unions.

2. Statistics for public security institutions, procuratorates, courts, and judicial authorities cover the cases accepted and settled by public security organs, courts and procuratorates, the statistics on traffic accidents, safe production, and the information on lawyers, notary, mediation provided by juridical bureaus.

3. Statistics for social security mainly consist of the social security benefits level and the social security participation.

4. Supervisory data on women and children development programs are mainly composed of women's social security, participation in decision making and management, education, health, family building, and legal protection etc. as well as children's health, education, environment, legal protection, and so on.

23-1 历届北京市人代会代表人数性别构成及议案、建议数 NUMBER AND SEX COMPOSITION OF DEPUTIES, NUMBERS OF PROPOSALS AND SUGGESTIONS OF ALL THE PREVIOUS BEIJING MUNICIPAL PEOPLE'S CONGRESS

项目 Item	代表人数(人) Number of Deputies (person)			性别比例(%) Sex Percentage (%)		议案立案数(件) Number of Proposals on Record (case)	建议数(件) Suggestions (case)
		女性 Females	男性 Males	女性 Females	男性 Males		
第一届 1st	564	106	458	18.8	81.2		
第二届 2nd	619	142	477	22.9	77.1		
第三届 3rd	618	162	456	26.2	73.8		
第四届 4th	745	202	543	27.1	72.9		
第五届 5th	751	203	548	27.0	73.0		
第七届 7th	1195	325	870	27.1	72.9		
第八届 8th	973	252	721	25.9	74.1	55	6644
第九届 9th	880	217	663	24.7	75.3	86	7921
第十届 10th	885	224	661	25.3	74.7	156	7281
第十一届 11th	763	197	566	25.8	74.2	166	9717
第十二届 12th	762	235	527	30.8	69.2	276	9859
第十三届 13th	771	236	535	30.6	69.4	153	7576
第十四届 14th	771	257	514	33.3	66.7	157	6136
第十五届 15th	771	296	475	38.4	61.6	262	4018
第十六届 16th	774	309	465	39.9	60.1		

注：1.北京市人大常委会是经北京市七届三次人民代表大会选举成立的，故一至七届人代会无议案及建议数。
2.代表人数为届首选举数，议案立案数及建议数均为本届五年会上及平时议案立案及建议的合计数。
资料来源：北京市人民代表大会常务委员会。

Note: a) Standing Committee of Beijing People's Congress was established upon election at the 3rd Session of Beijing 7th People's Congress. As a result, there were no proposals and suggestions at the 1st-7th People's Congresses.
b) Deputies were those first elected for that term. Number of proposals on record and suggestions included those at the meeting of the term and/or at ordinary times.

Source: Standing Committee of Beijing Municipal People's Congress (BMPC).

23-2 历届北京市政协会委员人数及提案立案数
NUMBER OF MEMBERS AND PROPOSALS OF ALL THE PREVIOUS BEIJING CPPCC

届别 Term		起止年月 Beginning-ending Month	委员人数（人） Number of Members (person)			提案立案数（件） Number of Proposals on Record (case)
				女性 Females	男性 Males	
第一届	1st	1955.04-1959.09	270	40	230	37
第二届	2nd	1959.09-1962.12	463	84	379	13
第三届	3rd	1962.12-1965.09	519	92	427	884
第四届	4th	1965.09-1977.11	529	88	441	23
第五届	5th	1977.11-1983.03	779	161	618	1610
第六届	6th	1983.03-1988.01	766	168	598	3122
第七届	7th	1988.01-1993.01	703	179	524	4276
第八届	8th	1993.01-1998.01	740	185	555	4975
第九届	9th	1998.01-2003.01	782	203	579	6240
第十届	10th	2003.01-2008.01	824	226	598	6871
第十一届	11th	2008.01-2013.01	737	233	504	5354
第十二届	12th	2013.01-2018.01	758	237	521	5410
第十三届	13th	2018.01-2023.01	761	261	500	6514
第十四届	14th	2023.01-	760	237	523	1092

资料来源：中国人民政治协商会议北京市委员会。
Source: The Chinese People's Political Consultative Conference Beijing Committe.

23-3 公安、法院、检察院收案、结案情况(2005-2022年)

项　目	Item	2005	2006	2007	2008	2009
公安机关办理案件	Cases Handled by Public Security Departments					
刑事案件立案情况	Criminal case filing status					
立　案 (起)	Cases Put on File (case)	107988	120554	127446	90045	98750
法院办理案件	Cases Handled by Courts					
刑事案件收、结案情况	Criminal Cases Accepted and Settled in Courts					
收　案 (件)	Cases Accepted (case)	17488	17725	19592	20024	18819
结　案 (件)	Cases Settled (case)	17624	17701	19536	20004	18773
婚姻家庭、继承纠纷案件收、结案情况	Marriage and Inheritance Dispute Cases Accepted and Settled in Courts					
收　案 (件)	Cases Accepted (case)	26739	27860	28089	30402	33056
结　案 (件)	Cases Settled (case)	27002	27845	27916	29499	32902
合同纠纷案件收、结案情况	Contract Dispute Cases Accepted and Settled in Courts					
收　案 (件)	Cases Accepted (case)	133534	141485	135099	144948	153766
结　案 (件)	Cases Settled (case)	135612	141439	134829	140512	152128
权属、侵权纠纷及其他民事案件收、结案情况	Ownership, Infringement Dispute and Other Civil Cases Accepted and Settled in Courts					
收　案 (件)	Cases Accepted (case)	42690	44890	46892	53864	58057
结　案 (件)	Cases Settled (case)	43166	45005	46372	51668	57135
检察机关办理案件	Cases Handled by Procuratorial Organs					
审查逮捕案件	Arrest Cases to Be Examined and Approved					
收　案 (件)	Cases Accepted (case)	17441	18137	19126	16584	17593
结　案 (件)	Cases Settled (case)	16398	16795	17210	16562	17606
审查起诉案件	Cases of prosecution to be reviewed and made					
收　案 (件)	Cases Accepted (case)	19672	19869	21462	20137	20453
结　案 (件)	Cases Settled (case)	17899	18517	20394	19047	19989

资料来源：北京市公安局、北京市人民检察院、北京市高级人民法院。

CASES ACCEPTED AND SETTLED BY PUBLIC SECURITY DEPARTMENTS, COURTS AND PROCURATORATES (2005-2022)

2010	2011	2012	2013	2014	2015	2016	2017	2018	2019	2020	2021	2022
104327	142835	145724	140498	153334	174374	150312	140250	138696	138291	137728	144711	116575
19824	19574	22168	19109	20556	19980	16737	18584	17091	20320	16440	21513	12082
19870	19423	22084	19012	20357	19667	16905	18628	17062	19582	15796	20837	12468
36799	35251	35418	37347	39390	43869	43141	50467	52675	49077	35187	48507	33101
37160	35149	35201	35296	38565	40436	43606	51800	52950	49402	34753	43256	32411
148655	144433	145017	149237	162893	237850	253456	279287	347240	343861	261610	334410	259513
153130	144766	143153	141642	155472	207012	255852	285872	346884	338714	261681	296185	268087
64379	65972	62736	64747	69541	85554	100574	114284	109296	119759	119735	173375	134058
65763	66405	62235	61688	67444	76644	100399	115125	110443	118326	119037	148058	135679
18060	18279	18563	16861	16594	14880	14307	16651	17359	19995	14525	20195	13920
17946	18208	18644	16860	16606	14840	14265	16663	17318	19992	14507	20347	13932
20982	20986	23553	21798	22251	20181	18786	21039	20311	24023	17850	25164	17491
19825	20293	21980	20684	22455	19935	18361	20807	19688	22825	18297	25276	17149

Source: Beijing Municipal Bureau of Public Security, the People's Procuratorate of Beijing, and the People's High Court of Beijing.

23-4 公安机关刑事案件立案情况
STATISTICS FOR CRIMINAL CASES PUT ON FILE BY PUBLIC SECURITY ORGANS

单位：起 (case)

项目	Item	立案 Cases Put on File	
		2022	2021
刑事案件	**Criminal Cases**	**116575**	**144711**
杀人	Homicide	142	165
伤害	Injury	1433	1866
抢劫	Robbery	63	90
强奸	Rape	514	661
盗窃	Larceny	13424	26758
诈骗	Fraud	78660	83316
其他	Others	22339	31855

资料来源：北京市公安局。
Source: Beijing Municipal Bureau of Public Security.

23-5 公安机关治安案件查处情况
STATISTICS FOR CASES AGAINST PUBLIC ORDER INVESTIGATED AND HANDLED BY PUBLIC SECURITY ORGANS

单位：起 (case)

项目	Item	查处 Cases Investigated and Handled	
		2022	2021
治安案件	**Cases Against Public Order**	**709385**	**637283**
扰乱公共场所秩序	Disturbing Orders in Public Venues	15089	14224
寻衅滋事	Causing Quarrels and Making Troubles	20579	18500
阻碍执行职务	Obstructing Government Officials in Performing Their Duties	1602	2208
殴打他人	Battering Other Persons	113789	119187
盗窃	Larceny	152525	159435
抢夺	Robbery and Snatch	216	187
伪造、变造、倒卖有价票证、凭证	Forge, Alter, Scalp Valuable Coupons or Certificates	63	201
诈骗	Fraud	100426	91918
卖淫、嫖娼	Prostitution or Soliciting Prostitutes	7291	8634
赌博	Gambling	8807	7525
其他	Others	288998	215264

资料来源：北京市公安局。
Source: Beijing Municipal Bureau of Public Security.

23−6 检察机关办理各类案件情况(2022年)
STATISTICS FOR CASES HANDLED BY PROCURATORIAL ORGANS (2022)

项 目	Item	受案(受理) Cases Accepted		审结案合计 Cases Settled	
		件 Case	人 Person	件 Case	人 Person
审查逮捕案件	**Arrests to Be Examined and Approved**	**13920**	**20060**	**13932**	**20104**
批准逮捕	Approved			6681	8763
不批准逮捕	Disapproved			7251	11341
审查起诉案件	**Prosecution to Be Reviewed and Made**	**17491**	**22110**	**17149**	**21735**
起 诉	Prosecuted			12218	15452
不起诉	Non-prosecution			4863	6190
附条件不起诉	Conditional Non-prosecution			68	93
举报案件	**Reported Cases**				
控告案件	**Complaints**	**651**		**562**	
申诉案件	**Appeal Cases**	**5776**		**5160**	
民事检察案件	**Civil Cases**	**10823**		**10534**	
行政检察案件	**Administrative Cases**	**3203**		**3066**	

资料来源：北京市人民检察院。
Source: The People's Procuratorate of Beijing.

23−7 法院行政案件收、结案情况(2022年)
STATISTICS FOR ADMINISTRATIVE CASES ACCEPTED AND SETTLED BY COURT (2022)

单位：件 (case)

项 目	Item	收 案 Cases Accepted	结 案 Cases Settled	#判 决 Judgment	#裁 定 Mediation
合 计	**Total**	**31107**	**28625**	**20825**	**7125**
公 安	Public Security	1377	1406	610	749
资 源	Resources	495	516	172	336
城 建	City Construction	1394	1452	465	957
工 商	Industry and Commerce	883	926	269	381
专 利	Patents	1802	1610	1442	163
劳动和社会保障	Labor and Social Security	371	428	292	131
教 育	Education	92	93	25	60
其 他	Others	24693	22194	17550	4348

注：法院行政案件收结案为一审审结数。
资料来源：北京市高级人民法院。
Note: The statistics for administrative cases accepted and settled by court refer to the number of concluded cases at the first trial.
Source: Higher People's Court of Beijing Municipality.

23-8 法院刑事案件收、结案情况(2022年)
STATISTICS FOR CRIMINAL CASES ACCEPTED AND SETTLED BY COURT (2022)

项目	Item	收案(件) Cases Accepted (case)	结案(件) Cases Settled (case)	判决发生法律效力 Judgment with Legal Forces 件数(件) Number of Cases (case)	人数(人) Number of Persons(person)
合计	**Total**	**12082**	**12468**	**12679**	**16277**
#危害公共安全罪	Offences against Public Security	3324	3357	3527	3591
破坏社会主义市场经济秩序罪	Offences against the Socialist Market Economy Order	1099	1347	1400	2679
侵犯公民人身权利、民主权利罪	Offences against Civil Personal Rights and Democratic Rights	1683	1721	1695	1831
侵犯财产罪	Offences against Property	3239	3254	3290	4255
妨害社会管理秩序罪	Offences against Social Administration	2479	2545	2522	3662
危害国防利益罪	Offences against National Defense Interest	18	20	22	25
贪污贿赂罪	Crimes of Corruption and Bribery	197	179	193	201
渎职罪	Crimes of Misconduct in Office	33	30	26	29

注：法院刑事案件收结案为一审审结数。
资料来源：北京市高级人民法院。
Note: The statistics for criminal cases accepted and settled by court refer to the number of concluded cases at the first trial.
Source: Higher People's Court of Beijing Municipality.

23-9 法院婚姻家庭、继承纠纷案件收、结案情况(2022年)
STATISTICS FOR MARRIAGE AND FAMILY AND INHERITANCE DISPUTE CASES ACCEPTED AND SETTLED BY COURT (2022)

单位：件 (case)

项目	Item	收案 Cases Accepted	结案 Cases Settled	#判决 Judgment	#调解 Mediation
合计	**Total**	**33101**	**32411**	**10944**	**12182**
婚姻家庭纠纷	**Marriage and Family Disputes**	**22341**	**22224**	**8267**	**7427**
离婚	Divorces	14042	13777	4927	5137
同居关系	Cohabitation	187	180	71	39
抚养纠纷	Upbringing Disputes	1980	2057	905	601
扶养纠纷	Maintenance Disputes	43	44	17	12
赡养纠纷	Support Disputes	679	643	342	93
分家析产	Family Property Division	2546	2566	799	895
其他	Others	2864	2957	1206	650
继承纠纷	**Inheritance Disputes**	**10760**	**10187**	**2677**	**4755**
继承	Inheritance	3007	2843	746	1381
法定继承	Legal Inheritance	5848	5623	1237	2848
遗嘱继承	Testamentary Inheritance	1315	1157	444	417
其他	Others	590	564	250	109

注：法院婚姻家庭、继承纠纷案件收、结案为一审审结案数。
资料来源：北京市高级人民法院。
Note: The statistics for marriage and family and inheritance dispute cases accepted and settled by court refer to the number of concluded cases at the first trial.
Source: Higher People's Court of Beijing Municipality.

23-10 法院合同纠纷案件收、结案情况(2022年)
STATISTICS FOR CONTRACT CASES ACCEPTED AND SETTLED BY COURT (2022)

单位：件 (case)

项　　目	Item	收　案 Cases Accepted	结　案 Cases Settled	#判　决 Judgment	#调　解 Mediation
合　　计	**Total**	**259513**	**268087**	**137691**	**38688**
买卖合同纠纷	Trade Contracts	27145	26314	10078	5664
房地产开发经营合同纠纷	Real Estate Development & Operation Contracts	43	43	30	1
供电、水、气、热力合同纠纷	Electricity, Water, Gas, Heating Supply contracts	8874	8583	1958	513
借款合同纠纷	Loan Contracts	57316	58639	36061	8567
租赁合同纠纷	Lease Contracts	23011	23586	11355	3696
建设工程合同纠纷	Construction Contracts	9132	8819	3952	1748
承揽合同纠纷	Contracts for Hire of Work	3007	3045	1256	653
运输合同纠纷	Transportation Contracts	1047	1051	533	193
土地承包经营权合同纠纷	Contracts for the Right to Land Contracting and Management	698	859	469	57
劳务合同纠纷	Labor Contracts	8700	8770	3434	1925
服务合同纠纷	Service Contracts	28963	33874	16855	4453
其　他	Others	91577	94504	51710	11218

注：法院合同纠纷案件收结案为一审审结数。
资料来源：北京市高级人民法院。
Note: The statistics for contract cases accepted and settled by court refer to the number of concluded cases at the first trial.
Source: Higher People's Court of Beijing Municipality.

23-11 法院权属、侵权纠纷及其他民事案件收、结案情况(2022年)
STATISTICS FOR OWNERSHIP, TORTIOUS DISPUTES AND OTHER CIVIL CASES ACCEPTED AND SETTLED BY COURT (2022)

单位：件 (case)

项目	Item	收案 Cases Accepted	结案 Cases Settled	#判决 Judgment	#调解 Mediation
合计	**Total**	**134058**	**135679**	**59494**	**17717**
所有权纠纷	Ownership Disputes	2966	2785	1242	429
票据纠纷	Disputes on Bills	3410	3161	1561	579
证券纠纷	Disputes on Securities	3560	4359	70	10
与公司有关的纠纷	Disputes Relating to Companies	5070	4926	2524	300
不正当竞争纠纷	Unfair Competition Disputes	783	706	234	72
人格权纠纷	Personality Disputes	4764	4623	2658	620
侵权责任纠纷	Tort Liability Disputes	24036	23502	13066	3720
适用特别程序案件(一级案由)	Special-proceeding Cases (Primary Cause of Action)	5191	4709	2994	26
其他	Others	84278	86908	35145	11961

注：法院权属、侵权纠纷及其他民事案件收、结案为一审审结数。
资料来源：北京市高级人民法院。
Note: The statistics for ownership, tortious disputes and other civil cases accepted and settled by court refer to the number of concluded cases at the first trial.
Source: Higher People's Court of Beijing Municipality.

23-12 离婚、青少年刑事案犯情况
STATISTICS FOR DIVORCE AND JUVENILE CRIMINAL CASES

项目	Item	2022	2021
婚姻家庭纠纷案件数(结案) (件)	Marriage and Family Disputes (Closed) (case)	22341	28751
#离婚案件数	Divorce Cases	14042	15760
#调离案件数	Cases of Divorce Reconciled	5101	5518
判离案件数	Cases of Divorce Judged	2361	2564
青少年罪犯人数 (人)	Teenager Offenders (person)	1765	2675
14周岁以上不满16周岁罪犯人数	Teenager Offenders 14-16	8	9
16周岁以上不满18周岁罪犯人数	Teenager Offenders 16-18	76	107
18周岁以上不满25周岁罪犯人数	Teenager Offenders 18-25	1681	2559
青少年刑事案犯占全部刑事案犯的比重 (%)	Teenager Criminal Offenders as % of Total Criminal Offenders (%)	10.9	10.5

注：婚姻家庭纠纷案件数为一审审结数。
资料来源：北京市高级人民法院。
Note: The number of marriage and family disputes refers to the number of concluded cases at the first trial.
Source: Higher People's Court of Beijing Municipality.

23-13 律师工作
STATISTICS FOR LAWYERS

项目		Item		2022	2021	2022年为2021年% 2022 as % of 2021
律师事务所	(个)	Law Firms	(unit)	3297	3108	106.1
执业律师	(人)	Number of Practicing Lawyers	(person)	46971	42163	111.4
专职律师		Full-time Lawyers		42057	37590	111.9
兼职律师		Part-time Lawyers		2132	1420	150.1
公司律师		Company Lawyers		1049	1231	85.2
公职律师		Government Lawyers		1733	1789	96.9
法律援助律师		Legal Aid Lawyers			133	
担任法律顾问	(家)	Legal Counsel	(unit)	33217	30278	109.7
民事诉讼代理	(件)	Civil Case Litigation Agencies	(case)	142721	164134	87.0
行政诉讼代理	(件)	Administrative Case Litigation Agencies	(case)	27956	28625	97.7
刑事诉讼辩护及代理	(件)	Criminal Case Litigation Agencies	(case)	21994	25043	87.8
非诉讼法律事务	(件)	Off-court Cases	(case)	133671	188676	70.8

资料来源：北京市司法局。
Source: Beijing Municipal Bureau of Justice.

23-14 调解工作
MEDIATION

项目		Item		2022	2021	2022年为2021年% 2022 as % of 2021
人民调解委员会个数	(个)	People's Mediation Committees	(unit)	7849	7779	100.9
调解员人数	(万人)	Mediators	(10000 persons)	4.2	4.1	104.0
调解各类纠纷件数	(万件)	Disputes Mediated	(10000 cases)	20.7	22.4	92.3
#调解各类纠纷成功件数		Disputes Mediated Successfully		10.7	13.8	77.8
人民调解组织排查纠纷	(次)	Disputes Investigated by People's Mediation Organization	(time)	394195	370611	106.4
预防纠纷	(件)	Disputes Prevented	(case)	8648	7462	115.9

资料来源：北京市司法局。
Source: Beijing Municipal Bureau of Justice.

23-15 公证工作 NOTARIZATIONS

项 目		Item		2022	2021	2022年为2021年% 2022 as % of 2021
公证机构个数	（个）	Notary Offices	(unit)	24	24	100.0
执业公证员人数	（人）	Certified Notaries	(person)	429	429	100.0
总办证数	（件）	Certificates Issued	(case)	526650	539284	97.7
国内公证业务		Domestic Notarial Services		351612	376901	93.3
涉外公证业务		Foreign-Related Notarial Docummients		170462	158549	107.5
涉港澳公证业务		Hong Kong, Macao Affairs		2731	2574	106.1
涉台公证业务		Naiwan Notarial Services		1845	1260	146.4

资料来源：北京市司法局。
Source: Beijing Municipal Bureau of Justice.

23-16 法律援助工作情况 STATISTICS FOR LEGAL AID

项 目		Item		2022	2021	2022年为2021年% 2022 as % of 2021
法律援助机构个数	（个）	Number of Legal Aid Agencies	(unit)	17	17	100.0
法律援助机构人员数	（人）	Number of Legal Aid Persons	(person)	110	105	104.8
承办民事法律援助案件数	（件）	Civil Cases Aided	(case)	23436	21517	108.9
承办刑事法律援助案件数	（件）	Criminal Cases Aided	(case)	5359	8985	59.6
承办行政法律援助案件数	（件）	Administrative Cases Aided	(case)	56	71	78.9
法律援助机构接待咨询人次	（万人次）	Consultations by Legal Aid Agencies	(10000 person-times)	189.5	173.9	109.0
得到法律援助机构援助的妇女人数	（人次）	Females Receiving Aids from Legal Aid Agencies	(person-times)	11820	10128	116.7
得到法律援助机构援助的未成年人数	（人次）	Juveniles Receiving Aids from Legal Aid Agencies	(person-times)	570	573	99.5

资料来源：北京市司法局。
Source: Beijing Municiapl Bureau of Justice.

23-17 司法鉴定工作情况
STATISTICS FOR JUDICIAL APPRAISAL

项　　目	Item	2022	2021
司法鉴定机构个数　（个）	Judicial Appraisal Organizations (unit)	90	84
司法鉴定人员数　（人）	Judicial Appraisal Personnel (person)	1172	1057
司法鉴定业务量　（件）	Judicial Appraisal Cases Proceeded (case)	104900	111712

注：本表中司法鉴定机构数为北京市司法局审核登记的全部司法鉴定机构个数。
资料来源：北京市司法局。
Note: In the table, the number of judicial appraisal organizations is the number of all judicial appraisal organizations approved by and registered with Beijing Municipal Bureau of Justice.
Source: Beijing Municipal Bureau of Justice.

23-18 生产安全情况
STATISTICS FOR SAFE PRODUCTION

项　　目	Item	2022	2021
单位地区生产总值	Per Unit of GDP	0.96	1.15
生产安全事故死亡率　（人/百亿元）	Death Rate of Work Accidents (person/10 billion yuan)		
道路交通万车死亡率　（人/万辆）	Road Traffic Death Rate per 10000 Vehicles (person/10000 vehicles)	1.48	1.62
食品安全	Up-to-standard Rate of Food Security	98.52	98.52
抽检合格率　（%）	Supervision Spot Checks (%)		
药品抽验合格率　（%）	Up-to-standard Rate of Drug Spot Checks (%)	100.00	100.00

资料来源：北京市应急管理局、北京市公安局公安交通管理局、北京市市场监督管理局、北京市药品监督管理局。
Source: Beijing Emergency Management Bureau, Beijing Traffic Management Bureau, Beijing Municipal Administration of Market Supervision, Beijing Municipal Medical Products Administration.

23-19 消防建设情况(1996-2022年)
STATISTICS FOR FIRECONTROL (1996-2022)

年 份 Year	消防站数 (支) Number of Fire Stations (unit)	消防站消防车辆数 (辆) Number of Fire-fighting Vehicles of Fire Station (unit)	企业专职消防队队数 (支) Number of Full-time Fire Brigades in Enterprises (unit)	企业专职消防队人数 (人) Persons of Full-time Fire-fighters in Enterprises (person)
1996	36	180	101	1865
1997	38	190	104	1885
1998	41	210	108	1993
1999	44	236	120	2447
2000	47	259	120	2447
2001	50	266	120	2447
2002	52	296	112	2228
2003	56	303	112	2147
2004	57	381	120	2477
2005	57	342	120	2477
2006	64	357	109	2269
2007	69	401	109	2269
2008	77	558	109	2269
2009	86	572	109	2269
2010	91	664	109	2269
2011	98	604	87	1766
2012	107	670	76	1405
2013	122	735	76	1405
2014	125	799	76	1405
2015	134	858	78	1410
2016	143	916	65	1307
2017	145	924	65	1307
2018	211	1066	65	1307
2019	250	1177	65	1307
2020	270	1198	66	1040
2021	304	1272	66	1040
2022	377	1332	66	1040

资料来源：2017年及以前数据来源于北京市公安局消防局，自2018年起数据来源于北京市消防救援总队。

Source: Data for and before 2017 were from Fire Department of Beijing Municipal Bureau of Public Security. Data since 2018 are from Beijing Fire Rescue Corps.

23-20 火灾及损失
FIRE ACCIDENTS AND LOSSES

项 目	Item	火灾起数(起) Fire Accidents (time)		直接经济损失(万元) Direct Economic Losses (10000 yuan)	
		2022	2021	2022	2021
火灾起数 (起)	**Fire Accidents (case)**	**6846**	**7490**	**8290.7**	**10417.4**
特别重大火灾	Extraordinarily Serious				
重大火灾	Serious				
较大火灾	Big Fire	3	5	1748.1	2125.3
一般火灾	Relatively Big Fire	6843	7485	6542.6	8292.1
起火原因	**Cause of Fire**				
电 气	Electricity and Gas	2634	2585	3999.7	6323.0
生产作业	Violation of Operation	171	175	280.0	857.4
生活用火不慎	Carelessness in Fire Use	1071	877	2081.0	307.9
吸 烟	Smoking	667	787	245.5	270.5
玩 火	Fire Playing	34	48	4.9	14.6
自 燃	Spontaneous Combustion	68	132	83.9	491.7
雷 击	Thunderstroke	2	1	0.2	0.02
静 电	Static	2	5	0.3	61.4
放 火	Incendiarism	69	71	177.2	73.1
其 他	Others	2128	2809	1418.0	2017.8
受伤人数 (人)	**Number of Injuries (person)**	**106**	**103**		
死亡人数 (人)	**Number of Deaths (person)**	**62**	**59**		

资料来源：北京市消防救援总队。
Source:Beijing Fire Rescue Corps.

23-21 交通事故及损失
STATISTICS FOR TRAFFIC ACCIDENTS AND LOSSES

项　　目		Item		2022	2021	2022年为2021年% 2022 as % of 2021
交通事故		**Traffic Accidents**				
交通事故发生数	（起）	Number of Traffic Accidents	(case)	5249	5362	97.9
受伤人数	（人）	Number of Injuries	(person)	4087	4416	92.5
死亡人数	（人）	Number of Deaths	(person)	1052	1112	94.6
机动车事故		**Motor Vehicle Accidents**				
机动车事故发生数	（起）	Number of Motor Vehicle Accidents	(case)	3768	4374	86.1
受伤人数	（人）	Number of Injuries	(person)	2698	3448	78.2
死亡人数	（人）	Number of Deaths	(person)	728	918	79.3
直接经济损失	**（万元）**	**Direct Economic Losses**	**(10000 yuan)**	**3171.6**	**5291.9**	**59.9**
每万辆机动车死亡人数	**（人）**	**Persons Died Per 10000 Motor Vehicles**	**(person)**	**1.48**	**1.62**	**91.4**

资料来源：北京市公安局公安交通管理局。
Source: Beijing Municipal Bureau of Traffic Management.

23-22 社会保障相关待遇标准(1994-2022年)
LEVEL ON SOCIAL SECURITY BENEFITS (1994-2022)

单位：元/月 (yuan/month)

年份	Year	职工最低工资 Minimum Wages of Employed Persons	失业保险金最低标准 Minimum Unemployment Insurance	城乡最低生活保障标准 Minimum Subsistence Allowance for Urban and Rural Residents
1994		210		
1995		240	174	
1996		270	189	170
1997		290	203	190
1998		310	217	200
1999年第一次	First-time in 1999	320	224	210
1999年第二次	Second-time in 1999	400	291	273
2000		412	300	280
2001		435	305	285
2002		465	326	290
2003		465	326	290
2004年第一次	First-time in 2004	495		
2004年第二次	Second-time in 2004	545	347	290
2005		580	382	300
2006		640	392	310
2007		730	422	330
2008		800	502	390
2009		800	562	410
2010		960	632	430
2011年第一次	First-time in 2011		752	
2011年第二次	Second-time in 2011	1160	782	500
2012		1260	842	520
2013		1400	892	580
2014		1560	1012	650
2015		1720	1122	710
2016		1890	1212	800
2017		2000	1292	900
2018		2120	1536	1000
2019		2200	1706	1100
2020		2200	1816	1170
2021		2320	2034	1245
2022		2320	2034	1320

注：表中2017年及以前“城乡最低生活保障标准”为“城市居民最低生活保障标准”数据。
资料来源：城乡最低生活保障标准由中共北京市委社会工作委员会北京市民政局提供，其他资料由北京市人力资源和社会保障局提供。
Note: Data on minimum subsistence allowance for urban and rural residents of 2017 and before in this table refer to the data of minimum subsistence allowance for urban residents.
Source: Data on minimum subsistence allowance for urban and rural residents are provided by Social Work Committee of Beijing Municipal Committee of the Communist Party of China Beijing Municipal Civil Affairs Bureau, other data are provided by Beijing Municipal Human Resources and Social Security Bureau.

23-23 参加社会保障情况(1995-2022年)

单位：万人

年 份 Year	参加企业职工基本养老保险人数 Number of People Participating in Basic Pension Insurance for Enterprise Employed Persons	参加职工基本医疗保险人数 Number of People Participating in Basic Medical Care Insurance for Employed Persons	参加失业保险人数 Number of People Participating in Unemployment Insurance	参加工伤保险人数 Number of People Participating in Work-related Injury Insurance	参加生育保险人数 Number of People Participating in Maternity Insurance
1995	261.1		219.8		
1996	252.0		214.5		
1997	264.3		214.0		
1998	359.2		222.9		
1999	379.0		289.0		
2000	391.6		287.8	212.0	
2001	425.9	210.2	287.2	212.7	
2002	436.2	353.8	299.5	221.0	
2003	448.5	436.1	306.6	242.9	
2004	460.0	484.0	308.0	259.0	
2005	520.0	574.8	394.6	328.9	226.1
2006	604.1	679.5	482.2	465.3	263.3
2007	671.7	783.0	535.3	609.2	290.6
2008	758.1	871.0	614.3	666.5	324.1
2009	827.7	938.4	675.7	747.1	346.8
2010	982.5	1063.7	774.2	823.8	372.2
2011	1091.9	1188.0	881.0	862.4	395.3
2012	1206.4	1279.7	1006.7	897.2	844.7
2013	1311.3	1354.8	1025.1	920.3	883.2
2014	1392.6	1431.3	1057.1	961.0	915.6
2015	1424.2	1475.7	1082.3	1020.1	941.6
2016	1459.1	1517.6	1117.5	1060.2	981.0
2017	1514.3	1569.2	1170.2	1117.9	1035.2
2018	1591.5	1628.9	1240.7	1187.0	1104.0
2019	1651.6	1682.5	1294.8	1242.2	1164.4
2020	1679.9	1741.6	1318.4	1267.2	1341.1
2021	1725.1	1486.0	1359.0	1307.2	1082.7
2022	1764.7	1499.4	1391.4	1337.0	1077.5

注：1.自2001年起设置基本医疗保险指标，以前年份为大病统筹，2000年参加大病统筹人数为232.6万人。
2.参加城乡居民基本医疗保险人数2017年及以前数据为参加城镇居民基本医疗保险人数，下同。
3.自2006年起，农村居民最低生活保障人数不含农村五保供养人员。
4.自2021年9月起，“参加职工基本医疗保险人数”统计口径进行调整，去除6个月及以上未缴费人员，按调整后口径计算，2020年参加职工基本医疗保险人数为1450.7万人。历史年份数据未按新口径进行调整。

资料来源：城市居民最低生活保障人数和农村居民最低生活保障人数来源于中共北京市委社会工作委员会北京市民政局，其他资料来源于北京市人力资源和社会保障局、北京市医疗保障局。

SOCIAL SECURITY PARTICIPATION (1995-2022)

(10000 persons)

参加城乡居民基本养老保障人数 Number of People Participating in Basic Pension Security for Urban and Rural Residents	参加城乡居民基本医疗保险人数 Number of People Participating in Basic Medical Care Insurance for Urban and Rural Residents	参加新型农村合作医疗人数 Number of People Participating in New-type Rural Cooperative Medical Care	城市居民最低生活保障人数 Number of Residents Receiving Subsistence Allowances in Urban Areas	农村居民最低生活保障人数 Number of Residents Receiving Subsistence Allowances in Rural Areas
			0.9	
			0.9	
			2.8	
			4.3	1.2
			6.7	1.6
			7.8	1.8
			12.0	5.4
			16.1	6.7
		234.0	16.1	7.5
		250.4	15.5	7.8
		261.0	15.2	7.1
		268.5	14.8	7.8
		272.5	14.5	7.9
		274.9	14.7	8.0
	143.7	278.5	13.7	7.7
	159.8	276.8	11.7	7.0
	151.9	267.5	11.0	6.3
	160.1	254.4	10.4	6.0
	173.0	242.6	8.9	5.1
	181.0	223.9	8.5	4.9
215.7	191.2	211.9	8.2	4.7
213.1	202.2	186.9	7.8	4.4
209.0	392.2		6.7	3.8
204.7	400.1		6.5	3.8
200.4	398.3		7.0	4.0
192.4	400.8		7.1	3.9
187.5	404.3		7.0	3.7

Note: a)The basic medical care indicator was set from 2001. Before that it was called general healthcare program for major diseases which cover 2.326 million people in 2000.

b)Figures on residents participating in urban and rural basic medical care in and before 2017 referred to that of residents participating in urban basic medical care, the same below.

c)Residents receiving subsistence allowance in rural areas excluded rural persons enjoying five guarantees from 2006.

d)Since September 2021, the statistical coverage of the "number of people participating in basic medical care insurance for employed persons"was adjusted and removed those who failed to make payment for 6 months or more. Calculated according to the adjusted coverage, the number of people participating in basic medical care insurance for employed persons totaled 14.507 million in 2020. Data for the previous years were not adjusted according to the new caliber.

Source: Figures on residents receiving subsistence allowances in urban areas and residents receiving subsistence allowances in rural areas are from Social Work Committee of Beijing Municipal Committee of the Communist Party of China Beijing Municipal Civil Affairs Bureau; other data are from Beijing Municipal Human Resources and Social Security Bureau and Beijing Municipal Medical Insurance Bureau.

23-24 城镇职工参加社会保险情况(2022年)

PARTICIPATION OF EMPLOYED PERSONS FOR SOCIAL SECURITY INSURANCE PROGRAMS IN THE URBAN AREA (2022)

项目	Item	参加企业职工基本养老保险 Participation of Basic Pension Insurance for Enterprise Employed Persons		参加职工基本医疗保险 Participation of Basic Medical Insurance for Employed Persons	
		单位个数 (个) Number of Entities (unit)	人数 (人) Number of Persons (person)	单位个数 (个) Number of Entities (unit)	人数 (人) Number of Persons (person)
合计	**Total**	**823706**	**17647413**	**766203**	**14993630**
按登记注册类型分	**By Registration Type**				
国有	State-owned	5873	1197816	5768	1012327
集体	Collectively-owned	5235	185240	4262	155435
其他	Others	812598	16264357	756173	13825868
按隶属关系划分	**By Affiliation**				
中央单位	Central	7123	1626088	6692	1284243
地方单位	Local	816583	16021325	759511	13709387

资料来源：北京市人力资源和社会保障局、北京市医疗保障局。
Source: Beijing Municipal Human Resources and Social Security Bureau, Beijing Municipal Medical Insurance Bureau.

23-24 续表 Continued

项目	Item	参加失业保险 Unemployment Insurance		参加工伤保险 Industrial Injury Insurance		参加生育保险 Maternity Insurance	
		单位个数 (个) Number of Entities (unit)	人数 (人) Number of Persons (person)	单位个数 (个) Number of Entities (unit)	人数 (人) Number of Persons (person)	单位个数 (个) Number of Entities (unit)	人数 (人) Number of Persons (person)
合计	**Total**	**813779**	**13914474**	**834199**	**13369984**	**752147**	**10774726**
按登记注册类型分	**By Registration Type**						
国有	State-owned	15992	2059100	16740	2256914	5097	827973
集体	Collectively-owned	4509	101961	4710	116751	3416	85239
其他	Others	793278	11753413	812749	10996319	743634	9861514
按隶属关系划分	**By Affiliation**						
中央单位	Central	6858	1529855	7302	1497671	6132	1079004
地方单位	Local	806921	12384619	826897	11872313	746015	9695722

资料来源：北京市人力资源和社会保障局、北京市医疗保障局。
Source: Beijing Municipal Human Resources and Social Security Bureau, Beijing Municipal Medical Insurance Bureau.

23-25 城乡居民参加社会保险情况(2010-2022年)
PARTICIPATION OF RURAL AND URBAN RESIDENTS FOR SOCIAL SECURITY INSURANCE PROGRAMS (2010-2022)

单位：万人 (10000 persons)

年 份 Year	参加城乡居民基本养老保障人数 Residents Participating in Urban and Rural Basic Pension Security	参加城乡居民基本医疗保险人数 Residents Participating in Urban and Rural Basic Medical Care Insurance	学生儿童 Students and Children	城乡老年人 Rural and Urban Senior Citizens	劳动年龄内居民 Residents of Labor Age
2010		143.7	121.3	17.7	4.7
2011		159.8	135.5	19.1	5.3
2012		151.9	128.6	18.5	4.8
2013		160.1	137.5	18.8	3.7
2014		173.0	149.8	19.7	3.6
2015		181.0	157.7	19.8	3.4
2016	215.7	191.2	168.0	19.9	3.3
2017	213.1	202.2	179.2	19.9	3.2
2018	209.0	392.2	221.9	111.8	58.6
2019	204.7	400.1	232.5	114.3	53.3
2020	200.4	398.3	239.2	112.3	46.8
2021	192.4	400.8	246.1	110.3	44.4
2022	187.5	404.3	254.6	111.5	38.2

注：2017年及以前“参加城乡居民基本医疗保险人数”为“参加城镇居民基本医疗保险人数”数据。
资料来源：北京市人力资源和社会保障局、北京市医疗保障局。
Note: Figures on the number of people participating in basic medical care insurance for urban and rural residents in and before 2017 referred to the number of people participating in basic medical care insurance for urban residents.
Source: Beijing Municipal Human Resources and Social Security Bureau, Beijing Municipal Medical Insurance Bureau.

23-26 妇联组织状况
STATISTICS FOR WOMEN'S FEDERATIONS AND ORGANIZATIONS

项 目	Item	2022	2021	2022年为2021年% 2022 as % of 2021
妇联组织数 （个）	**Number of Women's Federations and Organizations (unit)**			
区妇联数	Number of Women's Federations in Districts	16	16	100.0
乡、镇妇联组织数	Number of Women's Federations in Townships	177	177	100.0
街道妇联组织数	Number of Women's Federations in Subdistricts	163	163	100.0
社区妇联组织数	Number of Women's Federations in Communities	3404	3399	100.1
村妇联组织数	Number of Women's Federations in Villages	3602	3600	100.1
妇联干部人数 （人）	**Number of Cadres in Women's Federation (person)**			
区妇联干部数	Cadres in Women's Federations in Districts	317	318	99.7
乡、镇、街道妇联干部数	Cadres in Women's Federations in Townships, Towns and Subdistricts	680	563	120.8
各类妇女联谊组织数（个）	**Number of Women's Sodalities (unit)**	**38**	**38**	**100.0**

资料来源：北京市妇女联合会。
Source: Beijing Women's Federation.

23-27 工会组织建设情况(2022年)
STATISTICS FOR LABOR UNIONS (2022)

项 目	Item	基层工会组织 (个) Grassroot Labor Unions (unit)	职工人数 (人) Number of Employed Persons (person)	会员人数 (人) Number of Members (person)
合 计	**Total**	**32562**	**5597102**	**4834114**
按单位类别划分	**By Registration Type**			
国有企业	State-owned Enterprises	910	414566	393277
集体企业	Collectively-owned Enterprises	1283	127595	114348
股份合作企业	Joint-equity Cooperative Enterprises	337	34418	32246
联营企业	Associated Enterprises	35	3971	3894
国有独资公司	Solely State-owned Enterprises	776	322586	315938
其他有限责任公司	Other Limited-Liability Companies	12322	1634099	1236203
国有控股公司	State-holding Companies	336	237507	234423
其他股份有限公司	Other Holding Companies	991	215909	194015
私营企业	Private Enterprises	4864	460741	376279
其他内资企业	Other Domestically-invested Enterprises	61	18509	15857
港澳台商投资企业	Hong Kong, Macao and Taiwan-invested Enterprises	444	123718	84835
外商投资企业	Foreign-invested Enterprises	870	298961	258500
事业单位	Public Institutions	3138	552569	518442
机关	Governmental Agencies and Organizations	1665	335488	321897
其他	Other	4530	816465	733960
按系统分	**By System**			
工业国防工会	Labor Unions for Industry and National Defence	715	270741	264960
工 业	Industry	699	260944	255222
国 防	National Defence	16	9797	9738
建筑工会	Construction	881	407601	337446
本 市	Local	469	258198	245560
市 外	Non-local	412	149403	91886
服务业工会	Services	651	260567	240206
交通运输工会	Transportation	227	228937	227802
政法卫文工会	Politics, Law, Health Care and Culture	247	129947	128552
教育工会	Education	78	205992	179867
金融工会	Finance	70	134255	133403
市直机关工会	Institutions under Direct Municipal Leadership	453	57142	56698
区工会	Labor Unions in Districts and Counties	29240	3901920	3265180

资料来源：北京市总工会。
Source: Beijing Federation of Labor Unions.

23-28 北京市妇女发展规划监测统计资料
SUPERVISORY STATISTICS FOR WOMEN DEVELOPMENT PROGRAMS OF BEIJING

项　　目	Item	2022	2021
参加职工基本养老保险人数（万人）	Number of People Participating in Basic Pension Insurance for Employed Persons (10000 persons)	1867.8	1826.8
#女　性	Females	855.6	838.0
参加职工基本医疗保险人数（万人）	Number of People Participating in Basic Medical Insurance for Employed Persons (10000 persons)	1499.4	1486.0
#女　性	Females	712.5	699.0
参加失业保险人数（万人）	Number of People Participating in Unemployment Insurance (10000 persons)	1391.4	1359.0
#女　性	Females	610.0	596.7
参加工伤保险人数（万人）	Number of People Participating in Work-related Injury Insurance (10000 persons)	1337.0	1307.2
#女　性	Females	571.5	563.6
参加生育保险人数（万人）	Number of People Participating in Maternity Insurance (10000 persons)	1077.5	1082.7
#女　性	Females	480.0	477.4
参加城乡居民养老保障人数（万人）	Number of People Participating in Pension Security for Urban and Rural Residents (10000 persons)	187.5	192.4
#女　性	Females	103.7	106.6
市人大代表中女性比例（%）	Share of Females in Deputies to Municipal People's Congress (%)	39.1	39.1
普通高中在校生中女生所占比例（%）	Share of Female Students in Total Enrollment in Regular Senior Secondary Schools (%)	49.9	50.4
中等职业教育在校生中女生所占比例（%）	Share of Female Students in Total Enrollment in Schools for Secondary Vocational Education (%)	42.5	41.7
高等职业本专科在校生中女生所占比例（%）	Share of Female Students in Total Enrollment of Undergraduates and Junior College Students in Higher Vocational Schools (%)	47.5	47.2
高等学校在校生中女生所占比例（%）	Share of Female Students in Total Enrollment in Institutions of Higher Education (%)	46.9	47.6
孕产妇系统服务率（%）	Rate of Systematic Service for Pregnant and Lying-in Women (%)	99.4	99.3
宫颈癌人群筛查率（%）	Screening Rate of Cervical Cancer Population (%)	51.5	46.5
乳腺癌人群筛查率（%）	Screening Rate of Breast Cancer Population (%)	65.9	57.6
艾滋病母婴传播率（%）	Mother-to-Child Transmission Rate of AIDS (%)		
开展婚姻家庭服务指导的婚姻登记机构比例（%）	Share of Marriage Registration Agencies Providing Guidance on Marriage and Family Services (%)	100.0	100.0
法律援助妇女人数（人）	Number of Women Receiving Legal Aid (person)	10580	8858

资料来源：北京市人力资源和社会保障局、北京市医疗保障局、北京市人民代表大会常务委员会、北京市教育委员会、北京市卫生健康委员会、中共北京市委社会工作委员会北京市民政局、北京市司法局。

Source: Beijing Municipal Human Resources and Social Security Bureau, Beijing Municipal Medical Insurance Bureau, the Standing Committee of Beijing Municipal People's Congress, Beijing Municipal Education Commission, Beijing Municipal Health Commission Social Work Commission of the Beijing Municipal Committee of the CPC and Beijing Municipal Civil Affairs Bureau, Beijing Municipal Bureau of Justice.

23-29 北京市儿童发展规划监测统计资料
SUPERVISORY STATISTICS FOR CHILDREN DEVELOPMENT PROGRAMS IN BEIJING

项　目		Item		2022	2021
孕前优生健康检查目标人群覆盖率	(%)	Coverage Rate of Target Population for Pre-pregnancy Eugenic Checkups	(%)	97.33	100.00
产前筛查率	(%)	Prenatal Screening Rate	(%)	93.39	95.58
新生儿死亡率	(‰)	Neonatal Mortality Rate	(‰)	0.67	0.90
婴儿死亡率	(‰)	Mortality Rate of Infants	(‰)	1.26	1.44
5岁以下儿童死亡率	(‰)	Mortality Rate of Children Under 5 Years Old	(‰)	1.93	2.24
3岁以下儿童系统服务率	(%)	Rate of Systematic Service for Children Under 3 Years Old	(%)	96.66	96.08
7岁以下儿童健康服务率	(%)	Rate of Health Service for Children Under 7 Years Old	(%)	99.24	99.03
5岁以下儿童肥胖率	(%)	Obesity Rate of Children Under 5 Years Old	(%)	3.29	3.49
5岁以下儿童超重率	(%)	Overweight Rate of Children Under 5 Years Old	(%)	11.25	11.29
5岁儿童乳牙龋患率	(%)	Rate of Deciduous Tooth Caries for Children of 5 Years Old	(%)	58.50	
0-6岁儿童眼保健和视力检查覆盖率	(%)	Coverage Rate of Eye Care and Optic Examination for Children of 0-6 Years Old	(%)	98.91	98.87
卡介苗疫苗接种率	(%)	Rate of Inoculation of BCG Vaccines	(%)	99.01	99.32
脊髓灰质炎疫苗接种率	(%)	Rate of Inoculation of Poliomyelitis Polio Vaccines	(%)	99.98	99.97
百白破疫苗接种率	(%)	Rate of Inoculation of Pertussis, Diphtheria and Tetanus Vaccines	(%)	99.97	99.96
含麻疹成分疫苗接种率	(%)	Rate of Inoculation of Vaccines with Measle Ingredients	(%)	99.90	99.97
普惠性幼儿园覆盖率	(%)	Coverage Rate of Inclusive Kindergartens	(%)	91.00	89.00
少先队实践教育营地(基地)数量	(个)	Number of Practice Education Camps (Bases) for Young Pioneers	(unit)	182	117
少年法庭数量	(个)	Number of Juvenile Courts	(unit)	21	21

注：孕产妇死亡率为常住人口口径。
资料来源：北京市卫生健康委员会、北京市教育委员会、共青团北京市委员会、北京市高级人民法院。
Note: The mortality rate of pregnant and lying-in women is of the statistical coverage of permanent population.
Source: Beijing Municipal Health Commission,Beijing Municipal Education Commission, China Communist Youth League Beijing Committee, Beijing Municipal High People's Court.

主要统计指标解释

参加职工基本养老保险人数 指报告期末按照国家法律、法规和有关政策规定参加企业职工基本养老保险并在社保经办机构已建立缴费记录档案的职工人数，包括中断缴费但未终止养老保险关系的职工人数和参加基本养老保险的离休、退休和退职人员的人数。不包括只登记未建立缴费记录档案的人数。

参加职工基本医疗保险人数 指报告期末按国家有关规定参加基本医疗保险的人数。包括参加保险的职工人数和退休人员数。

参加失业保险人数 指报告期末按照国家法律、法规和有关政策规定参加了失业保险的城镇企业事业单位的职工及地方政府规定参加失业保险的其他人员的人数。参加失业保险人数为参加失业保险的职工人数。

参加工伤保险人数 指报告期末参加工伤保险的职工人数。

参加生育保险人数 指报告期末参加生育保险的职工人数。

参加农村新型合作医疗人数 指截止报告期末乡镇已参加农村新型合作医疗的总人数。农村新型合作医疗制度是由政府组织、引导、支持，农民自愿参加，集体、个人和政府多方筹资，以大病统筹为主的农民医疗互助共济制度。

城市居民最低生活保障人数 指报告期末家庭平均收入在当地规定的最低生活保障线以下的城镇居民数。包括“三无”对象、失业人员和在职、下岗、退休人员等。

农村居民最低生活保障人数 指报告期末在建立农村最低生活保障制度的地区，得到当地政府或集体给予最低生活保障的农业人口家庭人数。

律师 指受聘参加律师事务所工作，提任法律顾问、刑（民）事代理人、刑事辩护人，办理非诉讼事件、解答法律询问，代写法律事务文书等主要从事律师业务的专职法律工作者和兼职律师。

公证人员 指在国家公证机关依法办理公证事务的司法人员。包括公证员、助理公证员和在公证处工作的其他人员。

调解人员 指人民调解委员会担负调解民间一般民事纠纷和轻微违法行为所引起的纠纷的工作人员。包括调解委员会的委员和调解小组调解员。

参加城乡居民养老保障人数 指报告期末参加城乡居民养老保险和享受老年保障福利养老金的人数合计。

市人大代表中女性比例 每一届当选的市人大代表中女代表中所占比例。

普通高中在校生中女生所占比例 指普通高中中具有学籍并在本学年初进行学籍注册的学生数中女生人数占总学生数的比例。

中等职业教育在校生中女生所占比例 指具有中等职业教育学籍并在本学年初进行学籍注册的学生总数中女生所占比例。

高等职业本专科在校生中女生所占比例 指具有高等职业教育本专科学籍并在本学年初进行学籍注册的学生总数中女生所占比例。

高等学校在校生中女生所占比例 指高等学校中具有高等职业本专科、普通本科、研究生、成人本专科、网络本专科学籍并在本学年初进行学籍注册的学生总数中女生所占比例。

孕产妇系统服务率 指年内孕产妇系统管理人数与活产数之比。

宫颈癌人群筛查率 指适龄妇女(35—64岁)中接受宫颈癌筛查的妇女所占比例。

乳腺癌人群筛查率 指适龄妇女(35—64岁)中接受乳腺癌筛查的妇女所占比例。

艾滋病母婴传播率 指艾滋病病毒(HIV)感染孕产妇所生儿童中因母婴传播途径感染的人数所占的比例。

开展婚姻家庭服务指导的婚姻登记机构比例 指在婚姻登记机构中，开展了婚姻家庭服务指导相关业务的婚姻登记机构所占比例。

法律援助妇女人数 指年满 14 周岁及以上女性公民年内获得法律援助机构组织提供的法律援助案件辩护、代理等服务的人次。

孕前优生健康检查目标人群覆盖率 指年内孕前优生检查总人数与计划怀孕夫妇人数之比。适用范围是孕前优生健康检查目标人群。

产前筛查率 指年内孕产妇产前筛查人数与产妇数之比。

新生儿死亡率 指年内出生至 28 天内(0—27 天)死亡的新生儿人数与活产数之比。

婴儿死亡率 指年内不满 1 周岁的婴儿死亡人数与活产数之比。

5岁以下儿童死亡率 指年内不满5周岁的儿童死亡人数与活产数之比。

3 岁以下儿童系统服务率 指该统计年度内 3 岁以下儿童在本年度内按年龄要求接受生长监测或4:2:2 体格检查（身高和体重等）的总人数与某年某地 3 岁以下儿童数之比。

7岁以下儿童健康服务率 指该统计年度内7岁以下儿童接受 1 次及以上体格检查（身高和体重等）的总人数与某年某地 7 岁以下儿童数之比。

5 岁以下儿童肥胖率 对照 WHO 标准的身高（长）别体重参考值，计算 5 岁以下儿童在该统计年度内至少有一次测量身高（长）别体重大于或等于同年龄标准人群身高（长）别体重中位数加 2 个标准差的人数与某年某地 5 岁以下健康管理人数之比。

5 岁以下儿童超重率 对照 WHO 标准的身高（长）别体重参考值，计算 5 岁以下儿童在该统计年度内至少有一次测量身高（长）别体重大于或等于同年龄标准人群身高（长）别体重中位数加 1 个标准差，且小于同年龄标准人群身高（长）别体重中位数加 2 个标准差的人数与某年某地 5 岁以下健康管理人数之比。

5 岁儿童乳牙龋患率 指 5 岁儿童根据乳牙龋坏牙数 (dt) 计算的患龋人数占总受检人数的百分率。参照国家第四次口腔健康流行病学调查方法完成抽样和现场调查。

0—6 岁儿童眼保健和视力检查覆盖率 指年内 0—6 岁儿童眼保健和视力检查人数占 0—6 岁儿童的百分比。

纳入国家免疫规划的疫苗接种率 指年内实际接种某国家免疫规划疫苗(某剂次)人数占应接种该国家免疫规划疫苗(该剂次)人数的百分比。

普惠性幼儿园覆盖率 指公办幼儿园和普惠性民办幼儿园(班)在园(班)幼儿数占在园(班)幼儿总数的百分比。

少先队实践教育营地（基地）数量 指街道(社区)、乡镇(村)少先队组织利用辖区内的各类党群阵地、文化场馆、社会资源建设的少先队校外实践教育营地(基地)数量。

少年法庭数量 指人民法院为维护未成年人合法权益、预防矫治未成年人犯罪而建立的少年法庭数量。

Explanatory Notes on Main Statistical Indicators

Number of People Participating in Basic Pension Insurance for Employed Persons refers to the number of employed persons participating in basic pension insurance for enterprise employed persons and keeping insurance premium payment records with social security organizations in accordance with provisions in national laws, rules and relevant policies at the end of reporting period, including the number of employed persons suspending the payment of insurance premium without terminating the pension insurance relation as well as retired employed persons participating in basic endowment insurance, excluding the number of persons only registered but having no insurance premium payment records.

Number of People Participating in Basic Medical Insurance for Employed Persons refers to the number of persons participating in basic medical insurance programs at the end of the reporting period in accordance with relevant national regulations, including the number of employed persons and retired persons participating in the insurance.

Number of People Participating in Unemployment Insurance refers to the number of employed persons in urban enterprises and public institutions participating in unemployment insurance programs at the end of the reporting period in accordance with provisions in national laws, rules and relevant policies, as well as other persons specified by local governments to participate in unemployment insurance. The number of people participating in unemployment insurance program is the number of employees employed persons who participate in unemployment insurance.

Number of People Participating in Work-related Injury Insurance refers to the number of employed persons participating in work-related injury insurance programs at the end of the reporting period.

Number of People Participating in Maternity Insurance refers to the number of employed persons participating in maternity insurance programs at the end of the reporting period.

Number of People Participating in New-type Rural Cooperative Medical Care refers to the total number of rural residents who have participated in the new-type rural cooperative medical care programs at the end of the reporting period. The new-type rural medical care system is a system of mutual aid in medical care for rural residents that is organized, guided and supported by the government, in which the rural residents voluntarily participate. It is a system of multi-party financing by collective entities, individuals and the government, and is mainly based on social pooling for serious disease.

Number of Residents Receiving Subsistence Allowances in Urban Areas refers to the number of urban residents whose average family income is below locally provided minimum living standard at the end of the reporting period, including elderly persons, minors, psychotic patients and disables who have no statutory guardian, no fixed pocketbook, no labor ability, unemployed persons, on-the-job persons, laid-off persons, and retired persons, etc.

Number of Residents Receiving Subsistence Allowances in Rural Areas refers to the number of persons in agricultural families covered by subsistence allowances of local government or collective entities in an area where rural minimum living standard guarantee system is established, at the end of reporting period.

Lawyer refers to a full-time legal worker and part-time lawyer joining a law firm, serving as a legal consultant, criminal (civil) proxy, criminal counsel, handling non-lawsuit events, answering legal questions, writing legal documents for others, and other lawyer business.

Notary refers to any judicial person handling notarization matters in national notarization agencies according to laws, including notaries, assistant notaries, and other personnel working in notarization offices.

Mediator refers to working personnel responsible for mediating general civil disputes as well as disputes caused by slightly illegal acts in any people's mediation committee, including members of people's mediation committees and mediators of mediation teams.

Number of People Participating in Pension Security for Urban and Rural Residents refers to total number of people participating in pension insurance for urban and rural residents and enjoying old age security benefit pension at the end of the reporting period.

Share of Females in Deputies to Municipal People's Congress refers to the share of female deputies in the elected deputies to the Municipal People's Congress of each session.

Share of Female Students in Total Enrollment in Regular Senior Secondary Schools refers to the share of female students in the total number of enrolled students in regular senior secondary schools who have student status and have registered their student status at the beginning of this academic year.

Share of Female Students in Total Enrollment in Schools for Secondary Vocational Education refers to the share of female students in the total number of enrolled students who have the student status for secondary vocational education and have registered their student status at the beginning of this academic year.

Share of Female Students in Total Enrollment of Undergraduates and Junior College Students in Higher Vocational Schools refers to the share of female students in the total number of enrolled students who have the student status for undergraduates and junior college students for higher vocational education and have registered their student status at the beginning of this academic year.

Share of Female Students in Total Enrollment in Institutions of Higher Education refers to the share of female students in total number of enrolled students in institutions of higher education who have the student status for higher vocational undergraduates and junior college students, general undergraduates, postgraduates, adult undergraduates and junior college students, or undergraduates and junior college students enrolled in Internet-based courses, and have registered their student status at the beginning of this academic year.

Rate of Systematic Service for Pregnant and Lying-in Women refers to the ratio of the number of people under the management of the system for pregnant and lying-in women to the number of live births in the year.

Screening Rate of Cervical Cancer Population refers to the proportion of women undergoing cervical cancer screening in the women of appropriate age (aged between 35 and 64 years old).

Screening Rate of Breast Cancer Population refers to the proportion of women undergoing breast cancer screening in the women of appropriate age (aged between 35 and 64 years old).

Mother-to-Child Transmission Rate of AIDS refers to the proportion of newborns infected due to mother-to-child transmission in the newborns given birth by the pregnant and lying-in women infected with HIV.

Share of Marriage Registration Agencies Providing Guidance on Marriage and Family Services refers to the proportion of marriage registration agencies carrying out marriage and family service guidance related service in the marriage registration agencies.

Number of Women Receiving Legal Aid refers to the person-times of legal aid case defense, representation and other services provided by legal aid organizations and received by female citizens aged 14 and above in the year.

Coverage Rate of Target Population for Pre-pregnancy Eugenic Checkups refers to the ratio of total number of couples having pre-pregnancy eugenic checkups to the total number of couples preparing for pregnancy in the year. The scope of application is the target population for pre-pregnancy eugenic checkups.

Prenatal Screening Rate refers to the ratio of number of pregnant and lying-in women undergoing prenatal screening to the total number of lying-in women in the year.

Neonatal Mortality Rate refers to the ratio of the number of newborns who die within 28 days (0-27 days) after birth to the number of live births in the year.

Mortality Rate of Infants refers to the ratio of deaths of infants under one year old to the number of live births in the year.

Mortality Rate of Children Under 5 Years Old refers to the ratio of deaths of children under 5 years old to the number of live births in the year.

Rate of Systematic Service for Children Under 3 Years Old refers to the ratio of the total number of children under 3 years old who have undergone growth monitoring or a 4:2:2 physical examination (height and weight, etc.) required by age during the statistical year to the number of children under 3 years old in a given year and a given area, within the statistical year.

Rate of Health Service for Children Under 7 Years Old refers to the ratio of the total number of children under 7 years old who have undergone physical examination (height and weight, etc.) for one or more times during this statistical year to the number of children under 7 years old in a given year and a given area.

Obesity Rate of Children Under 5 Years Old refers to the ratio of the number of children under 5 years old who have a measured weight for height (length) that is greater than or equal to the median of standard weight for height (length) of children of the same age plus 2 standard deviations, for at least one time during the statistical year, to the number of children under 5 years old with healthy weight management in a given year and a given area, calculated by reference to the standard reference value of weight for height (length) of WHO.

Overweight Rate of Children Under 5 Years Old refers to the ratio of the number of children under 5 years old who have a measured weight for height (length) that is greater than or equal to the median of standard weight for height (length) of children of the same age plus 1 standard deviation and is less than the median of standard weight for height (length) of children of the same age plus 2 standard deviations, for at least one time during the statistical year, to the number of children under 5 years old with healthy weight management in a given year and a given area, calculated by reference to the standard reference value of weight for height (length) of WHO.

Rate of Deciduous Tooth Caries for Children of 5 Years Old refers to the percentage of children of 5 years old with caries calculated in terms of the number of decayed deciduous tooth (dt) in the total number of children of 5 years old undergoing examination. Sampling survey and field survey are completed by reference to the methods of the fourth national oral health epidemiological survey.

Coverage Rate of Eye Care and Optic Examination for Children of 0-6 Years Old refers to the percentage of children of 0-6 years old undergoing eye care and optic examination in the total number of children of 0-6 years old in the year.

Rate of Inoculation of Vaccines Included in National Immunization Program refers to the percentage of people actually vaccinated against a national immunization program vaccine (a dose) in the number of people supposed to be vaccinated against the said national immunization program vaccine (the said dose) in the year.

Coverage Rate of Inclusive Kindergartens refers to the percentage of children enrollment in public kindergartens and inclusive private kindergartens (classes) in the total number of children enrollment in all kindergartens (classes).

Practice Education Camps (Bases) for Young Pioneers refer to the number of off-campus practice education camps (bases) for Young Pioneers built by sub-district (community), township (village) Young Pioneers Organization by making use of the positions of various party groups, cultural venues, and social resources within the jurisdiction.

Number of Juvenile Courts refers to the number of juvenile courts established by the people's courts to protect the legitimate rights and interests of minors, and prevent and correct minor crimes.

24

北京统计年鉴2023　BEIJING STATISTICAL YEARBOOK 2023

开发区
DEVELOPMENT ZONES

简要说明

一、主要内容

本章资料主要反映北京市开发区基本情况、招商、生产情况，重点介绍了北京经济技术开发区和中关村国家自主创新示范区的主要情况。

二、统计范围

根据 2012 年《国务院关于同意调整中关村国家自主创新示范区空间规模和布局的批复》，自 2013 年起，中关村国家自主创新示范区的统计范围在原有的海淀园、丰台园、昌平园、电子城科技园、亦庄园、德胜园、雍和园、石景山园、通州园和大兴生物医药产业基地的基础上，增加了平谷园、门头沟园、顺义园、房山园、密云园、怀柔园和延庆园七个园区。同时，“电子城科技园”更名为“朝阳园”；“德胜园”更名为“西城园”；“雍和园”更名为“东城园”。

北京首都国际机场临空经济区于2022年4月29日揭牌，由原北京天竺综合保税区和原北京临空经济核心区 2 个单位整合组建而成。

中关村国家自主创新示范区亦庄园在中关村国家自主创新示范区与北京经济技术开发区中为重叠部分。

Brief Introduction

I. Main Content

Statistics in this chapter mainly show the basic condition, attraction of investment and production of development zones in Beijing, the business invitation, capital contribution, investment, and production status. This chapter mainly focuses on the situation of Beijing Economic-Technological Development Area、 and Zhongguancun National Independent Innovation Demonstration Area.

II. Scope of Statistics

According to the *Official Reply of the State Council on Approving the Adjustment of Spatial Scale and Layout of Zhongguancun National Innovation Demonstration Area* issued in 2012. Since 2013, the statistic scope of Zhongguancun Area has been enlarged to include Pinggu Sub-park, Mentougou Sub-park, Shunyi Sub-park, Fangshan Sub-park, Miyun Sub-park, Huairou Sub-park and Yanqing Sub-park to supplement Haidian Sub-park, Fengtai Sub-park, Changping Sub-park, Electronic Science & Technology Park, Yizhuang Sub-park, Desheng Sub-park, Yonghe Sub-park, Shijing Sub-park, Tongzhou Sub-park and Daxing BioPharma Industry Base. At the same time, Electronic Science & Technology Park was changed into Chaoyang Sub-park, Deshengyuan Sub-park into Xicheng Sub-park and Yonghe Sub-park into Dongcheng Sub-park.

The Beijing Capital International Airport Economic Zone, integrating the two units of the former Beijing Tianzhu Free Trade Zone and the former Beijing Airport Economic Core Zone, was inaugurated on April 29, 2022.

Data of Zhongguancun Yizhuang Sub-park is counted in both Zhongguancun National Independent Innovation Demonstration Area and Beijing Economic-Technologic

24-1 开发区基本情况(2022年)
STATISTICS ON DEVELOPMENT ZONES (2022)

项目		Item		2022
开发区个数	(个)	Number of Development Zones	(unit)	3
区规划总面积	(公顷)	Total Planned Area of Development Zones	(hectare)	48563.6
累计已开发土地面积	(公顷)	Accumulated Area of Developed Land	(hectare)	36196.9
累计已供应土地面积	(公顷)	Accumulated Area of Supplied Land	(hectare)	30815.7
累计已建成城镇建设用地面积	(公顷)	Accumulated Area of Completed Land for Urban Development	(hectare)	27924.0
累计招商项目企业个数	(个)	Accumulated Number of Enterprises of Business Inviting Programs	(unit)	162059
总收入	(亿元)	Total Revenue	(100 million yuan)	95331.8
工业总产值(当年价格)	(亿元)	Gross Output Value of Industry (at current prices)	(100 million yuan)	14484.1
利润总额	(亿元)	Total Profits	(100 million yuan)	6933.4
应缴税金	(亿元)	Total Taxes Payable	(100 million yuan)	2317.3

注：1.本表中的开发区仅包括国家级开发区情况，下同。
2.表内“累计”指自开始至年末的累计数。

Note: a) Development zones in this table include those at national level only, the same below.
b) Accumulative data in this table refer to the accumulation from the beginning to the end of this year.

24-2 开发区土地开发情况(2022年)
LAND EXPLOITATION OF DEVELOPMENT ZONES(2022)

单位：公顷 (hectare)

名　　称	Item	规划总面积 Total Planned Area	累计已开发土地面积 Accumulated Area of Developed Land	累计已供应土地面积 Accumulated Area of Supplied Land	累计已建成城镇建设用地 Accumulated Area of Land for Urban Development
国家级开发区	**State-level Development Zone**	**48563.6**	**36196.9**	**30815.7**	**27924.0**
北京经济技术开发区	Beijing Economic-Technological Development Area	6579.9	5259.0	4604.0	4155.0
中关村国家自主创新示范区	Zhongguancun National Independent Innovation Demonstration Zone	46311.7	29267.0	25112.0	22725.4
海 淀 园	Haidian Sub-park	17430.6	15626.9	14065.9	13643.6
丰 台 园	Fengtai Sub-park	818.0	470.0	444.9	440.7
昌 平 园	Changping Sub-park	5140.3	2809.0	2044.7	1863.1
朝 阳 园	Chaoyang Sub-park	2610.0	1471.9	1447.1	1067.4
亦 庄 园	Yizhuang Sub-park	6235.0			
西 城 园	Xicheng Sub-park	1000.0	1000.0	1000.0	1000.0
东 城 园	Dongcheng Sub-park	603.0	288.8		288.8
石景山园	Shijingshan Sub-park	1334.0	459.6	459.6	339.6
通 州 园	Tongzhou Sub-park	3434.6	2342.3	1992.8	1292.9
大 兴 园	Daxing Sub-park	2025.1	849.0	597.3	503.4
平 谷 园	PingGu Sub-park	508.0	227.7	109.4	85.2
门头沟园	MenTouGou Sub-park	189.0	175.0	130.0	120.0
房 山 园	FangShan Sub-park	1572.6	869.7	686.2	625.7
顺 义 园	ShunYi Sub-park	1208.5	898.8	589.6	406.1
密 云 园	MiYun Sub-park	1000.8	699.3	645.1	466.0
怀 柔 园	HuaiRou Sub-park	711.0	693.1	664.3	359.2
延 庆 园	YanQing Sub-park	491.2	386.0	235.2	223.8
北京首都国际机场临空经济区	Airport Economic Zone near the Beijing Capital International Airport	1907.0	1671.0	1099.8	1043.6

注：1.中关村国家自主创新示范区亦庄园数据在中关村国家自主创新示范区与北京经济技术开发区中为重叠部分。
2.表内“累计”指自开始至年末的累计数。

Note: a) Data on Yizhuang Sub-park of Zhongguancun National Independent Innovation Demonstration Zone are overlapped in Zhongguancun National Independent Innovation Demonstration Zone and Beijing Economic and Technological Development Area.
b) "Accumulated" in this table refers to the accumulation from the beginning to the end of the year.

24-3 开发区经营情况(2022年)
OPERATING OF DEVELOPMENT ZONES (2022)

名称	Item	自年初累计 Accumulative Number from Year-beginning 总收入(万元) Total Revenue (10000 yuan)	利润总额(万元) Total Profits (10000 yuan)
国家级开发区	**State-level Development Zone**	**953317988**	**69333995**
北京经济技术开发区	Beijing Economic-Technological Development Area	202769014	13300192
中关村国家自主创新示范区	Zhongguancun National Independent Innovation Demonstration Zone	874629423	69009621
海淀园	Haidian Sub-park	370218392	25394243
丰台园	Fengtai Sub-park	75688743	5822784
昌平园	Changping Sub-park	52577124	5179492
朝阳园	Chaoyang Sub-park	96702478	6749931
亦庄园	Yizhuang Sub-park	91580381	8552532
西城园	Xicheng Sub-park	46010122	1547218
东城园	Dongcheng Sub-park	33570796	2926794
石景山园	Shijingshan Sub-park	41952541	7309972
通州园	Tongzhou Sub-park	10603357	311592
大兴园	Daxing Sub-park	8237784	703222
平谷园	PingGu Sub-park	1898289	94021
门头沟园	MenTouGou Sub-park	5662528	55513
房山园	FangShan Sub-park	6686745	211618
顺义园	ShunYi Sub-park	21274128	1424631
密云园	MiYun Sub-park	5394990	212159
怀柔园	HuaiRou Sub-park	4604313	266370
延庆园	YanQing Sub-park	1966714	2247529
北京首都国际机场临空经济区	Airport Economic Zone near the Beijing Capital International Airport	34835858	-1735405

注：1.中关村国家自主创新示范区与北京经济技术开发区、北京首都国际机场临空经济区存在重复单位，在国家级开发区汇总时已剔除重复部分。
2.中关村国家自主创新示范区统计范围为全部入区法人单位，其他开发区统计范围为规模(限额)以上法人单位。

Note: a)There are repetitive units among Zhongguancun National Independent Innovation Demonstration Zone, Beijing Economic-Technological Development Area, and Airport Economic Zone near the Beijing Capital International Airport. The repetitive parts have been eliminated when summarizing the data on state-level development zones.
b)The statistics for Zhongguancun National Independent Innovation Demonstration Zone cover all legal entities in the zone, while the statistics for other development zones cover the legal entities above designated size.

24-4 北京经济技术开发区主要经济指标
MAIN ECONOMIC INDICATORS FOR BEIJING ECONOMIC-TECHNOLOGICAL DEVELOPMENT AREA

项　目		Item		2022	2021
规划面积	(公顷)	Area Planned	(hectare)	6579.9	5960.0
开发区生产总值	(亿元)	Gross Output Value	(100 million yuan)	2456.4	2766.2
工业总产值		Gross Output Value of Industry		5128.7	5712.1
(当年价格)	(亿元)	(at current year's prices)	(100 million yuan)		
#高新技术企业		High and New Technology Enterprises		4112.3	4767.1
销售(营业)收入	(亿元)	Sales (Business) Revenue	(100 million yuan)	20276.9	19914.3
利润总额	(亿元)	Total Profits	(100 million yuan)	1330.0	1696.4
进出口总值	(亿美元)	Total Value of Imports and Exports	(USD 100 million)	259.0	315.4
出　口		Exports		72.4	127.7
进　口		Imports		186.6	187.6
一般公共预算收入	(亿元)	General Public Budget Revenue	(100 million yuan)	372.4	362.7
实际利用外商直接投资	(亿美元)	Actual Use of Foreign Direct Investment	(USD 100 million)	3.9	3.6
固定资产投资增速	(%)	Growth Rate of Fixed Assets Investment	(%)	10.7	17.1
从业人员期末人数	(人)	Year-end Number of Employed Persons	(person)	475342	442005
从业人员工资总额	(亿元)	Total Wages of Employed Persons	(100 million yuan)	910.8	762.1

注：1.工业总产值(当年价格)、销售(营业)收入和利润总额指标的统计范围是规模(限额)以上法人单位。
2.一般公共预算收入为地方级口径。
资料来源：北京经济技术开发区经济发展局、经济社会调查队。
Note: a) The statistics for gross output value of industry (at current prices), sales (business) revenue and total profits cover the legal entities above designated size.
b) The data on general public budget revenue are of the local level standards.
Source: Bureau of Economy and Development and Economic and Social Survey Team of Beijing Economic-Technological Development Area.

24-5 中关村国家自主创新示范区企业经营及科技活动情况(2008-2022年) OPERATING ACTIVITIES AND SCIENCE ACTIVITIES OF ENTERPRISES IN ZHONGGUANCUN NATIONAL INNOVATION DEMONSTRATION ZONE (2008-2022)

项目	Item	2008	2009	2010	2011	2012	2013	2014
总收入 (亿元)	**Total Revenue (100 million yuan)**	**10222.4**	**13004.6**	**15940.2**	**19646.0**	**25025.0**	**30497.4**	**36057.6**
技术收入	Technological Revenue	1693.4	2093.6	2478.3	2845.9	3403.1	4032.4	4837.7
产品销售收入	Products Sales Revenue	5229.2	5923.6	6889.6	7809.4	8741.2	10788.4	12474.2
商品销售收入	Commodity Sales Revenue	2398.9	3689.4	5032.2	7161.9	10077.4	11339.6	12832.6
其他收入	Other Revenues	900.9	1298.0	1540.1	1828.9	2803.4	4337.0	5913.1
利润总额 (亿元)	**Total Profits (100 million yuan)**	**726.3**	**1122.4**	**1298.9**	**1533.9**	**1788.6**	**2264.8**	**3031.5**
专利情况	**Statistics on Patents**							
期末有效发明专利数 (件)	Number of Patents in Force at the End of the Period (unit)	9836	11611	13988	15232	23198	35000	44870
当年专利授权数 (件)	Number of Patents Licensed in the Year (unit)	9050	10512	13151	12951	17969	22308	25065

24-5 续表 Continued

项目	Item	2015	2016	2017	2018	2019	2020	2021	2022
总收入 (亿元)	**Total Revenue (100 million yuan)**	**40811.9**	**46047.6**	**53025.8**	**58830.9**	**66422.2**	**72276.4**	**84402.3**	**87462.9**
技术收入	Technological Revenue	6623.6	7580.4	9369.6	11174.3	13450.8	16027.4	20419.4	22502.6
产品销售收入	Products Sales Revenue	13300.0	14752.5	15934.2	17058.7	19085.2	19784.8	23524.5	20676.1
商品销售收入	Commodity Sales Revenue	13339.5	14522.4	16406.1	17878.0	20253.9	21752.8	23682.0	24616.7
其他收入	Other Revenues	7548.9	9192.3	11315.9	12719.9	13632.3	14711.4	16776.5	19667.5
利润总额 (亿元)	**Total Profits (100 million yuan)**	**3404.5**	**3732.5**	**4321.1**	**4413.3**	**4182.6**	**6344.7**	**7725.3**	**6901.0**
专利情况	**Statistics on Patents**								
期末有效发明专利数 (件)	Number of Patents in Force at the End of the Period (unit)	63171	82890	114469	141486	170772	186511	206767	267471
当年专利授权数 (件)	Number of Patents Licensed in the Year (unit)	32327	37629	46046	56374	61221	74928	90434	98300

24−6 中关村国家自主创新示范区企业经营活动情况
OPERATING ACTIVITIES OF ENTERPRISES IN ZHONGGUANCUN NATIONAL INDEPENDENT INNOVATION DEMONSTRATION ZONE

单位：亿元 (100 million yuan)

项　　目	Item	2022	2021
工业总产值(当年价格)	Gross Output Value of Industry (at current year's prices)	13190.4	15369.1
总收入	Total Revenue	87462.9	84402.3
技术收入	Technological Revenue	22502.6	20419.4
产品销售收入	Products Sales Revenue	20676.1	23524.5
商品销售收入	Commodity Sales Revenue	24616.7	23682.0
其他收入	Other Revenues	19667.5	16776.5
利润总额	Total Profits	6901.0	7725.3
减免税总额	Reduced and Exempted Tax	1264.0	978.7
#增值税	Value Added Tax	331.7	242.2
所得税	Corporate Income Tax	748.3	661.4
应交增值税	Value Added Tax Payable	1028.3	1069.5
出口总额	Foreign Exchange Created by Export	3202.3	3893.8

24−7 中关村国家自主创新示范区企业研发活动情况
SCIENTIFIC ACTIVITIES OF ENTERPRISES IN ZHONGGUANCUN NATIONAL INNOVATION DEMONSTRATION ZONE

项　　目	Item	2022	2021
研究开发活动情况	**Statistics on Research and Development Activities**		
研究开发人员合计 (人)	Total Number of Research and Development Personnel (person)	1005583	978381
#全职人员	Full-time Personnel	904721	894831
研究开发费用合计 (亿元)	Total Research and Development Costs (100 million yuan)	4952.4	4600.2
#人员人工费用	Labor Cost	2695.6	2530.6
委托外部研究开发费用 (亿元)	Costs of Research and Development Conducted by External Units Entrusted (100 million yuan)	704.9	635.8
#委托境外机构	Entrusted Overseas Institution	13.7	13.0
研究开发产出情况	**Research and Development Output**		
专利情况	Statistics on Patents		
期末有效发明专利数 (件)	Number of Patents in Force at the End of the Period (unit)	267471	206767
当年专利授权数 (件)	Number of Patent Licensed (unit)	98300	90434
论文、著作情况	Statistics on Papers and Writings		
发表科技论文 (篇)	Number of Published Scientific Papers (unit)	16910	18972
技术改造和技术获取情况	**Technical Rennovation and Acquisition**		
技术改造经费支出 (亿元)	Expenditures on Technical Rennovation (100 million yuan)	11.0	11.1
引进境外技术经费支出 (亿元)	Expenditures on Introduction of Foreign Technologies (100 million yuan)	2.8	8.0
引进境外技术的消化吸收经费支出 (亿元)	Expenditures on Absorption of Imported Technologies (100 million yuan)	1.1	0.1
购买境内技术经费支出 (亿元)	Expenditures on Purchasing Domestic Technologies (100 million yuan)	6.6	7.4

24-8 中关村国家自主创新示范区企业人力资源情况
HUMAN RESOURCES OF ENTERPRISES IN ZHONGGUANCUN NATIONAL INNOVATION DEMONSTRATION ZONE

单位：人 (person)

项　目	Item	2022	2021
从业人员年末人数	**Number of Employeed Persons at the Year End**	**2790210**	**2849075**
#留学归国人员	Returned Students Studying Abroad	63209	59827
#在岗长期职工	On-the-post Long-term Employed Persons	2660637	2700884
按文化程度分	**By Educational Background**		
#博士及以上	Doctor Degree and Above	31727	32369
#留学归国人员	Returned Students Studying Abroad	3701	3606
硕　士	Masters	399185	390833
#留学归国人员	Returned Students Studying Abroad	48801	44834
大　本	Undergraduates	1385864	1403416
大　专	Junior College	527386	556537
按年龄分	**By Age**		
#29岁及以下	Age 29 and Below	837137	
从业人员平均人数	**Average Number of Empolyed Persons**	**2816894**	**2839965**

24-9 中关村国家自主创新示范区企业财务状况
FINANCIAL STATUS OF ENTERPRISES IN ZHONGGUANCUN NATIONAL INNOVATION DEMONSTRATION ZONE

单位：亿元 (100 million yuan)

项　目	Item	2022	2021
资产总计	Total Assets	198746.6	170177.3
流动资产合计	Total Current Assets	98721.7	91887.1
累计折旧	Accumulative Depreciation	10885.9	10237.8
负债合计	Total Liabilities	121923.9	93255.8
所有者权益合计	Total Owner's Equity	76821.1	77205.2
实收资本	Paid-up Capital	36549.8	30886.5

主要统计指标解释

已开发土地面积 指在规划范围内达到“七通一平”标准的，具备进行房屋建筑物施工或出让条件的土地面积。

已供应土地面积 指开发区内通过各种方式获得土地使用权的土地面积，包括出让、划拨、租赁等。

已建成城镇建设用地面积 截至报告期，已经建设并通过竣工验收的国有建设用地。包括已建成的住宅用地、工矿仓储用地、多功能用地、交通运输用地、商服用地、公共管理与公共服务用地，以及其他城镇建设用地等。海关特殊监管区域的已建成城镇建设用地包括现状围网范围内已建成的城镇建设用地，及开发区四至范围与围网范围间的海关专属办公用地。

累计招商项目企业个数 指自开始至报告期末累计招商入区，并经工商管理机关注册取得法人营业执照的企业个数。

总收入 指企业全年的生产产品销售收入、技术性收入和与本企业产品相关的商品的销售收入、其它收入等各种收入的总和，总收入等于主营业务收入加上其他业务收入。总收入应按不含增值税的价格计算，不包括补贴收入、营业外收入、投资收益。

出口总额 指直接出售给外商的产品、商品、技术或服务的总金额。包括来料加工装配出口，境外技术合同实现金额及在国内以外汇计价的商品出售和技术服务的总额等。

留学归国人员 指出国学习，取得学位的归国人员。

Explanatory Notes on Main Statistical Indicators

Area of Developed Land refers to the area of land that meets the standard of "seven connections and one leveling" and is qualified for construction or sale.

Area of Supplied Land refers to the area of land whose right of use is acquired in the development zones by various means including sale, transfer, and lease.

Area of Land for Urban Development refers to state-owned construction land that has already gone through construction and acceptance check by the end of the reporting period. It includes land for complete residential buildings, land for industrial, mining and storage use, multi-functional land, land for transportation, land for commercial services, land for public administration and services and other lands for urban development. Land for urban development under special administration of customs includes urban development land completed inside the current seine and land for office buildings of customs inside the development zones and between the seines.

Accumulated Number of Enterprises Involved in Business Inviting Programs refers to the total number of enterprises invited to development zones and awarded with business licenses for legal persons from the administration for industry and commerce from the beginning to the end of the reporting period.

Total Revenue refers to the sum of income earned by enterprises from sales of their own products, technological income, and income from selling commodities related to their own products, and other income. Total revenue is the sum of main business income and other business income. Total revenue shall be calculated at VAT-excluded prices, and exclude subsidies, non-operating income and return on investment across the year.

Total Export refers to the total amount of products, commodities, technologies or services directly sold to foreign traders. It includes the value of export of investor's raw materials processed and assembled, the value of technical contracts completed at home and abroad, and the total value of domestic commodity sales and technical services measured in foreign currency.

Returned Students Studying Abroad refer to persons who have come home after studying abroad and been conferred with academic degrees.

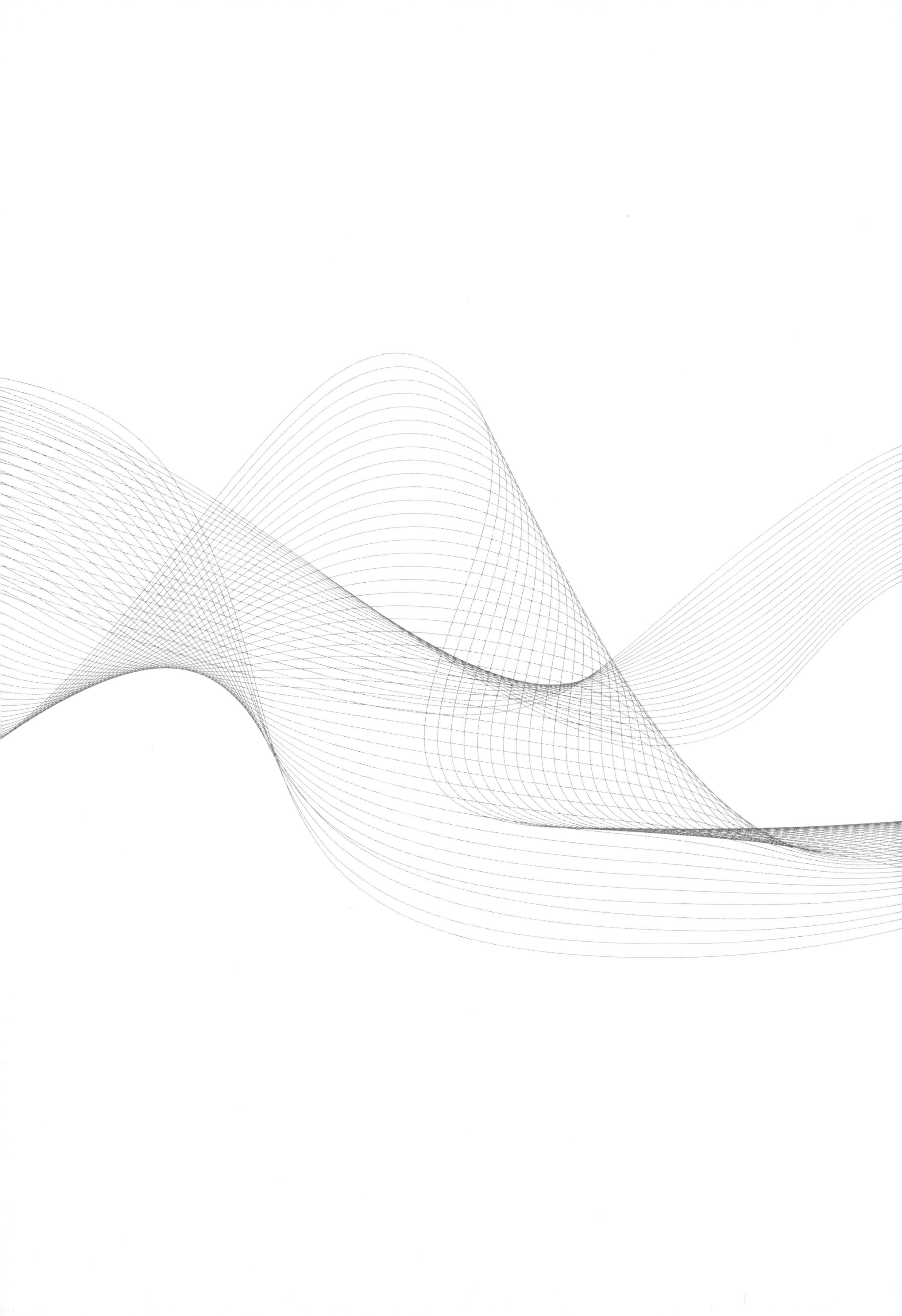